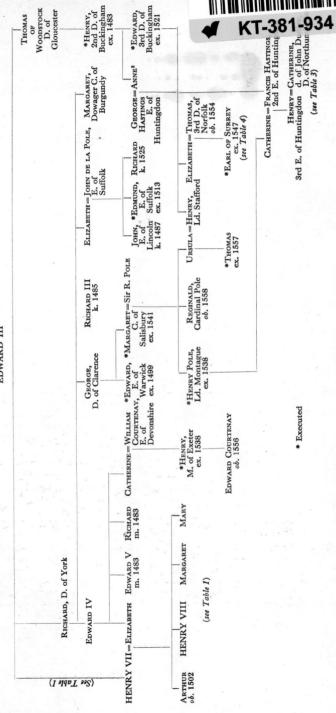

TABLE II.—THE TUDORS AND THEIR RIVALS

WHO'S WHO IN HISTORY

VOLUME TWO: ENGLAND
1485 to 1603

WHO'S WHO
IN HISTORY

Vol. II. England
1485 to 1603

by

C. R. N. ROUTH

General Editor: C. R. N. Routh

BASIL BLACKWELL
OXFORD
1964

To my pupils at Eton College (1921–1957),
who always taught me so much more than
I could ever teach them.

PRINTED IN GREAT BRITAIN BY
BILLING AND SONS LIMITED, GUILDFORD AND LONDON

GENERAL INTRODUCTION

DISRAELI once wrote in *Contarini Fleming*, 'Read no history, nothing but biography, for that is life without theory'—a sound piece of advice for the general public in the twentieth century, when theory is all too apt to swamp experience and when there is, perhaps, a greater demand for genuine history for the general public than ever before. Not a bad piece of advice, within limits, for the student of history in the public, grammar and secondary modern schools today; not without a wholesome reminder for students at the universities.

The *Dictionary of National Biography* is one of the great literary and historical achievements of British historians. Sir Thomas Browne was apt to enshrine a profound truth in the language of the seventeenth century—'diuturnity is a dream and folly of expectation'. Not even the *D.N.B.* can escape that devastating truth, and in fact the *D.N.B.* needs to be completely revised. *Who's Who in History* does not pretend to provide that revision and the authors of the four volumes wish to acknowledge their great debt to the *D.N.B.* Any criticisms are made only in the hope that they may further historical knowledge and scholarship and help to bring up to date the still invaluable articles of the *D.N.B.*

Three general objectives have been kept in view in the writing of the biographies—that they should be as accurate as possible, as up to date as possible and as full as space allows. Where space is limited there is bound to be a conflict between the length of the biographies and the number of the biographies. We have tried on the one hand to avoid scrappy biographies and on the other not to omit any name which everybody would expect to find in a biographical dictionary.

The difficulties begin when the hard core of 'inevitables' has been satisfied: clearly, not everybody will agree with the final selection of the 'rest'. In making this selection, we have been guided to some extent by the decision to try to make each volume a portrait of the age with which it deals and the four volumes something like a general outline history of Britain. Each generation alters its historical perspective; the hard core remains the same, but the personalities in the second rank change from time to time. We have ruthlessly cut down the enormous number of ecclesiastics who swell the volumes of the *D.N.B.*, while we have tried to lay more stress on those classes of people who are now recognized to have been immensely important in their own day—*e.g.* the merchants and travellers of the sixteenth century.

The decision to make each volume a portrait of its own age compelled another decision, to abandon the traditional alphabetical sequence and to adopt a chronological sequence which has sometimes in the later volumes had to be modified by a grouping of subjects, so that the general portrait of the age will also provide a portrait of each section of that age. To overcome the obvious defects in that method, the index of each volume has been prepared with the utmost care, and alphabetical indexes at the ends of the volumes should greatly help readers to find what they are looking for easily and quickly.

The ground-plan for the four volumes is as follows:

Volume 1, Roman and Medieval down to 1485, by W. O. Hassall.

Volume 2, Tudor down to 1603, by C. R. N. Routh.

Volume 3, Stuart and early Georgian, by P. Hill.

Volume 4, late Georgian and Victorian, by B. Rees and E. W. Gladstone.

There is bound to be a spill-over from one age to the next. We have as a general rule included each biography in the volume which covers the years of a man's greatest importance—for example, Sir Walter Raleigh appears in the Tudor volume, although he was executed in the Stuart period, while Robert Cecil, Earl of Salisbury, appears in the Stuart volume although he was born in the Tudor period. Such names appear in the index of both volumes.

Biographies are to a great extent verbal portraits which come more easily to life with the help of a painted portrait. These volumes are liberally illustrated: great care has been taken to select only authenticated portraits and to make sure that the present location of each one is accurately stated.

In each volume there are one or two genealogical trees, a glossary of technical terms, and very short general bibliographical notes of the standard text books which may prove useful to the general reader. At the end of most biographies one or two suggestions for further reading are added, which may be helpful to the student.

C. R. N. R.

INTRODUCTION

THE second volume of *Who's Who in History* covers the years 1485 to 1603 and deals with England and Wales. These years form one of the great creative periods in English history, comparable, for example, with the nineteenth century. Both experienced a tremendous revolution: in the Tudor age an ecclesiastical and doctrinal revolution, the Industrial Revolution in the Victorian age: both saw the British people travelling to the ends of their known world in search of wealth and trade: in both there was a great flowering of English literature: to each a woman on the throne bequeathed her name. The problem has been to know whom to include and whom to omit in this selection of Tudor biographies. Although the size of the book has been considerably increased beyond the original intention, space could not be found for all the men and women who might be thought to have strong claims to be included. Very reluctantly, in order to avoid scrappy biographies, I have left out all Scottish and Irish characters, the printers, the musicians, most of the writers and all the lesser statesmen or politicians. It may be possible to bring all these omissions together in another volume later on.

Four important books have been published recently, which appeared too late for me to be able to use them fully. Had I been able to read V. J. K. Brook's admirable life of Matthew Parker, I should in my own article have laid more emphasis on Parker's interest in antiquities and on his work for education. Jasper Ridley's fine biography of Cranmer has not, I believe, upset what I have written on Cranmer, but in view of his chapters on the Recantations I think I should have written more harshly of Mary I and of Cardinal Pole. Hester W. Chapman's life of Lady Jane Grey supplies some information about Abbot Feckenham which I should have been very glad to use. Dr. G. R. Elton's pamphlet for the Historical Association on Henry VIII has caused me to modify slightly what I had written about Henry's part in the Reformation.

Every effort has been made to ensure that the lists for Further Reading are as useful and as up to date as possible. Where possible historical novels (H.N.) have been included and I am grateful to Mr. Kenneth Charlton for his help in providing these titles. It did not seem necessary to include all the standard text-books.

It is not easy to be certain of the authenticity of sixteenth-century portraits, nor of the present location of them. I am very grateful to Mr. Kingsley Adams, C.B.E., Keeper of the National Portrait Gallery, for the advice and help which he has so generously given me in solving these difficulties. The portraits of Arthur, Prince of Wales, Catherine Howard, William Warham, John Colet, Henry Fitzroy, Sir Thomas More, John Fisher, Edward VI, Lord Darnley, have been reproduced by the gracious permission of Her Majesty the Queen. I have to thank the owners of the other portraits for their kind permission to reproduce them, and most especially the Duke of Buccleuch and his secretary, Miss MacEchern, for much kindness and help and for an unforgettable day at Boughton.

I wish specially to thank the Librarian and his staff of the Public Library at Stratford-on-Avon for their unfailing help, courtesy and co-operation. They have spared no trouble to meet my incessant and often baffling demand for books. No doubt there are many other towns as well catered for as Stratford-on-Avon: I have not met them.

Above all I must thank Professor Joel Hurstfield and Mr. Christopher Morris for their great kindness in reading this book in typescript. Their time and scholarship has been put at my disposal most generously and their conscientious reading and penetrating criticisms have saved me from innumerable errors. What errors remain are mine and not theirs. I am grateful also to Mr. William Baring Pemberton for reading the page-proofs.

Finally, it is a very great pleasure to me to put on record how much I have appreciated the unfailing patience, courtesy and friendship of Mr. J. A. Cutforth.

LIST OF PLATES

1. Henry VII. Bust by Torrigiano. (Victoria and Albert Museum)

2. Arthur, Prince of Wales. (H.M. The Queen. Windsor Castle)*
   Margaret, Countess of Richmond. Detail, Torrigiano. (Westminster Abbey)

3. Henry VIII. Attr. to Holbein. (Earl of Warwick, Warwick Castle)

4. Anne Boleyn. Holbein. (Earl of Bradford, Weston Park, Shifnal)
   Jane Seymour. Attr. to Holbein. (Duke of Buccleuch)*
   Catherine of Aragon. Attr. to Holbein. (Duke of Buccleuch)
   Anne of Cleves. Holbein, on an ivory box. (Victoria and Albert Museum)
   Catherine Howard. Holbein. (H.M. The Queen, Windsor Castle)*

5. William Warham. Detail, Holbein. (H.M. The Queen, Windsor Castle)
   Mary Tudor and Charles Brandon, Duke of Suffolk. Attr. to Mabuse. (Earl of Yarborough)

6. Erasmus. Holbein. (Earl of Radnor and the Royal Academy)
   John Colet. Detail, Holbein, from the bust by Torrigiano. (H.M. The Queen, Windsor Castle)

7. Henry Fitzroy, Duke of Richmond. (H.M. The Queen, Windsor Castle)
   Cardinal Wolsey. (Duke of Buccleuch)

8. Thomas Howard, 2nd Duke of Norfolk. Detail (Duke of Norfolk, Arundel Castle)
   Thomas Cromwell, Earl of Essex. Detail, after Holbein. (N.P.G. No. 1727)

9. Sir Thomas More. Detail, Holbein. (H.M. The Queen, Windsor Castle)
   John Fisher. Detail, Holbein. (H.M. The Queen, Windsor Castle)

10. Edward VI. (H.M. The Queen, Windsor Castle)
    Edward Seymour, Protector Somerset. Attr. to N. Hilliard after the Holbeinesque original. (Duke of Buccleuch)

11. Thomas Cranmer. Gerlach Flicke. (N.P.G. No. 535)

12. Lady Jane Grey. Engraving in Holland's *Herowologia**
    John Dudley, Duke of Northumberland. (Viscount de L'Isle,
    V.C., G.C.M.G., Penshurst)

13. Richard Fox. Detail, Corvus. (The President and Scholars,
    Corpus Christi College, Oxford)
    Cuthbert Tunstal. Detail, attr. to Hans Asper. (Brigadier
    R. C. J. Chichester-Constable, Burton Constable)

14. Mary I. Detail (Sir Montgomerie Fairfax-Lucy Bart., Charle-
    cote Park, Warwick)

15. Edmund Bonner. Detail from a woodcut at the N.P.G. An
    illustration in the 1st edition of Foxe's *Book of Martyrs*
    Stephen Gardiner. Detail (The Master and Fellows, Trinity
    Hall, Cambridge)

16. Reginald Pole, Cardinal. Detail (Lambeth Palace)
    Cardinal Allen. Detail (The President, Ushaw College,
    Durham)

17. Elizabeth I. Detail (Academia di Belli Arte, Siena)

18. William Cecil, Lord Burghley. (Bodleian Library, Oxford)

19. Sir Thomas Gresham. Detail, attr. to A. Key. (N.P.G. No. 352)
    Sir Francis Walsingham. Detail (N.P.G. No. 1704)

20. Nicholas Hilliard. Self-portrait, miniature, in his 30th year.
    (Duke of Buccleuch)
    Sir Christopher Hatton. Nicholas Hilliard. (Victoria and
    Albert Museum, No. P155–1910)
    Robert Dudley, Earl of Leicester. Detail (Viscount de L'Isle,
    V.C., G.C.M.G., Penshurst)
    Robert Devereux, Earl of Essex. Isaac Oliver. (H.M. The
    Queen, Windsor Castle)
    Hans Holbein. Self-portrait, in his 45th year. (Duke of Portland)

21. Mary, Queen of Scots. Nicholas Hilliard. (Duke of Portland)
    James Hepburn, Earl of Bothwell. Detail (N.G. of Scotland,
    No. PG869)
    Henry Stuart, Earl of Darnley. Detail (H.M. The Queen,
    Windsor Castle)

22. Edmund Grindal. Detail (The Master and Fellows, Pembroke
    College, Cambridge)
    Matthew Parker. Detail (The Master and Fellows, Corpus
    Christi College, Cambridge)

23. John Jewel. Detail (The President and Scholars, Corpus
    Christi College, Oxford)
    John Whitgift. Detail (Lambeth Palace)

24. Richard Hooker. Detail, monument at Bishopsbourne.
    John Foxe. Detail (N.P.G. No. 24)

25. Sir John Hawkins. Detail (The City Art Gallery, Plymouth)
    Sir Francis Drake. Rabel. (The Hakluyt Society)

26. Lord Howard of Effingham. Detail, Daniel Mytens. (N.M.M.,
    Greenwich)
    Sir Richard Grenville. Detail (N.P.G. No. 1612)

27. Sir Martin Frobisher. (Bodleian Library, Oxford)

28. Sir James Lancaster. Detail (The Master and Company of
    Skinners, Skinners' Hall)
    Sir Humphrey Gilbert. Detail (Commander W. R. Gilbert,
    Compton Castle, Paignton, Devon)

29. Sir Philip Sidney. Detail (N.P.G. No. 2096)
    The Earl of Cumberland. Nicholas Hilliard. (N.M.M.,
    Greenwich)

30. William Shakespeare. Soest. (Shakespeare Birthplace Trust,
    Stratford-on-Avon)*

31. Sir Walter Ralegh. Nicholas Hilliard. (N.P.G. No. 4106)
    'Dr.' John Dee. Detail (Ashmolean Museum, Oxford)

32. Sir John Harington of Kelston. Detail (J. Harington-More
    Esq. Sutherland)
    Bess of Hardwick. Detail (N.P.G. No. 203)

* The authenticity of the sitter has been questioned. The Soest
portrait of Shakespeare is almost certainly the one referred to by
George Vertue which he stated was painted by Lely for Sir Walter
Clarges. (Walpole Society, Vertue MSS, vol. IV, p. 13)

MARGARET BEAUFORT, COUNTESS OF RICH-MOND, mother of Henry VII, was born in 1433 and died in 1509, in the same year as her son, aged 76. She was the daughter of John Beaufort, first Duke of Somerset, and granddaughter of John of Gaunt. In 1455 she married Edmund Tudor, Earl of Richmond, half-brother on her mother's side to Henry VI. Her husband died in 1456 before their son, Henry, was born. During the Wars of the Roses she and her child lived at Pembroke Castle, after she had married Henry Stafford, Duke of Buckingham. Because she was a Lancastrian, after the Yorkist victory in 1461 she was kept there in honourable confinement, and when in 1470 the Lancastrians came back to power for a short while, she was released and went to Court. The final triumph of Edward IV at Tewkesbury, and the extinction of the direct Lancastrian descent from Henry IV, left her young son, Henry Tudor, Earl of Richmond, a possible claimant to the Lancastrian title. He was therefore sent abroad. His mother was of strong character, politically shrewd, highly educated, intelligent and ambitious, at any rate for her son. She was reconciled with Edward IV and on the death of her husband, Buckingham, she married the king's minister, Lord Stanley, later Earl of Derby. She took an active part in planning the rising of 1483 against Richard III, which was a failure, and in planning that of 1485 which brought her son to the throne as Henry VII. The Beaufort family had been excluded by an Act of Parliament from succeeding to the throne, but if that Act were to be ignored, the legal Lancastrian heir would be Margaret and not her son. All her life she remained on good terms with him, but she always signed her letters Margaret R., Countess of Richmond, as if to remind people of her true status.

It is disputable what part she took in politics after the accession of Henry, nor is it certain how often she went to Court. That she was a remarkable and excellent woman all were agreed. Fisher in his funeral oration extolled her many and Christian virtues: Polydore Vergil calls her 'a wise woman' and 'a most worthy woman whom no one can extol too much or too often for her sound sense and holiness of life. Henry allotted her a share in most of his public and private resources, thus easing her declining years.' (*Angl. Hist.*, bk. xxvi, Camden Soc., vol. lxxiv, p. 7.) Stubbs has called her 'a pious and noble mother', 'strict and stately, a woman of great experience, of many husbands and good advisers'. He says further, 'she kept her son straight and the court fairly pure both during his wife's life and after her death, when the discipline was so close that poor Katherine of Aragon had to write home to her father that she could not get a mouthful of meat in Lent'. (*Lectures on Mediaeval and Modern History*, pp. 395–6.) Perhaps her chief claim to be remembered is her generosity to the universities of Oxford and Cambridge, where the Lady Margaret Professorships of Divinity perpetuate her name, and at Cambridge Christ's College and St. John's College are her visible memorials.

E. M. G. Routh, *Lady Margaret*, 1924.   (*Plate 2*)
H. O. Everrett, *The Clergy Review*, May 1935.

HENRY VII, King of England 1485–1509, was born at Pembroke Castle on January 28th, 1457. He died at Richmond on April 21st, 1509, when he was 52 years old. He was the son of Edmund Tudor, Earl of Richmond, and Margaret Beaufort, great-granddaughter of John of Gaunt. His father was the son of Owen Tudor and Henry V's widow, Catherine of France. His father died before Henry was born, so that from birth he was Earl of Richmond. His early years were spent in Wales and much care was lavished on his education. When the Yorkist Edward IV recovered the English throne in 1471 during the Wars of the Roses, it was thought unsafe for the Lancastrian Henry to remain in England, and he was removed to Brittany, where he lived until Edward IV's death in 1483. The murder of the Princes in the Tower left Henry the only possible leader of any movement against the usurper, Richard III. A rebellion was organized by Henry Stafford, Duke of Buckingham, and John Morton, Bishop of Ely, which Henry was to join with the help of the Duke of Brittany, but a storm dispersed his fleet and he was forced back to Brittany (October, 1483). When Richard

III demanded that the Duke of Brittany should hand Henry over, Henry escaped to the court of the French king, Charles VIII. Here he was joined by many English refugees and an invasion of England was planned. On August 1st, 1485, Henry embarked at Harfleur and arrived a week later at Milford Haven with only 2,000 men. He relied for an army on his Welsh compatriots. After much hesitation Sir William Stanley joined Henry. On August 22nd, 1485, was fought the battle of Bosworth in which Richard was killed. The crown of England was found on a bush* and placed on Henry's head by Lord Stanley, Sir William's brother and Henry's step-father, for he had married the Lady Margaret Beaufort.

On October 30th Henry was crowned King in London, and on January 18th, 1486, he fulfilled his promise, made two years before in Brittany, to marry the Princess Elizabeth, daughter of Edward IV.

When Henry came to the throne his position was far from secure. He had no legal claim. His claim through descent from John of Gaunt was barred by an Act of Parliament which excluded the Beaufort family from the throne. Financially he was bankrupt: he had neither army nor navy; he was opposed by the wealthy and powerful Yorkist party, of whom the chief trouble-maker was to be Margaret, Dowager Duchess of Burgundy, sister of Edward IV. It was she who in 1487 was the real organizer of Lambert Simnel's invasion of Ireland and who had a major share in arranging the more dangerous invasion by Perkin Warbeck in 1491-7. Henry was able to defeat both these threats, as he also defeated the rising led by Lord Lovell and the Staffords in 1486. Henry therefore had three principal aims—to accumulate wealth, to cut away support for the Yorkist pretenders, and to strengthen his dynasty by making marriage alliances for his children. The measure of Henry's statesmanship is the skill with which he

* It is doubtful whether this story is true. It does not occur in any sixteenth-century account of the battle. But the thorn-bush, often with a crown, occurs among other Tudor symbols in the heraldic emblems in the tracery of the small lights above the large windows of the King's College Chapel, Cambridge. The windows were put in between 1515 and 1531. The story must by then at least have had a recognisable meaning.

used his foreign policy to further his domestic policy. For example, when he made the Treaty of Medina del Campo with Ferdinand of Aragon in 1489, by which his son, Arthur, was to marry Ferdinand's daughter, Catherine, Henry saw to it that a clause was inserted by which Ferdinand undertook not to harbour rebels against the English king. A similar clause was included in the Treaty of Etaples (1492) with the French King. Or again, James IV of Scotland had given help to Perkin Warbeck. After the episode was finished, Henry married his daughter, Margaret, to the Scottish king.

Similarly, Henry's financial policy was dovetailed into his foreign policy. Taxation was so unpopular as to be dangerous, as was shewn by the rising of the Cornishmen in 1497 against the subsidy voted by Parliament for defence against the Scots. Henry therefore relied on extra-Parliamentary methods—fines, loans, benevolences and feudal dues. Morton and Bray began the system which was developed by Empson and Dudley. It probably had a political as well as a financial purpose—to depress the nobility. Justice was subordinated to the pursuit of wealth. But Henry also extracted large sums of money out of his foreign allies: Catherine of Aragon had to bring a dowry of 200,000 crowns; the *Intercursus Magnus* of 1496 and the *Intercursus Malus* (*malus* from the Netherlands' point of view) of 1506 brought immense trading advantages to England. Henry also managed in 1492 to get Parliament to grant him money for a war with France and then he extracted a large indemnity from the French King for not having carried out his purpose. In 1497 the Milanese ambassador reported that Henry had more than six million golden ducats to which he was adding at the rate of 500,000 a year. When he died, he left to his son a treasure between one and two millions.

In many ways Henry VII was a modern-minded man, as is shewn by his patronage of the Cabots' explorations to Newfoundland, but in religion he was a mediaevalist, an orthodox churchman, who maintained good relations with the Papacy. His administration, although strong, was also mediaeval in structure. Francis Bacon draws a grim portrait of Henry, 'a wonder for wise men'. Henry could be dour and silent, miserly, subtle, cautious, but also bold and high-handed. Yet he had many more human qualities. He was a good son devoted to his mother, a faithful husband and a kindly father. He spent money as well as hoarded it, often on amusements; he loved the open air life and sports, especially hawking and hunting; he was interested in books and in architecture, as his own chapel in Westminster Abbey proves, and he loved music. He had a kind of sardonic sense of humour which appears in his treatment of Lambert Simnell. He must be rated one of the ablest of all English kings. He seized the throne by his boldness, he held it for twenty-four years by his statesmanship and he handed it on to his son secure, well-endowed and popular.   (*Plate 1*)

Bacon, *History of the Reign of King Henry VII.*
Pickthorn, *Early Tudor Government, Henry VII*, 1949.
C. Morris, *The Tudors*, 1955.

ELIZABETH OF YORK, wife of Henry VII, was born at Westminster on February 11th, 1465, and she died giving birth to a daughter on her birthday in 1503, having completed her thirty-eighth year. She was the daughter of Edward IV and Elizabeth Wydeville (or Woodville). When she was five years old she was to have married George Neville, eldest son of John, Earl of Northumberland, later Marquess of Montagu, and Neville was created Duke of Bedford, but his father switched sides against the King, Bedford was deprived of all his titles and Elizabeth's betrothal was cancelled. In 1475 Edward planned to marry her to Louis, the French Dauphin, but Edward soon discovered that Louis had no intention of keeping his obligations and therefore the engagement was broken off. Bernard Andréas, the blind poet laureate and historian, hints that Edward offered Elizabeth to Henry of Richmond, later Henry VII and her husband to be, but that Henry declined, suspecting that the offer was a trap to put him into the King's power.

Edward IV died in 1483. His Queen, suspicious of Richard of Gloucester, put herself with her younger son and her five daughters into sanctuary at Westminster. Elizabeth was at the time just eighteen. The Duke of Buckingham, having broken with Richard of Gloucester, made a plan for Elizabeth to

marry Henry of Richmond, who was then abroad. The Lady
Margaret, Henry's mother, highly approved the plan. Henry,
on Christmas Day, 1483, at the cathedral of Vannes in France
swore to marry Elizabeth as soon as he had secured the throne.
This oath he honoured on January 18th, 1486.

Elizabeth is one of the least important, though not the least
attractive, of the queens of England. Little is known about her.
What evidence there is suggests that the relations between
Henry VII and his Queen were happy. There is a pathetic
account in Leland's *Collectanea* of how Henry VII broke the
news of Prince Arthur's death to his wife and how Elizabeth
'with comfortable words' said to him that 'my Lady his mother
had never had no more children but him only, and that God . . .
had left him yet a fair prince, two fair princesses; and that
God is where he was and we are both young enough.' She
seems to have been beautiful, gentle, kind, generous to her
relations, her servants and benefactors. Her income never
covered her expenses. She was fond of dancing, of music,
dicing, hunting, she kept greyhounds, and she may have been
fond of archery—at any rate she bought arrows and broad-
heads, perhaps for hunting. She is still commemorated as the
model for the queen on our playing cards.

N. H. Nicolas, *Privy Purse Expenses of Elizabeth of York*, 1830.
Leland, *Collectanea, v.* 373–4.

ARTHUR, PRINCE OF WALES, the eldest son of Henry
VII and his wife, Elizabeth of York, was born on September
20th, 1486, and died on April 2nd, 1502, in his sixteenth year.
Henry, in order to strengthen his claim to the throne, set the
genealogists to work to trace his descent back to Cadwallader
and the ancient British kings: he identified Winchester with
Camelot, and therefore he sent his wife to Winchester to have
her baby and the boy was named Arthur after King Arthur of
the Round Table—one example of Henry's consciousness of
being Welsh. He was christened in Winchester Cathedral, his
godfathers being the Earl of Oxford, who arrived late for the
ceremony, and the Earl of Derby. When he was three he was
made Prince of Wales. When he was five, he was made a

Knight of the Garter, having been made a Knight of the Bath at his christening.

Henry saw to it that his son should have the best education which the revival of learning could provide. Arthur's first tutor was one John Rede, but later he was instructed by the blind poet laureate, Bernard Andréas, who wrote an unfinished life of Henry VII, in which he asserted that by the age of fifteen Arthur was familiar with all the best Greek and Latin authors. Arthur was probably never a strong child and there is no evidence that he was ever an athlete like his younger brother, Henry, but it is possible that he may have shown some aptitude for archery.

In 1488, when Arthur was only two years old, negotiations had begun for his marriage to Catherine of Aragon. Ferdinand of Aragon was clearly not going to commit himself until he saw whether the Tudor dynasty was going to be securely settled on the throne, therefore he held back for some years; but after the execution of Perkin Warbeck and the Earl of Warwick in 1499 he agreed to the marriage. For two years the Prince of Wales from Ludlow Castle was writing letters in formal Latin and still more formal terms at the age of fourteen to a girl two years older than himself whom he had never seen. The letters are characterized rather by politeness than by passion. At last in 1500 the terms of the marriage were settled at a meeting outside Calais, and on May 21st, 1501, Catherine embarked at Coruña for England. The voyage took five months, but she arrived safely at Plymouth on October 2nd, 1501.

The marriage took place in St. Paul's Cathedral on November 14th. Arthur and Catherine then went to Ludlow and set up court there as Prince and Princess of Wales. They were thought, however, to be too young to cohabit. On April 2nd, 1502, Arthur suddenly died before the marriage was consummated. This fact was to have momentous results, not only for Catherine but for England and the Papacy, when Henry VIII, having married Catherine, later sought to have the marriage annulled by the Pope. (*Plate 2*)

There is not enough material to warrant a life of Prince Arthur. The sketch in F. Maynard Bridge's *Princes of Wales* adds little to the account in the *D.N.B.* and is very inaccurate in dates.

MORTON, JOHN, Archbishop of Canterbury and Cardinal, was born probably in 1420 at Milborne St. Andrew, near Bere Regis in Dorset. He died in 1500, aged approximately 80 years. He was the son of Richard Morton, of a Nottingham family, and Elizabeth, daughter of Richard Turburville and Cecilia Beauchamp, being the eldest of five sons. He was educated at the Benedictine Abbey at Cerne, from which he went to Balliol, Oxford. He took up law, but he also took orders, and in 1446 he appears among the vice-chancellors of Oxford, known also as commissaries. He moved to London and practised as a lawyer principally in the Court of Arches, and became a Privy Councillor and Chancellor of the Duchy of Cornwall. From this moment he became a great pluralist and might almost be said to have collected offices and livings. All these appointments were ecclesiastical, but Morton's work was almost wholly legal or political, and there is little evidence that he resided in any of his livings.

During the Wars of the Roses Morton was mainly on the Lancastrian side, but he managed to keep in with the Yorkists when they were in the ascendant. He was present at the battle of Towton and at one point had to fight for his life: he was wrongly reported to have been taken prisoner (1461). He escaped to the north and sailed for Flanders, not to return to England for ten years. He was in 1461 attainted, convicted of treason and sentenced to lose all his possessions. While he was abroad he attended the Queen Margaret, first at Bruges and later at Louvain. He played a large part in reconciling Warwick and Clarence to the Lancastrians and when they sailed for England (1470), Morton went with them, landing at Dartmouth on September 13th. He was present at the battle of Barnet (April 1471), after which he hurried to Weymouth to meet the Queen and her son, who were expected there. He took them to Cerne Abbey and thence to Beaulieu.

The battle of Tewkesbury put paid to Lancastrian hopes and Morton now (1471) reconciled himself with the Yorkists. Edward IV evidently looked on Morton as a trustworthy and valuable servant, he reversed the attainder and in 1472 appointed him to be Master of the Rolls. In a short time

Morton held many prebends and five archdeaconries. One sign of the King's confidence in Morton may be seen in the embassy which Edward entrusted to him to bring the Emperor and the King of Hungary into an alliance against the King of France, Louis XI (1474). The next year he was one of the negotiators of the Treaty of Pecquiny where peace was made with Louis XI, and he received as his share of the spoils a pension of £2000 a year.

In 1478 he was appointed Bishop of Ely. On the day of his enthronement, after a night of prayer, Morton walked from Downham to Ely with his head uncovered, bare-footed and bare-legged, with his beads in his hand, saying his Pater-nosters. He now gave up the Mastership of the Rolls and to a great extent devoted himself to religious duties. He also became tutor to the Prince of Wales. At his palace in London he held reading parties both for young and promising scholars and also for men of learning, English and foreign: he set about reforming his diocese and he revived his connection with Oxford. When Edward IV died in 1483, Morton was one of his executors, but he refused to act on the grounds that he was not given large enough powers to act effectively.

When Richard of Gloucester began to scheme to seize the throne from his young nephew, Edward V, Morton was in a difficult and dangerous position. He was present at the council meeting at which Richard's plans began to make themselves known, a meeting made famous by Richard's reference to one of Morton's favourite hobbies, the growing of fruit:

> My Lord of Ely, when I was last at Holborn,
> I saw good strawberries in your garden there:
> I do beseech you send for some of them.
> (Richard III, iii, iv.)

That Morton at once went to order some did not save him from arrest: he was put into prison, but he was released on a petition from Oxford University on behalf of 'our dearest son' and allowed to reside with Buckingham at Brecknock Castle. Buckingham had already been forming his own plans against Richard, which he now divulged to Morton. Morton himself had almost certainly come to the conclusion that the hopes for the country rested now, not on Richard, but on Henry Richmond. He approved of Buckingham's plans and he became the intermediary between Buckingham and Reginald Bray, and this brought him into touch with Margaret Beaufort, Countess of Richmond, mother of Henry Richmond, later Henry VII. It is almost certain that it was Morton who first implanted in Margaret Beaufort's mind the idea that her son should marry Elizabeth of York, daughter of Edward IV, and thus end the feud of the Roses. If this is true, it goes a long way to establishing Morton, rather against the factual evidence, as being a clear-sighted and honest man, who did his best in the most difficult times for his country. A rising was planned to take place in the West. Morton decided that he ought to be at Ely: it is possible that he distrusted the success of a purely local rising and wanted to be in the east of England to raise forces there. Buckingham was suspicious of allowing so important a personage to leave his side. Morton escaped secretly by night and went to Ely. Shakespeare records for us Richard III's feelings:

> Ely with Richmond troubles me more near
> Than Buckingham with his rash-levied strength.
>
> (Richard III, IV, iii.)

Buckingham's rising failed, Henry Richmond's expedition from Brittany had to turn back, Buckingham was arrested and executed. Morton had gone to Flanders and was there till after Bosworth, except for a visit to Paris where he met Richard Fox, later Bishop of Winchester, and won him over to Henry's side. Morton was able to warn Henry that the Duke of Brittany meant to betray him to Richard III and thus to advise him to fly into the realm of the King of France.

In 1485 Henry Richmond invaded England and won the throne. Morton came back, his attainder was again reversed, he was made a Privy Councillor, in 1486 he was Chancellor and Archbishop of Canterbury. From that point on until his death in 1500 Morton was, under Henry VII, the most important and powerful man in the kingdom. He was supreme, except for the King, in Church and State. He now set himself to remedy the abuses in both, immorality in the monasteries, over-mighty subjects in the state. He reformed clerical abuses, even down to the form of dress: he ordered residence for those with care of souls: bishops were to take trouble in selecting curates. He set out on visitations (1490) to Lichfield, Coventry, Bath and Wells, Winchester, Lincoln, Exeter. He petitioned the Papacy to canonize Henry VI, in which he failed, and Anselm was canonized instead. In 1493 Morton was made a Cardinal. His position now was something like a foreshadow of Wolsey's position later on: Morton was head of the Church as Primate and Cardinal: he was chief administrator in the State as Chancellor of England, especially in the law: he was chancellor of Oxford university: he opened Parliament for the King and defended policy, especially taxation, in speeches more like modern speeches than those in the past: he received foreign embassies: he persuaded the Pope to allow some modification in the laws governing sanctuary.

In the realm of finance there seems little doubt now that Morton's position was extremely difficult. The King had to have money and left to himself Henry would have pursued a much more heavy-handed and even tyrannical policy than he did: he was restrained by Bray and by Morton. 'Morton's Fork' or 'Crutch' has passed into history, but it looks as if he accepted all the unpopularity for financial measures which would have been worse but for him, in order to save the reputation of the King. And he had to bear the burden of unpopularity for the many 'benevolences' which were raised out of the nobility.

In one respect Morton was a herald of the future: he was an indefatiguable builder. He repaired the palace at Canterbury; the Manor House at Lambeth, where the Gateway is his work; the episcopal residences at Maidstone, Aldington Park, Ford, Charing: his arms are on the tower at Wisbeach: he built what is now the old part of Hatfield House: restored Rochester Bridge; put the splendid roof on to the nave of Bere Regis church. In addition he cut a great canal from Peterborough to Guyhirne near Wisbeach, known as Morton's Leame, which brought the High Fen into cultivation amounting to 4,387 acres: this canal was 40 feet wide, 4 feet deep, with new outlets to the sea, and 40 miles in length. It lasted until 1725.

In legislation his most famous act is that of 1497 to protect from the penalties of Treason those who act under a *de facto* King, in order to protect all who had supported or were serving Henry VII.

It is not easy to decide whether Morton was a patriot or a self-seeker.* Bacon records of him that 'he was a wise man and an eloquent, but in his nature harsh and haughty, much accepted by the King, but envied by the nobility and hated of the people'. In that tribute there is nothing to persuade us that Morton was not a highly valuable statesman in harsh and difficult days. But Sir Thomas More, who as a boy was brought up in Morton's household, puts into the mouth of Hythlodaye in *Utopia* a more generous tribute: 'a man not more honourable for his authority than for his prudence and virtue. . . . In his speech he was fine, eloquent and pithy. In the law he had profound knowledge; in wit he was incomparable; and in memory wonderfully excellent. These qualities, which in him were by nature singular, he by learning and use had made perfect. The King put much trust in his counsel: the weal public also in a manner leaned upon him.'

The general opinion nowadays is that Morton was not, and Sir Thomas More was the author of *The History of Richard III*, both in the Latin and English versions. (Chambers, *Thomas More*, p. 55.)

Morton died on September 15th, 1500, at Knowle in Kent.

T. Mozley, *Henry VII, Prince Arthur and Cardinal Morton*, intro. 1878.
R. I. Woodhouse, *Memoir of Morton*, 1895.
Neither of these accounts differs at all from that in the *D.N.B.*

* This expression is really an anachronism. Society was not based on a sense of the nation as a unit, it was based on what at that time was called 'degree' and 'order'. When men observed their due 'degree' or place in society and maintained the established 'order', then good government was possible and resulted in law and order. If men broke the accepted order, chaos ensued. Such was the theory of the time (see the speech of Ulysses in *Troilus and Cressida*, Act I, sc. iii). Richard III was guilty of 'jumping the queue', abusing his 'degree', by snatching at one higher than was his in the established 'order'. Morton might claim to be a disinterested statesman, if he was trying to re-establish the accepted order.

FOX, RICHARD, Bishop of Winchester, Lord Privy Seal, was born between 1446 and 1448 at Ropesley in Lincolnshire, the son of yeoman stock. He died in 1528 aged about eighty. His early education is unknown, but he went to Oxford to Magdalen College where he studied law, then to Paris University where he took the degree of Doctor of Canon Law and was ordained. This close connection between the law and ordination was typical of the time and dictated Fox's future career.

While he was abroad in Paris he became secretary to Henry Tudor, Earl of Richmond, the future Henry VII of England. That he was already a known man is proved by Richard III's order prohibiting Fox from being appointed to the vicarage of Stepney, on the grounds that he was with 'that great rebel Henry ap Tuddor'. Fox obtained the living in 1485.

In that year he accompanied Henry on his invasion of England, was with him at Bosworth, and when Henry became King, Fox was made principal secretary of state and Keeper of the Privy Seal: at the same time he was appointed to the see of Exeter. For the next thirty years Fox was the typical ecclesiastical statesman of the type of which Gardiner was probably to be the last. In 1491 Fox was translated to Bath and Wells, in 1494 to Durham (probably because it was valuable to Henry to have him resident on the ever-dangerous Scottish border), in 1501 to Winchester. He never attended to his ecclesiastical duties until his retirement from politics, but he appointed a suffragan to do the work. During this period Fox was concerned in negotiating all the main treaties; he had a major hand in the treaty with Scotland in 1487, in the treaty of Etaples (1492), in the *Intercursus Magnus* in 1496, in the marriage treaty of Margaret Tudor and James IV (1502), and in the abortive marriage treaty for Mary Tudor and Charles of Castile in 1508. His work also included such military exploits as organizing the harbour works at Calais, and the defence of Norham Castle when Perkin Warbeck was in Scotland (1497). He was also an executor for Henry VII's will. When Henry died (1509), Fox was still in favour with Henry VIII, but the rise of Wolsey (about 1513) marks the end of Fox's pre-eminence. He was still used by the King and he went with Henry VIII to France in 1513 and was present at Thérouenne, but he was now a sick man, 'much hurt by the kick of his mule, and for some days he could neither sit nor stand', as the diarist John Taylor recorded. Fox disapproved of the new foreign policy and he found the campaign very distasteful. He wrote to Wolsey, who was just about to cross over to France, that unless he took with him a good supply of beer, he would have 'a cold stomach, little sleep, pale visage, and a thin belly', as he himself had.

In 1516 Fox resigned the Privy Seal and retired to look after the spiritual needs of his diocese. By 1518 he was seriously blind, yet he had ten more years to live. He seems genuinely to have regretted and even repented of his neglect of his bishoprics while he was 'meddling with worldly matters'. 'I have no little remorse in my conscience, thinking that if I did continual penance for it all the days of my life, though I shall live twenty years longer than I may do, I could not yet make sufficient recompence therefor.' He died on October 5th, 1528.

Fox may be remembered principally for his founding and building of Corpus Christi College, Oxford, but he was also a benefactor of other colleges both at Oxford and Cambridge. The screen and chantry which he built at Winchester display his well-known device of a pelican. He was also a Humanist and had contacts with Erasmus when that scholar visited England.

(Plate 13)

G. H. Blore, *Richard Fox, Bishop of Winchester*, 1501–1528, The *Record* of the Friends of Winchester Cathedral, 1947.

E. C. Batten, *Fox's Register for Bath and Wells*, 1889.

P. S. and H. M. Allen, *Letters of Richard Fox*, 1929.

SIMNEL, LAMBERT, impostor, was born probably in 1475: he died in 1525, aged about fifty. He was the son of Thomas Simnel of Oxford, variously described as a joiner, an organ builder, a shoemaker or a baker.

Polydore Vergil, the source of all later accounts, records that Simnel was a 'comely youth and well-favoured, not without some extraordinary dignity and grace of aspect'. An Oxford priest, Richard Symonds, conceived the idea of setting up Simnel as Richard, Duke of York, the younger of the two princes murdered in the Tower. Later, when the rumour spread that the Earl of Warwick, son of 'false, fleeting, perjured Clarence', had died in the Tower, Symonds changed Simnel's claim to that of being the Earl of Warwick.

Symonds secured the support of the Yorkist leaders— Margaret, Dowager Duchess of Burgundy, sister of Edward IV, implacably hostile to Henry VII, mainly because he had stopped the pension which her brother had paid her; Lord Lovell, who had fled to her court in the Netherlands; John de la Pole, Earl of Lincoln, who joined the Irish rebels. Margaret supplied Simnel with 2,000 German mercenaries under Martin Schwarz.

Simnel was taken to Ireland, where Yorkist sympathies were strong; he was accepted by Kildare and all Ireland (except Waterford); he was proclaimed King as Edward VI and was crowned in Dublin Cathedral. The rebels then crossed to England, landed in Lancashire and marched towards London. But they received no support. They met the King's army at Stoke-on-Trent on June 16th, 1487, and after a hard fight they were totally defeated. Lincoln, Lovell and other Yorkist leaders were killed: Symonds and Simnel were both taken prisoner, Symonds was imprisoned for life, but Henry behaved with much politic leniency towards the young and gentle Simnel. He turned him into his scullion and Simnel later rose to be his falconer. Later still he was transferred to the household of Sir Thomas Lovell. He died in 1525.

Polydore Vergil, *Anglica Historia*.
D. Scott Daniell, *The Boy They Made King*. Cape. 1959. (H.N.)

WARBECK, PERKIN, was born probably in 1474 and he died in 1499, at the age of about twenty-five. He was the son of John Osbeck, of Tournai, and his wife Catherine de Faro. (Osbeck is a variant spelling of Werbecque, anglicized into Warbeck.) After a restless career which included a year in Portugal with the wife of Sir Edward Brampton, a Yorkist supporter, he sailed for Ireland in the service of a Breton named Pregent Meno.

Warbeck landed in Ireland in 1491, dressed splendidly in silk clothes belonging to Meno. The Irish, remembering

Lambert Simnel, hailed Warbeck as the Earl of Warwick. Warbeck denied this on oath before the mayor. The Irish then said that he was Richard, Duke of York, which he again denied, but in the end he weakly allowed himself to accept this role. He was then taught to speak good English and, as far as possible, royal manners.

The next step in this drama of political chicanery was that Charles VIII of France saw a chance of using Warbeck in his quarrel with Henry VII. He invited Warbeck to France in 1492. The Treaty of Etaples (1492) ended this plot and Warbeck was compelled to leave France and to go to Margaret, Dowager Duchess of Burgundy, who accepted him as her nephew and set about properly educating him as a royal Yorkist. Henry VII thereupon broke off trading relations with the Netherlands, but this was a two-edged weapon which hit England as hardly as it hit the Netherlands and it had to be called off.

In 1493 Warbeck went to the court of the Emperor Maximilian I, who recognized him as Richard IV of England. Maximilian's son, Philip, turned the Netherlands into a centre for the conspiracy against Henry VII. Henry was soon aware of and dealt with the ramifications of the plot in England. Among the victims was that Sir William Stanley who had been largely responsible for the victory at Bosworth Field.

The next stages of the plot can be quickly summarized. In July 1495 Warbeck landed most of his forces at Deal, but he sailed away, after these had been dealt with by Henry, to Ireland. There Warbeck failed to capture Waterford, therefore he made up his mind to go to Scotland. James IV received him kindly and in 1496 a Scottish force invaded England. It was a small force and it rapidly withdrew. Warbeck left Scotland for Ireland in 1497, but Kildare was very cautious and Warbeck made up his mind to try his luck in Cornwall, where there had been trouble over taxation for the military expedition against the Scottish invasion. In Cornwall Warbeck met with strong resistance and slunk away to sanctuary at Beaulieu, where in 1497 he surrendered himself to Henry. Henry was always averse from making unnecessary martyrs, therefore he

contented himself with keeping Warbeck in honourable confinement.   In 1498 Warbeck tried to escape, was captured and
was imprisoned more severely.   In 1499 he tried again to
escape.   It is possible that Henry was a party to this escape,
because he wanted to deal with the real menace, the Earl of
Warwick.   Anyway, Warbeck did not escape and was hanged,
and the Earl of Warwick was executed.

Gairdner, appendix to *Richard III*, 1898.

T.S.I.H., vol. 2, pp. 7–11.

EMPSON, SIR RICHARD, financial statesman and lawyer,
was said by Bacon to be the 'son of a sieve-maker'. In fact, he
was the son of a well-to-do citizen of Towcester, but like his
partner later in administration, Edmund Dudley, belonged
to the rising middle class.   He was educated for the Bar
and became well known as a lawyer.   He was M.P. for
Northamptonshire in the 1491 Parliament and was elected
Speaker on the nomination of Henry VII.   But as early as 1485
he was a financial agent for the Crown and was hand in glove
with Dudley in the administration of the Crown's financial
policy.   He was arrested and with Dudley was accused of
treason and was executed on August 17th, 1510.

DUDLEY, EDMUND, financial statesman and lawyer, was
born probably in 1462 and he died on the block in 1510.
Bacon says that he was 'of a good family', being descended from
the mediaeval and baronial family of Sutton, but he was not a
member of the nobility.   Trained as a lawyer, he attracted the
notice of Henry VII by his legal knowledge.   True to his policy
of excluding from the Government the old nobility, Henry
employed the rising middle class.   Dudley was a Privy Councillor at the age of 23.   By 1497 he was entirely in the confidence
of the king.   In the sixteenth century the Speaker of the House
of Commons was the king's representative in the House, there
to run the Government's business and to look after the interests
of the Crown.   In 1504, on Henry's nomination, Dudley was
elected Speaker.

It was necessary for Henry to increase his revenue and therefore he established an agency to ascertain outstanding and con-

cealed sources of revenue. Dudley, helped by Sir Richard Empson, carried out this work. Men who had committed breaches of the law, incurred debts or failed to carry out certain duties were fined. Instead of paying the full amount straight-away, they entered into recognizances to pay, and many took a long time to clear themselves. In the meantime, taxes and feu-dal dues were ruthlessly collected, wherever possible. What made these two men so unpopular was that not only were they strenuously enforcing this policy, but they were lining their own nests very comfortably.* This policy was also an important method of keeping down the over-mighty subject. By the time Henry died in 1509 Empson and Dudley had amassed for the king between one and two million pounds.

When Henry VIII came to the throne, it was a swift and easy step to popularity to have these 'two ravening wolves', or 'caterpillars' of the Commonwealth (Naunton), arrested. Dudley was arraigned on a charge of treason for having sum-moned his friends to arms while the old king lay dying—a perfectly sensible precaution by a much hated man who saw himself bereft of his only protector, but one which was twisted into an attempt on the dying king's life. Dudley was attainted by Parliament and executed on August 18th, 1510. While he was in prison he wrote a book, *The Tree of Commonwealth*, in favour of absolute monarchy, in which it looks as if he was planning an attack on the property of the Church. He was the father of John Dudley, Duke of Northumberland.

Elton, *England under the Tudors*, ch. 3, for the financial system, 1955.
Hurstfield: *The Queen's Wards*, 1958.
Dudley, *The Tree of Commonwealth*, ed. by D. M. Brodie, C.U.P., 1948.
D. M. Brodie, *R.H.S. Transactions*, 4th Series, Vol. XV, 1932.

HENRY VIII, king of England 1509–47, was born at Greenwich on June 28th, 1491: he died at Westminster at midnight on January 28th, 1547, in his fifty-sixth year. He was the second son of Henry VII and Elizabeth of York.

* This accusation is denied by D. M. Brodie in her article on Dudley in R.M.S. Transactions of Series Vol. XV 1932.

Like all the Tudors he was given an excellent education, and like all the Tudors he made the most of it. Lord Herbert of Cherbury in his *Life of Henry VIII* records that 'his education was accurate, being destined (as a credible author affirms) to the Archbishopric of Canterbury, during the life of his elder brother Prince Arthur; that prudent king his father choosing this as the most cheap and glorious way for bestowing of a younger son', but he does not cite the authority for this improbable statement. All the same, Henry proved himself more than once a far from contemptible theologian: he could speak French, Italian and Spanish, and he was, of course, proficient in Latin. His book against Luther (1521) was almost wholly his own work. He was also passionately devoted to music, and the Venetian ambassadors have left it on record that he practised the lute, organ and harpsichord (probably the virginals) 'day and night'. He also, according to these Italians, 'acquitted himself divinely' as a dancer. Physically he was above average height, enormously strong and of great courage. He excelled in all athletic sports: nobody outdid him in jousting: he drew the best long-bow of his age and he could defeat the tallest archers in his own guard. He was an accomplished player of tennis and he was a strenuous rider to hounds, able to tire out eight or ten horses in the course of a day's hunting, mounting one after the other as they were exhausted. He had a love for finery and display, he was generous (but sometimes mean-spirited), handsome, hot-tempered and the idol of the country. His morals were neither better nor worse than those of Charles V, infinitely better than those of Francis I, Charles II or Louis XIV (Pollard, p. 186). Such was the paragon who ascended the throne in 1509. The portrait was to change during the next thirty-eight years.

Henry VIII and the succession (see also under biographies of his wives). Every schoolboy knows that Henry had six wives, but the usual deduction that Henry was therefore a lascivious Bluebeard is wide of the historical truth, for it leaves out of account what for a hundred years was the nightmare for all the Tudors, the problem of the succession, the provision of a male heir to the throne. Everyone agreed that a woman on the throne was unthinkable. If the Princess Mary were to succeed, whom could she marry without bringing the realm in danger, danger from abroad, if she married a foreigner, danger from a second Wars of the Roses, if she married at home? By 1524 Catherine of Aragon, whom Henry married in 1509, was forty years old and it was clear that she would have no more children. She had borne Henry seven children, including four sons, but only Mary survived. Henry began to search for other means to provide a male heir. In 1525 he brought out of retirement his illegitimate son, Henry Fitzroy, and showered honours on him, probably with a view to nominating him as his heir. He even contemplated for a moment marrying him to Mary, half-sister to Fitzroy. But Henry himself was only thirty-four years old and he had fallen in love with Anne Boleyn. But it was essential that their children should be legitimate in order to provide an indisputably legal male heir to the throne. That his love for Anne was genuine is proved by the series of love letters which he wrote to her in his own hand. He married her in 1533. By 1536 she had given the king only one daughter, Elizabeth. In that year Catherine of Aragon died. Henry was already casting eyes on Jane Seymour. When Anne's second child was still-born (1536), the problem of the succession was no nearer a solution. The execution of Anne followed inevitably.

Jane Seymour gave Henry the son that he wanted (1537), but in doing so Jane herself died. The boy was delicate, and who could be sure that he would survive? Left to his own inclinations, it is possible that Henry would not have married again. But when in 1538 Thomas Cromwell wanted a Protestant alliance with Cleves, the king showed no liking for Cromwell's policy or for his proposal, but he reluctantly agreed. When Anne of Cleves arrived in England (1539), he showed even less liking for the lady and within six months the marriage was dissolved.

Meantime Bishop Gardiner had brought to court Catherine Howard, whom he intended to set up as a Catholic rival to the German Protestant queen, Anne of Cleves. Anne had helped in no way to solve the problem of the succession and

Plate 1

Henry VII

Plate 2

Margaret Beaufort, Countess of Richmond

Arthur, Prince of Wales

now Parliament petitioned Henry to marry again and thus to strengthen the line of succession. He married Catherine Howard (July 1540), but in November 1541, much to the sorrow of the king, the story of her many indiscretions and misdemeanours was revealed and she was executed, in February 1542, before she had borne any children to Henry.

In 1543 Henry married again and for the last time. His last wife was Catherine Parr, who survived him by less than two years. There were no children by this marriage.

Henry VIII and the Divorce. On June 11th, 1509, a few months after he succeeded to the throne, Henry married Catherine of Aragon. She had already been married to Henry's elder brother, Arthur, who died in 1502. This former marriage put Catherine within the forbidden degrees of relationship with Henry. The canon law was based on Leviticus, xx, 21, 'If a man shall take his brother's wife, it is an unclean thing . . . they shall be childless' (but see Elton, *England under the Tudors*, p. 98, n. 1). To get over this canonical prohibition a dispensation was sought and obtained from Pope Julius II. When by 1524 Catherine had given Henry no male heir, Henry began to meditate upon Leviticus xx. 21 and to doubt the validity of his marriage, for only one child had survived out of seven. This happened to coincide with Henry's falling in love with Anne Boleyn, but in fact from the very first doubts had been expressed on the validity of the marriage, even by Pope Julius himself. An egoist like Henry must always have his own way, he is not capable of listening to argument. For argument Henry substituted his conscience and his conscience was of the kind which always convinced him that what he wanted must be right. What Henry wanted was an undisputed male heir and Anne Boleyn: he could only obtain both by being rid of Catherine: hence the divorce was indispensable: Henry turned to Wolsey to obtain it for him. Wolsey was in a dilemma: if he got the divorce, he would put into power his arch-enemies, the anti-clerical Boleyns; if he failed to get the divorce, Henry would rid himself of Wolsey, and might break with Rome.

c—(2)

On May 17th, 1527, Wolsey collusively summoned Henry before him to explain why he had married his brother's widow. On the 31st Henry told Catherine that they were living in sin and must separate. He then set about trying to convince the clergy, but Fisher, Bishop of Rochester, would have none of it, although most of the clergy professed themselves to be convinced. Suddenly the news came that Charles V's troops had sacked Rome and Pope Clement VII was a prisoner in the hands of Catherine's nephew. For two years the question of the divorce came to depend on foreign policy and on the success or failure of the French armies against Charles V. In 1528 the French king, Francis I, was having it all his own way and the Pope felt sufficiently independent of Charles to send Campeggio to England to try the case with Wolsey and to pronounce sentence. The two Cardinals opened their court on May 31st, 1529. Three weeks later, before any decision could be arrived at, Charles had destroyed the French army at Landriano (June 21st), Clement and Charles made peace at Barcelona (June 29th) and Charles and Francis at Cambrai (August 5th). Campeggio adjourned the court to October 1st. It never met again. Clement revoked the case to Rome. The fall of Wolsey followed inevitably.

Having failed to obtain the divorce by cooperating with Rome, Henry now made up his mind to put pressure on Rome. In November he called Parliament in order to use its anti-clericalism to force the Pope's hand. He intended also to subject the Church completely to his own authority. He began to take the opinions of the universities of Europe on the question of the divorce, a suggestion first made by Cranmer (August 1529). He followed this up by threatening to call a General Council. His policy was a failure, yet throughout 1530 and 1531 Henry continued to try to obtain Papal sanction for the divorce and Papal approval for his marriage to Anne Boleyn.

Between 1532 and 1534 a series of measures was passed which brought about the Reformation in England and the breach with Rome. On January 25th, 1533, Henry secretly married Anne Boleyn. The Act of Appeals (March 1533) forbade any appeals from the Archbishops' courts to Rome in cases involving wills or marriages. The divorce could now be legally settled in England. In the previous January Cranmer had been appointed Archbishop of Canterbury. He opened his court on May 10th, 1533, and on the 23rd he declared Henry's marriage with Catherine void and his marriage with Anne valid. On June 1st Anne was crowned and on September 7th her daughter Elizabeth was born. On March 23rd, 1534, the Pope at long last declared in favour of Catherine, but it was too late for any effect in England. Henry had outfaced Pope and Emperor, he had got his own way, but he was no nearer solving the problem of a male heir.

Henry VIII, the Royal Supremacy and the Reformation: the divorce was not the real cause of the Reformation in England, but it was the match which fired the powder. The word Reformation in Henry VIII's reign covers the abolition of some abuses in the Church, the transferring of the government of the Church from the authority of Rome into the hands of King and Parliament, transferring ecclesiastical property to the Crown, and severing all political and financial relations between the Church in England and the Papacy. Henry did not challenge religious doctrine.

There was much anti-clericalism among the laity, as had been shown in 1515 by the cases of Hunne and Standish. Henry determined to use this anti-clericalism to strengthen his own position at the expense of the Church and to secure Papal consent to the divorce.

As soon as Parliament met in 1529 the attack on the Church was launched in a group of acts which at the same time reformed some of the abuses in the Church. The Probate and Mortuaries Act limited the charges which the clergy could make in administering wills and the size of mortuary fees (1529). The Pluralities Act (1529) dealt with the evil of holding more than one benefice at the same time. A further act greatly reduced the evils of sanctuary and of benefit of clergy (1531).

The attack was also made on a wider front. Wolsey had been brought low by using against him the old statute of Praemunire (1393) which forbad the introduction into

England of any papal letters, excommunications or anything which affected the position of the King or his realm. This act was now (1530) turned against the whole of the clergy for having recognized Wolsey's legatine authority—which the King himself had recognized. The clergy surrendered at once, rather than lose its corporate property. The province of Canterbury bought its pardon for £100,000, York for close on £19,000. They were also compelled to recognize Henry as 'singular protector, only and supreme lord, and as far as the law of Christ allows even supreme head' of the Church (1531). 'Infinite clamours' continued in Parliament against the Church and in 1532 the Commons presented to Henry *The Commons' Supplication against the Ordinaries*, which complained of the Church's right to independent legislation and of many abuses in the ecclesiastical courts. Henry sent the petition on to Convocation, the clergy appealed to him for protection against the laity, and Henry thus became the mediator between the two sides. He demanded from the clergy their assent to the reform of ecclesiastical law, the surrender of the right to make laws independently of Parliament and their recognition that all existing canons must be approved by the Crown. The clergy again surrendered in what is known as the 'Submission of the Clergy', and in doing so the Church accepted the King in place of the Pope as its supreme legislator (1532). This submission was embodied in an act (1534) by which the clergy also lost the right of finally deciding ecclesiastical cases in the archiepiscopal courts: appeals were now allowed from those courts to the King in Chancery. In the same year (1534) the Act of Supremacy legalized all Henry's claims, laid down that the King 'is and ought to be Supreme Head of the Church of England', and gave him power to carry out visitations, which until now had been within the competence of the Church. The way to the dissolution of the monasteries was now clear.

In the meantime the direct attack upon the Papacy had been opened. In 1532 an act was made forbidding the payment to Rome of annates, the first year's full profits when a man was appointed to an ecclesiastical office. Henry postponed enforcing the act for a year—a hint to the Pope what he might expect, if he did not grant the divorce. The Pope ignored the hint and the act was enforced in 1533. By another act the Pope was deprived of Peter's Pence (1533). The Act in Restraint of Appeals (1533) laid down that in future all cases dealing with wills, marriages, tithes and similar 'spiritual' cases were to be settled in England and were not to go to Rome. This meant that the divorce could now be legally settled in England and need no longer wait upon the Pope's pleasure. This also meant that the supply line for finance from England to Rome was irreparably cut. The Act further laid down in clear cut terms that 'this realm of England is an empire... governed by one Supreme Head and King'. The Royal Supremacy was now legally and indisputably established. The Papal authority in England was wholly eliminated.

Pollard, *Henry VIII*. 1919.
H. Maynard Smith, *Henry VIII and the Reformation*. 1948.
G. R. Elton, *Henry VIII*, H.A. pamphlet GS51, 1962.

Henry VIII and the Church of England: after the breach with Rome the Catholic Church *in* England became the Church *of* England, the Royal Supremacy replaced the Papacy, Henry replaced the Pope—but he never claimed priestly or spiritual powers, he never claimed the right to celebrate the Mass nor to ordain priests. Short of this Henry was supreme: he controlled legislation and administration, he defined doctrine and he regulated ritual. For the time being at any rate he relied on Convocation, not Parliament, to carry out his ecclesiastical policy in matters spiritual. His purpose was to establish the spiritual independence of the Church of England from Rome. Henry had in 1521 attacked Luther and defended the Catholic Church in his book *Assertio Septem Sacramentorum*, for which he had received from the Pope Leo X the title of *Fidei Defensor*. He was no more inclined in 1536 to accept Lutheran doctrine, but he was perfectly ready to define the doctrine of the Church of England, a need which the Pilgrimage of Grace was to underline.

In July 1536 there appeared the *Ten Articles*, which were so

orthodox that even Reginald Pole could find nothing objection-
able in them. As a compromise they satisfied nobody. Henry
was cited to appear before a General Council in 1537. His
reply was to compel Convocation to declare that no General
Council could be convened without the consent of all Christian
princes—an early example of the use of the veto as we have seen
it in the United Nations. In August 1536 Cromwell issued the
Injunctions enforcing the *Ten Articles* and instructing the clergy
to place a Bible in Latin and English in every parish church.

The Pilgrimage of Grace (1536) persuaded Henry that a
clearer and even more conservative definition of doctrine was
required. In 1537 there was issued *The Institution of a Christian
Man*, commonly known as *The Bishops' Book*. Henry strongly
disapproved of it and filled the copy sent to him with criticisms,
but he allowed it to be published in 1538. There was nothing in
it of which a good Catholic then or now could disapprove. Thus
it failed to please the reforming party and by the mere fact that
it was new it disturbed the ordinary Englishman. (See Maynard Smith, *Henry VIII and the Reformation*, pp. 158–64, 365–70.)

Henry's position may be stated thus: he was in complete
control of the Church, but he preferred to go cautiously. He
would not acknowledge the Pope, he accepted a few minor
reforms, such as the use of an English Bible, but he stuck to the
orthodox doctrines of the Catholic Church. He greatly wanted
religious unity throughout the country and he tried to achieve
it all through his reign. When in 1539 the Statute of Six
Articles, which was very conservative, met with opposition
in the House of Lords from Cranmer and others, Henry went
down in person and 'confounded them all with God's learning'.
This 'whip with six strings' laid down severe penalties—death
was the penalty for denying transubstantiation—but these
were removed in 1540. There were various persecutions and
executions of both Catholics and Protestants during the last
years of his reign, but Henry was more concerned to create
unity than to exact punishments. He came to think that
unrestricted reading of the Bible was dangerous and in 1543
an Act was passed condemning all 'craftye false and untrue'
translations of the Bible, including that by Tyndale, and the

reading of the Bible in the approved version was much restricted. On May 29th, 1543, was published *The Necessary Doctrine and Erudition of Any Christian Man*, commonly known as *The King's Book*, a very conservative description of orthodox views, except on the Papacy.

Henry was no bigot. In 1543 he married Catherine Parr who had Protestant tendencies, and he unswervingly supported his Archbishop, Cranmer, who was much more 'modern' in his theology than the King. Three times, in 1543, 1544 and 1545, Henry by his personal intervention saved Cranmer from charges of heresy. And it was Henry who ordered an English Litany and who accepted from Cranmer what is still our own Litany (1544).

Henry had none of the rock-like faith of his first wife, Catherine of Aragon, nor of his first daughter, Mary, but he had a conventional affection for the Catholic Church in which he had been brought up. In days when religion and politics were very much the same thing Henry had also a highly developed flair for politics. It was the combination of flair and affection which enabled him to carry through the English Reformation without the civil wars and the destruction which religious change brought upon other countries.

Maynard Smith, *Henry VIII and the Reformation*, 1948.
Mackie, *The Earlier Tudors*, 1952.
E. G. Rupp, *The English Protestant Tradition*, 1945.
L. B. Smith, *Tudor Prelates and Politics*, 1953.

Henry VIII and Wales. On the death of Rhys ap Thomas in 1525 he was succeeded by his grandson, Rhys ap Gruffydd, but he was not given any of the offices held by Thomas. Walter Devereux, Lord Ferrers of Chartley, was appointed Chief Justice and Chamberlain of South Wales. The two men soon quarrelled and Rhys ap Gruffydd was arrested in 1530 and executed the next year. The President of the Council in the Marches was Voysey, bishop of Exeter, but he was an ineffective ruler and it became clear that an entirely new policy was necessary for Wales, where law and order had ceased to exist. It was also necessary to secure Welsh support for the revolution in church and state which had been carried out between 1529 and 1536 in the Reformation Parliament. It was Thomas Cromwell who recognized that action in Wales was essential. In 1534 Voysey was succeeded by Rowland Lee who was sent to Wales in order to restore good government. A series of acts was passed to re-establish order: one aimed at preventing felons from crossing the Severn to, or from, South Wales and the Forest of Dean; another inflicted a year's imprisonment on any person who assaulted those who tried to arrest him; a third act tried to ensure that jurors would convict guilty defendants; a fourth prohibited the carrying of arms when attending Courts and gave full power to officers of an English shire to arrest and indict any person who was accused of murder or felony in a neighbouring Marcher lordship. The general authority of the Lord Marchers was still recognized, but in 1535 an act was made to bring the administration of the Welsh shires into line with that of the English shires. It also entrusted local government to Welshmen, of which Rowland Lee did not approve. In 1536 the Act of Union was passed by which Welshmen became citizens of the new kingdom of England and Wales, English methods of law and administration were extended to Wales and the English system of shires and hundreds became the basis of local government. Wales was represented in Parliament and English became the official language. Monmouthshire became an English shire. The many adjustments made in the following half dozen years were summed up in detail in the act of 1543 which completely assimilated Wales to England. If Tudor policy was antagonistic to Welsh nationalism, it did at least provide the Welsh with security, law and order.

J. F. Rees, *Tudor Policy in Wales*, 1935.
W. Rees, *An Historical Atlas of Wales*, 1951.

Henry VIII and the Navy. Henry VII had been concerned mainly with securing his dynasty at home and in avoiding foreign entanglements, and therefore no great fleets were necessary for him. With the accession of his son, policy was changed and Henry VIII wanted to play a leading part in foreign affairs: therefore a change in naval policy was necessary. Francis I adopted an aggressive naval policy by moving his fleets from the Mediterranean to the Channel and by beginning to build more ships. The union of Brittany with the French crown gave France Channel ports and a race of seamen. The union of Spain, the Netherlands and the Empire under Charles V created a danger to England from Spanish ships, and the existence of a Scottish navy to back the Franco-Scottish alliance was a further threat to England. It was obviously sound policy for Henry to strengthen his fleet, and Henry had much personal interest in ships and in sailing.

Henry VIII inherited from his father 7 ships. By the end of 1512, in 3½ years, 17 new vessels had been added to the navy either by construction or by purchase. By 1546 the navy numbered 85 vessels (excluding 13 row-barges), of which Henry had built 46, purchased 26 and obtained 13 as naval prizes. At his death in 1547 the navy consisted of 53 ships with a total tonnage of 11,268, carrying 7,780 men and 2,087 guns. The best-known ship is the *Henry Grace à Dieu*.

Henry's achievement was considerable. He built the largest and most powerful navy in the world, he revolutionized its armament—the moment is marked when the curtall, a heavy gun of 3,000 lbs., hitherto used only as a siege-piece on land, was transferred to ships: the *Sovereign* was rebuilt in 1509 and given four. He improved its fighting and sailing qualities and he himself invented or adapted a type of ship suitable for the narrow seas. He enlarged the existing dockyard at Portsmouth and made two new ones at Woolwich and Deptford, and he also built forts for the defence of the coast. Henry may well be called the founder of the Royal Navy.

M. Oppenheim, *The Administration of the Royal Navy*, 1896, 1948.
M. Lewis, *The Navy of Britain*, 1948.

Henry VIII and the coinage: the sixteenth century saw a revolution in the price-level and this made the existing methods of public finance totally inadequate to meet the needs of government. Like their colleagues all over Europe, Tudor financiers were faced with inflation on a very large scale, the result first of all of the increased silver mining in Austria, and from the 1540s of the growing flood of silver from the Spanish New World.

In 1526 Henry VIII and Wolsey *devalued* the coinage—*i.e.* they increased the amount of money in circulation by reducing the weight of the silver coins. This was a sensible and reputable operation, because all it did was to bring the English coinage into a proper relationship with the continental coins.

In 1542, when Henry was virtually his own minister in every sphere, in order to meet his financial difficulties, which arose from his wars and other extravagances, he embarked on a policy which he kept up until his death in 1547, of *debasing* the coinage—*i.e.* he put more alloy into each silver coin, thereby altering the weight and adulterating the fineness of the silver coinage (the proportion of metal to alloy) to such a degree that he reduced the value of the silver coin to one sixth of what it had been in the time of Henry VII. The silver thus left over could be recoined at an enormous profit—about £500,000. This of course only increased inflation and drove up prices. Henry thus left severe economic problems to his successors, but it should in fairness be added that there was in his day no science of taxation and Parliament would not vote enough money to cover the needs of modern government when the value of money was falling.

It is difficult to recommend further reading on economic subjects when knowledge is changing every day. It is safe to recommend:

F. C. Dietz, *English Government Finance*, if it is remembered that some of his statistics are faulty.

G. N. Clark, *The Wealth of England* (1946), as an introduction of great value.

Henry VIII: summary. No other English king is better known or more quickly recognized in his portraits than Henry VIII. The gigantic figure with the broad shoulders, no doubt a little exaggerated by the fashion in dress at the time, the feathered cap set slightly atilt, the strong legs set wide apart, planted firmly, even arrogantly, on the ground, the

general air of commanding self-confidence, make Henry VIII
easily identifiable and give an immediate key to his character.
This is indeed a regal figure. A closer inspection, especially
in the later portraits, raises some doubts: that small and narrow
mouth, those pigmy eyes suggest meanness and even cruelty.
Henry was as much a Renaissance prince as was ever Francis I
or Lorenzo Il Magnifico. He could be affable, affectionate, as
he was at one time to Sir Thomas More; generous, as he was to
Reginald Pole before their quarrel or to Wolsey after his fall,
and always to Cranmer. He was highly intelligent and highly
talented; he loved books and games, pictures and music, fine
clothes and rich jewellery, as his portraits prove. He could also
be completely selfish, mean and treacherous, as he was to
Robert Aske and the rebels in the Pilgrimage of Grace: ruthless, as he was to the clergy in 1530; relentless, as he was to
Sir Thomas More and John Fisher in 1535, although it is fair
to add that there is some evidence that he disliked and regretted
the execution. If Henry is to be judged by the constancy of
morals, his character will not stand up to much cross-examina-
tion. If he is to be judged by the standards of his own times,
he must be recognized as a great and to a large extent a
successful king. The splendid young man who came to the
throne in 1509, by 1547 had become a revolting, swollen mass
of putrifying flesh, too heavy for his legs to bear and suffering
agonies from an ulcerous leg as he was wheeled in a chair from
place to place. Yet he was still (and even more so) his old self,
arrogant, self-centred, merciless, still full of affection for his last
wife, still popular with his people, even while they dreaded him.

As a statesman Henry must rank high. Not much has been
said in this biography about his foreign policy, which cannot
be simplified successfully for brief treatment. Too often his
foreign policy was vitiated by his natural bellicosity and by
his desire to play a leading and active part on the Continent.
This is especially true of his warlike policy in the last decade
of his reign and of his most unwise treatment of Scotland
(Mackie, *Henry VIII and Scotland*, R.H.S. Trans., 1947). But he
lived in dangerous times and by his realism, his capacity
for seeing things as they really were, by his invincible

courage and by his genius for ruling, he triumphantly rode out every storm and kept his kingdom free from foreign invasion and from the civil wars which beset continental countries.

At home Henry showed greater judgment. Nothing is more remarkable than the way in which he made Parliament into his ally. It is difficult to say now how far Parliament was 'packed'. What is certain is that Henry knew exactly how to 'manage' the House of Commons, both through the Lords and through the able servants of the Crown who sat in the Lower House. He had an uncanny understanding of the feelings of the Commons, so that the relations between the Crown and Parliament were on the whole very satisfactory. Always Henry remained the supreme authority and to him Parliament was only a support for the Royal Supremacy, but that did not prevent him from declaring that 'WE be informed by our judges that we at no time stand so highly in our estate royal as in the time of parliament'. His daughter Elizabeth inherited her father's wisdom and popularity: the Stuart kings never understood this Tudor alliance betwixt Crown and Parliament (Mackie, *The Earlier Tudors*, 441–3).

Henry left many problems to his successor—religious, economic and social, but his achievements were outstanding and invaluable. He made the English people aware of themselves: he gave them the English Bible: he built and manned for them the finest navy in the world: he implanted in them a respect for government and an affection for the Crown as head of that government: he guided a great politico-religious revolution along conservative lines so that for the most part he carried the nation with him—as Somerset and Northumberland in the next reign failed to do. He had none of the spiritual strength which marks out Sir Thomas More in glaring contrast, but in an age when material dangers threatened even the survival of the state, and when only strong government could have provided salvation, Henry provided what was needed courageously, ruthlessly and effectively.   (*Plate 3*)

G. R. Elton, *Henry VIII*, H.A. pamphlet GS 51.
Pollard, *Henry VIII*. 1919.

C. Morris, *The Tudors*. 1955.
R. Sutcliffe, *The Armourer's House*, O.U.P., 1951. (H.N., *Henry VIII's London*.)

CATHERINE OF ARAGON, first wife of Henry VIII, was born in 1485, the youngest child of Ferdinand of Aragon and Isabella of Castile, and she died in 1536, aged 51. Spain was the rising country in Europe: in search of powerful allies, Henry VII sought a marriage alliance with one of the Spanish royal family. In 1489 at the treaty of Medina del Campo Arthur, Prince of Wales, (aged 3), was betrothed to Catherine (aged 4). Not until 1501 did Catherine arrive in England and see Arthur. The marriage took place at St. Paul's on November 14th, 1501. Arthur was now 14, his wife nearly 16. They went to live together in Wales, but they were thought to be too young for cohabitation. On April 2nd, 1502, Arthur died: the marriage had never been consummated. At the age of 16 Catherine was a widow and remained so for the next seven years. Those seven years were a foretaste of what was to come later on.

Henry VII refused to allow her to return to Spain and negotiations were at once begun to marry her to his second son, Henry, in 1503. Before the plan was completed, Henry's wife died and he suggested that he should marry his daughter-in-law. This may have been merely a move in the diplomatic game; if so, it was successful. Isabella was so shocked that the marriage with Prince Henry was agreed to quickly. It was not to take place until he had reached his fourteenth birthday, which would be in 1505. So valuable a pawn did Henry VII find an unmarried Catherine in the business of international diplomacy that he refused to allow the marriage to take place, and it was not till after his death and Henry VIII's accession that the wedding took place (1509). For seven years Catherine's father left his daughter in England penniless and in debt, while Henry VII refused to finance her. She was wretchedly attended, scarcely ever allowed to see her future husband, and falling ever deeper into debt. During these years she shewed herself to be a diplomat of a very high order, all the time working to maintain the Anglo-Spanish alliance with a shrewdness and skill not belonging to the official Spanish ambassadors. On June 11th, 1509, she and Henry VIII were married, and both were crowned on the 24th.

From 1509 to about 1525 Henry and Catherine led a happily married life. The king was not always faithful, but she was a devoted and wise wife, who could shut her eyes to momentary lapses, while Henry treated her with affection and courtesy.

But in the sixteenth century a queen was expected to provide male heirs to the throne. Between 1510 and 1518 Catherine bore six children, of whom only one survived, a girl, the Princess Mary. These disappointments may have weakened Henry's affection: the perfidious behaviour of his father-in-law, Ferdinand, weakened his desire for a Spanish alliance: his conscience began to wonder why the children died: a male heir to the throne was a necessity: incidentally, also, Henry had become infatuated with Anne Boleyn. For five more years, from 1526 to 1531 Henry and Catherine remained together on friendly, but deteriorating, terms. On July 14th, 1531, Henry slipped away from Windsor without saying goodbye and never saw Catherine again. From that moment her life became more and more wretched. She was commanded to abandon the use of the word queen, she refused. Continual pressure was brought to bear on her to acknowledge that her marriage with Henry had been illegal from the start, she refused. She was assailed to accept the Act of Supremacy and to take the oath, she refused. She was moved from house to house, her daughter was forbidden to visit her. Her household was whittled away, her income reduced, even at last the curtains were taken down, the beds dismantled, the furniture removed, until she lived virtually in one room. And all the time she was in deadly fear of poison. She could get no help from her nephew, Charles V, the Emperor. For five years she warned the Pope that unless he pronounced in her favour on the question of marriage, the English church would break from Rome. Clement VII took no notice. At last on March 23rd, 1534, he gave his verdict that the marriage was valid. It was too late. Anne Boleyn had been declared queen by Parliament and the breach with Rome was complete.

Catherine was a woman of great intellectual ability. She was a strong supporter of the New Learning and of the Classical Revival—Erasmus found her scholarship more impressive than Henry VIII's. She was a shrewd diplomatist and a most formidable debater—as Henry VIII found to his cost. But she was much more than that—she was a heroine. In all her later troubles she had only one friend, Chapuys, the Imperial ambassador. She relied on him and he did all he could for her. But she relied on her religious faith much more. She never deviated from the line she adopted at the start. She declared she was Henry's legal wife and always had been, and she would never admit she was not. She was Henry's loving wife and she seems to have retained some affection for him even to the end. In her last letter to him she said, 'Lastly, I make this vow, that mine eyes desire you above all things'. She was Henry's loyal subject, she would obey him in everything, except that she would not disobey God and her conscience. Thomas Cromwell said of her that 'Nature wronged the Queen in not making her a man. But for her sex she would have surpassed all the heroes of history'. The people of England loved her and demonstrated their affection on every possible occasion.

Catherine died on January 7th, 1536. Polydore Vergil records that her last letter (quoted above) brought tears to the eyes of Henry VIII. Chapuys—admittedly a hostile witness—records that the king, dressed from top to toe in yellow with a white feather in his cap, gave a ball at Greenwich and went about among the revellers with the Princess Elizabeth in his arms, crying out, 'God be praised, the old harridan is dead'.

G. Mattingley, *Catherine of Aragon*, 1942.   (*Plate 4*)

ANNE BOLEYN, second wife of Henry VIII and mother of Elizabeth I, was born in 1507 and died on the scaffold on Friday, May 19th, 1536, in her twenty-ninth year. She was the second daughter of Sir Thomas Boleyn, afterwards Earl of Wiltshire and Ormond. Some of her early years were spent in France, but by 1522 she was home and living at the Court of Henry VIII. She had many admirers, although she seems not to have been very beautiful and had an incipient sixth finger on her left hand, which led her enemies to talk of her as a witch. She was on the point of marrying Lord Henry Percy, heir to the earldom of Northumberland, but by the king's command Wolsey put an end to this proposed marriage. It is not known for certain at what point Henry fell in love with Anne. It was not until 1527 that he began seriously to contemplate divorcing his wife, Catherine of Aragon. By that time Anne was living at Greenwich with the king, and by 1531 she was openly going about with him, to the fury and detestation of the English people. At Easter 1533 it became known that Henry and Anne had been married on January 25th. Anne had already for some months been pregnant. It was vital to all Henry's hopes for a male successor to the throne that the child should be legitimate, therefore Archbishop Cranmer pronounced the marriage with Catherine of Aragon to be null and void and that Anne was the king's lawful wife. But already Henry's passion was cooling: and he was complaining of her arrogant behaviour. On September 7th, 1533, Anne gave birth to a daughter, the future Elizabeth I. The king's disappointment was tremendous. Probably by 1534 he was in love with Jane Seymour. On January 7th, 1536, Catherine of Aragon died. Only one thing could have saved Anne—the birth of a male heir. On January 29th she was delivered of a son: it was still-born. On May 2nd she was arrested, and on May 19th, 1536, she was executed on charges of adultery which have never been satisfactorily proved to be true. Decapitation by a sword was a method of execution customary in France but unknown in England, therefore an executioner had to be brought over from St. Omer.* Anne spent the last night before her execution in the same room in the Tower as she had occupied the night before her coronation.

The only life of Anne Boleyn is in two volumes by P. Freidmann, published in 1884. (*Plate 4*)

JANE SEYMOUR, Henry VIII's third wife, was born probably in 1509 and died on October 24th, 1537, aged about 28. She was the eldest of eight children born to Sir John Seymour

* Mackie p. 379 gives Calais.

Plate 3

Henry VIII

Plate 4

Anne Boleyn

Jane Seymour

Catherine of Aragon

Anne of Cleves

Catherine Howard

of Wolf Hall, Savernake, Wiltshire, and his wife, Margaret, daughter of Sir John Wentworth, who claimed distant relationship with the royal family. She was the brother of Edward Seymour, later Duke of Somerset and Protector in the reign of Jane's son, Edward VI, and of Sir Thomas Seymour, Lord High Admiral, who was executed in 1549 by the reluctant command of his brother.

Little is known for certain of Jane's life, especially of her early life. Before Catherine of Aragon ceased to be queen, she was one of her ladies-in-waiting, and after Anne Boleyn married Henry VIII, she was in the service of the new queen. Probably it was in 1534 that Henry fell in love with her, and from that moment he paid much attention to her, to the fury of Anne Boleyn. Jane behaved with the greatest discretion and propriety, refusing all the king's advances until he was able to marry her. While the trial of Anne was pending, Jane lived with her brother and his wife and Henry undertook to see her only in the presence of her friends. Two days before Anne's execution Cranmer declared his marriage with Anne null and void and on the day of execution (May 19th) he issued a dispensation for Henry to marry Jane without publication of banns. They were married on May 30th, 1536.

Her married life lasted a little more than a year. During that time she was able to reconcile Henry with his daughter, Mary, and to win golden opinions from all who came in contact with her. She seems to have had no sympathy with the Reformation: Luther called her 'an enemy of the gospel', Cardinal Pole declared that she was 'full of goodness'. It is said that during the Pilgrimage of Grace she pleaded with Henry to restore the monasteries, but that he warned her not to meddle in affairs of state, if she wanted to avoid Anne Boleyn's fate. On October 12th, 1537, she gave birth to a son, Edward, later Edward VI, but she herself died on October 24th.

Jane Seymour appears to have been the best loved of Henry's wives. He went into mourning for her, which he did for none of his other wives, and he ordered that his own body should be buried beside hers in St. George's Chapel, Windsor. Owing to her frail health she was never crowned queen.   (*Plate 4*)

D—(2)

ANNE OF CLEVES, Henry VIII's fourth wife, was the daughter of John, Duke of Cleves: she was born on September 22nd, 1515, and died on July 16th, 1557 aged 42. Plain, ungraceful, ill-educated, this unfortunate German woman appeared for a moment on the chess-board of European politics, a pawn in the foreign policy of Thomas Cromwell. In 1538 the Emperor Charles V and Francis I of France were drawing together, a league had been made against the Turks, and it looked to Pope Paul III and to Cardinal Pole as if the time was ripe for an attack on the king of England. Cleves, situated on the lower Rhine, was strategically a threat to the Emperor. The then Duke of Cleves, William, was not himself a Lutheran, but he was allied with Lutherans and was as much an Erastian as was Henry VIII. Cromwell, therefore, proposed a marriage between Henry and Duke William's sister, Anne. Politically there might be something to be said for the policy: but no one could have been less suitable to wed the English king than Anne, who could speak no language but her own, had no manners and could neither sing nor play any instrument. Henry was averse from the match from the first, but he was deluded by a flattering portrait of Anne painted by Holbein.

Anne arrived in England on December 27th, 1539. Henry took an immediate dislike to her; 'Is there no remedy, then,' said the king, 'but that I must needs put my neck in the yoke?' They were married on January 6th; in the morning Henry said to Cromwell, 'My lord, if it were not to satisfy the world and my realm, I would not do that which I must do this day for none earthly thing.' The marriage was soon seen to be unnecessary, for the French king and the Emperor were falling out once more. Cromwell's policy was utterly discredited, he was arrested and executed (June 1540). July 9th Convocation declared the marriage null and void. Anne was set aside and pensioned off with lands to the value of £3,000. She accepted her fate calmly and lived out the rest of her life quietly in England. If in private Henry called her the 'Flemish mare', in public he treated her with courtesy and consideration, and when she had to give up the title of queen, she was accorded that of the king's 'sister'.   (*Plate 4*)

CATHERINE HOWARD, fifth wife of Henry VIII, was the daughter of Lord Edmund Howard, victor at Flodden Field, himself a younger son of the second Duke of Norfolk. The date of her birth is unknown: she was executed on February 13th, 1542, possibly in her nineteenth year. Largely owing to the poverty of her father she had a bad upbringing and was much neglected as a child, and when her father married a second time, Catherine went to live with her grandmother, the old Duchess [Agnes] of Norfolk. Very soon the girl's irresponsible and volatile character revealed itself. She allowed a musician named Mannock (or Manox) to treat her with much familiarity, probably in 1536. A more serious affair occurred between her and Francis Dereham, who was related to Catherine. The two became engaged and called each other husband and wife, although the engagement was hidden from the outside world, According to the views of the times, such an engagement would invalidate any other marriage in the future. When Catherine went to Court, the intimacy between them was ended, and Dereham went off to Ireland. He returned before she married Henry VIII and heard that she was engaged to marry a cousin of hers, Thomas Culpepper, a report which Catherine denied to Dereham.

In 1540 Henry VIII married Anne of Cleves, but from the first sight of her he hated the marriage. There is little doubt that he was soon attracted by Catherine Howard, as little doubt that Bishop Gardiner hoped to set her up as a Catholic rival to the queen. On July 9th, 1540, Anne was set aside and on the 28th Henry married Catherine privately at Oatlands. In July, 1541, Henry and Catherine went on a progress to the north of England. They arrived at Pontefract in August and stayed there until the beginning of September. It was here that Catherine, with the help of Lady Rochford, had several meetings with Thomas Culpepper, and she also appointed Francis Dereham as her secretary. In November the royal party was back at Hampton Court.

On All Saints' Day the king gave thanks to God for the good life he led and hoped to lead with his new queen, 'after sundry troubles of mind which had happened to him by marriages'.

The next day Cranmer revealed to Henry the story of his queen's indiscretions. An investigation was ordered by the king, who was deeply unhappy at the news. The principal witness against Catherine was Dereham, who confessed to having often lain with her. Catherine herself denied all the charges until denial was no longer possible. Legally she had committed adultery by marrying Henry after her engagement to Dereham. No proof was forthcoming of adultery after her marriage to the king. Torture was employed to wring further evidence from Dereham and Culpepper: probably a charge of adultery was not provable, only assumable with some degree of certainty in the case of Culpepper, who denied it to the end. Lady Rochford was arrested and went out of her mind. Legal and constitutional considerations prolonged the proceedings. Ultimately a 'pitiful confession' was made by Catherine and she and Lady Rochford were executed on the same spot as had been Anne Boleyn.   (*Plate 4*)

Lacey Baldwin Smith, *A Tudor Tragedy*, 1961.

CATHERINE PARR, Henry VIII's sixth and last wife, was born in 1512 and died on September 7th, 1548, at the age of 36. She was the daughter of Sir Thomas Parr, controller of the household to Henry VIII. Her father died in 1517 and Catherine was brought up by her mother, who was 22 years old at the time of her husband's death. Her education was careful and thorough and she became an accomplished scholar in Greek and Latin and modern languages.

When she was 12 years old an offer of marriage was made for her for Lord Scrope's son, but the offer was declined as not fulfilling the conditions laid down in her father's will. At some unknown date later she married Edward Borough, of whom nothing is known. Her second husband was John Neville, Lord Latimer, who had already been twice married and had two children by his second wife. He took some part in the Pilgrimage of Grace, but he escaped punishment and was held in favour by the king. He died in 1542 or 1543 and Catherine was at once sought in marriage by Sir Thomas Seymour, brother of Jane Seymour. She intended to marry him, but she was 'overruled by a higher power', which was in fact Henry VIII, whom she married on July 12th, 1543. Catherine was physically a small woman, but she had character, spirit and much shrewdness, besides great kindness of heart. She managed Henry more successfully than any other of his wives: she persuaded him to restore to Mary and Elizabeth the rank of Princess, which had been taken away from them as being bastards: she interceded for the victims of the persecution under the Six Articles: and she took much interest in the education of Elizabeth and of Edward, her step-children. For three months in 1544, while Henry was abroad invading France, she was Regent of England.

Henry's temper in his last years was very unreliable, for he was irritated by religious dissensions and in constant pain from an ulcer on his leg. Catherine nursed him and sometimes discussed religious questions with him. Once she differed from him. 'A good hearing it is', Henry said, 'when women become such clerks; and a thing much to my comfort in mine old days to be taught by my wife.' It is said that a charge of heresy was brought against her and was signed by the king without her knowledge. But she got to know of it and fell ill with anxiety. Henry sent his doctors to her and also visited her himself. When she recovered she went to see the king and explained that she had only meant 'to minister talk' and not to assert opinions of her own. 'Is it so, sweetheart? Then are we perfect friends', said Henry. But the next day she was walking with him in the garden at Hampton Court when the Lord Chancellor arrived with forty of the King's Guards to arrest her. Henry took the Chancellor aside and all that Catherine could hear was 'knave! beast! and fool!' Catherine interceded for the Chancellor, if he had done anything wrong. 'Ah poor soul!' said Henry, 'thou little knowest, Kate, how ill he deserveth this at thy hands. On my word, sweetheart, he hath been to thee a very knave.'

Henry VIII died on January 28th, 1547. At once Sir Thomas Seymour, who had lately been created Baron Seymour of Sudeley, asked Catherine to marry him. Their engagement is certain and Seymour passed several nights with her at Chelsea.

Royal assent had not been yet asked for: when it was, the Protector was hostile to the marriage, but Edward VI in the end took Seymour's part and the Protector became reconciled to the event. On August 30th, 1548, Catherine gave birth to a girl, but she died on September 7th from puerperal fever. Catherine lies buried in the chapel at Sudeley Castle.

Jean Plaidy, *The Sixth Wife*, Hale, 1953. (H.N.)

MARY TUDOR, Queen of France, Duchess of Suffolk, grandmother of Lady Jane Grey, was born probably early in March 1496, and she died in 1533, aged approximately 35. She was the third daughter of Henry VII and Elizabeth of York, therefore sister of Henry VIII. In 1507 she was betrothed to Charles of Castile, afterwards the Emperor Charles V. In 1509 her father died and her brother succeeded as Henry VIII. In 1514 arrangements were all but completed for her marriage to Charles, but the Emperor Maximilian I, Charles's grandfather, played false and the marriage never took place.

Henry VIII was not the man to lie down under such an insult. Swiftly and secretly he made peace with France and compelled his sister, who was eighteen years old, to marry Louis XII of France, an enfeebled and sickly old man of fifty-two. Mary was much in love with Charles Brandon, Duke of Suffolk, and she only agreed to marry Louis XII on condition that, were he to die, she should be free to marry whom she would. Her marriage with the French king lasted only eight months, for Louis died on January 1st, 1515. Left alone in France, Mary was in a perilous position. To save herself from being compelled to make another political marriage either by Francis I or by Henry VIII, she persuaded Suffolk (who had pledged his word to Henry not to marry Mary without his consent) to marry her secretly in Paris, probably in the last week of February 1515. Henry was furious, not because he disliked the marriage, but because Suffolk had broken his word and the marriage was made without Henry's consent, and he was only placated by a present of £24,000 and 200,000 French crowns and all the plate, jewels and rich clothing which had formed part of Mary's dowry.

The marriage was generally unpopular in England and therefore the Duke and Duchess retired into private life in Norfolk. During a short visit to London in 1516 Mary gave birth to a son. A year later she entertained Catherine of Aragon on her way to Walsingham (March 1517). In July she was at court, thence she moved to Hatfield, where she stayed in order to have her second baby, Frances, who became the mother of Lady Jane Grey. The King's anger over the marriage was short-lived: he had a deep affection for his sister Mary, much more than he had for his other sister, Margaret, the Queen of Scotland, and Mary was frequently at court. Her health was never strong and she was from time to time seriously ill, but was able to meet her one-time affianced husband, Charles V, when he visited England in 1520; she was able also to accompany Henry VIII to the Field of Cloth of Gold, during which a treaty was made with Francis I which restored to her a great part of her dowry, so that her annual tribute to Henry VIII was halved.

When Henry entered on his divorce from Catherine of Aragon, Mary was strongly on the side of the Queen, largely because she could not tolerate seeing Anne Boleyn, once one of her ladies-in-waiting, raised to the position of Queen above herself, who had once been a Queen.

The rest of her life is historically unimportant. She died on June 24th, 1533, at Westhorpe in Suffolk and was buried in the abbey of Bury St. Edmunds. That monastery was dissolved in 1538 and the coffin was moved into St. Mary's church. It was opened in 1784 and Horace Walpole and the Duchess of Portland took away some locks of Mary's hair.

Mary Tudor was an exceptionally beautiful woman, not only physically but also in character. Her beauty of face was known throughout Europe: she never lost the deep feelings which Henry had for her: she won the hearts of all France by her devoted treatment of Louis XII. Her family life with Suffolk was one of untarnished happiness. Like all the Tudors she loved music and was an accomplished musician. She had a gay nature and a light step for dancing, she adored beautiful clothes and enjoyed to the full the fun and pageantry of the life into which she was born. She had also strength and courage to tell her formidable brother just how far he could go, and to fight for what she thought to be due to the meanest of her servants. No wonder that Mary Tudor has gone down in history and in modern literature as the most romantic of a hard-bitten family.

M. A. E. Green, *Lives of the Princesses of England*, vol. 5: an admirable essay.

M. C. Brown, *Mary Tudor, Queen of France*, 1911.

Beatrice White, *Royal Nonesuch*. (H.N.)   (*Plate 5*)

MARGARET TUDOR, Queen of Scotland, was the eldest daughter of Henry VII and Elizabeth of York. She was born on November 29th, 1489, and she died on October 18th, 1541, at the age of 52. She was two years older than Henry VIII. She was not so well educated as the rest of the Tudors, but she could write, though only what she called 'an evil hand', and she could play on the lute and the clavichord. In 1495 Henry VII tried to arrange a marriage for Margaret with James IV of Scotland, in the hopes of thus cutting off Scottish support for Perkin Warbeck. This attempt failed, but after long negotiations the marriage was finally arranged in 1502, the espousals took place in 1503. Margaret left England for Scotland on June 27th, 1503; she arrived at Edinburgh on August 7th and the marriage took place on the 8th. An amusing account of her journey northwards will be found in Leland, *Collectanea*, iv, 258 *sqq.*, written by John Young, Somerset Herald, who was a member of her train. A letter betraying much home-sickness which Margaret wrote to Henry VII is printed in M. A. E. Green's *Lives of the Princesses of England*, vol. iv, p. 100. That biography is thorough, scholarly and very interesting.

After her marriage to the Scottish king, Margaret ceases to play a major part in English history, but on the death of James IV at Flodden Field in 1513 Margaret became the Regent of Scotland and the rest of her life is bound up with the history of Scotland. It will be fully dealt with in a later volume of these biographies devoted to Scotland and Ireland.

FITZROY, HENRY, DUKE OF RICHMOND, was the natural son of Henry VIII by his mistress Elizabeth Blount, a lady-in-waiting to Catherine of Aragon. He was born in 1519 and died in 1536, aged 17. His birthplace was the manor of Blackmore in Essex 'reported to have been one of Henry VIII's Houses of Pleasure and disguised under the name of Jericho. So that when this lascivious Prince had a mind to be lost in the embraces of his courtesans, the cant word amongst the courtiers was, that he was gone to Jericho'. (Morant, *Hist. of Essex*, ii, 57.) He was given the best possible education under Richard Croke, a famous Greek scholar, and John Palsgrave, author of the first French grammar in the English language. The king's affection for him was deep and lasting, he called him 'my worldly jewel'. The boy showed great aptitude at his books and he was much 'inclined to all manner of virtuous and honourable inclinations as any babes living' (Palsgrave to Elizabeth Blount). He developed into a fine horseman and was also a good musician, like all the Tudors. He had beautiful handwriting in a clear Italian hand.

When he was six years old he suddenly blazed into the public notice. On June 15th, 1525, he was created Duke of Richmond —the title may be significant, for it was that held by Henry VII before he was king. He had already a week before been made a Knight of the Garter. Other offices were showered upon him, including that of Lord High Admiral. He became also Lord-Lieutenant of Ireland and Warden of the Cinque Ports, and it was thought that Henry intended to make him King of Ireland. All this at six years old. The favour shown to him and the magnificence of his household contrasted glaringly with the treatment meted out to the Princess Mary, who was three years older. Catherine of Aragon watched with anxiety, and she had reason, for undoubtedly already the king was seriously disturbed by his failure to obtain a male heir from Catherine. That he had it in mind to advance his son even to the throne is suggested by the fact that two years before the divorce is said to have occurred to Henry, he was considering with the council to entail the succession on his illegitimate son, Henry Fitzroy.

Several proposals were made for marrying Fitzroy to a foreign princess, but in 1533 he married Mary Howard, daughter of the third duke of Norfolk by his second marriage and the sister of the Earl of Surrey, the poet. He was present at the execution of Anne Boleyn in May 1536, but on July 22nd he died, not without rumours that he had been poisoned by Anne Boleyn and her brother, Lord Rochford. He lies buried in St. Michael's church, Framlingham.   (*Plate 7*)

J. G. Nichols, *Camden Misc.*, vol. 3, 1854.

WARHAM, WILLIAM, Archbishop of Canterbury, was born probably in 1450 and he died in 1532, at the age of 82. He came of a Hampshire family, he was educated at Winchester and at New College, Oxford, where he became a Fellow in 1475, a post which he held for thirteen years. He directed the school of Civil (Roman) Law in the university until he left Oxford in 1488 to practise as an advocate in London in the ecclesiastical Court of Arches. By 1490 he was one of the most considerable lawyers in the country, and in that year he travelled to Rome on business for the Bishop of Ely. In 1491 he was in Antwerp settling a dispute with the merchants of the Hanse: in 1493 he was again in Flanders, with Sir Edward Poynings, on an embassy to persuade the Dowager Duchess of Burgundy to abandon Perkin Warbeck. Although the mission failed, it is said that Warham's speech was an immense success. On September 21st, 1493, Warham was ordained as sub-deacon at the age of forty-five and he now received many preferments. In 1494 he was made Master of the Rolls, in 1496 he negotiated the marriage of Arthur, Prince of Wales, with Catherine of Aragon, and from now onwards he was used in many important diplomatic cases by Henry VII, who trusted him completely. In 1502 he was consecrated Bishop of London, and in 1504 he became Archbishop of Canterbury and Lord Chancellor. The year 1506 saw him Chancellor of Oxford, and two years later he set about reforming some of the abuses in the Court of Audience. In 1509 he crowned Henry VIII and Catherine of Aragon and was appointed by the Pope to present to Henry the Golden Rose.

The first part, the happiest and the most successful, of Warham's life was now finished. The accession of Henry VIII and the arrival of Wolsey marked the end of the Middle Ages in England. New men and new methods, new policies also, were now to destroy the position of trust which Warham had enjoyed under Henry VII. By the time Wolsey became a Cardinal in 1515 Warham's position both as a statesman and as Archbishop was growing increasingly difficult. In that year Warham resigned from the Chancellorship and he retired almost completely from the Council. For a while he still appeared on state occasions—in 1520 he was present at the Field of Cloth of Gold—but in ecclesiastical matters he represented an old and out-worn system. In 1512 he had quarrelled with Fox, Bishop of Winchester, over alleged encroachments by Canterbury on the jurisdictions of the suffragans. In 1523 he was to quarrel with the encroachments which Wolsey was making on the rights of Canterbury. And indeed Wolsey was totally ruthless and unreasonable. No doubt Warham was a stiff and upright man, who stood rigidly upon the old order, but Wolsey humiliated the Archbishop in every sort of way. After 1515 no cross was carried in front of the Archbishop, even in his own diocese. At the ceremony when Wolsey received his Cardinal's hat, Warham had to play a minor part, and the arrival of Campeggio further diminished his importance. It is difficult to say what were the real relations between Warham and Wolsey. In his letters Warham is always protesting how much he values Wolsey's kindnesses to him, but the language smacks strongly of the sycophantic style of the times. On the other hand, when Warham was once ill, Wolsey offered him quarters at Hampton Court.

There is no difficulty in judging the relations between Warham and the King. Once the divorce had been mooted and as soon as the Reformation Parliament met in 1529, Warham disliked most of Henry's policy. He declined to give a decision on the question of the validity of Henry's marriage: he was appointed one of the counsel for the Queen, but Catherine had the lowest opinion of Warham's efforts on her behalf. Warham watched the development of the attacks on the Church with consternation. It was he who suggested the addition to the title of Supreme Head of the Church in England of the words 'so far as the law of Christ allows'. The demand for the Submission of the Clergy (1532) was too much for Warham. Up to that point he had not proved himself a true defender of his Church: he had proposed and agreed to far too many damaging compromises. He was an old man now: he had shirked advising Catherine on the plea that *Ira principis mors est*. But now at the last moment he roused himself to make a valiant stand. He gave notice at his last appearance in the House of Lords that he would in the next session move the repeal of all the statutes passed against the Church since the beginning of that Parliament. Henry's answer was to serve Warham with a writ of *praemunire*. The archbishop saw clearly enough that the fate of Sir Thomas More now awaited him. Broken in health and too ill to leave his bed, he began to dictate the speech which he would make in the House of Lords. 'I intend to do only that I am bound to do by the laws of God and Holy Church and by mine order and by mine oath that I made at the time of my profession.' He refused to admit a royal claim which had brought about the martyrdom of Thomas Becket, 'which is the best death that can be . . . I think it better for me to suffer the same, than in my conscience to confess this article to be a praemunire for which St. Thomas died'. Warham was always a better speaker of words than doer of actions. It was merciful that he should have died before any action was needed, on August 23rd, 1532.

Erasmus, whom Warham had more than once helped with generous gifts of money, has left a literary portrait of his friend in his *Ecclesiastes*. He tells us that Warham would give 'sumptuous entertainments, often to as many as two hundred guests, he himself ate frugal meals and hardly tasted wine: he never prolonged the dinner above an hour, but yet was a most genial host: he never hunted or played at dice, but his chief recreation was reading'. His income was very large, but he spent £30,000 on repairs and building of new houses, so that when he died he was so poor that there was hardly enough money to pay for his funeral.

The fine portrait by Holbein at Lambeth, and perhaps even more the beautiful drawing for that portrait which is in the collection of drawings at Windsor, give a vivid picture of the archbishop in old age.   (*Plate 5*)

Hook, *Lives of the Archbishops of Canterbury*, New Series, vol. 1, 1868.

Dr. Gairdner in the *D.N.B.*

WOLSEY, THOMAS, Cardinal-Archbishop of York, Lord Chancellor and virtual ruler of England from 1515 to 1529, was born about 1473 and died in 1530, aged about 57. Rumour held it that he was the son of a butcher in Ipswich: Cavendish, his gentleman-usher and eventual biographer, says that he was 'an honest poor man's son'. He went up to Magdalen, Oxford, where he became famous as the 'boy-bachelor' who took his B.A. degree at the age of fifteen. He became a fellow of his college, was ordained priest in 1498 and became bursar of the college in 1499, an office which he was compelled to resign for applying moneys to the completion of Magdalen Tower without the sanction of the college authorities. He became chaplain to Archbishop Deane of Canterbury and on his death chaplain to Sir Richard Nanfan, the Deputy of Calais. Nanfan died in 1507, but he had recommended Wolsey to Henry VII, whose chaplain he now became. Two years later Henry died and probably owing to the influence of the Lady Margaret Beaufort, who had small opinion of Wolsey, it was some months before Henry VIII gave him any office (1509).

1512 marks the first moment when Wolsey took a major part in deciding governmental policy. He supported the war against France to aid Pope Julius II. The war was a fiasco. The expedition of 1513 was the work of Wolsey, who took into his own hands the entire organization of the war. He was triumphantly successful, and the campaign which brought to the English armies the victories at Therouenne and Tournai and at the battle of the Spurs convinced Henry that Wolsey was indispensable.

Wolsey had two great objectives—the accumulation of power into his own hands and the accumulation of wealth with which

to sustain that power in all the pomp which he deemed necessary. The two went hand in hand. He became Dean of Lincoln
in 1509, of Hereford in 1512, Bishop of Tournai in 1513, Bishop
of Lincoln in 1514, the see of which he relinquished on becoming Archbishop of York in the same year. In 1515 Pope Leo
X made him a Cardinal and in 1515, when Warham resigned
from the Chancellorship, Wolsey was made Lord Chancellor
in his place. In 1519 he achieved his great ambition when he
was created *legatus a latere.* He also possessed at various times
the Abbey of St. Albans, the richest abbey in England: the
Bishopric of Bath and Wells (1518), exchanged for that of
Durham (1524), exchanged for that of Winchester (1529), the
richest see in England. Between 1515 and 1529 Wolsey,
although he was always ultimately dependent on the will
of the king, was to all intents and purposes the sole ruler
in the country. He governed the state through the chancellorship, the church through his legateship. In those fourteen
years he became the most powerful minister England has
known. Parliament was dissolved in 1515 and only met once
again during Wolsey's ministry. He also became the most
hated man in the kingdom. Every piece of policy he adopted
alienated one more of the great vested interests.

Wolsey's *financial* policy was not only universally detested,
but it was radically unsound. His foreign policy demanded
much more money than the country could produce. Wolsey
made no attempts to improve the finances by improving trade,
his only method was to browbeat Parliament. His new tax of
a 'subsidy' (1513) of 1s. in the £ on land and wages was hated:
his forced loan in 1522 infuriated the wealthy: his policy of
'anticipating' the subsidy granted by Parliament in 1523 by
ignoring the condition laid down by Parliament that the tax
was to be spread over several years and by demanding immediate payment made him still more unpopular: his Amicable
Grant of 1523 raised such a storm of protest that the king cancelled the levy. It was left to Cromwell later to provide more
effectively a substantial revenue for the Crown.

Wolsey's *social* policy, by which he tried to deal with the
problem of enclosures, made enemies of the country gentry. In

1517, 1526 and 1528 he tried to enforce the existing laws and sent out commissions to investigate what enclosures had taken place. He then proceeded to pull down hedges and to restore open fields, without curing what was really an economic problem, and only succeeding in making himself more unpopular. The cloth merchants, too, were infuriated by his attempts to maintain employment in a period of depression by forcing the clothiers to keep men at work (1528).

Wolsey's *legal* policy has a good deal more to be said for it, yet even that policy roused passions against him. Wolsey was not a lawyer by training, but he did excellent work in the court of chancery. He greatly increased the amount of work done there, he speeded up decisions and he saw to it that they were enforced. The cases dealt with in this court were civil matters of property, trusts, wills, etc. In the court of Star Chamber he dealt with criminal cases and enormously enlarged the power and importance of this court. Here it was that he disciplined those who thought they were above the law, that he ensured justice to the poor, and speedy justice at that. But by trying to concentrate all legal power in his own hands he alienated the common lawyers, and by his outrageous behaviour towards the better-to-do and by his hectoring and insolent manner, as in the case between Sir Hugh Vaughan and Helier de Carteret (see *T.S.I.H.*, vol. 2, p. 19–22), he aroused the hatred and contempt of powerful lords such as the Duke of Norfolk. It is, however, fair to add that of all Wolsey did or tried to do, only his work in chancery and Star Chamber endured.

Wolsey's *ecclesiastical* policy was a total failure. He recognized that there was a problem and he saw that some reform was overdue. It must be emphasized that Wolsey was no modern radical, he was essentially a conservative and mediaeval churchman. He was aware that such abuses as the benefit of clergy, sanctuary and the state of the monasteries needed attention: but he was also aware that the violent anti-clericalism roused by the cases of Hunne and Standish contained a threat of reform by the laity. Wolsey was determined that the Church should be reformed by itself, or rather by himself. This meant a delegation of authority to Wolsey from the Pope.

With great perseverance, determination and courage Wolsey made himself into the one supreme ecclesiastical authority in the kingdom, so that after he became *legatus a latere* the province of Canterbury even was subject to his control, although he was never Archbishop of Canterbury. Unhappily Wolsey exemplified in himself glaringly those very abuses with which he in his power might have coped: he was the greatest of pluralists, the most obvious example of the non-resident incumbent, he accepted bribes, he most obviously sought first riches and magnificence, and a long way afterwards the kingdom of God: he, a priest, had at any rate one son and a daughter, and in that son Wolsey displayed to the full his nepotism. The boy held sixteen rich benefices and Wolsey tried to get for him the Bishopric of Durham, but Henry VIII stuck at that. Into whose pocket went all this wealth? So hateful became his policy and the Papacy whom he personified as Papal Legate that, when he fell, he left the Church in England defenceless against the laity. Hence in the eyes of some people Wolsey was the author of the Reformation.

Much has been written about Wolsey's *foreign* policy. The subject is too long and too complicated to be dealt with satisfactorily here. The reader is recommended to turn to the chapter in Pollard's life of Wolsey, where he will find the most acute and the most impartial investigation. Pollard is probably right in thinking that Wolsey's policy was actuated wholly by his desire to keep in with and ultimately to obtain for himself the Papacy. Wolsey always regarded the Papacy as the source of all his 'high honour'. Every change in the policy of the Papal Curia was followed by a similar change in Wolsey's policy. It was Julius II who brought England away from peace with and into war against France in 1511: Leo X was responsible for peace in 1514, followed by the marriage of Mary, Henry VIII's sister, to Louis XII. It was the need for English support against the French expedition into the Milanese (1515) which secured for Wolsey a cardinal's hat: when the Pope made peace with France (1517-8), Wolsey followed suit: when Leo joined Charles V (1520), Wolsey made an alliance with the Emperor (1521). It has also to be remembered that Wolsey

Plate 5

Mary Tudor and Charles Brandon, Duke of Suffolk

William Warham, Archbishop of Canterbury

Plate 6

John Colet, Dean of St. Paul's

Erasmus

was a loyal servant of the Crown and Henry was a loyal son of the Catholic Church. This almost subservience to the Papacy, and the fact that Wolsey was the Papal representative in England for life, in the end caused his ruin. Once Henry was involved in the problem of the divorce from Catherine of Aragon, Wolsey's days were numbered. On June 24th, 1529, he lamented 'the Pope has refused all the concessions which, relying on him, I had promised the King . . . and that will be my ruin'.

Having failed to win for Henry the divorce Wolsey was no longer of any use to Henry. Between August and October 1529 it was clear that Wolsey was rapidly losing favour. On October 9th he was indicted for *praemunire*. On the 18th he gave up the great seal. On the 22nd he confessed his guilt. The king had for fourteen years given Wolsey his unstinted confidence and now at his fall Henry dealt generously with him. When the new Parliament on November 3rd launched a grand attack on Wolsey and arraigned him on forty-four charges, Henry refused to take any action and saved him from being imprisoned. Wolsey was allowed to retain some of his benefices and property and to retire to his archbishopric of York. It is a comment on Wolsey's views of an ecclesiastic's duties that he had never visited York since he was appointed archbishop fifteen years before. Nor did he in fact ever reach York. He moved northwards at a snail's pace and got no farther than Cawood. During this time he entered into most indiscreet correspondence with Rome and this became known to the government. Wolsey had taken with him on his journey northwards six hundred horsemen in his train, intending to make his enthronement at York a splendid spectacle. The government was determined to prevent him. On Friday November 4th, 1530, he was arrested and ordered to London. On the 24th at Leicester he died.

Wolsey is one of the great failures of history. Endowed with splendid gifts of intellect and administrative ability, he failed through the defects in his character. He was a born orator, eloquent and subtle, but Cavendish says that he had a 'filed tongue'. He was of 'rare and unheard of affability', said

E—(2)

Erasmus, but Shakespeare held that he was 'lofty and sour to them that lov'd not him', although 'to those men that sought him sweet as summer'. He had an unquenchable thirst for work, but also for wealth and power. Ambitious, aggressive, overbearing, proud, ostentatious and vulgar, his morals were not those of a good churchman, nor his policies those of a good statesman. He accomplished the impossible in serving two masters, but they were not God and mammon, rather mammon and Henry VIII. Had he lived and been in power he would have done his best to see that Parliament disappeared and that the English monarchy reproduced in England the monarchy to be found in seventeenth-century France. 'Glorious was he very farre above all measure, and that was great pitie; for it dyd harme and made him abuse many great gifts that God hadde given him', was the verdict of his great enemy, Sir Thomas More. Even so, he succeeded in providing for himself a magnificent memorial in his foundation of Cardinal College, which survives to-day as Christ Church, Oxford, and in his palace at Hampton Court. It should also be remembered to his credit that he was one of the earliest and strongest supporters of the 'new learning': he made great efforts to ensure that his foundations at Ipswich and Oxford were staffed by the best and most modern scholars. (Zeeveld, *Foundations of Tudor Policy*.) (*Plate 7*)

Cavendish, *Life and Death of Cardinal Wolsey*. *Ed. by Sylvester*, 1959.

Pollard, *Wolsey*, 1919.

T.S.I.H., vol. 2.

VERGIL, POLYDORE, historian, was born at Urbino in Italy about 1470, he died there in 1555, aged about 85. He was educated at two universities, Padua and Bologna, he was for a time secretary to Guidobaldo, Duke of Urbino, and he was ordained at some date before 1496. His relation, Adriano Castelli, Cardinal of Corneto, became the official collector of Peter's Pence under Henry VII and was given the bishopric of Hereford. In 1502 Polydore came to England and joined Adriano: most of his life was thenceforward spent in England. He received the living of Church Langston in Leicestershire

(1503), a prebend in Lincoln cathedral and in Hereford cathedral (1507), he was appointed archdeacon of Wells (1508) and was given the prebend of Oxgate in St. Paul's (1513), all owing to the influence of Adriano. In 1504 he was prosecuted for illegal speculation in foreign currency. In 1510 he secured a Papal bull for the foundation of St. John's college, Cambridge. In 1514 he went to Rome to try to get a Cardinal's hat for Wolsey. On his return he was put in the Tower by Wolsey with Adriano, whom Wolsey blamed for his failure to become Pope (1515), but when Wolsey was made a Cardinal that year, Polydore was released a few months later. The rest of his life was devoted to writing. He signed the denial of Papal supremacy, he accepted the articles of 1536 and communion in both kinds in 1547. In 1553 he returned to Italy and died at Urbino in 1555.

In his own day Polydore's fame rested on his *De Inventoribus Rerum*, which was published in Venice in 1499. This book was written in three months and described the 'first begetters' of all human activities, e.g. the origin of the gods, language, religion, etc. In 1521 he greatly enlarged the book and dealt with the origins of Christianity, but because he traced some ceremonies back to pagan superstitions, the book was put on the Index. He had earlier written a small book, *Proverbiorum Libellus*, which brought about a quarrel with Erasmus. In 1525, Polydore edited the works of Gildas (see *T.S.I.H.*, vol. 1, p. 10).

Today Polydore is chiefly remembered for his *Anglica Historia*. In 1506 Henry VII (or perhaps, more probably, Richard Fox, Bishop of Winchester) had suggested to him that he should write a history of England. The first printed edition appeared in 1534, a folio with illustrations by Holbein. The book was written in Latin and covered the history of England down to 1537. Down to 1540 the history is not much more than a compilation based on the old classical texts, such as Caesar, Polybius, Livy, Tacitus, etc., and on mediaeval histories such as Gildas and Bede, and on chroniclers such as William of Newburgh, William of Malmesbury, Geoffrey of Monmouth, etc. He also drew on MS. sources, so that his book is in some respects a work of research. From 1450 down to 1537 Vergil's book becomes increasingly valuable as an original source, especially for the reign of Henry VII. His avowed purpose was two-fold, to tell the truth and to justify the rise of the Tudor family. On the whole Polydore was an accurate historian, but now and again he allows his passions to colour his writing—for example, in book xxvii, where his hatred for Wolsey undermines his respect for the truth.

Vergil was an exponent of the new methods of writing history, he tested his authorities and he based his judgements on rational commonsense. He was a bold writer and he did not hesitate to criticize some English customs and institutions, such as the universities, the monasteries, the lawyers, for which he incurred much odium.

> Maro and Polydore bore Vergil's name;
> One reaps a poet's, one a liar's fame.

He was even accused of destroying his original sources. He hated and deplored the growing nationalism, especially in France, which was causing such suffering to his own country of Italy through the Italian wars of Charles VIII and Louis XII.

Denys Hay, *Polydore Vergil, Renaissance Historian and Man of Letters* (1952).

Polydore Vergil, *Historia Anglica*, A.D. 1485–1537. Ed. D. Hay, Camden Series, Vol. LXXIV, 1950.

CAVENDISH, GEORGE, gentleman-usher to Cardinal Wolsey and author of *The Life and Death of Cardinal Wolsey*, was born probably in 1499 and died probably in 1562, aged about 63. He was the son of Thomas Cavendish and Alice Smyth, both of well-to-do families in Suffolk. Thomas held the office of Clerk of the Pipe under Henry VII and Henry VIII, an office connected with the Exchequer, and it is probable that it was through his father's official position that George was introduced into the service of Wolsey. Little is known for certain about his early life, but he was at Cambridge in 1510, when he was about 11 years old, and he came down without a degree.

He was twice married: first, to a member of the wealthy Spring family of Lavenham, and secondly in the early 1520s to Margery Kemp, a niece by marriage of Sir Thomas More, a connection which was later to cause him some embarrassment when he was writing his life of Wolsey.

Cavendish was in Wolsey's service by 1522. His duties were to 'attend personally upon my lord', to act as his messenger or courier on important occasions, such as when Wolsey was paying a visit abroad, to look after the Cardinal's household and to organize his magnificent entertainments.

On Wolsey's fall in 1529 Cavendish did not desert him, but continued to work for him. On the Cardinal's death in 1530 he retired from public life to his home in Suffolk. Here he carried out a few duties in local affairs, but the chief work on which he was engaged, and the one on which his claim to be remembered is based, was the writing of *The Life and Death of Cardinal Wolsey*. The book was begun probably in 1554 and completed probably in 1558. It is impossible now to know how much he used previous chroniclers, such as Hall, but it is certain that his book is essentially a record of his own experience and his own first-hand knowledge of Wolsey. His book contains some errors of fact and errors in the sequence of events, probably due to mere forgetfulness. Curiously, he tells us little of Wolsey's private life, but on the whole he succeeds in convincing us that he himself was both honest and accurate as a historian. One curious point is that, although he was married to Sir Thomas More's niece and must have known More intimately, he never mentions him in his book. Both were orthodox catholics, but More was extremely hostile to Wolsey, and it looks as if Cavendish wanted to avoid giving offence by attacking More's views as set out in the biographies which were then beginning to appear. As a literary work the *Life* is a masterpiece, for Cavendish had a real genius for writing, his narrative is lively, colourful and always interesting. Its historical value is proved by the fact that no later writer on Wolsey has been able to do without Cavendish's *Life and Death*, which gives us an admiring, sympathetic, but not adulatory portrait of the Cardinal.

The Life and Death of Cardinal Wolsey, by G. Cavendish, ed. by R. S. Sylvester for the Early English Text Society, 1959. *T.S.I.H.*, vol. 2, pp. 16–19.

SADLER, SIR RALPH (the usual spelling is nowadays Sadleir, but Sir Ralph himself usually dropped the i: the form Sadleyer is also found), diplomatist and statesman, was born in 1507 and died in 1587, aged 80 years. Little is known of his early life, but while still young he was taken into the family of Thomas Cromwell, later Henry VIII's great minister and Earl of Essex. Probably in 1536 Sadler was made a gentleman of the king's privy chamber, and he at once made so good an impression on the king that Henry VIII sent him on a most delicate and important mission to Scotland, to try to find out how much truth there was in the complaints made by his sister, Margaret, the Queen-Dowager, against her son, James V, and to investigate the relations between the king of Scotland and the French. He succeeded in reconciling Margaret with her son after a visit to James in France, and he reported that the second question depended on the decisions made by the king when he returned from Paris.

So pleased was Henry VIII with Sadler's work that in 1540 he sent him again to Scotland to try to separate the king from the advice and policies of Cardinal Beaton, who was wedded to a Franco-Scottish alliance. Sadler was also to advise James V to take to himself the wealth of the Scotch church, as Henry had done in England. The mission was a failure, but Sadler had done the best that could be done. In 1541, he was again in Scotland to try to persuade James to agree to a meeting with Henry VIII. Again he failed, but that Henry was satisfied with Sadler's work is shewn by his making him one of his principal secretaries of state. He was also knighted and made a privy councillor and he entered parliament as member for Hertford (1541).

After the battle of Solway Moss, which was immediately followed by the death of James V, Sadler was sent to Scotland as resident ambassador. He was specially charged to arrange a marriage alliance between the new queen, the baby Mary, and Henry's son, Edward, Prince of Wales, in order to prevent any recovery of influence by the Cardinal Beaton, who had been imprisoned by the Protestant regent, Arran. The treaty was made, one clause of which provided that the queen should be brought up in Scotland under the care of 'an honourable knight and lady of England'. Henry proposed that Sadler and his wife should undertake this charge, but Sadler succeeded in avoiding this task. Party feelings broke out again in Scotland and at one point Sadler's house in Edinburgh was besieged by the mob and he narrowly escaped death from a musket bullet as he was walking in the garden. Sadler retired to Tantallon Castle (1543), an episode which Sir Walter Scott commemorated in *Marmion*, canto v. Sadler soon returned to England, but all his work was undone when war between England and Scotland broke out (1543). Sadler accompanied the Earl of Hertford on his campaign as treasurer to the army, an office which he filled again in the 1545 campaign.

Owing to his frequent absences on diplomatic missions, Sadler was not able to carry out his duties as secretary of state and he was replaced by Paget (1545), but he himself was given the post of Master of the Grand Wardrobe. When Henry died in 1547, he left Sadler a legacy of 200 gold marks and appointed him a member of the council to which the government of the country was entrusted during Edward VI's minority. When Somerset set out for the Pinkie campaign (1547) Sadler again went with him as High Treasurer of the Army. After the battle, in recognition of his outstanding services during the fighting, Sadler was raised to the rank of knight-banneret, a dignity which Holinshed calls 'above a knight and next to a baron'. Sadler was present when bishop Gardiner was arrested (1548) and he was also with the force which put down Ket's rebellion (1549). During Mary's reign Sadler remained in retirement at his home at Standon, near Ware in Hertfordshire.

In Elizabeth's reign Sadler, as a sound Protestant, became one of Cecil's most trusted servants. He was sent once more to Scotland with secret orders to arrange an alliance with the Protestant party. When hostilities broke out at Leith, he was at the camp and had a chief share in making the treaty of Leith (1560). In 1568 he was appointed Chancellor of the Duchy of Lancaster, a highly lucrative office. When Mary, Queen of Scots, fled to England, Sadler, very much against his will, was one of the commissioners appointed to meet the Scotch commissioners to deal with the problem of the Scots' queen. He it was who made the *précis* of the Casket Letters for Cecil. He it was also who was sent to arrest the Duke of Norfolk at the time of the Rising of the Northern Earls. And Sadler it was who twice found himself warder over the Queen of Scots, at Sheffield in 1572 and at Wingfield in 1584. He hated these appointments and never ceased applying for release, but before it came he had had to transfer the Queen from Wingfield to Tutbury. He was relieved in 1585. The next year, after the Babington Plot, Sadler was one of the commission which condemned Mary to death.

Sadler was a man of much importance in his own day. He was loyal, courageous and shrewd; his abilities were indeed greater than the offices which he held suggest. Everybody trusted him and he was well rewarded by the sovereigns whom he served. When he died on March 30th, 1587, he was said to be the richest commoner in England. He had sat in eight parliaments, he was a privy councillor under three sovereigns for close on fifty years: he knew more about Scotland than any other Englishman. He was a brave soldier, he was also 'a most exquisite writer' (Lloyd, *State Worthies*), and his state papers are now invaluable historical sources. He was a little man, devoted to field sports, especially to hawking. He was married and had three sons and four daughters.

The State Papers and Letters of Sir Ralph Sadler, ed. by A. Clifford, with a memoir by Sir Walter Scott, 2 vols., 1809.

T. U. Sadleir, *A Brief Memoir of the Rt. Hon. Sir Ralph Sadleir* (*1907*).

HUNNE, RICHARD, (died in 1514), was a well-to-do merchant tailor in London, a freeman of the city and a liveryman of the Merchant Tailors' Company. Sir Thomas More called him 'a fayre dealer among his neighbours', and

he approved of his 'worldly conversation', but he also wrote
that he was 'highe mynded and set on the glorie of victorie'.
He calculated Hunne to be 'well worth a thousand marks'.
It has been asserted that Hunne was in trouble for heresy
before 1514, but this is certainly untrue. It was not until after
his death that he was charged with heretical views on transubstantiation. In 1514 Hunne had a baby out 'at nurse' in
Whitechapel: the child died when five weeks old and was
buried by the priest of St. Mary Matfellon, Whitechapel. The
priest demanded the child's bearing-sheet (*i.e.* christening
robe) as a burial fee, but Hunne refused to pay. The priest,
Thomas Dryfield, sued Hunne in the consistory (ecclesiastical)
court and won his case. Hunne thereupon sued Dryfield in the
King's Bench court under *praemunire*, on the grounds that he
had been had up in a 'foreign' court, since the consistory court
only sat by authority of the bishop. The ecclesiastical authorities then arrested Hunne. His house was searched and some
forbidden books were found with marginal comments. He
was examined by FitzJames, Bishop of London and he made
a qualified admission of heresy, but he refused to withdraw
the action of *praemunire*. He was therefore sent to the Lollards'
Tower at St. Paul's. Hunne was an important person and the
ecclesiastical authorities were considerably embarrassed, for
the city of London was very anti-clerical. Two days later
Hunne was found hanged in his own silk girdle with clear
indications that he had been strangled and had his neck
broken before he was hanged. Was it murder or suicide?
Anti-clerical London was convinced that it was murder by the
Church authorities. The Coroner's inquest sat for two days,
heard the evidence, which included a confession by Charles
Joseph (extracted by 'payne and durance',) one of the
Chancellor Horsey's servants, and inspected the body in the
Lollards' Tower. A verdict of wilful murder was returned
against Dr. Horsey, the Bishop's Chancellor, and two of his
servants. Horsey was shut up in the FitzJames's palace and
FitzJames wrote to ask Wolsey to intercede for him. In the
meantime FitzJames had been proceeding against the body
of Hunne, which was exhumed and burnt as that of a heretic

(December 20th, 1514). On March 3rd, 1515, a bill was introduced into Parliament to restore all Hunne's property to his children, which was violently opposed by FitzJames as tending to discredit the ecclesiastical court.

Hunne's Case exacerbated the quarrel between the laity and the clergy, between the ecclesiastical and the civil courts. It perhaps played some part in the later declaration of the royal supremacy, the abolition of mortuaries and a curtailment in benefit of clergy. Horsey seems to have escaped with a fine.

Arthur Ogle, *The Tragedy of the Lollards' Tower*, Part I, 1949.
E. Jeffries Davis, *Eng. Hist. Rev.*, July 1915, vol. 30.
Pollard, *Wolsey*, 1929.

STANDISH, HENRY, Bishop of St. Asaph, died in 1535, the date of his birth is unknown. Very little is known of his early life, except that he studied both at Oxford and Cambridge. He became warden of the Franciscan house, Greyfriars, in London. Somehow he won the favour of Henry VIII and became a frequent preacher at Court. In 1515 he suddenly leaped into fame as the most popular man in London.

The arrest of Dr. Horsey, the Bishop of London's Chancellor, on a charge of murdering Richard Hunne put the Bishop and the ecclesiastics in a difficult position. If Horsey were brought to trial, he would almost certainly be found guilty. It was of paramount importance to prevent his being tried. FitzJames, the Bishop, very rashly determined to try to save him by confusing the issue. Parliament was just about to assemble and would be very anti-clerical. The Bishop appointed Richard Kidderminster, Abbot of Winchcombe, to preach at St. Paul's, and he instructed him to defend the thesis that no cleric could be cited in any secular court. The sermon raised violent passions, it was criticized in Parliament, where the Commons were engaged in trying to re-enact a temporary law of 1512 which subjected criminous clerks in minor orders to the secular courts. An appeal was made to the king, who agreed to a debate at Blackfriars at which he would be present (March 10th, 1515). Henry Standish defended the secular view with much success. The City of London showed its gratitude by repaving the church of the Greyfriars. Standish was summoned before Convocation and he appealed to the king for protection. A second debate at Blackfriars was held, in the presence of Henry VIII, where Standish again defended his point of view. The judges decided that in citing Standish before them, Convocation was guilty of *praemunire*. The ecclesiastics had been defeated.

Standish was soon rewarded with the Bishopric of St. Asaph (1518). He remained popular at Court and was employed on several less important diplomatic missions. At one point he quarrelled with Erasmus, of whose translation of the New Testament he disapproved. He was one of Catherine of Aragon's counsellors in the matter of the divorce, but she never trusted him, not unnaturally thinking that he was really on the king's side. He took part in the coronation of Anne Boleyn and he was one of the three bishops who consecrated Cranmer Archbishop of Canterbury. He died on June 9th, 1535, at an advanced but unknown age.

Pollard, *Wolsey*, 1929.
H. Maynard Smith, *Pre-Reformation England*, 1938.

CROMWELL, THOMAS, chief minister to Henry VIII from 1533 to 1540 (in his own day the usual spelling of his name was Crumwell), was born probably in 1485 at Putney, the son of a smith and fuller. He was executed in 1540 at the approximate age of 55.

The details of his early life are much disputed and most of the amusing stories told of him on his travels are apocryphal. He was probably very badly brought up and he himself once told Cranmer 'I was a ruffian in my young days'. At some point he quarrelled with his father and went abroad. Perhaps he took part in the Italian wars, certainly he became a merchant and traded with Antwerp, as certainly he acquired legal knowledge and became an attorney. He had also learned some foreign languages while he was on the Continent. He was back in England in 1512 and in 1520 he entered the service of Cardinal Wolsey, to whom he is likely to have recommended himself by his legal knowledge, his command of foreign languages and by his experience as a man of business. He was employed by Wolsey especially in the destruction of some of the smaller monasteries, in which work his ruthless methods caused him to be much hated.

On Wolsey's fall from power in 1529 Cromwell did not desert his master, as did Stephen Gardiner: he continued to serve him and he spoke in opposition to the bill of attainder in the House of Commons. But he used Wolsey's affairs to bring himself to the notice of the king. In November 1529 he entered Parliament with the expressed approval of the king. He spoke in support of the government's policy in the anti-clerical debates (1529), entered the king's service and was sworn of the council in 1530. His rise was not, as is often said, sudden and dramatic. He won the king's confidence by his exceptional administrative ability, displayed in a variety of offices which he gradually accumulated between 1532 and 1536. In 1532 he became Master of the King's Jewels, then clerk of the hanaper (1532), chancellor of the exchequer (1533), principal secretary (1534), Master of the Rolls (1534), Lord Privy Seal (1536). The turning point in his career was 1532, when he became the king's closest adviser in the crucial matter of the divorce. The first three offices were relatively minor offices, all connected with finance, which set up Cromwell as a finance minister. The other three offices were more important and gave him control of the whole bureaucratic machine. By 1536 he had an assured but by no means large income, an official house in which to live as Master of the Rolls, great prestige as Lord Privy Seal, and the complete confidence of the king. From 1533 to 1540 he was the king's most powerful minister, but he was always dependent on the support of the king.

The most modern view of Cromwell is that set out by Dr. G. R. Elton in his *The Tudor Revolution in Government*. Briefly, he argues that from the fall of Wolsey (1529) to 1533 Henry VIII had no consistent policy: in 1533 Cromwell appears on the scene with a ready-made plan for the divorce of Catherine of Aragon, for the subjection of the clergy, the establishment of the Royal Supremacy, for the breach with Rome and for the attack on ecclesiastical property. Further, he regards Cromwell as having carried out a complete revolution from mediaeval, personal and household government to a modern system of bureaucratic departments which functioned independently of the monarch. This view is effectively challenged by Professor Wernham in *The E.H.R.*, January, 1956. Dr. Elton holds that 'Cromwell not Henry, was really the government'. Professor Wernham holds that it was 'the minister and not Henry who did as he was told'.

There can be no doubt that Cromwell played a leading part in the great questions of the divorce, the Reformation and foreign policy while he was chief minister. In the attack on the monasteries Cromwell, as Vicar-General (1535), was the leading spirit. He began with a statistical survey of Church property, *Valor Ecclesiasticus*, the first survey of Church wealth since 1200, and still the most up-to-date in 1836. Cromwell's agents to collect the evidence were men as hard as diamonds, and very rough diamonds. The bill of 1536 attacked only the smaller monasteries, but it may be assumed that it was intended to destroy the whole system. The Court of Augmentations was set up to transfer the wealth from the Church to the Crown. In 1538, a second visitation was begun. By the act of 1539 the wealth of the monasteries was legally transferred to the Crown, and in the same year the friaries were destroyed. In 1540 the local branches of the Order of St. John were disendowed.

Cromwell was a man blessed with many talents and he made good use of them. He was a first class administrator and much of his work lasted. The Court of Delegates remained the supreme ecclesiastical court until it was superseded by the Judicial Committee of the Privy Council in 1832. The six new bishoprics established by Cromwell were the first to be created since the time of Henry II and the last until the reign of Queen Victoria. The parish registers, which are still maintained and which have proved a most valuable source of information to the historian, were first made compulsory under Cromwell.

It was impossible that such an efficient and such a ruthless monopolizer of power should be popular. Cromwell had steadily concentrated into his own hands the administration of the whole realm—lay administration through the offices enumerated above, ecclesiastical through the office of Vicar-General. In religion Cromwell was by conviction neither old-fashioned Catholic like Henry VIII, Norfolk or Gardiner, nor new-fangled Protestant like Cranmer. He once told some Lutheran envoys that 'as the world now stood he would believe even as his master the king believed', which might be taken to mean 'as the king might at any moment believe'. On the whole his sympathies probably lay with the Protestants. After the Royal Supremacy was established Cromwell had to deal with two parties, one which wanted a Catholic church without the Pope, and another which wanted a reformed church. Cromwell's ecclesiastical policy was intimately bound up with foreign policy. Broadly speaking, when France and the Empire were at loggerheads, there was no danger to England from the Continent: when these two countries showed signs of coming together, Cromwell tended to look to an alliance with the German Lutheran states. The king disliked close alliances, especially a Protestant alliance, and Henry was always a better judge of the international situation than was Cromwell.

Norfolk and Gardiner were representative of the conservative point of view and they were always opposed to Cromwell (who had ejected them from office) on personal grounds and on grounds of policy and religion. They could hope for the king's support. The struggle between the two sides was long and bitter. In the early months of 1539 it looked as if Cromwell was beaten. By midsummer he had apparently wholly recovered the lost ground. In 1540 he made a fatal mistake by forcing the king into an alliance with Cleves and into a marriage with Anne of Cleves. Henry hated the alliance and disliked the lady. Norfolk set up at Court his niece, Catherine Howard, as a rival to Anne in the king's affections. Cromwell could not get rid of Anne for Henry without installing in her place the nominee of his rivals, the Howards. (Wolsey had been in a similar quandary over Anne Boleyn.) His fall seemed certain, yet on April 17th he was made Earl of Essex and Great Chamberlain of England. On May 23rd he suddenly arrested one of the conservative leaders, Sampson, Bishop of Chichester. On June 10th as suddenly he himself was arrested. An act of attainder was rapidly passed and Cromwell was sent to the Tower, where he was kept until July 23rd—presumably in order to provide the necessary evidence for the separation from Anne of Cleves. On that day he was executed with barbarous inefficiency.

The reasons for Cromwell's fall have been minutely investigated, but no satisfying explanation has yet been found which covers his sudden arrest following so quickly on his being created Earl of Essex. Cromwell was a successful innovator, a destroyer, but also a builder. He was not crueller than most people of his own day, he seems not to have been vindictive, rather to have been devoid of passion. But it is difficult to have much sympathy with a man who could write such letters as he wrote to the Princess Mary Tudor. He has frequently been called a disciple of Machiavelli and is said to have read *Il Principe*, but it is doubtful whether his policies owed much to the direct influence of Machiavelli. Had he enjoyed all the resources of modern civilization, he might well have been a twentieth-century dictator of the most extreme kind. (*Plate 8*)

G. R. Elton, *The Tudor Revolution in Government*, 1953.
R. B. Wernham, *The E.H.R.*, January 1956.
R. B. Merriman, *Life and Letters of Thomas Cromwell.*
C. Mawson, *Ramping Cat.* (H.N.)

COLET, JOHN, Dean of St. Paul's, founder of St. Paul's School, was born in London either in 1466 or 1467: he died in 1519 at the age of about fifty-three. He was the son of Sir Henry Colet of the Mercers' Company, who was twice Lord Mayor of London, and his wife, Christian Knyvet of Ashwellthorpe in Norfolk, who had connections with the Grey de Ruthyn family and with the Stafford (Buckingham) family, so that John came of an extremely wealthy and distinguished family. Christian bore her husband eleven sons and eleven daughters, but only John survived infancy, and his mother survived both her husband and her son. The Colets lived in the country outside London at Stepney, a house and neighbourhood for which they all had much affection and where Christian continued to live after the death of her husband in 1505 and her son in 1519.

John was educated at the well-known school of St. Anthony in Threadneedle Street, where were also educated Sir Thomas More, Nicholas Heath (later Archbishop of York) and John Whitgift, Elizabeth's Archbishop of Canterbury, her 'little black husband'. In 1483 he went up to Oxford, almost certainly to Magdalen College. He took his M.A. in 1490 and then he travelled abroad into Italy, and on his way home at Paris he first heard the name of Erasmus, with whom he was later to form a lifelong friendship. He was back in England in 1496 and he had made up his mind to be ordained. He was ordained deacon in 1497 and priest in 1498; the next year Erasmus arrived in Oxford and their long friendship began. According to the custom of the time John was provided with a number of wealthy benefices, but far fewer than such a well-connected young man might have expected.

Between the years 1496 and 1505 Colet was at Oxford and gained an immense reputation for the lectures which he gave, first of all on the Epistle to the Romans. There can be no doubt that Colet owed a good deal to the studies in Platonism of Marsilio Ficino and Pico della Mirandola, and also to the writings of Plotinus. But his lectures broke new ground in the style and methods which he adopted. He abandoned the traditional style of taking the Scriptures sentence by sentence, word by word, the allegorical interpretation and the belief in verbal inspiration. Instead, he expounded the meaning of St. Paul's writing as a whole, he illustrated his lectures with comments on the life of St. Paul and his personal character, and he made many references to the historical conditions in which the Epistles were written. Colet was in fact working a revolution in teaching the Scriptures, and doctors and abbots were to be found at his lectures armed with notebooks.

About the same time, Colet was much influenced by and lectured on the alleged writings of Dionysius the Areopagite. The Reader in Divinity at Magdalen was the great scholar Grocyn, who came to the conclusion that these writings were

Plate 7

Thomas Wolsey, Cardinal, Archbishop of York,
Lord Chancellor

Henry Fitzroy, Duke of Richmond

Plate 8

Thomas Cromwell, Earl of Essex

Thomas Howard, 2nd Duke of Norfolk

not the work of Dionysius. It is a proof of Colet's intellectual
honesty that he at last accepted Grocyn's view. Colet was
always concerned as a scholar with arriving at the truth.

In 1504 Colet was made a D.D. and for a few years he held
the very valuable benefice of St. Dunstan and All Saints,
Stepney. But he was not concerned with the revenues, for he
employed both a vicar and a rector and on the death of his
father in 1505 he resigned the living.

In that year Colet was appointed Dean of St. Paul's and he
held this post until his death in 1519. His time at St. Paul's was
marked by his attempts to reform the Chapter and by his
frequent sermons in the cathedral. The first made him very
unpopular with the cathedral clergy. They resented the
simplicity of Colet's life, the plain dress which he wore and the
simple style of living which he adopted, and still more the
attacks which he directed upon the abuses which he found in
the church at large and in the London clergy in particular.
His sermons took the form of a series of lectures preached from
the pulpit on the New Testament, often delivered in English,
and he also invited outside divines to preach in the cathedral.
It was his firm belief that the abuses in the church existed
because men were not concerned with holiness, that holiness
could only be attained by an understanding of the Scriptures,
and to attain to that it was necessary for the Scriptures to be
expounded rationally.

On the death of his father Colet became a very wealthy man.
He made up his mind to devote the whole of that wealth to the
cause of education. By 1509 he was planning to found a new
school, to be known as St. Paul's. By 1510 the building was
finished and in 1518 Colet framed the statutes for the government of the school. His ideas were unorthodox—for example,
he placed the management of the school not under the clergy,
but under the Mercers' Company. Already some of Colet's
sermons had seemed to the Bishop of London, FitzJames, to be
more than unorthodox and to lay him open to a charge of
heresy, and in 1510 Colet was charged with heresy, for having
preached against the worship of images, the large revenues of
the bishops, and for having translated the Lord's Prayer into

F—(2)

English. Warham, the Archbishop of Canterbury, dismissed the charges as frivolous, but this did not put an end to the persecution which FitzJames kept up against Colet. As a result Colet grew weary of life at St. Paul's and he was planning to retire to the Carthusians at Sheen. He actually built a house there for himself, but in 1518 he had three attacks of the sweating sickness which so enfeebled him that on September 16th, 1519, he died.

Today Colet is remembered principally as the founder of what has grown into a great English public school. In his own day he was remarkable, not only for his scholarship, but also for the originality of his methods in preaching. His courage in attacking what he felt to be wrong was invincible; in 1512 he preached the opening sermon at the meeting of Convocation and took the chance of inveighing against the worldliness of the church in England. In 1512 and again in 1513 he was commanded to preach before Henry VIII, who was about to go to war against France; Colet openly denounced war in front of the King. Henry bore him no grudge, asked him to meet him at Greenwich and had an amicable talk with him, only in the end asking Colet to explain more clearly his views, in case his sermons might have undermined the courage of the soldiers whom Henry was about to lead to war. Erasmus records that after Colet had left Henry turned to his courtiers and said: 'Let every man have his own doctor; and let everyone follow his own liking; but this is the doctor for me.'

It is difficult to say how far Colet would have supported the Reformation in England. He was strongly anti-papal and it is reasonable to think that he would have approved of the legislation for the reform of the Church in the 1529 parliament. It is not possible to know now whether he would have taken the oath of supremacy or would have taken sides with More and Fisher and lost his head. There was a practical side to Colet's saintliness which put him further on the side of reform than, for example, Fisher would have approved. There is an amusing and lively account written by Erasmus of a pilgrimage which he and Colet made to Canterbury, in which he records the irritation, disrespect and finally the angry rudeness with which

Colet treated the ridiculous relics which were shown to the visitors. It is typical of him that when he was drawing up the statutes for his new school he inserted permission for the Mercers' Company to alter them when it seemed good to them to do so. In his last will there is a charming phrase in which he begs the boys of his school to 'lift up their little white hands' for him. It is notable that in that will Colet made no reference to the Virgin Mary and the saints, and that he left no money to provide masses for his soul.

The beautiful drawing of Colet made by Holbein cannot have been made from life, since Holbein did not come to England until 1525. It is almost certainly made from the sculpture on Colet's monument which was later destroyed in the Great Fire of London.   (*Plate 6*)

Seebohm, *Oxford Reformers*. 1887.
Froude, *Life and Letters of Erasmus*. 1894.
T. H. Lupton, *Life of Colet*. 1887.

GROCYN, WILLIAM, 'the patriarch of English learning' (Hallam, *Lit. of Mod. Europe*, i, 386), the first man to introduce Greek literature into England and to profess it publicly at Oxford, was born in 1446 (not 1442, as is often said) and died in 1519 at the age of 73. It is pretty certain that his father was a copyholder at Colerne, near Bath, where William was born (not at Bristol, as is frequently asserted). The boy went to Winchester in 1463, he went on to New College in 1465 and was admitted as a full Fellow in 1467, (for all these dates see Burrows, *Collectanea*, II, pp. 332 sqq. 1890).

A biography of Grocyn must inevitably consist mostly of a list of his offices and the dates when he acquired them. For example, he resigned his Fellowship in 1481 on being preferred to the living of Newton Longueville near Bletchley in Buckinghamshire. In the same year he became Reader in Divinity to Magdalen College and he took a distinguished part in a disputation before Richard III and Bishop Waynflete in 1483. He resigned the Readership in 1488.

In 1488 he left Oxford and travelled to Italy to learn Greek from those Greeks who had settled in Italy after the Turkish

capture of Constantinople (1453). He had already learned the
rudiments of the Greek language in England from Vitelli, who
had been appointed as Praelector of New College not later
than 1475. Grocyn met the great classical scholars, Poliziano
and Chalcondyles, and from them perfected his knowledge in
the Greek tongue and literature.

Vitelli left England for Paris in 1489. The way was clear for
Grocyn when he reappeared in Oxford in 1491. He now
rented rooms in Exeter College until 1493. In that year he
resigned from Newton Longueville and devoted his time to
daily lectures in public in Greek. His reputation grew and
when Erasmus arrived in England on his first visit in 1497, he
quickly made friends with Grocyn and his circle, which
included More, Colet and Linacre. His admiration for Grocyn
was almost unbounded. He wrote that Grocyn held 'the first
place among the many learned men of Britain'. 'Who can
help admiring the unbounded range of his scholastic
knowledge?'

It is not known when Grocyn finally left Oxford. In 1496 he
was appointed to the living of St. Lawrence, Jewry, but the
probability is that he did not reside. Perhaps the appointment
of his friend Colet to the deanery of St. Paul's in 1505 brought
Grocyn to London, for after that date he was frequently there
and often preached in St. Paul's at the invitation of Colet.
One proof of Grocyn's scholarship and critical mind is that he
had studied the supposed writings of Dionysius the Areopagite
and had come to the conclusion that they were spurious, a
decision which modern scholarship has confirmed. Colet had
accepted the writings, but he was at last persuaded by Grocyn
to the right view.

How close and intimate was this circle of friends may be seen
from a letter written by Sir Thomas More in 1504 to Colet:
'Grocyn is in your absence, as you know, the master of my life,
Linacre the director of my studies, Lily* the dear companion
of my affairs.'

Grocyn was a considerable pluralist and at one time held as

* The first Headmaster of St. Paul's School.

many as four preferments. Probably the reason was that while at New College he had acted as tutor to Warham, and when Warham became Archbishop he was generous in giving preferments to Grocyn. These livings brought in a very large income and Grocyn grew to be a wealthy man. He was also a very generous man and hospitable. In 1514 Erasmus wrote, 'I do not see what arrangement can be made for my residing here (in London) with anyone except with Grocyn, and certainly there is no one I should more like to live with, but I am ashamed to live at his expense, especially since I can make no return, and he is so kind that he will allow no payment from me . . . his extreme scrupulousness quite affected me. Give my heartiest salutations to Dr. Grocyn, the patron and preceptor of us all'.

Grocyn died in 1519, after being struck with paralysis. He is a somewhat shadowy figure, but he seems to have been a man of dry humour, simple, plain-speaking. Lily wrote of him that 'he lived content with a little, charming people by his exquisite urbanity, though his manner of speaking was simple and almost rustic'. Erasmus suggested that Grocyn was impatient of blunders, and that he 'greatly despised the divine genius of Plato in his laudations of Aristotle'. He left all his great wealth to Linacre to be used 'for the weal of my soul . . . and all Christian souls as it shall please him.' It happens that a list of Grocyn's books has been discovered at Merton College, written in Linacre's handwriting, together with an account of his expenses. Linacre fulfilled the wishes of Grocyn by relieving the poor and by purchasing books at Louvain to be distributed among Oxford scholars, and he gave 'Master Lily' forty shillings to buy Greek books to give away.

Montagu Burrows, article in *Collectanea* II, 1890, pp. 332–80.

LINACRE, THOMAS, physician and classical scholar, was born probably in 1460 and died in 1524, aged about 64. Nothing is known for certain about his family origins or his early life. About 1480 he went to Oxford, but to which college is not known. He became a Fellow of All Souls in 1484. It is possible that he learned the elements of Greek from the Italian scholar Vitelli, who was then at Oxford, and that he attended lectures given by Grocyn, with whom he became an intimate friend.

Perhaps Linacre obtained his earliest education from William de Selling, Prior of Canterbury, who may have been his uncle. We know for certain that Linacre accompanied Selling when the latter travelled to Rome in 1485 as Henry VII's ambassador. Probably they parted company at Bologna and Linacre attached himself to the great Italian classical scholar, Poliziano, and went with him to Florence. Linacre at once attracted attention by his quick and intelligent mind. He shared his studies with Lorenzo de Medici's two sons, one of whom later became Pope Leo X and did not forget this early friendship.

At some unknown date Linacre visited Rome, where he met the classical scholar, Hermolaus Barbarus, and it is more than probable that it was Barbarus who first turned Linacre's attention to the study of medicine. It may have been Barbarus also who gave Linacre his accurate and critical knowledge of Aristotle.

In 1495 Linacre was in Venice where he lived with Aldus Manutius, the founder of the Aldine Press and the greatest of the Italian printers. Aldus was devoted to Greek scholarship, especially to Aristotle rather than to Plato. He published the the first volume of the Aldine edition of the works of Aristotle in 1495: the third volume appeared in 1497 with a tribute in the preface to the scholarship of Linacre. Aldus paid a further tribute to him when he published in 1497 Linacre's translation of Proclus's work *de Sphera*.

Linacre was at Padua, the most famous university in Europe for medicine, late in 1495. On August 30th, 1496, he took his M.D. at Padua and Richard Pace has recorded the vivid impression which Linacre made on his examiners by his learning and his quickness. The next year he set out for England and on his way he visited at Vicenza the greatest of the Italian medical scholars, Leonicenus, who was the author of the first treatise on syphilis, the new disease which was beginning to attack Europe.

The precise date of Linacre's return to Oxford is not known, but after he was back, on the strength of his degree in medicine at Padua, he was given an M.D. at Oxford. He soon established a high reputation as a lecturer on medical subjects, and he probably also lectured on Greek subjects, especially on Aristotle. From Linacre Thomas More learned Greek, Erasmus owed much to his friendship and inspiration, and Colet was one of his closest friends until an unfortunate quarrel over a Latin grammar which Linacre wrote for Colet's new school of St. Paul's. It is not improbable that Linacre spent a time at Cambridge, according to Dr. Caius (the refounder of Gonville Hall under the name of Gonville and Caius College), and the fact that Linacre founded a lectureship at Cambridge suggests that he had some reason for remembering that university.

In 1500 or 1501 Linacre became tutor to Prince Arthur, but the prince died in 1502, so that Linacre's post was a short-lived one. In 1509 he was appointed physician to Henry VIII at a salary of £50 a year. This entailed his leaving Oxford and living almost exclusively in London, where he soon acquired a large and distinguished practice as a doctor: his patients included Wolsey, Warham, Fox, Colet, More, Erasmus and many others.

It is probable that Linacre was ordained deacon in 1511, but he was not admitted priest until 1520. Even before 1511 he was receiving many ecclesiastical benefices, and after 1520 he was given many more. He never resided in them: it was a common thing to present these livings to distinguished men who then sold them to clergy who were willing to pay for a living. Thus Linacre built up a considerable fortune which later he decided to use for the public advantage. About 1520 Linacre gave up his medical practice so as to have more time for literary work. Sir John Cheke tells a story that late in life Linacre took up the New Testament for the first time in his life and on reading the Sermon on the Mount exclaimed, as he threw the book away, 'either this is not the Gospel or we are not Christians'.

In 1523 he was appointed tutor to the princess Mary, when she was five years old. But he died on October 20th, 1524,

and was buried in the old cathedral of St. Paul's. He died of
the stone, the medical name for which was *calculus*. Linacre
was a noted grammarian, and it is likely that it was Linacre
whom Browning had in mind when he wrote his *Grammarian's
Funeral*:

> 'Back to his book then; deeper dropped his head;
>   Calculus racked him.'

Although Linacre was a priest, although he was a very
considerable classical scholar with great interest in Latin
grammar, he cannot be called typical of the Oxford humanists
who were his contemporaries, for his chief interest was not in
theology but in medicine. His principal claim to fame lies in
the immense amount he did to further medical knowledge in
the sixteenth century by translating several of the medical works
of Galen out of Greek into Latin, thereby making them more
widely understandable, and to make possible further advances
in medical knowledge by his founding the College of Physicians
in 1518, and by the foundation of two lectureships in medicine
at Oxford and one at Cambridge. In his own day it was as a
classical scholar that he was revered by such men as Erasmus.
His most important contribution to scholarship was his treatise
De Emendata Structura Latini Sermonis, published in the year of
his death, 1524, printed by Richard Pynson.

The Queen owns a portrait which is said to be of Linacre and
to have been painted by Quentin Matsys.

R. Weiss, *Humanism during the Fifteenth Century in England*.

J. N. Johnson, *Life of Linacre*, 1835.

J. F. Fulton, *Early Medical Humanists*, New Eng. Jour. Med.
ccv, 1934.

W. Osler, Linacre Mem. Lect: Camb, 1908.

R. J. Mitchell, *Thomas Linacre*, E.H.R. 1, 1935, pp. 696–8.

ERASMUS, DESIDERIUS, the greatest of all the Humanists,
the man who restored the Latin language to Western Europe:
his name occurs so often in the biographies of the English
Humanists that a sketch of him may justifiably be included in
this volume. He was born on October 27th, 1466, at Rotterdam

and he died at Basle on July 12th, 1536, aged 70. He was an illegitimate son of Roger Gerard, a monk. He was christened Erasmus, the Greek form of the German Gerard, and he himself took the additional name of Desiderius, the Latin form of Erasmus, in 1496. All three words mean 'longed-for'. He first used the full form of Desiderius Erasmus Roterdamus in 1506. Much against his will he took monastic vows in 1488, he was ordained in 1492. His first visit to England took place in 1499, when he came with one of his pupils, Charles Blount, the young Lord Mountjoy. He stayed there for rather less than a year, some of which time he spent at Oxford. It was there that he met the English Humanists, especially Colet, and it was Colet who first influenced Erasmus to make theological study the chief purpose of his life. He soon recognized that he would have to learn Greek. He became also an intimate friend of Sir Thomas More. He seems to have approved of England and especially of the charming English girls who accompanied all handshakes with a kiss. Unfortunately he was misinformed by More about the laws governing the export of currency, with the result that when he left England he had all his money confiscated by the customs officials at Dover (1500).

In the autumn of 1505 Erasmus again visited England and at once renewed his old friendships with Mountjoy, Colet and More, and became intimate also with Fox, Bishop of Winchester, Fisher of Rochester and Warham, Archbishop of Canterbury. He also was promised ecclesiastical preferment by Henry VII, which did not materialize. In 1506 he left for Italy.

Erasmus's third visit was a longer one, lasting from 1509 to 1514, and during this time he gave lectures on divinity and Greek at Cambridge, residing at Queens'. Warham proved a generous and helpful patron and gave him a prebend in Kent. Many countries in Europe were now vying to attract Erasmus to live among them. Gradually Cambridge began to pall, the plague appeared, Erasmus suffered from kidney-trouble, which he attributed to English beer. By 1514 he had made up his mind to leave England. He paid three more very short visits to England, but he never again lived there.

It was in 1509 that Erasmus composed his most popular

work, *The Praise of Folly* (*Moriae Encomium*: the title is a play
upon the name of Sir Thomas More). The book was in fact
a satire on contemporary society in which Erasmus singled out
the ecclesiastical hierarchy for his most bitter and scathing
attacks. The book went through seven editions in a few months
and twenty-seven in a few years. Written originally in Latin,
(illustrated by Holbein), it was translated into most European
languages. Two other books had enormous success—the
Adages of 1500, a collection of ancient thoughts and proverbial
sayings and witticisms, with Erasmus's comments on them,
and the *Colloquies* of 1516, of which twenty-four thousand
copies were sold in a few months, a book of wonderful humour,
wit, sarcasm and criticism, containing his account of his visit to
Canterbury and Walsingham and his views on the superstitions he found there. In the course of his life he produced a
stream of editions of various works by the classical authors—
Cato, Cicero, Aristotle, Demosthenes, Josephus, a Greek text
with Latin translation of the New Testament, Latin translations
of Euripides, Isocrates and Xenophon; and he translated the
works of the early Fathers of the Church—Hilary, Jerome,
Cyprian, Ambrose and Augustine. The quality of his Latin
prose was said by his contemporaries to be superior to that of
Cicero himself.

Erasmus was essentially an international figure, having no
fixed home of his own, moving restlessly from town to town,
from country to country, happy in none, happiest perhaps in
England. He was a small man, thin, frail and timid, not being
made, as he himself said, for martyrdom. He was querulous
and ready to take offence, he was always cadging money, in his
early years having none of his own, he was a martyr to the
stone and he had so weak a stomach that the smell of fish
would make him ill for days. If we judge him by his letters, we
must form a very poor opinion of him. But he must have had a
genius for friendship, otherwise such men as Colet and More
and Linacre and Warham could never have held him in such
affection as they did. The greatest scholar and theologian of
his time, he was looked upon as the outstanding figure in
Europe. He played a leading part in reviving Greek learning

to supersede Latin: and he more than anybody else succeeded in getting scholarship applied to scripture and the Fathers, as if they were classical texts. The Catholic Church looked to him to champion the old faith, the leaders of the Reformation expected him to take their side. It was an unenviable and impossible position. Erasmus was no hero and no leader. What he was, was a man who believed implicitly in Liberty of thought, in Charity as 'the greatest of God's commandments', and in solving problems by the use of reason and moderation.

Preserved Smith: *Erasmus*.   (*Plate 6*)

J. Huizinga, *Erasmus of Rotterdam*, Phaidon, 1952.

F. M. Nichols, *The Epistles of Erasmus*—an English trans. of most of his letters. 3 vols. 1901–18.

H. R. Trevor-Roper, *Historical Essays*, 1957, pp. 35–60.

FISHER, JOHN, Bishop of Rochester, martyr, was born in 1469 at Beverley in Yorkshire, the son of Robert Fisher, a well-to-do mercer. John Fisher died on the scaffold in 1535, aged 66. (A papal dispensation of 1491 states that Fisher was then in his twenty-second year, which settles the date of his birth and his age when he was executed. The date given in the *D.N.B.* is wrong by ten years.) He was educated at the collegiate church attached to the Minster: about 1482 he went to Cambridge to Michaelhouse, at the approximate age of 12 to 13: he took the preliminary degree in grammar in 1483, his B.A. in 1488, his M.A. in 1491, in which year he was elected a Fellow of Michaelhouse. In 1494 he became a Proctor and in 1497, at the age of twenty-eight, he was elected Master of the college. He became a D.D. in 1501, in which year he was made vice-Chancellor of the University. From 1504 to 1514 he was annually made Chancellor, and in 1514 he was elected Chancellor for his lifetime. In 1504 he was appointed to the bishopric of Rochester, the smallest and poorest diocese in England, and he was never translated to any more lucrative see.

The turning-point in his life was when he became (probably in 1500 or 1501) one of the chaplains to the Lady Margaret Beaufort, mother of Henry VII. They became the firmest of friends, Fisher was soon advanced to be her confessor, and it was this intimacy between them which resulted in Fisher's advising her on her plans for endowing professorships of divinity at Oxford and Cambridge and for building the two new colleges of Christ's and St. John's at Cambridge. Fisher preached the funeral oration on the death of Henry VII and a few months later he delivered the funeral speech on the Lady Margaret with his deeply felt eulogy of his best friend. (1509)

During the whole of his life Fisher remained a devoted friend to Cambridge University. He was the first Lady Margaret Reader at Cambridge, 1503: in 1505 he became President of Queens' College at the instigation of the Lady Margaret, but he resigned the post three years later. In 1525 he made an endowment at Christ's College, and it was he who persuaded the Lady Margaret to found a second college at Cambridge. He himself gave to St. John's £500 and nearly 1,500 acres out of the lands which she had given to him. He also bequeathed to this college his large and valuable library, but unfortunately the books were wilfully destroyed at the time of his execution. At the age of 48, under the influence of Erasmus, Fisher learned Greek, and at the age of 50 he was taught Hebrew by Robert Wakefield. When he drew up his statutes for St. John's College, he ensured that junior students should learn Greek and senior students Hebrew. He laid stress on the religious purpose of the college, especially on the duty of preaching and the study of theology. Indeed, Fisher's main purpose and hope was that these two colleges would prove a recruiting ground for future priests and raise the quality both of learning and also of preaching among the clergy in England, which he felt had fallen very low of recent years. Fisher was himself a noted and popular preacher, preaching in the vernacular and using a style and a diction which could be understood by everybody, however humble.

In an age which was much given to controversial writings Fisher was a man of his age. Being confronted with a Lutheran book which sought to prove that the claims of the Popes were false because St. Peter had never been at Rome, Fisher wrote a reply which was published in 1522. But the most notable passage in it is that in which he forthrightly attacks the scandalous behaviour of the Church in Rome: 'Nowhere else is the life of Christians more contrary to Christ than in Rome, and that, too, even among the prelates of the Church'. Opposed as he was always to Luther and the Lutherans, he was yet clear-sighted enough to see and bold enough to denounce the vices of the Church at that time. When Wolsey ordered a public burning of heretical books at St. Paul's Cross, Fisher was appointed to preach the sermon, which took two hours to deliver. When Luther published his *Assertio* (1520), Fisher replied with his *Confutatio* (1523), a work of 200,000 words, which was written, as were all Fisher's controversial writings, in Latin. This book was filled with all Fisher's profound learning, but it makes much more dreary reading than does Sir Thomas More's *Dialogue against Heresies* which is enlivened with wit and humour. Fisher also wrote a *Defence of the Priesthood* and a *Defence of the King's Assertion* in reply to Luther's attacks on the Mass and on Henry VIII's book on the seven sacraments. Fisher always emphasized that the Scriptures by themselves are not enough: to understand them rightly they must be read in the light of interpretations made by the Early Fathers and of the teaching of the Church throughout the ages (1525). In this same year he wrote one more book, *De Veritate Corporis*, against the Lutheran, Oecolampadius of Basle. The book was much too long to be successful and the fact that it was written in Latin confined its circulation to the learned. At the same time Fisher was involved in the controversy over Robert Barnes (*q.v.*).

It was not, however, only on religious matters that Fisher stood out against what he held to be wrong. In the Convocation of 1523 he had strongly withstood Wolsey's demand for a high tax on clerical incomes, and it is more than probable that this attitude had brought Fisher to the notice of Henry VIII in no very good light, so that the king was already prejudiced against him when Fisher found himf dseleeply and fatally involved in the matter of the king's divorce. Throughout the whole of this long business Fisher and Sir Thomas More are revealed as men of integrity, courage and determination. On

the question whether the Pope had the power to grant a
dispensation for a man to marry his deceased brother's wife,
Fisher never wavered in asserting that the Pope had that power.
He was equally steadfast in his opposition to the royal
supremacy. It was largely owing to him that the wording of
the consent of Convocation was modified by inserting the
phrase 'as far as the law of God allows'. In 1528 he was
appointed to be one of the counsellors to Queen Catherine
of Aragon and in the next year he spoke boldly on the side of
the queen, asserting that the marriage could not be dissolved
by any power, divine or human. This speech infuriated the
king, who wrote a reply full of violent abuse of Fisher's
character and motives. When the clergy surrendered to the
king, only Fisher spoke in opposition, and Sir Thomas More
gave up the Great Seal (1532). It was Fisher who led the
opposition in the Lords to the Act in Restraint of Appeals,
for which insubordination Henry had him confined under the
care of Gardiner, Bishop of Winchester (April 1533), but in
June he was allowed to go to Rochester.

Just at this time Fisher most foolishly allowed himself to
become embroiled in the episode of the Nun of Kent, Elizabeth
Barton. The Act of Attainder (1534) included the name of
Fisher, and he was found guilty of misprision of treason, the
penalty for which was imprisonment at the king's pleasure
and the forfeiture of all his goods. In the end Fisher was let
off with a fine of £300, one year's revenue of his bishopric.

The first session of the 1534 Parliament established the royal
supremacy and settled the succession to the throne of the
children of Henry and Anne Boleyn. It also enacted that an
oath must be taken to accept and defend 'the whole effects
and contents of this present Act'. On April 13th, 1534, Fisher
was summoned to Lambeth to take the oath. He refused to
take it and was given a few days to think over the matter. On
the 17th April he again refused and was sent to the Tower.
Both Fisher and More were ready to take the oath to the
succession to the throne: both refused to countenance any
diminution in the supremacy of the Papacy. Both were
attainted for misprision of treason and Fisher was deprived of

his bishopric. The passing of the Act of Treason in 1535 turned Fisher and More's refusal into treason, for by this Act a refusal to take the oath could be construed as an attempt to deprive the king of his title, which was treason. Many attempts were made to get Fisher to accept the oath, but all failed. Up to this point Fisher had made no direct declaration of his views, he had merely refused to take the oath. But on 7th May he was tricked by a messenger from Cromwell into believing that Henry was truly desirous of hearing his genuine views and the reasons for them, and he was given a solemn promise that no harm should come to him as the result of anything he said. Fisher therefore declared openly and fully his views and thereby he provided the government with the plainest evidence against him.

Even so it is possible that Henry would not have put Fisher to death, if at that moment the Pope had not made Fisher a Cardinal. This drove Henry to ungovernable rage and sealed Fisher's fate. On June 17th, 1535, he was brought to trial and condemned to death for high treason, and the penalty was that he should be drawn on a hurdle to Tyburn and there be hanged, drawn and quartered. This penalty was remitted and he was allowed to be executed by beheading. The sentence was carried out on June 22nd. Sir Thomas More was executed on July 6th.

When the news reached the Continent, Europe was horrified and bewildered. Both Fisher and More were men of international reputation, partly through their controversial writings, partly by the eulogies of them which Erasmus had spread abroad—More for his legal and theological learning, his piety, his wit and his happy family life: Fisher for his scholarship and holiness of life. Erasmus described them as 'the wisest and most saintly men England had'. The Pope wrote to Francis I of France of the 'innocence and holiness of' Fisher and 'of his learning, both famous and spread throughout the whole world, for the defence of the Catholic faith'. Many leaders in Europe had visited More, many called on Fisher at Rochester which lay on the main road from Dover to London, and among them Campeggio in 1518.

Fisher was the most conscientious bishop of his time. He looked after his diocese with pastoral care, investigating cases of heresy, always trying to raise the quality of the clergy, visiting the sick, giving alms which he could scarcely afford and entertaining visitors at his table, although his own personal standard of living was almost ascetic. There is no record of any heretic in the diocese of Rochester being sent to the stake, but Fisher maintained in his *Confutatio* that it was lawful to hand over relapsed heretics to the secular arm.

In his religious views and in his religious behaviour Fisher was essentially a mediaevalist—he kept a small closet where he would spend many hours in secret prayer and where he would scourge himself with whips. He was essentially also a spiritually-minded man. The portrait of him by Holbein (plate 9) reveals a steady, calm and sympathetic man, gazing a little beyond this world: but the strong modelling of the face, the firm and broad nose, the square chin, the flexible line of the mouth combined with the firm set of the lips, all speak of conviction built upon faith. He stood the representative of the old order, Henry VIII represented the new, modern world. In that world there was no room for both Henry and Fisher, just as in the new world of the United Provinces there was to be no room for both Maurice, Prince of Orange and Oldenbarnefeldt (1619). Old, tired, desperately ill, short of money, denied his books of devotions and writing materials, always cold and often hungry, Fisher endured his imprisonment in the Tower with unfailing courage and embraced death with cheerful calm. He and Sir Thomas More were canonized in St. Peter's, Rome, on May 19th, 1935, as martyrs for the Catholic faith.   (*Plate 9*)

Bridgett, *Life of Blessed John Fisher*, 1888.
E. E. Reynolds, *Saint John Fisher*, 1955.

MORE, SIR THOMAS, Lord Chancellor, was born in 1478 and died in 1535 at the age of fifty-seven. He was the son of the Judge Sir John More by his first wife, Agnes Graunger. After beginning his education at St. Anthony's school in

Threadneedle Street, he was then put to live in the household
of Archbishop Morton, who was also the Lord Chancellor.
More would have been about twelve years old then and he
spent two years in the Morton family, where he soon made
a reputation for his intelligence, wit and liveliness.   Years
afterwards he paid a tribute to the Archbishop, for whom he
always had much affection and respect, in his *Utopia.* (*T.S.I.H.*,
vol. 2, p. 5.)   About 1492 More went to Oxford, almost
certainly to Canterbury College, later to be incorporated into
Christ Church. Here he came under the influence of the New
Learning, was friends with Grocyn and Linacre, studying
Greek and Latin and French, theology and music. After two
years or less he returned to London to study law (1494), he
became an intimate friend of Colet and in 1497 was first
introduced to Erasmus who became his lifelong bosom friend.
He began his legal life at New Inn, but in 1496 he was transferred to Lincoln's Inn where he had a rapidly successful career.

  In 1499, however, More began to have doubts whether he
ought to follow a legal career and ought not to become a priest.
For some four years he seriously examined this possibility and
for a time lived in close touch with the brothers of the Charterhouse. In the end (1503) he abandoned the idea of an ecclesiastical life and turned with renewed energy to the study of law,
in which he was quickly and brilliantly successful.

  In 1504 he was elected to Parliament, but his constituency is
not known. It is said that in this year 'as a beardless boy' he
opposed and 'clean overthrew' the King's demands for a huge
sum of money to cover the marriage of the Princess Margaret
to the King of Scotland. Henry in fury revenged himself
by keeping John More in the Tower until he paid a fine of
£100. (Pollard in his *Wolsey* denies this story.) The next year
(1505) More married Jane Colte and settled in London in
Bucklersbury. During the next six years he lived a quiet and
enjoyable life, rejoicing in his four children, dividing his
leisure time between developing his home and literary pursuits.
Twice Erasmus came to visit him: in 1508 More went to Paris
and Louvain, but he returned convinced that Oxford and
Cambridge were superior universities. In 1511 his wife died

and within a month he had married again, this time a widow, Alice Middleton, who had one daughter. Alice was seven years older than More and proved to be a capable housekeeper rather than a sympathetic wife. More now moved from Bucklersbury to Crosby Place in Bishopsgate Street, where he remained until he bought land in Chelsea and built for himself what was to become one of the famous houses of England.

All this time he had been proving himself a notable lawyer: he was made under-sheriff of London (1510) and he soon came into close relations with the new and young King Henry VIII, who professed for More much affection. More never allowed himself to be blinded by this and he never put much trust in the King's protestations. 'If my head should win him a castle in France, it should not fail to go.'

The year 1516 saw the publication of *Utopia*, a literary masterpiece which, under the guise of representing an ideal society, was in fact a bitter attack on the political and social evils of the day. In 1521 he was called in by the King to help him in writing his book on the seven sacraments against Martin Luther. Later Henry was to accuse More of having 'villainously and traitorously' provoked him to write this book in defence of the Papacy and thereby to put a sword in the Pope's hands to fight against himself. More replied that he had been 'a sorter out and placer of the principal matters' after the book was finished, 'wherein when I found the Pope's authority highly advanced, and with strong arguments mightily defended, I said unto his Grace "I must put your Highness in remembrance of one thing, and that is this. The Pope, as your Grace knoweth, is a prince as you are, and in league with all other Christian princes. It may hereafter so fall out that your Grace and he may vary upon some points of the league, whereupon may grow breach of amity and war between you both. I think it best therefore that that place be amended, and his authority more slenderly touched". ' In 1523 More became Speaker of the House of Commons. Up to this point More had himself been in favour of reform, but he always envisaged the reform of the church as coming from within and he was utterly opposed to reform by revolution. For this reason he himself wrote a letter against Luther, and in 1528 he wrote his *Dialogue* against the English reformers, especially against Tyndale.

On the fall of Wolsey in 1529 More was appointed Lord Chancellor. He must be regarded as one of the greatest of Chancellors, both for the unassailable integrity with which he conducted his court and also for the unequalled rapidity with which he discharged the cases. It has been charged against him that he was implacable against heretics and sent some of them to the stake. It is true that he was stern against *seditious* heretics, those who stirred up strife against the state. To others, he was lenient and helpful, as he was to his future son-in-law, Roper. It is beyond doubt certain that Thomas More, as a layman, never could have legally and never did in fact send a man or woman to the stake (see Chambers, *Life*, pp. 274–82).

More was the first layman to hold the office of Lord Chancellor: he held it until 1532, when he resigned (he was not dismissed) because he found himself increasingly out of sympathy with the King's policy over the divorce and the anti-papal legislation. For the next two years he wrote many controversial letters and pamphlets, in some of which he sank to the lowest depths of vulgar abuse and vindictive wit, especially against Tyndale. Most of his writing was in Latin, including *Utopia*, but after his death an English edition of his works was published in 1557. In 1533 he became for a short while embroiled in the episode of the Nun of Kent, Elizabeth Barton, and his name was included in the Bill of Attainder, but it was removed at the third reading. More himself said that his danger was only postponed, not removed, and when on March 30th, 1534, a new Act of Parliament required an oath to the succession of Anne Boleyn's children, More knew that his end was very near. He was willing to accept the oath to the succession, as a matter within the right of Parliament to deal with, but he refused to take the oath repudiating the papal supremacy, and he refused to say that the Princess Elizabeth was legitimate. He was committed to the Tower (April), charged with high treason and tried at Westminster on July 1st, 1535. He was of course found guilty and was executed on Tower Hill on July 6th. It is a characteristic of victims under an autocratic government that they nearly always die confessing their disobedience, not protesting their innocence. Thomas More is an exception to that general rule, for he died protesting that he was 'the King's good servant but God's first'. He was canonized by Pope Pius XI in 1935.

Of More's execution it must be said that the law was strained to breaking point in order to secure a 'legal' conviction. An Act of Parliament had to be passed to legalize retrospectively the oath for refusing which he was imprisoned. Even so, it is possible on purely political grounds to make out a case on Henry's side. Henry was always a political realist and never a man of moral principle. The need for an indisputably legitimate heir to the throne, and a male heir at that, was paramount in his and in most people's view. More was a 'wise, righteous and brave man who went to his death for his conscience' (J. D. Mackie, *History*, June 1936). He was a first-class scholar, a man of the highest principles, a practising Christian, a faithful husband, a devoted father; his capacity for friendship, his wit, his hospitality, his kindness to servants, his love of music, his affection for animals as his menagerie at Chelsea proves, his powers of conversation, made and still make him a great and good and lovable man. But More was also a saint, and like many other saints there was in him a hard core of granite, a fibre strong as steel, which made him a formidable opponent in controversy, a severe critic where he felt his principles to be outraged, and which gave his saintliness that almost fanatical desire for martyrdom which one sees in men like Southwell. It was not that he was impervious to the reasonable arguments of his friends and of his beloved daughter Meg: rather, he simply declined to listen to argument; one almost has the feeling that he feared he might lose the martyr's crown. It is claimed for him that he died in order to save the Papacy and the unity of Christendom. Yet there is a curious letter which he wrote to Cromwell when he was in prison in which he urges the King to pursue his idea of a General Council on the grounds that the present Pope might be deposed and a new Pope appointed with whom His Highness might be well content; 'never thought I the Pope above the

General Council' (Eng. ed. of More's works, 1557, p. 1427). Perfection is not given to man and More was not perfect. The shock which his execution caused throughout Europe is the measure of his status and reputation in his own day. *(Plate 9)*

W. Roper, *Life of Sir Thomas More.*
R. W. Chambers, *Thomas More*, 1935 (*cf. History*, N. S. XXI, 81, pp. 60 *sqq*).
E. E. Reynolds, *Margaret Roper*, 1960.
J. W. Hexter, *More's Utopia. The Biography of an idea.*
H. R. Trevor Roper, *Historical Essays*, 1957, pp. 91–7.
Jean Plaidy, *St. Thomas' Eve*, Hale, 1954. (H.N.)
R. Bolt, *A Man for All Seasons* (H. play).
The Clergy Review, May 1935.

LEE (or LEGH), ROWLAND, Bishop of Coventry and Lichfield and Lord President of the Council in the Marches of Wales, was the son of William Lee of Morpeth, Northumberland, and of Isabel Trollope of Thornley in Co. Durham. The date of his birth is unknown: he probably died in 1543. He first entered public life in 1528 under Wolsey. He shared with Stephen Gardiner and Thomas Cromwell in the suppressing of those monasteries whose wealth Wolsey required for his foundation of Cardinal College at Ipswich. After Wolsey died, Lee stuck to Cromwell, who put his son under Lee's charge, and he became one of the principal agents between the King and Cromwell and the clergy, and in the matter of the king's divorce; and for his many services he received frequent preferments. It is possible that it was Lee who secretly married Henry VIII and Anne Boleyn on January 25th, 1533. His final reward was the Bishopric of Lichfield and Coventry, known in those days as Chester, on January 10th, 1534. This appointment caused much offence to at least one person. Stephen Vaughan, a close friend of Cromwell's, wrote to him: 'You have lately holpen an earthly beast, a mole, and an enemy of all godly learning, into the office of his damnation, *a papist*, an Idolater, and a fleshly priest'. (Ellis, *Original Letters*, 3rd series, ii, 285.)

In May 1534 he was appointed President of the King's

Council in the Marches of Wales with the object of restoring law and order, which had broken down under Voysey, Bishop of Exeter. He owed his appointment to Cromwell, who seems first to have recognized the need for a new and consistent policy in Wales. Lee proved himself a man of loyalty and of resolute energy, 'stowte of nature, readie-witted, roughe of speeche, not affable to any of the Walshrie, an extreme ponisher of offenders, desirous to gain credit with the Kinge and comendacon for his service'. (Gerrard to Walsingham.) There is some evidence, not above suspicion, that he hanged five thousand criminals.

When Henry VIII began to carry out a reorganization of government in Wales and introduced the shire system from England and appointed Welshmen as J.P.s, Lee opposed the policy, since he did not think Welshmen would be impartial in administering justice and he himself was not 'of that perfectness to know what shall chance in time coming'. We know little about the last three years of his Presidency and very little of interest about the last years of his life. He died at Shrewsbury probably on January 28th, 1543, and is buried there in the church of St. Chad's.

J. F. Rees, *Tudor Policy in Wales*, Hist. Assoc. pamphlet, 1935.

HOWARD, THOMAS, EARL OF SURREY, 2nd DUKE OF NORFOLK, soldier and statesman, was born in 1444 at Tendring Hall in Stoke-by-Nayland: he died at Framlingham in 1524 at the age of eighty. His father was Sir John Howard, 1st Duke of Norfolk, who was killed at the battle of Bosworth (1485), and his mother was Catherine, daughter of Lord de Moleyns. He was educated at Ipswich Grammar School, but when the Wars of the Roses broke out, he became a page to the Earl of March, afterwards Edward IV, and he fought beside him at the battle of Towton Field (1461). When Edward became King, Thomas Howard was attached to his court and soon revealed exceptional skill in the use of arms. At the coronation of Edward's queen in 1465, Howard acted as Deputy Earl Marshal of England at the age of twenty-one, a proof of how greatly the King esteemed him. A further proof of Edward's high opinion of Howard may be seen in his advising Sir John Howard to send his son abroad to the court of Charles the Bold, Duke of Burgundy, at Dijon, where the young man could develop his exceptional gifts for a military life.

For two years Howard remained at Dijon. In 1468 he returned to England and was appointed an esquire of the body to King Edward IV, an office which entailed his constantly attending the King in person. When war broke out between Edward IV and Warwick the King-Maker (1469), and Edward had to go into exile, Howard was prevented from accompanying Edward by a surprise attack of the Lancastrian ships, which compelled Howard to take sanctuary at Colchester. On the return of Edward to England, Howard broke sanctuary, joined the Yorkist leader and fought for him at Barnet (1471).

In 1472 Howard married a rich heiress, Elizabeth, daughter of Sir Frederick Tilney of Ashwell Thorpe in Norfolk and widow of Humphrey Bourchier, (son of Lord Berners), who was killed at Barnet. (In the article in the *D.N.B.* on Thomas Howard, the chronology at this point has been much confused.) In 1475 he accompanied Edward IV to France and was present at his meeting with Louis XI at Picquiny. On his return to England he went to live at Ashwell Thorpe as a country gentleman and became sheriff for Norfolk and Suffolk (1476-7). On January 18th, 1478, he was knighted by the King at the marriage of Richard, Duke of York, to Lady Anne Mowbray, only child of the 4th Duke of Norfolk who died in 1476. Anne died before the marriage was consummated and thereby the direct line of the Mowbrays became extinct. Sir John Howard was the next of kin and he became the Duke of Norfolk, while his son, Sir Thomas Howard became the Earl of Surrey, by which name he will now be known in this article, until he in his turn became Duke of Norfolk in 1514. In 1483 he was made a Knight of the Garter and became a Privy Councillor.

It might almost be said that from this moment Surrey became the prototype of those Tudor statesmen who later accepted the royal supremacy and adhered loyally to the person and the policy of whoever sat on the English throne. Surrey had supported the Yorkist cause in the person of

Edward IV: he supported, but did not intrigue and plot with, Yorkist Richard III and he fought on his side at Bosworth Field. He then accepted the Lancastrian Tudors. At Bosworth his father was killed and he himself was badly wounded and was taken prisoner.

Henry VII, desperately in need of money, seized all the Norfolk estates and on November 7th, 1485, the dead Norfolk and the living Surrey were attainted, but Surrey's life was spared. After Henry had married the Yorkist Elizabeth, Surrey accepted the Tudor right to the throne, and when the Earl of Lincoln raised rebellion against Henry VII, Surrey refused to profit by it and declined the offer of the Lieutenant of the Tower of a chance to escape. He was not, however, released from prison until a year later (1488), when the attainder was reversed and Surrey was given back some part of his estates, for Henry saw the value of such a man.

The first use which the King made of him was to send him in 1489 to put down a serious rising in Yorkshire, which he did successfully and humanely. As a reward he was created Lieutenant-General of the North and deputy to the young Prince Arthur as Warden of the Eastern and Middle Marches towards Scotland. He put down another rising at Pontefract (1492) and by obtaining pardon from the king for all the rebels he won the affection of the people as well as the confidence of the King.

Surrey's principal duty now was to watch the Scottish border, which was being threatened by James IV and Perkin Warbeck. In 1497 he compelled James to abandon the siege of Norham Castle and to retreat home again. Surrey pursued him and took Ayrton Castle, but he himself had to withdraw owing to bad weather. In 1501 he was made Lord High Treasurer and a Privy Councillor. The King again shewed his confidence in Surrey by sending him to arrange a marriage between the Princess Margaret and James IV of Scotland. Two years later (1503) Surrey escorted the Princess to Scotland and on August 8th he gave the bride away on behalf of Henry VII.

In 1507 Surrey's wife died: two years later he married Agnes Tilney, a cousin of his first wife, Elizabeth Tilney. Just before his second marriage he was in Antwerp negotiating a marriage between Princess Mary and Charles of Castile, afterwards the Emperor Charles V, which never took place. Henry VII now made Surrey an executor of his will and just before he died he restored to Surrey all the property of the Mowbrays, Bigods and Howards which he had seized in 1485 and retained since then (1509).

When Henry VIII came to the throne in 1509 Surrey was sixty-five years old. His age, his experience, his reputation for disinterested loyalty and—to a young man like Henry—most especially his military reputation, all marked out Surrey as the chief member of the Privy Council. He still had fifteen years to live. Those years were embittered by his long duel with Wolsey, whose social origins he despised and whose policy he wholly distrusted. He lost that duel in the sense that he never acquired a commanding position in the Council over policy: that fell to Wolsey. In another sense he won his fight in so far that Henry paid no attention to Wolsey's great efforts to poison the King's mind against his rival. To the end Henry seemed to preserve his respect and liking for this loyal servant. Those years were sweetened by Surrey's tremendous military victory over James IV at Flodden in 1513, when Surrey was seventy years old, although there is some evidence that it was the advice of his son, Sir Edward Howard, which at a critical moment ensured a decisive victory. At least, the old general recognized and acted on the good advice. As a reward, on February 1st, 1514, Surrey was created Duke of Norfolk and Earl Marshal of England, a title and an office which have remained conjoined to the present day. He was given twenty-six manors in Norfolk and Suffolk which brought him an income of £40 p.a., and he was given an augmentation of his heraldic arms which included a part of the royal arms of Scotland.

In an age which set great store by name, fame and glory, Norfolk found himself frequently called upon to fulfil functions and duties which much irked, and even deeply wounded, his sensitive nature. He was hotly opposed to Wolsey's policy of marrying the King's sister, Mary, to Louis XII of France, yet it fell to him to conduct the Princess to France for the wedding. More personally distasteful and humiliating, he found himself compelled to conduct Wolsey from the high altar to the West door of Westminster Abbey, when Wolsey was formally invested with the Cardinal's hat. In 1517 Surrey was called on to put down the rising of the London apprentices, which he did with all his old skill. In 1520 Henry VIII went to France to the Field of Cloth of Gold and he left Norfolk in charge of his kingdom, a high enough honour and responsibility for any man. But a more terrible duty followed. In 1521 he was appointed Lord High Steward to preside over the trial of Edward, Duke of Buckingham, on a charge of high treason. Buckingham was Norfolk's oldest friend, father of the wife of Norfolk's eldest son. It is incredible to us of the twentieth century that Norfolk should have been appointed, that Norfolk should have agreed to serve; the more incredible when we remember that in the sixteenth century treason trials had only a foregone conclusion. 'With tears streaming down his face Norfolk passed sentence of death on a man with whose sentiments he entirely agreed, but had his reward in a grant of manors from Buckingham's forfeitures.' (*D.N.B.*)

Norfolk never after this made more than an occasional appearance at Court. His last appearance was in 1523, 'when he had a short and apparently affectionate conversation with the King'. (*House of Howard*, i, 109). He died on May 21st, 1524, in his eightieth year at his historic castle of Framlingham. He was buried at Thetford Priory, where an elaborate monument was erected over his tomb, on which was engraved a long biographical history, largely the work of his own hand, which remains a chief source of information about the details of his life. At the dissolution of the monasteries the tomb disappeared, but the inscription has been preserved. The bones of the Duke were translated to the Howard Chapel at Lambeth. Norfolk's second wife, Agnes Tilney, survived him for more than twenty years and she greatly damaged the Howard family by her lax guardianship of Katherine Howard, the fifth wife of Henry VIII. She was buried beside her husband at Lambeth.

Thomas Howard, second Duke of Norfolk, was first and foremost a soldier. He was a modest man and a humane man in an age when humaneness and modesty were fast disappearing.

Henry VIII had a good deal of respect for him, the English people as a whole admired and even loved him. Polydore Virgil summed up the general opinion '*vir prudentia, gravitate et constantia summa*,' (a man of the utmost wisdom, solid worth and loyalty).   (*Plate 8*)

Brenan and Statham, *The House of Howard*, a useful book, but unscholarly and heavily weighted against the Tudors, written in melodramatic language.

Polydore Virgil, *Anglia Historia*, ed. by Denys Hay, 1950.

ASKE, ROBERT, leader of the Pilgrimage of Grace, was born about the beginning of the century: he died in 1537, aged approximately thirty-seven. Little is known of his early life. He was in the service of the Earl of Northumberland and in 1527 he was admitted to Gray's Inn. He became a lawyer with 'great businesses' in London and he was clearly a gifted orator. His personal appearance was exceedingly plain and he could boast of only one eye. He was a man of considerable physical strength, who could spend day after day in the saddle with little time for food or sleep. He was also a man of absolute integrity and uncommon courage, but was too trustful of others for the treacherous times in which he lived.

The Pilgrimage of Grace began at Louth in Lincolnshire, (October 1537), where a rising took place against the suppression of the monasteries. Other motives added fuel to the fire, but the rising was quickly put down. At once another and much more serious rising broke out in Yorkshire. It was of this rising that Aske became the leader. It was a conservative and in no way a revolutionary rising in a backward area of England which resented the rise of 'new men' like Thomas Cromwell, the suppression of the religious houses, taxation and some of the ecclesiastical changes. The King promised a pardon to all and an inquiry into their grievances. On Henry's personal invitation Aske went to London to discuss the grievances. Henry sent him back home with assurances which were held to be enough to satisfy the rebels. Aske was able to settle another rising, under Sir Francis Bigod, for which loyal work he received the personal thanks of the King. But Henry was only biding his time. By May 1537 Aske was in prison in London. He was examined and sentenced to be hanged, drawn and quartered. Henry was determined that all the prisoners should be executed in their own counties. Aske was sent north to Yorkshire and was executed within the city of York. He had begged the King that he might be hanged until he was dead before being disembowelled. Henry granted this favour, but he kept his word by ordering Aske to be hanged in chains from the church tower until he died of starvation.

M. H. and R. Dodds, *The Pilgrimage of Grace*, 2 vols, 1915.
Pickthorn, *Early Tudor Government, Henry VIII*, 1934.
H. F. M. Prescott, *The Man on a Donkey*, 1952. (H.N.)

DARCY, THOMAS, LORD. Statesman and rebel, a leader of the Pilgrimage of Grace, was born in 1467 and died in 1537, aged seventy. He was the son of Sir William Darcy and his wife Euphemia, daughter of Sir John Langton. In 1488 he succeeded to the ancient family lands in Lincolnshire and Yorkshire, the family home being Templehurst. He was twice married, first to Sir Richard Tempest's daughter Dousabella, who was the mother of his four sons; secondly to Edith, widow of Lord Neville and mother of the young Earl of Westmorland, the steward of whose lands Darcy became in 1505. In that same year he was raised to the peerage. His family lands, his new title, and especially the new connection by marriage with the great northern family of Nevilles, greatly strengthened his position and prestige in the north. Between 1488 and 1511 he received many appointments in the north and on the border, such as the Captain of Berwick and the Warden of the East Marches. He was second only in importance to the Earl of Northumberland.

In 1511 Darcy, at his own request, was given command of a force of English archers which Ferdinand of Aragon had asked Henry VIII to supply for the invasion of France. Five companies of 250 men each sailed from Plymouth in May and arrived at Cadiz on June 1st. Unfortunately the English troops were quarrelsome and ill-disciplined and Ferdinand soon got rid of them—they were only in Spain for a little more than a fortnight. The journey home was long and stormy and Darcy had to spend much money on victualling his men and paying their wages. He complained bitterly to Wolsey later, but the Spanish ambassador dealt with him very liberally and appeased his anger.

In 1513 Darcy accompanied Henry VIII on his French campaign and was present at the battle of Thérouenne, where he had some accident which caused a rupture from which he suffered for the rest of his life. On returning home from the war he was once more employed in governing the borders. In 1529 he did not scruple to prepare the indictment against his friend Wolsey which led to the fall of the minister. At first he was on the King's side in the matter of the divorce and he appeared as a witness at the Queen's trial. But it is likely that he was beginning to see whither Henry was tending. In 1532, in reply to a speech by the Duke of Norfolk, Darcy boldly supported the view that such causes as divorce were spiritual causes and ought to be settled by the Papacy. For the next three years Darcy was kept in London and not allowed to go home to the north. He was unemployed and he began to hate the growing despotism of the Cromwellian policy.

By 1534 he was hand in glove with Lord Hussey, and the two of them began to plot with Chapuys, the Imperial ambassador, for the Emperor Charles V to invade England and rid the country of a tyranny which was destroying the Church. He told Chapuys that if only he could get home to the north he would prepare for a general rising. At last he was allowed to go and he was at Templehurst by November 13th, 1534, or more probably late in the next year, 1535.

It was in October 1536 that the first outbreak of the Pilgrimage of Grace occurred in Lincolnshire. It soon spread into Yorkshire. Only Pomfret Castle seemed capable of holding out against the insurgents, and Darcy was in command there. The castle was in disrepair and short of supplies. Darcy cannot be blamed for this, since he had been detained in London for three years. The rising was mainly caused by the suppression of the monasteries, of which Darcy strongly disapproved. It was aimed not against the King but against Cromwell, and

Darcy sympathized with the view that the minister and not the King was responsible. In other words, all his instincts made him favourable to the rebels. He hesitated to join them only because he detested the thought that he would be branded as a traitor. At 7 o'clock in the morning of Saturday, October 21st, he surrendered the castle to Robert Aske and took the Pilgrims' oath.

When Henry sent his representatives to deal with the situation, they were instructed to offer Darcy a safe conduct to London or a pardon, if he would submit. Darcy wrote a letter to Henry to explain his conduct. The King then sent him a pardon, but on January 6th, 1537, he summoned Darcy to London. Darcy pleaded that he was too ill to go. Meantime the Pilgrimage of Grace was ended, but immediately another rising under Sir Francis Bigod took place. Darcy and Aske were able to deal with that, for which services they were sent the thanks of the King. But soon after Darcy was arrested, taken to London, charged with high treason and condemned to be hanged, drawn and quartered (May 15th, 1537). The sentence was commuted to one of beheading, and Darcy was beheaded on Tower Hill on June 30th.

M. H. and R. Dodds, *The Pilgrimage of Grace*, 2 vols. 1915.
K. Pickthorn, *Early Tudor Government: Henry VIII.* 1834

ELIZABETH BARTON, the Nun of Kent, was born in 1506 and was hanged at Tyburn on April 20th, 1534. She was a domestic servant in the family of Thomas Cobb at Aldington, in Kent. In 1525 she fell ill of some intestinal disease. On her recovery she was seized with religious mania, fell into trances and cried out with 'marvellous holiness in rebuke of sin and vice'. Cobb, Richard Masters, the parish priest, and Warham, Archbishop of Canterbury, believed her to be inspired by the Holy Ghost. Dr. Bocking, the cellarer of Christ Church, Canterbury, was sent to investigate. He saw a chance of exploiting the girl as propaganda for the old beliefs and customs of the Catholic Church. Having taught her what to say in the trances which she could now simulate at will, and having arranged a 'miracle' in the Chapel of Our Lady in the next village, he removed her to the priory of St. Sepulchre at Canterbury (1527).

Her fame as a prophetess spread rapidly and she became a source of income to the monks of Christ Church. Wolsey, Fisher, Bishop of Rochester, and Sir Thomas More became persuaded that she was genuine, and even some exalted ladies at the Court had contacts with her. But as soon as it was known that Henry VIII was planning to divorce his wife and to marry Anne Boleyn, the Nun of Kent began to inveigh against the king and to prophesy that, if he married Anne, he would die 'a villain's death' within a month and should no longer be 'king of this realm'. Henry took no notice of the prophecy and married Anne. He was not dead within six months. Instructed by Bocking, the Nun announced that Henry, like Saul, was no longer king in the eyes of God and that his subjects were freed from their allegiance. This was high treason. The Nun, Bocking, Masters and six other persons were arrested. All admitted the imposture. In January, 1534, an Act of Attainder was brought in against them, and both More and Fisher were included in it. Proceedings against these two were dropped. On April 20th Elizabeth Barton, Bocking and the other priests were hanged—Bocking, it is said, with abominable cruelty.

Froude, *History of England*, vols. I and II.

BILNEY, THOMAS, martyr, was born probably in 1495 and died at the stake in 1531, aged approximately 36. His family name was derived from the Norfolk villages of Bilney. While still very young he went up to Trinity Hall, Cambridge, in order to study Law, and he did in fact take a Bachelor degree in civil and canon law. But by temperament he was much more religiously than legally minded. From his own account he was for some time unhappy and went through a spiritual conflict, but when Erasmus's version of the New Testament in Latin, not Greek, appeared, Bilney bought a copy 'and at first reading (as I well remember) I chanced upon this sentence of St. Paul (O most sweet and comfortable sentence to my soul) in I Tim. i: "It is a true saying and worthy of all men to be embraced that Christ Jesus came into the world to save sinners, of whom I am the chief and principal". I seemed unto myself inwardly to feel a marvellous comfort and quietness, insomuch that my bruised bones leaped for joy.' He abandoned the law and in 1519 was ordained priest.

Bilney was one of the group of Cambridge men who gathered at the White Horse to discuss the new learning and from that to go on to religious disputes, hence the White Horse came to be known as 'Little Germany'. Here he became friends with such men as Hugh Latimer (whom he took as his Confessor), Robert Barnes (whom he converted), Matthew Parker, to be later Archbishop of Canterbury. Everybody loved 'little Bilney', so small, so modest, so friendly, and he became almost the leader of the Cambridge reformers.

Whereas many of his friends became gradually more and more heretical, Bilney remained orthodox on all the main doctrines of the Catholic Church, so orthodox that it is a misnomer to call him a Protestant martyr. Bilney was not without some eccentricities. He detested music: 'coming from the Church where singing was he would lament to his scholars the curiosity of their dainty singing which he called rather mockery with God than otherwise': and when Dr. Thirleby, at that time a scholar with rooms below Bilney's (later he was the first and only Bishop of Westminster), began to play upon his recorder, Bilney 'would resort straight to prayer'. Luther would not have approved of this hatred of music.

Bilney's sermons provoked a great deal of opposition because he stressed the direct access of the individual to God without the need for pilgrimage or the intercession of saints, and he came to be looked on, quite unfairly, even if naturally, as a Lutheran. In 1526 Wolsey himself examined Bilney at Cambridge. He seems to have exacted from him an oath that he did not hold and would not propagate Lutheran doctrines. But the next year (1527) Bilney preached a series of sermons in London denouncing the idolatry of saints and complaining of the idolatry of the Christian Church, but for which the Jews would have been converted. Inevitably he was had up before a panel of bishops presided over by Cuthbert Tunstal, Bishop of London. Bilney was in the most perilous position, for as the law stood he had recanted before Wolsey in 1526; now he was facing a charge of being a relapsed heretic, for which the only penalty was to be burned at the stake. Tunstal behaved with the most Christian patience and gentleness, obviously wholly anxious to save Bilney. He suspended the trial to give Bilney a chance to think again in private: Bilney refused to recant. On the fourth day Tunstal convicted him of heresy, rather on the accusations of his opponents than on his own answers, but he postponed sentence till the next day, when he again implored Bilney to consult his friends, and gave him till the afternoon to decide. Bilney refused to recant, Tunstal gave him two more days in which to consult his friends. On the seventh day of the trial Bilney recanted. He was sentenced to carry a faggot at St. Paul's, to refrain from saying Mass publicly and from preaching until he was given permission to do so. He was also to remain in prison until he was set free by Wolsey (December 1527). Wolsey released him in November 1528.

Bilney returned to Cambridge a broken man, tortured by the memory of his recantation. Latimer has recorded that so inconsolable was Bilney that his friends dared not leave him alone. At last he made up his mind. One night he left Cambridge, telling his friends that he was going 'up to Jerusalem'. He went to Norwich, where his unpopularity was greatest. He preached in the open fields and gave a copy of Tyndale's *New Testament* to the 'anchoress of Norwich', probably Dame Agnes Edrygge. Reluctantly the bishop of Norwich ordered Bilney's arrest. What else could he do? Bilney was tried as a relapsed heretic and was burned at the stake.

A controversy sprang up after his death over whether he had at the last moment made a complete recantation. So nearly completely was he orthodox that any statement he made would look like a recantation. The whole problem is examined in *The Recantation of Thomas Bilney* by E. G. Rupp, London Quarterly, April 1942. It is unlikely that any convincing answer can be produced now. When all is said and done, the orthodox 'little Bilney' lit as long-lasting a candle in England as did the reformers, Latimer and Ridley.

E. G. Rupp, *The English Protestant Tradition*, 1949.
H. Maynard Smith, *Henry VIII and the Reformation*, 1948.
C. Sturge, *Cuthbert Tunstal*, 1938.

FRITH, JOHN, Protestant martyr, was born in 1505 at Westerham in Kent and he was burned at the stake in 1533 at the age of 28. He was the son of an innkeeper, he went to school at Eton College and at the age of fifteen went to King's College, Cambridge. There was another Etonian at King's, Edward Fox, the great friend of Stephen Gardiner, which may be the reason for Frith's becoming Gardiner's pupil—a fact which was to have tragic consequences later. Inevitably this clever and scholarly young man frequented the White Horse Tavern, taken there no doubt by Gardiner and Fox. What Frith there imbibed became for him the truth, for which he suffered partly at the hands of Gardiner, who even so did his best to save his pupil.

Frith was well known for his personal beauty and for his wit and friendliness. He was also a young man of great abilities and a fine scholar. It is just possible that he may have met Tyndale at Cambridge. He took his degree in 1525 and the next year he was transferred to the new foundation at Oxford, Cardinal College—in itself a tribute to his scholarship, for Wolsey was on the look out only for the best in the new learning. But these young men from Cambridge were already infected with heresy from the meetings at the White Horse Tavern. Frith was arrested and put into prison, whence he was rescued by Wolsey, who forbad him to go more than ten miles from Oxford. Frith disobeyed and went abroad (1528) to Antwerp, not to Marburg as is usually said. He was certainly in close touch with Tyndale, but it is untrue that he helped Tyndale in the translation of the New Testament, for that book was published two years before Frith went abroad. It is possible that he helped in the revision of the 1534 edition, which was published after his death.

Henry VIII was very anxious to help Frith and to save him from heresy. Cromwell wrote to his close friend, Stephen Vaughan, who was trying to persuade Tyndale to return to England, that the King heard good reports of Frith's learning and laments that he should use it in furthering the 'venomous and pestiferous works, erroneous and seditious opinions of the said Tyndale'. Henry hoped that Frith was not 'so far yet inrooted' in such evil doctrines and he wished Vaughan to try to persuade Frith to return to England. But Frith would not renounce his opinions.

In 1530 he came back to England, but he was arrested in Reading and put in the stocks, from which he was rescued by the local schoolmaster.

Probably he went abroad again and returned in 1532, but perhaps he was here for two years and then tried to escape abroad. In any case, in 1532 he was arrested in Essex and put into the Tower, on what charge is not known. In the Tower he was well treated and was even allowed to go out to dine with friends. While he was in prison he formulated his religious views on paper, exactly what Tyndale had begged him not to do. His views on transubstantiation were highly heretical.

After five months in the Tower Frith was brought up in front of a commission of bishops, presided over by Cranmer, all of whom were only anxious to save Frith—Cranmer interviewed him alone 'three or four times to persuade him to leave that imagination'. It is possible even that Cranmer arranged for him to have a chance to escape abroad, but Frith would not take it. Gardiner, his old tutor, also did his best, but all to no avail. Frith refused to recant anything and revealed himself as undoubtedly a heretic by the standards of the times. He was condemned and was handed over to the secular arm to be burned.

He was burned at Smithfield on July 4th, 1533, bound back to back with a young tailor's apprentice, Andrew Hewet, at the same stake. Dr. Cooke, a London parson, told the people, while Frith was burning, that it was as wrong to pray for the heretics as it was to pray for a dog. 'The Lord forgive thee' were Frith's last words. His doctrine of the Sacrament is that now adopted in the Book of Common Prayer.

The article in the *D..N.B.* is very inaccurate.
Maynard Smith, *Henry VIII and the Reformation*, 424–431, 1948.

FOREST, JOHN, martyr, was born in 1470 (perhaps 1474) and died in 1538. He became a friar Observant at Greenwich. Henry VIII greatly respected these friars, which may be the reason why Forest was appointed Confessor to Catherine of Aragon. When Wolsey determined to visit the house at Greenwich, the friars strongly opposed him, but Forest persuaded them to agree. After Henry began his search for a divorce from Catherine, the Provincial, Peto, preached a bold sermon in the presence of Henry forthrightly denouncing the divorce. As a result, Forest was made Provincial in Peto's place. No doubt Henry expected that Forest would take his side, but instead Forest began to preach quite as strongly as Peto against the divorce. In 1533 he was dismissed and put into prison. In October 1534 the Greenwich Observants were dispersed and it would be about this time that Forest made some sort of submission. Hall says that Forest at his later trial stated that 'he took the oath with his outward man, but his inward man was never consented thereunto'. Latimer gave a more respectable version: 'Laws must be obeyed and civil ordinances I will follow outwardly, but my heart in religion is free to think as I will.'

For about two years Forest was free from prison, but he went about exhorting people to stand firm in the old forms of religion and he produced a book *De Auctoritate Ecclesiae et Pontificis Maximi* in which he vehemently attacked the claim that the King could be head of the Church in spiritual matters. In 1538 he was arrested on a charge, not of treason, but of heresy. Under examination Forest's courage gave way and he made a full submission. When the recantation was brought to him, he recovered his nerve and refused to accept it. He was handed over to the secular arm to be burned as a relapsed and obstinate heretic.

Forest was burned at Smithfield on May 22nd, 1538. Care was taken to make the scene specially memorable. Cromwell, Lords of the Council, the Lord Mayor and many other important personages were present. Latimer made a long speech urging Forest to recant. Forest's answer was, 'I will die. Do your worst upon me. Seven years ago you durst not for your life have preached such words as these; and now, if an angel from heaven should come down and teach me any other doctrine than that I learned as a child, I would not believe him.

Take me; cut me in pieces, joint from joint. Burn, hang, do what you will, I will be true henceforth to my faith.'

In a chapel in Llan Dderfel in Wales there had been a wooden figure of an ancient Welsh saint, Dderfel Gadern, which had for long been a lucrative shrine for the parish. Cromwell had ordered this image to be sent to London to be destroyed. One of its alleged attributes was that it could destroy a forest by fire. The image was now broken up and was used as faggots with which to burn Forest. Over the pyre was slung a kind of bed made of chains. In this bed Forest was laid and was slung above the flames to be slowly roasted to death.

Froude, *H. of E.*, vol. iii, 105 sqq.
Maynard Smith, *Henry VIII and the Reformation*, 442 sqq., 1948.

LAMBERT, JOHN, (his real name was Nicholson, but he took the name of Lambert, on his own shewing for fear the bishops might murder him), martyr, was born at some unknown date in Norwich and was burned at the stake at Smithfield in November 1538. Educated at Cambridge, he became a Fellow of Queens' College in 1521. It is said that Thomas Bilney converted him to Protestantism, but Bilney was never really a Protestant. Lambert, who frequented the White Horse in Cambridge, was ordained priest and had for a time a living in Norfolk, but he was in some trouble through reading forbidden books. The Merchant Adventurers then sent him to be their chaplain in the English House at Antwerp. In 1529 Sir Thomas More and Bishop Tunstal passed through Antwerp and no doubt heard about the Protestant propaganda which Lambert was carrying on. This may well be the reason why More, when he became Lord Chancellor, had Lambert sent back to England (1532).

Lambert was summoned to Lambeth and was confronted with forty-five articles which he answered with great skill and learning. Archbishop Warham saved him and kept him at his own house at Otford. Warham died in August 1532 and Lambert was free. He took up teaching Latin and Greek to children, resigned his priesthood and thought of marrying, he also entered the Grocers' Company. But Lambert was a man who simply could not avoid controversy. He was soon in trouble. In 1535 he was arraigned before Cranmer and Latimer on a charge of denouncing the worship of saints. Latimer was said to be 'most extreme against him', but Lambert won his point that it was not necessary to eternal salvation to pray for the intercession of the saints and therefore it could not be heresy to abstain. But he would not learn: freed from prison on Friday, he was there on Saturday trying to reopen the whole discussion: as a result he was put into prison for a very short time.

Freed again, again Lambert asked for trouble. When Bishop Taylor of Lincoln, almost a Lutheran, preached a sermon on the Real Presence with some of which Lambert did not agree, Lambert was there at the foot of the pulpit and tried to start a dispute there and then. Taylor refused to listen and told Lambert to put his criticisms into writing. Lambert did this and produced a point of view very near to that of the Swiss reformer, Zwingli. At this moment Robert Barnes was sitting on a commission charged with the duty of extirpating these 'Sacramentaries'. Taylor sent Lambert's paper to Barnes who passed it on to Cranmer. Lambert was summoned to appear before Cranmer: very rashly he appealed from Cranmer to the Supreme Head of the Church, Henry VIII himself.

Henry was at this moment anxious to prove to the world that, although he had repudiated the Papacy, he had not repudiated the Catholic faith. What more convincing way than by personally presiding over the trial of an alleged heretic? The trial took place and Henry presided. The trial was not an edifying spectacle. Only the bishops behaved decorously. The King magnificently dominated the scene, but the occasion and perhaps the too similar characters of King and defendant combined to bring out the worst side of Henry's bullying character. Lambert kept his end up for some time, but after standing for five hours he was too weary to make any answers at all. The conclusion was inevitable. To Henry's question, 'Do you believe that in the Sacrament of the Altar is the Body of Christ?', Lambert infuriated the King by replying, 'St. Augustine. . . .': 'I do not want to know what St. Augustine says. What do you believe?' Lambert answered, 'I deny that it is the Body of Christ.' There was no answer to that except the flames of Smithfield.

The present writer knows of only two biographies of Lambert, the one in the *D.N.B.* and the short, but vivid portrait drawn by H. Maynard Smith in his *Henry VIII and the Reformation*. This article owes everything to both.

BARNES, ROBERT, Protestant martyr, was born at Lynn in Norfolk in 1495 and was burned at the stake in 1540, at the age of 45. Very early in life he became an Augustinian friar and joined the Austin friars at Cambridge. Soon after he went abroad to study at Louvain, and on his return he was made Prior of the Austin house. Barnes's enthusiasm for learning soon turned his house into a centre of classical reading and learning. It is most probable that he met Erasmus, but there is no evidence that he did so. One of his pupils was Miles Coverdale. In 1523 he took his D.D. and he became much interested in theological questions, partly as a result of coming under the influence of Bilney, who claimed to have converted Barnes. Soon Bilney, Barnes and Latimer were the leading members of that group of 'modernists' who met at the White Horse in Cambridge and discussed the views of Luther.

Barnes first fell foul of the Cambridge authorities over a sermon he preached on Christmas Eve 1525 in which he attacked with much amusing scurrility the litigiousness of the age. The charge brought against Barnes was that he had preached the doctrine of the Anabaptists that lawsuits were unlawful between Christians. In fact, he had never said this. His error lay in his never realizing that, the law of England being what it was, he had put himself into a perilous position. He was examined in Cambridge, but his case was remitted to Wolsey in London.

Thanks to the friendly help of Gardiner and of Fox, Barnes was given a private interview with Wolsey. Wolsey did all he could to save Barnes from the effects of the law. Barnes was unhelpful and Wolsey at last warned him that if he persisted in his attitude 'then you must burn' (February 1526).

At his own request Barnes was next formally tried by a panel under the Bishop of Bath. Barnes was argumentative and tedious. On being at last told that he must either recant or burn he recanted and abjured all the articles preferred against him, none of which (it is fair to add) had the remotest connection with the main doctrines of the Catholic Church. A wiser man than Barnes would have spotted this. He was commanded to make his recantation in public. Barnes has left a vivid account of the ceremony, but one is justified in thinking that he was more concerned with the sense of the ridiculous than of the shame. Gardiner once described Barnes as 'a trim, minion friar Augustine, one of a merry scoffing wit, friarlike, and as a good fellow in company well loved of many'. A later historian has written of him 'he was the man who called for drinks'. (Cooper, *Athenæ*, i, 215). But Barnes was also a conceited, vain man, one who overrated his own abilities and who loved to stand in the limelight. The sixteenth century was not an age in which it was safe to stand in the limelight. It may redound to Barnes's credit that he was ready to be burned for his convictions: it does not necessarily follow that those convictions were worth burning for, or that he need ever have burned for them, had he been a wiser and no less honest man.

After the trial Barnes was not allowed to return to Cambridge: he was put into house-arrest in London, but he was left free to work and to teach. He was not a staid enough man to take clear stock of his position. He now sold copies of Tyndale's *New Testament*, a forbidden book, and it is likely that he behaved in other indiscreet ways. Barnes was now sent to close confinement at Northampton. There his friends advised him to leave feigned evidence of suicide, which he did, and while the authorities dragged the river, Barnes escaped overseas to Wittenberg (1528). He had now put himself into the position of a relapsed heretic.

At Wittenberg he was welcomed by the German reforming theologians and he lived in the same house as Martin Luther. Here under the name of Antonius Amarius or Anglus he wrote his *Articles of the Christian Church*, published in German in 1531, which provided full evidence that he was a heretic. (See Rupp, *The English Protestant Tradition*, pp. 39–40.) His *Supplication unto the most gracious prynce Henry VIII* appeared in the same year (1531) and a copy was sent to Henry. Henry and Cromwell at this time were in need of Protestant help against the Papacy and sent for Barnes to come to England under a safe conduct. Barnes paid a short visit to England. Sir Thomas More, the Lord Chancellor, would have put him into prison again—'Barnes but for the King's safe conduct should have standen in peril to be burned and his books.'

In 1535 Barnes dedicated his *History of the Popes* to Henry VIII in the hopes of obtaining some preferment, but all he got was a Welsh prebend worth £18 a year, although he had been employed by Henry and Cromwell on diplomatic missions. The probable truth is that Henry cordially detested Barnes. About this time Barnes took to saying the Mass and *Te Deum* in English, but he strenuously opposed the Anabaptists and the Sacramentaries, those who denied transubstantiation. He was put on to a commission to 'extirpate Sacramentaries' and in the course of this work he delated John Lambert to Cranmer, with the result that Lambert was burned at Smithfield.

In 1539 Barnes was sent to Germany to negotiate the marriage with Anne of Cleves: his success can not have made him any more popular with Henry. In the Catholic reaction of 1540 Barnes soon found himself in serious trouble. He preached a sermon at St. Paul's in which he scurrilously attacked Bishop Gardiner for some criticisms Gardiner had made against the friars. Gardiner complained to the King, an examination was ordered and Barnes abjectly broke down. Gardiner behaved generously and offered Barnes a pension and to have him to live with him in his own house for instruction. Barnes signed a very mildly worded recantation and was ordered to preach again in London. He did so and Gardiner was present. Barnes preached such an ambiguous sermon that the Lord Mayor asked Gardiner if he should not commit Barnes to prison. Barnes was sent to the Tower, he was condemned by an Act of Attainder without trial and he was burned at the stake on July 30th, 1540.

The above account is based on the article by Gardiner in the *D.N.B.* corrected in details by E. G. Rupp's *The English Protestant Tradition*.

BARLOW, WILLIAM, Bishop, was one of four sons of John Barlow, who was a member of the Essex-Hertfordshire branch of the family and who was implicated in the rebellion of Perkin Warbeck. There was also a sister, Elizabeth, who became a lady-in-waiting to Margaret Tudor, wife of James IV of Scotland. Professor Rupp has shewn in his *The English Protestant Tradition* that the articles in the *D.N.B.* and other dictionaries 'conflate the careers of two, three, and possibly four persons besides being embellished with details proper to the career of his brothers John and Roger'. There are errors also in the 1958 edition of the *Oxford Dictionary of the Christian Church*, the *Dictionary of English Church History*, and in H. Maynard Smith's *Henry VIII and the Reformation*. The following account is written subject to any correction which future research may make necessary.

There is no evidence for the date of William Barlow's birth: none that he was ever at Oxford or Cambridge, and none that he was ever consecrated a bishop, probably because the Canterbury Register was carelessly kept. There is no doubt that he held a series of preferments as Canon or Prior, including Prior of Bromehill in Norfolk (1525). This house was dissolved in 1528 and the endowments transferred to Wolsey's new college at Ipswich. Probably Barlow was compensated with employment in Wolsey's household: he was sent to Italy in 1528 on the matter of the King's divorce. In 1534 he became Prior of the Canons Regular at Haverfordwest, a post which he owed to the patronage of Anne Boleyn. By this time Barlow was a strong reformer and he fell foul of the clergy in the district, who maltreated his servants and threatened him with persecution. Barlow wrote to Cromwell bewailing the blindness and ignorance of the Welsh clergy, saying that 'no diocese is so without hope of reformation'. He was transferred from Haverfordwest to Bisham, but in 1535-6 he was sent by Cromwell on an embassy to the court of James IV, no doubt because his sister was lady-in-waiting to the Queen.

Perhaps as a reward for his service he was made Bishop of St. Asaph's (1535), but he was almost at once translated to St. David's (1536) and probably never even visited St. Asaph's. At St. David's he at once fell out with the canons, who delated him to Roland Lee, the Lord President of the Marches of Wales, for having preached against purgatory and confession and for claiming that when two or three persons, even 'cobblers and weavers were in company, and elected, in the name of God, that there was the true Church of God'. Barlow became impatient with one of his 'chaunters' and had him put into prison. He then refused to pay the fine which Roland Lee imposed on him. At last Barlow tried to remove his cathedral seat away from St. David's to Caermarthen. But Barlow was genuinely interested in the education of his people and he obtained the grant of the endowments from some suppressed houses to found Christ's College, Brecon.

In 1548 under Edward VI Barlow attracted the favourable attention of Protector Somerset by a sermon against images. As a reward he was translated from St. David's to Bath and Wells. On the accession of Mary, Barlow resigned his see and fled the country to Germany. When Elizabeth came to the throne he returned and assisted in the consecration of Matthew Parker as Archbishop of Canterbury. He was made Bishop of Chichester in 1559 and a prebend of Westminster. He died in 1569 and was buried at Chichester.

William Barlow was not the author of the *Burial of the Mass* nor of the *Lutheran Factions*. These two pieces of vituperative propaganda were the work of Jerome Barlow, who had no connection with William. William was the translator of part of the Apocrypha for the *Bishops' Bible*, a new translation commanded by Matthew Parker and published in 1568, which remained the official version until the Authorised Version of 1611. Barlow was a typical Erastian bishop of his time on the reforming side, violent in his opinions, unwise often in his treatment of opponents, (as in Wales), and sometimes lacking in seriousness. Cranmer once said of him that 'Brother Barlow has spoken the truth, but in half an hour he will teach the world to believe that it was but in jest'. One unique achievement he may claim, that he married his five daughters to five Anglican bishops.

E. G. Rupp, *The English Protestant Tradition*, 1949.
L. B. Smith, *Tudor Prelates and Politics*, 1953.

TYNDALE, WILLIAM, (the family also used the surname of Hutchyns), translator of the Bible, was born almost certainly at Slimbridge in Gloucestershire, where is now established the Wildfowl Trust. It is possible that he was born on the west side of the Severn in Monmouthshire: certainly he was not born at North Nibley, where his monument now stands. The date of his birth is also uncertain, perhaps 1491, 1492, 1495. He was put to death at Louvain in 1536 when he was between 41 and 45 years of age. We know little of his early life and next to nothing of his family, which may possibly have tended towards Lollardy. Tyndale went to Magdalen, Oxford, in 1508 or 1510, under the name of Hychyns. He took his B.A. degree in 1512, his M.A. in 1515, and in 1518 he migrated to Cambridge to learn Greek, probably because Croke, the greatest teacher in Europe, had just returned to Cambridge and Tyndale wanted to read the New Testament in the original Greek. In 1521 for financial reasons he left the university and became tutor to the children of Sir John Walsh at Little Sodbury in Gloucestershire. He stayed there about two years and left at his own request. He had quarrelled with the local clergy and the visitors at Sir John's table, where he tactlessly aired his modern theological views, learned at Cambridge— so much so, that he was arraigned before the Archdeacon of Gloucester as a dangerous heretic. (The Bishop of Gloucester was an Italian absentee, Julio de'Medici, later Pope Clement VII.) Tyndale was cleared of the charge of heresy, but it was better for all that he should leave the district. Sir John recommended him to Sir Henry Guildford who introduced him to Tunstal, Bishop of London. Tyndale had made up his mind that he must translate the New Testament into

English as an antidote to the sickness from which he believed the Church to be suffering. 'If God spare my life, ere many years I will cause a boy that driveth the plough shall know more of the scriptures than thou dost.' His plan now was to become chaplain to the Bishop of London, to live in his palace and there to translate the New Testament. But Tyndale was wholly unqualified for the post of chaplain and Tunstal told him that he had four chaplains already and had no room for any more.

Tyndale now fell in with a Gloucestershire man named Poyntz, a relation of Sir John Walsh, who arranged for him to preach at St. Dunstan-in-the-West. Here he became acquainted with a rich cloth merchant, Henry Monmouth, who had him to live with him for the next six months. Tyndale soon grew weary of London, he was disgusted with the London 'praters', despised the pageantry of the Church and was outraged by the magnificence of Wolsey. He made up his mind to go abroad, 'as there was no room in My Lord of London's house to translate the New Testament; also there was no place to do it in all England'.

It was while he was in London that Tyndale was first influenced by Lutheran ideas and it was here that he met and became friends with the future martyr, John Frith. When, therefore, he went abroad, he was already infected with heretical opinions. He set out with the intent to find some town where he could in peace translate the New Testament from the original Greek into vernacular English. The town he selected was Hamburg. Since he was destitute of money, somebody must have financed him. It must surely have been the Merchant Adventurers in London, of whom Henry Monmouth was one. They had agencies at Antwerp and Calais and were closely connected with Hamburg and Lübeck merchants in London. These wealthy, middle-class merchants were much interested in Lutheranism, were strongly anti-clerical and hoped for a Lutheran reformation in England, largely in order to get rid of ecclesiastical laws which hampered their trade. They saw in Tyndale the right man for their purpose. They sent him to Germany where he could translate and have printed the New Testament in English which they would arrange to smuggle into England.

At Hamburg Tyndale went to the house of a Protestant widow, Margaret von Emmersen, whose nephew was about to go to Wittenberg. Tyndale went with him, or as Sir Thomas More put it, 'gat him to Luther straight'. On May 27th, 1524, there matriculated at the university a certain Gulielmus Daltin, who was in fact William Tyndale with the syllables reversed. He was probably the first Englishman to arrive at Wittenberg. He remained there from May to December 1524, when he returned to Hamburg to pick up a sum of money which had been sent to him by Henry Monmouth. In January 1525 he was back in Wittenberg where he met a 'plausible but penniless' scoundrel named Roye, an apostate English friar, who now became Tyndale's amanuensis. In six weeks Tyndale's translation of the New Testament from Greek into English was copied out and the two of them went to Cologne to get the book printed (August 1525). Peter Quentel, a Catholic printer, was ready to print the book for the English market: a contract was made for a quarto volume with references, marginal notes and a prologue. It was a dangerous undertaking: Roye talked too much and the municipal authorities forbad any further printing. Only a fragment, less than half of the quarto as far as it had gone, is to-day in the British Museum, which is all that has survived of the gospels of St. Matthew and St. Mark which Quentel had printed before the work was stopped.

In September 1525 Tyndale and Roye went to Worms and started their work all over again. So rapidly did they work that the new complete version, printed by Schoeffer, in octavo, not quarto, was on sale in London early in March 1526. This edition was a plain text without glosses, references or prologue: the book was thus the less controversial, smaller and easier to smuggle, and cheaper to sell.

From 1526 to 1529 Tyndale was in Antwerp, where the Merchant Adventurers were strongly established, communications with England were easy and heretics escaping from persecution could foregather. In 1529 he went to Hamburg and on the way he was shipwrecked off the coast of Holland and lost all the MSS of his translation of the Old Testament. Once again he had to start afresh, this time helped by Miles Coverdale. In 1530, hearing of the death of Wolsey, which made Antwerp a safer place, Tyndale returned thither and his translation of the Pentateuch from the original Hebrew text—Tyndale had taught himself Hebrew in two years—was issued from Hochstraten's press, although the imprint is of Lufft at Marburg. Unfortunately Tyndale rashly and unnecessarily added glosses to the text which laid him and his book open to the charge of heresy and alienated all orthodox people, especially the Anglican bishops.

When the New Testament was distributed in 1528, Sir Thomas More wrote as a counterblast his *Dialogue Concerning Heresies and Matters of Religion*, a statement of Catholic doctrine running to some 170,000 words. Tyndale replied in 1530 in his *Answer unto Sir Thomas More's Dialogue*. This was an able piece of criticism, but it was spoiled by its intense bitterness and grossly unfair personal attacks on More. Unhappily More replied with his wearisome *Confutation* in which he sank to unaccustomed scurrility and abuse. 'This contest of Tyndale and More was the classic controversy of the English reformation. No other discussion was carried on between men of such pre-eminence and ability and with such clear apprehension of the points at issue. To More's assertion of the paramount authority of the church Tyndale replied by appealing to scripture, with an ultimate resort to individual judgment, (*D.N.B.*).

During this period Tyndale published four other works of importance. In 1528 there appeared *The Wicked Mammon*, a work which owed almost everything to Luther: *The Obedience of a Christian Man* (1528), again largely inspired by Luther, being a defence of despotic government and an attack on personal freedom. It is difficult not to feel that Tyndale allowed himself to be overwhelmed by Protestant influences, difficult to believe that these two books represent his real views and feelings. His *Practice of Prelates* (1530) was both a forthright attack on the Papacy and also on Wolsey and the divorce proceedings. Before this last book reached England Cromwell had read the *Christian Obedience*, with the views of which both he and Henry VIII agreed so strongly that they tried to persuade Tyndale to return to England. The negotiations, which were carried out by Cromwell's friend, Stephen Vaughan, failed and Henry was so infuriated by one answer that Tyndale sent him that he tried to have Tyndale kidnapped (1531). Tyndale therefore left Antwerp for two years: when he returned in 1533 he went to live in the 'English House', a building set aside by the local authorities for the Merchant Adventurers in England.

Tyndale was now very near the end of his life. A handsome, unprincipled young man turned up in Antwerp and made friends with Tyndale. This was Henry Phillips, the son of a wealthy landowner in Dorset. Probably because he was desperately in need of money and hoped to recoup his fortunes by serving Charles V against the Protestants, Phillips, by means of the lowest forms of treachery, caused Tyndale to be arrested in Antwerp (1535). Tyndale was imprisoned in the state prison of Vilvorde, where he remained for eighteen months. In September Thomas Cromwell tried to get lenient treatment for him, but to no avail. In 1536 Tyndale was brought to trial, degraded from his ecclesiastical orders as a heretic and condemned to death. He was executed on October 6th, 1536, being strangled before his body was given to the flames to be burnt. At the stake he is said to have cried out, 'Lord, open the King of England's eyes'. Years before he had written, 'If they shall burn me, they shall do no other thing than I look for'.

Tyndale ought to be looked upon as one of the great heroes in English history. He described himself as being 'evil favoured in this world and without grace in the sight of men'; it is true also that he was apt to attribute to his opponents the lowest motives, although they were honourable men like Sir Thomas More. But his life was one of 'utter disappointment and struggle—persecuted in one city, fleeing to another' (Chambers). Only a man of the toughest fibre and the most invincible faith could have achieved what Tyndale achieved.

Plate 9

John Fisher, Bishop of Rochester

Sir Thomas More, Lord Chancellor

Plate 10

Edward VI

Edward Seymour, Duke of Somerset, Protector

Fundamentally, he was a simple and reasonable man, never a very good judge of character (or he would never have taken up with Roye or been taken in by Phillips), a very remarkable linguist and a wonderful writer of English prose. He died a martyr and he had his reward, in the most ironical manner. Those who had persecuted him as a heretic for translating the New Testament at last came to the conclusion that an authorized version of the Bible must be made available to the people. In 1537 Henry VIII commanded that Matthew's Bible should be placed in every parish church. This book was a composite work 'truly and purely translated by Thomas Matthew'. Matthew was in fact Rogers, the first victim of the Marian persecutions. But who had made most of the translations? Part of the Old Testament was the work of Miles Coverdale: part of the Apocrypha was translated by Rogers; the Pentateuch, the book of Jonah, almost certainly Joshua to II Chronicles, and the whole of the New Testament were the work of Tyndale. When the compilers of the Authorized Version in James I's reign came to do their work, it was to Tyndale that they turned, so that our Authorized Version to-day is mainly the work of Tyndale. Has any other one man given as great a gift to his own country, and as the centuries go by, to millions beyond his own country? Tyndale's Bible laid the foundations of the English literary language and his words and phrases have become part and parcel of the everyday speech of Englishmen.

Tyndale's Works: Parker Society.
J. F. Mozley, *William Tyndale*, 1937.
W. E. Campbell, *Erasmus, Tyndale and More*, 1949.
Maynard Smith, *Henry VIII and the Reformation*, 1948.
R. W. Chambers, *Man's Unconquerable Mind*, 1939.
C. Morris: *Political Thought in England, Tyndale to Hooker*, 1953.
J. H. Maclehose, *The Burnished Sword*, Blackie, 1956. (H.N.)

COVERDALE, MILES, first translator of the entire Bible into English, Bishop of Exeter, was born in Yorkshire—hence perhaps his name, Cover-Dale, in Richmond—almost certainly in 1488. It is as well here to make plain that exact details of

Coverdale's life, especially in the early years, are a matter of conjecture. He went to Cambridge, studied theology, was ordained priest and (1514) entered the convent of the Austin Friars at Cambridge. Coverdale was never a very strong character, was too apt to fall under the influence of the immediately stronger character than himself. He fell under the influence of Robert Barnes, Prior of the Austin Friars, and as a result frequented the White Horse tavern to discuss modern theological problems. Barnes must have been pretty well what we should call 'left wing' in theological matters, for he was summoned to London on charges of heresy and Coverdale went with him to help him prepare his defence. In London he made the acquaintance of Thomas Cromwell—it is now pretty certain that he did not make the acquaintance of Sir Thomas More—and the two became good friends. This must have been about 1526, before Cromwell was of any importance in politics, but when he was of importance in the City. The next year Coverdale got a grant from the government, presumably through Cromwell, to buy books for his theological studies. The next year (1528) Coverdale apostasized from his order, became a secular priest and took to preaching heretical views— that the Sacrament was only a *remembrance* of Our Lord's death: that auricular confession should be avoided: that worship should not be made to images. He had become a complete heretic. Thomas Cromwell, who was a careerist, if ever there was one, abandoned Coverdale as an unsafe man.

At this point dates are specially difficult. It is said that he took the degree of Bachelor of Common Law at Cambridge in 1531. On the other hand it seems fairly certain that he was out of the country from 1528 to 1534. Probably he went to Antwerp and there met Tyndale, and went with him to Hamburg, where he helped in the translation of the Pentateuch. In 1529 he seems to have been in Antwerp and to have joined Jacob von Meteren, a well-known Protestant printer of the time. Von Meteren paid Coverdale to translate the Bible into English, possibly because he had already heard that Cromwell in England was ready to back such a translation.

Certain it is that the House of Commons petitioned in 1534

that an authorized version of the Bible should be put into every parish church. It is not improbable that Cromwell turned to his old friend, Coverdale, to provide such a book. More than that cannot be said.   What is known is that a complete translation of the Bible was introduced into England. It was not printed in Antwerp, that was too dangerous: it was printed in Zurich by Froschover. There was in England a law against the sale of foreign books, therefore an English colophon was inserted: in 1536 Nycholson printed a new frontispiece with the words 'faithfully and fully translated into English' instead of the original 'translated out of Douche (German) and Latyn'. The first issue contained a dedication to Henry VIII and included the words 'your dearest wife . . . Queen Anne', but in no time the new queen was Jane Seymour and the word Anne was changed to Jane, in some copies by pen.

Coverdale was anxious to commend his book to Henry, and he wrote in his dedication words which strongly upheld the royal authority. For this reason, having the divorce in mind, he translated Deuteronomy xxv, 5, as 'her kynsman' and not as 'her husband's brother shall go in unto her'. Coverdale's reading is still the alternative reading in the Authorized Version.

Coverdale was not the fine linguist that Tyndale had been, nor did he pretend he was. His translation of the Bible was not made from original sources, as had been Tyndale's, but he used (as he said) 'five interpreters' in German and Latin. He also used Tyndale, but he was not the purist for strict accuracy that Tyndale was. Coverdale often chose a more dramatic word, he would add a word to improve the music of his prose, he would paraphrase the source, if he thought a paraphrase would make the meaning clearer. His translation of the Psalms is very far from accurate, but it is the version we use today in our Psalter and it is by far the best for singing. It is to be noted that Coverdale was more extreme in his Protestant views than was Tyndale, but he was a much wiser man and avoided the glosses and comments which Tyndale had added to his translation, thereby laying himself open to charges of heresy.

Coverdale was employed by Cromwell to help with the Great Bible of 1539, in which year he came to England to complete the work. On the fall of Cromwell he went abroad again and during the reaction of the 1540s his Bible was prohibited by proclamation (1542).

For a few years Coverdale lived at Tübingen, where he took a doctorate of divinity. In 1545 he was schoolmaster and pastor at Bergzabern. In the meantime he had defied Henry VIII's Six Articles and married Elizabeth Macheson. On the death of Henry he came back to England (it is possible that he was in England before Henry died). In 1548 he was staying at Windsor Castle, when Cranmer was there, preparing his First Book of Common Prayer. He had been appointed almoner to Queen Catherine Parr, but she died soon after her marriage to Lord Seymour and Coverdale preached the funeral sermon (1548). He was an excellent and popular preacher, and in 1551 he was appointed to the see of Exeter in the place of Bishop Voysey, who had reached the age of nearly 90. He took an active part in all the reforms of Edward VI's reign, but on the accession of Mary he was deprived of his bishopric, on the grounds of his marriage, and he went abroad. The King of Denmark, at the suggestion of Coverdale's brother-in-law (who rejoiced in the name of Maccabaeus McAlpine), invited him to go to Denmark and he was given a free pass to leave England with two servants—one was said to be his wife—and to take his baggage unsearched. For a time he preached to the English refugees at Wesel, and then, on the invitation of Duke Wolfgang, he returned to his old work at Bergzabern. In 1558 he was at Geneva and is said to have had a hand in the production of the Geneva Bible.

In 1559 he returned to England. He did not resume his bishopric, but he took part in the consecration of Parker as Archbishop of Canterbury, clad in a black gown, for his increasing Protestantism did not allow him now to wear vestments. In 1563 he refused the offer of the see of Llandaff and he began to pay little attention to the Act of Uniformity. Nobody seemed to mind until 1566, and then he resigned his living of St. Magnus near London Bridge rather than conform.

He continued to preach and he always drew large congregations. He died in February 1568 and was buried in St. Bartholomew's: when this church was pulled down in 1840, Coverdale's remains were translated to St. Magnus.

Coverdale was never as great a man as Tyndale. He was neither such a fine scholar nor such a good linguist: his literary style was more ornate than Tyndale's, but perhaps more musical. But he was essentially a good man, a good Christian and a most conscientious priest and bishop.

Conyers Read's bibliography of the Tudor period lists no biography of Coverdale. There is a long, full and excellent article on him in the *D.N.B.*, though a little confused in arrangement: The *Encyc. Brit.* contains an admirable article by A. F. Pollard. See also Maynard Smith, *Henry VIII and the Reformation.* 1949

ASKEW, ANNE, Protestant martyr, was born in 1521 and died in 1546, aged twenty-five. She came of an old Lincolnshire family, being the second daughter of Sir William Askew (or Ayscough) of Stallingborough, near Grimsby. She was very well educated and gave much of her time to studying the Bible and to disputing with the clergy of Lincoln Cathedral. Her sister was betrothed to one Thomas Kyme of Kelsey, but she died before the marriage could take place, whereupon Anne's father compelled her to marry Kyme, which she did much against her will. She had two children, but the marriage proved unhappy and Kyme turned her out of the house, to her great content.

In 1545 she was charged with heresy on account of her views on the Sacrament. Bonner did his level best to save her and she was in the end acquitted for want of witnesses against her. Soon afterwards she was summoned before the Council at Greenwich: she refused to make any recantation and was put to the rack, because it was thought that she was being secretly encouraged by important people whose names she might reveal under torture. She herself recorded that Lord Chancellor Wriothesley and the Solicitor-General, Rich, turned the screws with their own hands.

In 1546 she was charged again with heresy along with Dr. Shaxton, formerly Bishop of Salisbury, and two others. Shaxton recanted, Anne would not, and she and the others were burned at Smithfield on July 16th, 1546. So crippled was she from the rack that she had to be carried to the stake in a chair. Shaxton was appointed to preach the sermon before the fires were lighted and at the last moment Wriothesley offered Anne a pardon if she would recant. She again refused and went to the fire with the utmost composure and resolution. Her sufferings were shortened by bags of gunpowder which were hung round her body.

C. Wriothesley's *Chronicle*, Camden Society.
Foxe, *Book of Martyrs*.

BOCHER, JOAN, often known as Joan of Kent, Anabaptist martyr, died in 1550; the date of her birth is unknown. She first came into prominence as a 'great dispenser of Tyndale's New Testament' in about 1540 to the ladies of Henry VIII's court. She was a friend of Anne Askew who was burned for heresy in 1546. In 1542 she had been examined by Cranmer, but she was released, according to the Catholics in Canterbury, with Cranmer's connivance. In 1549 the Council was informed by the Justices of the Peace in Kent that Joan was at work again, spreading extraordinary opinions which the Justices could not well understand. One thing was certain, that she was an Anabaptist. It seemed that she was spreading abroad that Christ had not taken flesh of the Virgin, but had 'miraculously passed through the Virgin as through a glass' (Burnet's *Records*, v. 246–7). This was clearly heresy, but unfortunately the Acts against heresy had just been repealed and the Justices did not know what action ought to be taken. The Council gave orders for Joan to be arrested. She was examined and behaved defiantly before the Commission. All attempts to get her to recant failed and she was excommunicated. There was no statutory power now to burn heretics, but heresy could not be tolerated. Happily the Lord Chancellor discovered that heretics had been burned in England before any law against them had been passed (1401). Joan was condemned to be

burned, unless she recanted. The government did all they could
to persuade her to recant and her execution was postponed for
more than a year, perhaps because *de heretico comburendo* had
been repealed, and Somerset was a tolerant man (May 1549
to May 1550). Every day for a week Cranmer and Ridley
visited her to argue with her, but their efforts all failed. Joan
was defiant and abusive and she was at last burned on May 2nd.
She interrupted the sermon preached before her execution with
screams and curses, so that the general opinion was that it
would have been better to send her to Bedlam than to the stake.
There is not the least evidence for the story that Edward VI
viewed her execution with horror and only agreed to sign the
warrant very reluctantly.

Burnet, *History of the Reformation*, vol. v, 246–9.
Pollard, *England under Protector Somerset*, 1900.

EDWARD VI, King of England 1547–53, was born at
Hampton Court on October 12th, 1537, and died on July 6th,
1553, in his sixteenth year. He was the third child and only
legitimate son of Henry VIII; his mother was Henry's third
wife, Jane Seymour. Archbishop Cranmer was one of his godfathers. His mother died on October 24th and the heir to the
throne, 'His Majesty's most noble jewel', was brought up
'among the women' with every kind of precaution to ensure
his good health. The traditional view has been that Edward
was all his short life a frail and unhealthy child, but the latest
biography of him (H. W. Chapman, *The Last Tudor King*)
reveals him as a normally strong and healthy boy until the
last three years of his life, fond of athletic exercises. When
peace was made with Scotland in 1543, one of the terms was
that Edward, who was less than six years old, should marry
Mary, Queen of Scots, who was not yet seven months old.

At the age of six Edward was placed under his first tutor,
Dr. Cox. A year later Sir John Cheke was brought from Cambridge to help in the boy's education, and Sir Anthony Cooke
and Roger Ascham also shared in the teaching. Edward
proved himself an apt pupil, thanks largely to the enlightened
methods of Cheke, who soon became wholly responsible for

Edward's education and for whom Edward developed great affection, the only person on whose behalf he is known ever to have shewn any emotion. He quickly became proficient in Latin, Greek, and French, it is possible that he also spoke Italian, and he had the Tudor love for music and much interest in astronomy. Many boys of his own age and standing shared their education and recreations with him, on terms of equality, of whom his favourite was Barnaby Fitzpatrick, the son of Lord Ossory, and with him he continued to correspond all his short life.

Henry VIII died on January 28th, 1547. The new king was 9 years old. Henry had nominated a Council of Regency, of which the chief members were Edward's uncle, Edward Seymour, Earl of Hertford, later Duke of Somerset, and John Dudley, Viscount Lisle, later Earl of Warwick and Duke of Northumberland. The history of Edward's reign is rather the story of the struggle for power between these two councillors than of the acts of King Edward VI. But the young king was not the priggish, tiresomely precocious and unimportant child which historians have painted him. As a result of his own nature—he was not for nothing a Tudor and the son of Henry VIII—and his intensive education he matured quickly, too quickly. He soon revealed the Tudor capacity for bearing himself with dignity in public and for winning the affection of the people. Under Somerset the public appearances were frequent, long and exhausting, and the boy-king lived under too great pressure. He himself was intensely interested in religion and theology, he would listen to interminable sermons, making notes on them and discussing them afterwards. He became as fanatical a Protestant as his half-sister, Mary, was a fanatical Roman Catholic, and he strongly supported the doctrinal reformation which Cranmer, Somerset and Northumberland carried through and forced on the nation.

On the fall of Somerset and the victory of Warwick Edward was even more hardly pressed. Northumberland (as Warwick became) deliberately used the emotions and ambitions of the king to further his own selfish ends. Under the strain the boy's physical health gave way. 'Forced into the mould of a saviour and a genius, while being treated as a catspaw, he died in the process: probably because of it.' (Chapman, *ib*.) In April, 1552, he was attacked by measles and perhaps smallpox at the same time, but by May he had recovered. In September he was visited by Girolomo Cardano, the famous physician and astrologer from Milan, who has left a vivid picture of Edward's powers of argument, and who cast the king's horoscope—wrongly. (*T.S.I.H.*, 2, 42.)

In January, 1553, Edward was again ill, this time with consumption from which he never recovered. He was well enough to take seriously Ridley's frequent sermons on the poverty of the people. He discussed the problem with Ridley, sent for the Lord Mayor and finally handed over to the Corporation of London Bridewell Palace, which became Christ's Hospital, as 'a place of correction for the idle and vagabond', which later became an orphanage. St. Thomas's was to be rebuilt and endowed, and Grey Friars was to be used for poor relief.

By June the king's condition was beyond hope. He was now persuaded by Northumberland to agree to altering the succession, to cut out his two step-sisters, Mary and Elizabeth, in favour of Northumberland's daughter-in-law, Lady Jane Grey, and on June 14th the law officers were summoned to witness the king's 'devise'. On July 6th Edward died. The news of his death was suppressed until July 10th to give Northumberland time to complete his plans. The body was neither embalmed nor coffined during the nine hectic days before Mary ascended the throne on the failure of Northumberland's plot. It was not until August 8th that Edward was buried in Westminster Abbey.

The accounts left to us by foreign ambassadors of their audiences with the king leave no doubt that Edward was a highly intelligent youth; they prove also that he had a mind of his own, strength of character to insist on his own way, and even at that early age diplomatic skill, as in his dealings with the Emperor Charles V recounted by himself in his diary. Some of the state papers which he himself drew up, such as his memoranda for the Parliament of 1552 in twelve 'bills' for a reorganization of the government, with their many divisions and sub-divisions, suggest that had he lived, he might have become an able administrator. But the intensity and the narrowness of his religious views suggest also that, if that had happened, the Church of England might well have been a very different thing from what it became under Queen Elizabeth, and much less well adapted to the genius of the English people.

H. W. Chapman, *The Last Tudor King*, 1958.   (*Plate 10*)
S. T. Bindoff, 'A Kingdom at Stake', *History Today*, September, 1953.
C. Morris, *The Tudors*, 1955.

SEYMOUR, EDWARD, 1st EARL OF HERTFORD, DUKE OF SOMERSET, Protector, was born probably in 1506. He was executed on Tower Hill on January 22nd, 1552, at the approximate age of 46. He was the brother of Jane Seymour, Henry VIII's third wife. He led the normal life of a sixteenth-century courtier who had secured the good opinion of the king, holding various minor offices and amassing a very large number of estates, steadily advancing in the peerage, but for some time having little influence in politics. On the fall of Thomas Cromwell, Hertford (as he became in 1537) continued to rise in the king's favour. In 1542 he became Lord High Admiral, but he relinquished the post almost at once. In March, 1544, he was in command of the force sent to Scotland which pillaged Edinburgh, and in 1545 and 1546 he saw further military service in France, where he won a brilliant military success over de Briez at Boulogne in 1545. Signs of his increasing importance were his appointment in 1544 as Lieutenant of the kingdom during the king's absence in France and his diplomatic missions to the Emperor Charles V.

The jealousies between Hertford and the powerful Howard family (Norfolk and his son Surrey) came to a head in 1546. It is not possible to say that the dramatic fall of the Howards in January, 1547, was Hertford's work, but when on January 28th the king died, Hertford was by far the most important man in the kingdom. He succeeded in keeping the news of Henry's death secret until he had got possession of Edward VI, then the news was published, but the most inconvenient clauses of

Henry's will were suppressed. In spite of some opposition in the Council, Hertford was made Protector, and on February 16th he became Duke of Somerset. For the next two years he exercised virtually royal authority. In one prayer used by him he speaks of himself as 'caused by Providence to rule', and he even wrote to the king of France as 'brother'.

The problems which faced Somerset were many and difficult —a nation divided over religion, a war in Scotland and social discontent everywhere, were the chief evils waiting urgently to be cured.

Scotland. Somerset envisaged a peaceful union of the two countries in one 'empire' of Great Britain—a statesmanlike objective. He wanted the 'consent' of the Scots: his method was to go to war—a far from statesmanlike action. He won the Battle of Pinkie in September, 1547, and lost thereby all hope of reconciliation with Scotland. Mary Queen of Scots was sent to France and married the Dauphin instead of Edward VI.

Religion. Somerset was a hot and advanced Protestant and he at once set about making England into a Protestant country. He began by claiming to exercise the Royal Supremacy and enforcing the use of English in church services, a measure which Gardiner and Bonner opposed and they were therefore sent to the Tower. The heresy laws of Henry VIII and the treason laws were repealed, a sign of his moderation, but an act was passed dissolving the chantries—another step in secularizing church property. Parliament authorized the Communion to be administered in both kinds (the bread *and* the wine) and the marriage of priests was allowed. The first stage in this revolution culminated in the Book of Common Prayer of 1549 and the Act of Uniformity. This book was a compromise in the hope that the Catholics would accept it, and as such it was a failure. It led to a rising in Cornwall, but it had no influence in provoking Ket's Rebellion in East Anglia.

Social Discontent. Agrarian discontent was rife all over England and the discontent was made worse by inflation. High prices, enclosures for pasture and encroachments on the common land were the chief symptoms. The chief mouthpiece of discontent were the clerics and preachers, men such as Latimer and John Hales of Coventry, who persuaded Somerset that the enclosures were the work of hard-hearted and tight-fisted landowners. Hales in 1547 tried to cure the evil by three bills presented to Parliament, but the House of Commons, where sat the landowners, rejected them all. Somerset in 1548 condemned enclosures by proclamations and set up commissions to enforce the laws against them. All over England minor riots took place: Ket's rebellion (1549) brought things to a head.

Somerset had clearly failed to provide good government. His position was already shaken by his having sent his brother, Lord Admiral Seymour, to the block on a charge of treason. In October, 1549, Somerset was arrested, but was soon released. His chief rival, Warwick, for two years bided his time. In October, 1551, he acted. Somerset was arrested on a faked charge of treason and in February, 1552, he was executed.

The reasons for his failure are not difficult to understand. From the very first his position, constitutionally, was unsound, for it was known that he had usurped power against the wish of Henry VIII by suppressing the king's will. That might have been forgiven him, if he had provided sound government. Unhappily he was the wrong man in the wrong place at the wrong moment. Like other public men of his day he was ambitious, as his seizing power proves—and he was rapacious for wealth. He made a huge fortune out of the spoliation of the church property. His great extravagance in the building of Somerset House gave general offence. He even destroyed an aisle of St. Paul's Cathedral to provide the material.

On the other hand he had many and considerable merits of a kind rare in statesmen of his day. He was a genuine lover of liberty, he had a sincere and warm affection for the poor, his mind was original and in some respects far-sighted, as in his plans for a union with Scotland, and his personal life was lived on a high plane of morality. He was a refined and sensitive man in a rough and brutal age: in all his letters there is never a coarse nor a brutal word such as disfigured the letters of Thomas Cromwell. He looked on duelling as 'a heathenish custom'. He was well read and a good linguist, but he had no artistic sense and he was an inconoclast. He hated extreme measures and there were no burnings under his government. Yet he was a failure and a disastrous failure.

The truth is that, if he was far-sighted, he was not at all clear-sighted. However admirable his intentions may have been, his methods were deplorable. He ruined his plans for Scotland by his lack of imagination and his impatience. It was madness in the sixteenth century to repeal all the strong weapons which Henry VIII had forged exactly at the moment when Somerset was planning a religious revolution in a country already divided and turbulent. He forgot that Edward VI was a minor and that, even if the country would accept a Royal Supremacy, it would not easily accept a mere Ducal Supremacy. Noble-minded, generous, he may have been, but he was impetuous, impatient, and at times violent and headstrong, obstinate and self-willed. In short, he was no statesman at a moment when only the highest form of statesmanship could have saved the situation to which he had called himself as saviour. (*Plate 10*)

The only biography of Somerset is that by A. F. Pollard, which draws a very favourable portrait. For an alternative view of him, see G. R. Elton, *England under the Tudors*.

DUDLEY, JOHN, EARL OF WARWICK, DUKE OF NORTHUMBERLAND, soldier, sailor, statesman, was born probably in 1502 and died in 1553, aged about fifty-one. He was the son of that Edmund Dudley, Henry VII's financial minister, who was executed by Henry VIII, and Elizabeth Grey, daughter of Edward Grey, Viscount Lisle. In 1512 Edmund Dudley's attainder was repealed and John Dudley was restored in blood when he was about eleven years old.

Dudley soon made a name for himself at court by his physical courage and his daring and skilful horsemanship both in tourney and in military exercises. In 1523 he was knighted by the Duke of Suffolk, in whose army he was serving at Calais. During the next fifteen years he received many minor appoint-ments and in 1538 he became deputy governor of Calais. In 1542 he was created Lord Lisle and was also made lord high admiral for life. He was with the Earl of Hertford (later Protector Somerset) when he ravaged the lowlands of Scotland and burned Edinburgh to the ground (1544); he became a Privy Councillor in 1543; he led the assault on Boulogne in 1544 and was governor of Boulogne from 1544 to 1546. In that year he was made Earl of Warwick and the next year he was one of the executors of Henry VIII's will and a member of the commission which Henry provided to govern during the minority of his son, Edward VI. Warwick, however, readily agreed to Somerset's monopolizing all the power as Protector (1547).

The next two years greatly increased Warwick's fame and reputation. He resigned the office of lord admiral which went to Somerset's brother, Thomas Seymour. When Somerset invaded Scotland in 1547, Warwick was lord-lieutenant of the army which won the battle of Pinkie, largely through Warwick's military genius. He next became President of Wales (1584–50): he served again in Scotland (1549): and he crushed Ket's rebellion at Dussindale outside Norwich (1549).

As his fame and reputation mounted, so mounted also his greed and ambition. On October 13th, 1549, Somerset was driven from office and put in the Tower, leaving Warwick supreme in the Council. He seized most of the principal offices of state and in 1551 he became Duke of Northumberland. Somerset was now accused of plotting against Northumberland's life; he was tried, condemned and executed (1552).

Supreme without any rival, Northumberland acquired a dominating influence over Edward VI. Early in 1553 the King fell ill. Northumberland saw his chance of altering the succession in favour of his own family. He persuaded Edward to make a will in which he cut out his sisters Mary and Elizabeth and left the crown to Lady Jane Grey, daughter of the Duke of Suffolk and wife of Northumberland's son, Guilford Dudley. The Council was coerced into agreeing and Northumberland saw himself as sole ruler on behalf of his daughter-in-law, a young girl who was horrified at the prospect of being Queen.

The plot failed. Edward died on July 6th and Lady Jane Grey was proclaimed Queen, but Northumberland failed to get hold of the person of the Princess Mary, the legitimate Queen. The whole country sided with Mary and ultimately Northumberland himself had to declare for her. He was arrested, taken to the Tower on July 23rd, and on August 18th he was tried for high treason and condemned; and on the 22nd he was executed on Tower Hill, asserting on the scaffold that he was and always had been a Catholic. He lies buried near the high altar in St. Peter's within the Tower, between Anne Boleyn and Catherine Howard and near to Protector Somerset, whom he hounded to death.

Northumberland is perhaps the only character in English history for whom nobody (except Bishop Hooper) has had a good word to say. In 1550 Hooper wrote to Bullinger a letter in which he called Northumberland 'fidelissimo ac intrepido militi Christi', an expression which exposes Hooper's total lack of understanding. Three years later a far different, but a truer, description was written of him: 'Keep that close which thou hast: the world is dangerous. The great devell Dudley ruleth: (duke I shuld have said); well, let that pass, seeing it is owte, but I trust he shall not longe' (*Epistle of Poor Pratte*). Northumberland was a man totally lacking in principle, whose only object in life was his own personal advancement and gain. He is the arch representative of that New Nobility which had cast greedy eyes on the remaining wealth of the Church after the dissolution of the monasteries. The reason why Northumberland threw overboard the religious compromise of 1549 and went bald-headed for a Protestant revolution (the Second Book of Common Prayer, 1552, was the outcome of Northumberland's policy) was that he entered into an unholy alliance with the more extreme Protestant clergy, men like Hooper, who were ready to sell their episcopal lands to the New Nobility in return for their support in forcing Zwinglianism on the Church of England. Hooper received the see of Worcester in addition to that of Gloucester and he then handed over to Northumberland the revenues of Gloucester, in return for which he was let off paying his first-fruits.

The most outrageous example of Northumberland's tyranny was his treatment of Tunstal, Bishop of Durham. Northumberland meant to secure the wealth of Durham for himself. After many intrigues and plots, in 1553 he hurried a bill through Parliament which dissolved the see of Durham, set up two new sees of Durham and Newcastle, endowed them with 2,000 and 1,000 marks per year respectively, and the old revenues of Durham went to the King, who gave them to Northumberland.

But if Northumberland was a bad man on the make, there is another side to the medal. He was a fine soldier, a fine sailor, and he did try to stop the rot which set in in naval administration at the end of Henry VIII's reign: he did not accomplish much, but he did build the Chatham dockyard which was to play so important a part in the revival of the navy in Elizabeth's reign. He did also try to deal with the serious problem of inflation. He recognized the evil of a debased coinage, and although he made some mistakes in tackling the problem, he did take some steps to stabilize currency and prices which enabled Elizabeth to cure the evil by about 1560 (see Elton, *England under the Tudors*, pp. 209–10, 226–9, 354–5). All the same, he must be reckoned as a disastrous ruler who did infinite harm, politically, morally and spiritually.   (*Plate 12*)

There does not seem to be any biography or study of Northumberland beyond the article in the *D.N.B.* There is much need for one.

Pollard, *England under Protector Somerset*, 1900.

S. T. Bindoff, 'A Kingdom at Stake', *History Today*, September, 1953.

F. G. Emmison, *Tudor Secretary*, pp. 104–111, 1961.

GREY, LADY JANE (more accurately, but less familiarly Lady Jane Dudley), 'the Nine Days' Queen', was born at Bradgate Old Manor in Leicestershire early in October 1537 and she died on Tower Hill on February 12th, 1554, in her seventeenth year. She was the eldest surviving daughter of Henry Grey, Marquis of Dorset and later Duke of Suffolk, and his wife Frances, daughter of Charles Brandon, Duke of Suffolk, and Mary Tudor, sister of Henry VIII, the widow of Louis XII of France. Jane was thus cousin to Edward VI, to the Princess Mary and the Princess Elizabeth. Were

Plate 11

Thomas Cranmer, Archbishop of Canterbury

Plate 12

John Dudley, Duke of Northumberland

Lady Jane Grey

Edward VI to die without issue, were Mary and Elizabeth to do the same or to be in any way debarred from the succession; then Jane Grey stood in the direct line to succeed to the throne. From this one fact and from the unscrupulous use made of it by ambitious and unprincipled politicians arose the misery of Jane's life and the tragedy of her death.

When she was nine years old Jane entered the service of Queen Catherine Parr, and she was much at court up to the death of the Queen in 1548. After Henry VIII's death in 1547 Catherine married Thomas Seymour, Lord Sudeley, brother of Protector Somerset. This unprincipled schemer purchased the wardship of Jane Grey from her father, assuring him that he would marry her to the King, Edward VI. But Protector Somerset was planning to marry the King to his own daughter (another Jane), and to marry his own son, the Earl of Hertford, to Lady Jane Grey. Already she was a pawn in the political game, but her life in the household of Thomas Sudeley was perhaps the happiest that she knew: she had much affection for Sudeley, who treated her with a good deal of kindness. The fall of Thomas Seymour and his execution in 1549 meant that Jane had to return to her own family at Bradgate: she was never again to know any happiness.

One reason for her unhappiness was the extreme severity of her parents. Jane was a girl of unusual beauty both in her personal appearance and also in her mind and character— gentle, amenable, highly intelligent and a very apt pupil. Her parents are said to have been more severe 'than needed to so sweet a temper' (Fuller), and Jane herself told Roger Ascham that she had to endure 'pinches, nips and bobs'. Ascham found her sitting indoors at her books while the rest of the household were out hunting. 'I wis', said Jane, 'all their sport is but a shadow to the pleasure that I find in Plato.' Her education was liberal and she responded eagerly to the teaching of her tutor, John Aylmer, who entered the Dorset household after Edward VI came to the throne, probably in 1549 when Jane was twelve years old. Aylmer (he became Bishop of London in Elizabeth's reign) was in touch with the German and Swiss reformers, so that it was doubtless through him that Jane corresponded with

K—(2)

Bullinger, chief pastor at Zurich, and his pupil, Ulmer or Abulmis. Ulmer came to Bradgate in 1550 and spent his vacations from Oxford there, when he gave Jane and her sister lessons in Latin and Greek. By the time she was fourteen Jane was proficient in both those languages, and it is possible that she also knew some Italian and French, but that she also added the Hebrew, Chaldean and Arabian tongues is mere flattery. Her immense reputation abroad as a scholar went far beyond her deserts. It is probable that the Protestant reformers on the Continent were only too anxious to keep in with and to magnify the abilities of the girl who might one day be Queen of England.

In 1551 Jane's father became Duke of Suffolk and she made her first appearance at the court of Edward VI. This was followed by a visit to the Princess Mary which lasted for nearly a month. Suffolk saw that the King's days were numbered and he took care to be on good terms with the heir to the throne.

The fall of Somerset put the political power into the hands of John Dudley, Duke of Northumberland. His purpose was to alter the succession and to secure the throne for his son, Guilford Dudley. He therefore first married his son to Lady Jane Grey—almost certainly against her will, for she wanted to marry the Earl of Hertford, but she was coerced into marrying Guilford Dudley by her ambitious father, who even used physical violence upon his daughter. The marriage took place on May 21st, 1553, in the Dudley's London house. Jane was then compelled to live with her husband's family, and so cordially did she come to detest her father-in-law that she fell seriously ill; she herself was convinced she had been poisoned, but in fact she suffered a nervous breakdown.

Northumberland's second purpose was to persuade the King before he died to cut out both the Princess Mary and the Princess Elizabeth from the succession and to leave the throne in his will to Lady Jane Dudley. This he succeeded in doing. Edward died on July 6th, 1553, but news of his death was not published until the 8th. The next day Jane was informed by the Council that she was now Queen. She fainted at the news, but it cannot have come as a complete surprise to her, for some time earlier the Duchess of Northumberland had blurted out the possibility to her, and she records that when she came into the Council the Lords 'began to make me complimentary speeches, bending the knee before me, their example being followed by several noble ladies, all of which ceremony made me blush. My distress was still further increased when my mother and my mother-in-law entered and paid me the same homage.'

For nine days, from Sunday, July 9th, to Wednesday, July 19th, Lady Jane Dudley was Queen. During this time she resided in the Tower. She signed a few documents, perhaps six in all, she dined once in state, she received the Regalia, she made one or two appointments, and she resolutely refused the request of her husband and the violent demand of her mother-in-law that Guilford Dudley should be made King. It was a parody of Tudor monarchy. The whole country favoured the Princess Mary. By Tuesday the 18th Jane's cause (it was in reality Northumberland's cause) was all but lost; on the next day Mary triumphed and Jane was no longer Queen.

Mary herself wished to save the life of Lady Jane Dudley and it is probable that she would have done so, but Jane's father, the Duke of Suffolk, weakly took part in Wyatt's Rebellion and this sealed her fate and that of her wholly innocent husband. Both were executed on February 12th, 1554, Guilford first outside the Tower, because he was not of royal blood: then Jane, being of royal blood, within the precincts of the Tower. On her way to the block she met the headless body of her husband being brought back into the Tower for burial.

It is easy to be sentimental and romantic over the fate of such a pathetic figure as Lady Jane Grey. But it has to be remembered that she was a staunch Protestant and that, had she lived, she might well have been used by the Protestant party in an attempt to be rid of Catholic Mary and to re-establish the Protestant religion of Edward VI. Lady Jane was thus a potential danger: it is possible to justify her execution on purely political grounds.   (*Plate 12*)

J. G. Nichols, *The Chronicle of Queen Jane and Two Years of Queen Mary*, Camden Society, 1850.

H. W. Chapman, *Lady Jane Grey*, Cape, 1962.

T.S.I.H., vol. 2, pp. 48–52.

R. Davey, *The Nine Days' Queen*, 1909. A mine of most interesting information, but the author is apt to moralize.

S. T. Bindoff, 'A Kingdom at Stake', *History Today*, September, 1953.

KET, ROBERT, rebel, was put to death in 1549; the date of his birth is unknown. He came from an old Norman family (the name appears down the years as Le Chat, Cat, Kett, Ket, Knight), one branch of which had settled at Wymondham in Norfolk. Robert and his brother William were well-to-do tradesmen who were also landowners. Robert held the manor of Wymondham from John Dudley, Earl of Warwick, the man who in August, 1549, came to suppress the rising which now goes by Ket's name. It was only by an accident that Ket became its leader.

On June 20th, 1549, a small riot took place in south Norfolk, when the men of Attleborough, Eccles and Wilby threw down the fences with which the lord of the manor of Beckhall in Wilby had recently enclosed part of the common land over which these men had grazing rights. Trouble was also brewing further south, but it was not until July 6th–8th that all these men joined hands in a series of attacks on the hedges in various manors. Robert Ket had a long-standing feud with John Flowerdew, a lawyer who had become a landowner. After the Dissolution of the Monasteries the splendid priory church of Wymondham had been bought from the Crown by the inhabitants. Flowerdew, who lived in the neighbourhood, stripped the lead off the roofs and carried away the bells. The Kets resented this. When in July Flowerdew's closes had been thrown down, he bribed the rioters to go and do the same to Robert Ket. On July 9th or 10th Robert Ket led the rioters back in a reprisal on Flowerdew's fences, and thus by accident he became the leader of the insurgents, and he was joined by his brother William.

Ket marched on Norwich, throwing down hedges as he went. On being refused admission into the city Ket moved to Mousehold Heath, where he and his men encamped for the next six weeks. He soon had 16,000 men under his command. Good order was maintained, law-courts were established and chaplains said prayers every morning, using the new Book of Common Prayer—a clear proof that the rising was not religious in origin.

On July 21st Ket rejected the Government's offer of a pardon, on the grounds that 'Kings were wont to pardon wicked persons, not innocent and just men'. Ket now seized Norwich. William Parr, Marquess of Northampton, was sent with 1,400 men to recover the, city which he did without opposition. But on August 1st Ket attacked and after a grim struggle he secured the place. Becoming now more ambitious, he tried to capture Yarmouth, but he failed.

On August 23rd the Earl of Warwick arrived at Norwich, where he was joined by Lord Willoughby of Parham. Their joint forces amounted to some 12,000 men, many of them German troops. The offer of a pardon to all but Robert Ket was rejected. On the 24th Warwick got into Norwich. On the 25th the rebels left their camp, since their lines of communication were cut. On the 27th Warwick saw his chance and launching his German troops at the rebels he utterly destroyed them. The Kets fled, but were soon captured. Robert was hanged in chains from Norwich Castle, William from Wymondham steeple.

Religion played no part in the rebellion: Norfolk was a county always in favour of Lollardy, Lutheranism and Puritantism, therefore it was not likely to rise against Somerset's Protestantism. Nor did enclosures play a large part: as far as present-day knowledge goes, enclosures had not advanced far in Norfolk, and the rebels' demands contain only one obscure reference to enclosures. Why, then, did Ket allow himself to head the rising? The answer would seem to be that he never regarded the movement as a rising against the Government.

The Tudor system worked well so long as there was sound government, both centrally and locally. Somerset was not providing sound central government. In Norfolk local government had broken down with the sudden fall of the Howard family, and no county was worse governed than Norfolk. Ket and his followers expected the central government to back them up in teaching the local magnates a lesson. It is probable that if Somerset had been left to himself, the story might have ended differently, for he was notorious for being sympathetic with the downtrodden poor. It is significant that Somerset was himself in the first place going to take command of the government force, but on or a little before August 17th he was replaced by the Earl of Warwick. It is likely that the Council was apprehensive that 'the good Duke' would be too lenient to the rebels.

S. T. Bindoff: *Ket's Rebellion*, Historical Association, pamphlet G 12.1949.

HALES (or HAYLES), JOHN, author, died in 1571. It is not known when he was born. He was the son of Thomas Hales of Hales Place in Halden, Kent. He never went to the university, but he knew Greek, Latin, French and German. At some time he became lame through an accident and he was often known as 'club-foot Hales'. When the monasteries were dissolved, Hales obtained large grants of land in Coventry, but he converted St. John's Hospital into a free school, the first to be established in Edward VI's reign. For the use of the scholars in this school Hales wrote a Latin grammar, *Introductiones ad grammaticam*, partly in Latin and partly in English.

In 1548 Hales entered public life. He was already prominent as an opponent of enclosures, and in this year he became a member of Somerset's commission to enquire into the progress of enclosures in the midlands since 1489. He was, indeed, Somerset's right-hand man in his whole campaign against enclosures. (It is probable that Hales was Clerk of the Hanaper, although the *D.N.B.* specifically denies this.) In this same year he was elected member of Parliament for Preston in Lancashire, but he was not returned again until 1562 for Lancaster.

Hales was a Protestant, but he was also a conservative reformer (Bindoff, *Tudor England*, p. 131), and he set about trying to put his ideas into practice through three bills which he introduced into Parliament—one for the rebuilding of decayed houses, one for maintaining tillage, a third against the regrating and forestalling of markets. All three failed. Hales was also very active over the Subsidy Act of 1548. This Act, the equivalent of our Finance Act today, contained a radical proposal, to put a tax on sheep and cloth. The immediate object was to allow the government to abolish the very unpopular custom of purveyance, by which the Crown purchased supplies from its subjects at low prices and on long credit (Bindoff, *ibid.*). The new tax was to compensate the Crown for its loss of purveyance. Hales believed that the great expansion of the cloth trade and the growth of sheep farming was ruining the economy of the nation by diverting too much of its output into a single channel and he proposed to attack the evil by the method of taxation, 'an early essay in the use of taxation as an instrument of economic planning' (Bindoff, *ibid.*). His plan was accepted by the Protector and also by Parliament, perhaps by the latter because the tax might prove easy to evade.

Hales was an energetic and strictly honest man, and he soon fell foul of Northumberland after Somerset had fallen from power. In 1552 he left the country and went to Strassburg, where he became active among the Marian exiles, especially in Frankfurt. In 1558 he returned to England, but in 1564 he was in disgrace with Elizabeth for having supported the marriage of the young Marquis of Hertford to Catherine Grey and for having written that, if the Queen were to die and leave no heir, the Crown should go to the Suffolk family.* He was put in the Fleet, but he was soon rescued through the help of Burghley. Hales died on December 28th, 1571.

It is almost certain that Hales was the author of *A Discourse of the Commonweal of this Realm of England*, written in 1549 and published in 1581.† The book consists of three dialogues between a Knight and a Doctor, with one or two minor characters taking part now and again. The probability is that

---

* A. F. Pollard in the *Political History of England 1547–1603*, p. 255, attributes this episode to John Hales's nephew, John.

† But H. R. Trevor-Roper in *Historical Essays* p. 86 is persuaded by Professor Hughes (*Bulletin of the John Rylands Library*, 1937) that Sir Thomas Smith is the author.

the original of the Knight is Hales and the Doctor is Latimer. The Dialogues set out very vividly the economic state of the country under Edward VI and, broadly speaking, attribute the troubles of the times to the debasement of the coinage. What makes the *Discourse* an important book is that in it for the first time the close connection between private business concerns and the welfare of the state is clearly recognized. Hales held that the pursuit of private gain was often to the advantage of the state. Unless subjects were prosperous, there was no source from which revenue could be obtained, therefore it was the duty of the state to give private enterprise as much chance to develop as possible, and if necessary to guide it into the channels most profitable for the welfare of the community as a whole. It was during Somerset's Protectorate that the expression 'commonwealth's man' came into general use to describe those people who tried to explain the commonweal and to carry out a policy to promote it. Hales was the chief exponent of this body of opinion.

The Commonweal of this Realm of England, ed. by E. Lamond, 1929.
S. T. Bindoff, *Tudor England*, Penguin, 1950.
A. F. Pollard, *England under Protector Somerset*, 1900.
Tawney, *Agrarian Problem in the Sixteenth Century.*

KNOX, JOHN, Scotch Protestant reformer and historian, was born not earlier than 1512 and not later than 1515. He was ordained priest in April 1536: he was an Apostolic Notary in 1540 and 1543: he may have been a clerk in Cardinal Beaton's employ in 1545. He came under the influence of Wishart, the first Protestant martyr, in Scotland, and his 'acceptable doctrine' and was then accounted an 'apostate priest'. He was saved from Wishart's fate of burning by Wishart's good advice, 'Nay, return to your bairns and God bless you. One is sufficient for a sacrifice.' He was in daily danger of arrest and eventually took refuge in the castle of St. Andrew's, which was held by the murderers of Cardinal Beaton. When that fell, Knox was sent by its French captors to the French galleys (1547–9). On his release he went to

England, where the Protestant reformation under Edward VI
was in full swing. He became a licensed preacher at Berwick
and then at Newcastle. Here he became acquainted with
Mrs. Elizabeth Bowes, wife of the captain of Norham Castle,
and here he courted her daughter, Marjory, whom he married.
But in 1550 he was up in front of Tunstal, Bishop of Durham,
to explain his doctrine. Tunstal was a conservative in religion:
Knox represented the most advanced side of the Reformation.
To him and to Northumberland the Book of Common Prayer of
1549 did not go far enough. In 1551 Knox was appointed one
of the six chaplains to Edward VI. He was all but offered
the see of Rochester, but he quarrelled with Northumberland
and was twice arraigned before the Privy Council. He could
have had the living of All Hallows in London, but he refused
it. That he had influence in ecclesiastical matters is proved
by his success in getting the Black Rubric added to the Second
Prayer Book of Edward VI, which laid down that to receive
the Communion kneeling did not imply adoration.

Knox disliked Northumberland and he also saw that the
Duke's days were numbered. On the accession of Mary, Knox
(1554) went overseas. From that moment he passes from
English into Scottish history and his further career will be
fully dealt with in the volume in this series of biographies to
deal with Scotland and Ireland.

Edwin Muir, *John Knox*, 1929.

Lord Eustace Percy, *John Knox*, 1937. An excellent, but
neglected, biography.

R. S. Wright (ed.), *Fathers of the Kirk*; W. Croft Dickinson,
John Knox, 1960.

J. D. Mackie, *John Knox*, H.A. pamphlet G.20, 1951.

MARY I, Queen of England 1553–8, was born in 1516 and
died in 1558 at the age of 42. She was the third child of Henry
VIII and Catherine of Aragon and the only one to survive
infancy. For the first years of her life she was given into the
charge of the Countess of Salisbury.

For the first twelve years of her life she was Henry VIII's
'pearl of his kingdom'. To begin with Catherine supervised her

education, but from 1523 Linacre and Vives (a Spanish scholar) prescribed the curriculum: Latin, Greek, music, modern languages, astronomy, geography, natural science, mathematics; much of her spare time was given to embroidery. In the end Mary spoke Latin, French, Spanish, and knew, but rarely spoke, Italian. Like all the Tudors she was an enthusiastic and competent musician.

Very early in life she became a pawn on the chess-board of international politics. In 1518 she was betrothed at the age of 2 to the newly-born Dauphin of France: that was broken off and she was promised to the 22-year-old Emperor, Charles V. Mary was then 6: Charles chose to marry Isabella of Portugal, whereon Mary was offered to James IV of Scotland and then to Francis I of France (he was 32 in 1527).

In 1526 Mary was sent as Princess of Wales to Ludlow, where a court was established for her, her education provided for, and instructions were given to the Countess of Salisbury, mother of Reginald Pole, and to Mary's chamberlain, John Dudley (who later as Northumberland was to try to prevent her from succeeding to the throne) that the Princess was to have plenty of good food, clean linen, dancing and open air exercise. It is likely enough that these next two years were to be the happiest in Mary's life.

In 1528 the first suggestions of the divorce were mooted. From 1528 to 1530 Mary hardly ever saw her parents. In 1531 she was separated from her mother, she was forbidden to write to her, and she never saw Catherine of Aragon again. The next year began the unhappiest part of Mary's life. In 1532 Henry VIII spent on his daughter one-fifth in the whole year of what he spent in one day on Anne Boleyn. In 1533 Mary was deprived of her title of Princess of Wales: when in the same year Elizabeth was born to Anne Boleyn, Mary was declared a bastard and cut out of the succession to the throne by Act of Parliament. Her household was broken up, the Countess of Salisbury was sent away, and Mary was relegated into the new household set up for the new Princess Elizabeth.

1534–6 were probably the most cruel years which Mary had to endure. Henry was determined to break what he called her

'Spanish Pride'—and in truth Henry was not far wrong in his description, however far he was from a fair interpretation of it. Mary had to endure every sort of petty persecution, of which to-day one may be justified in guessing that the worst part was having to receive such detestable letters from Thomas Cromwell. One friend she had, Chapuys, the Imperial ambassador. On the whole his advice was frequent, moderate and wise. In 1536 Catherine of Aragon died. Public demonstrations had been frequent and in favour of Mary. But when Catherine died, Mary capitulated to the demands Henry made upon her. She even acknowledged that 'the marriage heretofore between his majesty and my mother . . . was by God's law and man's law incestuous and unlawful'. She thereby acknowledged her own bastardy. She is not to be blamed. One may guess how great a support Catherine had been. She was dead. Mary's cousin, the Emperor, Charles V, advised her to yield. Nor is it right for us to forget that Henry VIII was faced with a tremendous national problem, the lack of an indisputable heir, especially a male heir, to the throne.

Mary's cup of sorrow was not yet quite full. Henry seemed very ready to restore Mary to his favour. The arrival on the scene of Jane Seymour brought her a good friend. And even Cromwell, always a swimmer with the tide, made her a present at the New Year. But there were still crosses to be borne. In 1540, her old tutor, Dr. Featherstone, and her mother's chaplain, Abell, were burnt at the stake. But worst of all was the wholesale attack made on the Pole family, so that among other sufferers Mary's best friend, the Countess of Salisbury, was executed.

That Henry's treatment of his daughter may have been only politic and even repugnant to him may be perhaps supported by his treatment of her after the execution of Anne Boleyn— which removed Mary's most bitter and dangerous enemy. It is said that Anne contemplated the murder of Mary by poison. At any rate from 1536 to 1547 Mary lived a life of ease and contentment, with apparently enough money to allow her to enjoy herself at the gaming tables and to indulge her love of giving presents to her relatives, friends, and especially her godchildren. (Madden, *Privy Purse Expenses of the Princess Mary, 1831.*)

Between 1547, when her father died, and 1553, when she ascended the throne, her difficulties were chiefly religious. She had much affection for Edward VI, little liking for his religion. Her quarrels were mostly with the Council, not with Edward. The Council demanded conformity to the new Protestant religion. Mary stood up superbly, imperturbably and invincibly to all the attempts made to bring her to accept the new Protestant religion. Her courage was only equalled by her dialectical skill. By the time Edward died Mary had conceded nothing and maintained her own position intact, without falling out herself with Edward VI.

In July 1553 Edward VI died and Northumberland made his desperate bid to substitute his daughter-in-law, Lady Jane Grey, in place of Mary as the new Queen. Mary was at Hunsdon when a message came from the Council telling her to visit her brother, who was very ill. On her way she was warned that the King was already dead. She rushed to her own house at Kenninghall in Norfolk, whence she wrote to the Council, promising a general pardon if she was proclaimed at once. Then she went with all the local supporters she could raise to Framlingham and there she proclaimed herself Queen. Her standard was hoisted over the Gatehouse and she announced that 'The Queen is not fled the realm, nor intendeth to do, as is most untruly surmised'. On the 19th July, so swiftly did the nation react to her courage, she was proclaimed in London. On August 3rd she entered London triumphantly as Queen, Northumberland having already been arrested at Cambridge. Her reign had begun and she had the whole nation at her feet.

The first few months of her reign were marked by Mary's moderate behaviour. Out of the sixty conspirators who had tried under Northumberland to prevent her succession, only seven were brought to trial and only three were executed. No attempt was made to influence the elections to Parliament. Inevitably Parliament annulled the divorce of Catherine of Aragon and established Mary's legitimacy; it repealed the ecclesiastical legislation of Edward VI's reign and restored things to what they were at the end of Henry VIII's reign. Parliament refused to rescind the Royal Supremacy and to restore the church lands. Thus far the new arrangements were acceptable to the nation as a whole.

How came it, then, that almost within weeks Wyatt's rebellion was on the move (1554), within months Mary's popularity was gone, and the most human, the most merciful, the most sincerely religious, the least worldly and the most moral of all the Tudors has gone down to history as Bloody Mary? The answer may be seen in the title under which H. F. M. Prescott rightly first published her life of Mary Tudor, *Spanish Tudor*. Mary was a Spaniard first and a Tudor second, and she was never a truly English Tudor: she never understood the English, it might be said that she never tried to understand them. Being Spanish, she made two fatal mistakes—she insisted on restoring the old Papal Catholic religion and she turned to Spain to find a husband. Thus in both directions she cut herself adrift from the main characteristic of her subjects, their growing sense of nationalism. She never saw that the English were not really a religiously-minded people— 'in thirty years they accepted five distinct changes in their religion without any great fuss about the matter'. (Conyers Read, *The Tudors*, p. 138.) Had she stopped when she restored things as they were at the end of her father's reign, all would have been well, for Henry's settlement, by eliminating the Pope, had fed the nationalistic feelings of the English. By restoring allegiance to the Papacy, she flouted English nationalism: she flouted it again by marrying a Spaniard: she outraged it by the loss of Calais: and in the end by her burnings she identified Papal Catholicism with persecution and with foreign interference in England.

For a moment she won golden opinions by her courageous stand against the Wyatt rebellion. Her Guildhall speech was inspired with all the old Tudor appeal (1554). But the marriage to Philip II (July 1554) was fatal. Fatal also was the policy of restoring Papalism when Reginald Pole arrived in England as Archbishop of Canterbury and Papal Legate (1554). Much blame must lie on the Parliament, which only acquiesced in this religious policy at the price of retaining the spoils of church property. Most fatal of all, perhaps, was the re-enacting of the statute *de heretico comburendo* (1555), which restored to the ecclesiastical courts the power to deal with heresy which Henry VIII had taken from them. Hence the persecutions.

In the long run Mary must accept responsibility for the burnings, if only because she could have stopped them if she had wanted to do so. So also could the Council, and therefore it must share her responsibility. Mary was neither cruel nor sadistic. Her love for children and her longing to have children of her own suggest that she suffered from a thwarted maternal complex. She died on November 17th, 1558, a desolate, deserted and disappointed woman. She had restored Papal Catholicism, but had failed to restore the church's property: she thought she had reconverted the whole people of England, but she had only ensured that England would become a Protestant country: she looked for a family life with Philip and he gave her none: she had deluded herself into thinking she was pregnant when she was in fact suffering from a tumour: she had longed for an heir who would be a Catholic and she died knowing that the Protestant Elizabeth would succeed her.   (*Plate 14*)

H. F. M. Prescott, *Mary Tudor* (first published as *Spanish Tudor*, 1940).

Conyers Read, *The Tudors*, 1936.

C. Morris, *The Tudors*, 1955.

C. H. Williams, *The Making of the Tudor Despotism*, 1928.

H. Clifford, *Life of Jane Dormer, Duchess of Feria*, ed. J. Stevenson, 1887.

M. Irwin, *Young Bess* and *Elizabeth, Captive Princess*. (H.N.)

F. Rush, *Apprentice at Arms*. (Wyatt's Rebellion. H.N.)

BONNER, EDMUND, Bishop of London, was born probably in 1500 and died in 1569, aged approximately sixty-nine. There is more reason to believe that he was the lawful than the illegitimate son of Elizabeth Frodsham and Edmund Bonner of Hanley in Worcestershire. About 1512 he went to Broadgate

Hall, Oxford, now Pembroke College. He became bachelor of both Civil and Canon Law in 1519, was ordained about the same time and in 1525 became Doctor of Civil Law. In 1529 Wolsey appointed him as his chaplain and Bonner was with him at Cawood when he was arrested. Between 1532 and 1543 Bonner was frequently employed by Henry VIII on diplomatic missions, especially to Pope Clement VII on the business of the divorce of Catherine of Aragon. During this period he received several minor ecclesiastical preferments, including the living of East Dereham, Norfolk, and the Archdeaconry of Leicester (1535). From 1537 to 1539 he was Prebend of St. Paul's, and in 1538 he superseded Gardiner, Bishop of Winchester, as ambassador in Paris. His behaviour in announcing his appointment greatly offended Gardiner, as did also his appointment to the see of Hereford in 1538, and the two men were never on good terms. Bonner could be arrogant and overbearing: he once used such language to Francis I that the King told him that only his own love for Bonner's master saved him from a hundred strokes with a halberd. Before Bonner could be consecrated to Hereford, he was translated to London (1539), where he was consecrated and enthroned in 1540.

As long as Henry VIII was on the throne Bonner accepted the Royal Supremacy and was able to be a loyal servant of the Crown. When the government went into the hands of Somerset and he insisted that during the King's minority the Royal Supremacy was vested in the Privy Council, Bonner could not accept that. He resisted the Visitation and Injunctions of 1547 and was sent to the Fleet prison for two months. In 1549 he was accused of being lax in enforcing the new Prayer Book and was ordered to preach at St. Paul's on points laid down for him, which included the Mass and the full powers of the King while still a minor. Bonner obeyed in every respect except one —he omitted the Royal Supremacy. After a lengthy examination he was deprived of his bishopric and sent to the Marshalsea, where he remained until the accession of Mary.

On August 5th, 1553, Bonner was restored to his see of London and became a leading figure in religious matters. The violent accusations brought against him by Foxe the martyrologist may be discounted. There is no doubt that Bonner was unpopular, especially in London, the centre of Puritanism, but that he enjoyed sending men and women to the fire is certainly untrue—indeed he was admonished by letter from Mary not to treat heretics as lightly as he had been doing. The number of burnings was appalling and inevitably so in his own diocese of London.

On the accession of Elizabeth, Bonner's position was impossible. For a while he retained his bishopric, but he would make no concession to the new policy. Even after the Act of Uniformity he still insisted on the old Use at St. Paul's, and not unnaturally he was again deprived of his see. He refused to take the oath under the Act of Supremacy, but by an ingenious piece of legal argument he saved himself from further trouble. He was left in peace in the Marshalsea where he died in September 1569. He was buried in St. George's, Southwark.

Bonner is the clearest example of the conservative bishops of the English Reformation. In his youth he was a humanist and a reformer. He had seen Pope Clement VII at Bologna and had had the greatest contempt for him. Bonner and his friends were well aware of the need for reform and they accepted the breach with Rome and the Royal Supremacy as long as Henry VIII was king. In July Bonner and the others changed their point of view and abandoned the ideals of their youth, because they saw that the Reformation was now a revolution. The great mistake he and they made was that they only realized too late that the Papacy was worth fighting for, even if the Pope was not; for the unity of Christendom could not be saved without the vital link of the Papacy.

First and foremost Bonner was a lawyer and he always saw the legal side of the Reformation as being at least as important as the spiritual. 'When anything is called into question, if ye dispute it, ye must see whether it be decent, lawful and expedient.' John Ponet told him 'thou . . . allowest nothing to be well done (by whatsoever authority it be done) except it be lawful nor nothing to be lawful that is not agreeing to thy canon law.' Cranmer was even more outspoken: 'Well, my Lord, ye be too full of your law: I would wish you had less

Plate 13

Cuthbert Tunstal, Bishop of Durham

Richard Fox, Bishop of Winchester,
Lord Privy Seal

Plate 14

Mary I

knowledge in that law and more knowledge in God's law and your duty.' It was this exalting of the law which made any alliance between the two sides impossible.

Bonner was a government official and he expected the individual to accept decisions made by the government. His defence of the Marian persecutions was 'in matters of state, individuals were not to be so much regarded as the whole body of the citizens'. It was this reliance on the rule of the majority in search of unity which caused the conservatives to compromise with their opinions and to comply with the Royal Supremacy. It was this which made Bonner so mistrustful of rash preachers who taught the 'zely (*i.e.* simple, ignorant) people' that individual judgment was of more value than the authority of the Church.

Experience came to his aid. He never really liked the use of the Bible in English and he not unnaturally attributed the rebellions and the economic troubles of the last years of Henry and the reign of Edward VI to the discontent caused by reading the Bible in English and by the idealism of men whom he looked on as fanatical idealists. He was ready to admit the benefits of an English Bible, but he could not agree with Sir Thomas More that a 'commodity ought not to be kept back for the harm that may come of it'.

It is difficult to tell how sincere Bonner was. He told Mary that 'fear compelled us to bear with the times, for otherwise there had been no way but one'—death. Was he speaking the truth? It was safer to admit compulsion through fear than acceptance through approval. On the other hand, in July 1547, when he first protested against the *Book of Homilies* and then changed his mind, he explained that he did so 'upon a better consideration of my duty of obedience and of the ill example which may ensue to others thereof', thinking that his resistance had been 'neither reasonable nor such as might well stand with the duty of a humble subject'. Within two years he was ready to go to prison for defying the state.

On the whole Bonner usually appears as a somewhat inhuman man. Yet there was another side to him. He deeply appreciated the arts and he had a collector's eye for the

L—(2)

anatomy of the human body. He once sent a print from Paris to Lord Lisk: 'this present, which of late was imprinted here' is said to be a fine example of French art. 'The anatomy of the man is judged here to be exquisitely done. The anatomy of the woman pleaseth me not so much; howbeit, Mr. Beckinsall that is married and hath had but one child, telleth me that that is the figure of women in travail; to whose judgement, because I am ignorant, I leave the matter, thinking that he took consultation with some midwife touching his sentence.' Was Bonner perhaps more human than he makes out? Like Thomas Cromwell, Bonner was an ardent gardener and he used to send Cromwell seeds from 'Rome, Bobonye and parts of Lombardy'.

L. B. Smith, *Tudor Prelates and Politics, passim*, 1953. (*Plate 15*)
S. R. Maitland, *Essays on the Reformation*, xvii–xx.

GARDINER, STEPHEN, Bishop of Winchester and Lord Chancellor, was born probably in 1482 and died in 1555, aged about 73. The son of a cloth merchant, he went to Cambridge where he distinguished himself in Greek and later in both canon and civil law. In 1525 he was elected Master of Trinity Hall, a position which he held until he was ejected in 1549. He was made tutor to the son of the Duke of Norfolk, and it was through Norfolk that he became secretary to Wolsey. In 1526 he took part in proceedings against heretics; in 1527 he entered the service of Henry VIII, and in 1529 became the king's secretary. For the rest of the reign he was largely employed in diplomatic missions abroad and in matters arising out of the divorce. Almost the entire time he enjoyed the king's confidence, so that Henry once said of him that when Gardiner was away, he felt he had lost his right hand. But once or twice, as notably over the spoliation of the monasteries, Henry detected in him 'a coloured doubleness', but Gardiner always returned to favour. He was extremely hostile to Catherine of Aragon and was a member of the court which pronounced her marriage with Henry null and void, and Gardiner it was who, with the Bishop of London, carried the robes of Anne Boleyn at her coronation. In 1531 he became Bishop of Winchester. On the 10th of February, 1534, he signed a declaration repudiating the papal jurisdiction in England. In 1535 he followed this up by publishing his *De Vera Obedientia*, which was regarded as the ablest defence of the Royal Supremacy. It is said that he caused it to be spread among the Roman party that he had written the book under compulsion and in fear of death.

All this time his relations with Cromwell and Cranmer were steadily deteriorating. In 1539 there was issued the Act of the Six Articles, which involved the persecution of the Protestants. This was said to be mainly the work of Gardiner. Cranmer fought strongly against it, but in vain. On the fall in that year of Thomas Cromwell, Gardiner was elected Chancellor of Cambridge university, where he much disapproved of the growing Protestantism which he found there. At this time he launched an attack on Cranmer for heresy, but Henry VIII would listen to no accusations against the archbishop, for Cranmer was the one servant whom Henry always entirely trusted. Gardiner disliked a good deal of Henry's treatment of the Church, but he was invaluable to the king as a proof to the outside world that the Church had not fallen away from the old faith. Cranmer was no less valuable in enforcing the Royal Supremacy.

In 1547 Henry died and Gardiner was not included in the Council of Regency. He was utterly opposed to the policy of Somerset and Cranmer, partly on principle and partly because violent changes were being enforced during the king's minority. The Supremacy was no longer that of the king but of the Council. For his opposition he was put in the Fleet, then released, then put in the Tower, where he remained for five years until the accession of Mary. In 1551 he had been deprived of his bishopric.

When Mary Tudor came to the throne Gardiner was released, restored to Winchester and made Lord Chancellor. At her coronation it was he who put the crown on the queen's head. He had much to explain away—*De Vera Obedientia*, his treatment of the queen's mother, his support of Anne Boleyn, his repudiation of papal jurisdiction. He had to undo much of his work in order to prove the queen legitimate and to bring the country back to the Roman faith and papal control. He was opposed to the return of Cardinal Reginald Pole, but this was more than probably based on jealousy; he was opposed to the Spanish marriage, but he himself negotiated it, for patriotic reasons, in order to secure the best terms he could for the country. Much of his behaviour is open to considerable criticism, most especially his treatment of the princess Elizabeth, whom at one moment he seems to have thought of having murdered.

It is difficult to assess Gardiner's degree of responsibility for the burning of Protestants. The revival of the heresy laws was his work, and it was he who revived *De Heretico Comburendo*. He sat in judgement on Hooper and others who finally went to the stake. On the other hand, he tried to save their lives by persuading them to follow his own course. Certainly he tried to save Cranmer and there were no burnings in his own diocese.

Gardiner has been abused almost as much as Cranmer—crafty, abject, vindictive, bloodthirsty, despicable, are adjectives which have been applied to him. Yet he remained in prison for five years rather than sacrifice his belief in Transubstantiation. There is no reason to think that he was not sincere. All men were inconsistent in the sixteenth century, and both Gardiner and Cranmer were Erastians—Gardiner a Roman Erastian, Cranmer a Prostestant Erastian. Gardiner was first and foremost a lawyer and an adminstrator, a man of the world, ambitious, self-confident, clear-sighted, with a practical attitude towards the Church typical of his times. He loathed irregularity, lack of order and discipline, he was horrified by the laxness of the German Protestants, not less by the chaos which ensued in England after the Second Act of Uniformity. The Royal Supremacy could supply the discipline and the necessary control. Reunion with Rome under the Marian Supremacy would ensure order in the English Church. Cranmer was a spiritual man in days when to be spiritual was highly dangerous. Cranmer did not see the chaos in German Protestantism, he only saw the value of German scholarship. Both he and Gardiner accepted the supremacy of the State, both had qualms of conscience. Both were driven back to

solve their difficulties by their own personal opinions. Cranmer's was the crueller dilemma and the crueller fate. There
was no love lost between the two. 'The man who seeks for
truth and the man who is certain he possesses it are never for
long likely to be of the same mind.* Gardiner had his reward
in his own day: Cranmer's was delayed but is imperishable.

Powicke, *The Reformation in England*, 1941.   *(Plate 15)*
Maynard Smith, *Henry* VIII *and the Reformation*, 1948.
For the Roman point of view, Hughes, *The Reformation in
    England*, vol. 1, 1952; vol. 2, 1953.
L. B. Smith, *Tudor Prelates and Politics*, 1953.

ROGERS, JOHN, first Protestant martyr in the Marian
persecution, was born about 1500 and died in 1555, aged
approximately fifty-five. He was the son of John Rogers of
Deritend, a parish of Aston, near Birmingham. He was
educated at Pembroke Hall, Cambridge, where he took his
B.A. in 1526, and in 1532 was appointed Rector of Holy
Trinity in the City of London. He resigned this living in 1534
and became chaplain to the Company of the Merchant Adventurers in Antwerp. At that time he was an orthodox Catholic
priest, but he now fell in with Tyndale and was soon converted
to Protestantism. Before he was arrested in 1535, Tyndale
handed over to Rogers his incompleted translation of the
Old Testament. Tyndale was burned in October 1535;
during 1536 Rogers devoted himself to completing the Old
Testament by adding to it Miles Coverdale's renderings
(published in 1535) of the untranslated books and of the
Apocrypha, and Tyndale's own translation of the New Testament (published 1526). Rogers's only original contribution
was the Song of Manasses in the Apocrypha which he found in
a French bible printed in 1535. Rogers was also responsible
for the preface, the marginal notes (the first English commentary on the Bible), and a calendar and almanack and other
additional matter. Rogers signed the title-page with the name
'Thomas Matthew' and the book came to be known as

---

* Maynard Smith. *H. VIII and the Ref.*: p. 214.

Matthew's Bible. This was the book largely drawn upon for the Great Bible of 1539–40.

While at Antwerp Rogers married, probably in 1537, Adriana de Weyden: Weyden means 'meadows' and when in 1552 he naturalized his wife and children by a special act of parliament, the name was anglicized into Pratt from the Latin form 'prata'.

When Edward VI came to the throne Rogers returned to England (1548). He was given two livings in London (1550) and in 1551 he was appointed to a prebend of St. Paul's by Nicholas Ridley and shortly afterwards became divinity lecturer at St. Paul's.

With his Protestant views Rogers naturally sympathized with Lady Jane Grey rather than with Mary Tudor. He preached two sermons for which he was had up before the Council, and in 1554 he was sent to Newgate. Here, in conjunction with Hooper, Bradford and others, he drew up a confession of faith of the most extreme Protestant type. He was again examined by Gardiner with much rudeness and even brutality and was condemned to death as a heretic. When he asked to be allowed to see his wife, he was refused, and it is said that he met her and his eleven children on the way to the stake. At the stake he was offered a pardon, if he would recant, but he refused and he was burned just outside the entrance to the church of St. Bartholomew in Smithfield. He was the first of the Protestant martyrs and his example had a widespread effect in encouraging others. Ridley confessed that the news of Roger's death had destroyed a 'lumpish heaviness' in his heart.

J. L. Chester, *Life of John Rogers*, London, 1861.
T. F. Mozley, *Coverdale and his Bibles*. 1754.

CRANMER, THOMAS, Archbishop of Canterbury, was born on July 2nd, 1489, he was burned at the stake on March 21st, 1556, dying in his sixty-seventh year. In his youth his education was severely scholastic, but he also became a courageous and skilled horseman. At the age of 14 he went to Cambridge, and after graduating he was elected in 1515 to a fellowship at Jesus College. When he married, he lost his fellowship, but his wife died within twelve months and Cranmer was re-elected. In 1529 the king's suit for a divorce from Catherine of Aragon had opened. Cranmer fell in with two of Henry's officials, Gardiner and Fox, and threw out the suggestion that Henry VIII ought to consult the divines at European universities. Henry sent for Cranmer and commanded him to write a treatise on the subject. He also arranged for him to live with the Earl of Wiltshire, the father of Anne Boleyn, as his chaplain. Between 1530 and 1533 he was employed on diplomatic missions to Germany, during which time, although now a priest, he married a German woman. In 1533 he was recalled by Henry to succeed Warham as Archbishop of Canterbury. Cranmer did his best to avoid this office, but in the end he most reluctantly accepted. From that moment his troubles began.

On the secular side he found himself involved mainly in two problems, the ever present difficulty for the Tudors of providing a male heir to the throne, and the enforcing of the Royal Supremacy after the breach with Rome. On May 23rd, 1533, he declared the marriage of Henry with Catherine of Aragon null and void and on the 28th he declared Henry's marriage with Anne Boleyn legal (he did not himself marry them). In 1536 he pronounced that second marriage null and void, but he made efforts to save the life of the queen, in which he failed. In 1540 he married Henry to Anne of Cleves and within six months arranged the separation. By 1535 the breach with Rome was complete and the Royal Supremacy took the place of papal headship of the Church in England. Sir Thomas More and Fisher, Bishop of Rochester, refused to acknowledge it. Cranmer did his best to persuade them to accept it, and when they persisted and were condemned to death, he did his best to plead for them with Henry, but again he failed.

On the religious side, he was occupied largely in making the church services intelligible to the congregations by gradually introducing the use of the English language in place of Latin. In 1538 injunctions were given by Cromwell for a bible in English to be available in every parish church, and in 1539 the Great Bible, based on Matthew's Bible, was issued. In 1544 Henry authorized the use in English of Cranmer's Litany.

But there was at this time a reaction against innovations in religion and there was passed in 1539 the Act of the Six Articles, which laid down severe penalties for any divergence from their demands. Cranmer fought strenuously against them, especially against the clause dealing with the marriage of clergy. He failed and was compelled to send his wife back to Germany. When in 1540 Thomas Cromwell fell from power, Cranmer pleaded courageously for his life, but again to no avail. When Henry died in 1547, Cranmer, much against his will, was nominated to the Council of Regency.

In Edward VI's reign the move towards Protestantism was accelerated, but at first Cranmer went cautiously. He said Mass for Henry's soul and he withstood a bill for the suppressing of all colleges and chantries. But in 1549 was issued his First Prayer Book and the first Act of Uniformity. This was modified in 1552, when a second Prayer Book and a new Act of Uniformity appeared. In 1553 were issued the 42 Articles of Religion to which all the clergy were required to agree. With the arrival of Northumberland in the place of Somerset Cranmer was faced with a set of ruffians who were bent on despoiling the Church still further of its wealth. Cranmer withstood boldly this attack on church property, just as he boldly withstood Hooper's attempt to force Zwinglianism on the Church. Had Edward VI lived any longer, Cranmer would probably have failed, but he died just in time.

The accession of Mary Tudor was for Cranmer no solution to any problem. At the last moment, wholly against his will and only because the king on his death-bed virtually commanded him to do so, he had agreed to the substitution of Lady Jane Grey on the throne for Mary. There was no hope of mercy from Mary. Catherine of Aragon, Bishop Fisher and the Roman religion must be avenged. Cranmer was arrested for treason and condemned. For a time his life was spared, because what was required was a public recantation of his heresies. Until March, 1554, he was in the Tower. He was brought out and at a disputation at Oxford he was commanded to recant. He refused and went back to prison. Alone and separated from all his friends and from all help and encouragement he was

examined and re-examined. He made four so-called recantations, of which none is a recantation, only a reaffirmation of his
acceptance of the Royal Supremacy. For three more weeks he
held out, then he collapsed and made two complete and ignominious recantations. This did not save his life. He was to be
burned outside Balliol College. Before this he was set up in
St. Mary's Church to recant publicly all his heresies. Instead he
recanted his recantations, denied any belief in Transubstantiation and rejected the Pope and all his 'enormities'. It was, he
said, his right hand that had offended and it should burn first.
He was hurried to the stake and when the fire was lighted, he
first thrust his right hand into the flames, crying 'this hand hath
offended', he met his death with a courage and patient endur-
ance which filled all who saw him with admiration. (*T.S.I.H.*,
2, 52 sqq.)

Cranmer's reputation has been grossly maligned by nineteenth-century historians. The strictures of Macaulay and
Gasquet and Dixon are really irrelevant, because they see him
only through nineteenth-century eyes and never against a
sixteenth-century background. He is charged with being a
timeserver, inconsistent, and a coward. There may have been
a streak of timidity on him, yet timid men do not make good
horsemen. It is necessary to remember that Cranmer was a
scholar called to high office in days when toughness rather than
scholarship was desirable. Further, he was an Erastian in
days when everybody was Erastian. Gardiner was an Erastian under Henry VIII, and he had much difficulty in explaining away his book *De Vera Obedientia*, written in 1535, when he
was restoring papalism in 1553. Cranmer was perfectly consistent in his accepting the Royal Supremacy, whether it was
exercised by Henry VIII or Edward VI or Mary. He was
consistent in his dislike of the Papacy. As early as 1525 he was
writing, 'I will never consent to the Bishop of Rome, for then I
should give myself to the devil; for I have made an oath to the
King, and I must obey the King by God's laws'. Nor was he a
coward in his daily life. 'He alone, as far as we know, tried to
save the monks of Sion from the block; he alone interceded for
Fisher and More; for Anne Boleyn and the Princess Mary, for

Thomas Cromwell and Bishop Tunstall. He told Henry VIII that he had offended God, and Cromwell that the Court was setting an evil example. He maintained almost unaided a stubborn fight against the Act of the Six Articles, and resisted longer than any one else the Duke of Northumberland's plot.' (Pollard.)

Thomas Cranmer ought to be remembered with gratitude and admiration. If for a moment his courage failed, at the end he recovered and more than recovered it and he died heroically. He was the founder of the Anglican Protestant Church and he gave it a liturgy unsurpassed by any other. He worked to try to unite all the Protestant churches in Europe, and he was always searching for the truth.   (*Plate 11*)

Pollard, *Cranmer.*
F. E. Hutchinson, *Cranmer and the English Reformation*, 1951.
Thomas Cranmer: Three commemorative lectures in Lambeth Palace, 1956.
J. Ridley, *Thomas Cranmer*, 1962.

RIDLEY, NICHOLAS, Bishop of London, martyr, was born at Willimotiswick Castle, South Tynedale, in Northumberland, in about 1503, he died on October 16th, 1555, aged about fifty-two. He was the second son of Christopher Ridley of Unthank Hall, Northumberland, and Ann Blenkinsop, having one brother, Hugh, and two sisters, Elizabeth and Alice. He was educated at Newcastle, but not at the Grammar School, which was not founded until 1525. He then went to Pembroke Hall, Cambridge. His uncle, Dr. Robert Ridley, was a Cambridge man, being a fine scholar who collaborated with Polydore Vergil and who taught Greek in the university, and he offered to pay Nicholas's expenses. Nicholas repaid his uncle's generosity by soon becoming an outstanding scholar both in Latin and Greek. He took his B.A. in 1522 and then turned to study philosophy and divinity. He was ordained probably early in 1524 and was offered a Fellowship at Oxford which he declined. In that year he was made a Fellow of Pembroke Hall and the next year (1525) he took his M.A.

Ridley was said to be a man of small stature, handsome, well built and clean-shaven. He was not a political priest like Wolsey or Gardiner, nor a saintly reformer like Bilney and Latimer: he was a scholar, an intellectual, living among books and disputations and preferring an academic life to any other. It was probably during this period that Ridley met and made friends with Cranmer. From 1527 to 1530 Ridley was abroad studying (again at his uncle's expense) at the Sorbonne in Paris (1527) and at Louvain for some six months in 1529. He was back in Cambridge in 1530.

In 1532 he was made chaplain to the university, a post which he held for four years together with that of Senior Proctor for part of the time. He resigned probably in 1537 when, having taken his B.D., he became private chaplain to Cranmer and left Cambridge to live at Cranmer's manor of Ford in Kent. It was almost certainly during this last period at Cambridge that Ridley changed from an orthodox Catholic into a Protestant. When in 1538 Cranmer presented him with the living of Herne, close to Ford, Ridley still believed in Transubstantiation and probably thought that auricular confession was beneficial and to be encouraged, but not essential to salvation, because he could find no scriptural authority for it.

The passing of the Act of the Six Articles changed the whole situation (1539). This was a conservative measure which put the brake on the trend towards Protestantism. The fall of Thomas Cromwell made the position of the Protestants extremely dangerous. Ridley was by that time the most able debater among the Protestants, even including Cranmer. In 1540 he was elected Master of Pembroke Hall, Cambridge, but he did not reside in the university, because he was helping Cranmer to bring about gradually the Protestant Reformation and this was not a moment when he could leave the Archbishop. Cranmer now appointed him to one of the prebendal stalls at Canterbury, but Ridley found life there far from pleasant, owing to the incessant quarrels between the Catholic and Protestant clergy, not only over religious matters, such as church services in English, but over petty questions such as the boundary between his garden and Dean Wotton's.

It was while he was at Herne that Ridley came to his decision on the question of Transubstantiation. He had certainly made up his mind by the end of 1546, although he made no public declaration until December 1548. When the Lutherans and the Zwinglians renewed their controversy in 1544, Ridley sat down to examine the whole question. He read Bertram of Corbie's treatise, which had been written in 840 for the Emperor Charles the Bald and which was published in 1532. That led him to examine the writings of the early Fathers. As a result he came to the conclusion that no change took place in the inward nature of the bread and wine after the prayer of consecration and that the flesh and blood of Christ were not corporeally present in the bread and wine: but he never denied the spiritual presence of Christ in the bread and wine. Ridley was now a heretic.

In October 1545 Ridley was made the Eighth Prebendary in the Cathedral Church at Westminster. On September 4th, 1547, he was designated Bishop of Rochester and he was consecrated at St. Paul's on the 25th. He had also just been given the living of Soham in Cambridgeshire. When he became a bishop he was allowed to retain all his preferments and to hold them *in commendam*. He was also chaplain to Edward VI.

From now onwards throughout the reign of the Protestant Edward VI Ridley was engaged with Cranmer in carrying through the English Reformation. The first problem which confronted them was that of images. The more extreme Protestants in London took the law into their own hands and removed the images in St. Martin's Church in Ironmonger Lane. Cranmer decided to support this action. On Ash Wednesday, February 23rd, 1547, in a sermon preached before Edward VI Ridley dealt with the question. The line he took was that as far as he could see it was wrong for images to be displayed in the churches, but he was open to be persuaded that he was wrong in his opinion. He made a cautious and tentative suggestion that both images and holy water should be dispensed with.

The question of the Mass was a far more important and difficult matter and at this moment Cranmer and Ridley had no intention of allowing any attacks to be made on it. The success which the extremists had won over images led them to think that they would be as successful, if they tried to force the government's hand over the Mass, which they now openly denounced as idolatry. In December 1547 Ridley preached at St. Paul's Cross and hotly attacked the fanatics. He did not indicate at all what was his own belief about the Real Presence, so that everybody assumed that he believed in it. Ridley was to be reminded of this sermon in 1554/5, when he was in prison and being tried for his life.

In November 1548 Cranmer produced the first draft of his Book of Common Prayer. There is no evidence that Ridley had any direct hand in the drafting, but it is reasonable to suppose that he was much consulted by Cranmer in its composition. It was clear that the Prayer Book struck at the very roots of Transubstantiation and therefore Cranmer and Ridley now came out into the open. A disputation was arranged in the House of Lords for December 17th and it lasted three days. Ridley was said to be at his very best and to have confounded the arguments of Heath and Day. It was just about this time that Ridley also spoke in favour of a bill to allow the clergy to marry.

During March and April 1549 Ridley was mostly in his diocese at Rochester, ensuring that the Book of Common Prayer was being accepted by everybody, but this work was interrupted by his being called on to deal with the ravings of Joan Bocher. He had been put on the commission of Visitors who were to ensure that the new religious policy was universally enforced in Cambridge. The Visitors arrived in Cambridge in May. Ridley found himself involved in a dispute over a proposal to suppress Clare Hall. Ridley firmly stood out against Protector Somerset and Clare Hall was saved. In June he presided over three disputations between Catholics and Protestants on the subject of the Mass. This was an academic exercise in the Philosophy Schools involving no political action afterwards. At the end Ridley summed up and decided against the doctrine of Transubstantiation: even the Catholics admitted that his speech was a wonderful performance.

Bonner was deprived of his bishopric in October 1549; in the following February Ridley was appointed to the see of London, but he was not installed until April 12th, when he himself was not there and he was installed by proxy. Ridley behaved with notable kindness to Bonner's family, allowing Bonner's mother and sister to reside in his palace at Fulham and frequently inviting them to dine with him, and treating Mistress Bonner with the utmost respect; he would seat her at the head of the table and would not allow her to move lower down, even when a member of the Council was at dinner.

London was a difficult see to administer, for it was the centre of the extreme Protestants and Anabaptists. Ridley was always a strict disciplinarian and he was determined to crush the extremists, and at the same time to see to it that the Reformation was enforced throughout his diocese.

The first problem he tackled was that of the altar—was there to be an altar for the communion service or a communion table? If a table, where was it to stand, at the east end or in the body of the church? Ridley had already in 1549 removed the altar in Rochester Cathedral and substituted for it a movable table which he placed for the time being in the position which the altar had occupied. In May 1550 he made a visitation of his new diocese of London which lasted for seven weeks. At the end of it not a single altar remained. During the visitation Ridley interviewed every vicar and curate in his diocese and insisted on each of them making a written submission to his Injunctions.

The second problem was that of vestments. John Hooper was about to be consecrated Bishop of Gloucester, but he refused to wear vestments. At that moment the wearing of vestments was prescribed by law, therefore Ridley strongly opposed Hooper and also the Council, which was inclined to give way. Ridley's line was that he himself did not care much for vestments, but he did not regard them as being of spiritual importance. On the other hand, the law said they must be worn and the law must be upheld. Hooper became defiant and unreasonable and at last he was put in the Fleet. A royal pardon was granted to Cranmer and Ridley if they consecrated

Hooper without vestments and thereby might incur *praemunire*. Ridley still stuck out, because he saw in Hooper's obstinate opposition a desire to place individual judgment above ecclesiastical authority; that could only create chaos, that sort of anarchy which was characteristic of the Anabaptists. In the end Ridley carried his point and Hooper was consecrated wearing vestments.

Meanwhile Ridley was employed in various ways: he was frequently examining and disputing with Gardiner, the deprived Bishop of Winchester who was in prison: he was a member of a commission which was sent to enquire into scandals at Eton College (1552): he met John à Lasco to discuss how best to solve the difficulties raised by the church services of the foreign Protestant exiles in London: he paid a visit to the Princess Mary and tried to persuade her to hear him preach, but he failed entirely (1552). In 1553 he preached before Edward VI a sermon on the poverty of the London poor, a sermon which did a great deal to move the King to reopen St. Thomas's hospital, which had been suppressed for its wealth by Henry VIII, to found St. Bartholomew's and to grant the revenues of the Savoy to St. Thomas's.

The death of Edward VI and the accession of the Catholic Mary left Ridley in a perilous position. He had signed the will of Edward VI by which the succession to the throne was altered so as to cut out Mary and bring in Lady Jane Dudley as Queen. On July 16th, not the 9th, Ridley preached at St. Paul's Cross to a crowd which was wholeheartedly in favour of Mary. Ridley attacked Mary resolutely and called both her and Elizabeth bastards, an attack which Mary never forgot nor forgave. Northumberland's plot failed, Ridley went towards Framlingham to try to make his peace with the Queen, but she had him arrested before he got there and sent him to London to the Tower. He was deprived of his bishopric and Bonner was reinstated. Wyatt's rebellion made things still more difficult for the Protestant prisoners, but what Mary wanted was for the Protestant leaders to make a public recantation. In 1554 Ridley, Latimer and Cranmer were sent to Oxford for a public disputation. At the close of a noisy and hostile session Ridley was declared a heretic and was excommunicated. Every effort was made to persuade him to recant, but Ridley stood firm. He spent his time in prison writing to his followers to encourage them to remain loyal to the Protestant cause: he wrote a series of treatises on various aspects of Protestantism which he smuggled out of prison and which were sent abroad and there printed and smuggled back into England for distribution. On October 15th he was formally degraded from the priesthood and handed over to the Mayor for execution. The next day, October 16th, he and Latimer were burned 'on the north side of the town in the ditch over against Balliol College'. Whereas Latimer died quickly and in little pain, Ridley's death was prolonged and agonizing. The fire had been badly laid and only burned slowly under the faggots, with the result that the flames did not reach the gunpowder which had been provided to hasten his death. Slowly the lower part of his body was burned away. Ridley screamed in his agony 'I cannot burn. For God's sake let the fire come unto me'. He was not burning at all above his waist, his shirt was not even scorched. At last a soldier hauled a faggot away and let the flames rise: they reached the gunpowder and Ridley's pain was over.

If Bonner may be looked on as the outstanding example of the uncompromising Conservative bishop; if Latimer stands for the plain, down-to-earth defender of what he felt to be right; if Hooper may be taken to represent the violent, irrational and extreme reformer; Ridley may well be taken as standing for everything which was best in the English Reformation. He was gentle by nature, devoid of rancour, kind to his opponents, firm in his opinions, bold in opposition, as good a scholar as Cranmer and less timid, a man of independent judgment and with an understanding of genuine statesmanship, of invincible faith and undaunted courage. The Anglican Reformation probably owes more to Ridley than to any other single man.

J. G. Ridley, *Nicholas Ridley*, Longmans, 1957.

LATIMER, HUGH, Bishop of Worcester, martyr, was born probably in 1485 at Thurcaston in Leicestershire. He died in 1555, aged about seventy. The clearest portrait of Latimer is to

Plate 15

Stephen Gardiner, Bishop of Winchester,
Lord Chancellor

Edmund Bonner, Bishop of London

Plate 16

William Allen, Cardinal

Reginald Pole, Cardinal, Archbishop of Canterbury

be obtained by allowing him to speak for himself. 'My father was a yeoman and had no lands of his own, only he had a farm of three or four pound a year at the uttermost and hereon he tilled so much as kept half a dozen men. He had walk for a hundred sheep and my mother milked thirty kine. He was able and did find the king a harness with himself and his horse. I can remember that I buckled his harness when he went into Blackheath field (1497). He kept me to school or else I had not been able to preach before the king's majesty now.' 'In my time my poor father was as diligent to teach me how to shoot as to learn me any other thing. He taught me how to draw; how to lay my body in my bow, and not to draw with strength of arms as other nations do, but with strength of the body.'

In 1506 Hugh was sent to Cambridge, where he was elected to a Fellowship at Clare College in 1510. At some date unknown he took holy orders and in 1524 he became B.D. That Hugh was still a believer in the old religion is proved by the sermon he preached that day against the teaching of Melancthon. One of his hearers was Thomas Bilney, who was so much struck by the sermon that he called on Latimer. 'Bilney was the instrument by which God called me to knowledge; for I was as obstinate a Papist as any was in England. Bilney heard me at the time and perceived that I was zealous without knowledge, and he came to me afterwards in my study and asked me to hear his confession. I did so, and by his confession I learned more than before in many years. So from that time forward I began to smell the word of God and forsook the school-doctors and such fooleries.' The use of such words as 'smell' and 'fooleries' is typical of Latimer's racy and arresting English, touched sometimes with what we today might regard as coarseness.

In 1525 Latimer preached in the university church and the Bishop of Ely was present. He suspected that Latimer had Lutheran tendencies and he inhibited him from preaching in the diocese. Latimer was also examined by Wolsey's chaplains, but he disowned all connection with Lutheranism and was given permission to preach throughout the kingdom. He was

M—(2)

soon again in trouble on account of two sermons he preached 'on the card', in which he explained allegorically how men could win salvation by playing trumps (*D.N.B.*). He had also given much offence by depreciating what he called 'voluntary works', such as pilgrimages, in comparison with works of faith, *e.g.* of mercy (1529). Nor was his popularity at all increased when it was known that he strongly favoured the King's side over the divorce of Catherine of Aragon. But he won the favour of Henry VIII when he denied the validity of the marriage before the committee which Gardiner took to Cambridge in 1530 to ascertain the opinion of the university divines. He was at once appointed to preach before the King (1530). As a reward he was given the living in Wiltshire of West Kineton, to which he was instituted in 1531. A few months later he preached in a neighbouring parish and gave much offence by denouncing all the bishops and clergy in England as being, not shepherds entering in by the door, but thieves whom there was not enough hemp in England to hang. In 1532 he was accused of preaching that the Virgin Mary was a sinner, of denouncing invocation of saints and denying purgatory and hell fire. The Bishop of Salisbury, in whose diocese West Kineton lay, was Campeggio, an Italian and an absentee. After a delay of almost a year Latimer was cited to appear before the Bishop of London. At first he refused to sign the articles which were presented to him, but ultimately he made a complete submission. Foolishly he wrote a letter denying that he had confessed to any error of doctrine, only to indiscretion. For this he was compelled to admit to Convocation that he had erred in doctrine.

In 1533 he was again in trouble over a sermon he preached at Bristol, and he was inhibited by the Bishop of London. But he had good friends at court and he regained the King's favour, so that he was commanded to preach before Henry on Wednesdays in Lent (1534), and in 1535 he was made Bishop of Worcester in direct succession to four consecutive absentee Italians. Perhaps he owed these favours to the support which he gave to the marriage of Anne Boleyn with Henry VIII.

From now onwards his preaching became more outspoken. In 1536 he denounced the luxury of the bishops, abbots and 'other strong thieves'. At a meeting of Convocation he asked the clergy what they had done to benefit the poor during the last seven years. They had burned a dead man (Tracy) and tried to burn a living one—meaning himself. More and more in his sermons he dwelt upon the poverty of the poor and the wealth of the rich. And he moved more and more towards Protestantism. It is to be noted that when the Pilgrimage of Grace broke out, the rebels repeatedly demanded that Latimer and Cranmer should be handed over to them.

In his diocese Latimer worked hard. He issued orders that every priest was to possess a whole Bible in English, or at any rate a New Testament: he commanded his clergy to pay first attention to preaching, to admit no one to the Communion who could not say the Lord's Prayer in English, and to instruct the children in their parishes to read English. He had a statue of the Virgin in Worcester cathedral—'our great Sibyl', as he called it—stripped of its jewels and ornaments, and was anxious for it to be burned: 'she herself with her old sister of Walsingham, her young sister of Ipswich, with their other two sisters of Doncaster and Penrice would make a jolly muster in Smithfield'.

In 1538 he was on a commission to examine John Forest, and at the execution he preached a sermon, or (as he put it either callously or in the Pauline sense of 'I speak as a fool') 'played the fool after my customable manner'. In the same year he sat on a commission to investigate the famous miracle of the 'Blood of Hailes' and found it to consist of a yellowish gum. When in 1539 there was passed the Act of the Six Articles, Latimer and Shaxton, Bishop of Salisbury, resigned their sees. For more than twelve months he was a prisoner in the house of Sampson, Bishop of Chichester. He was then released, but he was forbidden to preach in or to visit London, either university, or his late diocese. For the next six years his life becomes a blank: then in 1546 he was brought before the Council on a charge of having encouraged his friend Crome, who was in trouble over his preaching. Latimer was put in the Tower and remained there until he was released by the general pardon at the accession of Edward VI.

Latimer set to work at once. His servant said of him, 'then most of all he began to set forth his plough and to till the ground of the Lord and to sow the good corn of God's word . . . preaching for the most part two sermons every Sunday . . . For he being a sore bruised man and above three score and seven years of age took notwithstanding all these pains in preaching, and besides this every morning ordinarily winter and summer about two of the clock in the morning he was at his book most diligently.' He refused to go back to his bishopric, but he became the most notable of preachers. Of all his sermons the most famous is still that 'of the Plough', in which he attacked unpreaching and non-resident bishops, citing the devil as the best example of a diligent bishop: 'He is the most diligent preacher of all others; he is never out of his diocese; he is never from his cure; he is ever in his parish; the diligentest preacher in all the realm; he is ever at his plough', In another course of sermons he took as his main subject the oppression of the poor by the rich, and included eulogies of Somerset's government. Latimer worked in concert with Hales and the 'commonwealth men' on behalf of the poor. Nothing could more vividly picture for us the effect Latimer's preaching had on his congregation than the entry in the churchwarden's accounts at St. Margaret's, Westminster, in 1549, one shilling and sixpence paid for 'mending divers pews that were broken when Dr. Latimer did preach'.

When Mary came to the throne Latimer was well aware of the danger in which he stood. On September 4th, 1553, a summons against him was issued, but he was given six hours' notice beforehand to give him a chance to escape. He refused to take it. In March 1554 he, together with Ridley and Cranmer, was sent to Oxford to take part in a dispute on the doctrine of the Mass. He was condemned for heresy and was handed over to the secular arm to be burned. Ridley was at the same time condemned. On October 16th, 1555—after so long a delay—they were both led to execution in Oxford 'upon the north side of the town in the ditch over against Balliol College'. They were fastened to the stake with a chain round the middle of both. Bags of gunpowder were hung round their necks and the fire lighted. 'Be of good comfort, Master Ridley', said Latimer, 'we shall this day light such a candle, by God's grace, in England as I trust shall never be put out.' Latimer died quickly with little suffering.

Latimer was a man sincere, courageous and full of vitality. His manner was aggressive, his style of preaching extremely effective, his English racy, easily understood, arresting and prone to become even harsh. His mind was clear but not subtle, he saw things in black and white. Being supremely self-confident he was often rash in his decisions, bold but ill-advised in utterance. As a reformer he had no patience with conservative bishops who had been trained as lawyers in the canon law. He was perfectly right in thinking that these men, men like Bonner and Gardiner, would always see the lawyers' or legalistic side of the Reformation as at least equal with the doctrinal or spiritual. He could not tolerate their readiness to compromise and comply. On the other hand, he had no understanding at all of what was involved in government or diplomacy, which are based on compromise, and he misunderstood the nature of law, which aims not at prefection but at the enforcement of order. (L. B. Smith, *Tudor Prelates and Politics*.)

It was impossible for such a mind to yield to the will of the majority in order to achieve unity, at the expense of his convictions. That is why he opposed *The Bishops' Book*, which he looked on as a temporary expedient to secure unity. In his refusal to believe in purgatory he was wholly logical: 'The founding of the monasteries argued purgatory to be; so the pulling down of them argueth it not to be. What uncharitableness and cruelness seemeth it to be to destroy monasteries, if purgatory be!' His denunciation of images, pilgrimages and other traditions was not merely iconoclastic. The reformer Hilsey said of him, 'I have perceived that his mind is much more against the abusing of things than against the things itself.'

Latimer's attacks on enclosures and the new landed interest were not directed solely against their cupidity. He felt their actions to be immoral and irreligious. 'If ye bring it to pass that the yeomanry be not able to put their sons to school . . . and they be not able to marry their daughters to the avoiding of whoredom; I say ye pluck salvation from the people and utterly destroy the realm. For by yeoman's sons the faith of Christ's religion hath been maintained chiefly.' Yet for all his preaching, he probably achieved more for Protestantism by the nobility of his death.

R. Demaus, *Hugh Latimer*, 1869, abridged edition 1935. *Religious Tract Society.*

H. S. Darby, *Hugh Latimer*, Epworth Press, 1953.

H. R. Trevor-Roper, *Historical Essays*, 1957, pp. 85–90.

HOOPER, JOHN, Bishop of Gloucester and Worcester, martyr, was born late in the fifteenth century and died in 1555. Nothing is known of his life until in 1519 he took his B.A. degree at Oxford, and the name of his college is not known. It is probable that he was a Cistercian monk at Gloucester and it may have been then that he took Orders. When the monasteries were dissolved, Hooper went to London and became much impressed by the writings of Zwingli and Bullinger. He returned to Oxford in order to spread their reforming views, but when the Act of the Six Articles was passed (1539) he fled first of all to Paris, then he came back to England, but he soon fled again to Ireland and thence to Switzerland. In 1546 he married an Antwerp lady at Basle, and in the following March he went to Zurich, where he became intimate with Bullinger and corresponded with such reformers as Bucer and John à Lasco.

In 1549, when the Protestant reformation was being established, he came back to England and was made chaplain to Protector Somerset, and he now represented the more extreme views of Protestantism. He was much more sympathetic with Zwingli than with Luther: he objected to the Lutheran doctrine of the Eucharist and held that 'the minister gives what is in his power—namely the bread and wine, and not the Body of Christ; nor is it exhibited by the minister and eaten by the communicant . . . to eat the Body of Christ is nothing else than to believe, as He Himself teaches in the sixth of John.'

Hooper's time was now given to preaching, usually twice a day, when he drew huge audiences: in engaging in disputes on such subjects as Predestination, and divorce which he held to be legal for both parties in cases of adultery; in denouncing Bonner: and in denouncing the new 1549 Prayer Book on the grounds that he objected to vestments and to the form of the oath by the saints. After the fall of Somerset, Hooper became chaplain to Northumberland, by whom he was completely deceived into looking on him as an honest and sincere man.

The controversy over vestments landed Hooper in great trouble and eventually in the Fleet. In 1550 he was appointed Bishop of Gloucester, but he declined to be consecrated wearing vestments. His obstinacy and unreasonableness at last angered even Northumberland, but if it had not been for Ridley, it is probable that the government would have given in to Hooper. Ridley stuck out against Hooper and Hooper found himself in the Fleet. With good common sense, Hooper saw no advantage in remaining in prison unable to further the Protestant reformation. He therefore gave in and was consecrated Bishop of Gloucester (1551).

Hooper's record as a bishop was entirely creditable. He preached three or four times a day—one wonders whether quality may not have suffered at the hands of quantity: he tried to organize his diocese on the model of Zurich—in doing which he was running counter to the tide of Protestantism in England: he made a most illuminating visitation throughout his diocese, in which he discovered that out of 249 clergy 10 could not say the Lord's Prayer, 27 did not know who was its author, 30 could not tell where it was to be found (*E.H.R.*, xix, 1904, pp. 98–9).

In 1552 the sees of Gloucester and Worcester were amalgamated and Hooper was made bishop of both. He met with more opposition to his methods in the new part of his diocese in Worcestershire than he had in Gloucestershire.

The accession of the Catholic Mary Tudor to the throne meant, of course, that Hooper would be one of the first Protestant bishops to be attacked, in spite of the fact that he had opposed the attempt to put Lady Jane Grey on the throne. His im-

prisonment was specially severe: he was deprived of his
bishopric, he was excommunicated for refusing to recant,
he was degraded from his clerical orders and was handed over
to the civil arm to be executed. It was thought politic to have
him burned in his own diocese of Gloucester. There on
February 9th, 1555, he was put to death. Owing to a contrary
wind which blew the flames away from him, Hooper suffered
terribly, but he never flinched nor (as far as is known) uttered
a word. He had specially asked for a quick fire 'shortly to make
an end'.

Hooper is on the whole the least attractive of the Protestant
martyr bishops. By his writings as much as by his preaching he
did a tremendous amount to popularize the more extreme
Protestant views. But he was personally, although of the
highest moral character and generous to the poor, so austere,
so stern and unbending, that he frightened away many who
sought his help and whom he would have wished to help.

In his opinions he was uncompromising: he would never
dream of compromising his faith in order to arrive at a temporary solution agreeable to all (L. B. Smith). To him the salvation of the individual soul was far more important than mere
unity in church services or rule by the will of the majority
(*ib.*). He was wholly impartial in his denunciations, for he
castigated the enclosing landlords (men who 'hath enough
given them from God, yet are not content therewithal') as
severely as he attacked the common people (who 'live idle and
will not labour'). He believed passionately in the beneficial
effects of spreading knowledge of the Bible by giving it to all
in the English language, just as he believed that the social
discontents and riots were the direct result of ignorance of the
divine law. He could never easily admit himself to be in the
wrong, and like others who have absolute confidence in their
own opinions, he was easily gulled by those who pretended to
think as he did (*e.g.* Northumberland). In our own age of
compromise it is difficult to be sympathetic with so uncompromising a character; but also in our own age, when persecution is rife outside our own boundaries, we can hardly not
admire a bishop who would today have as willingly gone to

prison and 'brain-washing' as he went in his own day to the
fire in Gloucester.

L. B. Smith, *Tudor Prelates and Politics*, 1953.
J. G. Ridley, *Nicholas Ridley*, 1957.

FERRAR, ROBERT, Bishop of St. David's, martyr,
was born probably not later than 1504, perhaps as early as
1502, and he died in 1555. He came of a Yorkshire family and
was born at Ewood near Halifax, according to tradition for
which no evidence exists. He was educated perhaps for a
short time at Cambridge, certainly later at Oxford, where he
became an Augustinian Canon. He then came under the
influence of the Protestant Gerard, was involved in a charge
of heresy and was compelled to recant (1528). He accompanied Bishop Barlow on a mission to Scotland, after which he
became Prior of St. Oswald's, Nostell, near Pomfret.

When Edward VI came to the throne Ferrar became chaplain to Protector Somerset, who made him Bishop of St. David's
(1548), the first appointment to be made by letters-patent
without any election by the Chapter. Ferrar soon found himself in trouble with his Welsh diocese, which had made Ferrar's
predecessor Barlow's life a burden to him. The Chapter
brought a series of ridiculous charges against him, including
an accusation that he 'daily useth whistling to his child and
says he understood his whistle when he was but three days old,'
that he whistled to a 'seal-fish tumbling in Milford Haven',
and that 'he useth bridle with white studs and snaffle, with
Scottish stirrups, with spurs, a Scottish pad with a little staff
of three-quarters long'. Unfortunately Somerset fell from power
at this time and fifty-six charges were laid against Ferrar before
the Privy Council and a commission was set up to examine 127
witnesses. Ferrar was in prison until the accession of Mary,
when he was deprived of his bishopric, because he was a
married priest (1554). The next year he was examined by
Gardiner, who accused him of breaking his monastic vow by
his marriage, to which Ferrar replied that his vow was to live
chaste, not single. Gardiner sent him down to Carmarthen

to be tried by Morgan, the man who had become Bishop of St. David's when Ferrar was deprived. At his trial Ferrar was required to subscribe to a list of articles which he refused to accept. He was condemned as a heretic and was burned on March 30th, 1555, 'on the south side of the market Cross'. He told a looker-on that if he saw him 'once to stir in the pains of his burning, he should then give no credit to his doctrine'. Ferrar's sufferings were intense, but he never flinched nor moved until he was struck on the head by a man named Richard Gravell, to put him out of his agonies.

Ferrar was a simple, sincere and brave man, but he was no match for the greedy Welsh Chapter whose outrageous robberies he tried to end. Fuller says of him that he was 'not unlearned, but somewhat indiscreet or rather uncomplying, which procured him much trouble; so that he may be said, with St. Laurence, to be broiled on both sides, being persecuted both by Protestants and Papists'.

R. Bretton: Bishop Robert Ferrar in *Halifax Antiquarian Society*, vol. 31, 1934.

POLE, REGINALD, Cardinal and Archbishop of Canterbury, was born in March, 1500 and died on the night of November 17th, 1558, aged 58 years. He was the son of Sir Richard Pole who had married Margaret, Countess of Salisbury, the daughter of Edward IV's brother, George, Duke of Clarence. He was, therefore, one of the Yorkist claimants to the throne. (See genealogical tree, Table II). It was this relationship to the reigning king in England which made him so important in the eyes of foreign rulers. Henry VIII shewed him considerable kindness and made generous grants of money towards the cost of his education at the Carthusian school at Sheen, at Magdalen College, Oxford, and at Padua university. In addition he made over to him ecclesiastical revenues to ensure him an income equal to his rank. At Oxford his teachers were Linacre and Latimer, in Italy the great scholars Longolius, Leonicus and Bembo. He also corresponded with Erasmus, met John à Lasco, the Polish reformer, and paid a visit to Rome. He proved himself a man of great intellectual qualities, brilliant in debate, and ultimately an admirable teacher, but he was never a learned theologian.

Pole was in Italy from 1521 to 1527. He was back in England by 1529 and was cordially welcomed by the king. But Pole disliked life at Court and retired to Sheen to pursue his studies. Pole was much opposed to the divorce from Catherine of Aragon which Henry was planning, and when the king sought his advice, he got leave to go abroad to Paris. But when he was there, Henry demanded that he should obtain the views of Paris university. Thanks to the influence of Francis I the opinion was favourable. Recalled to England, Pole was, on the death of Wolsey, strongly urged to accept either the bishopric of Winchester or the archbishopric of York. Henry was anxious to have him on his side in his quarrel with Rome, but Pole would not accept on those terms. In an interview with the king, Pole behaved tactlessly and violently, the king lost his temper and almost hit Pole, finally leaving him dissolved in tears. The quarrel was soon mended and in 1532 Henry allowed him to go abroad to Avignon and then to Padua.

Up to 1536, the year in which Pole visited Rome and became a Cardinal, Henry made many attempts to win him over, for he recognized the danger to England which might come from a hostile Yorkist. But Henry's impatience and Pole's inflexibility always prevented a reconciliation, which was at last made impossible by the publication of Pole's *De Unitate Ecclesiae*, in which discretion was thrown to the winds and abuse was poured out on Henry. From that moment Pole revealed his inherent lack of political insight. He thought the Pilgrimage of Grace was symptomatic of all England; he was prepared to become a traitor to his own country and to urge France and Spain to invade England, and he advocated a commercial blockade of England. Henry retaliated by executing Pole's relations, he may even have tried to have Pole murdered, but it may be that Pole only imagined this. Henry also took all possible steps to prevent Pole's legatine missions from succeeding.

Foreigners also recognized the importance of Pole in the

diplomatic world. His dynastic position became a reason for trying to arrange a marriage between him and Mary Tudor, and the Pope gave him a legateship to sustain English rebels with money. Nor did the Pope underrate the value of Pole's scholarship. From 1536, when he became a Cardinal, to 1549, when it looked as if Pole was likely to succeed Paul III as Pope, Pole's career was distinguished and he was probably happier than he was either before or after. Twice he presided over the Council of Trent and he was made Governor of the Patrimony of St. Peter, while he enjoyed the friendship of the most famous woman of Italy, Vittoria Colonna. But in truth he was losing ground. He belonged to the liberal catholics, who hoped for reconciliation between Lutheranism and the Catholic Church, and when this party failed to secure control of the Church, and the more extreme party was successful at the Council of Trent, Pole's own influence began to wane. He bowed to the inevitable and accepted the papal authority. He was not a strong enough man to oppose the policy of the papacy on principle and risk exile a second time. He had been exiled from England for denying the Royal Supremacy, he now accepted the Papal Supremacy. He was within an ace of being elected Pope on the death of Paul III; but although he was supported by the Imperial cardinals, that inevitably put the French cardinals against him, while the Italian cardinals wanted an Italian Pope.

On the accession of Mary Tudor it was only a question of time before Pole would return to England. He was appointed the new Archbishop of Canterbury. But his return for various reasons was delayed and it was not until November 20th, 1554, that he landed in England. He at once set about restoring England to the Catholic fold, reorganizing the Church and preventing the later succession of Elizabeth. Up to this moment he was still only in deacon's orders; on March 20th, 1556, he was ordained priest and the next day, when Cranmer was burned, Pole as Archbishop celebrated Mass for the first time in his life. For two years the government of England was very largely in the hands of Pole, who busied himself both in religious and secular affairs. But although the ecclesiastical settlement of Henry was reversed by Act of Parliament and Pole enforced many reforms which he wanted, he failed in the end both in making England Roman Catholic and in keeping Elizabeth off the throne. He must accept his share of responsibility for the burnings. All his life he hated extreme measures, but he dared not oppose the persecutions. He died the same night as Queen Mary with his work unfinished.

Reginald Pole was a sincere and single-minded man, a passionate believer in the Christian religion, a man of perfect integrity and unblemished morals. He had a genius for friendship and he was intimate with the best spirits in Italy, men like Contarini, Priuli and Sadoleto, women like Vittoria Colonna. But he was intransigent and inherently weak, he dreaded holding public office, and although he was able to speak his mind fearlessly and even violently, as he did to Pope Paul IV, he often shirked his clear duty, as he did when he failed to withstand the Marian persecutions. Yet he saw clearly the dangers inherent in the growing modern State and he took his stand courageously and consistently in defence of religion and the Church. It is his chief claim to be remembered that he also saw the need for reform in the Catholic Church, tried patiently to achieve reform and by his example and work made the ultimate reforms of the Jesuits the easier to achieve.   (*Plate 16*)

K. B. McFarlane: *Cardinal Pole*, 1924.
W. Schenk: *Reginald Pole, Cardinal of England*, 1950.
P. Hughes: *Rome and the Counter-Reformation in England*, 1940.
W. G. Zeeveld: *Foundations of Tudor Policy*, 1948.

PONET, JOHN (variations in spelling are Poynet, Poinet and Ponnet, but he always used the form Ponet), Bishop of Winchester, was born in Kent in 1516 (not 1514) he died in 1556, aged forty. Little is known of his early life. He arrived at Cambridge at the Queens' College about 1528, took his B.A., became a Fellow in 1532, M.A. 1535, Bursar 1537–9, Dean 1541–2. He was ordained in 1536 and took his D.D. in 1547. At the time of his arrival at Queens' that college was the most advanced in the university in its theological opinions, but Ponet was a member of a group of young men who were more distinguished for their humanistic interests than for theological opinions. His friends included John Cheke, Roger Ascham and William Cecil.

Ponet made good use of his time at Cambridge. He was a man with considerable intellectual abilities, he had a mind which ranged over many interests and he had great facility in learning languages. 'It was no sluggish attention which he gave to learning languages—Latin, of course, Greek, Italian, and at last German' (Bale). He was said to be an excellent mathematician and he was greatly interested in astronomy. As bursar of Queens' he designed the complicated sundial which is still in their front court, and he gave a copy of it to Henry VIII for Hampton Court. 'It shows not only the hour of the day, but also the day of the month, the sign of the moon, the ebbing and flowing of the sea, with divers other things as strange'. In addition to all this he made a greater study of the scriptures and of the Church Fathers than any of his contemporaries with the exception of Cheke.

In about 1547 he became chaplain to Cranmer and he quickly acquired much influence with the archbishop. He was said to have advised him 'in the hidden secrets of divine mysteries' and there is no doubt that Cranmer came to rely on Ponet more and more.

In 1549 Ponet wrote a tract defending the marriage of the clergy (Cranmer was a married man). On February 23rd, 1550, he was nominated to succeed Bonner as Bishop of London, but in March he was nominated to Rochester and he was consecrated in June. Within a year he was translated to Winchester in place of the deprived Gardiner. He was compelled to surrender the enormously wealthy revenues of that see and he received in exchange a fixed income of 2,000 marks a year.

At some point he seems to have been married to a butcher's wife at Nottingham while her husband was still alive. Machyn in his *Diary* records: 'The 27th day of July (1551) was the new Bishop of Winchester divorced from the butcher's wife with shame enough', and he was ordered to pay the butcher an annual pension as compensation. Ponet then married again, and when Mary Tudor came to the throne in 1553 he was deprived of his bishopric as a married priest. He took part in Wyatt's rebellion and when he saw that it was a failure he fled overseas to Strasbourg.

Little is known of his life abroad. He became involved in a dispute with Dr. Martyn over the marriage of clergy (1556) and he also wrote in the same year his *Short Treatise of Politike Power*. He died in Strasbourg in 1556.

Ponet has acquired a bad reputation among historians. The *D.N.B.* calls him 'clever, but somewhat unscrupulous': Miss Garrett in her *Marian Exiles* writes that 'of John Ponet the man there is little good to be said: he was quarrelsome, avaricious, unscrupulous and a coward'. Later writers tend to take a more generous view of his character and a higher view of his importance. Probably he was rather above than below the average standards of his time in character and integrity. His literary style was pungent, his mind vigorous and even aggressive, but he had a generous spirit and much magnanimity of heart. He has been called 'the highest ranking English churchman in Germany' during his exile, in daily touch with the humanists like Cheke and Morison (Zeefeldt). His *Short Treatise of Politike Power* was the 'most important contribution of the exiles to the history of English thought' (Zeefeldt). 'He was laying down a principle which anticipated by almost a hundred years Milton's declaration of the individual's independence from the state' (*ib*): and the American John Adams calls him 'the theorist whose *Politike Power* contained every essential principle of liberty which was afterwards dilated upon by Algernon Sidney and John Locke'. Ponet's main thesis is that rulers, just as much as subjects, have the duties of Christians and of citizens to obey the laws of God, of Nature and of men. Their position is one of trust and it may be forfeited, for 'all laws do agree that men revoke their proxies and letters of attorney when it pleaseth them, much more when they see their proctors and attorneys abuse it' (C. Morris, *Political Thought in England: Tyndale to Hooker*, p. 152).

W. S. Hudson, *John Ponet, Advocate of Limited Monarchy*, 1942.
W. G. Zeeveld, *Foundations of Tudor Policy*, 1948.
J. W. Allen, *History of Political Thought in XVI Century*, ed. 1954.
C. Morris, *Political Thought in England: Tyndale to Hooker*, 1953.

ASCHAM, ROGER, author, was born in 1515 and died in 1568 in his fifty-fourth year. He was educated privately to begin with, as was the custom of the time, in the household of Sir Anthony Wingfield, where he learned not only English and the Classics, but also a love for sport, especially of archery, which never deserted him. He went on to St. John's College, Cambridge, where he became so proficient in Greek that he taught the language to other students while he was still himself an undergraduate. He became a strong and on occasion a violent Protestant. In 1538 he became a reader in Greek at St. John's and he greatly influenced the development of the study of Greek in Cambridge. His handwriting was so beautiful that he was used by the University to write its official letters. In 1545 he published his *Toxophilus*, a treatise in the form of a dialogue, written in English, on the sport of archery. Three years later he became tutor to the princess Elizabeth. He greatly admired her learning, but he found the life cramping. He soon quarrelled with the steward and fell out with Elizabeth, and as a result he resigned his post. In 1550 he was appointed secretary to the English ambassador to Charles V and up to 1552 he resided abroad at Augsburg. Later he became Latin secretary to Queen Mary and he was given the rare privilege of being allowed to continue as a Protestant. In 1558 he became private tutor to the new Queen, Elizabeth I. He married in 1554 and had three sons, of whom one died in 1568 and two survived him. The last years of his life were devoted to writing his *Scholemaster*.

It may well be asked why a man whose life was so comparatively undistinguished and unsuccessful should be worth remembering today. The reason probably is that Ascham was not only a typical product of the age in which he lived, but he was also always something a little bit more than that, always a little bit ahead of his own times. Like many men in the sixteenth century, Ascham suffered from perpetual ill health; like many others he was always short of money and his life was one long struggle to keep going. Therefore he pestered his patrons for pensions and presents even more than was the habit of the times. He was a first class scholar, in days when learning and scholarship were fashionable, and he had all the irritability which so often marks the Renaissance scholars. But Ascham was more than a mere pedant and he deserves to be remembered specially by two classes of people. All who love and revere English prose literature should recall that Ascham, classical scholar though he was, fought for the use of the English language. In the introduction to *Toxophilus* he pleaded for the use of the 'Englyshe tonge' rather than the Greek or Latin, and while he was secretary to the English ambassador at Augsburg he wrote all his letters in English and not in Latin. The style of *Toxophilus* is itself a remarkably early example of pure English prose. But most especially all boys ought to honour Roger Ascham for the enlightened views he held on education. In his *Scholemaster*, published in 1570 after his death by his widow, he denounces the use of force in teaching and urges that the pupil should be attracted to learning by the gentle persuasion of his teacher. Those students who today follow gladly a classical education will there find set out clearly for the first time those methods of teaching Latin which have been generally adopted by succeeding generations of 'scholemasters'. Not least may Ascham be remembered as the man who pleaded (in *Toxophilus*) that sport should find an important place in any system of sound education.

E. M. Nugent: *The Thought and Culture of the English Renaissance*, C.U.P., 1956.

UDALL, NICHOLAS, reformer, dramatist and schoolmaster, was born in 1505 and died in 1556, aged fifty-one. He was educated at Winchester and at Corpus Christi College, Oxford. While he was at Oxford he came strongly under the influence of the new learning and in religion he favoured the Lutheran point of view. He came into prominence at court at the coronation of Anne Boleyn when he was author, or part author, of the pageants and masques which formed a large part of the celebrations and which laid the foundations for his reputation as a literary man.

In 1534 he was appointed Head Master of Eton, soon after he had published a book entitled *Flowers for Latin Spekynge, selected and gathered out of Terence, and the same translated into Englysshe*. It was the custom at Eton for some of the boys to act the plays of Terence and Plautus under the direction of the Head Master 'about the feast of St. Andrew', a custom very acceptable to Udall.

In 1541 his career as a schoolmaster came to an end—only temporarily, as it proved. A theft of silver images and other plate was committed by two of the scholars with the help of Udall's servant. Udall was examined on suspicion of having been aware of the theft, but although he appeared to be innocent of the theft, he confessed to being guilty of a moral offence with one of his pupils. He lost his mastership and was sent to the Marshalsea, but he was soon released and was once again in favour at court, and he also received several church preferments.

In 1549 he was employed by the government to write the answer to the demands of the West Country rebels for the old religion to be restored. Udall's answer was a forceful and able reply to the Catholic arguments and he defended with spirit the royal authority in matters of religion. On the accession of Mary, Udall was one of the few Protestants who were retained in favour and in employment, so much so that in 1551 he was made a Canon of Windsor and in 1554, in spite of his past record, he was made Master of Westminster school. These appointments are a proof of Mary's respect for learning and ability. He died in 1556 and was buried in St. Margaret's, Westminster.

The importance of Udall lies in the fact that he combined in himself activities as a moderate Reformer, as a humanist and as an able dramatist. Only one of his plays remains to us, *Ralph Roister Doister*, which is generally regarded as the first genuine comedy in English literature. It was almost certainly written in 1553–4 and therefore must have been intended for the boys of Westminster School and not of Eton College. The play has close affinities with Plautus and Terence, but Udall has succeeded in making the characters recognizably English. There is only one early copy of the play in existence and it is in College Library at Eton.

W. D. Cooper, Shakespeare Society's edition of *Ralph Roister Doister*.
Maxwell Lyte, *History of Eton College*, 1911.
Cambridge History of English Literature.

CHEKE, SIR JOHN, tutor to Edward VI, scholar and Secretary of State, was born in 1514 and died in 1557, aged forty-three. He was the son of Peter Cheke, one of the esquire-bedels of Cambridge University, and his wife Agnes Dufford, according to Roger Ascham 'a venerable woman'. He was educated at St. John's College, Cambridge, where he acquired a high reputation for his knowledge of the classical languages, especially Greek. While he was at St. John's he absorbed the doctrines of the Reformation and he probably had much influence on the development of William Cecil, later Lord Burghley, who married Cheke's sister. He was generally regarded as the leader of Greek studies, and in 1540 he became the first Regius Professor of Greek. He became embroiled in a dispute with Stephen Gardiner over the pronunciation of Greek and he was compelled to practise the view held by Gardiner: his own pronunciation was much like that usually adopted in modern England up to very recent times. In 1544 he became tutor to Prince Edward and devoted himself to educating that intelligent boy in the reading of the classical authors, and Cheke seems to have been one of the very few people of whom Edward VI was really fond. He also taught the Princess Elizabeth. About the same time Cheke was made a canon of what is now Christ Church, Oxford; when Henry VIII turned the college into a cathedral, Cheke was given a pension as compensation for the loss of his canonry.

With the accession of Edward VI Cheke's fortunes rose: the new King loaded him with gifts of land, including one grant in Suffolk which Strype described as 'no question a good pennyworth'. He was made Provost of King's in 1548 and was knighted in 1552. During Edward's reign Cheke was an ardent supporter of the Reformation and had a hand in some of the religious changes which marked that period. On Edward's death Cheke accepted Lady Jane Grey as Queen and acted as an additional Secretary of State. With the accession of Mary he went into exile in Italy and Germany, but Philip II had him kidnapped and brought back to England, probably because Cheke was the chief propagandist among the Marian exiles. Faced with the fear of being burned for heresy, Cheke recanted publicly and ignominiously, which he so much regretted that he fell ill and died on September 13th, 1557. He was one of the most learned men of his time and the author of innumerable books. His life was written by Strype in 1705.

C. H. Garrett, *The Marian Exiles*, 1938.
W. G. Zeeveld, *Foundations of Tudor Policy*, esp. pp. 244–5, 1948.

ELIZABETH I, Queen of England and Ireland (1558–1603), daughter of Henry VIII and Anne Boleyn, was born at Greenwich on September 7th, 1533, and died at Richmond on March 24th, 1603, in her seventieth year. None of her predecessors had ever reached such an age. On May 19th, 1536, when she was three years old, her mother was executed and she and her sister Mary were declared illegitimate, when Henry VIII married Jane Seymour. Henry married three times more: his last wife, Catherine Parr, proved herself an excellent step-mother to Elizabeth, taking much interest in her education and in that of Edward, Prince of Wales. Both children were above the average intelligence and were good friends. Elizabeth had some instruction from Edward's tutor, Cheke, more from the young William Grindal, who died in 1548, but the mainspring of inspiration in her education was undoubtedly Roger Ascham, who had the highest opinion of her abilities. Like all the Tudors Elizabeth was fond of music and of dancing ('high and disposedly' in later years with Leicester), and she was also very proficient in Greek, Latin, French and Italian, and later she also learned Spanish. She knew, thanks to Ascham, something also about the writings of the early Church fathers.

In 1547, soon after Edward VI had come to the throne, Protector Somerset's brother, Thomas Seymour, the Lord Admiral, a worthless and self-seeking adventurer, offered marriage to Elizabeth. She prudently declined on the grounds that she was too young. Seymour at once married Catherine Parr, with whom Elizabeth was living. Seymour took advantage of this to carry on a vulgar form of romping with Elizabeth, which seriously offended Catherine. But she died within a year: at once Seymour renewed his plan to marry Elizabeth. As a result he lost his head for high treason and Elizabeth was in dire danger, but she skilfully extricated herself. Her cold comment, when she heard of the execution, was, 'this day died a man with much wit and very little judgment.'

Elizabeth had, of course, no part in Northumberland's plot to exclude Catholic Mary and herself from the throne, so that when Mary rode triumphantly into London as Queen, Elizabeth was at her side. But Mary knew her to be at heart a Protestant and Elizabeth's position throughout the reign was uneasy and sometimes perilous. She refused to have anything to do with Wyatt's rebellion, but when that failed she was put in the Tower. When she arrived there, she sat down in the pouring rain and burst into tears, no doubt fearing that her fate was sealed. Wyatt, however, before his execution, publicly cleared Elizabeth of any hand in the plot and her examinations in front of the Council produced no evidence to justify her being put to death. She was left in the Tower for two months and released in April, 1555. For the next two years she lived quietly, biding her time, sometimes at Court, always popular with the English people. On November 17th, 1558, Mary died and the long reign of Elizabeth I began.

The new Queen was 25 years old. She had need of the highest form of statesmanship. England was at war with France and Calais was lost. Her only ally was Spain and little trust could be placed in Philip II. Trouble was threatening on the Scottish border. The exchequer was bankrupt, heavy debts were owing to the Antwerp bankers, the currency was debased and inflation was hitting all classes. The nation was split by religious differences: there was no Archbishop of Canterbury: nine bishoprics were vacant: the Marian persecutions had sickened the people of Roman Catholicism, yet the heir to the English throne was Mary Stuart, a Roman Catholic and more French than Scotch. The navy had decayed and there was no efficient army. Such was the new Queen's inheritance. Her first act was to appoint Sir William Cecil as her principal secretary of state and she thereby created the longest and perhaps the most successful partnership in government in English history. In the last analysis, however, most decisions of policy were the Queen's.

The first thing was to make peace with France, which was done at Câteau Cambrésis, in March, 1559. The next most urgent problem was that of religion.

Elizabeth was almost devoid of genuine religious feeling, although she had the conventional reliance upon God which everybody professed. She had been a Henrician Catholic under Henry VIII, a Protestant under Edward VI and a conforming Roman Catholic under Mary. Her own feelings were conservative, but she recognized that practically all her subjects, Catholic as well as Protestant, wanted a national and independent Church, a wish which suited her own strong nationalism. She therefore hoped to achieve a conservative settlement based on the first Prayer Book of Edward VI (1549). This did not suit the Anglican divines who had been exiled during Mary's reign and who were now returning home with every intention of building a fully Protestant Church. In the end the House of Commons compelled Elizabeth to go further to the left than she cared for, so that the settlement was based on the second Prayer Book of Edward VI (1552) with a compromise in the words of administration in the Communion service to get over the problem of Transubstantiation. Elizabeth had succeeded in making a settlement without 'opening windows into men's souls', which for the time being maintained the unity of the country. In 1559 were passed the Acts of Supremacy and Uniformity, with the substitution of the word

Governor in place of the Henrician word *Head* of the Church. Matthew Parker was appointed Archbishop of Canterbury.

In foreign affairs Elizabeth, who was always her own foreign minister in the final decisions, had to watch three countries— France, Spain and Scotland. In 1558 Spain was her ally and Philip II offered her marriage. She declined: she was not going to repeat the mistake of Mary. She saw also that Philip could not afford to break with England while he was at war with France. The problem of France was closely knit with that of Scotland. The *de jure* queen of Scotland was Mary Stuart, but she was married to Francis of Valois, heir to the French throne. She was also heir to the English throne, she was already quartering the arms of England with those of Scotland and France, while her own kingdom of Scotland was being governed by the Regent, Marie de Guise, in the interests of France, and her Guise brothers in France were Mary's uncles. In 1559 Philip II of Spain married Elizabeth of Valois. At the same moment the King of France, Henri II, died and Mary became Queen of France as husband of Francis II.

The situation for Elizabeth was complex. The key lay in Scotland. There the Regent's French policy was most unpopular and Protestantism was spreading under the leadership of John Knox. The protestant Lords of the Congregation were soon at war with the Regent. Clearly Elizabeth had to support the Lords. In 1560 she sent a fleet to stop French reinforcements reaching Scotland and she sent troops to expel the French from Leith. By the Treaty of Edinburgh (1560) she cleared Scotland of the French and left the Protestant Lords in command and in alliance with England.

Thus by 1560 Elizabeth had preserved friendship with Spain, isolated France and bolted the back door from Scotland into England.

To the average Englishman the burning question was that of Elizabeth's marriage. Of course, she must marry, in order to ensure the Protestant succession. But she must not marry a foreigner, as Mary had done so disastrously. Whom could she marry at home? To marry a foreigner was to alienate her people: to marry an Englishman was to stir up civil war. As soon as she came to the throne foreign princes were swarming round her for her hand—the King of Spain, the heir to the Swedish throne, two sons of the Hapsburg Emperor, the Scottish Earl of Arran. Elizabeth would have none of them. Later in her reign, when she wanted to gain time, she played with the idea of marrying the French King, Charles IX, then two of his brothers. In the end she died unmarried. We shall never know whether she wanted to be married, or whether the idea of marriage physically revolted her: whether she was capable or incapable of bearing children. The odds are heavily that she wanted to marry Robert Dudley (*q.v.* for their relations), and was perfectly capable of having children, but she recognized that politically the marriage was impossible, and Robert was already married to Amy Robsart. Not to be married left her with a trump card for any trick: to use the card was to throw it away for ever. With marvellous dexterity she kept her wooers dangling at the end of a string, with equal dexterity she left the frequent petitions of her Parliaments to marry 'answered answerless'. And when Peter Wentworth in 1576 took her openly to task, she shut him up in the Tower. How important this question of marriage was may be seen from the panic in the country when in 1562 Elizabeth all but died of small pox.*

Francis II died in 1559 and in 1561 Mary Stuart returned to Scotland. During the next seven years, while Elizabeth was showering honours on Robert Dudley, visiting Cambridge (1564), where she made Latin speeches, visiting Oxford (1566), where she heard Edmund Campion disputing in Latin, while she was refusing Parliament's petitions to marry and to name her successor, and while she was behaving in the most miserly way to her Lord Deputy in Ireland, Sir Henry Sidney, Mary was ruining herself in Scotland. After her

---

* She was saved by a young German doctor who happened to be present when all the other doctors had given her up for lost. He asked for a red blanket in which he wrapped the Queen and set her in front of the fire. In a short while the spots had come out and the Queen's life was saved. There is a tradition that the colour red is the only one which does not aggravate small pox, and beds with red curtains are often called "small pox beds". Such a bed exists at Charlecote Park, Warwickshire.

defeat at Carberry Hill (1567) she was shut up in Lochleven
Castle, but she escaped in 1568 and fled to England to throw
herself on Elizabeth's mercy. Elizabeth was in a difficult
position: there had never been any love lost between them:
Elizabeth was committed to Protestantism in Scotland: Mary
had been driven out by those Protestants: but Mary was a
queen and Elizabeth held strong views on the sanctity of
monarchs. On the other hand, Mary was a Catholic and the
heir to the English throne. Nobody doubted that she had
just been a party to the murder of her husband and had then
married the actual murderer, Bothwell. Policy dictated to
Elizabeth that she should support the Protestant Lords; her
personal feelings urged her to protect the Scottish Queen. She
solved, or rather postponed solving, the problem by setting up
a commission of enquiry into the facts of the case. After the
Casket Letters had been produced she allowed no decision
to be come to, the case was said to be non-proven on both sides.
But what was to be done with Mary? To send her back to
Scotland was to send her to her death. To keep her in England
was to incur frightful risks for Elizabeth and the whole realm.
Probably the best course would have been to pack Mary off
overseas, for since the murder of Darnley her stock on the
continent had sunk to zero. But Elizabeth was hardly to know
that, and the risk of leaving the Catholic claimant to the
English throne loose in Europe for Philip or the Pope to use
against England at any moment must have seemed to Elizabeth
and Cecil to be the greatest risk of all. Mary remained in
England, an unwelcome and not even a paying guest.

The dangers of this policy were soon apparent. After
Elizabeth has been on the throne for ten years those who were
discontented with her many compromises became more active.
There were those who had always disliked her religious
settlement, the Catholics and the Puritans: the old families,
such as the Norfolks, resented her government through the
'new men', such as Cecil: the Northern Catholic families
detested her 'interference' with their old independence of the
central government, families such as the Westmorlands and
the Northumberlands. And in foreign affairs relations with

Spain were deteriorating. Hawkins's slave-trading voyages had roused tempers on both sides: the expulsion from Spain of the English ambassador had infuriated Elizabeth: Elizabeth's seizure of the Spanish pay ships when they took refuge in English ports (1568) infuriated Philip. Alva retaliated by taking over all English property in the Netherlands, and Elizabeth retorted in like manner in England. It was in these circumstances that a proposal was made that Mary should marry the Duke of Norfolk. The plan was backed by the Northern Catholic Earls and it had the approval of Spain. Its purpose was to marry Mary to Norfolk, to substitute the Mary-Howard (Norfolk) faction for Cecil and his party, and to restore Catholicism, which would inevitably have led to the deposition of Elizabeth. The situation was extremely dangerous and Cecil was almost in despair. This was one of the crises of the reign, but the Queen knew what was going on and warned Norfolk, who denied any share in the plot. The Northern Earls were thus let down and felt that they must rise at once or never at all. The rebellion was easily put down (1569) and there followed a fearful vengeance—some 600 insignificant rebels were hanged throughout the northern villages, while the leaders for the most part got away with surrendering their properties. Elizabeth was not Henry VIII's daughter for nothing.

One result of the mistiming of the rising was that Pope Pius V was made to look almost ridiculous. He had intended his bull of excommunication to coincide with the Catholic rising in the north, but when he issued the bull in 1570 the rising was over, and when the bull was nailed to the door of the Bishop of London, it passed almost unnoticed. Of course, ultimately it had much importance, for it compelled English men and women to decide whether they preferred to be good Catholics or good English subjects of the queen.

Norfolk had been lucky in 1569 in only being put in the Tower, but he was a weak man who learned nothing. In 1571 he allowed himself for the second time to be involved in a plot by which he was to marry Mary, a rebellion in England was to be aided by a foreign invasion, Elizabeth was to be deposed and Mary made Queen. This was the Ridolfi plot of 1571, as a result of which Parliament demanded the execution of Mary, but Elizabeth refused and refused also her assent to a bill depriving Mary of all interest in the English throne. For a moment she did agree to sending Mary back to Scotland to be put to death, provided that guarantees were given that she would not be kept there alive, and on no account was Elizabeth's name to be mentioned in the negotiations. But Elizabeth soon changed her mind and Mary remained in England. But Spain was now clearly hostile and the end of the third civil war in France left that country free to attack England. Elizabeth therefore resorted to the old time-saving (or time-wasting) device of marriage negotiations. The *Politiques*, the moderate Catholics, were now in power in France and were ready for an alliance with England as a counter-weight to Spain. It was proposed that Henry, Duke of Anjou, brother of Charles IX and heir to the French throne, should marry Elizabeth. Nothing came of this, as Anjou on religious grounds refused to marry a Protestant. Then came the Massacre of St. Bartholomew (1572), which looked as if it must put paid to any Anglo-French alliance. Elizabeth kept the French ambassador waiting for three days for an audience. When it took place, she received the ambassador in dead silence with her councillors and ladies standing round. In the end she accepted his explanation, for in truth she could not afford to break with France. Within a few months she and Catherine de Medici were negotiating a marriage between herself and Charles IX's younger brother, Francis, Duke of Alençon (later Anjou). He was more than twenty years younger than Elizabeth, a dwarf, ugly and pock-marked. From 1572 to 1584 she kept her 'frog' on tenterhooks, until he died in that year unmarried. This proposed marriage was very unpopular and was openly attacked by Sidney, and indirectly by Spenser (in *Mother Hubbard's Tale*).

Elizabeth's marriage negotiations with the Duke of Anjou were closely tied up with the revolt of the Netherlands against Spain which began in 1568. This produced inside the Spanish dominions a Protestant party corresponding with the Huguenot party inside France. From 1561 to 1563 Elizabeth had given some help to these Huguenots: she got little advantage out of it and she spent more money than she could afford. When the Netherlands revolted, there were statesmen in England, like Walsingham, who wanted Elizabeth to go all out in support of these continental Protestants. She refused, for she knew that a religious war could only split England from top to bottom. On the other hand, she recognized the opportunities which these revolts gave her to weaken her enemies abroad. She was therefore ready to give secret and limited aid, which later through force of circumstances became open and considerably greater, but she did this, not on religious grounds, but simply on grounds of policy. In the 1570s she helped the Dutch, because she did not want a Dutch Protestant victory as a result of French help—that would have subordinated the Netherlands to France and brought France much too near the English Channel ports. So it was that, when the Dutch turned to the Duke of Anjou for help against Spain, Elizabeth at once began her prolonged marriage negotiations with Anjou. The Queen was criticized for never giving enough help to bring victory to the Huguenots or the Dutch, but she never wanted them to be victorious. She was concerned much more to stoke the fires and keep the rebels fighting in order to weaken her enemies abroad. It was not the salvation of French or Dutch Protestantism which Elizabeth had in view, it was the salvation of England.

In 1584 things came to a head. Anjou died, which ended the marriage plans: William the Silent was murdered, which left Elizabeth the unwilling leader of Protestantism in Europe. Spain had apparently strengthened herself by the conquest of Portugal and Parma had all but finished off the Dutch revolt. Once Philip was free of the Dutch he would turn his attention to the invasion of England, with a convenient jumping-off ground in the Netherlands. Reluctantly Elizabeth realized there was nothing for it but to send immediate help to the Dutch—hence Leicester's expedition of 1585 and Drake's voyage to the Spanish Main. Leicester proved a complete failure, Drake was brilliantly successful. But at home difficulties were piling up. The Puritans were voicing their discontent, the Jesuit 'invasion' shewed all too clearly the potential danger from the Catholics. Persecution of the Catholics increased and the roll of Catholic martyrs mounted. Always Elizabeth tried to mitigate the severities and to separate religion from politics. But on the home front the root of the danger lay in Mary, Queen of Scots. She was the centre of every Catholic plot. The revelations made by Throckmorton (*q.v.*) in 1583 drove Cecil and Walsingham to entrap Mary beyond escape. The Babington plot of 1586 sealed her fate: she was tried, condemned and sentenced to death. The problem was to bring Elizabeth to sign the death warrant. For months she hesitated, then at last she gave way and on February 1st, 1587, she signed it. Mary was executed at Fotheringay on February 8th. Elizabeth flew into a passion: she went into mourning, she railed at her ministers, she sent her Secretary Davison to the Tower, and she protested that the warrant had been sent off without her knowledge or consent. But Davison's salary was paid all the time he was in the Tower. If this was play-acting, as most of it was, it was wasted effort, for scarcely a tremor appeared on any political seismograph in Europe. Elizabeth's hesitations had arisen from a struggle between her personal feelings and her political instincts. As usual, her political instincts triumphed, but as usual she did her best to get rid of the responsibility.

The execution of Mary Stuart immensely strengthened England, for it removed the only conceivable alternative to Elizabeth in the eyes of the English Catholics. Elizabeth's main objective was now achieved, England was united and able to meet the invader. When in 1588 the Spanish Armada came, the government had no need to worry about Catholic Quislings. The ships built by Hawkins, Drake's offensive expeditions before the battle and his seamanship during the battle, the co-operation and commonsense of Howard of Effingham, the stage-management by Leicester at the camp at Tilbury, and not least the heroic leadership of the Queen herself, saw England through the sixteenth-century Battle of Britain. Elizabeth's speech to her troops at Tilbury remains one of the greatest in the English language.

'My loving people, we have been persuaded by some that are careful of our safety to take heed how we commit ourselves to armed multitudes for fear of treachery. Let tyrants fear. I have always so behaved myself that, under God, I have placed my chiefest strength and safeguard in the loyal hearts and goodwill of my subjects. And therefore I am come amongst you, as you see at this time, not for my recreation and disport, but being resolved, in the heat and midst of the battle, to live and die amongst you all; to lay down for my God and for my kingdom and for my people my honour and my blood, even in the dust. I know I have the body of a weak and feeble woman, but I have the heart and stomach of a king, and of a king of England too; and think foul scorn that Parma or Spain, or any prince of Europe, should dare invade the borders of my realm. . . .'

For thirty years Elizabeth had striven to unify the country against foreign invasion. That invasion had come and been defeated. The Queen was at the height of her fame and popularity. But she had fifteen years more to live and to govern the country. These were to prove years of anti-climax. She was to remain, but her old friends and advisers were slipping away. By 1596 they had all gone—Leicester, Knollys, Hatton, Walsingham, Hawkins, Drake, Frobisher, and two years later Burghley died. The Queen was virtually alone, only Burghley's son, Robert Cecil, and Whitgift were there to help her. The Elizabethan system was beginning to creak as early as 1588, when the Martin Marprelate attacks were launched against episcopacy in general and Archbishop Whitgift in particular, Elizabeth's 'little black husband'. The religious feuds were to go on for the rest of the reign and to them were added quarrels between the Crown and Parliament in which Peter Wentworth appeared at last to be attacking, if not monarchy itself, at least the monarch, for which Elizabeth sent him to the Tower. The session of 1597–8 was rowdy enough and Elizabeth vetoed twelve bills of small importance: that of 1601 was even more violent—'more fit for a grammar school than a court of Parliament', said Robert

Cecil, while the Commons 'hawked, spat and hemmed'. The Queen also fell foul of the Commons over monopolies in 1597 and again in 1601, when she was compelled to give way, which she did with all her old skill and graciousness. War continued in the Netherlands, in France where she had to support Henry of Navarre, in Ireland where a long and expensive struggle showed few signs of ending. As a result the national finances became dangerously involved and Elizabeth had to call Parliament and ask for supplies, a course particularly odious to her. At court new and young men, impatiently waiting for new policies, for promotion and for opportunities for fame and fortune, spent their time quarrelling and building factions. In her old age the Queen tried desperately to recreate the atmosphere and relationships of her youth and she turned to Robert Devereux, Earl of Essex, on whom she lavished honours, offices and affection, only to find out—for her judgment of men never failed her—that he was worthy of none of them. In him was centred all the discontent of the young courtiers. His rebellion in 1601 was a direct challenge to the whole Tudor system and to the Queen herself. She met it with invincible courage—she was barely restrained at the age of 68 from going out into the streets to see whether any rebel dared fire a shot at her. The rebellion failed and Essex was executed in February, 1601. Once again she was forced to decide between her personal feelings and her public duty, and once again duty won, but it must have been a terrible blow to send to the block the stepson of her once beloved Robert Dudley, Earl of Leicester.

For another year Elizabeth remained in good health and good spirits, but by 1602 she was beginning to lose vitality and interest, she was convinced that she was going to die, she began to refuse food, to decline to take any medicine and even to go to bed. Finally she lost her power of speech, but not her wits and understanding. She died early in the morning of March 24th, 1603.

Elizabeth had reigned for forty-five years, the longest reign since Edward III's and until George III's. It was one of the great creative periods in English history—in the realm of literature, of music, of architecture, in the art of limning, if not in that of painting, in exploration and the expansion of trade. Men saw Elizabeth as the inspiration of their work and the idol of their worship. She became Gloriana, the 'Faerie Queen', and we still call those forty-five years the 'Age of Elizabeth', the 'spacious days of good Queen Bess'. And yet the writers got nothing out of her for all their flattering patriotism: the sailors could only expect her support, if their voyages caused no diplomatic trouble and—more important— produced a handsome profit. Nor would she risk money on 'plantations' overseas: Elizabeth was no expansionist. She was a conservative through and through, an admirable conservative builder in her early years, a dangerous and obscurantist conservative in her later years, with the result that she left to her successor, James I, a number of unsolved problems—the relations of Crown and Parliament, the desperate state of the national finances, the religious problem of the Puritans.

How, then, did this extraordinary woman succeed in identifying herself with the age in which she lived—for it was not only the English who recognized her qualities? Pope Sixtus V said of her, 'she is certainly a great Queen and were she only a Catholic she would be our dearly beloved. Just look how well she governs! She is only a woman, only mistress of half an island, and yet she makes herself feared by Spain, by France, by the Empire, by all.' The answer seems to be by skill and by character. The cult of monarchy reached its height in England in Elizabeth's reign. (By the end of the reign this idea was already a trifle *démodé*.) A semi-religious, almost a semi-deified idol was exactly what the English people needed, looked for and enthusiastically accepted as a rallying point for their national life and their individual patriotism. Elizabeth recognized this opportunity and exploited it to the full. It suited exactly her own sense of nationalism, her innate vanity and that vein of vulgarity which was never far below the surface of her character. At the same time, it called forth the best that was in her—her unfailing sense of duty and service, her usually invincible courage, her uncanny judge-

Plate 17

Elizabeth I

Plate 18

William Cecil, Lord Burghley, Secretary of State

ment of men, and her astonishing ability to remain regal and yet never to lose the common touch. Her love of dresses and jewels delighted her subjects, her enjoyment in showing herself to her subjects was only equalled by their enthusiasm at her progresses: her wit, her repartee, her eloquence and her graciousness were only heightened by her frequent loss of temper, her violent oaths, her beer-drinking and her conforming to the conventional habit of spitting. People felt that she was the finest example of one of themselves. In an age which was on the whole savage and cruel, she could be and was ruthless and savage—as after the rebellion of the Northern Earls. She could be furious, abusive and formidable, yet (as Sir John Harington said) her smile 'was pure sunshine'. She could be disloyal to her ministers, but she never lost their loyalty: she could speak the most bitter words, yet she could write the most enchanting and heart-warming letters. She could hesitate and vacillate, change her mind and be criminally cautious, yet she could take the most dangerous risks against the wishes of her ministers and prove herself right. She had a wonderful flair for politics and a most discerning eye in foreign affairs—more discerning than those of her ministers. Nothing is more remarkable about her than the immense impression she made, even in her old age, on the foreign ambassadors who visited her. They might remark on her black teeth and her low-cut dresses, they might feel that she was 'strangely attired', they might note her loss of temper and her restlessness, but they all recognized her extraordinary grasp and understanding of the European political stage. Much of her financial tight-fistedness was due to her recognition that taxation caused more discontent than anything else: much of her shirking of responsibility is to be explained by her recognition that on her depended the unity and safety of the country: better that ministers and bishops should bear undeserved unpopularity than that the *mystique* of royalty should be undermined. The secret of her astounding success she herself revealed in her last speech: 'though God hath raised me high, yet this I count the glory of my reign, that I have reigned with your loves.' (*Plate 17*)

o—(2)

Neale, *Elizabeth* and *Essays in Elizabethan History*, 1958.
Conyers Read, *The Tudors*.
C. Morris, *The Tudors*.
J. Hurstfield, *Elizabeth I and the Unity of England*.
C. Creighton, *Queen Elizabeth*.
T.S.I.H., vol. 2, pp. 65–108.
M. Irwin, *Young Bess* and *Elizabeth, Captive Princess*. (H.N.)
 Companion Book Club, 1953.

CECIL, WILLIAM, LORD BURGHLEY, statesman, was
born in 1520 and died in 1598 at the age of 78. He was the
son of Richard Cecil and his wife, Jane Heckington of Lincolnshire. His grandfather, David Cecil, had thrown in his lot
on the side of Henry VII at Bosworth Field and thus laid the
foundations of the family fortunes. He became a member of
Henry's Yeomen of the Guard and Richard held several minor
appointments at Court.

William was educated at the grammar school in Grantham
and then at the grammar school at Stamford. In 1533 he went
to St. John's College, Cambridge, where he proved himself
a first-class classical scholar and became friends with such men
as Cheke and Ascham. In 1542 he fell in love with and married
Cheke's sister, Mary, but his father looked askance at the
marriage, for Mary's mother was only an innkeeper in
Cambridge. There was one son of the marriage, Thomas, who
never got on well with his father, and it cannot be said that
William ever showed him much affection or consideration.
Later, he became the first Earl of Exeter. It may have been
because of this indiscreet marriage that William left Cambridge
without a degree.

Mary died in 1544. The next year William married a very
remarkable woman, Mildred Cooke, a noted Greek scholar
and Puritan, who was to influence William's life considerably
in the future. Mildred's sister, Anne, married Nicholas Bacon,
later Elizabeth's Lord Keeper and father of Sir Francis Bacon.

Richard Cecil's position at Court ensured William's being
noticed by Henry VIII, but the truth is that only a little is
known about William's life before he became Secretary of

State to Elizabeth I, when she came to the throne. Probably thanks to Cheke and Ascham, who were tutors to the King, Edward VI, and to the princess Elizabeth respectively, William entered the secretariat of Protector Somerset in 1547. He went with Somerset to Pinkie Cleugh: he was made Master of Requests during the winter of 1547, and in the next year he became Somerset's private secretary. About this time he entered Parliament for Stamford. He sat on a commission to enquire into Anabaptism and on another to review the books printed in England dealing with religious matters. On the fall of Somerset (1549) Cecil spent two months in the Tower (1550), but on his release he was appointed principal secretary of state by Northumberland. Cecil was now beginning to appear as one of those professional politicians who find their way into every successive government. It was in this year that princess Elizabeth appointed him her Surveyor (or estate agent), but the duties were carried out by a deputy and Cecil seems to have had little direct contact with Elizabeth. In 1551 he was knighted, in 1552 he was made chancellor of the Order of the Garter, a post which he had to surrender when Mary I came to the throne. When Northumberland hatched his plot for putting Lady Jane Grey on the throne, Cecil played a most ambiguous part. When he was compelled to sign the 'device', he protested that he signed only 'as a witness': during the nine days when Lady Jane was queen, Cecil seems to have done as much as he could secretly to thwart Northumberland's plans. So adroit was his conduct that Mary I gave him a general pardon and renewed his commission as Justice of the Peace for Lincolnshire. In the course of her short reign Cecil was twice employed on diplomatic embassies, once to fetch Cardinal Pole to England and once to share in the attempts to make peace between the Emperor and the King of France. He seems also to have played a fairly important part in the 1555 parliament, especially as a drafter of bills and over a bill to check enclosures.

For at least a fortnight before Mary died Elizabeth was making arrangements for her succession. She had already chosen her Principal Secretary of State, so that at the first meeting of her Privy Council she appointed William Cecil to that position with the well-known tribute, 'I give you this charge that you shall be of my Privy Council and content to take pains for me and my realm. This judgment I have of you, that you will not be corrupted by any manner of gift and that you will be faithful to the state; and that without respect of my private gain will you give me that counsel which you think best, and if you shall know anything necessary to be declared to me of secrecy, you shall show it to myself only. And assure yourself I will not fail to keep taciturnity therein and therefore herewith I charge you.' Thus began forty years of partnership between queen and minister, the longest in English history. Often Cecil criticized his mistress, often Elizabeth railed against her minister; after Mary, Queen of Scots, was executed her fury was so great that Cecil dared not go to Court. But through all the stresses and strains the trust was never betrayed and the support was never withdrawn, and when at last, worn out and dying, Cecil was visited by the Queen as he lay in bed, she fed him 'with her own princely hand'. A short while before she had written to him that he was 'to her in all things and shall be Alpha and Omega.'

During these forty years, from 1558 to 1598, Cecil held three chief offices of state. From 1558 to 1572 he was Principal Secretary of State. He had to handle all the routine business of the Council and its relations with the Queen: he was responsible for the administration of foreign policy, he had to be well informed about all matters of defence, of public finance, of public relations between the Crown and the country, of the Church of England and its enemies. This involved him with jealous colleagues, jealous courtiers and a very temperamental mistress (Conyers Read, i, p. 121). From 1561 until 1598 he was Master of the Court of Wards, a post of immense importance, since wardship was, or should have been, one of the chief sources of revenue to the Crown, and also the most lucrative post for its holder. It was through the profits which he derived as Master that Cecil built up the huge income which enabled him to live in style and to build his great houses of Theobalds and Burghley. (For a full discussion of Cecil's emoluments from this office, see Hurstfield, *The Queen's Wards*.) From 1572 to 1598 Cecil was Lord Treasurer, the most important of all the offices. As Lord Treasurer he administered the royal finances and he also presided over the Court of Exchequer. In this capacity, as well as in that of Master of the Court of Wards, Cecil filled an important place in the English judiciary.

A biography of Cecil, therefore, is really a history of England from 1558 to 1598, a period to which Froude devoted three solid volumes. Not much more can be attempted here than to indicate Cecil's political and religious views and policies and to try to show what sort of a man he was. And here one is met at once with a further difficulty. If there is an appalling mass of letters and memoranda available to the political biographer—over one hundred folio volumes at the British Museum, over two hundred folio volumes at Hatfield House, and an incalculable number of state papers at the Public Record Office—only a very small number of Cecil's outgoing letters survive, and of his purely personal and family correspondence only one doubtful letter to his wife.

In 1571 William Cecil became Lord Burghley, the only one of Elizabeth's ministers to receive a peerage. The next year he was made a Knight of the Garter. In 1558 he suffered a grievous loss in the death of his wife. He had ten more years of life ahead of him, during which he suffered much ill health, especially from gout, and was forced to ride round his estates on a mule (see plate 18): the last five years he grew increasingly feeble and had to be carried wherever he went; he was also extremely deaf. But his mental powers never decayed and in his seventy-eighth year he still sat with the Privy Council. His son, Robert, was made Principal Secretary in 1596 and for the last two years of Burghley's life Robert took over virtually all the routine business of government. Burghley died on August 4th, 1598.

'Perhaps the greatest of his achievements was that he managed by great tact, great wisdom and great integrity of purpose, along with a nice sense of what was practicable and possible, to advance from strength to strength' (C. Read, i, 122), so that he became indisputably the Queen's first minister.

Regarded as a 'new man', he was hated by the older families, but not even Leicester's attempts to drive him from office succeeded. One reason for the Queen's unfailing support was that her views on policy were very close to Burghley's views. Burghley was essentially a conservative, by instinct as well as by reason opposed to rash schemes and extreme methods. He saw as clearly as did Elizabeth that the two threats to the safety of England were in fact one and the same threat, that the dangers from foreign invasion were inextricably bound up with the religious dangers at home.

In foreign policy both saw that for England, geographically placed as she was in relation to France and Spain, both Catholic countries, war was to be avoided as long as possible. Both realized that the nation's resources were not equal to a prolonged conflict. Both believed that national unity was essential, if war came, and that to go to war on religious grounds would not produce national unity. Both understood that the survival of England was bound up with the survival of the Netherlands, and therefore both reluctantly accepted war with Spain in the Netherlands, when it became clear that diplomacy would no longer serve.

In religion Burghley was never publicly a Puritan—he quarrelled more often with the Puritans than he agreed with them, but nothing shows more clearly his common sense than his warning to Whitgift in 1584 not to attack the Puritans in a manner 'as I think the Inquisitors of Spain use not . . . to trap their prey'. He also made the Puritan Travers tutor to his children and protected his relation, Robert Owen, a Brownist.

As a financier Burghley was always a conservative. Indeed, it has been charged against him that, inheriting an old-fashioned and inefficient system of national finances, he did nothing to reform and modernize it, being content merely to improve where he could. Certainly as Master of the Court of Wards he accepted the conventions of his times by which salaries of state officials were supplemented by gifts and profits incidental to the sale of wardships, and by his efficiency he greatly furthered his own interests, even at the expense of the Queen.

But at the same time he was developing and putting into practice an economic policy of first rate importance. By 1561 with the help of Gresham, he had restored a sound currency with a new silver coinage, minted at a profit to the Crown. He set about reducing ordinary expenditure and also making the defences of the country independent of foreign sources for gunpowder and naval stores. He developed mining for copper and tin and the growing of hemp: he paid bounties on shipbuilding, repaired harbours and made the people eat fish, not only in Lent, but on two days a week all the year round, in order to expand the fisheries which in turn expanded the number of mariners. He looked on piracy as 'detestable', pinning his faith rather on the finding of new markets and on encouraging foreigners to migrate into England. His whole policy was codified in 1563 in the Statute of Labourers. Mediaeval usury laws were abolished and interest was legalized up to ten per cent. Indeed, Cecil was proving himself to be one of the earliest of the long line of Conservative reformers. (K. Feiling, *A History of England*, pp. 391, *sqq.*)

In one department of government Burghley was invaluable to the Queen—her public relations officer. He was an indefatigable writer of pamphlets and he would use foreign channels for promoting English policy. His literary style was unattractive, but his great merit was that 'he never sought to display his own cleverness . . . or to advance his own interests. He sought only to promote the cause and serve his mistress' (C. Read in *Elizabethan Government and Society*, 1961).

William Cecil, Lord Burghley, must be accounted one of the greatest of English statesmen. For forty years (together with Elizabeth, who always had the final say) he guided the country through a maze of dangers at home and abroad. But there was nothing of the saint or of the hero in him, little of the genius. Camden wrote of him that 'of all men of genius, he was the most of a drudge; of all men of business the most of a genius'. In religion he was an upright, God-fearing man, who held faithfully to the Christian faith, but who cared little about its particular form. He could never have survived the religious difficulties of his earlier years, if he had not been unheroically pliant in the days of Northumberland and Mary I—and it was as well for England that he did survive. He could never have maintained himself in office under Elizabeth I, if he had not been as wary and cunning as a fox. He could never have saved England from sedition, privy conspiracy and rebellion, if he had not been ready to use all the weapons available in his time, which included the use of torture—but he never condoned political assassination—and to be resolute to the verge of ruthlessness, as he was over Mary, Queen of Scots. By super-human industry, by devotion to his Queen and country and by subordinating himself to the service of both, he, as much as the younger Pitt, became the pilot that weathered the storm.

In his private life Burghley was a devoted son, a faithful husband and a loving father, except to the unsatisfactory Thomas. Although he lived in sumptuous style, he himself ate very little and seldom drank wine. His chief recreations were gardening and reading in Latin, French and Italian books (seldom in English), or riding upon his little mule (see plate 18). He was blessed with an unfailing memory, which enabled him to dispatch business quickly. To his friends he was by nature kind, courteous and affable, and very loyal, as Robert Browne, the Separatist, discovered. His whole life bears witness to the advice he gave his son, Robert: 'serve God by serving of the Queen, for all other service indeed is bondage to the devil'.   (*Plate 18*)

C. Read, *Mr. Secretary Cecil and Queen Elizabeth*, 1955. *Lord Burghley and Queen Elizabeth*, 1960. These two books are the only full scale biographies, but they are not of the same quality as his life of Walsingham.

J. Hurstfield, *The Queen's Wards*, 1958.

J. Hurstfield, *History Today*, December, 1956.

C. Read, William Cecil and Elizabethan Public Relations, in *Elizabethan Government and Society*, 1961.

WALSINGHAM, SIR FRANCIS, Secretary of State, was born in 1532 (not 1530 *D.N.B.*) and died in 1590, aged 58. He was the only son among the six children of William Walsingham of Footscray in Kent and of his wife Joyce,

daughter of Sir Edmund Denny of Cheshunt in Hertfordshire.
His father died in 1533, and Joyce married Sir John Carey,
uncle of the first Lord Hunsdon. Francis went up to King's,
Cambridge, in 1548 and came down probably in 1550 without
having taken a degree. The Denny family had strong Protestant
leanings and King's was one of the most Protestant colleges in
Cambridge, under its Provost Cheke: Francis must have been
influenced by his surroundings, the more so since his tutor,
Gardiner, was also a strong Protestant, and in 1549 Martin
Bucer arrived in Cambridge and became Professor of Hebrew,
being himself one of the greatest of the Protestant scholars.
Francis was to be all his life an ardent and uncompromising
Protestant.

Between 1550 and 1552 Walsingham was abroad learning the
French and Italian languages. He was by nature a facile
linguist and this gift was to be the foundation of his political
success when he entered the Queen's service in 1568. He was
entered as a member of Gray's Inn in 1552, but the next year
the Catholic Mary Tudor succeeded to the throne and Walsingham left the country, ostensibly on the grounds of religion.
Conyers Read suggests that possibly there were other reasons,
that he might have been involved in the Protestant plots of
Northumberland and Wyatt (*Sir Francis Walsingham*, i, 22).
During this exile he was at Padua University where he was
appointed Consularius of the English Nation in the Faculty
of Civil Law, a post he held from 1555 to the spring of 1556.
During his sojourn in Italy he not only perfected his Italian,
but also learned much law and studied the political systems
of continental countries. Most important, perhaps, for the
future, he became expert in the new Machiavellian statecraft,
which he saw in practice both in Venice and among the
Jesuits. Later he was to apply the methods of the Jesuits
in Roman Catholicism to English Protestantism. It is possible
that before he returned home he visited Switzerland and had
contacts with English Protestant exiles in Basle, Strasburg and
Frankfurt. He was certainly back in England in 1560, by
which time Elizabeth I was on the throne.

In 1562 (not 1560 *D.N.B.*) he was returned for the first

time as M.P. for both Banbury and Lyme Regis: he chose to represent Lyme Regis. In that year he married a widow, Anne Carleill, who died in 1564 and gave him no children. Two years later he married the widow of Sir Richard Worsley of the Isle of Wight, by whom he had one daughter, who married Sir Philip Sidney, and one who died early. In 1568 he entered the service of the Queen, and he remained her most loyal servant for the next twenty-two years, up to the day of his death.

No doubt it was Walsingham's knowledge of foreign languages and the contacts which he maintained with friends abroad which first commended him to Burghley. In 1568 Walsingham supplied Cecil with a list of all persons arriving in Italy who might be dangerous to the Queen and her government. In 1569 he was employed by the government's secret service in London and he played a part in unravelling the Ridolfi plot, although at one point he was completely hoodwinked by Ridolfi (for details see under RIDOLFI).

From 1570 Walsingham was employed almost entirely on foreign affairs. In that year he was in France trying to secure toleration for the Huguenots. He was engaged in the matter of Elizabeth's projected marriage with Anjou. And in December of that year he supplanted Norris as ambassador in Paris. In conjunction with Sir Thomas Smith he negotiated the unimportant Treaty of Blois (1572), but all hopes of friendship with France were shattered by the Massacre of St. Bartholomew (August 24th, 1572), which event left a lasting impression on Walsingham and much increased his Protestant fanaticism. In 1573 he left Paris and was made Secretary of State, a position he held until his death in 1590.

His administration of what we should now call the Foreign Office was shared to a large extent with Burghley, but it must be remembered that in foreign affairs the final decisions were Elizabeth's decisions. Broadly speaking, Burghley and the Queen saw eye to eye in foreign affairs, and broadly speaking their policy was to play for time and to avoid committing themselves to one side or the other. This was diametrically opposed to Walsingham's views. He was not, like Burghley, a politician who was ready to trim his sails to suit the weather. Walsingham was an ardent Puritan and a man of inflexible principle. He had made up his mind that the one thing necessary for the safety of the country was the utter defeat of Spain and the removal of Mary, Queen of Scots. He was, therefore, uncompromisingly in favour of an alliance with Huguenot France and active intervention in the revolt of the Netherlands against Spain. James VI and Scotland must be made into friends. He was fully convinced that the struggle in Europe was not one between nation and nation, but between Catholicism and Protestantism. Walsingham was wrong in this belief: Elizabeth and Burghley had a juster understanding of the true state of affairs, that nationalism was a stronger force in Europe than religion. Walsingham was fearlessly outspoken to the Queen in advocating his policy and trying to persuade her that hers was wrong, and Elizabeth was often driven to outbursts of fury against him. But she continued to use him in all her diplomatic business. At first sight this is inexplicable, but probably the reasons are these: first and foremost, she knew that she could trust Walsingham to do his best to achieve her policy, however much he himself was personally opposed to it. She never doubted his abilities or his loyalty. In 1578 he was sent to the Low Countries to pursue a policy which Elizabeth knew well enough was exactly the opposite to what Walsingham approved. Walsingham bitterly resented the vacillations and procrastinations of the Queen, yet he accepted, 'with never so ill a will', a mission to Scotland which might involve him in humiliation (1583). He must have had one moment of pleasure when in 1585 he was able to negotiate with the Dutch commissioner in London the terms on which the Queen was ready to support the Netherlands against Spain. But even then by her vacillation and parsimony Walsingham was 'utterly discouraged'. From first to last Walsingham never had any success with the Queen in advocating his policy and methods.

A second reason for using Walsingham was that he was always able to supply the fullest and most reliable information. His secret service was extraordinarily efficient. On it he spent the whole of his private fortune, so that he died in the utmost poverty. He had at times in his pay fifty-three agents in foreign courts and eighteen other spies. He would get the fullest information from thirteen towns in France, seven in the Low Countries, five in Spain, five in Italy, nine in Germany, three in the United Provinces, three in Turkey. He was both patient and ingenious in ferreting out the plots raised against Elizabeth, as, for example, the Parry and the Babington plots (for details see under PARRY and BABINGTON). Many of his agents were disreputable characters—he employed Christopher Marlowe—and Walsingham himself employed Machiavellian methods, but there is no conclusive evidence that he ever strained the law or justice against his victims. There was no cruelty in Walsingham: he regarded the Catholics as political dangers and as such they must be got out of the way, but he was strongly opposed to making them into martyrs: he preferred to have them detained or deported, and he once had an idea of founding an American colony for them. Only against Mary, Queen of Scots, 'that devilish woman', as he called her, was he determined to go to extremes, for he believed that she was the cause of all the trouble and that as long as she lived Elizabeth and the country were in the direst danger. After her execution he set about organizing the defences of the country against the Spanish invasion, which he clearly foresaw. Burghley told him 'you have fought more with your pen than many here in our English navy with their enemies'.

Ardent Protestant as Walsingham was, he was no fanatic. Camden called him 'a most sharp maintainer of the purer religion', but Walsingham himself understood that unity was essential, if English Protestantism was to survive. 'I would have all reformation done by public authority: it were very dangerous that every private man's zeal should carry sufficient authority of reforming things amiss.' He also held that men's consciences were 'not to be forced, but to be won and seduced by the force of truth, with the aid of time and the use of all good means of instruction and persuasion'. On the other hand, breaches of the law and peace and order he would have visited with the sternest measures.

Walsingham was a man who kept up with his times. He was a great supporter of all overseas adventures and he subscribed to Fenton's voyage in 1582-3: he took Richard Hakluyt into his pay and Hakluyt dedicated the first edition of his *Voyages* to him; he corresponded with Lane, the explorer of Virginia, with Grenville and with Gilbert. He was greatly interested in the literature of his time and he was known to all the leading men of letters. All forms of learning earned his admiration and often his patronage—he founded a Divinity lecture at Oxford and he gave a polyglot bible to King's College, Cambridge. Worldly honours did not much interest him, and Elizabeth was chary of rewarding her public servants —only Cecil was given a peerage, Walsingham's reward was a knighthood (1577). He was also made Chancellor of the Duchy of Lancaster (1587) and Chancellor of the Order of the Garter (1578).

Walsingham died on April 6th, 1590. The news reached Philip II of Spain in a letter from a Spanish agent in England, who wrote 'Secretary Walsingham has just expired, at the which there is much sorrow'. Philip scribbled in the margin 'There, yes! But it is good news here'. That would have satisfied Walsingham as his epitaph. (*Plate 19*)

Conyers Read, *Sir Francis Walsingham*, 3 vols., 1925. It is unlikely that this excellent biography will be superseded.

DUDLEY, ROBERT, EARL OF LEICESTER, was born on June 24th, 1533 (Elizabeth I was born on September 7th, 1533), and died on September 4th, 1588, at the age of 55. He was the fifth son of John Dudley, Earl of Warwick, Duke of Northumberland (executed 1553), and a grandson of Edmund Dudley, Henry VII's finance minister, who was also executed. At an early age he was brought into the society of Edward VI and of the princess Elizabeth, but there is no evidence that he shared his education with them, although Roger Ascham taught him Latin, as he did Elizabeth. Robert was well educated and showed a preference for mathematics.

On June 4th, 1550, he married Amy Robsart of Norfolk, a marriage which William Cecil described as 'begun in passion,

ended in mourning'. Robert was then seventeen; in 1553 he
became M.P. for Norfolk and he supported his father's attempt
to exclude Mary Tudor and Elizabeth from the throne in
order to make his sister-in-law, Lady Jane Grey, queen. On
the failure of this conspiracy Robert was arrested and put in
the Tower, where his wife was allowed to visit him—a sign
that she and Robert were then on good terms. In January
1554 Robert was sentenced to death, but in October he was
released and pardoned. In 1557 he was at the battle of
St. Quentin, where he held the post of Master of the Ordnance
to the English army. In return for his good services he was
'restored in blood'—*i.e.* he could once more claim to rank as
a duke's son, a privilege which had been destroyed by his
father's execution for high treason.

On the accession of Elizabeth I Dudley lost no time in
appearing at Court. On January 11th, 1588, he was made
Master of the Queen's Horse—a post for which he was pecu-
liarly suited by his knowledge of horses, his superb skill as a
horseman and his great administrative powers. On April 23rd
he was created a Knight of the Garter and was sworn of the
Privy Council. This rapid advance in the royal favour made
Dudley exceedingly unpopular with the older families, such
as the Duke of Norfolk and his friends, and their hatred was
only increased by the palpable fact that the Queen was
infatuated with this son of a man who had been executed for
treason. Already the Spanish ambassador was writing to
Philip II of Robert Dudley as 'the king that is to be'.

Most of Elizabeth's favourites were given nicknames by the
Queen. Robert Dudley she named her 'eyes', which explains
the symbol W W which he frequently used in his letters to
Elizabeth in place of his own name. Christopher Hatton used
the symbol /\ /\ /\ /\ to represent his nickname of 'lids',
i.e. eye-lids. (Brooks, *Sir Christopher Hatton*, pp. 95–6.)
Leicester's enemies called him 'the gypsy'.

There is plenty of evidence to prove that Dudley, throughout
the years 1558 and 1559 was on excellent terms with his wife,
but there were plenty of malicious tongues to suggest that
Amy was an obstacle in the way of Dudley's highest ambition

and that he was planning to be rid of her. On Sunday, September 8th, 1560, Amy was found dead at the foot of the stairs in her house at Cumnor, near Abingdon. Every kind of rumour spread like wildfire: the Spanish ambassador has been represented as writing to Philip II that the Queen had told him of the death the day before it happened. There is not a shred of evidence for this (Jenkins, *Elizabeth and Leicester*, pp. 62–4). Inevitably, Amy was said to have been murdered at the instigation of her husband. Again, there is no evidence to prove this. The most convincing discussion on the cause of her death is to be found written by Professor Ian Aird in the *English Historical Review*, 1956, where he uses modern medical science to show that the most likely cause of death was a fall brought about by cancer of the breast, from which it is known that Amy Robsart was suffering. Robert Dudley took all possible steps to ensure that the inquest was held before a wholly impartial jury, which returned a verdict of accidental death. This was not enough to clear Dudley in the eyes of the world, nor was he helped by the fact that his relations with the Queen became closer and closer after Amy's death.

In 1562 Dudley was chosen as High Steward of Cambridge University: two years later he was created Baron Denbigh and Earl of Leicester and became Chancellor of Oxford University. In the previous year (1563), when Mary, Queen of Scots, was in search of a husband, Elizabeth made the staggering suggestion that she should marry Robert Dudley, and it has been thought that the grant of an Earldom was a move in this diplomatic game, for it was urgent that neither a Spaniard nor a Frenchman should marry the Scottish sovereign. What were Elizabeth's motives, or how genuine was her offer, will never be known: what is certain is that Dudley had no intention of sacrificing his chances of marrying Elizabeth by accepting Mary Stuart, and he himself called the whole proposal a 'fetch'. The episode was closed when Mary married Darnley.

In 1564 the Archbishop of Canterbury, Matthew Parker, issued an ordinance to impose uniformity in church ritual and vestments. The Puritans at once turned to Leicester for help and it became apparent that he belonged to the Puritan sect.

His reasons for joining them are obscure: Strype believed that Leicester had joined that party 'on some displeasure with the Archbishop and for other ends'. (P. Collinson. *Letters of Thomas Wood 1566-77* intro.) From this time forward Leicester became a bitter opponent of the Catholics. Years later this was to cause him much grief. In 1566, when the Queen was being entertained by Oxford University, a young man of the name of Edmund Campion made a speech in front of her of such brilliance and charm that she specially commended him to Leicester. Leicester proved a faithful and generous patron, and Campion freely acknowledged the debt when he dedicated his *History of Ireland* to Leicester in 1571. In 1581 Campion was arrested as a Jesuit missionary. The Queen and Leicester both personally interviewed Campion and Elizabeth did her best to save the young man's life, but he refused all her generous offers. When he came to be hanged and quartered, the executioner had orders that Campion was not to be cut down from the gallows until he was dead. It seems likely that those orders came from Leicester.

The arrival in England of the Queen of Scots in 1568 and her imprisonment raised all kinds of difficulties for the government. In 1569 a plot was hatched to rescue Mary from her prison at Tutbury and to marry her to the Duke of Norfolk. For some reason Leicester supported the idea of her marrying Norfolk, but he was not privy to the Rising of the Northern Earls and he lost none of the Queen's favour through it.

About this time—perhaps as early as 1568, certainly by 1573—Leicester became embroiled in what was probably his worst indiscretion: he had a liaison with Douglas Sheffield, widow of Lord Sheffield and sister of Lord Howard of Effingham. In spite of all the attempts made later to prove that he had married Lady Sheffield, there is virtually no doubt that he never did marry her and that the relationship between them was perfectly well understood and accepted by Lady Sheffield. There was a son by this misalliance, who was named Robert and was recognized by Leicester as his son. He was given the best possible education and grew up to be 'a milder version' of his father (Jenkins, *ibid.*, p. 368). He eventually

Plate 19

Sir Francis Walsingham,
Secretary of State

Sir Thomas Gresham

Plate 20

Nicholas Hilliard

Sir Christopher Hatton,
Lord Chancellor

Robert Dudley, Earl of Leicester

Robert Devereux, Earl of Essex

Hans Holbein

married Alice Leigh, of Stoneleigh, in Warwickshire, by whom
he had several daughters. He left wife and children and went
to Italy in company with his lovely cousin, Elizabeth Southwell,
dressed as a boy, and made a name for himself as a navigator,
explorer and naval architect (Jenkins, *ibid.*, pp. 367–8).

On May 7th, 1574, the first royal patent granted to actors
in this country was given to Leicester for 'Lord Leicester's
Men', the chief of whom was James Burbage. He had already
in 1571 founded by Act of Parliament a hospital for twelve
poor men at Warwick, which still exists.

1575 saw the marvellous entertainment which Leicester
provided for the Queen at Kenilworth, and which Shakespeare
is supposed to have witnessed as a boy of 11 and to have
commemorated later in his *Midsummer Night's Dream* in
Oberon's vision (II, ii, 148 *sqq.*), with its hidden reference to
the Queen and Lady Sheffield:

> Cupid alarmed, a certain aim he took
> At a fair vestal throned by the west
> And loosed his love shaft smartly from the bow
> As if to pierce a hundred thousand hearts. . . .
> Yet marked I where the bolt of Cupid fell,
> It fell upon a little western flower,
> Before milk-white, now purple with love's wound
> And maidens call it Love-in-Idleness.

(for a fuller treatment of this subject, see Jenkins, *ibid.*, 207–10).

But Lady Sheffield was not Leicester's one and only mistake.
There had been staying at Kenilworth for the festivities Lettice,
the widowed Countess of Essex, daughter of Sir Francis
Knollys and mother of Robert Devereux, second Earl of
Essex, who was to become the favourite of Elizabeth in her old
age. Already Leicester was making love to her (1575) and in
1578, when he knew that Lettice was pregnant, he married
her secretly without the knowledge or the permission of the
Queen. Of course he was accused, falsely, of having poisoned
Essex. When the Queen heard the news, she was furiously
angry, but she soon recovered her temper and Leicester was
forgiven. Not so Lettice, for whom Elizabeth preserved an

P—(2)

undying hatred and whom she would refer to as 'that she-wolf'. There was one son by this marriage, Robert, who died at the age of three and lies buried in the Beauchamp Chapel in St. Mary's, Warwick, 'the noble impe . . . a child of great promise'.

Leicester's marriage to Lettice proves that he had by 1578 abandoned all hopes of marrying Elizabeth. But his ambitions were still enormous. He probably had hopes of becoming the ruler of the Dutch Protestant provinces: he proposed in 1582 that his small son Robert should marry Arabella Stuart, the niece of Mary, Queen of Scots, and first cousin to James VI of Scotland, whereby the crown of England might come into his own family. In 1583 he made the rash suggestion that one of the daughters of Lettice by her first marriage should marry James VI—a suggestion which roused the fury of Elizabeth in her hatred of the 'she-wolf'.

All this time the dangers from Catholic plots and Mary, Queen of Scots, were increasing. It is probable that Leicester was the originator of the idea to form an association for the protection of the Queen's life (1584). In the same year there appeared a virulent and malicious pamphlet, *The Copy of a Letter written by a Master of Art at Cambridge*, better known as *Leicester's Commonwealth*. It was probably written by Charles Arundell (Arch. Vat., *Nunc. Div.*, 264, f. 239). The pamphlet was published at Antwerp, it was a piece of shrewdly written and entertaining propaganda against Leicester, repeating all the old stories, rumours and gossip. As historical evidence the pamphlet is worthless, as a proof of Leicester's unpopularity it cannot be ignored. Sir Philip Sidney wrote a passionate defence of his uncle in reply.

In 1585 the United Provinces in the Netherlands offered Elizabeth the sovereignty of these states. She absolutely declined in any circumstances to accept. She saw clearly that England could only survive so long as both her enemies, France and Spain, survived, the one to balance the other. She saw as clearly that an independent Netherlands would be unable to withstand a powerful France, and she was proved right in the eighteenth century. Her policy was to try to restore all the Netherland provinces to their ancient liberties 'wherein they

lived before the persecutions and oppressions begun by the
Duke of Alva', but they must remain Spanish (*Elizabethan
Government and Society*, Wernham, pp. 345–6). Reluctantly she
agreed to go to war in defence of the Dutch Protestants and
she sent an expeditionary force under the command of Leicester.
He landed at Flushing on December 10th, 1585. He received
a tumultuous welcome which entirely turned his head, as his
letters home show. He wrote to Burghley that the Dutch
would serve under himself with a better will than they had
under William the Silent. And he publicly announced that
the total expulsion of the Spanish from the Netherlands would
be accomplished in one summer's campaign.

On January 1st, 1586, the States General offered him the
office of Supreme Governor of the United Provinces. Before
he left England the Queen had made perfectly plain to him
that he was not to take any oath of allegiance nor to accept
any powers which would involve her in responsibilities beyond
the limited ones to which she was committed. Leicester
accepted the offer of the States General. Elizabeth was
furiously angry; she wrote to Leicester, 'How contemptuously
we conceive ourselves to have been used by you. . . . We could
never have imagined, had we not seen it fall out in experience,
that a man raised up by ourself and extraordinarily favoured
by us above any subject in this land, would have in so contemptible a sort broken our commandment. . . .' She was at
least as angry that she had now been committed to detaching
the Netherlands from Spain (Wernham, *ibid.*).

It soon became evident that Leicester was utterly unsuitable
for the command of any army. He lacked experience, he was
so arrogant that soon the States General repented of their
action, and he proved himself totally unable to work with any
of his military commanders. He made no attempt to control
the finances of the campaign, which further inflamed the Queen.
In 1586 he returned to England and was able to make up his
quarrel with the Queen, but militarily his campaign had proved
a failure, its only successes being the capture of the forts of Zutphen and Deventer, at the price of the death of Sir Philip Sidney.

Leicester's return was said to be necessary so that he could sit in the 1587 Parliament, which was to settle the fate of Mary, Queen of Scots. Leicester was violently in favour of her being executed at once and when it seemed that the Queen would refuse to agree, Leicester is said to have advised 'the sure but silent operation of poison and sent a divine privately to Walsingham to convince him it was lawful'. (Camden.)

Things in the Netherlands were going from bad to worse, and when Sir William Stanley betrayed Deventer to the enemy and Yorke did the same at Zutphen, the States General urged that Leicester should be sent back. He went back, but he did nothing effective and was finally recalled home in November 1587. He was at once on the best of terms with the Queen and when preparations were being made to resist the Spanish Aramda, Leicester was put in charge of the camp at Tilbury with the title of 'lieutenant and captain-general of the Queen's armies and companies'. But once again he proved himself unable to work harmoniously with other men. All the same, it was he who saw the possibilities in the Queen's suggestion that she might visit the troops at Tilbury, it was he who stage-managed her arrival and her triumphant review of her army, culminating in what has become one of the most famous speeches in the English language.

At the end of August, 1588, Leicester decided to go to Buxton to take the waters. On his way he stopped at his house at Cornbury in Oxfordshire, and there on September 4th in the morning he died 'of a continual burning fever' (Camden), probably of malaria, at the age of fifty-five. He lies buried in the magnificent tomb set up by his wife, Lettice, in the Beauchamp Chapel of St. Mary's, Warwick.

Robert Dudley, young, handsome, athletic, charming, ambitious, self-confident, might have cast his spell on any young lady. Deliberately he aimed his shaft at the first lady in the land and the shaft went home. There can be no doubt that Elizabeth was deeply in love with him and he was as devoted to her. There can be equally little doubt that she was never his mistress. Hers was the more disinterested love, his may well have been tainted with ambition. Both longed for their love to be consummated, but what Elizabeth the woman would gladly have given and received, that Elizabeth the Queen saw clearly could not be. The unity of England depended on her remaining unmarried in every sense of the word. Dudley could and did find physical satisfaction with other women, but without love. The Queen could have love, but no physical satisfaction. Both were sacrificed to inexorable circumstances. Leicester, middle-aged, corpulent, red-faced and white-haired, arrogant, intolerant, touchy, still showed his devotion to Elizabeth and to the Queen: she returned it to the day of his death. What the strains and stresses of that rare courtship must have been we may partly guess from the wild tantrums of Elizabeth and the furious insolence or the black despair of Robert. When he died, she had still fifteen years of life ahead of her. Is it mere coincidence that in her old age she turned for comfort to Robert Devereux, Earl of Essex, step-son of Robert Dudley, Earl of Leicester?   (*Plate 20*)

There is no full length biography of Leicester.

Milton Waldman, *Elizabeth and Leicester*, 1944.

Elizabeth Jenkins, *Elizabeth and Leicester*, 1961. To be used with care.

B. R. Wernham, Elizabethan War Aims and Strategy. *Elizabethan Government and Society, Essays presented to Sir John Neale,* 1961.

Letters of Thomas Wood, Puritan, 1566-77, ed. by P. Collinson, 1960, contains a most self-revealing letter from Leicester, on pp. 12-16.

DEVEREUX, ROBERT, 2nd EARL OF ESSEX, favourite of Elizabeth I, was born on November 10th, 1567, and died on February 25th, 1601, aged 33. He was the son of Walter Devereux, Earl of Essex and his wife, Lady Lettice Knollys, daughter of Sir Francis Knollys and Mary, sister of Anne Boleyn. He was, therefore, a cousin of the Queen on her mother's side, a relationship which may in part account for the extreme favour and leniency which the Queen showed to him. He was also step-son to Robert Dudley, Earl of Leicester, which is more likely still to account for Elizabeth's affection for him. His father died in 1576 and thus Robert became Earl of Essex at the age of 9. His early years were spent in the household of Lord Burghley and he proved himself to be a genuinely able and precocious child. He went to Trinity, Cambridge, under Whitgift (1579), took his M.A. in 1581, and first appeared at Court in 1584. Two years later (1586) he was created a knight-banneret for his courage at the battle of Zutphen, where Sir Philip Sidney was killed. On his return home he at once attracted the notice and favour of the Queen and in 1587 was made her Master of Horse, a fact the more remarkable, because his mother had married Robert Dudley, Earl of Leicester, to the Queen's fury. In 1588 he was made a Knight of the Garter. But even so early on as this, there were quarrels and scenes between the Queen and Essex. Essex seems to have taken no part in the fight against the Spanish Armada.

In 1589 Essex joined himself to the party of Don Antonio, the Pretender to the throne of Portugal. He was unhappy at Court, quarrelling with Ralegh and the Queen, so much so that Elizabeth was saying 'by God's death it were fitting some one should take him down and teach him manners!' Therefore, when the Drake-Norreys expedition was sent against Spain in 1589, Essex determined to join it. He knew the Queen would veto his going. He slipped away privately and succeeded in joining the official expedition. He proved an encumbrance, achieved some distinction—his courage was never in doubt—but furious letters from Elizabeth entailed his immediate return to England. When he met the Queen, all was forgiven him.

In 1590 Essex married secretly Frances, the daughter of Walsingham and the widow of Sir Philip Sidney. This aroused another angry scene with Elizabeth, but in a few months Essex was again restored to favour. The next year (1591) he was given command of a force which was sent to help Henry of Navarre. He behaved with much courage and he succeeded in capturing Gournay. But he earned a reproof from the Queen for creating twenty-three knights, too large a number to please Elizabeth, who hated to see knighthood cheapened. Twice he was recalled temporarily to satisfy Elizabeth that he was not risking his life rashly, and then in 1592 he was finally summoned home.

Between 1592 and 1596 Essex set about building up his political reputation at Court. He became the rallying point for all those who resented the monopoly of power by the Cecils: chief among these was Francis Bacon. Essex had genuine affection for Bacon, but his persistent and often ill-judged attempts to obtain political promotion for Bacon led to further quarrels with Elizabeth. Essex concentrated on foreign affairs and made Anthony Bacon, brother of Francis, his chief adviser. He built up a well-organized system of intelligence and he drew information from all parts of the continent, corresponding with Henry of Navarre and James VI of Scotland. In 1593 he was made a Privy Councillor. The year before Don Antonio had arrived in England and attached himself to the Essex party. It was largely through him that Essex brought to the gallows Dr. Rodrigo Lopez, the Queen's physician, on a charge of plotting to murder the Queen (1594), but not before Elizabeth had called Essex 'a rash and temerarious youth'.

In 1596 Essex was appointed general-in-chief of the land forces and also put in command of one of the five squadrons which formed the Cadiz expedition under Lord Howard of Effingham. The expedition was a resounding success, the Spanish fleet was totally defeated and Essex landed his army and captured Cadiz (June 22nd, 1596). The fleet then sailed to Cape St. Mary, where Essex landed a force and entered the town of Faro. He got little out of it, but he came away with the library of Jerome Osorio, Bishop of Algarve. The books eventually passed to the Bodleian. Essex then tried to persuade Howard to attack Lisbon and intercept the Spanish treasure fleet, but Howard refused, and on August 10th Essex reached Plymouth, the generally recognized hero of the expedition.

Essex was now at the height of his fortunes. His very success made him enemies at Court and the Queen was angry that her share of the profits of the Cadiz expedition was so small. When the treasure fleet entered the Tagus two days after the English had left, Essex's judgement was vindicated. At once he was restored to favour with the Queen. He was popular in the country, his knowledge of foreign affairs was at least as well-informed as that of the government, and Essex House now became a miniature Court. Francis Bacon alone saw the dangers and he wrote a letter to Essex warning him not to underrate the Queen and not to overrate a military reputation. The advice was not heeded. From this moment Essex's star began to set.

In 1597 he was given command of the Islands' Voyage, an expedition sent out to capture the Spanish treasure fleet and the Azores. It was a failure, principally owing to Essex's incapacity as a commander. Again he was out of favour with the Queen. A peace was patched up and Essex was made Earl Marshal (1597). The peace was short-lived. In 1598 Essex aided the Earl of Southampton in his secret marriage with one of the Queen's maids of honour. The Queen was furious and scenes between her and Essex were frequent. When the question arose who should command the expedition to Ireland to deal with O'Neill, Earl of Tyrone, Essex behaved outrageously, turned his back on the Queen and (according to Ralegh) told her that 'her conditions were as crooked as her carcase'. Elizabeth boxed his ears, Essex drew his sword and flung out of the Court in high passion.

Once again the two were reconciled and Essex was given command of the Irish expedition (1599). He arrived at Dublin on April 15th, 1600. His whole reputation was now at stake. He had an army of 15,000 men and wider powers than had been given to any previous Lieutenant and Governor-General. He began with a minor campaign in Munster which merely wasted time, money and men. Elizabeth wrote him a scathing rebuke and forbade him to return to England. Essex then made a half-hearted advance into Ulster, but instead of fighting Tyrone he met him at a ford in the river Lagan and contrived an ignominious peace. The Queen was rightly furious. It is not impossible that Essex, who was already corresponding with James VI and knew the Queen could not live long, was gambling on his own accession to the English throne and was well contented to have a friendly Tyrone in Ireland backed by a military force. Suddenly in September Essex deserted his army, embarked for England and arrived in the early morning in the Queen's bedroom at Nonsuch. At first she received him kindly, but then she confined him to his own house. Essex was now politically ruined. He fell seriously ill, recovered and set about building up a political party out of all those irresponsible young men who found themselves excluded from office and who clamoured for war with Spain— men like Rutland, Sir Christopher Blount and the young Earl of Southampton.

By the New Year the government was aware of what was going on. On February 5th, 1601, Essex's friends arranged for Shakespeare's play of *Richard II* to be played at the Globe on the following Saturday, February 7th, and the deposition scene was to be included. On the 7th the Council shut up Essex and his friends in Essex House in the Strand. On the 8th Essex with 200 men broke out and rode through the city of London, but he failed to arouse any enthusiasm or support. He was compelled to surrender. On the 19th he was tried in Westminster Hall with Southampton, Edward Coke conducted the prosecution with great acrimony and Francis Bacon basely gave evidence against Essex, who was inevitably condemned to death. He was executed on the 25th, dying with great dignity and courage. The story that Elizabeth gave Essex a ring with a promise to pardon any offence, if he sent it to her when in danger, and that Essex sent the ring from the Tower by the Countess of Nottingham, who never delivered it, is wholly apocryphal.

Essex is one of the tragic failures in English history. Handsome, brave, impulsive, loyal to his friends, generous, he won the hearts of the English people. Shakespeare twice wrote of him, once while he was in Ireland when the play *Henry V* was produced for the first time:

> Were now the general of our gracious empress,
> As in good time he may, from Ireland coming,
> Bringing rebellion broached on his sword,
> How many would the peaceful city quit
> To welcome him:

and there is a reference to him in the words applied by Ophelia to Hamlet:

The courtier's, soldier's, scholar's eye, tongue, sword,
The expectancy and rose of the fair state,
The glass of fashion and the mould of form,
The observed of all observers. . . .

But he was passionate, undisciplined and politically destitute of
all the qualities necessary for statesmanship. He came of an
old, feudal family and his faction represents the last kick of a
feudal aristocracy* against the new rich, the Cecils and the
Walsinghams. His great mistake was that he never understood
that all his fortune depended on the favour of the Queen, and
he tried to control and in the end to undermine the source
from which alone his success could spring.   (*Plate 20*)

G. B. Harrison: *Robert Devereux, Earl of Essex.*
A. L. Rowse, 'Robert Devereux, Earl of Essex' in *The Great
Tudors*, 1933.
L. W. Henry, The Earl of Essex and Ireland, 1599. *B. of the I.
of H.R.*, May 1959.
J. O'Neill, *Chosen by the Queen*, 1917. (H.N.)

RALEGH, SIR WALTER (this spelling, pronounced
Rawley, was the one he mostly used after his father's death in
1581; although the whole family used more than 70 variations,
he himself is not known ever to have used the usual modern
form of Raleigh), poet, historian, explorer, sailor, soldier,
courtier, was born probably in 1552 and he was executed in
1618. He was the second child of Walter Ralegh by his third
wife, and he was thus half-brother to Sir Humphrey Gilbert,
his mother's son by her first husband. He went to Oriel
College, Oxford, and later fought as a volunteer in the Huguenot
army at the battles of Jarnac and Monconteur, 1569. In 1578
he joined with Humphrey Gilbert in fitting out an expedition
for the Azores and the West Indies against Spain. In 1580–1 he
saw military service in Ireland, after which he returned to
England to the court at Greenwich. The story that he spread
his cloak 'in a plashy place', 'whereon the Queen trod gently

---

* I am indebted to Mr. C. Morris, King's College, Cambridge, for this
vivid description.

over, rewarding him after with many suits for his so free and seasonable tender of so fair a foot cloth' does not occur before mid-seventeenth century. He remained at court for many years as a favourite frequently and richly rewarded. In 1584 he was knighted.

In 1583–9 he sent out at his own expense of £40,000 six expeditions to plant a colony overseas in America, and later he sent out others, the last in 1603, but all were failures, the only tangible result being that the potato and tobacco were introduced into England and Ireland.

In 1588 he took no active part in the fighting against the Armada. 1591 he published anonymously an account of Grenville's last fight in the *Revenge*, which later became the basis for Tennyson's poem. In 1592 he was imprisoned for misbehaviour with one of the Queen's maids of honour, Elizabeth Throgmorton, but he was soon released. They were married and lived at Sherborne. 1594 he sent an expedition to reconnoitre the river Orinoco, and in 1595 himself went in search of the fabulously wealthy city of Manoa in South America, known as El Dorado. The expedition was a failure. On his return he played a leading part in Essex's expedition against Cadiz. 1597 saw him back at court and reconciled with the queen. He then took part in Essex's expedition against Spain, but his conduct led to a violent quarrel which was never healed.

When James I came to the English throne his mind had already been poisoned against Ralegh, who soon found himself in the Tower on a charge of being implicated in Watson's plot 'to surprise the King's person'. Ralegh was tried for high treason, convicted, condemned to be executed, reprieved and shut up in the Tower from 1603 to 1616. During his imprisonment he wrote his *History of the World*, beginning at the Creation, but he only got as far as 130 B.C. In 1616 he was released in order to go on an expedition to find El Dorado, on the condition that, if he failed, he would return. He set sail from Plymouth on June 12th, 1617. The expedition was a disastrous failure, and a fight took place with the Spanish just at the time when James I was trying to negotiate a Spanish marriage for his son, Charles, Prince of Wales. True to his promise, Ralegh returned to England and James had him executed, largely at the demand of the Spanish ambassador. (October 29th, 1618.)

Ralegh was an intellectual genius, witty, brilliant, graceful, a poet and a great writer. He had a fearlessly independent mind, a bitter tongue and a scornful use of repartee. He was rapacious, restlessly energetic, ambitious for power and fame, an unscrupulous schemer in pursuit of success. Yet he was also extravagantly generous, adored by his wife, beloved by his servants. He never attained to political power, because the queen never trusted his judgement, however much she enjoyed his company. He was accused of being an atheist, whereas in fact he only refused to accept without criticism orthodox opinions, and his *History of the World* proves him to have been deeply religious. His ideas were ahead of his times—he held that colonies (he would have called them plantations) would absorb surplus population, reduce unemployment at home and stimulate trade. When he laid his head on the block on the scaffold somebody asked him if he would not rather lie with his head to the East of Our Lord's arising. Ralegh's answer was, 'So the heart be right, it is no matter which way the head lieth'. *(Plate 31)*

E. Thompson, *Sir Walter Raleigh*, 1935.

V. Harlow, Introduction to *The Discovery of Guiana*, Argonaut Press, 1928.

D. B. Quinn, *Raleigh and the British Empire*, Hodder and Stoughton, 1947.

A. L. Rowse, *Ralegh and the Throckmortons*, 1962.

HATTON, SIR CHRISTOPHER, Lord Chancellor, was born in 1540 and died in 1591 at the age of 51. He was the second son of William Hatton of Holdenby, Northamptonshire, and his wife Alice, daughter of Lawrence Saunders of Harrington in the same county. Holdenby was a parish in the Hundred of Newbottle: local pronunciation shortened the name to Holmby, and it is as Holmby House that Holdenby is now remembered, the house where King Charles I was imprisoned in 1646. Christopher's sister, Dorothy, married as her second husband William Underhill of Idlicote in

Warwickshire, and it was their son William who sold New Place to Shakespeare at Stratford-on-Avon.

In about 1555 Hatton went to St. Mary Hall, Oxford, the Head of which was Allen, later the English Cardinal in Rome. It seems certain that the Hattons were brought up as Catholics and that up to the time of the Armada Christopher's religion was similar to that of the Queen—he sympathized with the English Catholics and hated the Puritans. After the execution of Mary, Queen of Scots, he became virulent against the Pope and the Jesuits. In 1560 he was entered at the Inner Temple, and here he took part in the literary and dramatic activities of the young men, rather than applying himself to the study of law. It was probably at the masque which was acted in 1561 at the Inner Temple in front of the Queen that Hatton 'danced his way into the heart of Elizabeth' (Sir Edmund Chambers). He now became a favourite of the Queen, a position which he held to the last day of his life.

For the next sixteen years Hatton was a courtier who received many favours from Elizabeth. In 1564 he was made one of her Gentlemen Pensioners and he was granted many estates and offices and an annuity of £400. In 1566 he was one of the embassy which went to Scotland to attend the baptism of James VI. The proceedings were marred by the testy behaviour of some of the Englishmen (including Hatton) who took amiss a joke perpetrated by some of the Scots at an entertainment, when some satyrs 'put their hands behind them to their tails which they wagged with their hands in such sort as the Englishmen supposed it had been devised and done in derision of them', for everybody knew that Englishmen had had tails bestowed upon them as a divine punishment for the martyrdom of Thomas Becket.

In 1571 Hatton was returned as M.P. for Higham Ferrers and in 1572 and 1584 for Northamptonshire. He was at first a silent member and made no mark in the House. But further advancement came to him in 1572, when the Queen appointed him Captain of her Bodyguard. The next year a violent Puritan, Peter Burchet, attempted to murder Hatton on religious grounds, but he mistook John Hawkins for Hatton and only succeeded in wounding Hawkins. It may be a sign of Hatton's increasing confidence and prestige that in 1573, with the help of the Queen and by very high-handed action, he compelled the Bishop of Ely to surrender to him Ely Place in Holborn (now Hatton Gardens), an episode which is inaccurately commemorated in one of *The Ingoldsby Legends*, 'The House Warming'. The year 1577 saw Hatton made Vice-Chamberlain and knighted, and his period as little more than a courtier came to an end. From then on he was the mouthpiece of the Queen in the House of Commons, it was his business to pilot government bills through the House, to prevent waste of time and debates embarrassing to the government.

Hatton found himself involved in the difficult problem of Elizabeth's projected marriage with the Duke of Anjou: at first he was in favour of it, but once he had seen Anjou in person he was so strongly opposed to it that he besought the Queen with tears in his eyes to go no further in the matter. He took some part in examining the accused in the Parry, Throckmorton and Babington plots against the Queen's life. Most importantly, he was on the Commission for the examination of the Queen of Scots, and it was Hatton's wise, tactful and moderate arguments which persuaded Mary to accept the competence of the Court to try her (1586). There is little doubt that it was Hatton who succeeded in persuading the unhappy Davison (Elizabeth's secretary) to send off the warrant for the execution of Mary (1587).

These were testing times. Hatton seems to have acquitted himself so well that in 1587 he was made Lord Chancellor. This appointment has aroused passionate arguments among historians, the earlier of whom have seen in it nothing but the mere caprice of an infatuated woman, prepared to promote her favourite to the chief place in the realm, although he was wholly unsuited to the post. Later historians have taken the view that the appointment was a purely political and not a legal one. The legal side was provided for by the appointment of trained legal advisers to help Hatton on that side of his work. The view that this was a piece of sheer favouritism by the

Queen is disposed of by the fact that Elizabeth was both before and immediately after the appointment doubtful whether she had done right. What she needed was somebody of sufficient strength of character and loyalty to co-operate with the new Archbishop of Canterbury, Whitgift, in suppressing the Puritans and enforcing uniformity in the Church of England. The appointment was justified by the co-operation which Hatton maintained with Whitgift. He had had to wait for more than twenty years before the Queen advanced him to an important political office.

The next year, 1588, Hatton was given the Garter and also became Chancellor of Oxford University. He died in 1591 and was buried in St. Paul's.

Christopher Hatton's place in English history has not yet been fully treated. For centuries he remained a figure of fun, a dancer and a butt for the dramatists—as in Sheridan's *The Critic*. It is true that his relations with the Queen, as judged by his letters, give some grounds to modern times for regarding him as a sycophant and nothing more. But modern times are only judging by modern standards. The tone of Hatton's letters represents only an exaggerated form of what in Elizabeth's day was looked on as the right way of approaching the monarch. There is no shred of evidence that Hatton was Elizabeth's lover, but the Queen was genuinely devoted to Hatton and in his last illness she constantly visited him, taking him broths and feeding him with her own hand. She gave him the nickname of 'lids' (*i.e.* eye-lids), which he used in his letters under the symbol of four triangles. She also called him her bell-wether and her Mutton. Hatton himself was a man with an extremely kind heart, and many letters exist from men and women in trouble thanking Hatton for the help he has given them—such people as the Catholic Pound, who published Campion's *Challenge*, and poor old Lady Egerton of Ridley, who wrote to him, 'You are the sole person in court that hath taken compassion on me, and hath given comfort unto my careful heart and, under God, kept life within my breast . . . a poor, wretched, abandoned lady, no way able to yield you thankfulness worthy thereof. You are the rock I build on.' It is arguable that most of these men and women were Catholics and that Hatton was only indulging his own religious feelings, but there is plenty of evidence to show that in his examinations of accused persons, whatever their religion, Hatton used gentler and more considerate methods than most of his contemporaries.

Financially Hatton's life was a disaster. When he died he was in debt to Elizabeth to the sum of about £40,000. He spent his money largely on the most extravagant building, as at Holdenby, where his new house was looked upon as the greatest piece of building in his time. He had shares in Drake's voyage of circumnavigation, in Frobisher's voyages in search of the North-west Passage, in Fenton's voyage of 1584, and in the Cadiz expedition of 1589.

There is great need of a full-scale biography of Hatton to settle his true place among English statesmen. Scattered through the works of Conyers Read and Sir John Neale are to be found references to Hatton which go far to recognize him as a Parliamentarian of great ability and an orator much above the average. Neale calls him 'the invaluable Hatton', 'the respected, the supreme parliamentary manager' (*Elizabeth and Her Parliaments*, ii, 159), and in describing Hatton's speech in the House of Lords after the defeat of the Armada, Neale writes, 'for its eloquence, its emotion, and its stirring, confident, patriotism, as well as a withering contempt for the enemy, Hatton's speech is not unworthy of place in the treasury of England's best' (*ibid.*, 195).   (*Plate 20*)

Sir Harris Nicholas, *Memoirs of the Life and Times of Sir Christopher Hatton*, 1847, is a commentary on the transcripts of Hatton's letters.

E. St. John Brooks, *Sir Christopher Hatton*, 1946, in some ways an entertaining picture of life in the reign of Elizabeth, but inadequate on Hatton himself.

SIDNEY, SIR PHILIP, poet, statesman and soldier, was born in 1554 and died in 1586, aged thirty-two. He was the eldest son of Sir Henry Sidney and his wife, Mary, daughter of John Dudley, Duke of Northumberland. To his contemporaries he clearly resembled one of those heroes of Greek antiquity in whom all gifts and graces were congruously blended. Educated at Shrewsbury and Christ Church, and then travelling abroad for two years (when he was in Paris on the day of the St. Bartholomew massacre), he was soon employed about the court and sent on missions to more than one foreign potentate. To us his public career must seem one of promise rather than achievement, but there is no gainsaying the extraordinary love and admiration which he won from all who knew him. His biographer, Fulke Greville, had 'friend to Philip Sidney' inscribed on his own tombstone, and Thomas Thornton wanted it similarly recorded that he was Sidney's tutor.

Sidney's heroic death (brought about by his refusal to wear armour on his thighs, out of bravado), following the siege of Zutphen, fighting against Catholic Spain, when, dying himself, he gave his bottle of water to a dying soldier, was followed by an astonishing outburst of grief from all, including the Queen. Over two hundred poetic elegies (one of which came from his devoted friend Spenser) mourned the irreparable loss of one who combined in his own life and character the qualities of the ideal Englishman.

Sidney was not only a man of diplomacy and action. His enormous pastoral romance *Arcadia* was written in letters to his sister in 1580–1, when his courageous protest against the Queen's projected marriage with the Duke of Anjou temporarily estranged him from her court. He did not mean the work to be published (nothing of his was published till the 1590s), and on his deathbed he desired that it should be burnt.

The *Arcadia* is not now easy reading, being, as Horace Walpole harshly but not untruly called it, a jungle of pastoral, sentimental and heroical adventures, full of digressions and improbabilities, with much prose-poetry and tortuous convolutions. There are a few passages of rich beauty, but the main cause of the book's enormous popularity for a century and more was the newness of such a feast of romance and sentiment. Scattered among these letters—together with some disastrous experiments in classical metres—are some of Sidney's best poems, but his main contribution to English poetry was

Q—(2)

undoubtedly the sonnets which he wrote to Penelope Devereux, daughter of the Earl of Essex, entitled 'Astrophel and Stella'. Not all judges are agreed on the merits of these sonnets. Hazlitt, to the astonishment of Lamb, thought them 'jejune and frigid'; Saintsbury called the one beginning

'With how sad steps O moon, thou climb'st the skies'

the first perfectly charming sonnet in the English language.

The third work for which Sidney is known is his *Apologie for Poetrie* in reply to an abusive attack on the theatre by Stephen Gosson, an ex-playwright turned Puritan, who hoped to find Sidney on his side. Sidney replied with an eloquent exposition of his conviction of poetry's supremacy over all other studies, both for edification and delight. It is a work of much charm and considerable humour. The limitations of his judgment are shown by what he says of the theatre, where he insists on the rigid dramatic formalities which were shortly to be blown sky-high by Shakespeare and his fellows. But much may be forgiven the author of the famous and disarming declaration, 'I never heard the old song of Percy and Douglas that I found not my heart moved more than with a trumpet'. A critic who writes like that about poetry has the root of the matter in him.   (*Plate 29*)

Mona Wilson, *Sir Philip Sidney*.
E. J. M. Buxton, *Sir Philip Sidney and the Renaissance*.
H. Morris, *Elizabethan Literature*, pp. 58–66.

GRESHAM, SIR THOMAS, financier, founder of the Royal Exchange, was born probably in 1518, the son of Sir Richard Gresham, a well-known merchant and financier and once Lord Mayor of London, who was much employed in the business of the Crown and frequently lent money to Henry VIII. Thomas died in 1579, aged 61 years. The name Gresham means 'grass-farm', and the family took their name from the village of Gresham in Norfolk. Thomas was educated at Gonville and Caius College, Cambridge, where he had taken his B.A. by the time he was 16 years of age. He seems then to have gone into business under the instruction of his uncle. In 1543 he was elected a Freeman of the Mercers' Company and he was already being employed by the Crown to buy gunpowder. It is possible that he was lending the Crown money, or else providing money for the Crown by other means, for in 1544–5 some foreign mercenaries were paid with funds which had been received from Thomas Gresham. In 1544 he married the aunt by marriage of Francis Bacon. In 1549 Sir Richard died and Thomas and his wife moved from his father's house into a house in Lombard Street, 'at the sign of the Grasshopper', which was the emblem of the Gresham family.

In 1551–2 Sir William Daunsell, the royal agent or king's merchant was relieved of his post for having 'done his highness marvellous ill service'. Thomas Gresham replaced him and went to live in Antwerp, the centre of the international money market. (For the importance of Antwerp, see S. T. Bindoff, *New Cambridge Modern History*, vol. 2.)

From 1551 down to the death of Edward VI in 1553 Gresham was for the most part taken up with finding ways and means to alleviate the Crown's financial difficulties, although he also still looked after his own personal interests and business. He lived in the house of Gaspar Schetz (whose father had named his three sons after the Magi), the chief financial agent of Charles V. He had two London agents, John Elliot and Richard Candeler, and he also had many agents all over Europe. He was usually in Antwerp for three or four months at a time, but in Elizabeth's reign he once spent as long as a year there without returning to England. In his first two years in Antwerp he crossed the Channel forty-two times. His factor at Antwerp was Richard Clough, a very astute man in negotiating loans, smuggling arms, money and foreign goods from the Netherlands into England. Clough was in the habit of writing immensely long letters, filled with detailed accounts of current events in the Netherlands, funerals, pageants, etc., but also containing very valuable political information, which Gresham used to pass on to Cecil. Gresham appreciated the value of Clough and would praise him generously, but he warned Cecil that Clough was 'very long and tedious in his writing'.

The Crown's financial difficulties were very great, brought about by wars at the end of Henry VIII's reign, by Somerset's extravagance, and to a very great extent by the inflation (rise in prices and therefore the fall in the purchasing power of money) which marked the sixteenth century. It has to be remembered that in England by the middle of the century and for some time beyond there was no class of specialized financiers, nor any bankers: it was the rich merchants who gave credit and discounted bills, but their capacity was limited. It was therefore frequently necessary for the Crown to seek for loans in foreign countries, which on the whole meant in Antwerp. By 1552 the interest on the Crown's debts was £40,000 and the foreign capitalists had succeeded in bringing down the rate of exchange to 16/ Flemish for £1 sterling.

Gresham set about his work with a will, but in fact he had not any revolutionary ideas on how to help the Crown. He advised the Council to set aside £1,300 per week and to send this sum secretly to him in Antwerp for the redemption of debt. He would use this money to buy up small sums of sterling every day in such a way that 'it shall not be perceived nor it shall be no occasion to make the Exchange fall'—in fact, the steady demand would make it rise. He also suggested that the fleet of the Merchant Adventurers should only be allowed to set sail if the owners lent money to the king at one rate of exchange in Antwerp which could be repaid in London at another rate. The difference in the rates of exchange would operate to the king's advantage. This was a typical example of the harsh and high-handed measures which Gresham was ready to adopt against other merchants—no doubt because he himself got a 'rake off' from the profits made by the Crown. Further, he advised that the Crown by the use of its prerogative should create a monopoly for itself in lead, by forbidding anyone except the Crown to export lead. The greatly enhanced price would benefit the Crown considerably.

Not much came of this so-called 'design', mainly because the Council gave up remitting £1,300 per week—much the most sensible part of the 'design'—after eight weeks, and also rejected the proposal to create a monopoly in lead, because it would make the government very unpopular. Nevertheless, within two years Gresham claimed that he had succeeded in raising the rate of exchange at Antwerp from 16/ to 22/ and was discharging the Crown's debts at this figure. He achieved this partly by giving huge banquets to the creditors, but chiefly by insisting to the Crown that it must be punctual in repaying its debts. He wrote to Northumberland, 'It shall be no small grief unto me that in my time, being His Majesty's agent, any merchant strangers should be forced to forbear their money against their wills. . . . To be plain with Your Grace in this matter, according to my bounden duty, verily if there be not some other ways taken for the payment of His Majesty's debts, but to force men from time to time to prolong it; I say to you, the end thereof shall neither be honourable nor profitable to His Highness'.

Gresham and Edward VI were always on good terms. The king once gave him property worth £100 p.a., saying 'you shall know that you have served a king', and he also gave him lands from time to time, such as Walsingham Manor. Gresham once gave Edward VI a pair of long Spanish silk stockings, 'a great present', said Stow, ' . . . for Henry VIII did wear only cloth hose or hose cut out of ell-broad taffeta'. In 1556, he gave Mary 'a bottle of fine Holland (gin) in a case of black leather'.

Besides being used as a financial agent, Gresham also acted as a source of diplomatic and political information, which he gathered from his agents scattered all over Europe.

On the accession of Mary and the execution of his friend Northumberland, Gresham was relieved of his office. Dauntsey and Dansell were reinstated, but Sir John Leigh spoke up for Gresham, and as the Queen's business in Antwerp was being badly handled—all Gresham's work in reducing the rate of interest was undone—Gresham was restored and went back to Antwerp. His chief problem now was how to get the money out of the Netherlands and into England, for a ban had been put on the export of bullion by Charles V. To begin with

Gresham tried to smuggle it out in bales of pepper, but there was a limit to the amount of pepper which any one country could require and this method gave rise to suspicions. Gresham then used armour, packing the bullion in 1,000 demi-lancers' harness. How valuable this trade with England was becoming is shown by the panic into which the Flemish merchants fell at the news of Wyatt's rebellion (1554). In that year Gresham succeeded in securing from the Emperor a license and passport for exporting 500,000 crowns in bullion from Spain, with the proviso that 'I should convey this money with as much secrecy and as small bruit as I could achieve'.

For some reason or other in 1556 to 1558 Gresham retired into private life, but he was reinstated in Antwerp just before Mary died. Gresham hurried off to offer his services to Elizabeth—in itself a proof of how lucrative a business all this was for Gresham himself. Elizabeth received him cordially and promised as much land as any other monarch had given him and even more. Perhaps Gresham was a financier after Elizabeth's own heart—cautious, secret and above all successful. The position was very bad: debt was £226,910, whereas revenue was only £200,000: the needs of defence were heavy and expensive: what Gresham had to do was to raise loans abroad as cheaply as he could. But he himself insisted that the right policy was to borrow as little abroad as possible, to restore the purity of the coinage and to enforce the strictest economy. It is difficult to quarrel with this judgment. It is less easy to approve of his reiterated suggestion to restrict the sailing of the Merchant Adventurers' fleet, unless they agreed to what in fact was a forced loan.

During this period 1559–60 he worked hand in glove with Cecil—his letters were full of important political information. But Gresham's difficulties were very great. They were eased when Philip II recalled his troops from the Netherlands to Spain and when Elizabeth made the Treaty of Edinburgh with the Scots and French. At once the rate of interest fell at Antwerp to 10%. In 1562 Elizabeth for political reasons backed the Huguenots: Gresham wrote, 'this pen can not write you' the bad effect on credit.

Gresham had for some time urged that the coinage should be reformed. That the reform was undertaken was mainly his work. It was carried out under the supervision of Daniel Wolstrat of Antwerp. Elizabeth made a small profit out of the transaction.

In 1559 Gresham became temporary ambassador to the Regent of the Netherlands. To adorn this office with proper dignity he was knighted. His letters to Cecil are full of political information of the highest value: he clearly foresaw the revolt of the Netherlands against Philip II, and he was very successful in bribing the Spanish officials to provide him with the fullest information. The danger to England was very great. Military stores were sorely needed. Gresham found much difficulty in supplying them from the Netherlands. He urged the manufacture of gunpowder in England, but he also spread a rumour abroad in the Netherlands that England had 200 ships ready and well-armed. In the event, he secured large quantities of ammunition and exported them as 'velvets'. He also extracted 2,000 corselets out of the King of Spain's armoury at Malines. He was on the whole very successful in his efforts, but his financial transactions (out of which he made a pile for himself) and the secrecy of his correspondence with Cecil raised up many enemies against him who delated him to the queen, but she knew when she was 'on to a good thing', and paid no attention to the accusations.

In 1560 Gresham had a fall from his horse and broke his leg. This seriously affected his health and he was lame for the rest of his life. He was called home the next year in order to help his recovery, but he was soon going back and forth between England and Antwerp, mainly in order to raise loans, also sometimes on diplomatic missions.

When the government in 1568 seized the Spanish treasure, Gresham advised the Queen to have the treasure coined and put at the disposal of the merchants, from whom the government could borrow at low rates of interest. The advice was taken and Gresham arranged the whole business.

The importance of Antwerp had for some time been declining and Hamburg was taking its place as a mercantile centre. Gresham secretly supplied the Merchant Adventurers with money to keep two cloth fleets at Hamburg to strengthen Elizabeth's credit there. Between 1570 and 1574 Gresham was often writing to the government complaining of its dilatoriness in repaying the debts owed to English merchants. In 1574 he ceased to be the Queen's agent, as his health was bad and his leg was giving him much trouble.

Gresham does not seem to have incurred much personal risk in his loans: on the contrary, he made enormous profits for himself out of his work for the Crown and it is clear that he was often very unscrupulous in his methods. The audit of 1574 (the last audit had been made eleven years before) showed that he had received in the interval £677,248 4s. 3d. and had expended £659,099 2s. 1½d. After certain deductions and allowances had been adjusted, Gresham was found to owe the Crown £10,000, but he worked out the sum so as to put the government in his debt to the tune of £11,506 18s. 0¼d. The commissioners disputed his claim. Gresham got hold of a duplicate copy of his accounts, added a footnote acknowledging his claim, went off to Kenilworth where the Queen was staying and got her sanction to his claim. Armed with this, he compelled the commissioners to sign the acknowledgment.

Ten years earlier (1564) Gresham's only son had died. He therefore decided to use his immense wealth for the benefit of the public by building a bourse or Exchange. His father had originally suggested the scheme and Clough had urged Gresham to build it in 1562. In 1564 Gresham offered to build it, if a site were provided. The Merchant Adventurers and staplers put up the money for the site and in 1566 the foundation-stone was laid. Gresham employed a Flemish architect, one Henryke, who had a hand in some of the stone work at Burghley, which has since disappeared. The wood came from Battisford, near his own home at Ringshall in Suffolk. Clough saw to the exporting from Antwerp of most of the other materials. The building was ready for use in 1568. Two years later Queen Elizabeth visited the building and gave orders for it to be called the Royal Exchange. Gresham's building was destroyed by fire in 1666. (For an illustration, see

Summerson, *Architecture in Britain 1530–1830*, Pelican History of Art, plate 66A.)

Gresham also founded Gresham College in London where free lectures were to be given (1575). This caused a quarrel with Cambridge University. He bequeathed Gresham House to the college on the death of his wife, but the plan was never very successful, although lectures are still given there.

In 1569 Gresham was put in charge of Lady Mary Keys, sister of Lady Jane Grey, who had made an imprudent marriage. He hated the post and was continually asking to be relieved and he was replaced probably in 1573. He died very suddenly on November 21st, 1579, and was buried in St. Helen's, Bishopsgate.

Sir Thomas Gresham was a shrewd, level-headed, self-confident man, blessed with foresight, a great capacity for hard work, 'a jewel for trust, wit and diligent endeavour.' (quoted in *D.N.B.*). He does not seem to have been a genius, and his famous law, 'Gresham's Law', that 'bad money drives out good', did no more than epitomize what many shrewd men of commonsense fully understood. He had no original ideas, he never questioned the economic ideas of his times, but he was a wonderful bargainer in negotiating loans, he recognized the evil of a debased coinage, though he probably did not recognize the evil of having two standard metals, gold and silver. (see Salter, *Sir Thomas Gresham*). He was a staunch Protestant.

(Plate 19)

J. W. Burgon. *Life and Times of Sir Thomas Gresham*, 2 vols. 1839, still the standard life.

F. R. Salter, *Sir Thomas Gresham*, Roadmaker series, 1925.

PALAVICINO, SIR HORATIO, financier and diplomatist, was born at Genoa about 1540, the son of Tobias Palavicino, a member of the wealthy, aristocratic banking family in Northern Italy, which was closely connected with most of the powerful Italian banking firms. He died in 1600, aged about 60. The family business was based on handling the papal monopoly in alum, a commodity greatly in demand in the Netherlands and England for the cloth trade. In 1578 Horatio sold the family stocks of alum at Antwerp to the Dutch rebels in return for an import monopoly which excluded all future farmers of the papal alum monopoly. The Dutch did not pay cash: Queen Elizabeth of England underwrote the loan in order to keep the Dutch revolt against Spain alive. In other words, she borrowed from Palavicino £29,000. In 1579 Sir Thomas Gresham, the English government's chief financial agent, died. It was necessary to find a successor, a man who had intimate knowledge of international high finance, was an expert in currency exchange, who could handle the transfer of large sums of money from one financial centre to another, to ambassadors and secret agents, who could find the ready cash for subsidies to allies, who was ready and able to turn ambassador (or spy) himself, and whose reputation created confidence and credit. Only Horatio Palavicino fulfilled all these requirements, and on top of this he could at need act as a secret agent.

In 1586 he was given a full diplomatic mission as ambassador to the Protestant princes in North-Western Europe to raise an army for the invasion of Eastern France. He became a naturalized Englishman and was knighted by Elizabeth. He lost the queen's favour when she discovered the profits Horatio had made out of the 1578 loan. He had lent her £29,000: in 1592 she repaid him £4,425 of the capital, the only repayment she ever made. But by that time Horatio had cleared £41,053 in interest alone. Between 1594 and 1600 he was engaged in increasing his own wealth and investing it in land. His methods were ruthless, unsavoury and highly successful. He speculated in corn and earned great hatred for the distress he caused in time of famine by raising the price. He bought *objets d'art* for his clients; he arranged the ransom of prisoners, notably Spanish prisoners from the Armada; he lent money on the most exorbitant conditions; he tried to make a corner, but failed, in the world supply of pepper. By the time he died in 1600 he was the richest commoner in the land, worth at least £100,000, and he had accumulated 8,000 acres in three counties. He was interested in sheep-farming and devoted some 2,600 acres to pasture. At his home at Babraham in Cambridgeshire he was something of a pioneer in agriculture, in experimenting in irrigating his meadows.

Palavicino was an unpleasant man, ruthless in pursuit of wealth, harsh as a landlord. He was impetuous and emotional, but also cold and calculating. He remained on friendly and even affectionate terms with the Cecils and the Earl of Shrewsbury, yet he was notorious for the duplicity with which he treated his debtors. His intellectual powers were considerable, his abilities enormous. He spoke six languages, his interests were wide and varied—for example, he studied naval and military affairs and served at sea against the Armada. He began life as a Catholic and changed over gradually to the new faith, influenced by the cruel treatment meted out to his brother by the Pope at the time of the alum crisis in 1578 (his brother was tortured), but doubtless as much influenced by the £29,000 owed to him by a Protestant queen. After his death his second wife married Sir Oliver Cromwell of Hinchinbrook, his son Henry (aged 14) married Catherine, Sir Oliver's daughter by a first marriage, his son Toby married her sister Jane, and his daughter Baptina married her brother Henry. Sir Oliver was the great-uncle of Oliver Cromwell, the Protector.

Lawrence Stone, *Sir Horatio Palavicino*, 1956, O.U.P.

WENTWORTH, PETER, parliamentary critic of royal prerogative, was born about 1524 (not 1530, as in the *D.N.B.*), and died in 1596 at the approximate age of seventy-two. He was the elder son of Sir Nicholas Wentworth of Lillingstone Lovell, a village at that time in a piece of Oxfordshire surrounded by Buckinghamshire, but by the time Peter succeeded his father the village had been absorbed into Buckinghamshire. He was twice married; first, to Letitia Lane, whose mother was a cousin to Catherine Parr; secondly, to Elizabeth, sister of Sir Frances Walsingham. He entered Lincoln's Inn in 1542, but it was not until 1571, when he was just on forty-seven years of age, that he entered Parliament as member for Barnstaple. 'I was first stirred up to deal in it . . . by God's good motion, then by sundry grave and wise men unknown unto me, and also by lamentable messages sent unto me by men likewise unknown unto me.' He was to sit in six parliaments during the next twenty-two years, as member for Barnstaple, then Tregony, and lastly for Northampton. He was a man 'of a whet and vehement spirit', which got him into frequent and serious trouble with the Queen for the attacks he made upon her, although he had a passionate love and reverence for her.

In his first parliament of 1571 he was a member of the committee which was formed in the House of Commons to submit a bill dealing with the Articles of Religion to the Archbishop, Matthew Parker. Parker asked why the Articles for the Homilies and some other matters had been omitted. Wentworth's answer was, 'Surely sir, because we were so occupied in other matters that we had no time to examine them, how they agreed with the word of God.' 'What!' said Parker, 'surely you mistook the matter. You will refer yourselves wholly to us therein.' Wentworth retorted, 'No, by the faith I bear to God, we will pass nothing before we understand what it is, for that were but to make you Popes. Make you Popes who list, for we will make you none.' In this same parliament Sir Humphrey Gilbert made a speech defending the privileges of the Crown. Wentworth made a violent attack on Gilbert, noting 'his disposition to flatter or fawn on the Prince, comparing him to the chameleon, which can change himself into all colours saving white'.

The discovery of the Ridolfi Plot in 1571 necessitated the calling of another parliament. Wentworth was returned for the seat of Tregony. Great pressure was put on the Queen to execute Mary, Queen of Scots, or at least to attaint her: Elizabeth preferred to delay the attainder, but she sent for the committees of both Houses and treated them with such tact that the Commons moved a resolution that the thanks of the House be given to her. Wentworth opposed the resolution to return thanks, 'the which for my part I did not think her Majesty had deserved, so that my speech was to stay thanks'.

Parliament met again after an interval of three and a half years, in February 1575/6. During the interval Wentworth brooded on his experience in the Commons. He thought the

House was too subservient to the Queen. On the 8th Wentworth made a resolution on liberty of speech. He forthrightly attacked the Queen for the 'great faults' she had committed. 'It is a dangerous thing in a Prince unkindly to intreat and abuse his or her nobility and people, as her Majesty did the last Parliament...' Sir John Neale has called this 'the most remarkable speech hitherto conceived in the Parliament of England.... He was wrong, utterly wrong in his own generation; but the future hallowed his doctrine. He, indeed, as much as any of his colleagues, shaped that future' (*Eliz. and her Parlts.* 1559–1581, pp. 318–25). The House stopped him, committed him to the serjeant's ward and appointed a committee to examine him 'for the extenuating of his fault'. As a result Wentworth was sent to the Tower, where he remained for rather more than a month: then the Queen ordered his release and sent a very magnanimous message to the House of Commons. Wentworth was brought to the bar of the House, where he made a humble submission on his knees and was then allowed to take his seat again.

In 1579 Wentworth was in trouble with the Council. His bishop complained that many Puritans were resorting to his house at Lillingstone Lovell, where they received the Sacrament in Puritan fashion. Sir John Harington noted that Wentworth was 'a man of great accompt with all of that profession' in his neighbourhood.

Wentworth was not a member of the 1584/5 Parliament, but he was returned for Northampton to the Parliament of 1586/7, made necessary by the Babington Plot. An attempt to reform the Church along Presbyterian lines failed in the Commons, because the Queen put a stop to it. Wentworth held that she thereby infringed the rights of the House. He therefore determined to make the Commons define their own rights to freedom of speech and no longer accept a definition laid down by the executive. He proposed to the House a series of questions, the answers to which would remain as the rulings of the House. Once more Wentworth, and four others, were sent to the Tower, not apparently for any speech made by them in the House, but for 'conferences in matters of religion' held outside the House where privilege did not arise. In fact, an organized campaign against the Elizabethan church settlement was being made and the Queen would have none of it. The Puritans had only narrowly failed to win their case in Convocation in the '60s. They were now fighting in Parliament. Puritanism was also changing its character: in the past it had been a protest of Puritan clergy against religion being subordinated to politics. By Wentworth's time in the '80s it was beginning to be a protest of Puritan squires against control of the state by the bishops.

Up to this point Wentworth had been the champion of free speech, for he saw that the way for the Puritan cause to triumph was to make it a struggle for privilege in the House of Commons. If he could win freedom of speech there, the Queen could no longer put a stop to the attacks on the Church. From 1587, however, he ceased to think in terms of parliamentary privilege and became entirely taken up with the problem of the succession to the throne.

It is not known when Wentworth was released from the Tower. In 1587 he drafted *A Pithie Exhortation to her Majestie for establishing her successor to the crowne*. The tract urged the Queen to nominate the heir to the throne: it drew a fearful picture of what would happen to England if she were to die without having established her successor: and it also warned her of the dreadful fate which would befall her own body and her own soul. Wentworth failed to win any sympathy for his course of action, and, when the Parliament ended, nothing had been done. In 1590 he tried to interest the Earl of Essex in his plan, but news of what was in his tract leaked out and he was summoned before the Council and put in the Gatehouse (August 1591). For a second time he tried to use Burghley to bring the Queen over to his way of thinking, and of course failed. He was treated very leniently and was released on November 21st.

Ever an optimist, Wentworth was now convinced that the Queen would call a parliament and declare the name of the heir to the throne. When she did call a parliament in 1593, he fully expected this to happen. He prepared a campaign for the House of Commons and called some friends together to discuss his speech, the bill he had drafted, a petition to the House of Lords, a thanksgiving if the Queen agreed, and an attack on her if she refused. Few were ready to support Wentworth's scheme and then news of his intentions leaked out. He was summoned before the Council and once again found himself in the Tower. He never left that prison. He was not badly treated, he had considerable liberty and his wife was allowed to be with him. In 1594 he wrote his *Discourse containing the Author's opinion of the true and lawful successor to her Majesty* (published 1598). This was an answer to Father Parsons' *Conference about the Next Succession to the Crown of England*, in which the Jesuit repudiated the doctrine of divine hereditary right and argued that Parliament could make null the hereditary right of James VI of Scotland to the English throne. Wentworth refuted Parsons' arguments and supported the right of James to succeed Elizabeth. He had previously been against the Scotch claim, perhaps because he was opposed to the succession of Mary, Queen of Scots. Her execution removed this stumbling block, but Wentworth found himself opposing Parsons for over-exalting Parliament. (Neale, *Eliz. and her Parlts.* 1584–1601, p. 262). Efforts were made to secure his release, but these for unknown reasons failed. Wentworth died in the Tower in 1596.

The Queen's policy on the succession problem was subtle, characteristic and successful, not to take action when no action was needed, to keep the succession uncertain, to dangle it in front of James VI, 'to be given or withheld according to his behaviour' (Neale, *Eliz. and her Parlts.* 1584–1601, 251–2). Wentworth wanted to wreck that policy: Elizabeth could only treat him as she did. He was wrong from first to last, but he was a man of passionate conviction, passionately devoted to the Queen and to his country, but he totally lacked self-criticism. One of his contemporaries said of him that 'Mr. Wentworth will never acknowledge himself to make a fault nor say that he is sorry for anything he doth speak'. The Queen once said of him, 'Mr. Wentworth has a good opinion of his own wit'. In his fight for freedom of speech he was far ahead of his own times: but he would not have extended freedom of speech to his opponents: it was lucky for the Stuarts that Wentworth was not in the House of Commons in days when he would have found much more support than he found in his own day: it was lucky for Wentworth that he was dealt with by a comparatively lenient sovereign, for he would have had shorter shrift from Charles I than he got from Elizabeth. Wentworth was a symbol of his own age—the fiery spirit of Essex and Ralegh burned as high in him; but he was also a pointer to the future, a forerunner of Pym and Hampden, but not a progenitor of the Earl of Strafford.

Sir John Neale, *English Historical Review*, xxxix, 36 *sqq.*, 175 *sqq.*, *Elizabeth and Her Parliaments*, 2 vols.
The article in the *D.N.B.* is unreliable for dates.

MARY, QUEEN OF SCOTS, was born in 1542 and was executed in 1587, aged forty-five. She was the third child and only daughter of James V of Scotland and of his wife, Marie de Guise. The rout of the Scottish army at Solway Moss had taken place on November 24th and Mary was born either on the 5th or 8th of December. It is said that in his despair over the military defeat James V, on hearing the news of the birth of his daughter, cried out, 'it came with a lass and it will pass with a lass', and turned his face to the wall and died on December 14th. Mary was, therefore, one week old when she became Queen of Scots. Negotiations at once began for her marriage with Edward VI of England, but these were frustrated on religious grounds by Cardinal Beaton. On September 10th, 1547, Protector Somerset, determined to bring about the marriage, defeated the Scots at Pinkie Cleugh (*T.S.I.H.*, vol. 2, pp. 40–2). The Scots now made a marriage alliance with the French, and on August 7th, 1548, at the age of 6, Mary sailed for France to marry the Dauphin, Francis, son of Henry II and Catherine de Medici.

Mary was brought up at the French court with the children of the royal family. Her education was purely French, she learned neither English nor Scotch, which makes one suspect Neale's reference to her 'pretty Scottish accent' (Neale,

Elizabeth, p. 166).* The court was soon impressed by her intelligence, her charm, her beauty and personality. She was brought up a strict Roman Catholic in the midst of a cultured and far from strict court, but the freedom of the court would seem to have affected her more than the strict discipline of the Church, if one is to judge by her later history. Yet, in truth, her position was an impossible one. She had never known Scotland, yet she was Queen of that country: she married on April 24th, 1558, a weak and sickly husband, Francis, heir to the French throne. She might thus combine the two kingdoms of France and Scotland, and she was heir to the throne of England. Yet before her marriage she had signed away Scotland to France, on the terms that if she died without an heir, Scotland was to go as a free gift to the King of France, with all her rights to the English throne, and any assent she might be compelled to make to any different arrangement by the Scots was to be null and void from the start. That that was a betrayal of her native country cannot be denied, but what did her native country mean to a girl of 16 who had left it at the age of 6?

In the year when Mary married Francis (1558) Mary I of England died and the Protestant Elizabeth came to the English throne. Mary at once claimed the English throne on the grounds of Elizabeth's illegitimacy. She quartered the arms of England with those of France and assumed the style and titles of the ruler of England—and she used them even after her accession to the French throne, on the death of Henry II, in 1559. The English Queen was not unreasonably incensed.

On June 10th, 1560, Marie de Guise died, which removed the Regent and created a feeling in some Scottish minds that the real Queen ought to return. On December 5th Francis II died and Mary was left a widow at the age of 18, with no throne in France, excluded from court by the jealousy of the regent, Catherine de Medici, and with the prospect of return-

* But *cf.* Gore-Browne, *Lord Bothwell*, p. 112, n. 1. '*Scotice respondere cœpit*, when Master John Rivat was present to translate her French to Father Edmund Hay (J. H. Pollen, *Papal Negotiations with Queen Mary*, 17.)

ing to Scotland, where the Roman religion was proscribed and
the Reformation was in full swing under John Knox. The
Protestant lords were trying to arrange a marriage between
James, the second Earl of Arran, who was heir to the Scottish
throne after Mary, and Elizabeth of England. Scotland was
a wild, uncivilized and heretical country, turbulent and split
into factions. To return from France to Scotland was an act
of great courage, especially as few of the lords seemed to want
Mary. Elizabeth refused the Arran marriage: at once a
reaction in favour of Mary set in.

The period of the negotiations for her return shows Mary at
her best. She offered to forget all troubles of the past, she
wanted to be recalled by the Scots, and she agreed not to
interfere with the new Protestant religion of Scotland. But
even at that moment she was playing a double game. She had
not made up her mind to go back. She was desperately anxious
to marry. The Guises backed her, hoping to recover their
influence in French politics. But all proposals for Mary's
marriage were thwarted by Catherine de Medici. At last Mary
determined to go back to Scotland. It was an inauspicious
moment from the point of view of Elizabeth. Mary was heir
to the English throne: she was a Catholic, and the treaty of
Edinburgh between Elizabeth and the Scottish Protestant
lords was as yet unsigned. Trouble was bound to ensue.

Mary sailed from Calais on August 15th, 1561. She had a
cheerless journey, she was delayed outside Leith by a dense fog
(Knox saw in this 'the sorrow, dolour, darkness and all im-
piety' which her arrival betokened), and no preparations
had been made for her at Holyrood. Mass was said in her
private chapel on the first Sunday, which resulted in a stormy
interview between Mary and Knox, who came away impressed
only by 'her proud mind, crafty wit and indurate heart'. (Knox
is no reliable witness.) And indeed her passions—always so
much stronger than her political judgments—led her into a
great error. She had told Moray that she did not want to
interfere with the religion of Scotland: but in fact she had
already told the Pope that she meant to restore Catholicism to
Scotland. And now she burst out at Knox: 'Ye are not the

kirk I will nourish. I will defend the Kirk of Rome, for I believe it is the true Kirk of God.'

Mary's aims now were wholly selfish. She had no patriotism left for France: she had none for Scotland: she meant to get the English throne by hook or by crook. Her expressed desire for friendship with Elizabeth was as little genuine as Elizabeth's for hers. In the meantime, her government of Scotland won her golden opinions for her discretion, but some thought politics sat lightly upon her. Knox noted that 'in the council she kept herself very grave: but as soon as ever her French fillocks and fiddlers and others of that brand gat the house alone, then might be seen skipping not very comely for honest women': and he thought she preferred to hawk and to 'shoot at the butts'. Mary now wrote to Elizabeth to say that if her claims were not admitted, she would seek the remedies provided for those 'who have been enormously and excessively hurt'.

Mary's immediate objective was marriage. She wanted to marry Don Carlos, son of Philip II, and thus to combine in her own person the thrones of England, Scotland and Spain. To accomplish this she was ready to restore Catholicism in Scotland. But the Guises were opposed to and prevented the marriage. Elizabeth suggested Robert Dudley, Earl of Leicester, but in 1565 there arrived in Scotland Henry Stewart, Lord Darnley, the elder son of the Earl of Lennox and Margaret, daughter of Margaret Tudor, sister of Henry VIII, and the Earl of Lennox. Thus Darnley was heir to the English throne after Mary herself. He was aged 19, extraordinarily handsome, very athletic, of the meanest intelligence, arrogant, wilful and vicious. Whether Mary did in fact fall in love with Darnley has been disputed. That she did would seem to be her only justification. If the marriage was simply a political move to strengthen her claim to the English throne, her intelligence failed to reveal to her that Darnley, a Catholic, could only further bind together the English and the Scottish Protestants, could only alarm the Scottish Protestant lords for the safety of their lands, and threaten the hopes of the Hamiltons of reaching the throne of

Scotland (Rait, *History of Scotland*, p. 71). At any rate, she married him, perhaps secretly in March, certainly publicly in July 1565. From this ill-judged marriage sprang most of Mary's future troubles.

Darnley was hateful to the Scottish lords, largely on account of his arrogance, his imprudence and his viciousness. Hateful also was David Riccio, one of Mary's musical quartet whom she now raised to be her foreign secretary. Moray headed a rebellion, which Mary succeeded in putting down, but she had already found out her mistake in marrying Darnley. His discontent that she refused to give him the Crown Matrimonial (*i.e.* the reversion of the throne to him, were Mary to die first), his weakness of character, and his accusations that she was Riccio's mistress, soon turned her love to hatred. The murder of Riccio in 1566 (see *T.S.I.H.*, vol. 2, pp. 68–71) was followed by the imprisonment of the Queen by the lords, but Mary escaped with Darnley, with whom she put up as well as possible until her son was born in June 1566. It is at least probable that she was already in love with Bothwell and anxious to be rid of Darnley. (A fairly argued case, on the whole favourable to Mary, denying that she was in love with Bothwell, will be found in Schiern's *James Hepburn, Earl of Bothwell*, chapter iv, but even Schiern at the end admits that, if Mary was not in love with Bothwell, her subsequent behaviour is incomprehensible.) He had just married Jane Gordon, sister of the Earl of Huntly, but within a matter of weeks he had made up his mind to secure the Scottish throne by marrying Mary. When Darnley fell ill at Glasgow—it was said of small-pox, almost certainly of syphilis—Mary attended him frequently, then fetched him away to an isolated house outside Edinburgh, Kirk o' Field, where he might have better air than in the city, the arrangements being left in the hands of Bothwell. She left Darnley there late in the evening of February 9th, 1567, and went in the company of Bothwell to Holyrood. Early in the morning of the 10th the house at Kirk o' Field was blown up and the body of Darnley was found under a tree, uninjured by the explosion: he had been strangled before the explosion took place. There is no proof

that Mary had any hand in the murder of her husband, nor
that she even knew it was to take place, since the only pur-
ported evidence contained in the Casket Letters must on the
whole be rejected. Yet, if she was wholly innocent, her subsequent behaviour with the universally accepted murderer,
Bothwell, requires much more explanation than has so far
been forthcoming. (But see Gore-Browne, *Lord Bothwell*,
pp. 303–23, for a most ingenious piece of detective reasoning.)
She made no attempt to exonerate herself when the populace
was vociferously accusing her, as she went through the streets.
She showered favours on Bothwell, probably agreed to a
collusive abduction, and within three months of Darnley's
death she had married the by then divorced Bothwell, who was
the universally accepted murderer of Darnley (May 16th,
1567). Never had Mary behaved with less wisdom or discretion.

Once again Mary's passions had outrun her judgment—
or so one is justified in saying, until further evidence in her
favour is available. Fairly or unfairly, all Europe turned
against her—France, Spain, Pope and her own subjects. The
Scottish lords raised an army against her, Mary and Bothwell
gathered a small force (mostly adherents of Bothwell's) to meet
them. At Carberry Hill, seven miles outside Edinburgh
(June 1567), the two sides met, but Mary's army dwindled
away without any battle being fought. She was forced to
abdicate and was imprisoned in a castle on Loch Leven.
Bothwell escaped to Norway. In 1568 Mary escaped from
Loch Leven, raised a force to meet her half-brother, the
Regent, Earl of Moray, but she was defeated at Langside, fled
to England and threw herself on the mercy of her very unwilling
cousin, Elizabeth of England. A Commission was set up to
investigate her guilt in the murder of Darnley. Elizabeth
refused to accept the evidence of the Casket Letters; she held
that nothing had been proved either way; she refused to send
Mary back to Scotland, but she put her into prison of one sort
or another in England, where Mary remained for the rest of
her life.

Mary now became the centre, witting or unwitting, of every
Catholic plot against the life of Elizabeth. Without doubt the

extreme Catholics used her for their own ends: without doubt Mary was a party to half their plots. She came to approve political assassination too many times for Elizabeth to feel safe or for anybody to believe her protestations. When her brother Moray was murdered (1570), she wrote to Cardinal Beaton that 'she was the more indebted to the assassin that he had acted without her instigation': but she told Moray's widow that the murder was done 'against our will'. She agreed to the plot by which she was to marry the Duke of Norfolk: she was a party to the Ridolfi plot (1571) which was linked with Norfolk's plot: she was pleading with Elizabeth for kindness and at the same moment she was hand in glove with Throckmorton in his plot for the invasion of England and the taking off of Elizabeth (1583): by her own actions she hopelessly entangled herself in the Babington Plot (1586), for she dictated a letter to Babington which gave her consent to a rising on her behalf which was to include the murder of Elizabeth. Her arrest, trial and condemnation followed inevitably. For a long time Elizabeth refused to sign the death warrant, but at last she gave way and Mary was beheaded at Fotheringay Castle on February 8th, 1587 (*T.S.I.H.*, vol. 2, pp. 75–7).

Mary Stuart has been fortunate in her biographers beyond her deserts. Largely through her dignity and courage at her execution, the spell which she failed to exert on most of her contemporaries she has succeeded in casting on her modern biographers. Mary, Queen of Scots, has become a legendary figure, a shamefully wronged woman, beautiful (Clouet has done his very good best for her), pathetic, romantic and pitiable. Swinburne wrote of her that 'the world never saw more splendid courage at the service of more brilliant intelligence'. That is a travesty of the truth.

It is doubtful how much intelligence she had: it failed her over Darnley and over Bothwell. She had some courage, as in deciding to return to Scotland from France—but what other choice was open to her? That courage failed her after Carberry when, in the Provost's house in Edinburgh, she was seen at the window half-naked and screaming for help. It failed her again after Langside, when she fled to England as fast as a horse could carry her, before her cause was irretrievably lost (Acton, *Lectures on Modern History*, p. 149). And it is difficult not to feel that much of her behaviour in prison in England was unheroic.

It is easy to say that no woman, placed in Mary's circumstances, could have succeeded where she failed (Bowen, *The Great Tudors*, p. 398). It is as easy to say that in any other circumstances Mary would as surely have ruined her own life. She was a woman destitute of all moral sense, incapable of self-sacrifice, concerned only with her own selfish ends. It is not even true that she remained faithful to the Catholic religion: she abandoned it in order to get the Scottish throne; she would have abandoned it, if there had been the slightest chance of her winning the English throne through the English Protestants. And she, the Queen, had not enough authority or will to marry Bothwell according to the Roman ceremony. Mary, Queen of Scots, is pitiable in that she had not enough character to control her passions: it is only by falsifying values, Protestant or Catholic, that she can be called admirable.

(*Plate 21*)

R. S. Rait, *Mary, Queen of Scots, Her Life and Reign*, 1900.
T. F. Henderson, *Mary, Queen of Scots*, 2 vols., 1905.
G. Buchanan, *The Tyrannous Reign of Mary Stewart*, ed. by Gatherer, 1958: deliberately perverted history, but good reading with corrections *passim*.
Jane Oliver, *Queen Most Fair*. (H.N., 1960.)

STUART, HENRY, LORD DARNLEY, second husband of Mary, Queen of Scots, was born at Temple Newsam in Yorkshire in 1545 and was murdered in 1567. He was the second but eldest surviving son of Matthew Stuart, Earl of Lennox, and his wife, Lady Margaret Douglas, Countess of Lennox, daughter of Margaret Tudor, widow of James IV of Scotland, by her second husband the Earl of Angus: Margaret Tudor was the aunt of Elizabeth I, therefore Darnley, who had been born in England and was an English subject, was next legal heir to the English throne after Mary,

Queen of Scots, if Elizabeth were to die childless. In 1560 de Quadra, the Spanish ambassador, reported to Philip II that if that were to happen the English Catholics would put Darnley on to the English throne. The Countess of Lennox— 'a very wise and discreet matron' (Sir James Melville's *Memoirs*, 1929 ed., p. 99)—was at that time corresponding with the Scottish Catholic lords about marrying Darnley to Mary, Queen of Scots. The Countess and Darnley, therefore, found themselves shut up in the Tower for a time by Elizabeth, who thought it worth while to deny the legitimacy of the Countess on the grounds that her mother had got a Papal divorce from Angus (1527) and that the Scottish estates had declared her to be a bastard. Mother and son were soon released and Darnley was daily at Elizabeth's court.

In 1564 Sir James Melville was sent by Mary to Elizabeth to get permission for Darnley to visit Scotland in order to 'see the country'. At that moment Elizabeth was suggesting that Mary should marry Robert Dudley, Earl of Leicester, but she very well knew the real purpose of the visit, for she said to Melville, 'ye like better of yon long lad, pointing towards my Lord Darnley. . . . My answer was that no woman of spirit would make choice of such a man, who resembled more a woman than a man. For he was handsome, beardless and lady-faced' (Melville, *ibid.*, p. 92). All the same, probably because she feared that Mary might in fact marry Leicester, Elizabeth sent Darnley to Scotland, 'in hope that he being a handsome, lusty youth, should rather prevail, being present, than Leicester who was absent' (*ibid.*, p. 101).

Darnley arrived at Wemyss Castle on February 18th, 1565, where he stayed with Mary for two or three days. It is probable, though disputable, that Mary at once fell desperately in love with 'the properest, and best proportioned long man that she had ever seen: for he was of a high stature, long and small, even and straight' (Melville, *ibid.*, p. 107). Darnley was indeed handsome and notably athletic, by repute a good musician on the lute; but his intelligence was of the meanest and he was vain, arrogant, irritable and vicious by the time he was twenty years of age.

The marriage between Darnley and Mary was chiefly engineered by Riccio, who was by this time rapidly advancing in the Queen's favour and confidence. Darnley was knighted and created Earl of Ross, later Duke of Albany, and it is possible that he and Mary were secretly married in March 1565. In April Darnley fell ill of the measles and Mary was assiduous in her attentions to him. On July 29th their public marriage took place in the chapel of Holyrood (1565).

From the moment that he arrived in Scotland Darnley was hated by the Protestant lords, because he was a Catholic. In next to no time he was universally hated for his extreme unwisdom. He chose as his friends the most disreputable of the Scottish nobles, his pride was 'intolerable' and 'his words not to be borne'. Politically he was a menace, for he could not keep his tongue quiet—'few durst advertise him, . . . because he told all again to some of his own servants, who were not all honest' (Melville, *ibid.*, p. 145). Then he took to drink and treated the Queen so shamefully in public that she 'left the house in tears'. Mary knew now what a fatal marriage she had made. She refused Darnley the Crown Matrimonial and she began to advance Riccio to the political importance which should have been Darnley's. Darnley's position was becoming increasingly difficult and there were some of his relations who were offended by his humiliation.

Hated as Darnley was, Riccio was soon even more hated, as a Catholic, as a foreigner, and for his arrogant behaviour. He was virtually the Queen's Prime Minister and all business was conducted by him. Darnley's Catholic friends and Protestant enemies now combined for a moment to murder Riccio. Darnley was not only privy to the plot, but he insisted on being present at the murder, because so great had his hatred for his wife become that he accused her of being Riccio's mistress. Riccio had done him 'the most dishonour that could be to any man'. On Saturday evening, March 9th, 1565, Darnley admitted the conspirators—Moray, Morton, Ruthven and others—into Holyrood and led them up by the private staircase into the room where Mary was dining with Riccio. After the murder was committed it was Darnley's

dagger which was left in Riccio's side—borrowed for the
purpose by the nobles, who were determined to make him
appear as the instigator of and sharer in the deed (*T.S.I.H.*,
vol. 2, pp. 68–71).

For political reasons Mary could not at once break with
Darnley. She promised him his proper position as her husband.
Darnley told her 'all that he knew of any man' in the conspiracy. There was a brief reconciliation, but almost at once
Mary discovered Darnley's share in the plot. She never
forgave him, but she was pregnant and she would do nothing
to jeopardize the legitimacy of her child. She began to favour
Moray, Maitland and others who hated Darnley. His position
was impossible and he determined to leave the country. The
nobles met at Craigmillar and determined to be rid of Darnley.
Darnley refused to attend the christening of his son at Stirling,
left for Glasgow to find a ship to take him abroad, but he fell
ill, almost certainly of syphilis, and could not go. Mary was now
in love with Bothwell, but she brought about a reconciliation
with Darnley and persuaded him, when he was convalescent, to
go with her to Edinburgh. She took him to an isolated house at
Kirk o' Field, outside Edinburgh, left him there on the evening
of February 9th, 1566, and went to Edinburgh with Bothwell.
Early in the morning of the 10th the house was blown up.
Darnley's body and that of his page were found under a tree,
unmarked by the explosion: they had been strangled before
the house was blown up.

Darnley's body was buried in the tomb of James V in the
chapel of Holyrood.   (*Plate 21*)

A biography of Darnley is to be found in the *Life of Mary* by
  Chalmers. A detailed account of the Kirk o' Field murder
  is to be found in chapter v of Schiern's *James Hepburn, Earl
  of Bothwell*, translated from the Danish by the Rev. David
  Berry, 1880.

RICCIO (or **RIZZIO**), **DAVID**, secretary to Mary,
Queen of Scots, was born probably in 1533 and died in 1566
at the age of 33. Generally reputed in his own day and for
centuries since to have been the low-born son of a teacher of

music at Turin, David is now thought to have come of a noble and wealthy family in Piedmont, that of Riccio di Solbitro. If this is true, then his poverty may have been a pose and his true status well known to the Queen. He is said to have had a pleasing bass voice and to have played the lute (Sir James Melville in his *Memoirs*, p. 103, ed. 1929, calls him 'a merry fellow and a good musician'), to have spent some time at the court of the Duke of Savoy, and then at the age of twenty-eight to have arrived in Scotland in the wake of Morette, who was on a mission for the Duke (1561). Mary had three *valets de chambre* who sang in her private chapel and she was looking for a fourth to complete the quartette. Riccio applied for the post and was accepted. He held this position for some years and then in 1564 the Queen's French secretary, Raulet, was dismissed for having been corrupted by English gold and Riccio was appointed in his place. A hostile writer, Randolph, had it that Riccio 'croope in on suspicion gathered against Raulet'. Mary was at this point planning to take the direction of policy entirely into her own hands and she feared that her French secretary might betray her to her uncle of Lorraine. The new appointment cannot have been a great success, for Melville records that 'advices given by the Queen of England were misconstructed . . . partly because David Riccio, lately admitted to be French secretary, was not very skilful in inditing French letters, which she [Mary] did write over again in her own hand' (*ibid.*, p. 23). One of the grounds for Riccio's unpopularity was that many looked on him as a Papal agent (Melville called him to Mary 'a known minion of the Pope', *ibid.*, p. 106), but he was never acknowledged as such by the Papacy.

At this point two things are certain—first, 'the extraordinary favour [which Mary] carried to that man' (Melville, *ibid.*, p. 105): secondly, that it was Riccio who was the chief manipulator of the Darnley marriage. Melville again noted that Riccio was Darnley's 'great friend at the Queen's hand' (*ibid.*, p. 107). Darnley and Riccio were at first intimate friends, playing tennis together by day and sharing the same bed by night.

It is possible and perhaps probable that Riccio arranged a secret marriage before the public wedding on July 29th, 1565. After that date Riccio virtually became secretary of state. It did not take Mary long after her marriage to find out what a disastrous mistake she had made. Her hatred for the insufferable Darnley grew, and as it grew Riccio attained the position which should have been that of Mary's husband. He became the Queen's adviser on all matters, even in the presence of the Scottish lords. The only road to royal favour was Riccio. Darnley demanded the Crown Matrimonial, but he was refused that and treated with (perhaps well deserved) contumely. The arrogance of Riccio became insupportable to the Scottish lords, as it was insupportable to Darnley. And his arrogance was encouraged by the Queen. Darnley's jealousy at last reached the point that he accused Mary of being Riccio's mistress. Darnley thereby played into the hands of those lords who hated Riccio. The murder of Riccio was the inevitable result.

As so often happens in conspiracies, enemies find themselves on the same side, bound together solely by hatred of a common enemy. Catholic relatives of Darnley resented his treatment by Riccio: Protestant lords saw in Riccio a Papal agent for restoring the Catholic religion in Scotland: many of both parties saw in Riccio the chief proposer for the bill to come before Parliament for confiscating the lands of those lords who had rebelled against Mary at the time of her marriage with Darnley. Norton, Moray, Lethington, Argyle, Ruthven combined to slaughter Riccio. All had a common aim, to be rid thereby of Mary. All were determined to make the murder appear the work of Darnley. Thus it was that Darnley's dagger was left in the side of Riccio. The murder took place in the evening of Saturday, March 9th, 1566, in the palace of Holyrood. Riccio was dragged from the very presence of the Queen when they were at supper and struck down outside with fifty-six sword strikes. His body was buried at first before the door of the abbey: later, by Mary's orders, it was laid in the royal tomb at Edinburgh, but then it was transferred to another part of the church.

For the murder of Riccio, see *T.S.I.H.*, vol. 2, pp. 68–71.
Conyers Read lists no biography of Riccio.
W. A. Gatherer, introduction to G. Buchanan's *The Tyrannous Reign of Mary Stuart*, pp. 22–4, 1958.

HEPBURN, JAMES, 4th EARL OF BOTHWELL, third husband of Mary, Queen of Scots, was born almost certainly in 1535 and died in 1578 at the age of 43. He was the son of Patrick Hepburn, third Earl of Bothwell, known as the Fair Earl, and his wife Agnes, daughter of Henry Lord Sinclair. He was brought up mostly in the home of his relative, Patrick Hepburn, bishop of Moray, where he acquired a better education than was usual among the nobles of Scotland at that time. His father died in 1556 and James inherited his hereditary offices, which included Warden of the Scottish Marches and Lord High Admiral of Scotland. Bothwell was a Protestant, but he supported the policy of the Catholic Queen Regent, Marie de Guise, and opposed Arran and the reforming lords. In 1557 he commanded an expedition which raided the English border lands and for the rest of his life he was unalterably hostile to England. In 1559 the English secretly arranged to supply the Protestant lords with £3,000 to help them against the French influence of Marie de Guise. When the money was sent north, Bothwell waylaid the conveyer of the cash and went off with it to his castle of Crichton, intending to hand it over to the Regent. Her confidence in Bothwell was so great that in 1560 she planned to send him to France to secure help in men and money, but she died in June of that year, whereupon Bothwell went on a visit to Denmark. Here he met a Norwegian girl, Anna Throndsson, whom he carried off to the Netherlands and there abandoned in great penury. She was years later to play a disastrous part in the fate of Bothwell, by giving away to Frederick II of Denmark, when Bothwell was his prisoner, the story of their early relations.

In 1560 Bothwell was in Paris and on the death of Francis II Mary, Queen of Scots, sent him to Scotland as one of her commissioners. The next year he was made a member of the

Privy Council. He was, however, in perpetual trouble because of his turbulent behaviour, especially in his relations with Arran, the nearest heir to the Scottish crown, so much so that in 1562 he was accused of trying to carry off the Queen and was imprisoned in Edinburgh. He managed to break out and then made up his mind to go back to France. On his way he was driven by a storm into Holy Island and he was detained by the English for a few months (1564). He went to France, but he was back in Scotland in March, returned to France and was thence recalled by Mary, who wanted his help against the Earl of Moray. Elizabeth I made every effort to prevent his return and sent Anthony Jenkinson with some ships to cruise off the coast of Scotland and to stop him from landing. But Bothwell gave him the slip and from now onwards he came to have increasing favour with and influence over the Scottish queen.

In February 1565 Bothwell married Lady Jean Gordon, sister of George, fifth Earl of Huntly, which makes it clear that Bothwell had not yet formed any idea that he might marry Mary, Queen of Scots. The Huntly family was Catholic, but Bothwell remained a Protestant. He was in Holyrood on the night of the murder of Riccio (1566), but he had no knowledge of the plot and no hand in it. When he and Huntly heard the noise of the murder they went to the inner court, but they were ordered back to their rooms by Morton, who had taken control of the palace. They managed to escape by a back window and both of them went to Bothwell's home at Crichton. Mary was a prisoner in Holyrood, but she patched up a reconciliation with Darnley and they both rode by night to Dunbar, where they were joined by Bothwell. His resolute behaviour had won her admiration and her gratitude, so that from now on Bothwell's position grew more and more important. Knox wrote that Bothwell 'had now of all men greatest success and familiarity with the queen', and Sir James Melville's opinion was that Bothwell had 'a mark of his own that he shot at', to be King in the place of Darnley. In October 1566 Bothwell was severely wounded by an outlaw: as he lay ill at his castle, the Hermitage, the Queen rode over to see him and returned the same day—a distance of between fifty and sixty miles. Her love for Darnley was dead: with good reason she hated him. Had she transferred that love now to Bothwell? Was he captivated? Was he merely an adventurer in search of a crown? On an answer to these questions depends a fair historical judgment on the events which follow. We are unlikely now ever to know the real truth, since the evidence of the Casket Letters is worthless, and there is no genuine evidence on the other side. The generally accepted version of the events is as follows.

By the end of 1566 everybody was agreed that Darnley could no longer be tolerated as the Queen's husband. In December a conference was held at Craigmillar at which Bothwell favoured divorce, but the Catholic lords were not likely to agree to this. Later, a bond was said to have been signed by Bothwell, Huntly, Maitland, Argyll and James Balfour undertaking to get rid of Darnley 'by one way or other'. In January 1567 Mary went to Glasgow to see Darnley, who was ill of so-called smallpox—almost certainly it was syphilis (Gore-Browne, *Lord Bothwell*, p. 290)—and she was to take him to Edinburgh. In order that Darnley should have better air than he would get in the city, the plan was changed and an isolated house at Kirk o' Field was chosen by Bothwell, who made all the arrangements for housing Darnley. He had gunpowder brought from Dunbar and placed in the Queen's room below that of Darnley, with the intention of blowing up the house with Darnley in it. The Queen left the house late in the evening of February 9th in order to attend a ball at Holyrood and went in the company of Bothwell. Bothwell attended the ball, left about midnight and returned to Kirk o' Field, where he himself fired the train to the gunpowder. With his companions he then returned to Holyrood as soon as the explosion took place. The body of the king was found some distance from the house, without any mark from the explosion, and it was generally held that he had been strangled before the explosion took place. Bothwell himself said that the accident was 'the strangest that ever chancit, to wit, the fouder (lightning) came out of the luft (sky) and had burnt the king's house'. He then gave large presents to all his accomplices, telling them to 'hold their tongues for they should never want so long as he had anything'. There are some difficulties in accepting this version, and an ingenious attempt has been made to prove that it was Darnley who had the powder put in the house with the intention of blowing up the Queen, that rumour of this reached Holyrood during the ball, that Bothwell went to Kirk o' Field to investigate, found the powder in the downstairs room and fired the train to blow up Darnley: but Darnley woke and smelt the burning, rushed out of the house in his nightshirt into the arms of Archibald Douglas and his friends, who murdered him before the explosion took place (Gore-Browne, *ibid.*, ch. 28).

Public opinion was from the first convinced that Bothwell was the murderer, but his position at court was not in the least degree weakened. He obtained a formal acquittal in the law-courts and he received large grants of land from the Queen. There can be no doubt that by this time Bothwell was determined to marry Mary. On April 24th, 1567, the Queen was returning from Stirling to Edinburgh, when she was met by Bothwell with an armed force and was carried off to Dunbar. It is almost impossible not to believe that this so-called abduction was carried out with the knowledge and consent of the Queen. Meantime Bothwell had started a collusive action for a divorce between him and his wife, Lady Jean Gordon, on the grounds that there had been no dispensation granted when he married her within the forbidden degrees. There had been such a dispensation and it has been discovered at Dunrobin in Sutherlandshire. On May 7th the divorce was granted and on the 15th Bothwell and the Queen were married at Holyrood (1567), according to Protestant rites. The previous day Bothwell had been created Duke of Orkney and Shetland.

Arrogant, ruthless, self-confident, Bothwell had never been a popular man. What he had now done was in effect to have usurped the government: there was not the least chance that the Scottish lords would take that lying down. They determined to capture the Queen and Bothwell at Holyrood.

Plate 21

Mary, Queen of Scots

James Hepburn, Earl of Bothwell

Henry Stuart, Lord Darnley

Plate 22

Matthew Parker, Archbishop of Canterbury

Edmund Grindal, Archbishop of Canterbury

Forewarned, Bothwell and the Queen fled to Borthwick Castle: when it was surrounded by Morton and Home, Bothwell escaped to Dunbar, where he was joined by the Queen in a few days. Raising a force which was mostly composed of Bothwell's men and was not a proof of public support for Mary, they met the lords at Carberry Hill. There was little enthusiasm even among Bothwell's followers: no reinforcements arrived to back the Queen: both sides began to negotiate; at once the Queen's army began to melt away. Bothwell himself created a very strong impression on the French ambassador, du Croc, who thought that if the troops had remained loyal the Queen's cause would have won under Bothwell's leadership. Bothwell tried to hazard all on a challenge to single combat: the Queen would not accept that and persuaded him to escape. He rode off unpursued to Dunbar. Bothwell and Mary never met again.

After a sojourn at Spynie with his old guardian the Bishop of Moray, Bothwell escaped by sea, making first for Orkney, then for Shetland. He collected a number of ships and became for a time captain of a pirate fleet. Pursued by Kirkcaldy of Grange, he was arrested by a Danish ship off the coast of Norway, whence he was sent to Denmark. There he was imprisoned by Frederick II, first at Malmoe and later at Dragsholm (1573–8), where he died in abject misery, having almost certainly gone out of his mind. Mary obtained a divorce by Papal dispensation in 1570, when she was planning to marry the Duke of Norfolk.   (*Plate 21*)

F. Schiern, *James Hepburn, Earl of Bothwell*, trans. from the Danish by the Rev. David Berry, 1880: invaluable for Bothwell's time in Denmark, not much use for his life in Scotland.

J. Stuart: *A Lost Chapter in the History of Mary, Queen of Scots, Recovered*, 1874: deals with Bothwell's marriage with Lady Jean Gordon, the divorce and the marriage with Mary, Queen of Scots.

R. Gore-Browne, *Lord Bothwell*, 1937; a spirited and ingenious defence of a barely defensible man, much biased in favour

of Mary, well documented, wittily written, but in the end
far from convincing.
M. Irwin, *The Gay Galliard*. (H.N.)

HARINGTON, SIR JOHN, poet, courtier, inventor of the
water-closet, was born in 1561 at Kelston, near Bath, and he
died in 1612 at the age of 51. He was the son of John Harington
and Isabella Markham who were imprisoned in the Tower at
the same time as the princess Elizabeth. John the elder was
fined £1,000 for conveying a letter to Elizabeth from one of her
friends while they were in prison. When Elizabeth became
queen she never forgot the loyalty of Harington and in recognition of it she became godmother to the young John.

The boy went to Eton, where he seems not to have differed
much from modern Etonians. He recalled his teacher's
addressing him as 'thou varay lazy fellow'—one can hear the
imitation of accent. He was as disrespectful even of the Provost,
who 'brake his leg with a fall from a horse that started under
him. Whereupon some waggish scholars, of which I think
myself was in the quorum, would say it was a just punishment,
because the horse was given him by a gentleman to place his
son at Eton'.

From Eton to King's, Cambridge, where he described himself
as a truantly scholar who had taken little for his money. Yet
he also paid a no doubt well-merited tribute to his tutor 'to
whom I never came, but I grew more religious; from whom I
never went, but I parted better instructed'. There is a pleasant
sidelight on the Queen, who sent him a copy of her speech to
Parliament (March 15th, 1576), 'and I do this, because thy
father was ready to serve and love us in trouble and thrall'.

After Cambridge John turned to the study of law at Lincoln's
Inn. On the death of his father (1582) he abandoned the law
and went to Kelston to look to the building of the house there.
Here, perhaps for the first time, he revealed his flair for
mechanical inventions, not only in a fountain (originally
designed by Ariosto) worked by running water, but also in a
more useful, if less decorative device which was to cause himself
some trouble later with the Queen, but to earn him also much

gratitude with all succeeding generations, even in a short time with the Queen herself.

He was not always at Kelston, for he was frequently at Court. And here it may be noted that, in spite of two or three quarrels and dismissals, his royal godmother always had for him a deep affection, as John Harington always had for her. He was so brilliant, so gay, so witty, so clever, that he could not but charm her: but discipline had to be maintained and Elizabeth never allowed personal feelings to undermine discipline—unless it might be with Leicester. Harington's first escapade was concerned with a translation which he made of the improper story of Giacomo in the 28th book of Ariosto's *Orlando Furioso*. The manuscript was circulated among the maids of honour at the Court. It fell into the hands of the Queen. John was exiled from Court, but one sees a wink of the eyelid in the verdict, until he had translated the whole of Ariosto's poem into English. John accomplished this by 1592, when he presented a magnificently bound copy of the work to Elizabeth on her visit to Kelston in that year. The versification may not have been above moderately good, but the volume carried a frontispiece, a portrait of Harington engraved on copper plate and signed by William Rogers, the first man to practise this art in England, probably the first book in England to be illustrated with copper plates.

The next important moment in Harington's life was the publication in 1596 of *A New Discourse upon a Stale Subject*, with the sub-title of *The Metamorphosis of Ajax*. This was published under the author's pseudonym of Misacmos. There were in fact three sections to this dissertation, but the real point of the publication was that Harington described in detail and with diagrams, and with a good many none too savoury digressions, often aimed at particular and well-known men at Court, his invention of the water-closet, on which John Harington's chief claim to fame ought to rely. (Ajax was a pun on the words 'a jakes', jakes being the Elizabethan word for a privy.) The work was issued under the initials T.C., which stood for T.C. Traveller. He explained 'how unsavoury places may be made sweet, noisome places made wholesome, filthy places made cleanly', at a cost of thirty shillings and eightpence. The Queen was much displeased, not with the indecorous passages in the book, but with veiled allusions to the Earl of Leicester. At one moment Harington was in great danger of facing Star Chamber: it is almost certain that Elizabeth's affection for him saved him from that process. But the edict went forth that that 'saucey poet' leave the Court 'till he be grown sober' (1596). By 1598 the Queen had forgiven her godson and commanded that a Harington water-closet be installed at Richmond Palace.

The next year (1599) Essex set out on his ill-fated expedition to Ireland. The Queen never trusted Essex, least of all on this military venture. She therefore sent her godson as Master of the Horse with orders 'to take account of all that passes in your expedition and keep journal thereof, unknown to any in the company: this will be expected of you. I have reasons to give for this order'. Harington had so little warning that 'I had scant time to put on my boots'. The expedition proved a total failure and on returning to England Essex took Harington (whom he had knighted in Ireland) with him to his interview with Elizabeth. The Queen was in a furious temper and ordered Harington home to Kelston. 'I did not stay to be bidden twice. If all the Irish rebels had been at my heels, I should not have made better speed.' But before he left London he had another interview with his godmother at which he was 'cleared and graciously dismissed. . . . Until I come to heaven, I shall never come before a statelier judge again, nor one that can temper majesty, wisdom, learning, choler, and favour better than her Highness did at that time'.

In 1602 Harington saw the Queen for the last time and found her in 'most pitiable state'. Within three months she was dead. How deep was Harington's affection for the Queen breaks out in a letter to his wife: 'I can not blot from my memory's table the goodness of our sovereign Lady to me, even (I will say) before born; her affection to my mother . . . her bettering the state of my father's fortune (which I have, alas! so much worsted), her watchings over my youth, her liking to my free speech and admiration of my little learning and poesie, which I did so much cultivate on her command, have rooted such love, such dutiful remembrance of her princely virtues, that to turn askant from her condition with tearless eyes would stain and foul the spring and fount of gratitude'.

Already by 1602 everybody of importance was taking out an insurance policy with James VI of Scotland. Harington wrote a tract *On The Succession to the Crown* (1602) in which he supported the claim of James VI to the English throne. He sent a copy to the King and with it a New Year present of a lantern so devised as to symbolize the waning light of Elizabeth and the rising splendour of James. There was also a representation of the Crucifixion with the inscription, 'Lord, remember me when thou comest into Thy Kingdom'—a typically light-hearted piece of bad taste, if not of blasphemy. The King treated Harington graciously, made him a Knight of the Bath, gave to him the properties of Harington's Markham cousins, forfeited for Sir Griffin Markham's part in the plot to put Lady Arabella Stuart on the throne, added the advowson of the rectory to the manor of Kelston, and confirmed all the properties his father had obtained through his Tudor marriage to the family for ever (Grimble, p. 144).

Towards the end of his life, from 1602 onwards, Harington was involved in three major lawsuits and quarrels over properties to which he tried to lay claim and some of which he tried to secure by force. He was greatly in debt and in need of money, but his methods of repairing his fortunes shew him in the least reputable light. Indeed, he was at one moment imprisoned, having promised to stand surety for the debts of his cousin, Sir Griffin Markham. He was in prison for a year, then he escaped.

In 1609 he translated the *Regimen Sanitatis Salernitanum* and entitled his book *The Englishman's Doctor*, or *the Schoole of Salerne*, perhaps for the use of James I's son, the prince Henry, for whom he had two years earlier composed the *Brief View of the State of the Church*. If none of Harington's literary productions commands much attention to-day, (in his own day his epigrams were much admired), his letters mark him as one of the great letter writers in English literature. Harington was a shrewd observer, he had a wonderful gift for what would nowadays be newspaper reporting, he was always interesting, usually witty, sometimes Rabelaisian, often serious. Some of the most intimate, alive and even moving portraits that we have of Queen Elizabeth are to be found in his letters: to his letters we owe the most vivid and forthright pictures of James I and his court, especially his vivid account of a drunken orgy, quoted in D. H. Willson's *King James VI and I.*   (*Plate 32*)

Ian Grimble, *The Harington Family*, 1957.
D. MacDonald, 'Sir John Harington,' *History Today*, vi, 1956.
Rev. H. Harington, *Nugae Antiquae* (collected letters), 1769.
N. E. McClure, *Letters and Epigrams*. Philadelphia, 1930.

HARDWICK, ELIZABETH, 'Bess of Hardwick', was born in 1520 and died in 1608 at the remarkable age for Tudor times of 87. She was the daughter of John Hardwick of Hardwick Hall in the county of Derby, and of his wife, Elizabeth Leake. Bess was married four times: (1) to Robert Barley or Barlow in 1532, but he died early in 1533; (2) to William Cavendish in 1547, he died in 1557. By this marriage there were six children and the first purpose in Bess's life was to further their interests. William became first Earl of Devonshire and from him sprang the long line of the Cavendish Earls and Dukes of Devonshire. Charles had a son, William, who became the first Duke of Newcastle and commanded Charles I's northern army in the Civil War. Elizabeth married Charles Stuart, Earl of Lennox, and their daughter was Lady Arabella Stuart, who all but succeeded Elizabeth I as Queen of England. Mary married Gilbert Talbot, seventh Earl of Shrewsbury, and their three daughters married respectively William Herbert, Earl of Pembroke, Henry Grey, eighth Earl of Kent, and Thomas Howard, Earl of Arundel. (3) Bess married William St. Looe in 1559 and he died in 1564 or 1565; (4) George Talbot, sixth Earl of Shrewsbury, in 1567, and he died in 1590.

During her long and vigorous life Bess was twice imprisoned in the Tower under suspicion of crimes of which she was wholly innocent, the first time from August 1561 to March 1562, the second time from 1574 to 1575. For fourteen years she shared with her husband, Shrewsbury, the thankless, expensive and dangerous honour of acting as gaoler to Mary, Queen of Scots (1569–83). From 1578 to 1603 she devoted herself to trying to make sure that Arabella Stuart should secure the entire Lennox inheritance and should succeed Elizabeth on the throne. She failed in both objects.

If devotion to her family, with whom she frequently quarrelled, was her first passion, Bess had another purpose almost as dear to her heart: she was one of the great builders of the English Renaissance, and if her magnificent house at Chatsworth has disappeared, Hardwick Hall remains as the durable monument to a lady of character and genius.   (*Plate 32*)

P. M. Handover, *Arabella Stuart*, 1957.
E. Carleton Williams, *Bess of Hardwick*, 1959.
Turberville, *History of Welbeck Abbey*.

CARY, ROBERT, 1st EARL OF MONMOUTH, was almost certainly born in 1560, the seventh son and tenth child of Lord Hunsdon. His grandmother was a sister of Anne Boleyn, which made Robert a cousin of Queen Elizabeth, perhaps the reason for his intimacy with her. He died on April 12th, 1639, aged about 79. He will always be remembered as the man who rode at breakneck speed on horseback from London to Edinburgh—and took a severe fall on the way—to carry the news of Queen Elizabeth's death to James VI of Scotland. He may also be remembered as the writer of a short but vivid autobiography, in which he gives a first-hand account of the defeat of the Spanish Armada, against which he served; a miniature portrait of Queen Elizabeth in a tantrum, because he had married against her wishes; a lively picture of the Anglo-Scot borderland in which he was Warden of the Marches; an eye-witness' account of the death of Elizabeth; a self-accusing description of the place-seeking which went on in the Court of James I; a cameo of Charles I in his nursery days, to whom he was both Keeper of the Wardrobe and Chamberlain; he also tells how he was sent after Charles and Buckingham on their expedition to Spain. In all this he reveals himself as an extravagant, well-dressed man of fashion, shrewd and clever in the pursuit of his own and of his family's fortunes, with some understanding of diplomacy, a colourful and attractive personality.

Memoirs of Robert Cary, Earl of Monmouth, edited by G. H. Powell, 1907.

PARKER, MATTHEW, Archbishop of Canterbury, was born on August 6th, 1504, at Norwich, and he died in 1575, aged seventy-one. He came of a well-to-do family, but little is known of his origins and early life. He went to Corpus Christi College, Cambridge, in 1521, where he took his B.A. degree in 1525, perhaps in 1524. He was ordained in 1527 and in that year was elected a Fellow of the College, having refused an offer to migrate to Wolsey's new foundation of Cardinal College, Oxford. For the next seven years he studied the early centuries of Church history. During this period Parker consorted with the reformers who met at the White Horse Inn, and became firm friends with people such as Bilney and Latimer, but Parker differed from these Cambridge reformers in that he was never a controversialist. The debates and disputes in which he took part served only the more to turn him back to finding out historic facts, not other people's opinions. Too many of the reformers came to look on religion as a thing to be debated and not a life to be lived: Parker never fell into that error, 'he was never drawn aside into undisciplined enthusiasm' (Kennedy, p. 34). He became a popular and influential preacher in and around Cambridge, but he was once attacked before Lord Chancellor Audley for alleged heresy. Audley dismissed the charge and urged Parker to 'go on and fear no such enemies'. One other fact in Parker's early days at Cambridge was to have immense influence on his later life—he became the firm friend of William Cecil (Lord Burghley) and Nicholas Bacon.

In 1535 Parker was reluctantly persuaded to accept the office of chaplain to Anne Boleyn, who gave him the deanery of St. John the Baptist College, Stoke-by-Clare in Suffolk, where he spent what were probably the happiest years of his life training young secular priests and pursuing his interests as a scholar, improving the college and saving it from dissolution when Henry VIII attacked the monasteries. Anne also before her execution commended her daughter Elizabeth to his care. This peaceful and busy life went on until 1544 when Parker was appointed Master of his old college at Cambridge, Corpus Christi. He became Vice-Chancellor of the university and also Dean of Lincoln. His period as Vice-Chancellor involved him in some stormy episodes: he quarrelled with Gardiner, the Chancellor of Cambridge, over the performance of a scandalous play at Christ's College, and Gardiner never had a good opinion of Parker from that time onwards. He had to withstand an attack on the revenues of the Cambridge colleges by the Crown which he warded off with great tact and skill. But perhaps in the long run the most important single event in Parker's life took place on June 24th, 1547, when he married Margaret Harlestone of Mattishall in Norfolk. They had been betrothed for seven years, but as long as the law forbade the marriage of clergy Parker was doomed to celibacy: as soon as the law was amended by the Lower House of Convocation Parker married this remarkable and admirable woman. The marriage led them both into great difficulties when Mary Tudor came to the throne, and the outspoken objections of Elizabeth, when she became Queen, to married clergy caused both Parker and Margaret great pain and trouble. But Margaret proved herself equal to all occasions and roused the admiration of Nicholas Ridley to such a pitch that he enquired of Matthew Parker whether Margaret had a sister, for if he himself were ever to marry he could not hope for a better wife than a lady like Mistress Parker. Even Elizabeth I was compelled in later years to acknowledge the worth of Mistress Parker. Parker was a modest and far from self-confident man and much of his success was due to his wife: it is noticeable that when she died his powers began to fail quickly.

When Ket's rebellion broke out (1549) in Norfolk, Parker happened to be in Norwich. As the rebels used the English Prayer Book and allowed licensed preachers to address them, Parker went to the camp and preached a sermon from the 'Oak of Reformation'. He gave them excellent advice, not to destroy the crops, not to shed human blood, and not to distrust the King. It was a rash sermon to preach in the circumstances and Parker only escaped the fury of the rebels 'by the judicious raising of the *Te Deum*' (Kennedy, p. 62). His purpose probably was then, as always later when he was Archbishop, to support law and order.

It is not possible to deal fully here with Parker's relations with Bucer, but it is necessary to record that he became a great friend of the German theologian—Parker preached the sermon at Bucer's funeral—and there is little doubt that Bucer had considerable influence on Parker's views on the Sacraments. Both were by nature moderate men of the *via* media, gentle and sincere (see Kennedy, pp. 65–9).

When Mary Tudor came to the throne in 1553, Parker as a married priest was deprived of his preferments and he had to disappear into obscurity. He lived with a friend and thoroughly enjoyed his retirement from public life and administrative duties, but he suffered an accident when one day he fell from his horse, and for the rest of his life suffered from a strangulated hernia which brought him incessant ill-health and eventually killed him.

In 1558 the accession of Elizabeth opened a new chapter in Parker's life. He himself would have liked to return to Cambridge and restore the university which had fallen into decay. But the problem of the Anglican Church prevented this. Elizabeth and Cecil were faced with the difficulty of holding the balance between the old Roman Catholics who still accepted the Pope as head of the Church, the Henrician Catholics who accepted the Catholic religion but repudiated the Papal supremacy, and the extreme Protestants who were now returning from exile on the Continent. It was essential to find the right man as Archbishop of Canterbury. Only a man of balanced judgment, of deep learning, gentle yet firm, conciliatory yet courageous, could successfully fill the office: only Matthew Parker had all the qualifications. He tried desperately to avoid the responsibility, but the Queen and Cecil knew that he was the right man and they compelled him to accept. Years later Parker declared that 'if he had not been so much bound to the mother (Anne Boleyn), he would not so soon have granted to serve the daughter'. He was consecrated in Lambeth Palace Chapel on December 17th, 1559. This consecration by four bishops surviving in England, though without sees, is the connecting link between the old and the new succession of Orders in the Church of England. (For a discussion on this point, see Kennedy, appendix II.)

Parker's first important piece of work was the Metropolitical Visitation of the southern province in 1560–61 to investigate how far the Act of Uniformity and the Injunctions of 1559—a code of orders to protect the new Church from Catholic 'superstition'—*e.g.* the cult of saints, reverence for relics: to ensure that only sound Protestant doctrine should be taught: 'to plant true religion' (see for full details P. Hughes, *The Reformation in England*, vol. 3, pp. 114–17)—were being carried out and to correct moral offences among clergy and laity. At that moment things seemed to be quiet and the nation to be accepting the new order.

By 1563 signs of the coming storm were evident. Both Parliament and Convocation were worried by fears of papal intrigues, of the hostility of France in the south and of dangers from Mary Queen of Scots in the north. Measures against the Romanists were stepped up and Parker was much troubled by the prospect of religious persecution. He took pains to ensure that the measures were leniently enforced, so that for the first ten years of Elizabeth's reign life was not made too difficult for the Romanists.

With the revival of the Council of Trent, with the increase in papal propaganda by introducing into England controversial books, and with the Puritan propaganda which was being broadcast by the Protestant refugees and with which even some of the Anglican bishops were sympathetic, Parker set out to provide uniformity in doctrine for the Elizabethan Church. He accordingly reduced Cranmer's Articles of Religion (1563) from forty-two to thirty-eight in number (in 1571 they became the Thirty-Nine Articles) and various Homilies and Catechisms were also issued. All were intended to lay down the fundamental points of belief.

Another problem with which Parker had soon to deal was the dispute over ceremonial and ritual. There was a large party in

Convocation which would have liked to destroy the whole settlement about ritual made in the Prayer Book and the Injunctions. Many clergy were taking the law into their own hands and were pulling down rood-lofts, destroying chancels and some were even turning the organs out of their churches. Similarly there was no uniformity in the vestments which the clergy wore or refused to wear. In other words, Parker was now faced with the problem of Puritanism. For the rest of his life he was continuously harassed by the disobedience of many of the clergy, by the irresolution of the Queen, and by the hostility of such courtiers as the Earl of Leicester. Parker dealt with these conflicting opponents mercifully and reluctantly. His 'Advertisements' were a compromise on the question of vestments, laying down that the surplice should be worn in the parish church and the cope in the cathedrals. He then set about seeing that these instructions were carried out. 'Execution, execution, execution of laws and orders must be the first and the last part of good governance, although I yet admit moderations for times, places, multitudes.'

Each year the situation became more difficult, the Puritans increased in numbers and in fanaticism, the Papacy grew more aggressive. The Rebellion of the Northern Earls in 1569, the Bull of Excommunication (1570), the massacre of St. Bartholomew (1573), persuaded the gentle Parker that strong measures were necessary and that Mary Queen of Scots (by now a prisoner in England) would have to be eliminated: 'If that only desperate person were away as by justice soon it might be, the Queen's Majesty's good subjects would be in better hope and the papists' daily expectation vanquished.' By dint of patience, tact, firmness and adaptability Parker had saved the Prayer Book from the attacks of the Genevans; he had built a new Church delicately poised on the foundations of the old; a sterner policy was now needed to defend that Church, a Whitgift rather than a Parker to direct the battle.

One other achievement belongs to Parker, perhaps his greatest. He had always made it his business to see that this 'new' Church was not in fact a new Church, that it should be the old, original Church revived. His study at Cambridge of the early centuries of the Church's history, his refusal to be moved by anything other than historical facts, his study of the Anglo-Saxon language, his collecting of ancient documents, were all directed towards one end, to prove that the 'new' Church of England was in truth the Old Catholic Church purged from the abuses and innovations of the Middle Ages. In 1566 he paid out of his own pocket John Day to cut in brass the first Saxon type for the publications of *A Testimonie of Antiquitie*, showing, 'the ancient faith in the Church of England touching the Sacrament of the Body and Blood of the Lord . . . above 600 years ago'.* He proved that it was a medieval innovation which forbade the clergy to marry and which restricted the receiving at the Communion to one kind.

Between 1563 and 1568 Parker was a moving spirit in preparing the Bishops' Bible, although he had not much time to give to the actual translation. He was, as Strype said, 'a mighty collector of books', not as a mere bibliophile but for a practical purpose, to help the Church of England in its struggle against Rome and the Puritans. The historian Freeman once said of Matthew Parker that it was owing to him, more than any other man, 'that there is anything to edit and anything to read about the early history of England'.

Although Parker was a modest and retiring man, hating publicity and ostentation, he had a proper regard for the office of Archbishop and for his duty as a hospitable host. He himself was very sparing in his diet, but he entertained liberally and his home life was organized on a spacious scale: he was given special leave by the Queen to maintain a body of forty retainers in addition to his regular servants. Among the many visitors who came to Bekesbourne Parker was once compelled to entertain the French ambassador. Parker was highly suspicious of his guests, whom he looked on as religious and political spies. Parker was in many ways *naïve*, but he was also shrewd and he kept a close watch on the Frenchmen. After the party had left, Parker sat down and counted his spoons and was surprised to find that none had disappeared.

Parker died on May 17th, 1575, worn out by pain and toil.

* See Brook, p. 141, n. 1.

He had endured much, for the Queen left him to take all the blame when he carried out her orders and they proved unpopular. He was buried in Lambeth Church and his tomb was desecrated by the Puritans in 1648. When Sancroft became Archbishop, Parker's bones were recovered and reburied, with the epitaph, *Corpus Matthaei Archiepiscopi hic tandem quiescit*. He is not the best known of the archbishops, yet among the long line of St. Augustine's successors none has served the Church of England more faithfully and more profitably than this gentle, modest, wise and saintly man.

W. M. Kennedy, *Archbishop Parker*, 1908.

F. O. White, *Lives of Elizabethan Bishops*, 1898.

W. E. Collins, *Typical English Churchmen*, 1902.

E. W. Perry, *Under Four Tudors*, 1940. Valuable for the domestic life of Parker and his wife, but worthless on the ecclesiastical side. *cf.* *Church Quarterly Review*, cxxxvii, July-September, 1943.

Canon C. Smyth, *The Listener*, October 30th, 1947.

V. J. K. Brook, *Archbishop Parker*, 1962.   (*Plate 22*)

GRINDAL, EDMUND, Archbishop of Canterbury, was born in 1519 at Hensingham in the parish of St. Bees, Cumberland, the son of a well-to-do farmer. He died in 1583 at the age of sixty-four. When he was fifteen he went to Cambridge, first to Magdalene College, then to Christ's and finally to Pembroke, of which he became a Fellow in 1538. Ridley was his tutor and no doubt Ridley's influence turned him towards Protestantism. He was ordained in 1544 and in 1547 he read Bullinger's *Origin of Error*, which led him to reject Transubstantiation. When in 1549 the commissioners visited Cambridge for an inspection of the university, Grindal argued with great ability and success against this doctrine in the debate staged in front of the commissioners. In that year he became Lady Margaret preacher and Vice-Master of Pembroke College. Two years later Ridley made him his chaplain, and Grindal soon became chaplain to Edward VI. By this time his reputation was so high that he was likely to be made a bishop, but Edward VI died and the accession of Mary put an end for the time being to his success.

Taking the least heroic but the wisest line, Grindal fled abroad to Strasbourg and passed on to Frankfurt, where he was much employed in trying to compose the differences among the Protestant exiles. On the death of Mary, Grindal came back to England and arrived on the day of Elizabeth's coronation, January 15th, 1559. He became Master of Pembroke and then was made Bishop of London by Matthew Parker, the Archbishop. Grindal accepted with some hesitation, for he was really a Puritan and he disliked the use of vestments and of ceremonial. He consulted his friends abroad and at last accepted on the grounds that these things were 'indifferent' and the important thing was to save the English Church for Protestantism.

Grindal's ministry in London was a failure. The city was full of Puritans and Grindal was too sympathetic to their way of thinking to be able to enforce Parker's policy of achieving uniformity in church services. He would deal severely, even harshly, with Romans—he recommended that torture should be applied to a Romish priest named Haverd who refused to answer the questions at his examination. Parker found Grindal 'not resolute and severe enough for the government of London'. He solved the problem by recommending that Grindal should be Archbishop of York, a diocese where he would have to root out Catholic recusancy rather than Puritanism (1570).

For five years Grindal set about his work with resolution and perhaps with relish. But in 1575 Parker died and Cecil persuaded the Queen to translate Grindal from York to Canterbury. It was a mistake. Grindal and the Queen never saw eye to eye, for their views on politics and religious policy were diametrically opposed. They fell out eventually over the question of 'prophesyings', clerical meetings for the exposition and discussion of scripture. They were not 'revivalist' meetings, but rather 'refresher courses' (C. Morris, *Political Thought*). The Queen wanted them forbidden: Grindal felt that the meetings might have been abused, but that it was enough to cure the abuse and to maintain a form of study which he believed did much to raise the standard of the clergy. In 1576 the Queen straightly commanded him to suppress all prophesyings. Grindal refused and wrote her a polite, sensible and admirable letter explaining his reasons and reminding her that it was her duty to consult her clergy in matters of religion. The Queen's answer was an order to suppress the meetings. Grindal refused and the Queen suspended him from his office, although he was allowed to continue his spiritual functions, such as consecrating new bishops.

By this time Grindal was growing old and nearly blind. It was clear that he ought to resign, but he would not. Then he grew worse and was preparing to resign when he died on July 6th, 1583. He was a man able, learned and of much charm, he had many friends, among whom he counted Spenser and Whitgift, he liked music and was fond of gardening, and sent grapes to the Queen. But he was unsuited to high ecclesiastical office in the times in which he lived, because he refused to toe the official line. He always wanted to improve the standard of the clergy and he spent much money on educational benefactions. On the other hand, he never realized the immense dangers involved in giving way to the extreme Puritans. Such a policy could only result in the end in the disruption of the hard-earned ecclesiastical settlement of 1559, and the Queen had a clearer, if narrower, outlook than Grindal.   (*Plate 22*)

F. O. White, *Lives of the Elizabethan Bishops*.
C. Morris, *Political Thought in England, Tyndale to Hooker*, 1953.

WHITGIFT, JOHN, Archbishop of Canterbury, was born at Grimsby in 1530 and he died in 1604, at the age of seventy-four. His father was a wealthy Grimsby merchant, his uncle Robert was Abbot of Wellow, near Grimsby, and it was his uncle who took him under his care and sent him to St. Anthony's school in London, where had also been Sir Thomas More and Archbishop Heath. He lived with his aunt, but she threw him out because he refused to attend 'morrow mass', the first mass of the day, and would not be persuaded by some of the canons of St. Paul's.

On the advice of his uncle, his father sent John to Queens' College, Cambridge, but the boy soon migrated to Pembroke (1550), where Nicholas Ridley was the non-resident Master and Grindal was President, and also Bradford, later the Marian

Plate 23

John Whitgift, Archbishop of Canterbury

John Jewel, Bishop of Salisbury

Plate 24

John Foxe

Richard Hooker

martyr, was a Fellow, and became Whitgift's tutor. So promising a pupil did Whitgift prove that when his father's finances were affected by losses at sea, Ridley made the son a Bible Clerk, which enabled him to remain at Cambridge.

Whitgift justified the privilege. His success was swift and steady. 1553–4, B.A.; 1555, Fellow of Peterhouse; 1557 M.A., 1560 ordained: chaplain to Cox, the strongly anti-Roman Bishop of Ely; Rector of Teversham: 1563, B.D. and Lady Margaret Lecturer in Divinity: 1567, D.D., Master of Pembroke, and immediately Master of Trinity. This last appointment was made in order to strengthen the Heads of Houses to deal with the growing trend in Cambridge towards presbyterianism. In 1567 he became Vice-Chancellor and Regius Professor; 1568, prebend of Ely. Being now far better off than ever before, he resigned the Regius Professorship and was succeeded by the holder of the Lady Margaret Chair: the latter was succeeded by Cartwright, and thus Whitgift had unwittingly provided Cartwright, later one of the leaders of Presbyterianism in England, with the chance which he wanted. (An account of Whitgift's dealings with Cartwright will be found in the article on Cartwright.) In 1571 Whitgift became Dean of Lincoln and Parker gave him a dispensation to hold at one and the same time the Deanery of Lincoln, the prebend of Ely, the Mastership of Trinity and the Rectory of Teversham. In 1572 he became Prolocutor of the Lower House of Convocation (*i.e.* President). In this year there was published the very popular and successful *Admonition to the Parliament*, which advocated that the Church of England should be reformed on the presbyterian model. Whitgift's *Answer* was the most learned and powerful defence of the Anglican settlement until Hooker's *Ecclesiastical Polity*.

In 1577 Whitgift was made Bishop of Worcester and soon after Vice-President of the Marches of Wales, while Sir Henry Sidney was away in Ireland. He proved himself a diligent, courageous and successful bishop, and a most able administrator in difficult circumstances of the Welsh Marches.

In 1583 Grindal, Archbishop of Canterbury, died. He had been an unsuccessful Archbishop, and when Whitgift was appointed to succeed him, he found a difficult and dangerous situation, in which ecclesiastical law was ignored, uniformity did not exist and the foundations of the Elizabethan settlement were being undermined. Between his appointment and his death he had restored peace and quiet to the Church, at least for the time being, he had enforced the law, more often by tact than by violence, but he was never afraid to deal boldly with dangerous opponents, and he had made many improvements in the administration of the Church. Both the Queen and Burghley had complete confidence in him, as is shown by his being made a member of the Council, the first ecclesiastical member for a long time.

He saw that the first thing to be done was to enforce the law, which he set about doing by his Articles of 1583. He saw also that there were genuine grievances against serious shortcomings in the Church: he set about remedying these by his Articles of 1585. He was determined to repress noncomformity, but he was also determined not to create Puritan martyrs as Mary Tudor had created Protestant martyrs. As time went on, he gradually reduced the severity of his rule and treated the Puritans with sympathy and kindness—he even welcomed Cartwright, when that extremist went to Warwick to Leicester's Hospital, now known as Lord Leycester's. But the Puritans never ceased to revile and calumniate him.

The variety of his work was enormous. He saw to it that the five vacant bishoprics were filled: he defended pluralism in order to improve the low standard of living and the penury of the clergy: he set about reforming the ecclesiastical courts, which were very unpopular owing to their dilatory ways, their expense and their extortions: he enforced orderliness at the two hospitals at Canterbury and also at All Souls College, of which he was Visitor. He realized that it was part of the Church's duty to back up the social and economic policy of the government, so that in 1597–8 he instructed all the bishops to see that the laws against vagabonds and sturdy beggars were properly enforced. Being a bachelor and a wealthy pluralist, he had a good deal of money at his disposal, and this he spent lavishly, not only in entertaining on a scale worthy of his office, but on the relief of the poor, as when he founded the Hospital of the Holy Trinity at Croydon, and also on education, when he founded a free school at Croydon, still known as Whitgift School. He gave much attention to the training of young men both at Trinity, Cambridge, and at Lambeth: he founded a Bible Clerkship at Peterhouse.

Whitgift was essentially an administrator rather than a spiritual theologian. His work was to lay the foundations of a secure Church on which others could build. The last ten years of his life saw the beginnings of this building which was later to develop according to the more theological, spiritual and Catholic conceptions of men like Lancelot Andrewes (*Dict. of Eng. Ch. Hist.*). It is to Whitgift's great credit that he recognized both the need and the opportunities for this beginning and encouraged the younger men to use them. The most notable example is the backing he gave to Hooker in writing the *Ecclesiastical Polity.*

One remarkable characteristic of Whitgift was his ability to subordinate his own instincts and inclinations to the general needs of the times. He was himself, if he could have had his own way theologically, a Calvinist, but he saw clearly that it was not right to try to inject Calvinism into the Anglican Church as established in 1559. When the great attempt was made in 1595 by the Cambridge divines to get the Archbishop to pronounce clearly in favour of Calvinistic doctrines, Whitgift summoned a conference to Lambeth and as a result he issued the Lambeth Articles which, while they conceded a good deal to the Calvinists, made some significant alterations in the original proposals and prevented the attempt to read a full Calvinistic doctrine into the old Thirty-nine Articles (V. J. K. Brook, *W. and the Eng. Ch.*).

When Elizabeth realized that she was dying, she sent for her 'little black husband' and Whitgift was with her to the end. He himself was now over seventy and worn out. He took some part in the Hampton Court Conference, but the immediate future lay with Bancroft, and Whitgift died on February 29th, 1604. He was buried in the parish church at Croydon.

'He was of a middle stature, of a grave countenance and

brown complexion, black hair and eyes; he wore his beard neither long nor thick.' He lived in splendour with a large army of retainers and he was on great occasions served 'upon the knee,' 'for the upholding of the state that belonged unto his place'. Strype called him a 'man born for the benefit of his country and the good of his church'. His biographer, Sir George Paule, wrote, 'happy surely was it for that crazy state of the Church (for so it was at this Archbishop's first coming and long after) not to meet with too rough and boisterous a physician'. Queen Elizabeth, that shrewd and difficult lady, said 'She pitied him because she trusted him, and had thereby eased herself by laying the burthen of all her clergy-cares upon his shoulders; which he managed with prudence and piety.' Izaak Walton has drawn a characteristically friendly sketch of him—'he was noted to be prudent and affable, and gentle by nature.' Characteristically, Macaulay has dismissed him in a few lines which reveal his misunderstanding of Whitgift, 'a narrow-minded, mean and tyrannical priest, who gained power by servility and adulation, and employed it in persecuting both those who agreed with Calvin about Church government, and those who differed from Calvin touching the doctrine of Reprobation' (*Essay on Lord Bacon*). Perhaps those who knew him best may pass the final judgment. When about 1571 Whitgift had it in mind to leave Cambridge, the Heads of Houses wrote to Cecil, the Chancellor, that should the Vice-Chancellor leave, 'the whole body of the University would lament', for he was 'wise, learned and wholly bent to the execution of good laws and statutes.' 'They could not want (*i.e.* do without) him'. (*Plate 23*)

H. C. Porter, *Reformation and Reaction in Tudor Cambridge*, 1958.
Izaak Walton, *Lives*.
V. J. K. Brook, *Whitgift and the English Church*, 1957.

JEWEL, JOHN, Bishop of Salisbury, was born in 1522 and died in 1571, aged forty-nine. He was one of a family of ten, the children of John Jewel of Berrynarbor in North Devon. His education began at Barnstaple school, whence he went in 1535 to Merton College, Oxford. His tutor was Parkhurst, later

Bishop of Norwich, who recommended him after four years to migrate to Corpus Christi College. He took his B.A. degree in 1540 and became a Fellow of his new college in 1542. In 1547 Peter Martyr, a Florentine reformer who became Regius Professor of Divinity at Oxford, arrived in Oxford and Jewel came much under his Protestant influence. In 1552 Jewel took the degree of B.D. and became Public Orator just in time to have to make the oration congratulating Queen Mary on her accession. Weakly he subscribed to religious doctrines which he did not believe, gave up his Protestantism, and then fled abroad to Frankfurt (1555), where he acknowledged his weakness and recanted his recantation. He moved about among the Protestant exiles in Frankfurt, Strasbourg and Zurich, then toured Italy and spent a short time at Padua.

On the death of Mary, Jewel returned to England (1559) and in 1560 he was consecrated Bishop of Salisbury. By nature and instinct, by upbringing and education, Jewel was really a Puritan. He had a supreme contempt for what he called 'the scenic apparatus of divine worship'. Vestments he labelled 'theatrical habits' and 'ridiculous trifles': the cope was a 'comic dress', the linen surplice 'a vestige of error'. This 'rubbish' and these 'fooleries' he wished to see done away with, because they could only disturb 'feeble minds'. But what makes Jewel a notable figure in the history of his own times is that he was capable of seeing these 'trifles', not merely as trifles and therefore to be abolished, but also as trifles which mattered nothing in comparison with the vital necessity of preaching the gospel and the Word of Life. Therefore he put up with these 'fooleries', because he recognized that 'the doctrine (of the Anglican Church) is everywhere most pure' and must be maintained against the Romish errors. To this work the rest of his life was dedicated. Even so, he felt so strongly that everything must be done in a decent and orderly way that he was prepared to enforce things which in his heart he disliked against the Puritans with whom he had much in common.

To the defence of the established Church Jewel brought the help of his profound learning, his deep piety and his unselfish sense of service. He set great store by education and he tried by incessant preaching throughout his diocese to raise the standard of his clergy. His most important piece of writing was his *Apologia pro Ecclesia Anglicana* (written in Latin in 1562 and translated into English in 1564 by Alice Bacon, brother of Francis Bacon) in which he justified the position of the Anglican Church and transferred the accusation of innovations to the Church of Rome. The *Apology* did not define Anglican beliefs: that explanation had to wait for Hooker. Jewel was a gentle, kindly, hospitable man, generous and courteous, yet he was ungenerously discourteous to the Roman Church, whose clergy he assailed in vulgar terms and whose Pope he denounced as the 'hangman of the Church'.

Jewel was a great patron of friendless and needy scholars, and he kept a kind of school in his palace at Salisbury where he trained poor boys of intellectual promise: it was here that Richard Hooker found the encouragement and often the financial aid which enabled him to stay at Oxford. In appearance Jewel was worn and emaciated, and in his later years he seemed a living skeleton (*D.N.B.*). He wore himself out by going round his diocese preaching, maintaining that a bishop 'should die in his pulpit'. Being booked to preach at Laycock, although too ill to keep his appointment, he insisted on doing so. When the service was ended he rode to Monckton Farleigh, where he went to bed and died, September 23rd, 1571.

F. O. White, *Lives of the Elizabethan Bishops.*   (*Plate 23*)

WHITTINGHAM, WILLIAM, Dean of Durham, was born at Chester probably in 1524 and died in 1579, aged about fifty-five. He was educated at Brasenose College, Oxford. He became a B.A. and in 1545 a Fellow of All Souls, in 1548 Senior Student of Christ Church. At the age of twenty-six he was given leave by his college to travel in France, Germany and the Low Countries for three years. Most of that time was spent at Louvain University, where he married a strongly Protestant lady, and he became so proficient in the French language that he was often employed as an interpreter at the English embassy in Paris. There is no reason for accepting the idea that his wife was a sister of Calvin.

He returned to England just in time for the Nine Days' Reign of Lady Jane Grey. He was an extreme Protestant and the accession of Mary to the throne made it dangerous for him to remain in England. With some difficulty he escaped overseas via Dover to France. On being questioned by the innkeeper at Dover, Whittingham replied that he was going abroad 'because the Whore of Rome was again erected amongst them'. The innkeeper was on the point of sending the party to a magistrate, but he was in some way cajoled into describing his female dog as 'one of the Queen's kind', after which Whittingham was free to go on his travels.

He went to Frankfurt (June 1554), where he soon became involved in a violent dispute with other Protestants over the use of the Prayer Book. Most of the English exiles wanted to use Cranmer's Second Prayer Book, but Whittingham and John Knox wanted to start a new Church with a Prayer Book of its own, much more extreme than their opponents cared for. So violent was Knox that he was expelled from the city. Whittingham soon followed him to Geneva (April 1555) with his party of twenty-seven supporters. Here was 'erected' the sort of Church which Knox and Whittingham wanted. Whittingham was twice elected a 'Senior' or Elder of this Church (1555 and 1556); he was then appointed Deacon (1558) and in 1559 he succeeded Knox as Minister.

During this time Whittingham was largely taken up with producing a new translation of the New Testament (1557), notable for its being the first English Bible to be divided into chapters and verses. His chief literary work was the 'Geneva Bible', known more vulgarly as the 'Breeches Bible', and closely connected with the name of Coverdale, but there is no doubt that Whittingham was responsible for most of the translation of the New Testament (1560). This book was the first to omit the Apocrypha and it became the ordinary Bible in English households, even after the Authorized Version of 1611.

The Prayer Book, known as the Genevan-English Order, published in 1556, was remarkable for the metrical versions of the Psalms which were included for congregational singing. This practice became very popular and gradually there were introduced into the Book of Common Prayer metrical versions of passages from the Scriptures, such as those by Sternhold and Hopkins. Whittingham was the man who saved this practice from disappearing and who made it popular by his skill in selecting suitable tunes.

The accession of Elizabeth opened the way to a return to England. Whittingham was delayed by remaining in Geneva to complete the publishing of the Geneva Bible, but he was home in 1560 and attached himself to Ambrose Dudley, Earl of Warwick, and his brother Lord Robert Dudley, the future Earl of Leicester. In 1562 war broke out between England and France and Warwick was sent to defend Havre: Whittingham went as his chaplain. It is said that his diligence in preaching was only equalled by his 'vigilance in discovering stratagems'. He preached always in armour and 'as the old captains and soldiers of Berwick would say, many years after, that—when any alarum came whilst he was preaching, he would be on the town walls as soon almost as any man.'

The reward for this service by the Church Militant was the Deanery of Durham (1563). He proved in many ways to be an excellent choice: he paid strict attention to his religious activities, holding two services a day and giving three or four hours a day to teaching the children: he was socially a great success, living 'in the great love and liking of his neighbours, for his affability and bountiful hospitality': and when he saw the Rebellion of the Northern Earls about to break out, he made every effort to persuade the Bishop to take military measures in time, but he failed to move the timid Pilkington. He had better results at Newcastle, where by means of his efforts 'the rebels never dared attempt of the siege of that town'.

On the other hand, he ignored the Act of Uniformity and introduced into Durham Cathedral Genevan principles which he was compelled to abandon, when in 1566 Archbishop Parker published his 'Advertisements' to regulate such things as the out of doors dress of the clergy and the use of the surplice, as well as enforcing kneeling at the Communion. He also embarked on a policy of iconoclasm: he broke up the image of

St. Cuthbert in the cloisters, he removed grave-covers to use as paving-stones, stone coffins as cattle troughs and stoups for steeping 'their beef and salt fish in, having a conveyance in the bottoms for letting forth the water, as they had when they were in the Church'. He lowered the frater roof and sold the lead for £20, while his wife burned the banner of St. Cuthbert. These actions could be defended on the grounds that the Queen had re-enacted the Injunction of 1547 for the removal of superstitious ornaments.

Whittingham was a difficult man and one not easily handled. He flatly refused to succeed to the office of Secretary of State in 1572. He boldly and successfully withstood his own bishop when Sandys, the new Archbishop, ordered Barnes, Pilkington's successor, to visit the cathedral. Whittingham told the janitor to lock the door, the Bishop tried to prevent him, the Dean 'did a little interrupt him, taking hold of his gown', and kept the Bishop out. Whittingham was then involved in other disputes: he was accused of adultery and of drunkenness, neither charge being well established: it was brought against him that he had never been properly ordained—nor in fact had he been ordained in the strict sense of the word, only 'ordered' as a minister at Geneva. Before any decision was arrived at on this point, Whittingham died at Durham in 1579.

He remains historically as an excellent example of that type of extreme Protestant who had little patience with the *via media* which Elizabeth wished to follow in matters ecclesiastical.

James Wall, *The Church Quarterly*, cxxii, 243, April–June, 1936.
S. L. Greenslade, *Durham University Journal*, 38–40 N. S., 1945–8.
W. Whittingham, *The Troubles of Frankfurt*, ed. by E. Arber, 1908. At least part of it is by Whittingham. Contains a useful introduction and a life of Whittingham 'by a student of the Temple', *c.* 1603.

FECKENHAM, JOHN de, last abbot of Westminster, deserves a longer biography than the space available in this book will allow. The main facts of his life can be shortly stated. He was born probably in 1518 and he died in 1585 at the approximate age of sixty-seven. He was the son of poor peasants named Howman who lived in Feckenham Forest, Worcestershire. The parish priest spotted the boy's abilities and a place was found for him in the monastery at Evesham. After becoming a monk he was known as John of Feckenham. He went to Oxford to what is now Worcester College: he took the degree of B.D. in 1539 and went back to the monastery at Evesham. This foundation was dissolved in 1540. Feckenham was then appointed to the benefice of Solihull and became chaplain to Bishop Bonner. Under Edward VI, when Bonner was deprived, Feckenham was sent to the Tower. When Mary came to the throne he was released and made Dean of St. Paul's. In 1556 he was entrusted with restoring the convent at Westminster. When Elizabeth came to the throne Feckenham was a steadfast opponent of her ecclesiastical settlement; he refused the oath of supremacy and he and his monks were ejected (1559). Between 1559 and his death in 1585 Feckenham was almost the whole time in some sort of restraint. In 1560 he was sent to the Tower: in 1563, he was released and put under the eye of Horne, Bishop of Winchester, who thought he could convert Feckenham, but failed to shift him a single inch. Therefore Feckenham was sent back to the Tower (1564) and later to the Marshalsea. In 1574 he was released on bail, but the Bishop of London objected to his being free to corrupt Londoners and he was in 1577 sent to live with Cox, Bishop of Ely. In 1580 Cox petitioned that he might be relieved of this incubus, and Feckenham was sent to Wisbeach Castle, a damp, wretched and half-ruined place, where he spent the last years of his life in much more severe conditions. He died there in 1584. What makes Feckenham such an admirable and interesting man is that he never compromised with his conscience for a moment: he never wanted Protestants to be maltreated: he is alleged to have saved twenty-eight people from burning under Mary: he was a most accomplished preacher and acute debater: he never showed violence nor venom nor vulgarity in his sermons and disputations: and he took all that befell him with a wonderful serenity. He ministered to Lady Jane Grey before and at her execution.

But more than that: he seemed always to have command of

very large sums of money. These he spent wholly either indirectly relieving the poor or else in building for the benefit of everybody.

Feckenham must be looked upon, not as an important character in Tudor history, but as one of the most attractive and genuinely Christian churchmen of his times.

A most interesting, slightly biased, account will be found in E. L. Taunton, *The English Black Monks*, vol. 1.

DAVIES, RICHARD, Bishop of St. David's, was born in 1501 and died in 1581, aged eighty, He was the son of a Welsh vicar, was educated at Oxford and took his degree in 1530. Under Edward VI he was given two livings in the diocese of Lincoln, of which he was deprived by Queen Mary. He and his wife then went into exile at Geneva, where they suffered greatly from poverty. When Elizabeth came to the throne they returned to England and he became Bishop of St. Asaph in 1560. The next year he was translated to St. David's. He became the trusted adviser to Matthew Parker and to Burghley on Welsh ecclesiastical matters.

Davies was a good scholar and linguist and he is to be remembered as the man who gave to Wales the Prayer Book and the New Testament in Welsh (1567), but the translation of the New Testament was almost entirely the work of Salesbury. Davies and Salesbury shared the expenses of producing these books. They intended to bring out a Welsh version of the Old Testament, but they quarrelled over 'the general sense and etymology of some one word' and the plan was never realized. Davies also had a hand in the Bishop's Bible of 1568. He died on November 7th, 1581.

F. O. White, *Lives of Elizabethan Bishops*.

SALESBURY, WILLIAM, translator of the Scriptures into Welsh, was born about 1517 and died about 1600, aged approximately eighty-three. He came of an old and distinguished Norman-Welsh family and was educated at Oxford where he became a strenuous supporter of the reforming movement in religion. He published many books to further the

Reformation. In 1547 he published his English-Welsh dictionary, and in 1567 he collaborated with Bishop Davies in translating the New Testament and the Prayer Book into Welsh, he himself translating all the New Testament except the pastoral epistles and the Revelation. His printed Welsh had a very odd appearance owing to his theory that the Welsh words should be spelt as nearly like their supposed Latin originals as he could make them. He is said to have pursued his studies in a secret room which could only be entered by climbing up the chimney.

MORGAN, WILLIAM, Bishop of St. Asaph, was born about 1541 and died in 1604. He was educated at St. John's College, Cambridge, and between 1575 and 1588 he held four livings in Wales. He made a translation of the Bible into Welsh, but he met with much local opposition and he was delated to the Bishop, who refused to take any action. Morgan was then reported to Archbishop Whitgift and was summoned to Lambeth. He succeeded not only in convincing Whitgift that he was perfectly capable of making a sound translation, for he knew both Greek and Hebrew, but he also won the support of the Archbishop who promised to defray all the expenses of producing the book. The Bible was published in 1588, an independent translation made directly from the original. Many of the changes made in the English Revised Version were taken from Morgan's translation.

In 1595 Morgan was made Bishop of Llandaff and he was translated to St. Asaph in 1601. He proved himself an admirable bishop, a sound administrator and a firm and incorruptible man, but he seems to have had a good many quarrels with people who were less scrupulous than himself. He died on September 10th, 1604. There is a biography of him by C. Ashton published in 1888 to commemorate the tercentenary of the Welsh Bible.

F. O. White, *Lives of Elizabethan Bishops.*

NOWELL (or **NOEL**), **ALEXANDER,** Dean of St. Paul's, author of much of the Prayer Book Catechism, was born perhaps in 1507 or 1508 (1506, 1510, 1511 have also been given) at Whalley, in Lancashire. He died in 1602. He was educated at Brasenose College, Oxford, became a Fellow of the college, Public Reader of Logic in the university, and after he was ordained he became Master of Westminster School and Prebendary of the Abbey (1551). Being given a licence to preach, Nowell soon acquired a great reputation as a preacher, and during the reign of Edward VI he 'preached in some of the notablest places and auditories in the realm'. When Mary came to the throne Nowell was returned to Parliament as member for Looe in Cornwall, but he was not allowed to take his seat on the ground that 'having a voice in Convocation' he was not eligible to sit in the House of Commons. He then went abroad and joined the Marian exiles. On Mary's death Nowell returned to England and was made Archdeacon of Middlesex, a Canon of Canterbury and a Canon of Westminster.

In November 1560 he was recommended by Elizabeth 'for his goodly zeal and special good learning, and other singular gifts and virtues' for election as Dean of St. Paul's. Nowell soon afterwards married, and Archbishop Parker wrote that, if the Queen would have a 'married minister' for Provost of Eton, there was none comparable with Nowell. The Queen would not have a married minister. Some of Nowell's sermons were bold rather than tactful and he was in trouble more than once. On January 1st, 1562, he placed a richly bound prayer-book with pictures of the saints and martyrs, on the Queen's cushion in St. Paul's as a New Year's gift: Elizabeth sent the verger to fetch her old book, and after the service was over she went to the vestry and soundly rated the Dean for infringing her proclamation against 'images, pictures and Romish relics'. In 1564 he was preaching a Lenten sermon before the Queen and spoke slightingly of the crucifix. The Queen called out, 'To your text, Mr. Dean—leave that, we have heard enough of that', and so confounded was Nowell that he could not finish his sermon. His boldest sermon was that in which he took the Queen to task for not marrying and providing an heir to the throne, with the Queen sitting listening. 'All the Queen's most noble ancestors have commonly had some issue to succeed them, but Her Majesty yet none.' . . . 'If your parents had been of your mind, where had you been then?'

In 1562 he became Rector of Much Hadham, Canon of Windsor in 1594 and Principal of Brasenose in 1595. He died in 1602. He was twice married, but he had no children. He was a fine scholar, a skilful debater, a learned theologian: he was held to be an authority on educational matters and he endowed a free school at Middleton. He was also a devoted and accomplished fisherman and is said accidentally to have invented bottled ale, for when one day he was fishing in the Ash at Much Hadham he left a bottle of ale in the grass beside the river and a few days later found the contents effervescent.

Nowell is to be remembered as the author of three catechisms: (1) the 'Large Catechism' approved by Convocation in 1563 and printed in 1572: (2) the 'Middle Catechism', an abridged version of the Large: (3) the 'Small Catechism' of 1572 which was almost identical with that in the 1549 Prayer Book and of which Nowell was probably the author: he was also the author of the first part of our present catechism, the second part being added in 1604 as a shortened and altered version of Nowell's.

R. Churton, *Life of Nowell*.

TUNSTAL, CUTHBERT, Bishop of Durham, was born at Hackforth in Richmondshire (*i.e.* Yorkshire) in 1474. He died in 1559 at the age of 85. He was the son of Thomas Tunstal by his second wife, the daughter of Sir John Conyers, whom he did not marry until some years after the birth of the son. In 1491 at the age of 17 Cuthbert went to Oxford to Balliol College, but owing to an outbreak of the plague he left Oxford and migrated to Trinity College, Cambridge, where he stayed until 1499, when he travelled abroad to Padua. At Oxford he knew More, Grocyn, Linacre and Colet, and his chief academic interest was in mathematics. He became a Fellow of Trinity, and when he was at Padua he met some of the Renaissance leaders, such as the printer and publisher, Aldus Manutius. He was at Padua for six years and returned to England in 1505, after a visit to Rome.

By this time Tunstal certainly knew Greek and Hebrew, 'he was a very eloquent Rhetorician, a passing skilful mathematician (famous especially for Arithmetic, whereof he writ a work much esteemed), a great lawyer . . . and a profound divine . . . ' (Bishop Godwin). He was not ordained until 1509, but (as was quite usual) even before this preferments had been showered on him, so that he was both Prebendary of Lincoln and Archdeacon of Chester. In 1515 Warham made him his Chancellor and Tunstal's public life had begun. For the next seven years he was for the most part employed on diplomatic work. In 1521 he went on an embassy to the Emperor Charles V; the Lutheran movement was beginning and Tunstal came away with a very bad impression of what he had seen of the Reformation in Germany. In 1522 Warham appointed him Bishop of London because 'he was a man of so good learning, virtue, and sadness, which shall be right meet and convenient to entertain ambassadors and other noble strangers at that notable and honorable city in the absence of the King's most noble grace'.

In 1522 he published his work on arithmetic, *De Arte Supputendi*, which he dedicated to his best friend, Sir Thomas More. This was the first work wholly on arithmetic to be printed in England, but it was never translated into English, and of its eight editions only the first was printed at home.

In 1523 Tunstal was made Keeper of the Privy Seal and he was now one of the most important civil and ecclesiastical servants of the Crown. But he did not neglect his diocese, where he set about dealing with a revival of Lollardy under the influence of the Lutherans. He had already in 1523 refused Tyndale's application to become one of his chaplains. Now in 1526 he prohibited various heretical books, including copies of Tyndale's New Testament. Three years later (1529), so determined was he to root out heresy, he bought up all the copies he could find of Tyndale's book in order to burn them. In fact, he only thereby increased the financial profits for Tyndale and enabled him to go ahead with more printings. Tunstal could never be called worldly-wise.

Tunstal remained Bishop of London until 1530: in that

year he was translated to Durham by Papal Bull to succeed the fallen Wolsey. He was to hold this see from 1530 to 1552 and again from 1553 to 1559, being deprived in 1552 by Northumberland, reinstated by Mary, and deprived again by Elizabeth in 1559. He was essentially a conservative, in the true meaning of that word. Like nearly all the bishops of his time he accepted quite easily the abolition of the Papal jurisdiction in England: he could not at first accept the Royal Supremacy: but he was a loyal Englishman and it only needed a tactful letter to bring him round to Henry VIII's point of view. Henry wrote to him that he had no intention of usurping spiritual jurisdiction and Tunstal was satisfied (1536). In 1530 he had been made the first President of the Great Council of the North. When the Pilgrimage of Grace broke out in 1536—he described it as 'worse than the Turks'—he fled from Auckland. Tunstal was not a strong man and should never have been made President of the Council of the North.

When Edward VI came to the throne Tunstal conformed to most of the ecclesiastical changes up to the time of Northumberland. But like many conscientious and generous-minded men, anxious to be reasonable, there was a point beyond which Tunstal could not be moved. He voted against the First Act of Uniformity and in 1552 he was deprived of his bishopric and imprisoned. But, in fact, it was Northumberland's determination to secure the revenues of the see of Durham for himself and his friends which brought about the final breach between them.

On the accession of Mary I Tunstal was released and reappointed to the see of Durham. He went to Gravesend to welcome Reginald Pole to England, and he was at Mary's right hand at her coronation. When Elizabeth came to the throne (1558), Tunstal took no part in her coronation. In 1559 he refused the Oath of Supremacy and was deprived of his bishopric. He had also refused to take part in the consecration of Matthew Parker as Archbishop of Canterbury. He was inevitably deprived of his see and he was sent to live with Parker, who treated him with the greatest kindness. He died on November 18th, 1559. Too often he was a man whose strength of character never quite matched his first-class abilities: but in general he preserved holiness in very unholy times. (*Plate 13*)

C. Sturge, *Tunstal*, a work of extraordinary erudition and judgment, but almost unreadable, since the footnotes often exceed the text per page.

G. H. Ross-Lewin in *Typical English Churchmen*, series iii.

L. Baldwin Smith, *Tudor Prelates and Politics*, 1953.

HOOKER, RICHARD, author of the *Laws of Ecclesiastical Polity*, was born at Heavitree in Exeter in 1553 and died at Bishopsbourne near Canterbury in 1600, aged 47. He came of a good but not wealthy family. His uncle had been Chamberlain of Exeter and once M.P. for that city. It was thanks to his uncle's generosity that Richard was kept at school, and the boy proved so promising a scholar that his uncle introduced him to Jewel, Bishop of Salisbury. On him the boy made so good an impression that Jewel provided his parents with a pension and sent Richard to Corpus Christi College, Oxford (1568). This college was rather Puritan, but Hooker formed his own views.

At Oxford Hooker made excellent progress so that he soon acquired a reputation as a scholar and a tutor, and he was so diligent that he was only absent from College chapel twice in four years. In 1571 Jewel died, but the Master of the college saw to it that Hooker was able to remain at Oxford. In 1573 he was elected to a scholarship, in 1577 he took his M.A. and in the same year was elected a Fellow of Corpus. In 1579 he became Reader in Hebrew to Oxford University. In that year for some unknown reason Hooker and several other Fellows were expelled from the college, but they were reinstated on appeal to the Visitor. In 1581 Hooker was ordained and in the same year he preached at St. Paul's Cross.

From this point the story of Hooker's life has always been based upon the account given by Izaak Walton in his *Life of Mr. Richard Hooker,* but Professor C. J. Sisson in his *The Judicious Marriage of Mr. Hooker* (1940) has conclusively shewn that account to be radically wrong. Hooker was not married in 1581, but on February 13th, 1588, to Joan Churchman, in the

u—(2)

parish church of St. Augustine's, Watling Street, as is proved by the entry in the parish register. He is known to have been at Corpus Christi College in 1582: he was presented with the living of Drayton Beauchamp in 1584, but there is no evidence that he ever resided there. By 1584 the challenge launched by the Puritans against the established Church demanded an authoritative answer from a first-class scholar and writer. The leaders of the Anglican Church saw the right man in Hooker. His appointment as Master of the Temple in 1585 was the first step in this counter-attack. In 1584 Hooker left Oxford and went to live in London with John Churchman, the father of his future wife, Joan. There is dispute over Walton's amusing account of the Churchman family and of the disastrous results of Hooker's marriage. The Churchman family were well-to-do and reputable people, (John rose to be Master of the Merchant Taylors), and their house in Watling Street came to be the headquarters from which the counter-attack on Puritanism was organized and launched by Hooker's supporters in the form of *The Laws of Ecclesiastical Polity*. Hooker first went to live there in 1584, he lived there all the time he was Master of the Temple, and he continued to live there with his family after his marriage.

When Hooker became Master of the Temple he was confronted with Walter Travers, a violent Calvinist, who was the afternoon lecturer. Hooker was strongly opposed to the Calvinist system, so that 'the pulpit spake pure Canterbury in the morning and Geneva in the afternoon'. (Fuller). Relations between the two grew tense and Travers at last accused Hooker of heresy for saying that 'he doubted not but that God was merciful to many of our forefathers living in popish superstition, inasmuch as they sinned ignorantly'. In 1591 Hooker was given the living of Boscombe, near Salisbury. The Librarian of Salisbury Cathedral has lately revealed that Hooker did reside at Boscombe. So the books he needed for his work were in that library and are still there, heavily annotated, on the shelves given by Bishop Jewel. (*Times Lit. Supp.*) Izaak Walton is thus vindicated at the expense of Professor Sisson.

Hooker completed the first four books of the *Laws of*

Ecclesiastical Polity in 1593 and they were published in that year, not (as is usually stated) in 1594. Every political argument demanded haste in publishing his work, so that it should coincide with the passing of the *Conventicle Act* of 1593 which was aimed against 'seditious sectaries and disloyal persons' who assailed the ecclesiastical supremacy. The bill was thus aimed against the Puritans and not the Romanists. The printing of the *Ecclesiastical Polity* was completed on the very day on which Sandys* made a speech in the Commons urging that stronger measures should be added to the bill (March 13th, 1593).

Hooker's chief purpose was to defeat the Puritan demand that the Anglican Church should be organized on the Genevan system. Dr. A. L. Rowse in his *The England of Elizabeth*, (p. 476), writes, 'In the fifteen-nineties the fact that the Church had won its battle is witnessed by the flood of apologetic literature on its side, culminating in a great work, Hooker's *Laws of Ecclesiastical Polity*'. Yet the fact remains that Hooker was unable to find a publisher in 1593. The publishers held that religious works, especially on the episcopal side, would not sell. The generous Sandys came to the rescue and undertook to bear all expenses and to guarantee the publishers against any losses they incurred. And the publishers were right, for it took eleven years to sell 1,200 copies, whereas the Genevan Bible was selling at the rate of thirty-four editions between 1593 and 1603. (Sisson, pp. 50–70.)

Hooker's reward from the Queen was the living of Bishopsbourne, near Canterbury. Here he died on All Souls' Day, 1600, 'meditating the number and nature of the Angels'. The fifth volume of his book had been published in 1597 and at his death he left three more volumes very nearly ready for the printers. (For the story of the suppression of these MSS, see Sisson, and also R. A. Houk's edition of Book 8, Columbia, 1931).

Izaak Walton is not to be blamed for the errors in his biography, for he was given false information, but one may accept his description of Hooker as 'an obscure, harmless man,

* Sandys was the son of Edwin Sandys, Archbishop of York. He was a lawyer, M.P., a good business man, a strong Protestant and a generous friend.

a man in poor clothes, his loins usually girt in a coarse gown or canonical habit; of a mean stature and stooping, and yet more lowly in the thoughts of his soul'. Fuller noted his 'dove-like simplicity' and went on to describe his preaching. 'Mr. Hooker's voice was low, stature little, gesture none at all, standing stone-still in the pulpit, as if the posture of his body were the emblem of his mind, unmovable in his opinions. Where his eye was left fixed at the beginning, it was found fixed at the end of his sermon: in a word, the doctrine he delivered had nothing but itself to garnish it . . . His style was long and pithy, driving on a whole flock of several clauses before he came to the close of a sentence; so that, when the copiousness of his style met not with proportionable capacity in his auditors, it was unjustly censured for perplexed, tedious and obscure.'

Hooker's memorial is, of course, his *Laws of Ecclesiastical Polity*. What he did was not only to explain why the Anglican Church could not accept the Roman doctrine, but also to explain fully and clearly what was the doctrine of the Anglican Church. Further, he demonstrated that Puritanism was a danger as much to the political as to the ecclesiastical stability of the State. What marks out Hooker's book from all other controversial literature of his time is its 'utter calm, the great charity of the language, the peace in which it is all thought out' (Hughes, *The Ref. in Eng.*, vol. 3, p. 218). Eschewing the normal methods of violent language and vilification, Hooker brought reason to bear on theological matters. Relegating to the background ephemeral problems, he built his argument on the real fundamental points at issue. These he argued with courtesy and moderation. Nor was he afraid to concede points to the other side. While he could write, 'Think ye are men, deem it not impossible for you to err', he could also grant that 'the word Presbyter doth seem more fit, and in propriety of speech more agreeable than Priest with the drift of the whole Gospel of Jesus Christ'. But there is a firmness in his moderation and he is not afraid to use strong language: he denied that customs were necessarily dangerous simply because the Roman Church used them. But he also wrote, 'with Rome we dare not communicate concerning sundry her gross and grievous abominations, yet touching those main parts of Christian truth wherein they constantly still persist, we gladly acknowledge them to be of the family of Jesus Christ'.

The Anglican Church has been marvellously blessed in Cranmer's Prayer Book, in the Authorized Version of the Bible and in Hooker's *Laws of Ecclesiastical Polity.*   (*Plate 24*)

Best ed. of Hooker's works is that of J. Keble, 1836, revised by
    Church and Paget, 1888.
I. Walton, *Life of Mr. Richard Hooker.*
C. J. Sisson, *The Judicious Marriage of Mr. Hooker,* 1940.
C. Morris, *Political Thought in England from Tyndale to Hooker,*
    H.U.L., 1953.

FOXE, JOHN (or **FOX**), martyrologist, author of *The Book of Martyrs*, was born in 1516 or 1517 at Boston, in Lincolnshire; he died in 1587, aged seventy. He came of good middle-class stock; 'his father and mother were of the commonalty of that town' (Boston), but while John was still young his father died and his mother married Richard Melton, who came from the neighbouring village of Coningsby, whose rector was one John Hawarden: this Hawarden was also a Fellow of Brasenose College, Oxford; later he was to become the Principal. When Hawarden met John Foxe in 1533, he was so struck by the promise of the young man that he persuaded his stepfather to send him to Brasenose, Oxford, where Foxe arrived in 1534. It is likely that he learned Latin at Magdalen College School: he became a B.A. in 1537 and a Fellow of Magdalen College in 1539, an appointment which he held for about seven years. He became lecturer in logic in 1539 and took his M.A. degree in 1543.

During these years Foxe studied theology, and by the time he was twenty-five he had read the Greek and Latin Fathers and had acquired some knowledge of Hebrew. It might be expected that the next step would be ordination, but it was not so. Foxe gradually adopted the reforming views of the Reformation and therefore he came to reject the doctrine of the celibacy of the clergy: therefore he refused to be ordained and therefore he lost his Fellowship.

Out of employment, Foxe turned his mind to school-
mastering, but he could find no opening, therefore he accepted
an offer to become tutor in the household of William Lucy at
Charlecote Park in Warwickshire. He spent but a year here,
during which time he married Agnes Randall of Coventry
(1547). Thence he moved to London, destitute of money, but
suddenly an offer was made to him to become tutor in the
house of the Duchess of Richmond, widow of Henry FitzRoy,
Henry VIII's illegitimate son, to the children of her brother,
the Earl of Surrey, who had in that year been executed by
Henry VIII. Thus began the long friendship between John
Foxe and Thomas Howard, aged eleven, who was later to
become the Duke of Norfolk and himself to be executed under
Elizabeth. Another boy came under his care at the same time,
Charles Howard, later to command the English fleet against
the Armada as Lord Howard of Effingham.

In 1550 Foxe was ordained deacon by Nicholas Ridley—by
that time marriage of the clergy had been legalized—but he
was not ordained priest until 1560.

On the accession of Mary Tudor the Duke of Norfolk was
released from the Tower and recovered the guardianship of his
grandchildren, with the result that Foxe was once again out of
employment. Besides which, he was too well known as a
Protestant to be safe under the new government of the papist
Queen. Therefore with the help of his patron Thomas Howard,
now the new Duke of Norfolk, he escaped overseas to Strasbourg,
taking with him the manuscript in Latin of his history of the
Church from the time of Wyclif, which was in fact the nucleus
of his later book, *Actes and Monumentes* or *The Book of Martyrs*.
This history was published in Strasbourg in 1554. From
Strasbourg Foxe moved to Frankfurt and then to Basle and it
was here that he began an enlarged edition of the history. He
was involved to some extent in the quarrels among the English
Protestant exiles in Germany, rather as a peacemaker than as a
disputant, but his principal work was the making of his new
book on the Marian martyrs.

When Mary died in 1558 Foxe did not at once return to
England: he waited to see his book through the press. But in

1559 he was back in England, entirely penniless. His faithful friend and patron, the Duke of Norfolk, gave him lodgings in his London house in Aldgate, where Foxe mainly resided for the next ten years. In 1560 he was ordained priest by Grindal, Bishop of London. Three years later John Day published the magnificent English edition of the *Actes and Monumentes*. The book was immensely popular and the Queen commanded a copy to be set up in every parish church. The book was dedicated to the Queen, who in return presented Foxe with the prebend of Shipton in Salisbury Cathedral. But there were bitter opponents of the book who attacked it violently and abusively— 'that huge dunghill of your stinking martyrs, full of a thousand lies' (Stephen Harding). A second edition was published in two folio volumes in 1570, a third edition in 1576 and a fourth edition in 1583.

Modern historians have also criticized the accuracy of Foxe's stories, notably S. R. Maitland, J. S. Brewer, J. Gairdner and Sir Sidney Lee. Their attacks are mostly concerned with the pre-Marian section of the book, and it is true that Foxe in this part of the work was inaccurate and interpreted the episcopal registers wrongly, but in the way which he thought to be the truth. The Marian section is on the whole open to very little criticism. (For a short discussion on this point see the *Dictionary of English Church History*, p. 230: for a full discussion see Mozley, *John Fox and his Book*.) Professor Rupp maintains that 'Foxe's *Book of Martyrs* is not accidental to English Protestantism; it holds a unique place in the making of the English Protestant tradition, one by which the memorial of events became itself an event. Foxe's *Book* counted in English history as much as Drake's Drum' (*The Eng. Prot. Tradition*, p. 208). It was probably the only book besides the Bible which poor men read for a hundred years.

John Foxe was a most unworldly man, caring nothing at all for money, success, the pleasures of this life; eating little, sleeping little, studying much, praying much. He hated cruelty in every form and lost no opportunity of trying to stop it. 'I can scarce pass the shambles where beast are slaughtered, but that my mind secretly recoils with a feeling of pain.' In 1551 he wrote a tract against the death penalty for adultery—'I think it neither useful nor necessary . . . What sort of a remedy is it which takes away the life of a sick man?' He alone pleaded for the life of Joan Bocher, as he also pleaded for the lives of the Anabaptists in a personal letter he wrote to the Queen, a wonderful piece of pleading (1575). He tried to save the life of George van Parris, another martyr, in 1551, and he expressed the most severe disapproval of the burning of Servetus in 1553.

But Foxe was no crank and no weakling. He viewed with horror the misgovernment of Northumberland and wrote a tract arguing in favour of a revival of excommunication as a discipline for the times. It was high courage to write personally to the Queen on the burning of the Anabaptists. It was not less courageous in 1569 to write to his friend and patron, the Duke of Norfolk, warning him against the proposed marriage with Mary Queen of Scots, a letter in which plain speaking was in no way weakened by the courteous tone of the letter. Foxe visited Norfolk in the Tower and he attended him at his execution. Norfolk left him a pension of £20 a year.

Foxe died on April 18th, 1587, and was buried in St. Giles's, Cripplegate. (*Plate 24*)

T. F. Mozley, *John Fox and His Book*, 1940.

Simeon Fox, a memoir printed in the 1641 edition of the *Actes and Monumentes*.

S. R. Maitland, various articles in the *British Magazine* between 1837 and 1847, some of which have been reprinted in *Essays on Subjects Connected with the Reformation:* very hostile to Foxe.

H. Morris, *Elizabethan Literature*, H.U.L., 1958.

RIDOLFI, ROBERTO di, conspirator, was born at Florence in 1531 and died at Florence in 1612 at the age of eighty. He came of a good family, many of whom were senators and supporters of the Medici. Roberto was brought up as a banker and as such he built up a business with London merchants. After Mary Tudor came to the throne and had married Philip II of Spain, Ridolfi visited England and soon settled down there. He was a strong Catholic and became intimate with many of the leading Catholic families in England. In much the same way as Horatio Pallavicino, he established his reputation and integrity as a banker, not only with his business connections, but also with Cecil and the government, who often employed him in financial affairs. It is odd that the accession of Elizabeth in no way lessened Ridolfi's importance and influence. He was able to keep up a large correspondence with friends and agents in Italy, even with the Papacy, and he was in close touch with both the Spanish and French ambassadors in London. His banking facilities brought him into contact with the Duke of Norfolk and other leaders in the plot to marry Norfolk to Mary Queen of Scots, to secure her recognition as the heir to the throne and to restore Catholicism in England. This plan fitted in with Ridolfi's genuine sympathy with the discontent of the English Catholics, the more so because he had been charged by the Pope to act as his secret agent in England. Ridolfi set himself to form a league of English Catholic nobles. He was in the pay of both France and Spain, and thus he was in an excellent position to be the go-between among the Pope, the conspiring English peers, the French and Spanish ambassadors and Mary Stuart's agent, the Bishop of Ross.

In 1568 Ridolfi consulted with de Spes, the new Spanish ambassador, how the lot of the English Catholics could be improved. In December he gave a letter of credit for twelve thousand ducats to Sir Thomas Tresham for the use of an Englishman who was going abroad. In the autumn of 1569 he sent to the leader of the Northern Earls' Rebellion twelve thousand crowns from the Pope with a promise of a further ten thousand to come. Up to this point the English government was wholly ignorant of what was going on, but in October Cecil became aware that Ridolfi was receiving large sums of money from abroad and was distributing it among the Bishop of Ross and some of Norfolk's servants. On October 7th Ridolfi was arrested and sent to Walsingham for examination.

To Walsingham Ridolfi admitted that he had paid over money to the Bishop of Ross and to the Duke of Norfolk, and he further admitted that he had been 'made privy to the matter of marriage betwixt the Queen of Scots and the Duke'. On a second examination Walsingham failed to extract any further evidence against Ridolfi, whose house was now searched and his papers seized. Nothing more was discovered against him. He remained with Walsingham until November 11th, when he was released on condition that he kept to his own house at the Queen's pleasure and gave an undertaking not to meddle in affairs of state, and he had to provide bail of £1,000. In January 1570 he was returned his bail and completely freed. It is extraordinary that he got off so lightly. With great skill he had explained his disbursements of money as part of his normal business of banking. He could account for his connection with the Spanish embassy, because Cecil had employed him to negotiate over the seizure by England of the Spanish treasure ships in 1568. His connection with the French embassy does not seem to have been known. It is possible that Cecil and the Queen hoped to use so able and well-informed a man for their own purposes, a view which is supported by the fact that Cecil had Ridolfi to dine on June 22nd, 1569, to discuss the Spanish negotiations.

Ridolfi was now in a position to go ahead with his plans. He was trusted by everybody, except by Alva in the Netherlands, who never had any confidence in him. Ridolfi began to co-ordinate the plot for Norfolk's marriage with the Spanish plot for the invasion of England. He made a list of forty peers who, he was convinced, would rise against Elizabeth. Mary Stuart approved his plans: the two plots were fused: the English Catholics were to rise, an invading army was to overthrow Elizabeth and her government, Mary would marry Norfolk and replace Elizabeth on the English throne: this was what is known as The Ridolfi Plot, which was unravelled by Sir John Hawkins. Ridolfi went abroad in order to explain the new scheme to Alva, Philip II and the Pope, March 24th, 1571. Even now Cecil was believing that Ridolfi was working on the English side.

Ridolfi went first to Alva, who refused to move a single man until the English Catholics had actually risen in revolt. He then left for Rome, but he sent three letters to the Bishop of Ross, the Duke of Norfolk and Lord Lumley by Charles Baillie.

Baillie was arrested at Dover: the letters were in cipher, but Baillie's confession at last opened the eyes of the government to the truth about Ridolfi.

In Rome Ridolfi found the Pope encouraging and he went on to Spain bearing a written approval of his scheme from the Pope. In Madrid he was asked whether it would be possible to assassinate Elizabeth and Ridolfi assured Philip that it could be done. Philip finally agreed that as soon as Elizabeth was dead Alva should invade England. Ridolfi wrote triumphantly to Mary, Norfolk and the Bishop of Ross, but they never received the letters from de Spes, for in September the government had got all the information it needed. Norfolk and many others were arrested: Alva refused to stir in the Netherlands: it was impossible for Ridolfi to return to England. The Ridolfi Plot had failed.

Ridolfi went to live in Florence where he became a senator. He died on February 18th, 1612.

The article in the *D.N.B.* by Sidney Lee gives a clear account. Conyers Read, *Sir Francis Walsingham*, vol. 1, provides further details, 1925.

E. D'Oyly, *The Mired Horse*, 1951. (H.N.)

THROCKMORTON, FRANCIS, conspirator, was born in 1554 and was executed in 1584 at the age of thirty. He was a member of the large and well-known West Midland Catholic family, whose name sometimes appears as Throgmorton. The family seat was and is still at Coughton Court in Warwickshire. The Throckmortons intermarried with many of the leading, and especially Catholic, families, such as the Digbys and Catesbys, and their history is closely connected with that of the staunch Roman Catholic families of the sixteenth and early seventeenth centuries. Although they were not directly involved in the Gunpowder Plot—Mr. Thomas Throckmorton had prudently gone abroad—before going he had loaned Coughton Court to Digby, and it was there that the wives of the 1605 conspirators had waited for the news of the Gunpowder Plot. Long before that date, the family was directly and disastrously involved in what is known as the Throckmorton Plot, in the person of

Francis Throckmorton, although he was no more than the agent carrying out other men's instructions.

Francis was the son of Sir John Throckmorton of Feckenham in Worcestershire, and Sir John was the seventh of eight sons of Sir George Throckmorton of Coughton Court, Warwickshire, and the brother of Sir Nicholas Throckmorton, the Elizabethan diplomatist. Francis, after matriculating at Oxford in 1572, in 1576 was entered as a student of the Inner Temple. In 1580 he went abroad with his brother Thomas: as an ardent Catholic he visited the English Catholic exiles on the continent and he heard plans for restoring the Catholic religion in England by means of a foreign invasion. He heard the story in France, he heard it in Madrid: in Paris he met Charles Paget and Thomas Morgan, the agents of Mary Stuart, and imbibed the same story. Put shortly, the plan was one devised by the Duke of Guise: his armies would invade Scotland and England at one and the same moments. He had originally intended to murder Elizabeth, but he gave up that idea. The English Catholics were to be roused against the government and Mary Stuart was to be put on the throne. The whole cost of the adventure was to be financed by the Pope and the King of Spain. Guise himself was to lead the invasion on the south coast of England.

Walsingham was well aware that some such scheme was being planned, but he had no detailed information. He therefore set a spy to work in the French embassy, a Frenchman who signed himself Fagot. It was Fagot who gave Walsingham the clue that he needed, when he wrote to him, 'the chief agents of the Queen of Scots are Mr. Throckmorton and Lord Henry Howard. They never come to the ambassador's house except at night'. . . . 'On the 29th April le Sieur Frocquemorton visited the ambassador's house'. At once Walsingham set spies to work on Throckmorton and early in November Throckmorton was arrested and his papers seized: these contained a list of Catholic noblemen, a plan of harbours suitable for landing military forces and a number of 'infamous pamphlets against her Majesty printed beyond the seas'. There is no doubt that Throckmorton had also organized communication between

Morgan and Mary, Queen of Scots, and also the Spanish ambassador, Mendoza.

At his first examination Francis denied all knowledge of the papers, they had been 'foisted' upon him by the searchers of his house. Being urged to confess and being promised pardon if he would do so, he still refused to admit anything. He was then sent to the rack in the Tower, but he still refused to admit anything. Sent to the rack a second time, he collapsed and agreed to make a full confession. His confession did not in fact cover the whole conspiracy, but it probably covered all that Francis knew. The damning evidence against him was the confession that 'he had set down in his own hand certain special havens for the landing of forces' and had also 'noted the number of persons of power as he thought fit to be drawn to that action with the aptness of their dwellings to each port'. He also admitted that on this calculation the Duke of Guise had decided on Arundel in Sussex as his port of landing for the invasion of southern England.

In view of this confession and of the written evidence to support it, there could be no result but the execution of Throckmorton at Tyburn. One other result of this so-called Throckmorton Plot was the expulsion of the Spanish ambassador, Mendoza, from the kingdom, since he had known all the details and was deep in the whole design.

For the early life, the article in the *D.N.B.* by Sidney Lee is reliable. For Francis's part in the plot, see Conyers Read's *Sir Francis Walsingham*, vol. ii, 380 sqq., 1925.

A. L. Rowse, *Ralegh and the Throckmortons*, 1962, gives no new information.

PARRY, WILLIAM, conspirator, was the son of Harry ap David of Flintshire, a man of good family, and his second wife, Margaret, daughter of the Archdeacon of St. Asaph's. His original name was William ap Harry. According to his testimony, his father died about 1566, aged 108, leaving fourteen children by his first marriage and sixteen by his second. No date is known for William's birth. He was executed on March 2nd, 1585.

William was educated at a grammar school in Chester from which, after several attempts, he escaped and went to London. Here he married a widow, Mrs. Powell, who brought him some wealth. He entered the household of William Herbert, the first Earl of Pembroke, with whom he remained until the Earl died in 1570, when Parry entered the Queen's service. A second marriage with a widow, Catherine Heywood, brought him several manors in Lincolnshire and Kent, which involved him in some litigation in 1571. He was a profligate and extravagant young man and he very soon squandered all his resources and was being pursued by creditors. He therefore applied to Burghley to be employed as a spy abroad, doubtless in order to elude the creditors. He tried to ingratiate himself with the English Catholics abroad, to worm out of them their secrets which he could send on to Burghley. He returned home in 1577 and was constantly applying to Burghley for financial help. In 1579 he suddenly disappeared overseas without a licence to leave the country: he was home again in 1580. Pestered again by creditors, Parry violently assaulted one of them, Hugh Hare, for which he was convicted and sentenced to death, although he complained that the Recorder 'spake with the jury and the foreman did drink'.

Pardoned by the Queen, Parry in 1582 asked leave to travel abroad. He continued to pretend that he was searching out the secrets of exiled Catholics, but in fact he was beginning to take the Catholic side. He urged a more lenient policy towards them in England and he pleaded for a pardon for some of the best of the exiles. Then he fell in with Charles Paget and Thomas Morgan, agents in Paris of the Queen of Scots. After reading some of the writings of Cardinal Allen, Parry began to ponder on the lawfulness of murdering princes for the sake of religion, with special reference to Queen Elizabeth. But he still played a double game: on May 10th, 1583, he wrote to Burghley, 'if I am not deceived, I have shaken the foundation of the English Seminary at Rheims and utterly overthrown the credit of the English pensioners at Rome'.

In January 1584 Parry was again in England. He went straight to Court and had an interview with Elizabeth. To her he confessed that he had had dealings with the Pope, Paget and Morgan to attempt 'somewhat' against her life, but he protested that he had done this only in order to 'discover the dangerous practices devised and attempted against her Majesty by her disloyal subjects and other malicious persons in foreign parts'. In March he received a letter from Cardinal Como which gave some colour to this story. This letter Parry shewed to the Queen, who pardoned his offences and provided him with a seat in Parliament (1584). He at once got into trouble for violently opposing an anti-Catholic bill and he was imprisoned for a few hours until released at the command of the Queen.

Short once more of money, Parry took up spying again. He selected a man named Edmund Neville, who may have been a cousin of Parry's, and to him he proposed a plot to assassinate the Queen. It is possible that Parry was only trying to extract from Neville some admission which could be used against him. Neville, however, revealed Parry's suggestion to one of the courtiers, who at once went with the information to Elizabeth. Parry was arrested, accused of compassing the Queen's death, partly on Neville's evidence, chiefly on the evidence provided by Parry himself in his confession to the Queen in January 1584.

It is difficult to be sure that Parry was really guilty. That he was technically guilty in discussing the murder of the Queen without any authority from a minister to do so as a trap is certain. Whether he ever intended to murder the Queen is another matter. Parry was a vain, weak and vacillating man, with an inflated idea of his own importance. It is unlikely that he would ever have had the resolution to carry out such a deed. When he was examined by Walsingham, he passionately protested that he had never mentioned such a matter to anybody since his return from France. He spent the night at Walsingham's house: next morning he asked for an interview and told Walsingham that he now remembered that he had mentioned to a kinsman of his a statement he had read in a book about the lawfulness of killing princes for the sake of religion. Confronted with Neville, he denied again that he had talked of murdering

Elizabeth. Examined a third time, Parry made a full confession, wrote it out and confirmed it in a letter to the Queen. What is certain is that Parry was a bad and miserable creature who, behaving as he did, could not hope in the sixteenth century to 'get away with it'. The most charitable thing is to suspect that he was not entirely sane. He was hanged at Westminster on March 2nd, 1585.

The article by Pollard in the *D.N.B.* is an excellent biography.

Conyers Read, *Sir Francis Walsingham*, vol. ii, gives the fullest account of what has come to be known as 'The Parry Plot', 1925.

BABINGTON, SIR ANTHONY, conspirator, whose name has been given to the plot (*Babington Plot*) against Queen Elizabeth (although he was not the originator of it) because he appeared to be, and in many respects was, the leader of the English Catholics in it. He was born in October 1561 at Dethick in Derbyshire: he was executed at Tyburn on September 20th, 1586, when he was just short of his twenty-fifth birthday. He came of an ancient and wealthy family, with one branch of which in the nineteenth century the historian Thomas Babington Macaulay was connected. Anthony was the third child and eldest of three sons born to Henry Babington by his second wife, Mary Darcy, grand-daughter of Thomas, Lord Darcy, who was executed for his part in the Pilgrimage of Grace. Henry died in 1571 when his son and heir, Anthony, was ten years old. Anthony became the ward of his mother, but her second husband, Henry Foljambe, and Philip Draycot of Paynsley in Staffordshire, had most of the care of Anthony's education. All three families were at heart Catholics, even if they conformed outwardly to the new state religion, and Anthony was brought up as a Catholic, especially when he was staying at Paynsley. He was at Dethick until 1577, but he made many visits to Paynsley where he met and eventually married (1579) Margaret, Philip Draycot's daughter, when he was eighteen years old. Before his marriage he was for a short time in the household of the Earl of Shrewsbury at Sheffield, when Shrewsbury was gaoler of Mary Queen of Scots, where he acted as page to Lord Shrewsbury. Whether he ever met Mary Stuart is doubtful, but certainly he conceived a great admiration for her.

In 1580 Anthony made a six months' tour of France, spending his time chiefly in Paris and Rouen. It was here that he first met Chidiock Tichborne, a recusant English exile, who was later to be executed at Tyburn on the same day as Anthony (1586). In Paris he was visited by Thomas Morgan, one of Mary Queen of Scots' agents, who introduced him to her ambassador, the Archbishop of Glasgow.

On his return to London (1580) Babington entered as a student at Lincoln's Inn. He was a handsome, charming, intelligent and wealthy young man, popular at Court where he met other young bloods who were Catholic admirers of the Queen of Scots. Anthony lodged near Temple Bar. One day he received a letter from Queen Mary, conveyed to him by a Mrs. Bray of Sheffield (Staffs.). From this letter he learned that Morgan and the Archbishop of Glasgow had recommended him to the Scots Queen. Shortly afterwards he was visited by the secretary to the French embassy who brought him a packet from Morgan. In it was another packet which Morgan asked Babington to convey to the Queen of Scots. This packet he succeeded in getting to the Scots Queen, the first of a series, as Babington admitted in his final Confession, although he could not recall more than five letters in all. In 1585 the Scots Queen was transferred to the much more vigilant care of Sir Amyas Paulet at Chartley and Babington's work as a postman came to an end.

At this time he joined a secret society for the protection of Jesuit missionaries in England, formed when Campion and Parsons arrived in this country. Babington took an active and dangerous part in aiding their movements about the country from house to house.

A plan to travel to Italy and perhaps even to settle in that country came to nothing, because Babington was unable to get a licence to leave the country (1586). In the spring he moved his lodgings from Temple Bar to Hern's Rents, Holborn, near to Lincoln's Inn Fields. Twice he received packets from

x—(2)

Morgan to forward to Queen Mary, but he refused to help. Then, towards the end of May 1586, Ballard returned to England and called on Babington at his lodgings. They were well acquainted with each other. Ballard gave Babington an account of an interview he had had in Paris with Mendoza, the Spanish ambassador. He explained that there was a plot arranged for the rising of the Catholics in England, this was to be supported by a foreign invasion, that Queen Elizabeth was to be murdered and Mary Stuart was to be released and put on to the throne of England. At first Babington was sceptical: Ballard overcame his doubts. Babington discussed the plan with his young Catholic friends. He then decided he had better fly the country and he applied to Walsingham for a licence to travel abroad. This brought him into contact with Robert Poley, one of Walsingham's agents. Poley ingratiated himself with Babington and got from him many of the details of the plot. Babington discussed with him the lawfulness of murdering Elizabeth. All this information Poley passed on to Walsingham.

In April 1586 Morgan had written to Queen Mary advising her to send a friendly letter to Babington and enclosing a draft for such a letter. Walsingham intercepted this correspondence and kept it for future use. When Poley revealed to Walsingham that Babington was talking about the lawfulness of murdering Elizabeth, Walsingham at once sent on Morgan's letters to Mary. On June 25th, 1586, Mary wrote to Babington and he received the letter on the 29th—of course, after Walsingham had read it. Babington sent a reply and one of Walsingham's agents took it to Chartley where Mary received it on Saturday, July 9th, in a cask of beer—the machinery which Walsingham had devised by which all Mary's correspondence passed in and out of Chartley with the secret knowledge of Sir Amyas Paulet. Thus all Mary's letters were known to the government without Mary's suspecting. On July 18th Mary sent Babington an answer, which he received on the 29th. This was the letter which brought Mary Queen of Scots to the block. In brief it may be said that Babington had written to Mary details of the plot, including the plan to murder Elizabeth: Mary replied approving of everything, including the murder of Elizabeth. An enormous literature has grown up dealing with the question whether the whole of Mary's letter, as produced at the trial, was genuine or whether that part of it approving of the murder of Elizabeth was forged by Walsingham. On the whole the evidence is against Mary and in favour of Walsingham. (See Conyers Read, *Sir Francis Walsingham*, vol. iii, pp. 1-70 for a full discussion of the problem.)

Walsingham had now all the information he needed. He played the Babington fish for several days, anxious to extract from him the fullest information. He probably played one day too long (Conyers Read, *ib*.). When Babington heard of Ballard's arrest, he wrote a protest (according to Camden and there is no reason to disbelieve his version) to Walsingham, who replied that Babington would be in similar danger if he did not take refuge in Walsingham's house. Babington did so, but finding himself a prisoner, he invited Walsingham's servants to supper and, pretending to pay the bill, he escaped to St. John's Wood. There with a few friends he hid himself, until he was driven by hunger to the house of a friend. There he was captured and imprisoned in the Tower.

It is possible to sympathise with this romantic and generous-minded young man, but it is impossible to regard him as a hero, except at the moment of execution. He was a half-hearted conspirator and at the trial he played the meanest part of them all, (Conyers Read, *ib*.), putting all the blame on Ballard, which Ballard gallantly accepted. Sentence of hanging and quartering was passed. Babington wrote an abject letter to Elizabeth crying for mercy. He offered £1,000 to a friend, if he could secure his release. On September 20th, 1586, he was executed at Tyburn. To his credit it must be recorded that an eye-witness wrote that Babington, who had to watch the appalling execution of Ballard first, shewed 'a sign of his former pride' by standing, instead of praying on his knees, 'with his hat on his head as if he had been but a beholder of the execution'. When his turn came, he died in such 'diabolical tortures' that when Queen Elizabeth heard the story she ordered that the rest of the conspirators should be hanged until they were dead.

There are two views on the Babington Plot—the Catholic and the other view. The Catholic view has been made out in the most scholarly and as far as possible impartial manner by Father Pollen, in his *Mary Queen of Scots and the Babington Plot*. The most impartial and scholarly study is to be found in Conyers Read's *Sir Francis Walsingham*, vol. iii, ch. XII, 1925. The account in the *D.N.B.* is open to criticism on the grounds of its chronology.

Alan Gordon Smith's *The Babington Plot*, Macmillan, 1936, may be used with interest and pleasure, but must be used with great caution. Biographies of Mary Queen of Scots, such as that by Stefan Zweig, must be, on the Babington Plot, discounted altogether.

S. Ross, *A Masque of Traitors*, 1954.   (H.N.)

LOPEZ, RODRIGO, physician-in-chief to Queen Elizabeth I, came of a Portuguese Jewish family. Little is known of his early life. He married the eldest daughter of Gonsalvo Añes, more usually known as Dunstan Añes, by whom he had two sons and three daughters. His brother-in-law was Alvaro Mendez, councillor to Sultan Murad, who created him Duke of Metilli. Thus Lopez had distinguished relations in many parts of Europe. He was driven from Portugal by the Inquisition and settled in England in 1559. Lytton Strachey in *Elizabeth and Essex* calls him a practising Christian, but Lucien Wolf in his *Jews in Elizabethan England* quotes evidence to show that Lopez was a practising crypto-Jew and that Burghley was well aware of it.

Lopez set up in London as a doctor and was so successful that he became the first house physician at St. Bartholomew's Hospital. Leicester and Walsingham became his patients and in 1586 he was appointed physician-in-chief to the Queen, who treated him with great generosity. He was now a well-known and prosperous man, with a son at Winchester College, a house in Holborn, and an assured position at Court. His very success, however, and his being a foreigner and a Jew, brought him many malicious enemies.

After Spain had incorporated Portugal in the Spanish

Empire the pretender to the Portuguese throne was Antonio Perez, known as Don Antonio. Lopez, of course, sided with Antonio against Spain. It was largely on the advice of Lopez that Elizabeth sanctioned the Drake-Norris expedition of 1589 to restore Don Antonio to the throne. That expedition was a failure, and the Earl of Essex, who was the leader of the anti-Spanish party in England, brought Antonio back to England in 1590 to act as a cat's-paw in his political ambitions. Lopez got to know Essex at court and agreed to act as interpreter between the Earl and Antonio. Relations between Lopez and Essex soon deteriorated and in 1593 Lopez rashly criticized the Earl to Antonio, who passed on the criticism to Essex.

Spanish spies were all the while plotting to get Antonio's servants to murder Antonio and the Queen. Lopez became involved in the first part of the plan, but he showed no sympathy with the idea of murdering Elizabeth. The plot reached the ears of the Council, Lopez was at once under suspicion and Essex saw his chance to have his revenge on the Jew. When he examined Lopez's papers nothing incriminating was found, but that did not deter Essex. Some of Antonio's servants were arrested, and under torture they brought charges against Lopez which led to his arrest. He was put in the Tower (1594) and was tried by a special tribunal over which Essex himself presided. Inevitably Lopez was found guilty and condemned to death. For three months the Queen delayed signing the death warrant, but she gave way at last, and on June 7th Lopez was drawn on a hurdle to Tyburn, where he was hanged and quartered. Camden records that on the scaffold Lopez declared that 'he loved the queen as well as he loved Jesus Christ, which from a man of the Jewish profession moved no small laughter in the standers-by'. There can be little doubt that Lopez was sacrificed largely to satisfy the vanity of Essex, but a point of view more hostile to Lopez will be found in the *E.H.R.* 1894 ably argued by A. Dymock.

Apart from the dramatic interest of Lopez's rise and fall, he has a claim to be remembered on another score, for there are considerable grounds for thinking that Lopez is the original of Shakespeare's Shylock.

Lytton Strachey, *Elizabeth and Essex*, 1928.

S. L. Lee, The Original of Shylock: *Gentleman's Magazine*, vol. ccxlvi, Jan.–June 1880.

Lucien Wolf, Jews in Elizabethan England: *Trans. of the Jewish Hist. Soc.*, 11, 1924–27.

A. Dymock, *English Hist. Rev.*, 1894, pp. 440–72.

Martin Hume, *Trans. of the Jewish Hist. Soc.*, vi, pp. 32–55.

G. Marañon, *Antonio Perez*, 1954.

STUCLEY, SIR THOMAS (there are many variations in the spelling of his name), adventurer, was born probably some time before 1520: he died in 1578. He was the third of the four sons of Sir Hugh Stucley and his wife, Jane, daughter of Sir Lewis Pollard, a Judge of the Common Pleas. There is no reason for accepting the rumour that he was the illegitimate son of Henry VIII. Nothing is known of his education, but he was probably a retainer of the Duke of Suffolk until the Duke's death in 1545. He was present at the siege of Boulogne (1544–5) and on the death of Suffolk he attached himself to the Earl of Hertford, afterwards Protector Somerset. He then returned to Boulogne, where he held the post of King's Standard-bearer at a wage of 6s. 8d. per day.

Boulogne was surrendered to the French in 1550 and Stucley returned to England to the court of Edward VI and to the service of Protector Somerset. In May of that year he conducted the French Marquis de Maine to Scotland and back on a visit of condolence to Marie de Guise, the Scottish Queen, on the death of the Duc de Guise. In April 1551 Stucley was in France at the court of Henry II, where he made an excellent impression. It is a characteristic of Stucley that he always succeeded in making a good impression at the first meeting, but he never succeeded in retaining the favour which he acquired. This may be seen in his relations with Queen Elizabeth, Burghley, Pope Pius V, Pope Gregory XIII, Philip II of Spain and many other people. He came back to England as a supporter of Somerset, but the arrest of Somerset foiled his plans and Stucley fled back to France and entered the service of Henry II, whose confidence he at once won. Henry sent him home to England with a letter to Edward VI strongly recommending him to the King. Henry's real purpose was to obtain information which would help him in his projected attack on Calais, but Stucley used the opportunity to reconcile himself with the English government by betraying the true purpose of his mission. Northumberland, however, thought to win Henry's friendship by betraying to him Stucley's disloyalty, and he threw Stucley into prison and cancelled the previous promise to pay his many debts.

Stucley seems to have been released about 1553, but his debts drove him abroad again. Unable to return to France, he now went to the Emperor, Charles V, to whom Queen Mary had written a letter of commendation. He served under the Duke of Savoy until October 1554, when he came home with the Duke, who was paying a visit to England. Stucley was given a guarantee of freedom from arrest for his debts for six months, which enabled him to be at Court until 1555, but by then his debts had not been paid. It was essential to him that his fortunes should be repaired, therefore in that year he married an heiress, Anne, daughter of Sir Thomas Curtis, a rich City alderman. On May 13th a warrant for his arrest was issued on a charge of uttering false money. Stucley escaped overseas and again took service under the Duke of Savoy in the English force led by the Earl of Pembroke. He took part in the Duke of Egmont's victory over Henry II of France at St. Quentin in 1557.

Being still in financial difficulties and in search of quick wealth, Stucley now took to buccaneering and preyed on the French ships. Complaints against him were soon lodged with the Lord High Admiral, but Stucley's luck held and on July 17th, 1558, the Admiral reported that he did not 'find matter sufficient to charge Stucley withal'.

In 1561 Stucley was given a captaincy in Berwick where, in spite of his few resources, he lived sumptuously and gained a reputation for his 'royalty to men at arms'. In the same year he entertained lavishly and made great friends with Shane O'Neill, a friendship which was to have important results later. As a result of his extravagance Stucley had soon exhausted all the wealth of his wife and it was necessary to find a fresh source of income. Stucley therefore embarked on his famous plan for founding a colony in Florida. Once again his power to create a good impression helped him: he was able to persuade Queen Elizabeth to supply one of the ships. The plan to plant a colony was a mere blind to cover Stucley's return to piracy. For two years his exploits at sea 'were a scandal to Europe' (*D.N.B.*), so that Elizabeth was compelled to disown Stucley and to send some ships for his arrest. Once again he was acquitted, but he had lost the Queen money and thus he also lost her good opinion. She never forgave him.

The year 1566 was the turning point in Stucley's turbulent career. Shane O'Neill in that year asked the English government to send Stucley to him to be employed against the Scots in Ulster. Stucley went, with disastrous results. The Queen knew that Stucley hated her religious policy and that he had been carrying on treasonable correspondence for at least three years with the Spanish ambassador and that he had accepted a pension from Philip II. She strongly suspected that Stucley's motives in going to Ireland were also treasonable. In June 1569 Stucley was accused of high treason and was shut in Dublin Castle (June to October). He had certainly proposed to Spain an invasion of Ireland, but once more the evidence was not enough to convict him and he was released. From this moment Stucley became a whole-hearted traitor.

Already he was in touch with Richard Creagh, Roman Catholic Archbishop of Armagh, and with Guereau de Spes, Spanish ambassador in London. As soon as he was released, Stucley went to London and offered his services to Fénelon, the French ambassador, but he soon discovered that he could make a better bargain with Spain. He returned to Ireland, fitted out a ship and sailed for Vimiero on April 17th, 1570, arriving there on the 24th. Stucley was received with extraordinary favour by the King, who gave him 3,000 ducats, all his daily expenses, and then a further 6,000 ducats and an establishment which was reckoned to cost the King 30 ducats a day. Stucley now lived in the most sumptuous style: he was known as the Duke of Ireland and he asked Philip to create him Duke of

Leinster and his son a Marquis. It is a disputable point whether Philip did in fact knight Stucley. Some months later Stucley left Spain and moved to Rome. It is pretty certain that Philip had now become aware of Stucley's real character, partly through letters from Maurice Gibbon, Archbishop of Cashel, who wrote frequently to undermine Stucley's position. Stucley had been trying to intervene in The Ridolfi plot, but his plan misfired. On his way to Rome, by some means or other, he commanded three galleys at Don John of Austria's great victory over the Turks at Lepanto (1571) and he won great praise for his courageous behaviour in the battle. The kudos he thus gained did something to reinstate him in Philip's favour, to whose court he returned after Lepanto in 1572.

Between 1572 and 1578 Stucley was here, there and everywhere—in Spain, the Netherlands, in Paris, in Rome—trying to persuade the Pope and Philip II to embark on an invasion of Ireland. At last in 1578 Stucley's efforts succeeded, largely through the help of James Fitzmaurice, a Geraldine who was violently opposed to Elizabeth's government in Ireland. Stucley won the favour first of Pope Pius V, then of Pope Gregory XIII, of the Cardinal of Como, who was Secretary of State, and of the English clergy in Rome, notably Dr. Maurice Clenog, the Provost of the English Hospital in Rome, who wrote to assure the Pope that Stucley was 'a man sent from heaven' (*divinitus*) for the English enterprise. The Pope provided 600 Papal infantry which were conveyed to the port of embarkation, the Fortezza del Re Catholico at Port'ercole. Stucley was leader of the expedition and he sailed in the *San Giovanni Battista* (possibly a Spanish ship) early in January 1578.

It was not until April 4th that he reached Cadiz. His ships were so rotten that it was necessary to refit, but Philip refused to allow him to do this at Cadiz. Stucley stayed there from April 4th to the 14th, then he sailed for San Lucar and went on to Lisbon, where he arrived probably on April 17th. Here he found that King Sebastian had no ships to offer him: instead he offered Stucley a command in his Portuguese army which was about to invade Morocco. Stucley accepted and diverted the

Papal troops from the invasion of Ireland to the invasion of Morocco. He declared that he knew Ireland as well as the best, and there were only to be got there hunger and lice. He fought with great courage at the battle of Alcazar, but he was killed early in the day after a cannon-ball had cut off both his legs (August 4th, 1578).

'Of this man', wrote Burghley, 'might be written whole volumes to paint out the life of a man in the highest degree of vain-glory, prodigality, falsehood and vile and filthy conversation of life, and altogether without faith, conscience or religion.' Yet Stucley impressed many other people more favourably, even if wrongly and only for a time. He became the hero of more than one play and of several ballads and he appears in Chapter V of Kingsley's *Westward Ho!*

H. Simpson, *The School of Shakespeare.*
Z. N. Brooke, *E.H.R.*, xxviii, 1913.
J. H. Pollen, *The Month*, ci, 1903.

ALLEN, WILLIAM, Cardinal ('Cardinal of England'), was born in 1532 and died in 1594, aged sixty-two. He was the second son of John Allen of Rossall (where he was born) in Lancashire and of Jane Lister of Westby in Yorkshire.

In his early years he was educated at home, but in 1547 he went up to Oriel College, Oxford. He took his B.A. in 1550, he became a Fellow of his college in the same year and M.A. in 1554. His tutor was the Rev. Morgan Philipps, much skilled as a debater and an ardent Catholic, who later was a valuable help to Allen in the founding of Douai College. In 1556 Allen was elected Principal of St. Mary's Hall, Oxford, and he was also for a time Proctor. In about 1558 he was made a Canon of York and his future seemed assured. But the accession of the Protestant Elizabeth changed everything for the uncompromisingly Catholic Allen, so much so that in 1561 he deemed it wiser to leave England and to settle at Louvain University.

While he was at Louvain he wrote a treatise on Purgatory which he published a few years later (1565). He was tutor to a young Englishman of the name of Christopher Blount, who was later to be executed for his part in the Essex rebellion of 1600.

Blount contracted some disease which also infected Allen, and so ill did Allen become that the doctors urged him to return to England and see what his native air could do for him.

It was 1562 when Allen returned to Lancashire and his health at once improved. Up to 1565 he devoted himself to recovering relapsed Catholics from heresy, so successfully that he became, in the eyes of the government, a menace and he was forced to leave his own county of Lancashire and move to Oxford, thence to the household of the Duke of Norfolk in Norfolk. Here he wrote his *Certain Brief Reasons Concerning Catholic Faith.* His open opposition to the religious policy of the Queen forced him once again to go abroad and he left England in 1565 for the Low Countries, never to return. In 1567 Elizabeth issued a list of those who were to be apprehended for their 'contempt and obstinacy': 'Alen' headed the list as he 'who wrote the late booke of Purgatory'. In this year Allen was ordained at Malines and remained there teaching theology.

Now took place (1567) Allen's first journey to Rome, this time with Morgan Philipps and with Dr. Vendeville, Regius Professor of Canon Law at Douai, who wanted to persuade Pope Pius V to adopt his plan for converting the infidels. He failed in his object, but on the way home Allen persuaded him to take up the cause of Catholicism in England and the Netherlands. Allen proposed to him to found a seminary college for English students abroad.

In 1568 Allen founded such a college at Douai to enable English students abroad to have the benefit of collegiate training: to form a body of learned priests capable of restoring the Catholic religion in England: to instruct English youths in the Catholic religion who might go to Douai for their education. Allen hired a large house and began to live there in collegiate fashion with a few English and Belgian students. His great difficulty was lack of funds, but he also encountered a good deal of local opposition. His plan was, however, approved by Pope Pius V, and thus Douai became the first of those seminaries which had been ordered by the Council of Trent.

In 1569 Allen became a B.D. and in the following year the

Regius Professor of Philosophy at Douai University, and in
1571 D.D. It was characteristic of his selflessness that he gave
the whole of his salary of 200 gold crowns to the seminary
college to improve the food and to raise the number of students
which the college could accommodate.

Owing to the death of most of the Catholic bishops in
England or else because they were in exile, it became necessary
to find some responsible person to delegate the necessary
powers to those priests who might be sent on mission to England
from Douai. Allen was given, first by Pope Pius V and then by
Gregory XIII, extensive powers for this purpose. The latter
Pope also made a grant of 100 gold crowns a month to make
Douai College financially independent. Gregory also sent for
Allen to go to Rome to give him advice on a seminary college
for Englishmen in Rome which he was thinking of founding.
An agreement was come to by which students were to be sent
from Douai to Rome as soon as the new college was ready to
receive them. In 1576 Allen arrived back at Douai.

Just about this time the English students at Douai became
extremely unpopular with the Spanish in the Netherlands,
principally because they regarded the English as taking the
side of Philip II in the dispute between themselves and the
Spanish King. So unhealthy did things become that it was
deemed unsafe for Allen to remain at Douai and he withdrew to
Paris (November 1576). Two years later the English college
was expelled from Douai and had to establish itself at Rheims.
With some prescience Allen had seen this to be inevitable
and he had been preparing the ground at Rheims for the
move (1578).

Meantime things had not been going well at the English
College in Rome, where the English students were quarrelling
so violently with the few Welsh students and with the Welsh
head of the College that Allen in 1579 made his third journey to
Rome, partly to deal with the quarrels, partly to try to recruit
more seminary priests for England. His chief object was to
persuade the Society of Jesus to take over the College in Rome
and to send some of the sixty-nine English Jesuits in Rome to
England. The result was that in 1580 the first invasion of

England by the Jesuits took place, when Fathers Parsons and Campion arrived in June to lead the English mission.

Allen remained head of the College in Rheims until 1585, when he fell ill and had to go for treatment at Spa. His life was despaired of and he even destroyed his ciphers, but he made a rapid recovery at Spa and in 1585 he made his fourth journey to Rome. Probably Sixtus V had summoned him thither to take up again his share in the revision of the Vulgate which he had begun in 1579. On August 7th, 1587, Allen was created a Cardinal under the title of St. Martinus in Montibus, largely at the request of Philip II, who was hoping to make use of Allen in England when she had been overcome by the Armada. Allen had no money with which to support his new position, but the Pope and Philip II saw to it that he was adequately supplied with revenues.

Up to about 1582 Allen's efforts to restore the Catholic religion in England were confined to missionary work carried out by his seminary priests from Douai and Rheims. But he began to realize that purely scholastic and religious attempts were proving ineffective. He therefore turned to political methods and did not hesitate both to use intrigue and to advocate armed force. He was in correspondence with Mary, Queen of Scots, and with the Guises: he was well aware of Parsons' plans for getting rid of Elizabeth from the English throne: he was for a short time involved in the Guise plan for putting James VI of Scotland on the English throne: he then became a whole-hearted supporter of the plan for substituting Philip II for Elizabeth. When the conquest had succeeded, Allen was to go to England as Papal Legate and to become Archbishop of Canterbury and Lord Chancellor. It is often said that he actually went to the Netherlands to join Parma's army of invasion, but it is certain that he remained in Rome. In two particular ways Allen made himself specially obnoxious to the English—to the Catholics as much as to the Protestants. In 1587 he published a letter defending the surrender of Deventer, a Dutch fort, to the Spaniards by the English governor, Sir William Stanley, and of a fort near Zutphen by Rowland York. He also violently attacked Elizabeth herself in this letter. Secondly, there was published just before the sailing of the Armada from the Tagus a pamphlet entitled *An Admonition to the Nobility and People of England and Ireland, concerning the Present Wars* . . . This was a violent and detestable piece of writing, to which Allen was persuaded to put his signature and thereby he became responsible for it, however far its tone was from Allen's normal writing. The defeat of the Armada put an end to Allen's political career.

In 1589 Allen was made Apostolic Librarian and he took a large part in the revision of the Vulgate. He had also taken a share with Dr. Richard Bristow in revising Gregory Martin's English translation of the Bible, generally known as the Douai Bible. The New Testament was published in 1582 at Rheims while Allen was at the English College: the Old Testament was not issued until 1609 at Douai after Allen's death. He also intended to revise the text of the writings of St. Augustine, but he died before he could complete the work on October 16th, 1594, and was buried in the Church of the Holy Trinity attached to the English College in Rome.

Allen was without doubt the most important Englishman abroad so far as religion was concerned. He has been denounced as a traitor by English Protestants and described by Catholics as being 'graced by every species of virtue'. Everybody who met him loved him, there is no known instance of his quarrelling with anybody. He had the power to win the loyalty of all kinds of persons and to persuade all kinds of opposites to live together peaceably. He had high intellectual gifts and his religious faith was unshakable and even fanatic. His weaknesses were that he relied entirely on his own personality to achieve success: he had no ability to build a system of government for his colleges, so that, as long as he was there, things went swimmingly; when his personality was withdrawn quarrels at once broke out. Again, as long as he confined himself to purely religious and spiritual methods he achieved considerable success. But he was a disastrous politician and all his schemes failed. He never understood his own countrymen, and their unanimous support of their Queen when the challenge from Spain arrived was the measure of his failure to understand.

However much one may deplore some of his methods, there can be no doubt that his motives were entirely selfless and his ruling passion was the glory of God.   (*Plate 16*)

The article in the *D.N.B.* is a verbatim reproduction of parts of the historical introduction to the *First and Second Diaries of the English College, Douai* (edited by T. F. Knox for the *Records of English Catholics*), with additions from other sources, 1878.

A. O. Meyer (tr. by J. R. McKee), *England and the Catholic Church under Elizabeth.*, 1916.

J. H. Pollen, *The English Catholics in the Reign of Queen Elizabeth,* 1920.

T. F. Knox, *Letters and Memorials of Cardinal Allen,* 1882.

PARSONS, ROBERT (or **PERSONS,**) Jesuit, was born at Nether Stowey in Somerset in 1546, and died in Rome in 1610. He was the son of a blacksmith who had eleven children, of whom Robert was the sixth. He was educated at Stogursey, then at Taunton, went up to Oxford, first to St. Mary's Hall, then to Balliol, of which college he became a Fellow. At heart he was a Catholic, but he twice took the oath of Supremacy. In 1575 he left Oxford after a quarrel with his colleagues who are said to have resented his popularity with his pupils. For five months he lived in London, then he went to Padua to study medicine: after two or three months there he went on to Rome and on July 4th, 1575, he was received into the Society of Jesus.

Parsons was ordained in 1578 and was put in charge of the second year novices. It was probably Parsons who originated the idea of sending Jesuits into England. Much to his surprise he was among the first to go and was appointed the Superior of the party. Parsons, Campion and seven others set out from Rome on April 18th, 1580, mostly on foot, having only a few horses. They took six weeks to arrive at Rheims and here the party split up. Parsons travelled to St. Omer with Campion. 'He was dressed up like a soldier, such a peacock, such a swaggerer', wrote Campion, and in the disguise of a captain returning from Flanders, Parsons arrived at Dover on June 16th alone (Campion was to follow). He moved to Gravesend and thence by boat to London, where he failed to find any lodgings, therefore he went to the Marshalsea, where he knew there were many Catholics. One of them found him a home and he summoned a synod of Catholic priests in London to meet him at Southwark, where they discussed many points of importance to the Jesuit mission.

On July 18th Parsons and Campion (who had arrived safely) met by night to say goodbye to each other. They were joined by Thomas Pound, at whose suggestion Campion wrote his *Decem Rationes* (see under CAMPION) and Parsons wrote his *Confessio Fidei*. He then began his tour of Northampton, Derby, Worcester, Gloucester, preaching and administering the sacraments in house to house. In October he was back in London, but he found that the hue and cry after the Catholics was at its height, so that he never dared stop more than two days in any one place. At last he set up a home in Bridewell, which acted as a secret centre for Catholic priests. The persecution increased, for the government was faced with a Catholic rebellion in Ireland, backed by Spanish troops, Spain was now in possession of Portugal, there was a threat from Scotland and Catholicism was on the increase in England.

At this point (1580) Stephen Brinkley set up a secret printing press near Barking, and in spite of great difficulties and dangers he succeeded in printing Parsons' *A Brief Discourse containing certain Reasons Why Catholics refuse to go to Church*. The press was removed to Stonor, near Henley (1581), where Brinkley printed Campion's *Decem Rationes*, but this led to a search at Stonor and to the capture of Campion. Parsons was at the time in Windsor Forest and he thought it safer to retire to Sussex for a short while, after which he left England and arrived on August 30th at Rouen. Here he spent the winter, his chief activity being the founding of a school at Eu, near Dieppe, for English boys. This was the first of such schools: later it moved to St. Omer, and later still it became the College of Stonyhurst in England. But Parsons was immensely busy in other directions. He was writing incessantly, he was the first man to see the necessity for saving Catholicism in

Scotland, if it was to survive in England, and therefore he was negotiating with Lennox to send a Jesuit to Scotland. Meantime the Papacy and Spain were negotiating for the Enterprise—the invasion of England—without much success. Parsons determined to take a hand in the work.

From June 1582 Parsons was in Spain until April 1583, but his efforts to persuade Philip II to take active measures failed. He fell dangerously ill in Madrid and all but died. In May he was in Paris and then he met Allen (*q.v.*) at Rheims. He then travelled to Rome for three or four weeks, during which visit he extracted from Pope Gregory XIII two briefs, one to re-excommunicate Elizabeth, and one to make Allen Bishop of Durham, but these were neither published nor put into operation. In October he was in Paris, then he went into Flanders to advise the Duke of Parma about the number of English Catholics in that country and there he spent the winter. Most of 1584 was taken up in Paris with organizing the coming and going of English Catholics, sending off books, vestments, chalices, in close co-operation with Allen. It is said that at one point he was in great danger of being murdered at the instigation of the Earl of Leicester. For some months of 1585 Parsons was at St. Omer, but in September he and Allen went to Rome. The Pope was now Sixtus V and Parsons wanted to do his third year of probation before taking his final vows as a Jesuit. Allen went to discuss the financial difficulties of the seminary at Rheims; but there is no doubt that both went in order to persuade the new Pope of the importance of the Enterprise.

For the next three years Parsons was living in Rome, first at the English College and then as Latin Secretary to the General of the Society. He took his last vows in May 1587 and he became Rector of the English College in 1588. During these years he directed the Jesuit mission to England and it was he who sent Father Garnet to England. He poured out a good deal of advice to Philip II on the invasion of England, but in fact he had little influence in getting the Armada despatched. It was certainly through his activity that Allen was made a Cardinal. Less than a month after the news reached him of the destruction of the Spanish Armada Parsons left Rome and went to Spain, where he passed the next eight or nine years in founding and managing English seminaries there. He also spent much time in inciting Philip II to renew his attacks upon England, but he also warned him that no attack would be successful unless it was supported by a strong party of Catholics inside the island. He was perfectly well aware that some of the Spanish policy had only alienated English Catholics, but there are grounds for thinking that it was Parsons' intrigues abroad which greatly contributed to English Catholics' lukewarmness towards Papal and Spanish policy. In 1594 he published his *Conference about the next Succession*, in which he stated that the Pope's deposing power was an article of faith. The English Parliament made it high treason for anyone to possess a copy. Almost all English Catholics repudiated this doctrine and many foreign Catholics denounced it as impolitic.

In 1594 Cardinal Allen died; at once a quarrel broke out over his successor, in which Parsons was involved—probably unfairly—as a competitor.

When he became Rector of the English College in Rome, he used all his powers and influence to control the Jesuit mission in England. His appointment of Blackwell as Superior with unprecedented powers roused fury among the discontented English Catholics. They sent two delegates to Rome to dispute the appointment: Parsons dealt with them high-handedly and shut them up in the English College. All the time Parsons was also deeply involved in political intrigues— *e.g.*, that Arabella Stuart should marry the Cardinal Farnese (and the bride was a possible heir to the English throne), but there is not the least evidence that Parsons knew anything about the Gunpowder Plot. He died in Rome on April 15th, 1610, and lies buried beside Cardinal Allen in the church of the English College.

To the average English Protestant interested in Elizabethan church history Parsons is at best the least attractive, at worst the most conspiratorial and traitorous of the English Catholics. It is arguable that he is the most interesting. Father Philip Hughes (*The Reformation in England*, iii, pp. 333 *sqq.*) sets out

clearly in a series of quotations the normal view of the Protestant historians, that Parsons was merely 'a politician in
priest's disguise' (Froude). He counteracts this view with (to
a Protestant) a most unconvincing reply. Probably there can
be no reconciliation between the two views of divergent faiths.
A juster estimate of Parsons' importance will be found in
C. Morris's *Political Thought from Tyndale to Hooker*, chapter 7,
where he shews that Parsons was 'the real power behind
Cardinal Allen and behind all plots against Elizabeth, and he
had a genius not only for political organization, but also for
political thought'. Parsons certainly believed that the community acting as a whole had the right to depose 'a tyrannical
and especially an infidel ruler', and he regarded Elizabeth as
such a ruler. But what makes Parsons an unusual Catholic
thinker is that in the last resort he turns for the test of religious
truth, not as one would expect to the authority of the Catholic
Church, but to individual conscience (C. Morris, pp. 135–7).

Leo Hicks, Letters and Memorials of Father Robert Parsons,
S.J., vol. i, 1578–88. *Catholic Record Society*, xxix (1942).
J. H. Pollen, The Memoirs of Father Robert Parsons, *Cath.
Rec. Soc. Misc.*, ii (1905), iv (1907).

TOPCLIFFE, RICHARD, persecutor and torturer of
Roman Catholics, was born in 1532: he died in 1604 at the age
of 72. He came of a good county family, being the eldest son of
Robert Topcliffe of Sowerby*, in Lincolnshire, and his wife
Margaret, daughter of Thomas, Lord Burgh, of Gainsborough.
He entered Parliament in 1572 as member for Beverley: in
1586 he was returned by Old Sarum, a constituency which he
represented until shortly before his death in 1604.

He was taken into the service of Burghley in about 1573,
and there is extant a letter from Topcliffe, in his execrable, even
for those days, handwriting and spelling, in which he describes
with relish the harsh treatment meted out to the Papists of
Norwich.

From about 1586 and for the next twenty-five years Topcliffe

---

* Spelt, apparently, Sowerby, Somerby or Somerly.

became for his own contemporaries, Protestant or Catholic, what he has remained ever since, one of the most odious and detestable government officials in British history. 'Because the often exercise of the rack in the Tower was so odious and so much spoken of by the people, Topcliffe had authority to torment priests in his own house in such sort as he shall think good.' Topcliffe himself boasted that 'he had in his own home a machine, of his own invention, compared with which the ordinary rack was mere child's play' (*D.N.B.*). So loud were the complaints of both Protestant and Catholic that Burghley at one moment had Topcliffe arrested on the grounds that he had exceeded his instructions: but his imprisonment was short lived.

The most notorious cases in which Topcliffe played the part of the villain were those of Robert Southwell, the Bellamy family, Henry Walpole and Thomas Fitzherbert. The last proved such a scandal that Topcliffe found himself for a while in gaol, whence he wrote 'on Good or Evil Friday 1595' two letters to the Queen—'two more detestable compositions it would be difficult to find.' (Dr. A. Jessop, *One Generation of a Norfolk House.*)

When Topcliffe tired of work and wanted to retire in peace, he obtained from the Queen a grant of the Fitzherbert estates at Padley Manor in Derbyshire. Here he lived from 1603 until his death in 1604.

Those who want to pursue the details of Topcliffe's iniquitous and disgusting tortures may refer to the sources given at the end of the article in the *D.N.B.* For a less revolting, but also detailed account, the reader may be satisfied with an article by The Revd. Sir John O'Connell, *Richard Topcliffe*, in the *Dublin Review*, October 1934.

C. Devlin, *Richard Topcliffe*, in *The Month*, N.S. v, 1951, adds nothing to the above.

MAYNE, CUTHBERT, the first seminary priest to be executed in England, was born in the parish of Sherwell, near Barnstaple, in 1544, and he died in 1577 at the age of 33. He was sent to Oxford by his uncle, who had conformed to the

Anglican Church; he was at St. John's College, which was at that time much affected by the Catholic revival—Edmund Campion was at that college—and Mayne became a Catholic. He took his B.A. in 1566 and his M.A. in 1570, but when the Bishop of London, on evidence contained in some letters from Mayne's friends overseas, sent to arrest him, Mayne left Oxford and went abroad to the English seminary college at Douai. He spent three years there (1573 to 1576), was ordained priest in 1575, took his B.D. in 1576 and in April of that year he returned to England secretly on missionary work.

Arriving safely in England, Mayne went to his own west country and became chaplain to the Catholic Francis Tregian in his house, Golden, in Cornwall. For a year he lived there in safety, in the guise of Tregian's steward, and during this time he travelled about from house to house, administering the sacraments, comforting Catholic families and reclaiming the relapsed. Inevitably news of his presence in Cornwall leaked out. The Sheriff was Sir Richard Grenville. After consultation with the Bishop of Truro Grenville set off with an armed force for Golden: he knew the house well and had not any difficulty in arresting Mayne. He found him wearing an *Agnus Dei* (a wax imprint of a lamb). Mayne's papers were confiscated and among them was found a Papal Bull of Indulgence dated 1575, the Jubilee Year, 'divers other relics used in popery . . . with a special treatise against the Book of Common Prayer'.

Mayne's trial followed the usual course and he was condemned for treason for possessing the Bull. There was a difference of opinion among his judges, because it was claimed that the Bull expired in 1575, but the verdict went against Mayne. He was executed on November 30th, 1577, with all the horrible customs of those days.

Mayne was the first of the Catholic martyrs, neither the most distinguished nor the most important. but he was the simplest and the most forthright, he practised none of the equivocation of the later seminary priests. What Burghley and Walsingham needed to know was how Catholics would behave, if England were to be invaded by a Catholic power (*e.g.* Spain). Confronted with that question, Southwell and

Gerard refused to answer it. Mayne did not hesitate: at his final examination he said, 'If any Catholic prince took in hand to invade any Realm to reform the same to the authority of the see of Rome, that then the Catholics in that Realm invaded by foreigners should be ready to assist and help them.' Mayne was a brave man who died for his religion: he also provided the justification for the acts of a government responsible for the safety of the realm and of its religion as established by law. It is not possible for the seminary priests to claim that they were not meddling with politics and that they were put to death solely on grounds of religion.

Allen, *A Briefe History.* (I have not been able to consult this work.)

A. L. Rowse, *Tudor Cornwall*, pp. 347 *sqq.*, 1941.

A. L. Rowse, *Sir Richard Grenville*, pp. 134 *sqq.*, 1937.

PENRY, JOHN, martyr and founder of Welsh noncon-formity, was born in 1563 and was executed in 1593, aged 30. He came of a well-to-do family and in 1580 he went up to Peterhouse, Cambridge. In 1586 he transferred to Oxford, probably to join in a Puritan movement which was beginning there. He took to preaching, and finding that his native Wales was exceptionally backward and ignorant, he decided to approach the Government. From this moment he developed into a pamphleteer with a most forthright and rash style. He attacked those whom he believed to be the cause of the evils with violence and a total disregard for the possible consequences, including even the queen herself in his diatribes. Between 1587 and 1590 he printed in his secret press and published a series of pamphlets which, among other things, attacked especially severely the bishops. In 1588 there came from his press, and the proofs of it were certainly corrected by Penry, the first of the Mar-Prelate tracts, known as *The Epistle.* In the next twelve months several more appeared. Penry was helped by John Udall and Job Throckmorton. Nobody to this day has dis-covered for certain who Martin Mar-Prelate really was. Penry suffered persecution more than once, and he was ultimately arrested and condemned to death for treason, not for the Mar-

Prelate tracts. He himself denied that he was Mar-Prelate, and the evidence against him was to a large extent extracted from witnesses who had been put on the rack. The article in the *D.N.B.*, written between 1895 and 1896, accepts Penry as the author: this account should be compared with *The Notebook of John Penry 1593*, published by the Camden Society in 1944, where strong credence is given to Professor Dover Wilson's theory that the real author was Sir Roger Williams. Penry was an unwise, but a highly courageous, controversialist, who was ready to die for his opinions. He was tried for treason on May 21st, 1593, and was condemned to death. On the 29th May, while he was having his dinner, he was suddenly told that he was to die that day. At five o'clock in the afternoon he was hanged.

The Notebook of John Penry 1593, edited by A. Peel for the Camden Society, 1944.
Dover Wilson, in *The Library*, October, 1907.

SOUTHWELL, ROBERT, Jesuit martyr and poet, was born towards the end of 1561 and he died in 1595, aged thirty-four. He was the third son of Richard Southwell of Horsham St. Faith, near Norwich. His father was the illegitimate son of that Sir Richard Southwell who took a leading part in the destruction of the monasteries and whose unscrupulous and hard-bitten character is clearly revealed in the drawing by Holbein at Windsor Castle. The Southwells were cousins of the Cecils and the Bacons.

Robert's life began excitingly with his being kidnapped when he was an infant by a gypsy woman who was captivated by the baby's beauty in his cradle. The child was soon recovered and lived an uneventful life, the youngest in a family of three boys and five girls. In 1576 at the age of sixteen he left England with his cousin John Cotton and went to live at the English College at Douai, with the object of attending the Jesuit school near-by. Robert was at once attracted by the Jesuit order and applied for admission, which was refused him. He then moved to Rome and on October 17th, 1578, he was accepted as a candidate for the order of the Jesuits. His two years as a novice were spent chiefly at Tournai, he became a full-fledged Jesuit in 1580, returned to Rome, took holy orders and became Prefect of Studies at the English College in Rome. From this moment his heart was set on one thing—to be sent on the English mission to minister to the persecuted Catholics in England. This was certain to end in martyrdom, for the penal laws against Jesuits were appallingly severe. On May 8th, 1586, Southwell set out for England with Henry Garnett. They landed on the east coast in July, but Walsingham was well aware that they had arrived and from that moment Southwell was closely watched. Under the assumed name of Cotton he lived for the most part in hiding in London, but he moved about secretly into Sussex and the north country, comforting the persecuted, celebrating the Mass and making new converts to the Catholic religion, besides strengthening the weak and the relapsed. He soon won the reputation of being 'the chief dealer in the affairs of England for the papists'.

In 1589 he became chaplain to the Countess of Arundel, with whom he had rooms in her house at the Strand. Much of his time was spent in writing treatises to encourage his fellow Catholics or protests against the policy of the government, which he managed to have printed and distributed, of course anonymously, but Cecil and Walsingham were highly suspicious. Robert continued this dangerous and courageous life up to 1592, but on June 20th of that year he was arrested at the house of a Catholic friend, Richard Bellamy, who lived at Uxenden Hall, near Harrow-on-the-Hill. The Bellamy family were staunch Catholics and had been put under arrest as recusants. Southwell used to celebrate Mass there and instruct the sons and daughters. One daughter, Anne, was the first to be made prisoner and she was examined by Topcliffe. She gave away the means by which the Catholic priests were hidden in the house. Topcliffe made all arrangements to catch the next priest who arrived: that proved to be Southwell and he was easily taken. Topcliffe wrote to the Queen, 'I never did take so weighty a man, if he be rightly used.' He was imprisoned first in Topcliffe's house in Westminster, where he was brutally tortured. He was then moved to the Gatehouse where he lived in such filth and misery that his father begged the Queen either to release him or let him be imprisoned in better quarters. The Queen ordered him to be sent to the Tower, where he was allowed books and clothes and some friends to visit him. But he was thirteen times examined by members of the council and he was tortured ten times, not by the rack, but by new forms 'each one worse than death'.

In February 1595 he was put on trial for treason, condemned to death, and on the 21st he was drawn to Tyburn, where he was hanged. He was saved from the final agonies of quartering by Lord Mountjoy, who refused to allow the hangman to cut the rope before Southwell was dead.

Robert Southwell was a man of singular beauty both of face and of mind. Strong in his religious faith, free of all rancour, with his eyes set always on the heavenly crown which he felt assured would be his, gentle yet firm, a poet, yet also a man of action, endowed with almost superhuman courage, he remains for posterity probably the most beautiful of the Catholic martyrs—only Campion can rank with him. His latest biographer, Christopher Devlin, having written a whole book to prove that Southwell's one object in life was, not only to be martyred, but to be martyred with as much agony as possible, suddenly at the end of his book writes, 'Left to himself he would have asked nothing better than to die quietly, at peace with all.' One or other of Father Devlin's pictures must be false—there can be no doubt which Southwell himself would repudiate. Martyrdom of the most agonizing kind was what he sought: it is curious that he was deprived of the last agonies by the humanity of Lord Mountjoy. No one can say that even so Southwell did not have his fill of agony.

High claims are made for Southwell as a poet. The present writer's view is that Southwell lived too early to rise to the top class as a poet—English poetry had not developed to its full by the time he died. His claim to be remembered as a writer may rest more securely on his splendid English prose.

Christopher Devlin, *The Life of Robert Southwell*, 1956.
Pierre Janelle, *Robert Southwell the Writer*, 1936.

Dom Hilary Steuert, *Downside Review*, LIV, 1936.

H. Morris, *Elizabethan Literature*, pp. 78–9, 1958.

R.S., *An Humble Supplication to Her Majesty*, ed. R. C. Bold, C.U.P., 1953.

CAMPION, EDMUND, Jesuit and martyr, was born in January 1540 and died in 1581 at the age of 41. He was the son of a London bookseller and he was educated first at a London grammar school with help from the Grocers' Company, then at Christ's Hospital, and finally at the newly founded college of St. John's at Oxford. As a boy he had a precociously developed gift for disputation and oratory, so that he was selected to make a speech to Queen Mary on her entry into London in 1553.

At Oxford Campion became a junior fellow of his college in 1557 and took his M.A. in 1564. When Elizabeth I visited the university in 1566, Campion delivered such a successful oration to her that she commended him to Leicester, who for many years was a generous patron to him. In 1568 Campion was ordained deacon in the Anglican church, but he was at heart a Romanist. Uneasy in mind, at the invitation of James Stanihurst (father of one of Campion's most brilliant pupils) he accepted an invitation to go and live in Ireland, where Stanihurst was planning to revive the old Romanist college in Dublin. The English government, however, suspected Campion of being a Catholic, and therefore he fled in disguise to England in 1571 and thence overseas to Douai. There he was reconciled to the Catholic church, took his B.D., and in 1572 set off on foot for Rome to join the Society of Jesus. He spent his novitiate at Brünn and then worked at Prague. In 1580 he was ordered by Allen, head of the English Catholics in Rome, to accompany Robert Parsons on the first Jesuit mission to minister to the English Catholics. Campion knew full well that this was his death warrant.

Campion reached Dover on June 24th, 1580, Parsons having gone on ahead. The authorities were on the alert, but Campion escaped arrest and was taken by a Catholic, Thomas Jay, to a house in Chancery Lane, where he waited ten days for

Parsons. London was too dangerous a place for the two Jesuits to stay for any length of time and they agreed to separate. A Catholic of the name of Pound suggested that Campion should write an account of the reasons why they had come to England, which could be published if they were arrested. Campion wrote a letter to the Privy Council explaining that he and Parsons had come to England solely to preach and to minister to the Catholics, and that they were forbidden to have anything to do with politics. Pound was to keep this letter secret until an arrest took place; but Pound could not keep his tongue quiet: news of the letter spread, copies were circulated, and one reached the Bishop of Winchester, who passed it on to the government. As a result, the anti-Catholic laws were more rigorously enforced and a search was begun for Campion.

Campion now travelled from one Catholic house to another, largely in Lancashire. He preached to the families, heard confession, gave advice and encouragement, celebrated Mass and gave the Communion. In 1581 he wrote and Parsons arranged for the secret printing of a pamphlet setting out ten reasons (hence its name, *Decem Rationes*) why the Roman Church and not the Anglican, was the true Church. On June 27th everyone who went to the service in St. Mary's, Oxford, found a copy of the pamphlet in his place.

Campion's chances of escape were now nil. On July 17th he was taken at the house of a Mr. Yate at Lyford in Berkshire, through the treachery of a scoundrel named Eliot, who was suspected of murder and was trying to save his skin by betraying the secrets of the Catholics. Eliot arrived at Lyford on Sunday, July 16th. He met the cook, a friend of his, who took him upstairs where Campion was celebrating Mass. Eliot sat through the service, then sent to the local magistrate to come and arrest Campion. A first search failed to find him, but the next day a second search revealed him and two other priests hidden in a secret chamber above the gatehouse.

Campion was taken to London and put in the Tower. He was then examined in front of the Queen, who offered him a pardon and advancement, if he would attend Anglican services. Campion refused. The government then set out to find some political charge against Campion and invented a plot which, they said, had been hatched at Rheims to murder the Queen. Campion denied all knowledge of it. He was racked three times, and at the last time he seems, on his own admission, to have given away the names of some of the houses where he had stayed. His trial was a mockery of justice. The rack had so broken him that he could not raise his right hand to plead 'not guilty' (November 14th, 1581). On December 1st he was dragged on a hurdle through the rain and slush to Tyburn, where he was hanged before an enormous crowd. With unwonted humanity, the executioners waited until he was dead before carrying out the rest of the sentence.

Campion was the noblest of all the Catholic martyrs. A scholar, a gentleman, a priest, a man of genuine holiness, he was also a lovable, courageous and honourable Englishman. He had none of that passionate longing for martyrdom which sustained Robert Southwell in similar circumstances. Campion's was a simpler and perhaps a nobler attitude. He saw quite clearly that if the Catholic faith was to survive in England, then English priests must be sent from abroad to save it. He saw as clearly that he must be one of those priests. He never doubted what his fate would be, but he seems hardly to have bothered about that. Nor was he ever anxious to blame the government: he was only concerned with showing that it was for religion and for nothing else that he was being put to death. In the light of his pure religious faith, the natural and necessary political anxieties of his opponents appear almost mean and shabby.

R. Simpson, *Edmund Campion*, 1866.

C. Hollis, 'Edmund Campion, S.J.', *The Great Tudors.* A scrupulously fair historical essay. 1935.

E. Waugh, *Edmund Campion*, 1947. A brilliantly written eulogy, which sets out fully the Catholic point of view and concedes no points to the other side.

For the taking of Campion, see *T.S.I.H.*, vol. 2, pp. 82–5.

The *Decem Rationes* has been printed in a translation by the Manresa Press, 1914.

GERARD, FATHER JOHN, Jesuit, was born on October 4th, 1564, and died in Rome at the English College on July 27th, 1637, at the age of 73. He was the second son of Sir Thomas Gerard of Bryn in Lancashire and of his wife, Elizabeth Port, of Etwall in Derbyshire. He was educated first at Oxford, where he matriculated in 1575, and then in the English College at Douai (1577) and at Rheims (1578). It is possible that he did not go to Oxford till 1579, to Exeter College, whence he left for the Jesuit college of Clermont in Paris (1580–1). In the latter year he met Father Parsons at Rouen, but he was in England again in 1582. In 1583 he tried to leave England without a licence; he was arrested and put into the Marshalsea (March 5th), where he remained until he was released at Easter 1584. At the end of May 1586 he left England and on August 5th he arrived at the English College in Rome. He was ordained priest in 1588, entered the Society of Jesus and was at once sent back to England on missionary work (see Caraman's *John Gerard*, *Autobiography*, pp. 261–3).

Gerard was extremely active in ministering to the Catholics, bringing back to the Roman Church relapsed Catholics, and in converting Protestants to Catholicism. The government made every effort to capture him, but it was not until 1594 that he was arrested. He was then shut up in the Counter, the Clink and the Tower. In the Tower he was 'put to the manacles', that is, he was left suspended in mid-air by his hands with his arms fastened above his head. This excruciating torture he bore with the greatest courage and steadfastly refused to answer the questions put to him (*T.S.I.H.*, vol. 2, 86–8).

On October 4th, 1597, he made a dramatic escape by swinging himself along a rope over the ditch of the Tower (Caraman, *ibid.*, ch. 17). This would have been a remarkable feat for a young athlete in the best of training, but for a man on his thirty-third birthday who was all but crippled in his hands as a result of torture, the whole episode (the planning and contemplation of it must have been nerve-racking) can be called almost superhuman.

From 1597 to 1606 Gerard continued his missionary work, moving from house to house, usually living in secret, sometimes renting a house of his own. Nothing more clearly illustrates the limitations of police work in the sixteenth century than the failure of the government to recapture Gerard, in spite of its great efforts. When the Gunpowder Plot was discovered, Gerard was naturally assumed to be implicated, although the probability is that he knew nothing about it. The hue and cry after him was intensified, so that at last he made up his mind to leave the country. On May 3rd, 1606, he crossed to Belgium in company with the ambassadors of Spain and the Low Countries. He spent six weeks at St. Omer and then went to Tivoli for a rest. In 1607 he was appointed English Penitentiary at St. Peter's: in 1609 he was sent to Flanders to help found the first novitiate of the English Province at Louvain. In 1614 he became the first Rector of the new Jesuit college of philosophy and theology at Liège. In 1622 he went to Rome to obtain Papal support for the new Institute of Religious Women founded by Mary Ward. On returning to the Low Countries he was made Rector of the house of the English Jesuits at Ghent (1622–7). For the last ten years of his life (1627–37) he was confessor to the English College at Rome, where he died on July 27th, 1637. A list of his writings is to be found at the end of the article in the *D.N.B.*

On August 27th, 1601, an agent of Robert Cecil wrote a description of Gerard: 'of stature tall, high shouldered, especially when his cope is on his back, black haired, and of complexion swarth, hawk nosed, high templed, and for the most part attired costly and defencibly in buff leather garnished with gold or silver lace, satin doublet, and velvet hose of all colours with clocks corresponding, and rapiers and daggers gilt or silvered'. Topcliffe, the notorious torturer, recorded in his own spelling, unorthodox even for his century, that Gerard was 'Kewryoos in spetche If he do now contynewe his custome And in his spetche he flourrethe & smyles much and a falteringe or Lispinge, or doublinge of his Tonge in his speeche'.

Gerard's *Autobiography*, written originally in Latin, is a vivid

and at times exciting account of the kind of life endured by
a Catholic priest in the days of Elizabeth I. It reveals Gerard
as a man of invincible courage, of untiring energy and un-
questioning faith. It also reveals him (for example, in his
persistent use of equivocation) as one of those men who have
been the cause for the sinister meaning given to the word
jesuitical. He had none of the flaming passion of Southwell,
which wins our admiration: he had none of the nobility of
Campion, which commands our affection. There is a touch of
rancour in Gerard which is conspicuously absent in Campion
and Southwell. And as one reads his narrative, it is difficult
at times not to feel that for him strict observance of the Catholic
tradition is a sure passport into the kingdom of Heaven, even
at the expense of Christian behaviour.

John Gerard, *The Autobiography of an Elizabethan*, translated by
Philip Caraman, 1951.

CARTWRIGHT, THOMAS, Puritan divine, was born in
1535 and died in 1603, aged sixty-eight. His birthplace was in
Hertfordshire and he came of yeoman stock. In 1547 he matriculated as a sizar of Clare Hall, Cambridge. In 1550 he went
as a scholar to St. John's College, which was closely identified
with the new religious views of the Reformation. On the
accession of Mary, Cartwright left the university and went to
study law. When Elizabeth came to the throne, Cartwright
returned to Cambridge as a Fellow of St. John's, then of
Trinity; then he went back to St. John's as Lady Margaret
Professor of Divinity (1569). Two years before, he had been
elected a university preacher: his sermons were so effective
that 'the Sextone was faigne to take down the Windows' of St.
Mary's, so great was the crowd that came to hear. But it was
in his lectures on church government that Cartwright raised the
issue which involved him in a long struggle with the Vice-
Chancellor, Whitgift. Cartwright's view was that God had
revealed His will in the Scriptures only. The Scriptures laid
down a rule for church government. That rule was not
episcopacy as set up by Elizabeth in the English Church, but

Presbyterianism as conceived by Cartwright and his followers upon the model of the Calvinist Church at Geneva. Under Elizabeth's system the Church was ruled by bishops appointed by the Crown. Cartwright held that ministers must be chosen by the people.

Cartwright was now deprived of his professorship; he left Cambridge and went to Geneva, but at the urgent request of many friends he returned to Cambridge in 1572, only to find himself again in trouble with Whitgift. Cartwright went abroad again to Heidelberg, Antwerp and Middleburgh. It was in this period that he translated *The Book of Discipline*, written by Travers, which was the most important statement of the Puritan demands for church reform. The Latin text was circulated in manuscript about 1583: the English translation was not published till 1644. He fell ill in Holland and in 1585 he came back to England after Leicester and Burghley had pleaded for his return.

Cartwright was now appointed by the Earl of Leicester to be master of the hospital which he had founded in Warwick. He set himself to organize into a system the small Puritanical assemblies in England. He may have had some connection with the Martin Marprelate tracts. He almost certainly wrote the first *Admonition to Parliament*, but not the *Second Admonition*. He was arrested in 1590, but there was no conclusive evidence against him. He went to the Channel Islands where he remained until 1598. His last years were spent in Warwick where he 'grew rich and had great maintenance to live upon and was honoured as a patriarch by many'. But in 1603 he was in London in connection with the Millennary Petition. He was to have taken part in the Hampton Court Conference, but he died on December 27th, 1603.

Cartwright was 'unquestionably the most notable Puritan of his generation, and perhaps the most learned and cultured man the sect ever produced' (*Dict. of Eng. Church Hist.*). Hooker's *Ecclesiastical Polity* was directed against him by name, as also were some of Archbishop Whitgift's writings.

A. F. S. Pearson, *Thomas Cartwright and Elizabethan Puritanism*, 1925.

W. Haller, *The Rise of Puritanism*, 1938. Paperback 1957.
V. J. K. Brook, *Whitgift and the English Church*, 1957.
Knappen, *Tudor Puritanism*, Chicago, 1939.
C. Morris, *Political Thought in England: Tyndale to Hooker*, pp. 161–4, 1953.

BARROW or **BARROWE, HENRY,** Separatist, was born about 1550 and died in 1593, aged approximately 43. He was the third son of Thomas Barrow and his wife, Mary Bures of Shipdam in Norfolk. He was related to Francis Bacon and distantly connected with Lord Burghley. Bacon records that Henry Barrow was a 'gentleman of a good house'. Nothing at all is known of his early life until 1566, when he was at Clare College, Cambridge. He took his B.A. degree in 1569 or 1570. At the university he was according to Bacon a 'vain and libertine youth', an accusation which Barrow himself admitted. In 1576 he became a member of Gray's Inn, but he was never called to the Bar. In 1580 or 1581, 'walking in London one Lord's Day with one of his companions, he heard a preacher very loud as they passed by the church. Upon which Mr. Barrow said unto his consort, "Let us go in and hear what this man saith that is thus earnest". "Tush, "saith the other, "What! shall we go to hear a man talk?" But they went in and Barrow was so much impressed by what he heard that he wholly changed the course of his life. Giving up the law he turned to the study of the Bible and devoted himself thereafter to religion.

He soon came under the influence of John Greenwood, who had been ordained, but who had come to deny the scriptural authority of the English church and of episcopal government. Through Greenwood Barrow read the writings of Robert Browne, but he never met the founder of the Brownists. Barrow was now a Puritan, but by 1589 he had become a 'congregationalist', one who regarded each congregation as a Church in itself. Barrow has come to be known as one of the founders of the Separatists and thus of modern Nonconformity. To Barrow separatism meant that sinners must be separated from the saints and the Church must consist only of the saints: that the Church must be separated from the State: that each

z—(2)

congregation must be to some degree separated from central control. Barrow held that a man's conscience was the final court of appeal, but he believed firmly in non-resistance, and that rebellion would be 'most unlawful and damnable by the Word of God'.

On October 7th, 1586, Greenwood was arrested by the orders of Aylmer, Bishop of London. He was put in the Clink, where on November 19th Barrow visited him. Aylmer was on the lookout for him and Barrow found himself arrested. Between November 19th, 1586, and March 1589, Barrow was examined five times, and at the most important examination, when Burghley was present, Barrow alienated Burghley's sympathy by his intemperate language. Finally on March 11th, 1593, both Greenwood and Barrow were charged with circulating seditious books, they were convicted on the 23rd and were to be executed the next day. The execution was stayed only when the two victims were 'ready to be bound to the cart': on the 31st they went to the place of execution and were actually tied by their necks to the tree when a reprieve arrived. But the stay was only temporary and both men were hanged on April 6th, 1593. While Barrow was in prison he wrote many pamphlets and treatises, but there is no evidence that he was the author of the Marprelate Tracts.

F. J. Powicke, *Henry Barrow and the Exiled Church of Amsterdam*, 1900.

C. Morris, *Political Thought in England, Tyndale to Hooker*, 1953.

BROWNE, ROBERT, founder of the Brownists or Puritan Separatists, from whom are sprung the modern Congregational Noncomformists, was born in about 1550 at Tolethorpe Hall, near Stamford, in Rutland. He died in 1633, aged about 80. He was the third son of Anthony Browne and his wife, Dorothy Boteler, and he was remotely connected with Lord Burghley, who protected him more than once on the grounds of kinship. Browne went up to Corpus Christi College, Cambridge, in 1570 and took his B.A. in 1572.

His period at Cambridge coincided with the time when Cartwright was advocating a Presbyterian system for the

Church and Browne came much under his influence. On leaving Cambridge Browne turned to teaching (1572–5) in Northamptonshire, but he came to be depressed by the 'woful and lamentable state of the Church', gave up teaching and after a short time spent at his home, he returned to Cambridge and took to preaching, probably in 1579.

Browne was now a Congregationalist—he held that Christ was the only true Head of the Church, and next under Christ came, not the Crown nor the Bishops, but the Church collectively. For a time he compromised over the power of the Bishops, perhaps because his views were not fully settled. He grew more and more difficult and at last he went to Norwich, where he thought people were more 'forward'. Here he set up independent congregations (or conventicles), with the result that he was arrested and was for a short time in prison (1581). He was freed at the request of Burghley and returned to Norwich, where he organized the first Congregational Church and took it overseas to Middleburg in Zeeland (1581). The next two years were years of misery for all concerned. Browne was intolerant and difficult, but so also was his one-time friend, Harrison, who roused the Congregation against its founder. Browne left Holland in 1583 for Scotland, but he found a very cool reception there, came back to England and submitted to the Anglican Church (1585). The next year he became Master of St. Olave's school, Southwark, but he behaved outrageously, ministering to separatist congregations and yet also attending orthodox services.

In 1591 Browne was ordained deacon and priest in the Anglican Church and Burghley presented him with the living of Achurch-cum-Thorpe Waterville in Northamptonshire. In 1610 his wife died, but two years later he married again. The marriage was an unhappy one and Browne was sued for restoration of conjugal rights in 1623. He now let the parsonage fall into decay and he separated from his wife altogether. Between 1617 and 1627 he was suspended from clerical office, but suddenly one day he returned to full ministration. This led to many quarrels with his churchwardens and with the parishioners. In 1630 he assaulted a police constable who was his godson and he went to gaol for a short time. After his release he lived for two years in Northampton and he died in October 1633 and was buried in the churchyard of St. Giles's.

Browne was an unstable and not very courageous man, nor was he very clear-minded in his views. Cartwright had always held that in reforming the Church it was necessary to 'tarry for a Magistrate', and by a Magistrate he meant a Sovereign or a Lay Ruler. It was because Browne came to despair of the Magistrate's ever doing anything that he wrote his book, *Reformation without Tarrying for Any*, 1582. He then put his trust in the Christian Congregation, but experience made him despair just as much of the Congregation. Browne had two objectives in view. The first was to 'Separate': he began by wanting to separate the Church from the State and then each Congregation from the whole Church. His second object was to 'Reform' the Church. Here he began by wanting to get rid of all relics of Popery (vestments and ritual, etc.): then he went further and wanted to have only what he called a 'gathered Church'. This was really one aspect of Separatism, because Browne wanted to separate the sheep from the goats, the saints from the sinners, the inwardly converted from the outwardly conforming. (C. Morris, *Political Thought in England*, p. 165.) To achieve all this Browne began to emphasize the duty and powers of the Magistrates,so that he appeared in his own day, as he still appears to us to-day, inconsistent and unreliable.

F. J. Powicke, *Robert Browne, Pioneer of Modern Congregationalism*, 1910. Contains a list of Browne's writings with criticisms.
C. Morris, *Political Thought in England, Tyndale to Hooker*, 1953.

CABOT, JOHN, explorer, the dates of whose birth and death are unknown, was probably a Genoese by birth who became in 1476 a naturalized Venetian. He married a Venetian and had three sons, Ludovico, Sebastiano and Sancio. The names of all three appear in the letters patent issued by Henry VII in 1496, but Sebastiano is the only son of whom anything further is known.

The facts of John Cabot's life have been greatly disputed and even now we have to rely on deductions and guess-work.

But in 1956 research in the archives at Madrid revealed a letter from an Englishman, John Day, who was in Andalusia, to a Spanish notable who was almost for certain Columbus himself. The letter was written some time between December 1497 and spring 1498. This letter has settled one point finally: John Cabot's first voyage was made in 1496 and not in 1497: the 1497 voyage was his second. It also establishes for certain that the men of Bristol had already discovered the 'island of Brasil' (*i.e.* Newfoundland) before Cabot's first voyage. 'It is considered certain that the Cape of the said land was found and discovered in the past by the men from Bristol who found Brasil, as your lordship well knows. It was called the island of Brasil and it is assumed and believed to be the mainland that the men from Bristol found.' . . . . 'Since your lordship wants information relating to the first voyage, here is what happened: he (John Cabot) went with one ship, his crew confused him, he was short of food and ran into bad weather and he decided to turn back.' This voyage must have been after the patent was issued in 1496 and before the 1497 voyage.

John Cabot came to Bristol between 1490 and 1495. He had lived in Venice as a merchant engaged in the spice trade beyond the Levant. He developed an idea that these spices might be got hold of by a voyage westwards across the Atlantic to the east coast of Asia. Venice, who did not allow any competition against her eastern trade, refused to help him, as also did Spain and Portugal. Cabot therefore came to England. Bristol was a rich city and ambitious to take the place of Southampton as the chief port for the spice trade. Cabot knew all about that trade, he knew all about maps and globes and Renaissance geography: but he was not rich and he was in need of capital. Bristol supplied him with ships and crews and could tell him much about the Icelandic knowledge of northern geography.

Cabot had his plans ready before any news came of Columbus's success. Cabot was therefore an originator and not a mere imitator. When he heard of Columbus's claim to have discovered Cipango (Japan) and Cathay (China), he disbelieved the claim. He was convinced that the nearest point of Cathay lay in the same latitudes as the British Isles and that thence the continent sloped south-west down to the tropics. He believed that Columbus had not gone far enough to find the mainland, that he had only found the islands in mid-ocean. He himself intended to find the nearest point of the mainland and then to follow the coast to the tropics, thus avoiding Spanish possessions. His main objective was to extend the discovery by the men of Bristol of a valuable fishing coast into the discovery of new land which would act as a jumping-off point for a rich oriental trade in spices.

On March 5th, 1496, Henry VII issued letters patent giving Cabot and his heirs a monopoly of trade in the new lands and to the Bristol merchants the privilege of being the only port from which this trade could operate. On May 20th, 1497, Cabot in the *Matthew* of Bristol set sail, the first English ship to cross the Atlantic. (Is it possible that the ship's real name was *Mattea*, for that was the name of Cabot's wife, and he may well have called the ship after her?) The ship was 50 tons and was manned with a crew of some 18 or 20 men. On June 24th he sighted land and made a landfall on the Island of St. John—he gave it this name because he found it on St. John the Baptist's Day. It is not possible to say for certain exactly where the landfall was, but it was either in Maine or in Nova Scotia. He went ashore and formally took possession of the land, in the presence of perhaps a dozen men. He set up a cross, the banner of Henry VII, the banner of the Pope and of St. Mark, the patron saint of Venice. The little party did not advance more than a bowshot from the shore. They saw no inhabitants, but they found traces of them—a track, a burnt out fire, felled trees, snares for game, a carved stick like a netting-needle. Then, 'being in doubt, he returned to his ship'. This was the only landing he made. The passage home took fifteen days, with a fair wind and good weather. He made a landfall in Brittany and came home round Land's End—a course which was taken against his better judgement at the demand of others in the ship. He was back in Bristol by August 6th, and he had an interview with Henry VII on the 10th. He became a well-known and popular figure: the

King gave him a gratuity of £10 and a pension of £20; he came to be known as 'the great Admiral' and was followed in the streets by crowds of admirers; at Court he moved about splendidly dressed in silks and he gave lectures on the voyage and demonstrations of his instruments.

The third voyage of 1498 was to be a fully equipped expedition. Cabot's plan was to return to the place he had discovered, follow the coast down to the tropics and there carry on a lucrative trade with the mainland and with Cipango. The King provided one fully equipped ship, the Bristol and London merchants provided four other ships and the cargoes. These ships were provisioned for one year. It was said that the King promised a body of convicts to carry out the hard labour of planting a colony, but the evidence for this is far from convincing.

The fleet set sail from Bristol in early May 1498. Next to nothing is known about the voyage. One ship was damaged in a storm and had to put into an Irish port. It was probably Cabot's ship: if so, he must have sailed again after repairs. No direct news of Cabot and his other four ships has ever been heard from that day to this. It is most improbable that all five ships were lost; there are some reasons for thinking that some of the ships did in fact return. It may be deduced that Cabot did reach the coast of America and did follow it down into the tropics, perhaps entering the Caribbean. Whether he arrived home himself can not now be known: it is true that his pension was still being paid in 1499, but there is no proof that Cabot received it—probably it was paid to his wife.

Cabot was a remarkable man, for he had an original mind and considerable intellectual powers. He had read and understood Marco Polo and was thus able to refute the Spanish claim to have reached Asia. He had studied cartography and he knew how to make the best use of maps and globes. He could state a case clearly and persuasively, as is shown by the way in which he won Henry VII's approval for his schemes. He could win popular support and admiration. His reputation has suffered, because no trustworthy records have survived of all his doings.

The principal authority on both John and Sebastian Cabot is Dr. J. A. Williamson, and up to the present moment his book *The Ocean in History* and his pamphlet on *The Voyages of John and Sebastian Cabot* (Historical Association pamphlet 106, 1937) have been the standard works. The discovery of John Day's letter has necessitated a complete reappraisal of the Cabots. Dr. Williamson has undertaken this, and I am deeply grateful for his generosity in allowing me to read and use the introduction to his forthcoming book in typescript before publication.

CABOT, SEBASTIAN, cosmographer and cartographer, was born almost for certain in or near Venice not later than 1484, the second son of John Cabot. He was brought to Bristol probably in 1490 and he died almost for certain in 1557. There is great difficulty in ascertaining the true facts of his life, very largely because of his own character. (The account given in the *D.N.B.* must be used with care, for much of it has been rendered untrue by modern research. The most valuable modern study is that by J. A. Williamson in his *Maritime Enterprise* 1485-1558.) We know nothing about his early life, except that the voyages and discoveries before 1500 which have been attributed to him are certainly those of his father, John Cabot. Williamson says of him that he was 'a vain egoist, fond of giving vent to mysterious utterances containing a maximum of self-praise and a minimum of hard fact'. We know now that Sebastian was not guilty of deliberately perverting the truth, but he was guilty of suppressing the truth, where his father's voyages were concerned. 'It can not be denied that he shewed a strange want of generosity on the point'. 'In other matters he undoubtedly lied freely and frequently.' There is no evidence that he accompanied John on his voyages. What is certain is that he went to Spain in 1512 and returned to England in 1548.

Sebastian was really not a sailor nor a leader of men. When in 1505 Henry VII paid him a pension of £10 charged on the customs of Bristol, it was paid, not for any explorations, but for 'diligent service and attendance . . . in and about our town and port of Bristol'. He must have known all about the voyages which the Bristol merchants sent out in 1501 and 1502, and it seems certain that he did himself lead an expedition in 1508 or 1509, before Henry VII died, to discover the north-west passage. Sebastian had seized on the truth that 'the trans-atlantic land was a separate continent altogether distinct from Asia', and he had learned this from his father's voyage of 1498. When Sebastian sailed in 1509, he took two ships with him, partly at the king's expense, and he went to Labrador (as we know it and not Greenland, so called because a *labrador*, a ploughman or landowner, from the Azores first told the King of England of the country). Between 61° and 64° he found a strait going west: he went through it for some 10° of longitude, then it seemed to turn south and to open out. Sebastian felt sure that he had turned the limit of the New Found Land and was now in the Pacific. The sea was thick with floating ice and his men mutinied, so that perforce he returned home. Modern discovery corroborates his story and he certainly found Hudson's Strait. He may have gone as far north as Fox Channel and as far south as 38°.

Sebastian was certainly in England in 1512, when he was paid 20s. for making a map of Gascony and Guienne for the Marquis of Dorset's invasion of France. He accompanied Dorset's expedition and then transferred his services to Spain. He lived at Seville from 1512 to 1515, then we lose track of him until 1518, when he was appointed Pilot Major to Charles V. Ferdinand of Spain died in 1516, therefore it is possible that Sebastian came back to England for 1515 and 1517.

There is a story that he went on a voyage with Thomas Spert, who was master of the *Harry Grace à Dieu*, in 1516, but this is totally unsubstantiated. In 1521 Henry VIII planned an expedition to the west and proposed to put Sebastian in command of it. Sebastian did in fact pay a visit to England in that year, but the necessary subscriptions were not forthcoming and the voyage never took place.

For thirty-five years Sebastian was in the service of Spain, then suddenly he came back to England. He had tried to come back in 1538, but Henry VIII was not prepared to pay higher wages than those paid by the Emperor and no more was heard of the proposal. With the accession of Edward VI the government on October 9th, 1547, made out a warrant for £100 to bring Sebastian once again to England. He arrived in 1548. The next year Protector Somerset gave him a pension of £166 13s. 4d., payable quarterly. Charles V did his best to get Sebastian back to Spain, but the English government answered that Sebastian had no wish to go and as he was an English subject (he had almost certainly been born in Venice) he could not be compelled to go. Sebastian was always ready to claim to be an English or a Venetian subject as best suited his book at the moment. It has been said that he was appointed Grand Pilot of England, but the office and title did not then exist. It is said that he became governor of the Low Countries' Merchant Adventurers, which is wholly untrue, as it is also untrue that he was involved in the struggle with the Hansa. What is true is that he became the first governor of the newly formed Merchant Adventurers of England (1551), who sent out Willoughby's expedition of 1553. Sebastian drew up the ordinances for this and he was called 'the chiefest setter forth of this journey or voyage'.

The last picture we have of him is in 1556 when the Merchant Adventurers sent out their third voyage, which included a pinnace named the *Serchthrift* commanded by Stephen Borough:

> 'The 27th, being Monday, the right worshipful Sebastian Cabota came aboard our pinnace at Gravesend, accompanied with divers gentlemen and gentlewomen who . . . went on shore . . . and the good old Master Cabota gave to the poor most liberal alms, wishing them to pray for the good fortune and prosperous success of the *Serchthrift* our pinnace. And then at the sign of the Christopher, he and his friends banqueted and made me (Stephen Borough) and those that were in the company great cheer: and for very joy that he had to see the towardness of our intended discovery, he entered into the dance himself amongst the rest of the young and lusty company.'

There is no doubt that he died in 1557.

Sebastian Cabot was a 'man of good education and of a subtle and reflective mind', but he was a restless, vain creature, always thinking that his worth was not being properly appreciated. He was undoubtedly a considerable geographer, intensely interested in the shape of the world, and one of the leading authorities on the scientific side of navigation and the making of maps. He gave a most necessary and most valuable stimulus to English sailors when he returned to England in 1549. He himself made one of the finest maps of his time, his 'mappemonde', drawn on parchment and illuminated with gold and colours. The original has perished and of the drafts made from it only one now exists in the Bibliothèque Nationale in Paris. In E. G. R. Taylor's *Tudor Geography* opposite page 80 is a diagram which represents Sebastian's ideas about the shape of the polar regions and passages. The search for the north-west passage was originated by Sebastian Cabot. A portrait of him hangs in the ducal palace in Venice. The only relic which Bristol possesses is the Dun Cow, the rib of a whale, said to have been given to Bristol as a proof of the discovery of Newfoundland by Cabot, and preserved now in the chapel under the N. W. Tower of St. Mary Redcliff.

See for further reading under John Cabot.

WILLOUGHBY, SIR HUGH, navigator, was the son of Sir Henry Willoughby of Middleton, who was made a knightbanneret at the battle of Stoke in 1487 and died in 1528. The date of Hugh's birth is unknown: he died in 1554. He first saw military service in Hertford's (later Somerset) expedition to Scotland in 1544, when he was knighted at Leith on May 11th. From 1548–9 he was captain of Lowther Castle on the border. When Somerset fell from power, Willoughby lost a valuable patron: it may be either this or the suggestion of friends, among whom Sebastian Cabot would be one, which made him turn his thoughts to the sea.

By the middle of the sixteenth century the manufacture of woollen cloth in England had outstripped home consumption and the continental markets, owing to the deflation of the mid-sixteenth century, were also shrinking. There was great need to find new markets and the Far East seemed to be the most promising area. No doubt an additional, but subsidiary, attraction was the certainty of a valuable return cargo of pepper and spices. (Foster, *England's Quest of Eastern Trade*, pp. 5-6). The difficulty was how to get there without infringing the Spanish and Portuguese monopolies. In 1553 was formed in London a company of 200 shareholders with a capital of 240 shares of £25 each to open up trade with Cathay by sailing along the North-Eastern shores of Europe by the so-called North-East Passage. The company was given a charter by Edward VI and Sebastian Cabot became its first Governor.

The first expedition sent out by the company consisted of only three ships, of which the largest was the *Bona Esperanza* (160 tons), commanded by Sir Hugh Willoughby as Captain-General, with Richard Chancellor in the *Edward Bonaventure* as Pilot-General. The third ship was the *Bona Confidentia*. The fleet set sail from Ratcliffe on May 10th, 1553. In August after passing the Lofoten Islands, Chancellor was separated from the other two ships by a storm and he therefore made straight for the rendezvous at Vardö. Willoughby and his ships never arrived there. For weeks they wandered about in ice and fog: they probably sighted the coast of Novaia Zemlia: in September they reached the bay of Arzina on the coast of Lapland. Here they spent the winter, but although they were provisioned for eighteen months, the arctic cold and possibly also scurvy caused them all to perish miserably (1554).

In the spring some Russian fishermen found the two ships and the frozen corpses, together with Willoughby's will and journal which prove that the party was alive in January 1554. The vessels were recovered and, manned with new crews, were brought home. The journal was printed by Hakluyt and there is a manuscript copy of it in the Cottonian MSS (Otho E viii 10), but neither the original of it nor of the will can now be traced.

It was said that Willoughby's corpse was brought home for burial, but there is no proof of this at all. A tradition holds that his clothes were sent home and were used in painting the portrait preserved at Wollaton House as the only known authentic portrait of Willoughby: but this cannot be true, because the clothes belong to the seventeenth century. (C. R. Beard, *Connoisseur*, July 1931).

Hakluyt, *Principal Navigations*, i, 226–237.
Foster, *England's Quest of Eastern Trade*, ch. I.

CHANCELLOR, RICHARD, navigator; almost nothing is known of his early life and nothing of his family, except that he had two sons. We know that he was brought up in the household of Henry Sidney, father of Sir Philip, and that Henry Sidney had a very high opinion of him. What information we have about his later life comes from Hakluyt. Chancellor died in 1556.

Chancellor is said to have sailed with 'Roger Bodenham with the great Barke Aucher' on a journey to Candia and Chio, but he first comes into prominence in 1553 when he was appointed Pilot-General in the *Edward Bonaventure* in the 1553 expedition to Russia, led by Sir Hugh Willoughby. Chancellor was separated from Willoughby in a storm off the Lofoten Islands and therefore made for the rendezvous at Vardo. When, after a week of waiting, Willoughby had not turned up, Chancellor went on by himself and entered the White Sea (hitherto unknown to Western Europe) and anchored at the small port of Nenoksa, near the mouth of the river Dwina. He learned from the natives that he was in Russia, whereupon he journeyed to Moscow—a long and difficult journey overland—and there had an interview with the Tsar, Ivan IV, who received him with great kindness and welcomed the plan to establish trading relations between England and Russia. 'Your country merchants . . . shall have their free mart with all free liberties through my whole dominions.' Elated with his success, Chancellor returned to his ship and sailed home (1554). He wrote an account of the Russian Court and of the habits of the Russian peoples which was printed by Hakluyt and is the first such account to be given to the English people. His achievement was considerable, for he had found an all-sea route to Russia, a most valuable market for English goods and for equally valuable goods from Russia—furs, hides, tallow, wax, flax and hemp. In addition, it looked as if Moscow might well prove a valuable half-way house to the Far East, for Moscow is, in fact, farther East than Aleppo. (Foster, *England's Quest of Eastern Trade*.)

The promoters of this first enterprise now followed up Chancellor's success by obtaining a new charter from Mary Tudor to form the Muscovy Company, by which the Company obtained a monopoly in the area and trade which it sought to develop. In 1555 Chancellor sailed again in the *Edward Bonaventure* with another vessel accompanying him. One notable feature of this expedition was that it carried several merchants who were to remain in Russia to act as factors and to organize a regular trade. The great business acumen of the Company is shewn by its instructions to these agents to find out the best routes from Russia to Cathay.

Chancellor reached Moscow in October 1555. He was received again with much consideration by the Tsar, he was able to establish good relations and to obtain valuable trading rights, including exemption from customs dues. That the interest in this new trade was as great on the Tsar's side as on the Company's was shewn by the Tsar's sending home with Chancellor a special envoy, Ossip Grigorjevitsch Nepeja.

The return journey began in July 1556 and it proved a fearful disaster. Of the four ships which now formed the fleet, two were lost on the Norwegian coast: a third was forced to winter in Trondheim and only arrived in England in 1557. The *Edward Bonaventure*, with Chancellor and Nepeja on board, after four months reached the Scottish coast, but the ship was wrecked in Pitsligo Bay, Aberdeenshire, in November. Chancellor and Nepeja tried to land in a ship's boat, but this was quickly swamped. Nepeja and a few others made the shore, but Chancellor was never seen again.

Besides being a seaman Chancellor was also a mathematician who could hold his own with John Dee. He could also make and improve the instruments for navigation. In 1553 he collaborated with Dee in compiling a new table of ephmeerides or planetary movements. (E. G. R. Taylor, *Tudor Geography* 1485–1583, p. 91.)

No biography of Chancellor exists except that in the *D.N.B.* by J. K. Laughton.

GILBERT, SIR HUMPHREY, soldier, navigator, explorer, is generally thought to have been born in 1539, but it is possible that his birth was earlier. He died at sea in 1583. He was the second son of Otho Gilbert of Greenway on the river Dart and of Katherine, daughter of Sir Philip Champernoun of Modbury in Kent. Otho died in 1547 and his widow married Walter Ralegh of Fardell and Hayes in Devonshire, by whom she had three children, one of them a boy named Walter; thus Humphrey Gilbert was the half-brother of Sir Walter Ralegh. The difference in age between them was probably thirteen years.

Humphrey was educated at Eton and Oxford: at the university he is said to have studied navigation and the art of war. His earlier education must have been thorough and along classical lines, for his writings display an intimate knowledge of Greek and Latin philosophers and poets, and it is probable that he could speak both French and Spanish. After Oxford, he was attached to the household of the Princess Elizabeth, and later, for a short time, he resided in one of the Inns of Chancery.

He first saw military service under Ambrose Dudley, Earl of Warwick, at the siege of Newhaven (i.e. Havre in Normandy) in 1562–3, during the religious civil wars in France: he was wounded on June 5th, 1563—not on September 26th, as the *D.N.B.* states, by which date peace had been made.

In July 1566 he served in Ireland under Sir Henry Sidney in his campaign against Shane O'Neil. After four months on October 12th he was sent back to England with despatches for the Queen.

Gilbert was in Ireland again in July 1569, for he wrote to Cecil for leave to return to England 'for the recovery of my eyes'. Before that leave was granted Gilbert had made a name for himself by his so-called 'pacification' of Munster. To our modern way of thinking his treatment of Munster, of which province he was put in complete control, was revolting and uncivilized. Gilbert himself describes his ruthless methods of wholesale slaughter in a letter to Cecil without any apology for them. Sir Henry Sidney wrote highly praising Gilbert's services, for which he had knighted him on January 1st, 1570. The difference in standards between the sixteenth and the twentieth centuries may be judged by the following quotation: 'His manner was that the heads of all those (of what sort soever they were) which were killed in the day should be cut off from their bodies and brought to the place where he encamped at night, and should be laid on the ground by each side of the way leading into his own tent, so that none could come into his tent for any cause but commonly he must pass through a line of heads, which he used *ad terrorem,* the dead feeling nothing the more pains thereby; and yet did it bring greater terror to the people, when they saw the heads of their dead fathers, brothers, children, kinsfolk and friends, lie on the ground before their faces when they came to speak with the said Colonel.' (Thomas Churchyard, *General Rehearsal of Wars,* 1579.) Gilbert left behind him with the Irish a reputation second only to that of Oliver Cromwell.

If Gilbert had all the acquisitiveness of his times—that he had is proved by his petition in 1572 for the grant of all the south-east coast of Ireland—in his defence it may be said that out of his expenses in Ireland for nine months of £3,315 7s. he only received repayment of £600.

In 1570 Sir Humphrey married Anne Ager of Ottenden in Kent, a wealthy heiress, by whom he had five sons and one daughter. The next year (1571) he was returned as M.P. for Plymouth alongside Sir John Hawkins. It may be a proof of his loyalty to his queen or of his independent and combative mind that he at once fell foul of the House of Commons in general and of Peter Wentworth in particular, who called him 'a flatterer, a lyer and a naughtie man', for having defended the queen's prerogative in the unpopular question of royal licenses.

The year 1572 was an unfortunate one for Gilbert. He was sent to the Netherlands in command of 1,500 English volunteers to help the Zeelanders in their rebellion against Spain— probably Elizabeth's real purpose was to get possession of Flushing. The campaign was a failure and Gilbert came back to England disgusted with the quality of the troops which he had been given and with the Zeelanders' commander, t'Zaarets.

From 1573 to 1578 Gilbert lived at Limehouse, retired from public employment and devoted his time to writing. He polished up his old 'Discourse' on the North-West Passage, which his friend Gascoigne, the poet, published in 1576. He also had an idea of going to help John Oxenham, who had been cut off in the Panama isthmus with captured treasure, for he was now developing a plan for breaking up the Spanish empire. He sent to the government schemes for wrecking Spanish maritime power by seizing her Newfoundland fishing fleet, attacking the treasure fleet on its way to Europe and occupying the islands of Hispaniola and Cuba as permanent bases for this purpose. He embodied these ideas in another 'discourse' entitled *How her Majesty might annoy the King of Spain,* but the government was anxious at all costs to avoid war with Spain and Gilbert's approach was ignored (1577).

The rest of Gilbert's life was devoted to his plans for planting an English colony in North America. Other people were thinking along the same lines, men such as Richard Hakluyt the elder, who was to help Gilbert with advice and had been collecting information for some years. On June 11th, 1578, Gilbert obtained from the Queen a patent which authorized him to search for and to occupy with English settlers lands 'not actually possessed of any Christian prince or people'. The patent was valid for six years and he was to hold all the land he discovered from the Crown. He was already beginning to collect ships: he had as his chief partner Henry Knollys, son of Sir Francis Knollys, the treasurer of the household, but he turned for his main support to his own family. He sold some of his wife's property and he raised subscriptions from his brothers Sir John and Adrian Gilbert. He also brought in Walter Ralegh and his elder brother Carew. Five of Katherine Champernoun's sons were involved in the expedition besides some Champernoun and Carew cousins.

The fleet was to consist of ten ships, gathered together at Plymouth. Unhappily, during the delays in fitting them out quarrels broke out between Knollys and Gilbert: eventually

AA—(2)

Knollys deserted with three of the ships and sailed off into the Channel and Bay of Biscay where he took to piracy. On November 19th, 1578, Gilbert at last set sail with seven ships. He himself commanded the *Anne Ager* (named after Gilbert's wife), 250 tons, with the title of Admiral of the Fleet: the *Hope of Greenway*, 160 tons, was commanded by Carew Ralegh, the Vice-Admiral: Miles Morgan commanded the *Red Lion*, 110 tons: the *Falcon* of 100 tons was under the command of Walter Ralegh, she being the Queen's ship: the *Galleon* of 40 tons under Richard Veal, the *Swallow* of 40 tons under John Verney and the *Squirrel* of 10 tons carrying eight men, these completed the squadron.

The destination of the fleet is unknown, for the secret was well-kept, so that not even Mendoza, the Spanish ambassador, knew. When we remember to what dimensions the expansions of England overseas was to attain, the sailing of Humphrey Gilbert on the first attempt to plant Englishmen overseas is a notable event. In fact, the voyage was a failure from the very start. What evidence we have suggests that the plan was to cross the Atlantic by way of the Canaries to the West Indies and then to work up the coast of North America. The ships were heavily armed in order to repel attacks by Spanish ships. The voyage was to be one of reconnaissance to prepare for a later expedition for colonizing.

The fleet scattered after leaving Plymouth, probably owing to bad weather, and it never reassembled. Gilbert put into an Irish port where he took in more supplies, but he failed to find the rest of his fleet when he again put to sea, therefore he returned to port where he fell in with the *Hope of Greenway*, which had sprung a leak; Miles Morgan had slipped away to join Knollys in his piracy: later his ship, *Red Lion*, was lost at sea. Walter Ralegh with one or two other ships besides the *Falcon* set out on the course which had been planned, and made for the West Indies, but when he found he was short of food and had lost his right bearings, he turned for home near the Cape Verde Islands. Here he met and fought some Spanish ships which handled Ralegh's vessels very roughly. He reached Dartmouth in May 1579 in a battered condition, almost at the same moment as Gilbert returned to Plymouth. Both Gilbert and Ralegh wanted to try again in the summer of 1579, but they encountered difficulties with the government, which disapproved of piracy too near home and therefore forbade the expedition, although there is no evidence that either Gilbert or Ralegh indulged in piracy, whatever Knollys and some of Gilbert's men had done.

The last four years of Gilbert's life were given to almost feverish activity to accomplish his American schemes. In 1580 he sent out that Simon Fernandez who had accompanied Ralegh in the *Falcon* in 1578 to reconnoitre the American coast. In three months Fernandez returned with a great deal of first hand information. There was need for hurry, since Gilbert's patent expired at the end of 1584. Unfortunately, of all his old ships only the tiny *Squirrel* survived, and unfortunately also Gilbert was short of ready money. He therefore set about raising money by every device he could think of. One of the chief methods he employed was to sell in advance tracts of the lands he had not yet discovered. For example, Dr. John Dee purchased all the land north of parallel 50°. By dint of skilful advertising many other purchasers were found. Gilbert represented that a small investment might turn a simple English gentleman into a feudal lord of huge estates. The prospect of finding gold and jewels was held out, the possibility of finding new markets for raw materials and for manufactured goods was exploited. Especially did Gilbert seek to persuade the loyal Catholic gentry that they might create overseas a new state in which they could still serve their Queen and could at the same time preserve their Catholic religion. Between June 1582 and February 1583 Gilbert got rid of nearly nine million acres of land, all on paper, of which most went to the Catholic investors, led by Sir George Peckham and Sir Thomas Gerrard. These latter intended to send out an expedition on their own in 1582 to explore the territories and then to follow that up with a large colonizing expedition in 1583. Thanks, however, to the warnings of Catholic priests and the intriguing of the Spanish ambassador, Mendoza, most of the Catholics backed out, so that these two expeditions never took place.

Gilbert made an agreement with the Southampton merchants that they should have a monopoly of trade with the new colonies in return for financial help here and now. Even so, money was scarce and the expedition was delayed month after month.

In February 1583 the Queen created a difficulty. She had observed that Gilbert was 'a man noted of not good hap at sea' and she suggested that he should not accompany the venture in person. Elizabeth seems always to have liked Gilbert and she did not now forbid him to go, nor was she angry when he went ahead with his plans. Indeed, she sent Gilbert a message through Ralegh that 'she wished great good hap and safety to your ships as if she herself were there in person' together with a jewel of 'an anchor guided by a lady'.

Gilbert set sail on June 11th for Newfoundland. The fleet consisted of *Delight*, 120 tons, in which Gilbert sailed as Admiral: the *Bark Ralegh*, 200 tons: the *Golden Hind*, 40 tons: the *Swallow*, 40 tons: the *Squirrel*, about 10 tons. On the 13th the *Bark Ralegh* turned for home and went into Plymouth, probably owing to a shortage of victuals brought about by the numerous delays before sailing when the victuals were consumed in harbour. In a fog on July 20th *Swallow* and *Squirrel* lost touch with the rest of the fleet and did not recover it until they arrived at Newfoundland, when Gilbert found the *Swallow* in Conception Bay and on August 3rd he met with the *Squirrel* in the harbour of St. John's. Gilbert went ashore on the 4th (Sunday) and on the 5th he formally annexed the harbour and two hundred leagues every way in the name of the Queen and took possession of the land for himself and his heirs. He spent a fortnight prospecting and made up his mind that he would plant a colony here. One ship he sent home with all the sick, nor did he leave any garrison at St. John's when he sailed on August 10th for America. His stay at St. John's had discovered two things: that a great mistake had been made in recruiting the crews from pirates and prisoners, and that Gilbert was quite incapable of dealing with the lawlessness and discontent which immediately broke out. The discontent grew in the ships, especially after the *Delight* had run aground and was wrecked either on Sable Island or near Cape Breton. On August 31st, therefore, Gilbert turned back, having accomplished none of his main objectives. He himself was sailing in the *Squirrel* and he insisted on remaining in her in spite of heavy seas, although his friends tried to persuade him to go aboard the *Golden Hind*. On September 9th the *Squirrel* disappeared and was never seen again. The last sight that men had of Gilbert was sitting in the stern of the *Squirrel* with a book in his hand; whenever he came within hearing distance of the *Golden Hind* he was heard to say, 'we are as near to Heaven by sea as by land'.

It is not easy to assess the character of Sir Humphrey Gilbert. Probably the eulogies which have been showered upon him are as far from the truth as is most undiscriminating praise. That he was genuinely pious, patriotic and brave is not to be denied. He was said in his own day to be afraid of the sea, but the manner of his death gives that the lie. There are too many examples of his ungovernable temper for us not to feel he was an obstinate, jealous and self-opinionated man. He was a bad leader, unable to win the respect or the affection of his followers, incapable of dealing with mutiny and insubordination. According to Clark, the master of the *Delight*, the loss of that ship and most of its men was entirely due to Gilbert's refusal to take the advice of a better navigator than himself. When Gilbert asked him which course to take, Clark advised west-south-west, whereupon Gilbert at once commanded him to sail west-north-west. Clark explained that *Delight* would be on the sands before daylight; Gilbert accused Clark of being out of his reckoning and ordered him in the Queen's name to sail as Gilbert had said. Clark obeyed and *Delight* was on the sands by seven o'clock in the morning. (Clark's narrative is printed in W. G. Gosling's *Life*.) As a man of action, Gilbert was a failure, except perhaps in Ireland, and one may doubt what value his temporary success there ever had.

But as a man of intellect and imagination Gilbert must rank high. His was an original and creative mind, bold, far-seeing and extremely modern. His whole conception of overseas expansion was new, far ahead of the ideas of his time. And as a writer his reputation should be higher than it is. Among his works there is a 'discourse' entitled *The Erection of* [Queen Elizabeth's] *Academy in London for Education of her Majesty's Wards and others the youths of nobility and gentlemen.* Broadly it was a plea for a kind of university in London. How modern was Gilbert's mind may be seen in the rules which he suggested for the library of this academy: he laid down almost all the rules which are now generally accepted as necessary for a librarian to observe: he suggested that a copy of every book published should be placed in the library, as is now done, for example, in the British Museum: he anticipated the future law of copyright. Gilbert was a typical product of a brilliant but undisciplined age. (*Plate 28*)

D. B. Quinn, *Sir Humphrey Gilbert*, 1940.

W. G. Gosling, *The Life of Sir Humphrey Gilbert*, (ch. 6 in particular must be used with care).

Edward Hayes, (captain and owner of the *Golden Hind*), *A Report of the Voyage . . . by Sir Humphrey Gilbert*, printed in Hakluyt's Voyages, 1599, more easily accessible in E. J. Payne's, *Voyages of Elizabethan Seamen.*

CAVENDISH, THOMAS, (Hakluyt always used the form CANDISH), circumnavigator, was born at Trimley St. Martin in Suffolk in 1560. He died at sea in 1592, aged thirty-two years. Having wasted, not only the savings of his minority, but also a large fortune in extravagant living at Court, Cavendish turned to piracy to rebuild his ruined finances. His first voyage was made in a ship of his own which he contributed to Ralegh's expedition of 1585 which sailed under the command of Sir Richard Grenville in the first attempt to found the colony of Virginia in North America.

The next year Grenville planned an expedition of his own modelled on the lines of the immensely successful expedition of Drake in 1577–80. Two accounts of Cavendish's voyage exist: one is signed N.H. and was written under the eye of Cavendish on board the *Desire*: the other was partly written by Francis Pretty on board the *Hugh Gallant* before she was sunk in the Pacific owing to a shortage of crews to sail her home. Pretty's account seems to suggest that Cavendish bore the whole expense of the expedition, but there are grounds for thinking that the Lord Chamberlain, Lord Hunsdon, may have been his patron.

The second voyage, 1586: the expedition left Plymouth in July. It consisted of three ships under the command of Cavendish— he was only twenty-six years old—the *Desire,* his flagship (140 tons), the *Content* (60 tons) and the *Hugh Gallant* (40 tons). The crews totalled 123 and the ships were victualled for two years. The first landfall was at Sierra Leone in August, where eleven days were spent in procuring provisions and water. A call was paid at one of the Cape Verde Islands, then the fleet sailed on to Brazil. Three weeks were spent here near the island of San Sebastiano, 120 miles south-west of Rio de Janiero. Cavendish put to sea again on November 23rd and in mid-December he arrived at a Patagonian harbour which he named Port Desire after his ship. Here they stayed over Christmas, studying the habits and manners and arts of the Patagonians. Sailing was resumed on December 28th and on January 3rd, 1587, the expedition reached the opening of the Straits of Magellan. After losing an anchor in a great storm which lasted for three days, Cavendish entered the straits on January 6th. The next day they saw a party of twenty-three starving Spaniards, the remnants of 400 who had been left by Sarmiento in 1584 to defend the narrows. Cavendish took off one Spaniard, Hernando, all the rest perished.

The passage of the straits took forty-nine days. On the way through they saw the hull of a small barque which they took to be the *John Thomas,* abandoned there by Drake nine years before. On the whole Cavendish had good luck with the weather, but for a month 'we fed almost altogether on mussels and limpets and birds, or such as we could get on shore, seeking for them every day as the fowls of the air do' (Pretty).

On February 24th the fleet entered the Pacific and sailed up the coast of Chile as far as Quintero Bay, just north of Valparaiso. Here the Spaniard Hernando was put ashore to talk with three mounted Spaniards: suddenly he leaped up behind one of the horsemen and galloped away—a piece of singularly bad luck for Cavendish, for he would certainly warn the whole seaboard. One day a watering-party was attacked by 200

Spaniards and twelve men were killed, although the Spanish lost twenty-five (April 1st, 1587). Cavendish's main object now was to plunder as much as he could, but on the whole he did not have much success: the Spanish had learned a lot since Drake's attacks and they had organized a system of swift ships which carried the news of the English arrival ahead of the fleet. They also had many more men posted along the coastline, but their ships were not yet armed. Cavendish experienced a good deal of stiff fighting and, although he captured a few ships and burned a few towns, none gave him plunder enough to compensate for the loss of some thirty men, a loss which forced him to abandon the *Hugh Gallant* as he had not enough crews to sail three vessels.

With *Desire* and *Content* Cavendish went on to Costa Rica (July 1st). He captured and burned a ship from which he took a French pilot, but the Spaniards were well aware of his movements: he had a little before this taken a ship carrying letters to the Viceroy to warn him of Cavendish's approach. The letters were revealed by a Spaniard who by the command of Cavendish was 'tormented with his thumbs in a wrench'. Off the west coast of Mexico he learned that the *Santa Anna* of 700 tons was expected with a rich cargo from Manila and that her landfall would be at Cape St. Lucas, the most southerly point of California, 'very like the Needles at the Isle of Wight' (Pretty). For three weeks *Desire* and *Content* hung about the point: at last on November 4th they sighted the *Santa Anna*. She carried no heavy guns and therefore, in spite of a gallant resistance which lasted some six hours, she was compelled to surrender. Cavendish took his prize into a near-by harbour, where he put the Spaniards ashore with a supply of food. The treasure in gold *pesos* amounted to 22,000, but out of a total of 600 tons of merchandise Cavendish could only transfer to his two ships forty tons for each, so heavily laden were they already. The rest of the cargo and the Santa Anna herself were burned. Cavendish also took off the prize-ship two Japanese boys and three young native boys from Manila, and also Nicholas Roderigo, a Portuguese from China, from whom he probably got the large map of China to which Hakluyt referred at length in his book. Cavendish also obtained a Spanish pilot for the Philippines.

On November 19th the *Desire* and *Content* set sail for England, but the *Content* belied her name. There had been something like a mutiny among her crew, who were dissatisfied with their share of the plunder from the *Santa Anna*. She was slow in following *Desire* out of harbour and 'so we lost her company and never saw her after' (Pretty). Was she perhaps trying to go home independently by way of the North West Passage? She was never heard of again.

On January 3rd, 1588, Cavendish sighted the Ladrone Islands and on the 14th he was in the Philippines. He was by no means strong enough to attack Manila: indeed, Roderigo revealed to him that the Spanish pilot was trying to urge the Spanish in Manila to attack him. Cavendish at once hanged the pilot from the yard-arm. His course is a little disputed, but it is fairly certain that he sailed through the narrows between Java and Bali (March 1st) and arrived at a safe haven near the western end of the south coast of Java, probably Wijnkoopers Bay.

He set sail for the Cape of Good Hope in the middle of March which he sighted on May 16th (the *D.N.B.* says March 19th which is manifestly impossible). On June 8th *Desire* called at St. Helena and Cavendish became the first Englishman to have visited that island, which was occupied by the Portuguese. The ship was here cleaned and revictualled and then set out for home. Early in September Cavendish entered the English Channel: his track must have crossed that of Medina Sidonia who brought the defeated Armada into Santander three days after Cavendish entered Plymouth (September 9th, not the 10th, as the *D.B.N.* records).

Thus at the age of 28 Cavendish became the second Englishman to circumnavigate the globe. In a letter to Lord Hunsdon he claims that he had burnt and sunk nineteen ships; had burned and plundered all the towns on the Spanish littoral that he had touched at; had captured a galleon which was 'one of the richest of merchandise that ever passed those seas', had obtained intelligence concerning China 'such as hath not been heard of in these parts'; had ascertained that trade might be freely had in the Moluccas; and finally he had discovered the island of St. Helena (Foster, *England's Quest of Eastern Trade*). This was a wonderful achievement, the more so for so young and inexperienced a commander, one which might put him on the same pedestal as Drake. Yet it must be admitted that Cavendish lacked what Dr. J. A. Williamson calls 'the artist's touch by which Drake made things go easily'. Cavendish more than once used torture to elicit information which Drake would have drawn out over the dinner table and his gold plates, but Drake did use torture. Cavendish's third voyage was to reveal deeper and more fatal flaws in his character.

The third voyage, 1591: there can be no doubt that, at any rate after the taking of the *Santa Anna*, Cavendish had done well enough out of his expedition to wish to renew the voyage. Men like Robert Parke were already pressing the Chinese market for the English cloth trade as a result of Cavendish's enterprise (Foster *ib.*). In August 1591 Cavendish joined with John Davis in an expedition to China and the South Sea. They sailed from Plymouth in August. Davis had been persuaded to go by a promise that he should explore the North-West Passage from the Pacific side. Cavendish commanded a ship which had been known as the *Leicester*, but was now named the *Galleon*. Davis commanded Cavendish's old ship *Desire*; the two other vessels were the *Dainty* and the *Roebuck*, to which was added a small ship known as the *Black Pinnace*. On November 29th the fleet reached the coast of Brazil and took the town of Santos, hoping to obtain food: not much was forthcoming. It was not until January 24th, 1592, that Cavendish set out again on his voyage. This was too late in the season, the weather was unusually severe and during a storm Cavendish was separated from the rest of his fleet. He had forgotten to appoint a rendezvous, but Davis expected that Cavendish would make for Port Desire, which eventually he did. It was as late as March 18th when Cavendish rejoined Davis, who had picked up the *Roebuck* in a poor state. The *Dainty* had given up and returned home. In the meantime Cavendish had quarrelled with the officers of the *Galleon* and he now left that ship and went aboard the *Desire*, violently criticizing all in the *Galleon*, it seems without any reason for doing so. Indeed, there is ground for thinking that Cavendish had gone to pieces and that his mind was probably unhinged.

On March 20th they sailed for the Straits of Magellan which they reached on April 8th. The weather was so bad that by the 21st they were only half way through and had to take refuge in a small cove where they remained until May 15th, short of food and suffering much from the cold. And another grave danger began to appear: perhaps the capital for the voyage had been insufficient, for now the gear was rotten and the sails old and there were no spares to make good the losses. Davis advised that the ships should press on—but he was anxious to discover the North-West Passage. The men, too, were anxious to go ahead, since they were in search of plunder and spoil. Cavendish by now had lost all capacity for leadership and against the advice of all he proposed to turn back and try to reach the East Indies by way of the Cape. Davis dissuaded him, arguing that the ships were in bad condition, the crews were short-handed and the provisions almost finished. Cavendish thereupon left the *Desire* and went once more aboard the *Galleon* and gave orders to sail for Santos in Brazil. On the night of May 20th, 1592, he suddenly altered the course of his own vessel and deserted the others.

Cavendish soon fell in with the *Roebuck* and the two ships made for the Brazilian coast. An attack by a Portuguese force cost him twenty-five men, and he lost another twenty-five when he attempted to land at Espirito Santo. As a result the *Roebuck* left Cavendish and sailed for England. Cavendish tried vainly to persuade his men to tackle once more the Straits of Magellan, but they reluctantly agreed to make for St. Helena and there refit. The *Galleon* got within two leagues of the island, but she was driven away by contrary winds. Cavendish then made for Ascension Island, but he missed the way and turned for the Cape Verde Islands. The last record that we have of Thomas Cavendish is his last letter written to his executor, Sir Tristram Gorges, in which he reports the death of his cousin, John Locke, and his own imminent death. That the *Galleon* must have arrived at long last in some English port is proved by the fact that this letter reached its destination, but Cavendish died within a few days of Locke, but not before in his letter he had stigmatized Davis as 'that villain that hath been the death of me and the decay of this whole action, whose only treachery in running from me hath been an utter ruin of all'. This was the last and most bitter criticism of the many which he made of his friends, and it was of all the least justified.

The end of Cavendish was as the beginning: he who in his youth had squandered his wealth now, at the end of his short life, squandered the splended reputation he had won by his voyage of circumnavigation. He stands for posterity as a typical Elizabethan, one of that galaxy of brilliant stars which illuminate the Elizabethan firmament, but whose heat too often consumes their splendour. Thomas Cavendish shines in the same constellation as Robert Devereux, Earl of Essex, and Sir Walter Ralegh.

The accounts of his voyages are easily accessible together with his last letter in E. J. Payne's *Voyages of Elizabethan Seamen— second series*, 1900.

Dr. J. A. Williamson: *The Age of Drake*, 1946 ed.

Sir William Foster: *England's Quest of Eastern Trade*, 1933.

JENKINSON, ANTHONY, merchant, traveller and navigator: the date of his birth is unknown, he died in 1611. Practically nothing at all is known of his early life. It was the custom in his day for a boy who wanted to follow a career in trade to be sent to the Levant, and Jenkinson seems to have left England for the East in 1546. According to his own account, he travelled through Flanders, Germany, over the Alps into Italy, through Piedmont into France; he visited Spain and Portugal, thence to the Levant via all the principal islands, Malta, Sicily, Candia, Rhodes and Cyprus; he was in Greece, Morea, Corinth, Turkey and Syria; he went all over the Holy Land, he was also in North Africa; and all this he accomplished between 1546 and 1553. (The list of his travels is printed in Delmar Morgan's *Early Voyages and Travels to Russia and Persia*, Hakluyt Society, vol. ii, pp. 341–3.)

In 1553 Jenkinson was in Aleppo where he witnessed the entry of Suleiman the Magnificent on November 4th. He was granted an interview with that monarch and obtained from him a safe-conduct, which was in reality a guarantee of free-trade in all Turkish ports. It is not known for certain what was the purpose Jenkinson was pursuing, but almost certainly the merchants in England were preparing a plan for developing trade between England and the Levant in order to secure a regular supply of spices. Nor is it known whether Jenkinson followed up the privileges he had obtained from the Sultan. If he did, he gave up the hope of cashing in on Eastern trade by this method and turned his attention to developing the promising results which flowed from Chancellor's contacts with Moscow.

First journey 1557. In 1557 Jenkinson was admitted a member of the Mercers' Company, the same year in which the Russian ambassador Nepeja arrived in London after his shipwreck in Scotland. In April 1557 the Muscovy Company fitted out a fleet of four vessels to trade with Russia and explore the possibilities of reaching Cathay by land and it appointed Jenkinson—'a man well travelled whom we mind to use in further travelling'—as Captain-General of the fleet and as the Company's Agent at a salary of £40 a year for three years. The appointment was made, because Jenkinson was a skilful navigator who understood surveying as far as the science was known in the sixteenth century. His observations for latitude showed wide errors, but they were wonderfully accurate, if we consider how crude were the instruments available to him.

The ships set sail from Gravesend on May 12th, 1557, and Nepeja sailed with Jenkinson in the flag-ship, *Noble Primrose*. The Lofoten islands were reached on June 27th, the North Cape on July 2nd, the fleet then passed what Jenkinson called Lappia (Lapland) and Sviatoi Ness, named by Borough Cape Gallant. It entered the White Sea and anchored safely at St. Nicholas Road on July 12th, having covered 2,250 miles from London. Jenkinson and Nepeja then landed, went by boat up the Dvina river as far as Kholmogori and Vologhda and thence by land to Moscow, where they arrived on December 6th.

They were kindly received by the Tsar, Ivan the Terrible, with whom they dined on Christmas Day. They spent nearly five months at Moscow, and it was not until April 23rd, 1558, that the next stage of the journey was begun.

On that day Jenkinson, with letters of recommendation from the Tsar, set out from Moscow for Cathay, taking with him Richard and Robert Johnson—Richard had been with Chancellor on the 1553 voyage and with Borough in the *Searchthrift* in 1556—and an interpreter. Their first objective was down the Volga to Astrakhan at the head of the Caspian Sea, the farthest outpost of the Russian domains. They found the city in a ghastly condition, for after it had suffered from famine the plague attacked it, so that the Englishmen were met with thousands of corpses lying about in the streets (July 14th). Jenkinson here picked up what he called a 'wench' named Aura Soltana, whom he sent to England as a present to the new Queen, Elizabeth I. (Delmar Morgan, *ib.*, p. 109). Jenkinson now bought a boat and set sail from Astrakhan, the first Englishman to enter and navigate the Caspian Sea (August 10th, 1558). He explored the delta of the Volga and the north coast of the Caspian, and charted the northern shores. (His map of these parts was published in 1562.) During this time Jenkinson was exceedingly ill and he and his party were all but captured by robbers, who boarded the boat under the pretence of searching for infidels. Only hard swearing by the interpreter saved the four Englishmen. On September 3rd they reached the Mangishlak peninsula, where they landed, and set out on the 14th overland for Vezir.

Jenkinson now found himself in a land infested with robbers and marauders, wild tribesmen with whom it was impossible to have any dealings. In the end Jenkinson was only glad to pay their many exactions and to be rid of them. The caravan with which he was travelling numbered 1,000 camels. After five days travelling, they reached the domains of Timur Sultan, brother of Hakjim, the Khan of Khiva. His subjects stopped and plundered the caravan, but Jenkinson rode off to Timur and made his complaints so forcibly that he was given a horse worth half the value of the stolen goods and excellent entertainment.

He stayed in Vezir until October 14th, when he moved on to Urgendj. Here he spent six weeks, but he found that it was impossible to trade owing to the wild marauders of those parts, therefore he set out for Bokhara, which he reached on December 23rd, having had to repel an attack on the way.

At Bokhara Jenkinson was well received and he was granted an interview with Abdullah Khan on the 26th, to whom he presented the letters he had brought from the Tsar of Russia. Abdullah was much interested in the arquebuses which the Englishmen carried, and 'did himself practise the use thereof'. He also bought some of the travellers' goods, but before he had paid for them he set out on a military expedition and his servants refused to honour his debts, so that Jenkinson had to take what he could get.

So great was the anarchy and confusion of the country that it soon became clear to Jenkinson that it was impossible to pass from Bokhara to Cathay, which put an end to establishing trade with Cathay by this route. Nor did the inhabitants of Bokhara want the English exports. The only thing to do was to go back by the way he had come. On March 8th, 1589, Jenkinson left Bokhara with a caravan of 600 camels for the Caspian, where he arrived on April 23rd. He found his ship, but it was now without anchor, cable or sail. The travellers set about spinning a cable out of hemp and making a sail out of some cloth, and they were preparing to manufacture an anchor out of a wooden cartwheel, when a barque from Astrakhan arrived with a spare anchor. The three Englishmen, together with six ambassadors who were bound for Russia and twenty-five liberated Russian slaves, set sail and arrived at Astrakhan on May 28th. To his great disappointment, Jenkinson had learned that English cloth could not compete with a similar article imported via the Levant and Syria: he had also discovered that the Caspian area was unsuited to trade owing to its few harbours, its shortage of ships, the frequent ice, and the poverty of the people. Therefore on June 10th he left Astrakhan, went up the Volga for six weeks to Kazan, which he left on August 7th and arrived at Moscow on September 2nd, having been on his travels for one year, five months and nine days since he last left that city. He

stayed in Moscow until February 17th, 1560, when he set out
for home via the White Sea, arriving in London probably some
time in the autumn, after 'a journey so miserable, dangerous
and chargeable with losses, charges and expenses as my pen is
not able to express the same'.

It had been and still remains a memorable journey. In spite
of the robbers and their exactions, the voyage shewed a satisfactory financial profit. Jenkinson had proved conclusively that
further attempts to trade in Central Asia would be a waste of
time and money, a verdict 'which was accepted as final and
centuries passed before Bokhara saw another English visitor'.
(Foster, *England's Quest of Eastern Trade*, p. 22.) But there
seemed to be a chance that trade might be built up by exploiting
the hatred which existed between the Persian Shiah Mohammedans and the Turkish Sunni Mohammedans, who were
frequently at war. English goods might be injected through the
north. It might also be possible to persuade the Asian merchants to carry their goods for Syria and Europe to the Persian
markets and there to exchange them for English goods: or the
Russia Company might secure privileges to pass through
Persia and seek the Asian goods themselves. It was Jenkinson
who persuaded the Company to send a second expedition to
explore these possibilities. Hence the second journey, 1561.

The second journey, 1561. The instructions given to Jenkinson
by the Company were to obtain from the Tsar leave to carry
its trade through Russia into Persia, for which it was prepared
to pay a reasonable tariff. He was then to go on to Persia and
there to ask of the Shah—the Great Sophi, as he was known in
England—permission to trade freely in Persia, and also for a
guarantee 'for free passage also for us at all times to pass, as
often as we will, with our goods and merchandise into any part
of India, or other countries thereunto adjoining, and in like
manner to return through his dominions into Russia or
elsewhere'. (Delmar Morgan, *ib.*, i, 117.) Jenkinson was also
to carry letters from Queen Elizabeth to the Tsar and to the
Shah.

Jenkinson sailed from Gravesend in the *Swallow* on May 14th
and he arrived at Kholmogori on July 26th. From there he

went overland to Moscow, where he arrived on August 20th, having taken only thirteen days over a journey which usually took five weeks by water. He found the Tsar was celebrating his second marriage and there was considerable delay before an interview could be arranged. So little success did he achieve when at last he met the Tsar that he made up his mind to return to England. He sold the Company's cloth and other goods, received his passport and paid for the post-horses for the return journey; he was on the point of leaving when Nepeja called on him and persuaded him to cancel his arrangements and wait for a time further. Within three days Jenkinson received the permission to travel through Russia into Persia: he was promised letters of recommendation to the foreign princes through whose countries he would have to pass: he was also entrusted by the Tsar with some secret and very important political commissions: and the Tsar, to shew his gratitude, gave to the Company wider privileges than it had ever had before. On March 15th Jenkinson dined with the Tsar and also with the Persian ambassador, who travelled with him when he left Moscow on April 27th, 1562.

Astrakhan was reached on June 10th. The Persian ambassador here parted from Jenkinson, who remained in the city until July 15th, when he sailed into the Caspian. The voyage was beset with dangers from pirates and in one specially severe storm Jenkinson lost an anchor and his ship became very leaky, but he survived these perils and arrived at Derbend on August 1st. Derbend belonged to Persia and Jenkinson was the first Englishman to visit it. From Derbend he moved on to Shabran in the province of Shirvan under the rule of Abdullah Khan. Jenkinson set out to interview Abdullah at Shemakha and he was there entertained at a gigantic feast, 'with divers kinds of meats to the number of 140', which were followed by 'a banquet of fruits of sundry kinds with other banquetting meats to the number of 150 dishes'. Abdullah promised him a bodyguard to carry him safely to the Shah at Kazvin and early in October Jenkinson started for the Persian capital.

The ruling Shah was Shah Tahmasp (Jenkinson calls him Shaw Thamas) with whom Jenkinson had an interview on

BB—(2)

November 20th, when he presented 'the Queen's Majesty's letters' and also the presents which he had brought for the Great Sophi. The Shah asked in what language the letters were written: 'I answered in the Latin, Italian and Hebrew; well, said he, we have none within our realm that understand those tongues'. The Shah asked whether Jenkinson was a '*Gower*, that is to say an unbeliever, or a Muslim, that is of Mahomet's law'. Jenkinson answered that he was a Christian. 'What is that said he unto the King of the Georgians' son (who being a Christian was fled unto the said Sophi) and he answered that a Christian was he that believeth in *Jesus Christus*, affirming him to be the Son of God and the greatest prophet: Doest thou believe so said the Sophi unto me: Yea, that I do, said I: Oh, thou unbeliever, said he, we have no need to have friendship with the unbelievers, and so willed me to depart.' Jenkinson took his leave, but he was followed by a man with a basin full of sand which he 'sifted all the way that I had gone within the said palace, even from the said Sophi's sight unto the court gate'. At one moment it looked as if the Shah would put Jenkinson to death, but Abdullah Khan intervened on his behalf and 'the said Sophi changed his determined purpose and on the 20th day of March 1562 he sent me a rich garment of cloth of gold and so dismissed me without any harm'.

While he was at Kazvin, Jenkinson got into touch with some Indian merchants and arranged with them that, if he succeeded in establishing a permanent trade in Persia, they would supply him with as much spices as he was ready to take. On his way home he called again on Abdullah Khan who gave him most valuable concessions to buy and sell freely in Shirvan exempt from all customs dues.

Meantime the King of Georgia was being attacked by both Turks and Persians and he sent to Jenkinson to ask him to arrange with the Tsar to send him help. Jenkinson urged the King to send an embassy to the Tsar to make his request in person. He also sent one of his companions, Edward Clarke, to try to penetrate into Georgia from Arrash, the centre of the silk industry, and to get permission from the Georgian king for the Company to trade freely in his kingdom, but Clarke found

JENKINSON, ANTHONY   375

that this was impossible without jeopardizing the good relations
with Abdullah Khan. This is a striking example of the way in
which Jenkinson lost no opportunity of furthering the trading
interests of the Company.

On his arrival at Moscow Jenkinson had another interview
with the Tsar who gave him even more valuable privileges for
the Company than he had before, in return for the commissions
which Jenkinson had carried out for the Tsar in buying for him
jewels and silks and fulfilling the secret political negotiations
which he had entrusted to him (August 1563).

Jenkinson spent the winter in Moscow (1563/4) and he
organized a second expedition to Persia on which Cheinie and
Alcock set out probably in May 1564. On July 9th, 1564,
Jenkinson embarked for England in the *Swallow* and he arrived
in London on September 28th, after an absence of over three
years. His second journey is no less remarkable than the first
and was of great value to the Company, for he had for the first
time opened up the possibilities of trade with Persia. He had
also established a reputation as a trustworthy and successful
political agent.

Jenkinson, as a result of his own wide experience, was now
convinced that it would prove perfectly possible to navigate the
Polar sea and open the passage from West to East, provided
that the right time of year was chosen and proper planning
preceded the expedition. In May 1565 he wrote a petition to
the Queen urging her to finance such an exploit and offering
himself to lead the expedition. The thrifty Elizabeth was not
prepared to risk money on such a scheme and nothing came of
Jenkinson's proposal.

In the autumn of 1565 Jenkinson was despatched by the
government on a highly responsible mission. The English
Channel at this time swarmed with English adventurers who
were indistinguishable from mere pirates. They attacked
Spanish and French ships and the complaints of these foreign
governments at last alarmed Elizabeth to such an extent that
she made up her mind to put an end to their depredations.
On September 17th, 1565, Jenkinson sailed from Queenborough
in command of the *Ayde* (200 tons) with the Queen's commission

to stop the pirates. But he had also a more serious order: he was to prevent Bothwell, husband of Mary, Queen of Scots, and other Scotch lords from landing in Scotland: therefore he at once sailed for the Firth of Forth. Arriving at Berwick he heard that Bothwell had already landed, therefore Jenkinson turned his attention to the pirates. A certain Charles Wilson had been employed by the governor of Berwick to watch out for Bothwell, but he missed him. Wilson was in reality a pirate, and although he held Bedford's licence, Jenkinson captured him. Thereupon Bedford wrote furiously to the Privy Council describing Jenkinson as 'that vile man' and asserting that 'never was any so abused by a villain as (Wilson) had been by Jenkinson'. There is no record of how the episode ended (1565).

A few months later the Russia Company sent Jenkinson on a mission to Russia to safeguard its interests against an Italian merchant, Barberini, who had extracted from the Queen letters of recommendation to the Tsar and who, in the opinion of the Company, was infringing its rights granted by the Tsar. Jenkinson sailed from London on May 4th, 1566, in the *Harry*, and he arrived at Moscow on August 23rd: he had an audience with the Tsar on September 1st, when he delivered the Queen's letters and the normal presents. He was wholly successful in securing a complete monopoly of trade for his Company (1567) (Delmar Morgan, *ib.*, i, 48 sqq).

The Tsar seems to have been a mercurial creature. In 1571, in a temper against Elizabeth, he annulled the privileges he had granted to the Company: at once the Company sent Jenkinson to Russia to deal with the crisis. In the summer of 1571 Jenkinson was again in Russia. He arrived at St. Nicholas on July 26th to hear that the Tsar was furious with him and was threatening to cut off his head. With immense bravery Jenkinson set out for Moscow. He reached Kholmogori (August 1st, 1571), where he found the plague raging. A messenger of his was all but burnt for trying to force the cordon drawn round the city. He remained at Kholmogori until January 18th, ignored by the Tsar, destitute of money and ill-treated by the inhabitants. But at last the plague ended and

Jenkinson was ordered to go to Moscow, where he arrived on February 3rd. It was not until March 23rd that the Tsar admitted him to an interview and explained the reasons for his discontent. Jenkinson attributed everything to the incompetence of the Russian ambassador in England and to the bad behaviour of the Company's agents in Russia. On May 13th, 1572, Jenkinson saw the Tsar again and was well received. The Tsar went out of his way to compliment Jenkinson and he then restored the privileges to the Company. Jenkinson left Russia on July 23rd and arrived in England on September 10th. This was the last journey that Jenkinson undertook. For fifteen years he had devoted himself to fostering good relations between England and Russia and he had been entirely successful. 'And thus, being weary and growing old, I am content to take my rest in mine own house, chiefly comforting myself in that my service hath been honourably accepted and rewarded of her Majesty and the rest by whom I have been employed.'

Between 1572 and 1578 Jenkinson moved from London to live at Sywell in Northamptonshire. He was married probably in 1568 and he had twin daughters who died in infancy. A son who was born in 1580 also died as a baby, but there was another son who survived and gave to Jenkinson three grandchildren. He took much interest in the voyages of Frobisher. In 1577 he was sent on a mission to treat with the King of Denmark on the right of the English to navigate the northern seas. He sat on the commission which reported on the ore brought back by Frobisher in 1578. About 1600 he moved to Ashton in Northamptonshire and he died at Tighe in Rutland in 1611. From Anthony Jenkinson was descended Robert Jenkinson, second Lord Liverpool, who was Prime Minister in 1812 to 1827.

If Jenkinson is to be remembered as a traveller and trader and a diplomat, he ought not to be forgotten as a geographer. The vaguest and most inaccurate ideas prevailed in England and Europe about the East. The early voyages of Englishmen to the White Sea dispelled some of the erroneous notions; Jenkinson's travels greatly extended Western European geographical knowledge. He was the first man to describe from personal observation the eastern parts of Russia, the first to descend the Volga since it had become a Russian river, the first to navigate the Caspian Sea and to realize that it was a landlocked sea, the first to describe accurately the countries which lay along its coasts. Some of his descriptions of lands farther afield, especially of the rivers, were far wide of the mark, as when he tries to explain what he took to be the underground flow of the Oxus. His influence on geography was not always beneficial: his vivid descriptions were published in all the best collections of travels and his map was included by Ortelius in his famous atlas: thus Jenkinson's errors were perpetuated. All the same, he bridges the gap between Marco Polo in the thirteenth century and the English and Russian travellers of the eighteenth century. Jenkinson's map, which was published in 1562, has been attributed to William Borough, but there are good grounds for thinking that it was chiefly the work of Jenkinson. Borough may have done the drawing. (A full description will be found with a reproduction in Delmar Morgan's book. E. G. R. Taylor, *Tudor Geography 1485–1583*, pp. 29–30, 1930.)

Delmar Morgan, *Early Voyages and Travels to Russia and Persia*, Hakluyt Society, 2 vols, 1886.

Foster, *England's Quest of Eastern Trade*, The Pioneer Histories, 1933.

THE HAWKINS FAMILY, (the family spelt the name Hawkyns), lived in Plymouth and for three generations it was one of the most famous names in England. Between 1524 and 1622 three members played a leading part in local politics in Plymouth, in national politics in London, in overseas trade and naval warfare, or in all four at one and the same time. To some extent the Hawkins family was the creator of Plymouth, not only as the leading city in the south-west, but as the leading port for the new trade with the Americas.

HAWKINS, WILLIAM (first), merchant, politician and sailor, was born between 1490 and 1500, the son of John Hawkins of Tavistock and Joan, daughter of William Amydas of Launceston. He married Joan Trelawny and they had two sons, William and John, and one daughter. William Hawkins died in 1553 or 1554.

Hawkins was a man of much importance in Plymouth. He became Treasurer to the Corporation in 1524, he was Mayor in 1532 and again in 1538, and he sat in the 1539, 1547 and 1553 Parliaments as member for Plymouth. But it was as a trader that he is chiefly to be remembered. He began as an exporter of cloth and tin to western Europe, from whom he imported salt and wine from France, sugar and pepper from Portugal, soap from Spain and fish from the Banks of the 'newfoundlands'. Between 1530 and 1532 he sent several expeditions to Guinea and Brazil to develop the new Atlantic trade, especially in dyewood (Brazil means dyewood) for the English clothiers. On one voyage an Indian chief was brought back who was introduced to Henry VIII. The 1540 voyage proved how lucrative was this trade—the exports taken on the voyage were valued at £23 15s. 0d., the home-coming cargo of 'one dosen olyfantes tethe', 12 tusks (one cwt.) of ivory and 92 tons of Brazil wood at £615.

William Hawkins was a quarrelsome man, tough, resolute and uncompromising, very able, loyal to the government, but always looking after his own interests. He was more than once fined, but he never paid the fines: he was in prison once, but we now know that he was in the right. He laid the foundations of the new trade with the New World. And he was the father of the great Sir John Hawkins.

HAWKINS, WILLIAM (second), merchant, ship-owner and sailor, was born about 1519 and died in 1589, aged about 70 years. He was the elder son of William Hawkins (first) and brother of Sir John Hawkins.

The second William is a less national and heroic figure than his brother John, a less romantic figure than his nephew Richard, but in his own way he was a man of great local importance and he was often on the fringe of national and international events. In 1553 he was made a freeman of Plymouth; in 1558 he became a privy councillor of the borough; he was three times mayor of Plymouth, in 1567–8, in 1578–9 and in 1587–8. He built the new conduit which improved the water supply of Plymouth (1568–9), and in 1573 he and John farmed the town mills which were worked by power provided by the sea-tides.

It was through his ships and his trading ventures, usually carried out in conjunction with John, that he was brought into touch with the world of national politics. During the war against France in Mary's reign the Hawkins ships went privateering in the Channel, generally with profitable results. When the revolt of the Netherlands broke out, William repeated these tactics with the same success, to judge by the stream of complaints which poured in from France and Spain. Plymouth became the headquarters and William and John the mainspring of the unofficial war which went on between English and Spanish ships for two decades before the Armada set sail. It was William who organized the Protestant ships in the western Channel in cooperation with the Huguenots farther east towards Cowes in the Isle of Wight. It was William who had the chief hand in seizing the Spanish treasure at Plymouth in 1568. It was William who, when he heard (a false story) that John had been killed by the Spanish in the Indies, wrote to Cecil and requested that some of that treasure should be handed over to him, William, as compensation.

In 1582 he led an expedition, at the age of 62, to Brazil, and took with him his nephew Richard.

William Hawkins was mayor of Plymouth in the year of the Armada. He did not fight in the English fleet, but he helped to fit out seven ships from Plymouth to join the fleet, he collected reinforcements for the fleet, and he subscribed £25 towards the expense of defence.

He died on October 7th, 1589, and was buried in the church of St. Nicholas, Deptford.

Williamson, *Hawkins of Plymouth*, 1949.

HAWKINS, SIR JOHN, ('Achines' the Spanish called him) merchant, ship-owner, ship-builder, naval commander, naval administrator, was born at Plymouth in 1532 and died at sea on November 12th, 1595, aged 63 years. He was the second son

of William Hawkins (first): he was twice married, first to
Katherine Gonson, daughter of Benjamin Gonson, Treasurer
of the Navy (1559), and secondly to Margaret Vaughan. By
his first marriage he had one son, Richard, later Sir Richard
Hawkins.

When he was about twenty he killed a barber of Plymouth
named White, but he was judged by the coroner to have struck
White 'because he could not avoid him'. John was about
twenty-one when his father died, leaving his brother William
head of the family. John and William went into partnership
and worked together until probably 1560, when the business
was wound up. After that the two brothers worked separately,
but each invested in the ventures of the other. John certainly
spent a good deal of time at sea, voyaging principally to the
Canary Islands: as certainly he was by 1560 a wealthy man, for
when the partnership was broken, his share of the capital was
£10,000—a very large sum in those days. He was also a man
of importance, for in 1556 he became a freeman of Plymouth.
In the course of his travels to the Canaries he had learned the
possibilities of trading slaves between the Guinea coast of
Africa and the Spanish possessions in the West Indies. In 1559
or 1560 he left Plymouth and went to live in London, there the
more conveniently to further this new opening in trade.

The Slave-trading Voyages

(1) *The first slave-trading voyage* took place in 1562. A
syndicate was formed which included John's father-in-law,
Benjamin Gonson, and Sir William Wynter, Surveyor of the
Navy and Master of the Ordnance. This was intended to be a
comparatively small expedition to gain experience. Hawkins
sailed from Plymouth in October with the *Salomon*, the *Swallow*
and the *Jonas*, and possibly with a fourth vessel. He picked up
a pilot at Teneriffe and made for the Guinea coast. Here he
secured about 400 negro slaves and chartered a Portuguese ship
in which to transport the slaves. A Spanish friend had already
ascertained that his presence and his cargo would be welcome
in Hispaniola, although officially the Indies were forbidden to
trade with foreigners. In April 1563 Hawkins arrived at the

small ports on the north coast of the island—San Domingo was too public a place for him to sell his goods there. At Isabella, Puerto de Plata and Monte Christi he disposed of his English merchandise and his slaves, either in exchange for a little gold, a little sugar and a large lading of hides, or else for bills drawn upon Seville, since coined money was scarce in the Indies. He paid the normal customs dues in slaves, chartered a vessel from a Spaniard named Martinez, put Thomas Hampton in command of it and sent him off to Seville with part of the new cargo. He sent the Portuguese ship to Seville under its Portuguese captain and crew. From these actions it is possible to think that Hawkins felt assured that all he had done would be acceptable to the Spanish authorities in Spain and the Portuguese in Portugal. At Seville Hampton's cargo was seized by the Spanish: the Portuguese captain sailed his ship, not to Seville, but to Lisbon, where the cargo was impounded by the Portuguese Guinea traders. Hawkins arrived at Plymouth in August 1563, bringing with him by far the more important results of his trading with the Indies. When he heard what had happened at Seville he went straight to London to enlist ihe sympathies of the government on his side against Spain.

On this first voyage Hawkins had, deliberately and openly, broken the three great rules governing trade in the Spanish Indies. He had gone there without a licence to do so: he had traded without a licence: he had carried goods which had not previously been declared at Seville. He must have known the rules perfectly well. It is evident that Hawkins expected to get preferential treatment and that he was making this voyage into a test case. We do not know why he should have expected this, but it is possible that the answer lies in a curious episode when Queen Mary was on the throne. Hawkins was in Plymouth when the negotiations for the Spanish marriage were going on: some of the Spanish emissaries travelled through Plymouth and used the services of Hawkins and his brother. When Philip came to England in 1555 to marry Mary, one Spanish record avers that he knighted Hawkins. This is possibly not true, as we know that Hawkins was knighted during the fight against the Armada. But we also know that Hawkins often spoke of

Philip II as 'my old master': the word servant in that context meant something more than merely subject. Is it not likely that Hawkins had done some special service for Philip II which led him to think that Philip would give him privileged treatment in trading with the Spanish West Indies? If so, John Hawkins got his answer: he reckoned that he lost in Seville and Lisbon £20,000. Even so, the voyage paid a handsome dividend.

(2) *The second slave-trading voyage* took place in 1564. This was a much more important business than the first, for it had political as well as trading objectives.

The syndicate for the first voyage was now joined by three Privy Councillors, Cecil himself had much to do with supervising the expedition, and the Queen herself chartered to the leaders the largest vessel—it was the *Jesus of Lubeck* of 700 tons, but in a wholly rotten condition, (illustration in Williamson, *ib.*, p. 68)—and ordered that the fleet should sail under her own royal standard as well as the Cross of St. George. Probably what she hoped for was, first, to find out the exact position in Florida where a French colony had just been planted to the danger of the Spanish in the New World: and to rebuild the dying alliance with Spain against France: if Spain would allow England to trade freely with the West Indies, England would do what Spain appeared incapable of doing, protect the West Indian possessions, and she would thereby strengthen her own economy by the increase in trade and her defences against the French and Mary Stuart.

Hawkins at the age of 32 sailed from Plymouth on October 18th, 1564, in command of a fleet consisting of the royal ship, the *Jesus*, and three Plymouth vessels, the property of Hawkins, the *Salomon* (130 tons), the *Tiger* (50) and the *Swallow* (30, not the same as the ship on the first voyage). The total tonnage was 910: the total of the crews was 150, of which 80 sailed in the *Jesus*. Hawkins took only 1 man to every 6 tons, a great reduction on the normal, which resulted in his losing from disease not more than a dozen seamen. The orders he issued to the ships were 'Serve God daily (i.e. daily prayers), love one another (i.e. no quarrelling), preserve your victuals (i.e. no wasting), beware of fire and keep good company (i.e. sail close together)'.

After being delayed for five days at Ferrol by contrary winds he went to Teneriffe and thence to Sierra Leone to pick up slaves. He reached Dominica on March 9th, Margarita on the 16th and he called at Borburata in Venezuela. In all these places the Spanish wanted to trade, but the law was against them: therefore Hawkins had to go through the collusive farce of making a show of force so that the Spaniards could plead afterwards that they had been compelled to trade. Twice also, so treacherous were some of the Spanish governors, Hawkins had to make a real demonstration of force, notably at Rio de la Hacha where Hawkins landed an armed force, 'standing in doubt of their courtesy'. But he was able to sell all his goods, including the slaves, for which he was paid in gold and silver in lump and also in worked precious metals. At Curacao he took on board a large cargo of hides, which commanded a high price in England, to the value of £2,000.

When he arrived in Florida, he found the French settlement under Laudonnière in the direst want. He offered them a passage home, but Laudonnière refused it. He sold the *Tiger* to the French, and accepted payment in the form of a bill which he was never able to cash. Hawkins also gave them victuals. Laudonnière's gratitude took the form of a tribute that Hawkins 'has won the reputation of a good and charitable man, deserving to be esteemed as much of us all as if he had saved all our lives'.

Hawkins arrived home at Padstow on September 20th, 1565. Details of the profits made on this voyage are missing, but the Spanish ambassador reported to Philip II that the dividend was 60 per cent. The Queen was certainly satisfied, for she granted a coat of arms to Hawkins—sable, on a point wavy a lion passant or; in chief three bezants; for a crest, a demi-moor proper bound in a cord.

(3) *The Third Voyage*, 1567. Of the three voyages this one was by far the largest in size and organization, in its objectives the most hazardous, in its commercial and financial results a failure, and in its political results momentous: it is hardly too much to say that it marks the end of one epoch and the opening of another.

The Queen was once again a shareholder, this time contributing two ships. The syndicate was large and impressive and the whole affair was both an important joint-stock company trading for financial profits and also an act of state, part and parcel of the foreign policy of the government. Cecil, says Williamson, played almost the part of managing director.

The total ships were the *Jesus of Lubeck* (700 tons and even more rotten than in 1564, in spite of £500 worth of repairs) and the *Minion* (300 tons, built in 1536, and said to be 'spent and rotten'). The brothers Hawkins contributed four ships—the *William and John* (150), the *Swallow* (100), the *Judith* (50), the *Angel* (33). The total tonnage was 1333, the total personnel was 408, or one man to $3\frac{1}{4}$ tons, a higher proportion than Hawkins approved of. Among the officers were Hampton and Francis Drake, also a nephew of John Hawkins, a young man named either Paul Hawkins or Horsewell. Drake began the voyage in command of the *Jesus*, but he transferred later to another ship.

Before Hawkins sailed from Plymouth he had proof that he could not expect anything but hostility from Spain during his voyage. A Flemish admiral, de Wachen, entered Plymouth harbour, went into the Cattewater, where lay Hawkins's ships, refused to dip his flags and tried to get as near as he could to the royal ships. Hawkins at once opened fire: the episode was eventually peaceably disposed of. But the omen was clear.

On October 2nd, 1567, Hawkins set sail with his six ships and 400 men. About seventy of those men were to return. In Sierra Leone he was invited by the king to join in an attack on the town of Conga. Hawkins agreed and after some fairly stiff fighting he was able to sail westwards on February 7th, 1568, with a cargo of nearly 500 negroes. As an offset he had lost eight or nine men killed and a largish number of wounded.

He arrived at Dominica at the end of March and went on to Margarita, where he spent nine days and had a friendly reception from the governor. From there he sailed for Borburata in Venezuela. Here, contrary to all expectations, Hawkins was able to spend two months and to trade very profitably. From Borburata he set out for Rio de la Hacha. Here he met with organized opposition and was forced to take the town by direct assault. All the population and all the wealth of the town had been moved inland as soon as Hawkins appeared. But the booty was betrayed by a renegade negro slave and Hawkins had it all put aboard his ships. Then he had an interview with the governor, Castellanos, who gave in and paid 4000 gold *pesos* belonging to Philip II for sixty slaves and 1000 *pesos* of his own for another twenty, after which trade was opened to everybody. One of Hawkins's gunners, Job Hortop, was much interested in the wild life which he met with, and on this voyage he studied the habits of alligators, catching one with a dog as live bait on a hook and chain (Williamson, *ib.*, 128).

The next port of call was Santa Marta, small but able to trade. The farce of a collusive landing in force had to be used here, after which Hawkins was able to sell more than 100 slaves and some English goods and to revictual the fleet.

From Santa Marta to Cartagena: here it became clear that a landing was impossible, for the place was strongly fortified. Since leaving England Hawkins had increased his fleet from the original six to ten vessels. At Cartagena he reduced it to eight and set out on the homeward voyage not intending to land anywhere else in the West Indies. It was July and he was anxious to get the *Jesus* clear of the Caribbean (Williamson, *ib.*, 131). The *Jesus* was in such a parlous state that most commanders would have abandoned her. Hawkins did not. Nothing more clearly testifies to Hawkins as a loyal servant of the Queen than his dealing with the problem of the *Jesus*. She was the Queen's ship: if she were to be abandoned during the voyage, the loss would fall wholly on the Queen. If she had to be abandoned or repaired after returning home, the loss fell on the syndicate. (After the second voyage she had cost them £500.) As the Queen's servant Hawkins took a risk. It was essential to repair the *Jesus* and San Juan de Ulua was the only place to do it.

On September 15th Hawkins sighted San Juan. He was flying only the royal standard, but the colours were so faded that the Spanish officials mistook the flags for Spanish flags and assumed that the ships were the Spanish plate fleet. The anchorage was very small. An island of 240 yards lay parallel to the main coast and about five hundred yards from it, rising some three feet above the highest water level. On the island were some guns which commanded the port. If he was to be safe from treachery, Hawkins must get possession of the island. By good luck he did, because the port officials thought the fleet was the plate fleet and let it in without opposition. Hawkins arranged for victuals and for the payment for them: he sent word to Mexico to announce his arrival and to make clear that his intentions were peaceful (September 16th). The real plate fleet was not expected before the end of the month. Hawkins had time to repair his ship and be gone. Next morning the plate fleet arrived. To prevent it from entering its own harbour would be an act of war. To let it enter was to run grave risks. Hawkins decided he must let the fleet in. An amicable arrangement was come to with the new governor, Don Martin Enriquez, and hostages were exchanged. But Enriquez from the beginning was planning treachery. The wind was unfavourable for an entry until September 21st. When the fleet was inside there were twenty-eight ships in a much confined space. Enriquez plotted to transfer the pick of the Spanish crews on to a merchantman which could then be manhandled alongside the *Minion*. The English gunners on the island were to be surprised and knocked out and the guns turned on the English ships. Hawkins spotted the treachery and twice sent to Enriquez to protest against the movements which he saw taking place. The Viceroy arrested the English messenger the second time and blew the trumpets to launch his attack.

The ensuing battle lasted from ten in the morning to four in the afternoon. The Spaniards easily overran the English gunners on the island, but Hawkins got the *Minion* cleared from her anchors and withdrew from the island. It took longer for the *Jesus* to be hauled clear, but that too was accomplished. Hawkins then concentrated the fire of these two ships on the two Spanish fighting ships. He brought his guns to bear at point-blank range, sank the Spanish admiral and the vice-flagship was set on fire and burnt out. One merchantman also was destroyed. The Spanish sank the *Angel* and captured the *Swallow* and the Portuguese caravel. The *Grace of God* lost her mainmast and had to be abandoned. The *Judith*, commanded by Drake, got clear. The Spanish then tried to dislodge the English by means of fireships which caused a panic in the *Minion*'s men, who cast her off from the *Jesus*. As she began to move the men on the *Jesus* made a rush to get aboard the *Minion*: Hawkins was the last to leave the *Jesus*.

The *Minion* did not go more than a quarter of a mile, but she was out of range of the island guns. With her was the *Judith*. Next morning the *Judith* was gone, and no one has ever to this day discovered why Drake left Hawkins alone. Hawkins had no food and the *Minion* was leaking. It is not possible to know precisely what his casualties amounted to, but he seems to have left San Juan with about 200 men. After a fortnight he landed all the men who wanted to risk their lives rather on land than on sea. He sailed for home on October 16th: on December 31st he entered the port of Vigo where he bought victuals, but 'our men with excess of fresh meat grew into miserable diseases and died, a great part of them'. He picked up twelve new men from an English ship and set sail on January 20th, 1569. He reached Mount's Bay on January 25th, sent a message to his brother at Plymouth and got from him a new crew to bring the *Minion* home.

The voyage had been a disaster, but it was not a financial failure. The records in the Admiralty Court shew that Hawkins transferred nearly all the treasure from the *Jesus* to the *Minion* and brought it safely to England.

J. A. Williamson, *Hawkins of Plymouth*, 1949.
M. Lewis, *Fresh Light on San Juan de Ulua*, in *Mariner's Mirror*, July 1937.
I. A. Wright, *Caribbean Documents*.
Raynor Unwin, *The Defeat of John Hawkins*, 1960.

Hawkins and the Ridolfi Plot. Hawkins was left with a burning fury against Spain for the treachery at San Juan, the more inflamed by the treatment meted out (in Mexico and in Spain) to those of his crews who had been taken prisoners.

He was determined to have his revenge for the treachery and to get the prisoners released.

In February 1570 a letter reached Cecil from George Fitzwilliam, one of Hawkins's imprisoned crews at Seville, asking for the government's help to get them released. Hawkins at once had several interviews with the Spanish ambassador, Don Guereau de Spes. At this moment Fitzwilliam was released. Hawkins sent him to Madrid to interview Philip II (April 1571). Cecil was well aware that Spain was backing the Ridolfi plot for an invasion of England by Alva, the murder of Elizabeth and the enthronement of Mary, Queen of Scots, in her place. But he did not know the details. It was John Hawkins who unravelled the plot.

Hawkins succeeded in gulling the foolish de Spes into believing that he was an ardent Catholic, that he wanted to see Mary, Queen of Scots, on the throne of England and that at the moment of invasion by the Spanish navy he would desert with all his ships to the side of Spain. All this was done with Cecil's knowledge and approval. de Spes and Philip were completely hoodwinked. Philip gave Hawkins a patent of Spanish nobility and a pardon for his offences in the West Indies, with a promise to pay for the upkeep of sixteen ships and 1,600 men for two months. Having concerted with Philip the exact plans for the invasion, Hawkins at once passed them on to Cecil, who was now able to bring together all the pieces in the puzzle —the part Alva was to play, the complicity of Mary Stuart's ambassador, the Bishop of Ross, the treachery of the Duke of Norfolk. Ross confessed all, Norfolk was executed and de Spes turned out of the country. Hawkins, the tough naval commander, was now revealed as the subtle diplomatist.

Hawkins and the New Navy. In 1571 Hawkins became M.P. for Plymouth. In 1573 he was all but murdered. He was riding along the Strand, when suddenly a man named Peter Burchett stabbed him, mistaking him for Sir Christopher Hatton, not because of any physical resemblance between Hawkins and Hatton, but probably because both always had a liking for specially fine clothes. The wound was severe, but

cc—(2)

Hawkins recovered and suffered no ill effects afterwards. In 1577 he succeeded his father-in-law, Sir Benjamin Gonson, as Treasurer of the Navy. For the next ten years Hawkins was taken up with reforming both the administration of the Navy and also the building of the ships themselves.

The men who formed the Navy Board belonged to a generation which had only seen service in home waters. The only theatre of fighting which they could imagine was the Channel and the North Sea. For such fighting they believed in the old-fashioned ship, the floating castle, of which the *Jesus of Lubeck* was well known to Hawkins. These carracks rose high out of the water and were made very unwieldy by the top-heavy castles which were built at the bow and stern in order to repel the enemy, if they were able to board the ship. Hawkins had seen at San Juan de Ulua how unserviceable and dangerous such a ship could be. Further, Hawkins had no intention of confining the war against Spain to the Channel and the North Sea, he intended to fight in the Atlantic, at the Azores, on the coast of Spain and in the West Indies. For such warfare a new kind of ship was needed. Between 1570 and 1587 the design of the new ships was considerably modified. The evidence that this was wholly the work of Hawkins is not conclusive and some credit may have to be given to Wynter and the rest of the Navy Board. But it is difficult not to feel that the drive towards such a reform must have come from the experienced Hawkins. What Hawkins wanted was ships that could sail much nearer the wind than the old 'round ship' so that they could choose their own range for fighting. Therefore the length of the keel was increased and the ship was what we should call today stream-lined. The proportions of the ships built at the Deptford yard were usually three or three and a half times their breadth in the length on keel, or four times their breadth over the whole length of the ship. This gave speed and manoeuvrability, which was increased by cutting down the towering upper works on deck. These were only needed for close fighting, but Hawkins's plan was to increase the armament of the ships and to fight at long range. The ships, therefore, rolled less in heavy weather and greater use could be made of the gun-ports on the lower decks. The enemy was never to be allowed to board, therefore the guns in the upper works were unnecessary.

The ships were more heavily armed—an improvement which was probably the work of Wynter, but of which Hawkins highly approved. A typical example of this new sort of ship is the *Revenge*, which was built in 1575. She was of 450 tons, 92 feet long, 32 feet broad, carrying forty-six guns in all. She remained the model for all English ships for the next three hundred years.

In what may be called the interior economy of the ships Hawkins was a pioneer. He refused to crowd the ships with men. The normal ratio was one man to every one and a half tons, but Hawkins preferred one man to two tons. This reform made the seaworthiness of a fleet greater, since victuals and drink lasted longer. Victuals for one man for four months occupied one ton of stowage: guns, ammunition, etc. had to be allowed for: thus to reduce the number of men to one man for every two tons added fifty per cent. to the time a fleet could stay at sea.

Hawkins also increased the pay of the men from 6/8 to 10/- per month. He was greatly interested in hygiene. In 1586 he introduced into his own ships apples and pears and he kept live pigs and sheep on board. On his last voyage in 1595 he experimented with 'lasting victuals, a new kind of victuals for sea service devised by Mr. Hugh Platte, 4 barrels at £4. 10s. the barrel'. On this voyage he also took with him 927 'Brasill Beds', probably hammocks copied from a pattern used by the Indians in Guiana, which was looked on as part of Brazil— hence the name Brasill beds.

Hawkins and the Two Bargains. In 1577/8, just after he had become Treasurer of the Navy, Hawkins made a report to Burghley on the corruption which he found rampant in the dockyards. The Queen was being made to pay £9,000 for materials and not £4,000 worth was used in her service. The difference went 'for Sir William Wynter's commodity'. Similarly she was paying for good timber for repairs to her ships, but the repairs were being carried out in rotten timber, while the good

was used for other people's private ships. As a result of this
report a new system was instituted in 1579 in the First Bargain.

This Bargain comprised two agreements: one between the
Queen and Hawkins, by which Hawkins undertook to provide
at his own expense all the ropes, cables, hawsers and other gear,
for which he was to be paid £1,200 p.a. without having to
render detailed accounts, but his work was to be supervised
and a report sent in to Burghley: another between the Queen
and Pett and Baker, the master-shipwrights, who undertook a
regular routine of inspection and repairs of the ships at their
own expense, for which they were paid £1,000 p.a. and their
work was also to be supervised.

Hawkins saw that war was imminent. He wanted to save the
Queen £4,000 which was being wasted by dishonest contractors; to make her unsound ships into sound ships; and to fit the
fleet for trans-oceanic service. Naturally enough those who
lost by the new system never stopped accusing Hawkins of
robbing the Queen and of ruining the ships, but an enquiry
in 1583 into the state of the navy exonerated Hawkins.

The Second Bargain was struck in 1585. By it the agreement
between the Queen and the master-shipwrights was ended.
Hawkins now undertook to do all the repairs to ships afloat
or grounded, pay all the wages involved in administering this
work, to find all the materials, victuals and lodgings involved.
For this he was to receive £4,000 p.a. In addition he undertook
all heavy repairs and to find all the materials, wages, etc. For
this he was to be paid £1,714. 2. 2. p.a. Hawkins thus became
responsible for the upkeep of the whole Royal Navy, but the
armaments were not included. Again he was relentlessly
pursued by those who lost their illegal profits by his reforms.
The justification for his policy and the integrity of his character
were revealed in the efficient state of the fleet when it sailed
against the Armada.

Hawkins as a strategist. It is a mistake to regard Hawkins
solely as an active naval commander and an administrator in
business and commerce or of the Royal Navy. He was also a
man whose 'wide-ranging mind' (Williamson) included within

its purview the strategical conduct of the war. Hawkins held that Philip II depended on his American treasure to save him from bankruptcy. Therefore, if sea-power were brought to bear on the Atlantic trade routes, Philip would be ruined, England would be safe. Hawkins rejected all idea of military invasions, because England had no army and military adventures were expensive for a country which had no money to spare. He therefore relied on purely naval warfare, which might be made to a large extent to pay for itself.

Hawkins and the Spanish Armada. When the Armada set sail from Spain Hawkins could not at once leave the Navy Board and it was June before he joined the fleet at Plymouth. Here he took command of the *Victory*, one of his own new ships. He ranked third in seniority below Howard and Drake, and he was a member of the war council which Howard consulted 'on every question of moment'. When the fleet moved out towards Ushant, Hawkins was in command of the in-shore squadron towards the Scilly Isles. He took part in all the engagements with the Armada as it sailed up the Channel, and on Friday, July 26th, he was knighted by Howard on board the *Ark Royal*. The fight between Portland and the Isle of Wight had revealed weaknesses in the organization of the English fleet, which was now formed into four squadrons, one of which was under the command of Hawkins. By the time the English fleet left contact with the Armada and abandoned it to destruction by wind and wave, Hawkins's policy as Treasurer of the Navy had been fully justified: not one of the English ships had fallen out of the fight owing to damage by the sea or by the enemy.

Hawkins's post-Armada voyages. After the defeat of the Armada Hawkins had a year's leave in order to deal with the naval accounts. In 1591 his wife died, but he soon married again, Margaret Vaughan. In 1592 he founded an almshouse at Chatham, known as Sir John Hawkins's Hospital, and it survives today.

Hawkins made two voyages after the Armada. In 1590 he organized an expedition in two squadrons: one squadron of six of the Queen's galleons under Frobisher sailed for the Azores, victualled for four months, while a second squadron of six under Hawkins, victualled for six months, sailed for the Spanish coast. When Philip heard of it, he cancelled all sailings from the West Indies, so that Frobisher and Hawkins could only take a few prizes, which paid for some of the expenses of the fleets.

In 1595 Hawkins and Drake sailed in a fleet which was put under the joint command of both. This was a joint-stock company in which the Queen took shares. Its purpose was to land a force at Nombre de Dios, march across the isthmus and capture Panama. But in August news came which caused them to change their objective—that the flagship of the Plate fleet was lying damaged in San Juan de Puerto Rico. Hawkins and Drake sailed from Plymouth on August 28th with the intention of capturing the treasure and bringing it straight home. The voyage was a disaster. The joint command was a great mistake: Hawkins and Drake were men of wholly different character and they never succeeded in establishing a unity of command by which alone the voyage could succeed. They quarrelled, they wasted time and opportunities, and Spain meanwhile was taking counter measures. One of the English ships, the small *Francis*, was taken by the Spanish and her commander's written instruction fell into Spanish hands, revealing that Puerto Rico was the destination of the fleet. Spanish reinforcements sailed at once for Puerto Rico. The game was up. On October 31st Hawkins fell ill and he died on November 12th, 1595. He was buried at sea.

Character of Hawkins. Modern research has discredited the hostile views about Hawkins which appear in J. K. Laughton's article in the *D.N.B.* The nineteenth-century historians were writing just at the time when public opinion loathed the idea of slaves and slavery. If Hawkins was capable of trafficking in slaves, he was capable of any other sort of dishonesty and cruelty. But in fact in dealing in slaves Hawkins was only doing what public opinion of his own day approved. He was a product of the Tudor age, a man of diversified abilities. He was a consummate seaman, a bold and skilful navigator, a first-class business man, an original designer of ships and of strategy, in a corrupt age an uncorrupt administrator of the navy, a politician and diplomatist who could outwit a foreign ambassador, single-minded in his devotion to the Queen. He was also a man of fashion, well educated, able to write clearly technical memoranda for Burghley, finely dressed, one who moved as easily in the company of Kings and courtiers as he did with sailors and contractors. He could command strict discipline among his crews, yet at the same time command their affection and respect. In religion he was to begin with an orthodox Catholic, but as the years went by and the fierceness of the war increased, he became gradually more and more Protestant, so that his letters towards the end have a Puritan ring about them. Like most people of his time, at any rate in the later years, and like Oliver Cromwell after him, he identified the enemies of his country with the enemies of God. There is a steadiness about him, a determination to order things carefully and methodically, leaving nothing to chance, which contrasts strongly with the haphazard way in which Drake left everything to the inspiration of the moment. Drake was a genius whose exploits have won for him immortal fame, but it is doubtful whether he contributed more to the defeat of Spain and the salvation of England than his less famous, but not less devoted patriot, Sir John Hawkins.   (*Plate 25*)

The account in the *D.N.B.* must be used with caution. The above account is based on the most up-to-date authority, J. A. Williamson's *Hawkins of Plymouth*, (1949), which corrects and supplements, but does not supersede, his *Sir John Hawkins*, (1927).

HAWKINS, SIR RICHARD, merchant and naval commander, was born in 1560 and died in 1622, aged 62. He was the only child of Sir John Hawkins and his first wife, Katherine Gonson. Nothing is known of his early life, which must have been spent mainly among ships and commerce, until he appears in history as vice-admiral in command of a ship in the voyage made by his uncle, William Hawkins (the second) in 1582–3. In his *Observations*, which were written between 1602 and 1603 and which were being printed at the moment of his death in 1622, Richard records, 'In anno 1582, in the island of Margarita, I was at the dredging of pearl oysters, after the manner we dredge oysters in England; and with mine own hands I opened many and took out the pearls, some greater, some less, and in good quantity'. It was on this voyage that one of the captains reported his ship, *Bark Bonner*, to be leaking so badly that he advised she should be abandoned. A council of captains agreed, but Richard opposed them and undertook to sail the ship home with a crew of volunteers, on condition that they were paid one third of her value as salvage. The *Bark Bonner's* captain was shamed into sailing her home himself.

Richard next appears in command of the galliot *Duck* (20 tons) in Drake's expedition to the West Indies, 1585–6. All that is known of him on this voyage is that he suffered from a severe attack of fever, but he learned a valuable lesson from this experience, as also from his father's interest in hygiene. Of the Cape Verde Islands he wrote, 'in two times that I have been in them, either cost us the one half of our people with fevers and fluxes of sundry kinds'. When he himself came to lead an expedition (1593) he refused to land at the Cape Verde Islands.

It is likely enough that Richard accompanied Drake on his 1587 raid on the Armada ports in Spain, but there is no evidence that he did. In that year he sold some guns to Plymouth for its defence. He fought in the English fleet against the Armada in 1588 in command of the Queen's *Swallow* (350 tons). Two of his private merchantmen were used as fireships at Calais.

When his father, John Hawkins, sailed for the Spanish coast in 1590 Richard went with him, and we owe it to Richard that we know that the rate of mortality on that voyage during six months at sea was much below the average on previous voyages, a sure tribute to John Hawkins's foresight and understanding.

In 1592, according to Richard, there was afoot a project to capture Nombre de Dios and Panama. This plan came to nothing, but it spurred Richard on to build up an enterprise which was to eclipse all previous transatlantic expeditions. He had immediately after the defeat of the Armada (1588) laid down a galleon of his own of about 350 tons. His object was to make a complete survey of eastern Asia, where he was ambitious to plant an English trading empire. He planned to sail through the straits of Magellan, pay his overhead expenses by plundering the treasure towns of Peru, refit in California and then cross the Pacific to eastern Asia. Hawkins described his ship as 'pleasing to the eye, profitable for stowage, good of sail and well conditioned'. His mother, on being asked to christen the ship, gave it the name of *Repentance*, since for those seeking the port of Heaven repentance was the best ship. Later Queen Elizabeth insisted on the name being changed to *Dainty*. In April 1593 Richard sailed the *Dainty* from the Thames to Plymouth. Late in May he was ready to go, but a gale destroyed *Dainty*'s mainmast, so that he did not get away until June 12th, 1593. He was away ten years and never again saw his father.

He followed the normal course across the Atlantic, but he avoided the Atlantic islands after his experience in 1585. Presently he arrived at land which he took to be the Atlantic coast of *Terra Australis Incognita*, but it was in fact the Falkland Islands. He got through the Straits of Magellan in forty-six days (Drake had passed through them in sixteen days), and he intended to sail north until he was above Callao before attacking any Spanish towns. But his men were mutinous and compelled him to attack at once and win treasure. Richard does not seem to have had the complete control over his men which was one of the great gifts his father possessed. Richard gave in and attacked Valparaiso. Some gold was taken, but the news of his arrival in Spanish waters quickly spread. The Viceroy of Peru sent out six ships and 2,000 men against *Dainty* and her 75. The first encounter was lucky but ominous. Richard soon found that the Spanish had devised a new and faster ship for the defence of their towns than they had had in the pre-Armada days. They were heavily armed, much more heavily than *Dainty*. They were more nimble to manoeuvre and could easily take the weather gauge from Richard's ship. Thanks to good luck with the weather Richard escaped at the first meeting. The men were still out of hand and insisted on chasing worthless prizes. At the Bay of Atacames the Spaniards fell in with the English again. The result was a foregone conclusion. After a fearful battering at close range for three days on end *Dainty* was sinking and there were only twenty out of her seventy-five men left unhurt. Hawkins still fought on, but when nineteen of his men were killed and forty wounded, there was nothing for it but to surrender, which Hawkins did on condition that the men were sent back to England (June 22nd, 1594). Hawkins himself was severely wounded and he was taken as a prisoner to Peru. Here he lived for three years, loved by everybody. His men were sent to Spain and after three years were released. It is likely enough that while he was in Peru he conformed to the Catholic religion, but this was not a genuine conversion: once he got back to England he was soon hunting down Catholics. After three years in Peru he was transferred to Spain: he tried to escape and was caught and was imprisoned in Madrid. He was promised release if he would pay a ransom of £3,000. He had the money at home, but it was in the hands of his stepmother and she refused to remit any of it. Eventually the ransom was paid, perhaps through the good offices of Burghley, and Richard Hawkins was freed in 1602.

On the accession of James I Hawkins was knighted and made Vice-Admiral of Devon. He was Mayor of Plymouth (1603–4) and was one of the members of Parliament for the town. In 1622 he took part in a bungled expedition against the Barbary pirates and on his return he suddenly died. His widow, Judith, survived him for seven years.

A great deal of new evidence on Richard Hawkins became available after the article in the *D.N.B.* was written. This is summarized in J. A. Williamson's *Hawkins of Plymouth* (1949). The documents are printed by the Hakluyt Society, edited by Miss Wright. The *Observations of Sir Richard Hawkins* have been edited and published by J. A. Williamson (1933).

DRAKE, SIR FRANCIS, navigator and naval captain, was born at Crowndale near Tavistock in Devon, probably in 1543. He died at sea in 1596 at the approximate age of fifty-three. His father, Edmund Drake, had been a sailor, then a yeoman farmer and a staunch Protestant. After the rising in the south-west in 1549 the family escaped to Gillingham in Kent, where Edmund became a preacher to the sailors and naval workmen at the new naval station on the Medway, later to become Chatham. Francis was thus brought up among ships and sailors and he learned to become a fanatical Protestant.

The first voyage Drake made was in 1566. At the age of twenty-four he joined a small expedition, financed by his cousin John Hawkins, under the command of Captain John Lovell, which went to the Spanish Main. At Rio de la Hacha the governor tricked Lovell into landing ninety negroes and then refused to pay for them. Lovell meekly went home and Drake never forgot this experience of Spanish behaviour and of English weakness.

In 1567 Hawkins sailed on his third slave-trading voyage and took Drake with him in the *Jesus of Lubeck*. Drake does not appear to the best advantage, for after the battle was over he sailed home and left Hawkins to fend for himself. Hawkins accused him of deserting him, but the facts of the case are not now fully known and the quarrel was soon made up.

Drake now set himself to destroy the Spanish monopoly in the New World and to defend English Protestantism against Philip II. He early saw that Philip's strength depended on the treasure which he drew from Mexico and Peru. Drake also realized that the key to this treasure-house was the Isthmus of Panama, the only line of communication between the Peruvian port of Lima on the Pacific side and Nombre de Dios on the Atlantic side. If he could get control of Panama and Nombre de Dios the supply of Peruvian silver would dry up and the flow of Mexican gold could be seriously interfered with.

Drake's next three voyages were all directed to this main objective. That of 1570–1 was only a voyage of reconnaissance to discover the exact route of the treasure-train from Panama to Nombre de Dios. The voyage of 1572 aimed at the capture of Nombre de Dios and of the treasure-train. The town was easily taken, but Drake was wounded and carried off by his men before any of the treasure in Nombre de Dios could be collected. The attack on the train, after a first failure, was a complete success and when Drake arrived home at Plymouth on Sunday, August 9th, 1573, the whole congregation turned out of the church to greet him—'few or none remained with the preacher'.

Drake arrived just at the moment when the Queen was trying to patch up a reconciliation with Philip of Spain. The danger was that Philip might demand as one of his terms the return of all Drake's plunder and the execution of Drake as a pirate. Somebody warned Drake to disappear, which he did so successfully that we know nothing about him for the next two years. Then in 1575 he turned up in Ireland serving with Essex's army. In 1576 he returned to England, bringing with him Thomas Doughty, a friend of Leicester and soon to be an acquaintance of Burghley, perhaps even his spy in Drake's next voyage, the voyage of circumnavigation of 1577 to 1580.

This voyage was undoubtedly intended to carry the unofficial war into the Pacific Ocean and to the west coast of the Spanish-American colonies, whatever other reasons were made public, such as the shipping of currants from Alexandria. A summary of the probable understanding arrived at between the Queen and Drake, perhaps to the exclusion of Burghley, and involving the later disputes with Doughty, may be read in Dr. J. A. Williamson's *The Age of Drake*, chapter x.

The expedition consisted of the *Pelican* (120 tons and 18 guns), the *Elizabeth* (80+16), the *Marigold* (30+16), the *Benedict* (a pinnace), the *Swan* (50+5), a store ship, and in all about 160 men set sail from Plymouth in November, 1577. In the Atlantic Drake captured a Portuguese ship which he put in the charge of Doughty, a well-educated, but a crooked and unreliable man. Soon Drake was aware that Doughty was stirring up trouble in his ship; Drake therefore moved him to the *Pelican*, but there Doughty began to preach mutiny to the crew, whereupon Drake sent him as a prisoner to the *Swan*. Then came strange weather, fogs and calms alternating with gales. In accordance with the views of the times, Drake and many others were persuaded that Doughty was using magic to ruin the voyage. When Drake announced that the expedition was going to raid the Spanish coast, the gentlemen-adventurers grew discontented, having believed that they were going on a voyage of discovery and in search of trade. The safety of the whole expedition was at stake. Drake took stern measures. When they arrived at Port St. Julian, where Magellan many years before had executed the leaders of a mutiny, Drake set up a jury to try Doughty. He was found guilty of having betrayed the plan of the expedition to Burghley and of stirring up mutiny among the crews. He was sentenced to death: then, in the, to us, strange manner of the times, Drake and Doughty dined together and received the Sacrament and Doughty was then beheaded. The whole trial may have been very irregular, but there is no doubt that the sentence was just and saved the lives of many who would have perished, if mutiny had prevailed.

Some weeks later Drake dealt with the sailors and the gentlemen. At a Sunday service he preached the sermon himself. He openly attacked all in the fleet, the sailors for being mutinous, the gentlemen for shirking their share of the work. 'My masters, I must have it left. I must have the gentlemen to haul and draw with the mariner, and the mariner with the gentleman. I would know him that would refuse to set his hand to a rope.' Then, after this direct challenge, came the unexpected compliment, 'but I know there is not any such here'. He then dismissed all the captains and masters from their posts, and he told the men that any of them could go home who wanted to and he would provide a ship for the purpose, but absolute loyalty and obedience he would have from those who stayed. Not a man volunteered to leave him. The mutiny was quashed, peace restored, the officers reinstated. The whole episode illustrates Drake's character, his sternness where sternness was vital, his lack of rancour against the chief villain, his capacity for softening straight talk with a tactful compliment. By such means did he win the hearts of his followers.

On August 21st, 1578, the *Pelican* (now renamed the *Golden Hind* in honour of Sir Christopher Hatton, a principal share-

holder in the expedition, whose cognizance was a golden hind),
the *Elizabeth* and the *Marigold* entered the Straits of Magellan.
Luck must have been with him, for Drake got through in the
record time of 16 days. At once the weather deteriorated for
several weeks; the *Marigold* lost touch and was never seen again;
John Winter in the *Elizabeth* took refuge in the Straits and then
returned home. We now know that he did not desert Drake,
that he intended to try to meet him in the Pacific, but his men
refused and compelled him to go back to England.

When the weather improved Drake turned north to plunder
the Spanish colonies. At Valparaiso he took a ship heavily
laden with gold and on the way up the coast he took many
more. At Callao he heard that a great treasure-ship had just
sailed for Panama. This was the so-called *Cacafuego* (Spitfire).
He easily overtook and overpowered it, ransacked it, set it free
and gave its captain a safe-conduct, in case he fell in with
Winter. Going on northwards Drake reached Nicaragua and
had the *Golden Hind* careened at Guatulco. He then made for
California and reached a point somewhere between latitudes
42° and 48°, where in a now unknown harbour he refitted and
in July, 1579, set out for home. But before he went he took
possession of California in the Queen's name, called it New
Albion, and set up a brass plate announcing the annexation.

On the way home he called at the Moluccas and made a
treaty with the sultan of Ternate, promising to the English
a monopoly of the spice trade—a promise which influenced the
founding of the E.I.C. in 1600. After being almost wrecked
on a submerged reef, the *Golden Hind* reached Java and then
turned for home. Drake arrived at Plymouth in October 1580.
He had been away three years and he brought back with him
treasure which paid a dividend of 1,400 per cent. on the initial
outlay of the expedition.

Elizabeth was delighted with the financial success of the
voyage, especially as it was at the expense of Spain. She brought
the *Golden Hind* to London, where crowds came to see the ship.
She herself in April, 1581, went on board with the French ambassador who, at the Queen's command, knighted Drake, whose
reputation was now at its height. In 1584 it was clear that war

with Spain was likely and Elizabeth was ready to get in the first blow. A strong expedition was fitted out to attack the Spanish possessions in the West Indies and Drake was put in command. This was an official voyage and Drake sailed as the Queen's admiral, 1585. He had with him two of the Queen's ships and 27 other ships belonging to private investors in the venture. These carried 2,300 men, who included twelve companies of soldiers for service on land. Martin Frobisher went as second-in-command, Walsingham's son-in-law, Carleill, went as a soldier. The purpose of the expedition was to do the maximum amount of damage to Philip II's source of strength, the wealth from his colonial possessions. The treasure-fleet was to be captured, if possible: the towns on the Spanish Main were to be destroyed, and perhaps even a garrison might be left in one of them as a permanent threat to the Peruvian and Mexican treasure.

Drake sailed from Plymouth in September 1585, and he was home again late in July 1586. In that time, although he lost three hundred men from fever while he crossed the Atlantic, he sacked San Domingo, but succeeded in extracting only a small sum as ransom. His next objective was Cartagena, the most important of the towns on the Main. The attack was completely successful, Drake dismantled the defences and carried off the guns. He was paid £30,000 as a ransom and he left the town derelict. This would have been the place to garrison, but Drake rightly came to the conclusion that it would have been too difficult to reinforce it. He was most anxious to go on and capture Panama, but sickness broke out again among his men and he had to give up the idea. He set out for home through the Florida channel and would certainly have attacked Havana in Cuba, the point at which the plate-fleets assembled on their way home to Spain, but his fighting strength was so much reduced by death and sickness that again he had to abandon the idea. But he captured the Spanish settlement at St. Augustine on the mainland and took all the guns. It is reckoned that all told Drake brought away 240 Spanish guns and thereby seriously weakened* the armament

* But Professor Michael Lewis denies this in his *Armada Guns*.

of the Armada, for Spain could not herself manufacture guns and had to pay high prices for them in Italy or even to smuggle them out of England (Williamson, *Sir Francis Drake*, p. 89, Collins, 1951). On his way home he called in at Virginia and found Ralph Lane and his colonists in great distress, therefore he gave them a passage home.

The expedition did not pay for its expenses, but Drake had greatly damaged the Spanish. Had the Queen followed up this voyage with another swift attack under Drake on Panama, perhaps the Spanish invasion of England would not have been possible. But she did not and the Spanish American colonies were able to recover, as Drake and Hawkins found out in 1595. When, therefore, Drake was home again, it was clear to all that only a direct attack on the Spanish ports and shipping would, at best prevent, at worst delay the sailing of the Armada.

Of Drake's exploits, the voyage of circumnavigation was probably the most remarkable—it put England and Drake on the map. The attacks on the Spanish Main in 1585 were immensely valuable, but they were incomplete, through no fault of Drake's. The 'singeing of His Catholic Majesty's Beard' (1587), was probably the most audacious and the most valuable of all the deeds that Drake did for England. The audaciousness is testified to by the opinions of the Spanish; the value, by the time it gave England to meet the Armada. Everybody knew that 1587 was the advertised date for the sailing of the Armada. Drake compelled Philip to postpone the sailing until 1588.

Drake's orders in 1587 were to 'impeach' and 'distress' the King of Spain's ships inside his ports. Twenty-seven ships, including four of the Queen's, and about 2,200 men sailed from Plymouth in April, 1587, in so great a hurry that the victualling was not completed: Drake was afraid that the Queen might change her mind, as in fact she did, but too late—Drake was gone. He reached Cadiz on the 19th and at once sailed into the harbour and wrought immense havoc among the 80 ships he found there. His Vice-Admiral, Borough, was so outraged at such dangerous and unorthodox methods, taken without first summoning a council of war, that

Plate 25

Sir Francis Drake,
Admiral

Sir John Hawkins,
Treasurer of the Navy

Plate 26

Sir Richard Grenville,
Vice-Admiral

Lord Howard of Effingham,
Lord High Admiral

he took his ship out of Cadiz and refused to co-operate. The Spanish losses were at least 24 ships and may have been 37.

The larger part of the Armada was in Lisbon, but Drake knew that that was too strong a port to be captured. He therefore sailed to Cape St. Vincent in order to cut off supplies to that harbour. An attack on Lagos found that place too strong to be taken, but at Sagres Drake personally led the attack and captured the fort, which gave him a harbour near St. Vincent. Here again Borough refused to join in such unorthodox warfare and Drake made him a prisoner in the *Golden Hind*, Borough's ship. An attempt to lure the Spanish Admiral, Santa Cruz, out of Lisbon by taunts and insults failed, whereupon Drake went back to St. Vincent. Here he captured a whole year's supply of staves for making barrels, so that when the Armada sailed the casks were made of unseasoned wood and leaked badly. He also destroyed the tunney fisheries on which the Armada depended for its supply of fish.

Hearing of the approach of a plate-ship, Drake sailed for the Azores, where he fell in at exactly the right moment with the *San Felipe*, which he easily overpowered and he brought back to England her cargo, which was valuable enough to pay the costs of his expedition twice over. He arrived at Plymouth on June 26th, 1587. More valuable than the wealth and the papers which he had captured giving the secrets of the Indian trade was the delay he had imposed on the sailing of the Armada. Furthermore, he had now achieved such a moral ascendancy over the Spanish that they not only regarded him as the Devil, but they were convinced that he used a magic mirror which enabled him to watch the movements of men and ships in any part of the world. When the Armada sailed in 1588, it sailed with an inferiority complex. (J. S. Corbett, *Papers Relating to the Spanish War, 1585-7*, Navy Rev. Soc., xi, Intro., for the most interesting account.)

Undoubtedly Drake was now the greatest seaman in the world and one would expect him to have commanded the English fleet against the Armada. But in the sixteenth century by convention a commander of a national fleet had to be a

DD—(2)

grandee: and there was a sounder reason than mere convention: the great seamen like Drake, Hawkins, Frobisher, were men of the same social standing and would not necessarily be ready to take orders from one of their own class, whereas all would obey an outstanding member of the aristocracy. For this reason the Lord High Admiral, Howard of Effingham, was put in command of the English fleet and Drake accepted the appointment cheerfully and loyally.

Had Howard and Drake had their way, they would have sought out the Armada in Spain and fought it in Spanish waters rather than allow it to reach the Channel. The Queen disapproved; she feared the Armada might give the English fleet the slip and arrive in the Channel unopposed. The difficulty in victualling the ships and the vagaries of the wind also made it hazardous for the English to sail too far from the Channel. Between the first sailing of the Armada on May 18th, 1588, and its arrival off the Lizard on the 19th of July, Howard three times put out to sea to search for the Armada and three times was driven back by the wind. Drake was the most vehement supporter of the offensive and he was perfectly right, but he could not get his own way (Corbett, *Drake and the Tudor Navy*, ii, 171). That Drake was in favour of finishing a game of bowls on Plymouth Hoe before attacking the Spanish is so out of keeping with his impetuous character that the story must be rejected as sound history, but it may live on as a proof of Drake's unshakable confidence in the outcome of the battle.

The Armada was off Plymouth on the 20th and the English fleet was caught inside the harbour. Howard got the ships warped out during the night and was to windward of the Spanish in the early morning of the 21st. The Spanish fleet sailed, not in crescent formation, rather that of an arrow-head or fish-tail (or, as one foreign historian called it, an 'eagle'). The English were in one unit in close-hauled line ahead, while the Spanish were in three divisions, each line abreast. Medina Sidonia's instructions were not to engage the English, unless it became necessary, nor to land on the coast, though he might capture an English harbour, if that proved possible: his main purpose was to carry the Armada up the Channel in order to make contact with Parma in the Netherlands and to transport his army across the water to invade England. Howard could not know this, and he rightly feared a landing or an attack on one of the Channel ports. The fighting on the 21st achieved little more than 'we put them to leeward, kept the weather of them and distressed two of their best ships' (Howard). During the night Drake was to lead the English line and keep a light at his stern for the others to follow. Suddenly Drake put out his light and disappeared in the darkness: thus the English lost touch with the enemy. He was for long accused of having gone off in order to capture a Spanish ship (he did in fact capture the *Nuestra Senora del Rosario*, but he fell in with her the next day accidentally), but we now know that he saw some ships sailing to the windward and he thought they were Spanish ships trying to get the weather gauge of the English. He went to investigate and found they were neutral merchantmen (*The Fugger Newsletters*, 2, 168; *T.S.I.H.*, 2, 99–100).

The next engagement took place on the 23rd between Portland and the Isle of Wight. Drake played a leading part in this. The wind had been NNE, to the advantage of the Spaniards, but it suddenly shifted to SSW, Drake got to the windward of the Armada, flung himself at them, cut off Recalde and then joined Howard in attacking Sidonia. The Spanish fleet was soundly beaten, but the English gunpowder ran out and Howard had to break off the action.

Howard decided that the formation in which they had been fighting was too loose and uncontrolled. He reorganized his fleet into four squadrons: Frobisher was in command of the left, next to him was Hawkins, then Howard, with Drake in charge of the right. On the 25th Hawkins and Drake tried to drive the Spanish vanguard (*i.e.* the right rear ships) on to the Owers sandbanks and caused great havoc among them: unfortunately Howard and Frobisher were not so successful with the rearguard (*i.e.* the Spanish left rear ships) and the Armada was able to make its way on up the Channel. (The pace was very slow, not more than two miles an hour.) When the Armada reached Calais, Sidonia heard that Parma could not be ready for him for a week. He was compelled to anchor in the dangerous roadstead of Gravelines in bad weather. Lord Henry Seymour now left his watching of the Narrows and joined Howard. It was decided to dislodge the Armada by the use of fireships, and Drake was the first to offer some of his own ships for the purpose. Panic seized the Spanish, they cut their cables and fled in the utmost confusion. The English attacked at once, but the old-fashioned Howard broke out of the fleet in order to capture a galleass stranded on the French coast. Thus Drake led the attack, drew up to short range and poured his fire into Sidonia's ship, then turned NE to prevent the Armada from reforming, while Hawkins dealt with the rest of the ships. The defection of Howard was felt at this point, for alone Drake could not prevent some ships from reforming, but the bulk of the Armada was scattered to leeward along the French coast. A running fight ensued, but just at the moment when the English were about to destroy the Armada, a storm blew up from the W and the English had to break off the action. But the Armada was in fact defeated and when the wind shifted to the S the fleet had to crawl N, with its ships unworkable as a result of the last fighting and of the damage done in the confusion caused by the fireships. The English were now short of powder and short of food and therefore they turned for home, leaving the Armada to its fate on the Scottish and Irish coasts.

For once, Elizabeth was ready to follow up the victory with a view to preventing a second Armada. She wanted to intercept the Spanish treasure-fleet, as being the cheapest and most profitable method of warfare. Hawkins urged a permanent squadron cruising off the Azores. Drake argued for capturing Lisbon and putting Don Antonio, the claimant, on to the Portuguese throne. He was allowed to have his way, but his star was waning and he was never again to know the resounding successes which had been his up to the defeat of the Armada.

The Lisbon expedition of 1589 was a failure, but that was not the fault of Drake. From first to last his strategy and tactics were impeccable, but he was hindered by the fatal instructions given to him that the Spanish shipping in the northern ports was to be attacked first. Drake wanted to go straight for Lisbon, and he was right. The attack on Corunna only succeeded in warning Lisbon of what was coming to it. The soldiers were under the command of Sir John Norreys, and he never fully co-operated with Drake. The attack on Corunna wasted time and had no valuable results: the land battle at El Burgo was an arid victory: by the time the expedition reached Lisbon, which had been totally unprepared and must have fallen, if Drake had been allowed to go there first of all, it had put its defences in order and was ready for an attack. Drake realized this and strongly opposed Norreys's plan that the fleet should land the army at Peniche, that the army should then march 50 miles to Lisbon and raise the country in favour of Don Antonio, and Drake should take the fleet round by sea, enter the Tagus and be prepared to re-embark the army after it had taken Lisbon. Drake disliked being separated from the army; he argued rightly that, even if the wind were fair for the fleet to sail up the Tagus, it might change at any moment and leave the ships unable to get to sea again. And if the army by any chance came to grief, it might well need the help of the fleet before either of them reached Lisbon, or worse still after the fleet was in the Tagus and before the army was in Lisbon. Norreys insisted on his plan: Drake hung about Cascaes until he got news that Norreys was at Lisbon: he at once made plans for forcing the harbour and was on the point of entering when he got fresh news that Norreys was in retreat. Drake took the fleet to Cascaes and found the army there, in desperate straits. Norreys had lost so many men on the march to Lisbon that he had only 9,000 left, a third of whom were unfit for duty. The army's only artillery were the guns on the ships, and these he had left behind, therefore he could not breach the walls of Lisbon. He had no transport and he found no enthusiasm in Portugal for Don Antonio. Drake's judgment had been vindicated in every respect.

It was necessary for the expedition to pay for itself. Drake therefore set off for the Azores in hopes of capturing a treasure-ship. But a terrific storm broke up his fleet and he only just got back into Plymouth after a complete failure. He was court-martialled, but acquitted, but for the next five years he was in disgrace with the Queen. He retired to live at his Devon home of Buckland Abbey. Old age was settling down on all the great figures of the last thirty years, including in some respects the Queen herself. Spain was gradually rebuilding her energies, her morale and her ships, so that Philip was in a position twice again to threaten invasion: only bad weather destroyed his hopes. He and his commanders learned much about strengthening the defences of their overseas possessions. At last in 1595 Elizabeth agreed to an expedition to intercept the treasure-fleet and she gave the joint command of it to Drake and Hawkins. It was a fatal mistake—fatal to divide the command, fatal to share it between two men who were so wholly opposite in character and abilities, and fatal to organize the expedition so that in effect there were two fleets, one under Drake and one under Hawkins. They sailed from Plymouth in August 1595. Quarrels broke out at once. Drake had too many men for too few victuals and Hawkins declined to help him. When they reached the West Indies the plan was to try to capture Panama, strategically a sound plan. Unluckily the Spanish captured an English ship carrying written orders that Puerto Rico was to be the objective, because Drake had heard of a disabled treasure-ship in that harbour. The new and speedy methods of the Spanish soon carried the news to the governor. Hawkins now died and Drake was in sole command (1595). The attack on Puerto Rico failed and Drake made his way towards Nombre de Dios, which he easily captured. But the march to Panama ended in disaster and Drake never again 'carried mirth nor joy in his face'. He died at Porto Bello on January 28th, 1596, and was buried at sea.

Drake was a genius with all the merits and all the faults which go with genius. His intellect was brilliant and bold, his courage invincible, his patriotism deep and fiery. His Protestantism was genuine and even fanatical. He was an unrivalled sailor—only Nelson is comparable with him, and it is interesting to see how Nelson impressed himself first and foremost on his own countrymen, while Drake impressed himself on his enemies. He was a great commander-of men and he had all the attributes of a leader. He could be kind and generous, as he usually was, courteous to his enemies and yet ruthless in attaining his purpose. He was also overbearing and hasty, extremely difficult to work with, irritable and not above using the normal methods of his times—he employed torture in order to extract information from some prisoners, as any other commander would have done. His real greatness is to be seen in his original views on naval warfare. He was one of the greatest of all naval tacticians. He was the first to recognize that the ship was the fighting unit and not the soldiers on board: that manoeuvring and shooting were more important than boarding. He alone insisted on target practice, he alone recognized how much greater must be the supply of gunpowder to meet modern conditions of naval warfare. He was always for the offensive, never for the defensive, because he understood and preached that the destruction of the enemy's fleet was the first duty of the navy. And he was probably the first commander to understand and to put into practice the combined use of sea and land operations. (Corbett, *Drake and the Tudor Navy*, ii, pp. 133 *sqq.*) (*Plate 25*)

J. Corbett, *Drake and the Tudor Navy*, 1917. Needs some revision, but is indispensable.

J. A. Williamson, *The Age of Drake*, 2nd ed., 1946.

J. A. Williamson, *Sir Francis Drake*, Collins, 1951.

M. Lewis, *The Spanish Armada*, 1960.

G. Mattingley, *The Defeat of the Spanish Armada*, 1959.

FROBISHER, SIR MARTIN, navigator, was born in 1539 in the West Riding of Yorkshire, and he died in 1594, aged fifty-five. He was the son of Bernard Frobisher and his wife, a daughter of Sir John York, Master of the Mint and a well-known merchant adventurer in London. The family was in origin Welsh, but it had migrated from Chirk to Yorkshire in the middle of the fourteenth century. By the time Martin was born the family was one of the most important in the county. There are known to be over fifty variants in the spelling of the family name in the sixteenth century.

In 1542 Martin's father died and the boy was sent by his

mother to live with her father, Sir John York, who soon noticed that the boy was 'of great spirit and bold courage and natural hardiness of body'. Therefore Martin was sent to sea as a member of the 1553 expedition to the Guinea coast under the command of Thomas Wyndham. This voyage was disastrous in its loss of life—but Martin came home safely—yet it was triumphant in its financial profits. Therefore in 1554 John Lok led a second expedition to the Guinea coast and Martin went with it. One of the native chiefs demanded a hostage before he would trade: it would seem that, at his own request, Martin was left as the hostage in the Castle of 'Mayne' (Mina). He later fell into the hands of the Portuguese and was imprisoned, but after a while he was released and returned home. In 1559 Martin was on a voyage to the Barbary coast.

Between 1559 and 1576 (from twenty years of age up to thirty-seven) Frobisher was employed as a pirate, but he also had an interest in the coal trade. As a pirate he took many prizes, usually holding a commission from some Protestant Frenchman, such as the Prince de Condé, or from the Protestant William of Orange. He was arrested by the English government at least five times and was imprisoned for a short while, but he was never brought to trial on a criminal charge. Likely enough Elizabeth and the Council found him a useful, if unofficial, servant, and certainly Frobisher's name was both well known to and well hated by Philip II of Spain.

During this period three curious and not wholly explained episodes took place. In 1572 Frobisher was involved in a scheme planned by the Earl of Desmond to escape from London, where he was prisoner. It looks as if Frobisher agreed at first to help Desmond, but the plot was revealed, and it is not impossible that Frobisher gave it away to the government.

In 1573 Philip II approached certain Englishmen, among whom Frobisher was one, about a service which he believed they were ready to do for him—perhaps the capture of Flushing. The evidence is too incomplete to know what were Frobisher's intentions. On the whole, it is at least possible that he played with the idea of collaborating with Spain. There is no evidence that he did in fact do so.

In 1575 Frobisher may have been implicated in the nefar-
ious plans of Thomas Stuckley, that adventurer in Ireland.
It seems that Frobisher's wife got wind of this and intervened
. . . 'some jarre happened between Furbisher and her', but
we do not know the ultimate result. At this point Frobisher
seems to have abandoned piracy and turned to the search for
the North-West Passage. For more than fifteen years he had
been examining the possibilities, consulting with Portuguese
travellers and with English cosmographers such as Hakluyt,
Gilbert and Dee. Now, thanks mostly to the driving enthusiasm
and the financial backing given by Michael Lok, Frobisher
embarked on the first of the three voyages he was to make into
Arctic waters. He set sail on June 7th, 1576. His fleet consisted
of a newly built ship, the *Gabriel* (15 to 20 tons), under the
command of Christopher Hall: the *Michael* (20 to 25 tons),
commanded by Owen Griffyn: and a pinnace of 7 to 10 tons.
Frobisher was its admiral and pilot, the crew consisted of
35 men and boys. In 1558 a Venetian named Zeno had
published a map of the Arctic regions which was mostly either
inaccurate or frankly fictitious. Frobisher knew this map and
was thereby misled. Sailing up the North Sea, passing the
Shetlands and the Faroes, he sighted Cape Farewell, the southern
point of Greenland. This he took to be Friesland (or the Faroes)
as depicted on the Zeno map. He then lost company with the
Michael, which deserted him and returned to Bristol. Then
the pinnace was lost and Frobisher was left with only the
Gabriel and eighteen men. Hemmed in by 'monstrous great
ilands of ise which lay dryving all alongst the coast', enveloped
in thick fog, his ship all but in pieces, Frobisher showed what
a consummate seaman and man of courage he was, being
'determined rather to make a sacrifice onto God of his lyfe
than to return home without the discovery of Kathay. . . .'
After a time of extreme danger and hardship the ice was
'consumed and gone' and the *Gabriel* was able to sail on northwards. On August 11th the ship entered the 'strait', which
they named Frobisher's Strait, believing themselves to be in
the North-West Passage which would lead them to Cathay.
They thought the land on their right was Asia, that on their

left America. After exchanging gifts with the Eskimos and putting five of his men ashore, none of whom was ever seen again, Frobisher lifted an Eskimo and his boat out of the water and took him home to England. He arrived at Harwich on October 2nd, 1576. One of his men had brought with him a piece of black pyrites. The English goldsmiths denied that it contained any gold at all, but an Italian assayer insisted that there was gold in the stone. Thus was formed the Cathay Company with Michael Lok as its Governor. All the liabilities of the first voyage were transferred to the new Company, which expected to pay for the expenses of the first voyage out of the profits from gold from the second voyage.

The second voyage was on a bigger scale, the Queen lent a ship of 200 tons (the *Ayde*), supplies were for seven months and condemned criminals were to be taken and left in Friesland to make friends with the natives. The object of the expedition was not to find the North-West Passage, but to bring home as much of the pyrite as possible. Our knowledge of this voyage is drawn from two vivid accounts written by George Best, Frobisher's lieutenant on the *Ayde* or *Aid*, and by Dionyse Settle, a gentleman who accompanied Frobisher. The fleet sailed on May 27th, 1577, and it returned to England at Milford Haven on September 23rd, bringing with it some 200 tons of worthless pyrite and a native man, woman and child, all three of whom died within a month of reaching England. There was so much wrangling over the value of the ore that a third expedition was planned to bring back 2,000 tons of the pyrite and to establish a colony of 120 in the Arctic regions.

This third expedition consisted of fifteen ships. They left England on May 31st, 1578, and returned in October. The most notable event was that Frobisher entered what now is known as Hudson Strait, but which he called 'Mistaken Strait', because it proved not to be the one he was looking for. Historically the most interesting result of the voyage was that a box of nails was discovered, which has now been accepted as proving that there was a European trade with Greenland prior to the Frobisher voyages. There is every reason for believing that

Michael Lok was pretty well ruined by his investments in these voyages. Frobisher also lost *pari passu*. But he lost no time in recovering his losses.

In 1578 he took part in the expedition under Sir William Winter which was sent to put down the rebellion of Fitzmaurice and Desmond in Ireland. When this work was completed, Frobisher seems to have returned to his old game of piracy, if we are to judge by the frequent complaints which poured in from the Netherlands to the Council. That he was by 1582 again in funds may be seen from his subscribing £300 towards an expedition to the East Indies and Cathay. Frobisher was to have commanded it in conjunction with Fenton, but the two never got on well together and Frobisher withdrew— fortunately, as the voyage under Fenton was a failure. In 1585 Frobisher went as Vice-Admiral under Drake on the 1585 expedition to the Spanish West Indies, which brought home spoils worth £60,000. Frobisher was then in 1587 put in command of the Channel Fleet to guard the Channel against the Spanish invasion. He spent his time 'capturing everything which savoured of the Spaniard'. When the Armada did come in 1588, Frobisher was in command of the *Triumph* and fought under Howard in the battle up the Channel, in which he distinguished himself perhaps more signally than any other commander. When the fleet was reorganized into four squadrons, Frobisher was in command of one of them and for his splendid work he was knighted by Howard.

After the defeat of the Armada Frobisher was an outspoken supporter of Hawkins's theory that Spain ought to be ruined by England's cutting off her treasure from the Indies. Between 1589 and 1592 he went on three expeditions to the Azores and captured many valuable prizes, especially in 1592 the *Madre de Dios*, which was worth £150,000. Two years later, in 1594, he went in command of a small squadron which the Queen sent to help the French Huguenots, but he was killed at the storming of the fort at Crozon, near Brest.

Frobisher was a rough diamond in some ways, but his reputation as an impossibly bad-tempered and impetuous man probably derives from the abuse which Michael Lok poured out on him. He was as brave as a lion, a consummate seaman, much loved by his men and always very popular with the Queen. He was immensely strong physically and was noted for his feats of strength, and it should be remembered in his favour that he wanted to treat the natives in the Arctic regions with kindness. *(Plate 27)*

V. Stefansson, *The Three Voyages of Martin Frobisher*, 1938.
W. McFee, *Sir Martin Frobisher*, 1928.

GRENVILLE, SIR RICHARD, naval commander, was born on June 15th, 1542, and he died probably on September 12th, 1591, at the age of 49. He was the son of Roger Grenville and his wife, Thomasine Cole of Slade in Devon. His father died on Sunday, July 19th, 1545, when his ship *Mary Rose*, the second largest of Henry VIII's ships, capsized. His mother married again, Thomas Arundell of Clifton, and it is probable that Richard spent most of his early days at Clifton, that house to which Theodore Palaeologus, last descendant of the Byzantine emperors, retired, who lies buried in the church at Landulph.

At the age of seventeen (1559) Richard entered the Inner Temple to acquire a sound, general training with enough law to enable him to run his family estates. In 1562 he was involved in an affray in the Strand between Sir Edward Unton, Fulke Greville, Robert Bannester and their servants, and Richard Grenville, Nicholas Specott and their servants. Grenville ran Bannester through with his sword, left him dead in the street and fled. He was later pardoned, on what grounds is not known. In that same year he seems to have been returned as M.P. for Dunheved (Launceston), although he was still a minor, but it is possible that this may have been a different Richard Grenville. Not later than 1565 he married Mary, the daughter of Sir John St. Leger. He had two boys, Bernard and John, the former of whom was father of that Sir Bevil Grenville, who became famous during the Civil Wars in which he supported Charles I.

In 1566 Grenville went abroad to fight in the wars in Hungary against the Turks. He was home in 1568 and the next year he went to Ireland with Sir Warham St. Leger to arrange for the lands which had been mortgaged to St. Leger by the Earl of Desmond. Grenville's intention was to settle the lands in Munster as one form of investment, but the outbreak of the Fitzmaurice rebellion ruined his plans and his lands, so that he had to give up the proposition, though he was to return to it twenty years later.

Dr. A. L. Rowse has emphasized that Grenville came from an old established family, was an aristocrat and well aware of it, whereas the Drakes and Hawkins were new men. This may explain the curious episode in 1572, when information was laid against Grenville 'as a gentleman who belonged to the Earl of Arundel'. This was the year in which Cecil had defeated his opponents, that aristocratic faction, led by the Earl of Arundel and the Duke of Norfolk, which resented the new man's political monopoly of power. Norfolk had been executed and the accusation brought against Grenville was that he had said he 'feared the said Earl would prove himself a coward, for if he had not been one never a Cecil in England could have chopped off the Duke's head'. It is surprising to find 'this alignment of the forward-looking, undeviatingly Protestant Grenville with the conservative and Catholic earl' (Rowse, *Sir Richard Grenville's Place in English History*, p. 82).

Grenville was M.P. for Cornwall in the 1571 parliament: he was returned to the 1572 parliament as member for Launceston, and he did a certain amount of work in committees. But at this time he was mainly taken up with preparations for his South-Sea project. His plan was to sail through the Straits of Magellan into the South Sea, take possession of Terra Australis and find the western outlet of the imagined Straits of Anian, which would provide the most direct North-West Passage for England to Cathay. This was the first English attempt to break the Spanish monopoly of the Pacific by way of the Straits of Magellan, rather than by way of Baccalaos (Labrador), the route approved by Humphrey Gilbert. Grenville obtained his Letters Patent from the Queen in 1574 and by June he had leave to sail. But at that moment the government began a policy of appeasement towards Spain and as a result Grenville was forbidden to go on his expedition

(Rowse, *ibid.*, pp. 86–7). Three years later (1577) Drake set out on his voyage of circumnavigation, which was in reality a continuation of Grenville's plans.

Forbidden to sail the seas, Grenville turned his attention to local affairs and family interests. As Sheriff of Cornwall (1576–7) he was engaged in putting into practice in Cornwall the government's anti-Catholic policy. He arrested Father Mayne at the home of the Tregian family and he put a stop to the activities of other Cornish Catholic families—for which work he was knighted in 1577. It was at this time also that he went in for large building changes in the family home at Buckland Abbey near Plymouth.

In 1585 Grenville sailed from Plymouth in command of Ralegh's first expedition to plant a colony in North America. He landed a hundred men on the coast of what is now North Carolina, left Ralph Lane in charge and returned home, on the way capturing a Spanish ship, the *Santa Maria*, with a cargo of gold, silver, pearls, ginger and sugar, the sale of which more than paid for the expedition. Grenville's conduct on the voyage to Roanoke, where the colony was planted, was violently attacked by Lane, who accused him of 'intolerable pride and unsatiable ambition'. In truth, it was Grenville's firm leadership which enabled the colony to be planted at all.

The next year (1586) Grenville took three ships to Roanoke with supplies for the colonists. Meantime Drake, on his way home from plundering the Spanish Main, had arrived at Roanoke. Finding the colonists short of food and discontented with their lot, he gave them a passage home. When Grenville arrived there in July, the colonists were gone. He left fifteen men to hold the fort and set out home again. There was sickness among his crews, many died and he called at Newfoundland in order to rest and feed his men. Then he made for the Azores in order to capture some prizes to pay for the expedition, in which he was not so successful as in 1585.

The struggle between England and Spain was nearing the crisis. All 1587 Grenville was engaged in strengthening the defences of the west country, but he was also busy planning and building a third expedition to Roanoke. News that the

Spanish Armada was about to sail put an end to his hopes and plans; he was ordered to send his ships to join Drake's squadron off Plymouth. For a moment there was a chance that Grenville might have gone in command of an expedition 'to singe the King of Spain's beard', but it was doubtful whether Grenville and Drake could get on well enough together. At the moment when the Armada arrived, we have no information of what Grenville was doing. Apparently he did not serve at sea against the Armada, probably he was in command of the land forces in Cornwall.

When the danger was passed, Ralegh and Grenville were commissioned to keep watch at sea on the approaches to Ireland, in case the Spanish fleet returned. When the need for this precaution disappeared, Ralegh and Grenville turned their attention to Ireland. Grenville bought land in Munster, took over to Ireland some settlers from western England and set seriously to work to make a plantation in Munster to provide an estate for his younger son. He spent two years there and then was suddenly summoned to England by the government, whose plan was now to maintain a squadron at the Azores to waylay the Spanish treasure fleet. After his failure in the Lisbon expedition of 1589 Drake was in eclipse. Grenville was to be Vice-Admiral of the fleet under Lord Thomas Howard (1591). It is not possible here to retell the story of Grenville's last fight in the *Revenge*: that has been done superbly by Sir Walter Ralegh. It must suffice to record that the English fleet was caught unawares at Flores by the main Spanish fleet under Don Alonso de Bazan. After the strategic retreat (fully justifiable) by Lord Thomas with his five ships, Grenville, who had ninety-five men sick ashore, was left alone to face the fifty-three Spanish ships. Even if one allows that he ought to have tried to get away, it is extremely doubtful whether he could have done so. At any rate, it was not within the make-up of Grenville to fly, 'out of the greatness of his mind he could not be persuaded' (Ralegh). Between 3.0 p.m. on the 9th September to the morning of the 10th, *Revenge* beat off the attacks of and so much damaged fifteen Spanish galleons that they were 'far more willing to hearken to a composition than hastily to make any more assaults'. There could be only one end and it came. Surrender by the crew, not by Grenville (he wanted to blow up the ship): the death of Grenville, and then, a little later, a gigantic cyclone in which some sixteen ships of Bazan were destroyed, and down went also *Revenge*. The inhabitants of the Azores were fully convinced that as Grenville was a devil, all the devils rose from the bottom of the sea to avenge his death.

Grenville may well stand as the personification of the robuster side of Elizabethan England. Less intellectual than Ralegh, he was as tough as, but less rough than Frobisher: as competent as Hawkins, he was more boisterous: as brave as Drake, he was even more explosive. Unscrupulous in pursuit of his own interests, he was a loyal and honest servant of the Queen, but high-handed in carrying out his duties, as he showed in his method of arresting Mayne. The stories which have grown up round all these famous men reveal their character to us—Drake finishing his game of bowls on Plymouth Hoe, Ralegh spreading his cloak in a plashy place; Essex at Cadiz flinging his hat upon the waves; Grenville at dinner biting his glass and crunching the splinters in his mouth till the blood ran out. That last legend is the most revealing of them all. It is not the veracity of the story which signifies, it is that men should find it easy to believe such things of such heroes.   (*Plate 26*)

A. L. Rowse, *Sir Richard Grenville of the Revenge*, 1937. A piece of historical writing unlikely to be superseded.

A. L. Rowse: *Sir Richard Grenville's Place in English History*. The Ralegh Lecture, British Academy, 1957. Volume XLIII, Proceedings of the British Academy.

Sir Walter Ralegh, *A Report of the Truth of the Fight about the Isles of Açores*. Arber's *English Reprints*, 1871.

HOWARD, CHARLES, BARON HOWARD OF EFFINGHAM, EARL OF NOTTINGHAM, Lord Admiral of England,

commander of the English fleet against the Armada, was born in 1536 and died in 1624, aged 88. He was the son of William Howard, first Baron Howard of Effingham, who was the eldest son of Thomas Howard, second Duke of Norfolk. Charles

Plate 27

Sir Martin Frobisher

Plate 28

Sir Humphrey Gilbert,
Admiral

Sir James Lancaster

probably served at sea with his father (1544–6) and again (1554–7), and therefore he was not destitute of naval experience when later he became Lord Admiral. He became very popular at Court, where he resided for twelve years, a favourite of the Queen, whose cousin he was through Anne Boleyn. He saw military service under the Earl of Warwick, when he played a minor part in putting down the rising in the north in 1569. The next year he was given command of the naval squadron which escorted the young queen of Spain down the Channel, when she moved from Flanders to Spain. In 1573 his father died and he became Baron Howard of Effingham. In 1574 he was made a Knight of the Garter.

The turning-point in his career came in 1585 when he was made Lord Admiral. He was now 50 years old. The office combined in his one person responsibilities which to-day are divided between a Cabinet Minister, First Lord of the Admiralty, First Sea Lord and Chief of the Naval Staff, Second, Third and Fourth Sea Lords, Commander-in-Chief of the whole fleet always, and of the main fleet in wartime. (Lewis, *The Spanish Armada*, p. 35, 1960.) His appointment might be called quasi-hereditary, for his father, two uncles and a great-grandfather had held the office before him.

In 1586 he was one of the commission set up to try Mary, Queen of Scots. He was not, in fact, present at the trial, but William Davison, the Queen's secretary, declared that it was Howard who urged the Queen to sign the death warrant.

In 1587 he was appointed 'lieutenant-general, commander-in-chief and governor of the whole fleet and army at sea fitted against the Spaniards and their allies'. Later generations have wondered why Drake was not put in command. Howard's appointment caused no surprise to his contemporaries. Drake was a finer seaman, but to have elevated Drake to the top would have aroused jealousies among the other seamen. In the sixteenth century rank was of the highest importance and men of rank expected to command: men of lesser degree expected to serve under them. To have put 'gentlemen' to serve under Drake might well have led to a refusal to obey his orders. There was no need to run this risk. In Howard of Effingham

EE—(2)

the Queen could call on a man of the highest birth, of long experience, of unfailing commonsense, and one who recognized his limitations and was ready to take advice from others, but who never shovelled off the final responsibility. He and Drake worked together in perfect amity and with complete success.

Howard took command in the *Ark* (800 tons), a ship originally built by Ralegh and known variously as *Ark*, *Ark Ralegh*, *Ark Royal*. He joined Drake at Plymouth on May 23rd, leaving the defence of the Downs to Sir Edward Seymour. At Plymouth Howard set up a Council of War which he regularly consulted all through the campaign. He then tackled three urgent problems. First, he backed up Drake's incessant plea to the Government that the right strategy was for the English fleet to search out and destroy the Armada before ever it entered English waters. The Queen shilly-shallied and it was not until July 7th that the fleet was allowed to set sail for Corunna. On the 9th the wind changed and the fleet was forced to return to Plymouth, for Howard dared not run the risk of being by-passed by the Armada.

There was a second reason for turning back, which was the second problem facing Howard—there were not enough victuals. He had already written to Burghley pointing out the dangers which would arise, if the victuals ran short at the time of service. 'We shall now be victualled, beginning the 20th of this April unto the 18th of May, and the advertisement that giveth the largest time for the coming of the Spanish forces is the midst of May, being the 15th. Then have we three days' victual. If it be fit to be so, it passeth my reason'. This is the letter of a man who knows his business and is not afraid to pursue it.

The Queen's reluctance to allow the fleet to search out the enemy aroused in Howard's mind the fear that there was treachery about and that the Queen was being hoodwinked. On June 23rd he wrote to Walsingham, 'Let her Majesty trust no more to Judas kisses; for let her assure herself there is no trust to French King nor Duke of Parma'. And that same day he wrote to the Queen herself, 'For the love of Jesus Christ, Madam, awake thoroughly and see the villainous treasons round about you . . . and draw your forces round about you, like a mighty prince, to defend you. Truly, Madam, if you do so, there is no cause to fear. If you do not, there will be danger'. This is not the letter of a mere courtier and favourite.

Howard was a courageous man, but he was also a prudent one, and his conduct of the earlier stages of the fights against the Armada was sound and sensible. Ralegh wrote in his *History of the World* (book 5, ch. 1, sect. 6) that Howard was 'better advised than a great many malignant fools were that found fault with his demeanour'. Of course, he made mistakes, and one mistake in particular has rightly earned him much condemnation. On the night of Sunday, July 28th the English launched eight fire-ships against the Armada. Panic ensued and the formation of the Spanish fleet was broken. At dawn on the 29th Howard saw the Spanish *capitana*, *San Lorenzo*, stranded on the shore of Calais. At once he led his whole squadron to capture the prize. At the very moment when Drake, Hawkins and Frobisher were seizing the first oppor- tunity of attacking the now demoralized Armada, the Lord Admiral and all his ships were out of the fight. The truth is that Howard was to a large extent a mediaevally-minded man. War was still to him something of a stately ceremony. He had not grasped what Drake and his companions understood, that war was now an entirely new thing: the enemy must be annihilated by a concerted attack. Howard was content to 'pluck their feathers by little and little'. The *San Lorenzo* was a splendid feather.

Even before the fleet returned home to England disease had begun to ravage the crews. Their conditions grew worse as soon as demobilization began. One of the noblest traits in Howard's character was his unfailing interest in his men and his unremitting attempts to alleviate their distress—notably in his protests against the callous treatment by the Government, which even refused to supply Howard with pay for the men. (Stone, The Armada Campaign of 1588, *History*, N.S. XXIX, 110, Sept. 1944.) It was typical of Howard, Hawkins and Drake that in 1590 they cooperated in establishing the naval charity, 'The Chest at Chatham', which was later incorporated in the Greenwich Hospital. The actual chest is preserved in the Royal Naval College at Greenwich.

Howard continued as Lord Admiral, but he only took active part in one of the post-Armada expeditions—that of 1596, when he was joint commander with the Earl of Essex in the expedition against Cadiz. The Spanish fleet was totally defeated, but Essex landed in too great haste, which allowed many of the ships to escape. It was Howard who decided that the English fleet must return home and not carry the war to the other ports along the coast. This decision infuriated Essex, and the quarrel was exacerbated in 1597 when Howard was made Earl of Nottingham and in virtue of his office as Lord Admiral now took precedence over Essex.

As long as Elizabeth survived Howard retained her confidence and affection; it was to Howard that on her deathbed she nominated James VI as her successor. The new King treated Howard with as much respect and confidence as had the old Queen. There was no commission on which he did not sit: in 1605 he went to Spain to negotiate the treaty of peace; in 1613 he commanded the squadron which escorted the Princess Elizabeth to Flushing for her marriage to the Elector Palatine.

The office of Lord Admiral was for life and Howard clung to it far too long. He held it for thirty-four years, and thirty-one of them after 1588. Corruption set in among the offices for which Howard was responsible, and he did nothing to cure the evil. In 1619 at long last he was bought out by the Duke of Buckingham and retired with a pension of £1,000 a year. He died on December 13th, 1624, at the age of eighty-eight.

There is no evidence at all that Howard was ever a 'papist', a good deal of evidence that he was a staunch 'protestant'. (Laughton, *From Howard to Nelson*, pp. 38 *sqq.*)   (*Plate 26*)

M. Lewis, *The Spanish Armada*, pp. 33–7, 158–60, 1960.
J. K. Laughton, *From Howard to Nelson*, pp. 1–40, 1899.
J. Corbett, *The Successors of Drake*, 1900.

FENTON, EDWARD, soldier and sailor, came of a Nottinghamshire family. The date of his birth is unknown: he died in 1603. The first record of him shows that he sacrificed his patrimony to a preference for a military career. He held a command in Ireland under Sir Henry Sidney in the suppressing of Shane O'Neill's rebellion in 1566. In 1577 he was in command of the *Gabriel* in Frobisher's second voyage in search of the North-west passage and of Cathay: he seems to have performed a very small part in this expedition. In May 1578 he sailed as Lieutenant-General and second in command (in the *Judith*) of Frobisher's third voyage to Meta Incognita. He was home again by October. The next year he was again employed in Ireland. By far the most important event in his life was when he was made commander of the Earl of Leicester's expedition in 1582–3, which was intended to develop trade by way of the Cape of Good Hope, the Moluccas and China, and so home.

The voyage was a signal failure, partly and inevitably because it started too late in the year, partly owing to the most unusual weather experienced in the Channel, very largely because Fenton was entirely the wrong man to command such an expedition. By profession he was a soldier, but other soldiers have proved good commanders at sea: even so, the appointment bred great jealousy among the section of the crew which had lately been serving with Drake. The commission under which he sailed gave him powers which went to his head; he behaved frequently in the most high-handed way. He himself had planned first to make himself king of St. Helena, and from there to raid the Portuguese carracks. This ran counter to the ideas of the group of merchants who sailed with him; they only wanted peaceful trade. It is true that Fenton was circumscribed by a Council whose majority decisions were binding. But it is revealing that Fenton should have described an illness in his ship as 'only the scurvy' and that he should have quarrelled with everybody.

The expedition consisted of the *Leicester* (400 tons), the *Edward Bonaventure* (250 or 300), with two other small vessels of 50 and 40 tons. It left Southampton in May 1582, reached Sierra Leone in August, and then, there being no hope of reaching the Cape so late in the year, made its way towards Brazil. Fenton himself intended to go through the Magellan Straits, but he heard that these were now guarded by some Spanish ships. He therefore went to St. Vincent on the coast of Brazil, where the governor at first refused to deal with the English: later he allowed them to buy victuals and some sugar. A sudden attack by three Spanish warships resulted in a fierce fight in which one Spanish ship was sunk. Fenton was by now despairing of any financial success and decided to sail for home, which was reached in May 1583.

Our chief source of information for this voyage is the most interesting diary kept by one of the chaplains, Richard Madox, a very remarkable young man, well-read, familiar with the most up-to-date methods of navigation. He took with him an *Ephemerides*, that is, a book of astronomical tables, and 'a very perfect instrument', probably an astrolabe. He also seems to have known something about coastal survey. Madox was a man of intelligence and shrewdness, of perfect integrity, one who behaved courageously and sensibly in difficult circumstances.

In 1588 Fenton commanded the *Mary Rose* (600 tons) against the Spanish Armada. He died in 1603.

E. G. R. Taylor, *The Troublesome Voyage of Captain Edward Fenton 1582–1583*. The Hakluyt Society, 1959.

CLIFFORD, GEORGE, 3rd EARL OF CUMBERLAND,

naval commander, was born in 1558 and died in 1605, aged forty-seven. He was the eldest son of Henry, second Earl of Cumberland, whom he succeeded in the earldom in 1569/70. His mother was Lady Eleanor Brandon, daughter of Charles Brandon, Duke of Suffolk, and Mary Tudor, daughter of Henry VII, Dowager Queen of France, who had married Louis XII.

In 1571 Cumberland entered Trinity College, Cambridge. He remained there until 1574; he took his M.A. in 1576, having chiefly studied mathematics. His tutor was John Whitgift, later to be Archbishop of Canterbury. From Cambridge Cumberland moved to Oxford in order to study geography, a subject in which he was expert and 'took great delight'. In 1577 he married his cousin, Lady Margaret Russell.

Cumberland's naval life opened in 1586. Between that date

and 1598 he fitted out at his own expense twelve expeditions—1586, 1588, 1589, 1591, 1592, 1593, 1594, 1595, 1597, 1598—as well as commanding the *Elizabeth Bonaventure* (600 tons) against the Armada in 1588, he may have taken part in the Cadiz expedition of 1596. Of these expeditions the twelfth and last voyage was the most considerable, consisting of twenty ships. Cumberland took command of the *Malice Scourge*, led his fleet to Porto Rico and captured San Juan. The intention was to plant an English settlement there, but illness compelled him to abandon the attempt and the whole episode proved an expensive failure. Indeed, none of his voyages paid him a satisfactory dividend. At the start of his active life he was a very wealthy man, but when he died he was more than £1,000 in debt. Much of his money was wasted on mere gambling, dicing, betting and other forms of extravagant living, but his expeditions ruined him.

Cumberland was a man of action, his courage was invincible, his vitality enormous, and he was prepared to spend himself in order to share the burdens of storms, illness and shortage of food. He was a skilful and much beloved commander, and it would seem that he undertook his unsuccessful voyages principally in order to damage Spain and to benefit his own country. He was in high favour with the Queen, whose glove he wore in his hat, but he was an unfaithful husband and was separated from his wife for many years, although at the end he sought for and obtained her forgiveness. (*Plate 29*)

G. C. Williamson, *George, Third Earl of Cumberland*, 1920.

FENNER, GEORGE, naval commander, came of a Sussex family which had many connections with the sea. George was the most notable seaman of them all, but his cousin Thomas had almost as fine a record as George, and William was a worthy third in the trio. Thomas was with Drake in the Indies voyage of 1585 and took a leading part in the highly successful attack on Cartagena. He was present at Drake's attack on the Spanish Armada in Cadiz in 1587 and he played a distinguished part in the series of fights in the Channel against the Armada in 1588. William accompanied Drake and Norris in the Coruña expedition of 1589 and he died of his wounds on the voyage home.

Little is known of the early years of George's life, and even later, when he has become famous, there are many gaps in our knowledge of his life. He may have made a voyage to the Gold Coast, but nothing is known of it. He seems never to have accompanied Drake on any of his voyages. He comes into prominence first in 1566. John Hawkins was fitting out an expedition, but at the last moment the Queen refused to let him sail. In the last days of October 1566 George Fenner set sail from Plymouth with exactly the same number of ships as Hawkins had fitted out. Were there two voyages being prepared at the same moment, or did Fenner take over Hawkins's ships, men and stores? He was only allowed to sail after giving a bond that he would not injure the privileges of the King of Spain in the Indies. His first port of call was at Santiago in the Cape Verde Islands. During the night the Spanish attacked him and Fenner and his ships barely escaped by cutting their cables. A few days later, cruising alone in his *The Castle of Comfort* off the Azores while he was following a Spanish ship with the purpose, Fenner said, of 'borrowing a cable', he was set upon by three Portuguese ships, a galleon of 400 tons and two caravels. Fenner, by dint of splendid gunnery, beat off three separate attacks before night fell. At dawn the Portuguese were still in contact with him and had been reinforced by two more ships, making the odds five to one. Once again, by superb gunnery Fenner not only beat off the enemy, but he so badly mauled them that they withdrew and Fenner escaped, returning home to Plymouth.

For the next twelve years all that is known of Fenner's life is that he was a privateer who was continually complaining to the Privy Council against Spain or answering complaints from Spain and France. The Council seems to have ignored all the complaints impartially.

In 1587 George in the *Leicester* (400 tons, 160 men) with Thomas Fenner in the *Nonpareil* (500 tons, 250 men) patrolled the north coast of France on the look-out for the Spanish

Armada. When in 1588 the Armada came, George took a distinguished part in the fighting up the Channel and at Gravelines, and then up the North Sea to the Firth of Forth. In 1591 with Howard of Effingham he was in the *Leicester* once again, patrolling the coast of Brittany. In 1597 he and Howard were together again in the Islands Voyage led by Essex—a failure, but not through any fault of Fenner's. Later in the same year the two were watching out for the 'Invisible' Armada. Fenner was given false information with which he hurried back to Plymouth. He was sent off back to Brest: again he was given false news, again he took it to Plymouth, but his reputation was so high that he was not blamed. When at last real news came that five Spanish galleys had arrived, the government turned at once to George. 'Tarry not, good George, but do the best you can.' Howard was in the Channel, Fenner pursued westwards, but the galleys were two days ahead of him and he had no hope of catching them.

The article in the *D.N.B.* suggests that Fenner died perhaps in 1600. But there is one more record of him, for he became the first Brother or pensioner in Sutton's Hospital in the Charterhouse, where he died on October 26th, 1618.

George Fenner was 'one of the greatest English seamen even of the days of Elizabeth' (G. S. Davies). His fight against the Portuguese was the first example of the power of modern gunnery, to be followed later by Grenville in the *Revenge* at the Azores.

G. S. Davies, Master of the Charterhouse, *Cornhill Magazine*, 1920.

J. Corbett, *Drake and the Tudor Navy* (*passim*), 1900.

J. Corbett, *The Successors of Drake* (*passim*), 1917.

LANCASTER, SIR JAMES, mercantile captain, was born in 1554 or 1555 and died in 1618, aged approximately sixty-four. He was the son of James Lancaster of Basingstoke, husbandman. In 1571 he became an apprentice in the Skinners' Company, being 'prentice to Blasse from the feast of John the Baptist for ten years'. He was sworn a Freeman of the Company on

March 10th, 1579, on payment of 3s. 4d.* His early life was spent in Portugal.

When the Armada set sail, Lancaster commanded the *Edward Bonaventure* (250 tons) in the English fleet under Drake, but no details of his service seem to be known.

In 1591 he again commanded the *Edward Bonaventure* in the first English voyage to the East Indies. The general of the expedition was George Raymond in the *Penelope*. The fleet set sail on April 10th, much too late in the year, so that it did not arrive at Table Bay† until the end of July, the first visit of any English ships to that port. There was so much sickness on board that a month was spent here, but so many died that the *Merchant Royal* was sent home with 50 men and the rest of the crews were split between the other two ships. The story of the voyage is one of disaster on disaster. The *Penelope* was lost off Cape Corrientes (September 12th, 1591). On the 16th the *Edward Bonaventure's* mainmast was struck by lightning and four men were killed. She sailed on to Mozambique and the Comoro Islands, where she lost a third of her crew in a surprise attack by natives. At the end of November Lancaster reached Zanzibar and stayed there till mid-February 1592. His plan was to make for Cape Comorin and lie in wait for the shipping plying between Goa and the Portuguese eastern settlements. The ship lost her course, victuals ran short and Lancaster's attempts to make Sokotra, the Laccadives and the Nicobar Islands all failed. In June he reached Sumatra and then made for Penang in order to prey on Portuguese shipping. He lay there till the beginning of September, but his crew suffered much sickness and was reduced to 34 of which only 22 were fit for work. He succeeded in taking a Portuguese ship filled with pepper and another filled with rice, and then one from Goa with a varied cargo. He moved away to the Nicobar Islands to take in supplies and then to Ceylon, but his men now insisted

* I owe this information to the kindness of the Worshipful Master of the Skinners' Company, and to the help given me by the Clerk to the Company in searching the Court Books of the Company.

† The name Table Bay was not used until 1681: the name up till then was Saldanha Bay.

on going home. Lancaster was 'very sick, more like to die than to live', and in no condition to enforce his own wishes. In April 1593 they reached St. Helena, where provisions and nineteen days' rest restored the crew, but as their morale rose their discipline fell, they got out of hand and made for England. Foul winds delayed their passage, provisions again ran short and in desperation Lancaster made for Trinidad. No supplies were available here, but in June he reached Mona and was provisioned by some French ships. He then set sail for Newfoundland to make contact with the fishing fleets, but the wind drove him back to the West Indies and he was again at Mona in November. Lancaster and his second in command, Barker, landed in order to get supplies, leaving six sailors on board. These men cut the cable and sailed off to San Domingo where they surrendered the ship to the Spaniards.

For a month Lancaster and his party of eighteen were marooned with only vegetables to eat. Then twelve were taken off by two French ships, and Lancaster was one of them. They remained off San Domingo until April 1594, then Lancaster and Barker got a passage home in another French ship commanded by Jean Lenoir which reached Dieppe on May 19th. On the 24th Lancaster reached Rye in Sussex after having been away for three years. It is usually said that the voyage was financially a great success. There is not the slightest evidence that this was so (Foster, *Eng: Quest of E. Trade*, p. 134). What Lancaster had succeeded in doing was to penetrate into the Indian Ocean as far as the Malay peninsula without any opposition from the Portuguese. Out of the 198 men who set sail only twenty-five returned to England.

Within five months Lancaster was at sea again with three ships financed by London merchants. Lancaster commanded the *Consent* (240 tons), Barker commanded the *Solomon* (170 tons), and a third ship went with them, the *Virgin* (60 tons). The objectives of the expedition were to raid the Portuguese possessions in Brazil (Pernambuco) and to capture Spanish and Portuguese shipping throughout the voyage. This expedition was a great success and paid a high dividend. Pernambuco was reached on April 18th, 1595, and the town was taken and held until all the merchandise in the warehouses had been transferred to Lancaster's ships. The booty was far too great for his ships to accommodate all of it. At that moment by good chance Jean Lenoir turned up and joined his ships to Lancaster's. An arrangement was made with some Dutch ships to carry the rest of the spoils home and Lancaster was just about to sail when he heard that the Portuguese were building a redoubt at the mouth of the harbour. Lancaster was for ignoring it, but his companions thought it necessary to capture it. Lancaster was too ill to lead the attack himself, which he entrusted to Cotton, Barker and Lenoir with some three hundred men. He gave them strict orders never to go beyond the range of the English guns. The redoubt was easily taken, then the force began to chase the enemy and soon found itself faced with a superior force far out of range of the English ships. Cotton, Barker and Lenoir were killed and some thirty-five men. Lancaster set sail at once and reached England in July 1595 after a most profitable expedition.

For four years nothing is heard of Lancaster except that in 1598 he was one of the managers of Cumberland's twelfth expedition. Then in 1601 Lancaster was selected to lead the first expedition sent out by the new East India Company.

It is not possible here to give a detailed account of this long and dangerous voyage. It was an aggressive expedition planned with the object of spoiling the Portuguese, and it was much helped by the friendly co-operation of the Dutch, who hated the Portuguese quite as much as did the English (*Mariner's Mirror*, xviii, 4, October, 1932). Five ships were employed: Lancaster was 'General of the Voyage' and commanded the *Red Dragon* (this was Cumberland's old *Malice Scourge*, 600 tons). His crew numbered 202 men and the guns forty. In all 480 men set sail, of whom more than 180 died before the ships started back for England and at least half of the 480 never returned home.

The fleet sailed from Tor Bay on April 20th, 1601. By September it had reached Saldanha Bay, but all the crews were suffering from scurvy, 'the plague of the sea and the spoil of mariners' (Sir Richard Hawkins). Lancaster's crew was in much better shape than the others because he had taken bottled lime juice with him as an experiment—the first sailor to do this. By October 29th 107 men had died. By Christmas Day eighteen more were lost. Discontent grew among the men and five men stole a boat and tried to desert, but they were caught. The fleet reached Sumatra in June 1602 and here Lancaster had a most satisfactory interview with the nonagenarian King of Achin, Alauddin, who was delighted with the presents given to him and with the letters which Queen Elizabeth had sent him. Commercial privileges were easily granted to the East India Company, but very little pepper was to be had. However, on October 3rd a rich carrack was captured and the cargo was transferred to Lancaster's ships; the carrack was then returned to the Portuguese, who much appreciated this 'courtesy'.

Lancaster then sailed for Priaman, where he found the *Susan* ready to return to England with a large cargo of pepper and cloves. Sending her home independently, Lancaster moved on to Bantam, a thousand miles from Achin. The king here was a boy of nine years old, trading privileges were granted, in five weeks the ships were laden with a huge cargo, and the first 'factory' of the E.I.C. was settled at Bantam.

The return journey was made with the utmost difficulty: bad storms, contrary winds, leaky ships, rudders lost and the ever-present fear of mutiny justified Lancaster's description of the voyage on his return to England in September 1603, when he gave thanks that he had been 'delivered from infinite perils and dangers in this long and tedious navigation'.

Lancaster was knighted in 1603 and gave his time and attention to organizing the affairs of the E.I.C. He was also interested in the search for the North-west Passage, and Baffin gave the name of Lancaster to one of the sounds in the north-west (1616). Lancaster died on June 6th, 1618, a wealthy man. He left most of his money to charities (he was never married and therefore had no claimants), some of which are administered today by the Skinners' Company. (*Plate 28*)

Sir William Foster, *The Voyages of Sir James Lancaster*, Hakluyt Society, 2nd ser., lxxxv, 1940.
The Mariner's Mirror, xviii, 4, October, 1932.

NEWBERY, JOHN, traveller. Virtually nothing is known of the early life of this very interesting, intrepid and important man. There is a slight possibility that he was related to Ralph Newbery who published Hakluyt's *Principal Navigations*: he may also have been in his early years in Holland and have learned Dutch. (Foster, *England's Quest of Eastern Trade*, pp. 79 and 94.) He first appears in history in 1579 as a 'citizen and merchant of London', 'desirous to see the world'. He made three remarkable journeys which give him the right to a place in any dictionary of biographies: his only failure is not to have found a place in *D.N.B.*

The first voyage, 1579. Newbery left London in March and travelled overland to Marseilles. Thence he sailed to Tripoli in Syria, from there he took ship to Jaffa and then went on to Jerusalem where he visited 'the monuments of those countries'. The return journey to England was made via Jaffa, Tripoli, Marseilles, Paris to London. Newbery had been away for eight months.

The second voyage, 1580. Newbery left England on September 19th in an English ship bound for Tripoli. He arrived there in January, 1581, and went northwards to Aleppo. Here he dressed himself as a Mohammedan trader, provided himself with a Greek servant and on March 19th set out for the Portuguese port of Hormuz at the southern end of the Persian Gulf. The next day he was at Bir, where he took a boat down the Euphrates to Fallujah and thence by land to Baghdad (April 15th, 1581). After staying there for nine days he went by boat down the Tigris to Basra, (May). Here he changed boats and went down the Persian Gulf to the island of Kishm. On the way the party was all but taken and made into slaves. From Kishm Newbery crossed over to Hormuz, (June 22nd). At Hormuz he took a house and stayed there for six weeks. The Portuguese at that time had no objections to the English visitor, but the Venetian merchants were very jealous of him. One of them, Michael Stropene, seduced Newbery's Greek servant 'to understand my secret purposes'.

On August 1st, 1581, Newbery left Hormuz and made up his mind to go home by land through Persia. He knew a little

Arabic, but he had no European companion, only a servant, this time a Persian Jew. On this journey he carried with him a small stock of cloves as merchandise. On September 6th he reached Shiraz, where he spent sixteen days, and Isfahan on October 4th, where he stayed three days. He then travelled north to Kashen (October 12th) and he spent more than three weeks in this important trading centre. His next move was north-west to Tabriz, where he arrived on November 23rd. He left Tabriz on December 1st, 1581, for Julfa, arriving eventually at Erzerum on December 21st. Here he spent Christmas and arrived at Erzingan on January 3rd, 1582, and Constantinople on March 9th.

Most people would have taken ship for Venice and then have travelled to England overland, but that was too easy for Newbery. He decided to go straight across Europe northwards to Dantzig on the Baltic Sea and then home by ship along the northern European coast. On April 4th, 1582, he sailed into the Black Sea, where he encountered a violent storm. He reached Reni at the mouth of the river Pruth on April 25th, where he was fascinated by the methods of making caviare. On May 1st he left for Jassy, then on to Kaminietz on the Russo-Polish frontier. We know next to nothing about his journey from there to Dantzig, but we do know that he picked up a boat at Dantzig and reached London on August 31st, 1582. His journey had taken all but two years. By the end of it he was the first Englishman to have travelled down the valley of the Euphrates: probably the first, certainly the second, if not the first, to set eyes on the famous depot of Hormuz: the first to cross southern Persia and to visit Shiraz and Isfahan: the first to reach Constantinople from Persia *via* Asia Minor: the first to sail on the Black Sea and to travel through the Danubian countries to Poland and the Baltic.

The third voyage, 1583. In the autumn of 1582 a plan was formed by the New Turkey Company (later the Levant Company) for reaching Cathay by way of Hormuz and India. Newbery was selected to lead the party and to carry letters from the Queen to the Great Mogul and to the Emperor of China. No one was better fitted for the post, for Newbery could speak

Arabic, he was already on good terms with the governor of Hormuz, and his courage and business ability had been fully proved. The Hakluyts were involved in the plan and Newbery had been in correspondence with the younger Hakluyt, for he had written to him from Aleppo as 'Right wellbeloved and my assured good friend'. Hakluyt had given him a note from the writings of a Portuguese pilot, Fernando Fernandez, and a letter from Thomas Stevens to his father, containing valuable information about sailing by the Portuguese route round the Cape. Stevens was a Jesuit, which proved valuable later, for otherwise 'we might have rotted in prison' (Taylor, *Tudor Geography*, 1485–1583, p. 136). Newbery was also to find a second copy of *The Geography of Abulfeda*. He failed to find one in Syria, but he wrote hoping for success in Baghdad or Persia. Hakluyt did get a copy, probably not from Newbery.

Newbery was to lead a party of six to Baghdad: there, two were to stay with part of the stock-in-trade: the four were to go on to Basra, and there two were to stay to trade: Newbery and Ralph Fitch were then to take £300 or £400 worth of stock and 'so to go for the Indies'. There also accompanied the party a gem-polisher named William Leeds, and a painter of the name of James Story, who went at his own expense for the fun of it.

The party sailed from London in the *Tiger* on February 13th, 1583—('Her husband's to Aleppo gone, master of the *Tiger*', Macbeth, 1. iii), but a storm drove the ship into Falmouth, and it was March 11th before they got away again. They arrived at Tripoli in Syria at the end of April, stayed there for a fortnight and then went on to Aleppo. At the end of May they set out for Baghdad, travelling to Bir on camels, by boat down the Euphrates to Felujah, then on camels by night because of the heat to Baghdad, where two of the party remained. The rest reached Basra on August 6th, where two more remained with some of the stock: Newbery and Fitch set off with £400 in goods and money, accompanied by Leeds and Story.

In mid-August they embarked at Basra for Hormuz where they arrived on the 5th of September. Unluckily, there was a new Governor who knew not Newbery, and he had the party

Plate 29

The Earl of Cumberland

Sir Philip Sidney

Plate 30

William Shakespeare

arrested and thrown into prison. This was the work of Michael Stropene, who denounced them as spies, and the Governor sent the four travellers off to Goa to be dealt with by the Viceroy (November 29th, 1583). Here they were interrogated to see whether they were heretics, but nothing was proved against them, and they were released on bail. It was here that Thomas Stevens came to the rescue by helping to find the surety. Story had been taken up by the Jesuits, who persuaded him to paint their church and to join their order as a probationer, and he was free as air: Newbery, Fitch and Leeds were freed on condition they did not leave Portuguese territory. They now hired a house and began to trade and felt pretty confident that all was now well. After a few months they asked that their bail should be cancelled and the money returned to them. To their surprise the Viceroy threatened them that they 'should be better sifted before it were long and that they had further matter against' them. The three of them, therefore, turned their money into jewels, left their shop open with all the goods displayed for sale and slipped away (April 1584).

Newbery led his companions into south India to Bijapur, the capital of the kingdom of that name. They moved on to Golconda, famous for its diamond mines, in order to investigate the possibilities of trading in precious metals and stones, since Leeds was an expert in these things. We know nothing of what transpired there: the next matter of interest is that they came to Agra to the court of the great Emperor Akbar, but finding he was away at Fatehpur Sikri, they travelled the twenty miles and obtained an interview with Akbar and presented Queen Elizabeth's letter. We have to deduce a personal meeting from Fitch's account of the Emperor's dress and court, but he does not specifically state that they met the Mogul in person.

In September 1584 the trio separated: Leeds remained as an expert on jewels to the Emperor: Fitch went on down the Ganges and Newbery set off home to England to plan fresh travels. On the 28th September the three parted company. Newbery on his way home met a lonely death, nobody knows where or how. He deserves a memorial.

FF—(2)

There is no life of Newbery in the *D.N.B.* The above account owes everything to Foster's *England's Quest of Eastern Trade*, 1933, supplemented by E. G. R. Taylor's *Tudor Geography 1485–1583*, 1930.

FITCH, RALPH, traveller, was born probably in 1550 and he died in 1611. Little is known of his family or of his early life. Just before he started on his first journey in 1583 he made a will which shews him to have been a bachelor and in which he mentions a brother Thomas and a sister and niece both named Frances. He describes himself in that will as 'citizen and leatherseller of London', by which he means that he was a member of the Leathersellers' Company. Some details of his connection with the Leathersellers' Company are preserved in its records and have been printed by Sir William Foster in his *England's Quest of Eastern Trade*. But it is not until he joined Newbery's third expedition in 1583 that Fitch becomes important. His part in that journey will be found described in the article on NEWBERY up to the time when they parted company on September 28th, 1584.

When Newbery and Fitch parted company at Fatehpur Sikri, Fitch took boat with 180 other passengers down the river Jumna to Allahabad, then down the Ganges to Benares, Patna and Tanda, a trip which took five months during which Fitch studied with interest the search for alluvial gold at Patna and the trade in cottons, sugar and opium. From Tanda he moved northwards to Kutch Bihar, no doubt to investigate the trade from China which arrived in India *via* Tibet. This diversion occupied some two months or more, after which he came south again down the Ganges to Hugli, where was a Portuguese trading centre which was wholly independent of the Viceroy of Goa and which welcomed the English traveller and merchant. (For Fitch's experiences at Goa see under NEWBERY, third voyage.) Fitch stayed here until November 28th, 1586, but he moved about visiting Kachua, Sripur and Sonargaon in Eastern Bengal. Newbery had promised 'if it pleased God, to meet me in Bengala within two years with a ship out of England'. The two years were up and there was no sign of Newbery.

Fitch, therefore, embarked at Sripur in a small Portuguese ship which took him to Bassein, where he became the first Englishman to enter Burma. From Bassein he went by inland navigation of the Irrawadi delta to Syriam and thus to Pegu. Fitch made many sketches of Burmese life and he wrote a colourful description of the city and of the royal court, including the methods used for capturing wild elephants.

From Pegu Fitch moved to Chiengmai in the Siamese Shan states, a journey of more than two hundred miles which took him twenty-five days. Here he investigated the trade from China and he found Chiengmai 'a very fair and great town, with fair houses of stone, well peopled'. This must have been late in 1587, for on January 10th, 1588, he sailed from Pegu for Malacca, which he reached on February 8th. Here he remained for seven weeks, studying the trade with China and the Malayan Archipelago, until March 29th, when he set out for Martaban and back to Pegu, where he stayed until September 17th, when he took boat again for Bassein and thence to Bengal, which he reached in November 1588.

Fitch's account of his travels at this point becomes very obscure. It seems that on February 3rd, 1589, he shipped for Cochin on the Malabar coast in a crowded ship. The voyage was much delayed by many calms and it was made very uncomfortable by the heat and by the overcrowding, but eventually the ship arrived at Colombo in Ceylon, where five days were spent. Fitch arrived at Cochin only to find that the last boat of the season for Europe had sailed only two days before. For eight months he languished at Cochin, but at last on November 2nd he secured a passage to Goa. It was a dangerous business to revisit the Viceroyalty of Goa, but Fitch took the risk and he spent three days in the city, probably in disguise. From Goa he went to Chaul, and here once again he was delayed, this time for three weeks, when he got a boat for Hormuz. Hormuz was as dangerous for him as was Goa, and he had to remain there for fifty days before he could book a passage for Basra. Somehow he managed to avoid being recognized and he got away safely.

Undaunted by his adventures, Fitch scorned to go from

Basra to Aleppo by the direct route. Instead he went up the Tigris as far as Mosul, then to Mardin, Urfa and Bir. 'From Bir', he records, 'I went to Aleppo, where I stayed certain months for company, and then I went to Tripolis, where, finding English shipping, I came with a prosperous voyage to London, where, by God's assistance, I safely arrived the 29th April, 1591, having been eight years out of my native country'.

When he got home, he found that his family had given him up for dead and had already divided his estate. He set about writing an account of his journeys, but he had little skill in writing and he relied to a great extent for his descriptions of places on Thomas Hickock's English translation of Cesare Federici's *Viaggio* (published 1588). Hakluyt published Fitch's account in the second edition of his *Principal Navigations* and Purchas also used it in his *Pilgrimes*. In 1592 Fitch became a member of the newly incorporated 'Governor and Company of Merchants of the Levant'.

In August 1596 Fitch was again in Aleppo trading. His fellow-merchants made him consul, a post which he had already refused in London and which he now accepted very reluctantly. The appointment was cancelled in March 1597 by the Company, not out of dissatisfaction with Fitch, but on the grounds that the merchants in Aleppo had no right to make the appointment. Hakluyt records that Fitch was living in London in 1599. He was more than once consulted by the East India Company. In October 1611 he made a second will which was signed on October 3rd and proved on the 15th, which shews that Fitch died on some day between the 3rd and the 15th. Fitch must be accounted one of the greatest of the merchant adventurers.

Hakluyt, *Principal Navigations*.
Purchas His Pilgrimes.
Foster, *England's Quest of Eastern Trade*.

DEE, 'DR.' JOHN, mathematician, astrologer, alchemist, was born in 1527 and died in 1608 at the age of 81. He was the son of Roland Dee and his wife Joanna, daughter of William Wild, and he came of a Welsh family which claimed to trace its descent back to Roderick the Great, Prince of Wales. John was educated at Chelmsford Grammar School, and in 1542 he went to St. John's College, Cambridge. He took his B.A. in 1544, became a fellow in 1545, and when in 1546 Henry VIII founded Trinity College, Dee was made one of its original fellows. In this capacity he was responsible for producing several classical plays. In one of them a man and his basket were carried up to Jupiter's palace, 'whereat was great wondering and many vain reports spread abroad of the means how that was effected'. It was thus that Dee first acquired a reputation as a conjuror and magician which was to stick to him for the rest of his life.

In 1547 Dee went to the Low Countries and brought back to England the first astronomer's staff and ring made of brass which had been designed by Gemma Frisius, Cosmographer to the Emperor Charles V, and two globes constructed by Mercator. These instruments Dee gave to Trinity College when he left Cambridge the following year to go to Louvain. Before he left, he took his M.A. degree, which was in fact the highest degree he ever achieved, although he came to be known as Dr. Dee.

At Louvain Dee began to form a number of friendships which lasted all through his life. He was taught by all the great geographers of the time, either in person or by correspondence, by Gemma Frisius, Mercator, Pedro Nuñez, Ortelius, Finaeus, and all these men became his intimate friends. Later, Dee himself became the technical instructor of all the great English seamen—Chancellor, the Boroughs, Jenkinson, Frobisher, Gilbert, Ralegh, and probably also Drake. He was the friend of Stow, Camden and especially of Richard Hakluyt the elder and the younger. He was always popular with Queen Elizabeth, and he counted among his acquaintances the Emperors Maximilian II and Rudolph, Henry II of France, and had many other friends throughout Europe.

Dee remained at Louvain until 1550, in which year he moved to Paris and there he gave by invitation a series of lectures on Euclid, the first on that subject ever to be delivered.

He was listened to by enormous audiences, so large that many had to listen through the windows. On his return in 1551 to England he was introduced by Sir John Cheke (Edward VI's tutor) to Cecil and by Cecil to the King, who gave him an annuity of £100, which was later exchanged for the living of Upton-on-Severn.

In 1553 he was accused of trying to take Queen Mary's life by poison or by magic, and he was for a time in prison, but eventually he was acquitted by Star Chamber of treason, but he was sent to Bonner to be examined on a charge of heresy. At last, by the special favour of Philip and Mary, Dee was given his full liberty. The originality of Dee's mind is revealed by his petition to Mary to establish a royal library and to ensure the preservation of manuscripts and of historical monuments— a petition which unhappily failed.

When Elizabeth came to the throne, Dee was taken into royal favour, partly because he selected a fit day for the coronation by means of an astrological calculation. Unfortunately for Dee the royal favour did not go beyond the promise of many lucrative preferments which were never fulfilled. In 1562 Dee went to Antwerp to arrange for the printing of some of his writings, and he wrote to Cecil that he had bought a book called *Steganographia*, by John Trithemius, a treatise on writing in cipher, obviously a subject which would much interest Cecil. The next year Dee was in Venice and probably at this time he visited the island of St. Helena.

These were busy years for Dee. In 1563 he was in Hungary and met the Emperor Maximilian II. They were also years of renewed disappointment, for in 1564 he was granted the Deanery of Gloucester, but it went to somebody else, and he only narrowly missed the Provostship of Eton College. In 1571 he was in Lorraine; on his return he explained the appearance of a new star (1572). More than once he was summoned to an interview with the Queen, more than once the Queen visited Dee at his own house. On one occasion she listened for three days to his discourses on a new comet which had terrified the court, and once he was hastily summoned to cope with a crisis of the greatest importance—a wax figure of the Queen had been found in Lincoln's Inn Fields with a pin driven into the breast.

In 1584–5 Dee was employed by the government to make calculations to show the effects on England of adopting the Gregorian calendar. He made the most exact investigations and discovered that eleven days and not ten would have to be omitted. He was prepared to compromise on ten in order to get uniformity with foreign countries, but the Church, led by Grindal, would have nothing to do with such a Papistical innovation.

At about this time Dee took to experiments in alchemy, involving gazing into a crystal, summoning spirits and recording their answers. He fell in with a scoundrel of the name of Kelly, who exploited Dee shamelessly. In 1583 the Bohemian Laski met Dee and Kelly and promised to finance them in his own country. Dee and Kelly left England on September 21st, and the mob at Mortlake broke into his house and destroyed much of his books, furniture and instruments, looking upon him as a magician. The visit to Bohemia was a failure; Dee then had an interview with the Emperor Rudolph, but Rudolph soon saw through the impostures. A similar failure attended Dee's interview with the King of Poland in 1585, and he had to leave the country as a result of protests from the Bishop of Piacenza, apostolic nuncio at the Emperor's court. In 1586 the Emperor of Russia made a handsome offer to Dee, but Dee refused it.

One of Dee's interests was a search for the philosopher's stone. He is said to have transmuted into gold a piece of metal cut from a warming-pan and to have sent to Queen Elizabeth the piece of gold together with the pan with a hole in it which exactly fitted the piece of gold. At last Kelly carried the séances with spirits too far (1587) when he declared that the angels had announced that he and Dee must have their two wives in common. Dee actually consented to this, but the arrangement not naturally uncaused violent quarrels and Kelly parted from Dee. But they kept up a correspondence for some time.

Dee's finances had fallen into chaos and he made many

attempts to secure some preferment, especially the Deanery of Gloucester. At last in 1595 he was appointed Warden of Manchester College: it is hardly surprising to hear that he got on very ill with his staff. When James I came to the throne Dee unsuccessfully petitioned him that he might be tried and cleared of the charge of being a sorcerer (1604). Being in bad health Dee resigned from Manchester College (1604). He was now desperately poor and had to sell his books from time to time to keep body and soul together. What his family life can have been like it is impossible to imagine. He was twice married: the first time in 1565 to Katherine Constable, the widow of a London grocer (E. G. R. Taylor, *ibid.*, p. 107, n. 1), who died in 1574: the second time to Jane, daughter of Bartholomew Fromond, in 1577, by whom he had one son and ten other children. He died in December 1608, and was buried in Mortlake church.

Dee was a prolific writer and probably the second English Diarist, after Edward VI, Machyn being before Dee. Seventy-nine works by him are known, few of which were ever printed. (A list appears in the *D.N.B.*) He is said to have invented the phrase 'The British Empire'. Aubrey describes him as having 'a very fair clear rosy complexion; a long beard as white as milk; he was tall and slender; a very handsome man. . . . He wore a gown like an artist's gown, with hanging sleeves and a slit; a mighty good man he was.'   (*Plate 31*)

C. F. Smith, *John Dee*, 1527–1608, London, 1909.
J. O. Halliwell, *The Private Diary of John Dee*, Camden Society, XIX, 1842.
E. G. R. Taylor, *Tudor Geography*, 1485–1583, where Dee's contribution to geography and his connections with the seamen are admirably dealt with, 1930.
A. Ponsonby, *English Diaries*, pp. 61–6, 1923.

HAKLUYT, RICHARD, of Oxford, the Younger, author of *The Principal Navigations*, was born probably in 1552 or 1553 and he died in 1616 at the age of about 64. His family had been perhaps in origin Dutch, but it had been settled for centuries in Herefordshire. Richard was left an orphan and was looked after by his cousin, Richard Hakluyt the Elder, a member of the Middle Temple, well known to the Queen's statesmen, Burghley and Walsingham especially, as also to the businessmen of the City of London. His main interests were literary and intellectual and he was a friend of Ortelius and Mercator, the cosmographers, and of 'Dr.' John Dee, the mathematician. It was at his guardian's house one day that young Richard saw lying on a table a map of the world. Richard the elder explained the map and the developments which were taking place in geography: from that moment Richard the younger made up his mind to devote himself to the study of geography.

Richard was educated first at Westminster School and then in 1570 he went up to Christ Church with a school scholarship and an exhibition from the Skinners' Company. He took his B.A. in 1574 and his M.A. in 1577. He devoted all the spare time he could find from his university curriculum to reading the travels and voyages recorded in Greek, Latin, Italian, French and Portuguese books (Spanish he seems not to have learned for a long time), and after he had taken his degrees he gave lectures on these subjects at Oxford. At some point he took holy orders and in the course of his life he held a number of preferments. In 1583 he was chaplain to Sir Edward Stafford, brother-in-law of Lord Howard of Effingham and English ambassador in Paris. In 1586 he was prebendary of Bristol and in 1590 he became rector of Wetheringsett in Suffolk, where most of the work on the second edition of *The Principal Navigations* was done. In 1602 he was prebendary of Westminster and in 1603 Archdeacon. He was also chaplain of the Savoy and in 1612 he held the living of Gedney in Lincolnshire. He was twice married and left one son who did him little credit. He died on November 23rd, 1616, and was buried in Westminster Abbey.

Hakluyt's fame rests on his books and on one book in particular. In some ways Hakluyt was a practical man rather than a man of letters, a researcher and an editor rather than an original writer. In the making of his books he had before him a very clear objective—to urge the expansion of England overseas. His earliest piece of writing was an essay (1579–80) entitled *A Discourse on the Strait of Magellan*. His object was to demonstrate how easily England could plant a self-supporting colony there which would control the gateway into the Pacific. He also urged that an expedition should be sent to search for the North-East Passage in order to open a market for English woollens and a short route to the Spice Islands. Hence the voyage by Pet and Jackman in 1580 (E. G. R. Taylor, *Tudor Geography*, 1485–1583, ch. vii). This essay was never printed.

Hakluyt's first printed work was his *Divers Voyages to America* of 1582. This was a collection of all the documents bearing on Queen Elizabeth's title to newly discovered lands and the voyages so far made to America. The book established his place as a cosmographer and probably produced the offer of the chaplaincy to Sir Edward Stafford in Paris.

The six years in Paris revealed Hakluyt's unquenchable energy. He was tutor to Lady Sheffield's illegitimate son by the Earl of Leicester (she had since married Sir Edward Stafford): he acted as a Queen's messenger between Paris and London: he was engaged by Walsingham to discover what the French were doing in Canada, and to achieve this he would be off to St. Malo to interview sea captains who knew well the St. Lawrence and the Banks: he had an English translation made of Cartier's discoveries in Canada and he consulted Mercator on the North-West Passage. And all the time he was collecting more material for a manuscript which he wrote in 1584 entitled *A Discourse on Western Planting*. This was never printed until 1877, but copies were sent to the Queen, Walsingham and Leicester, all of whom treated it like a confidential diplomatic document (E. G. R. Taylor, *Late Tudor and Stuart Geography*, p. 6). This pamphlet once again illustrated the practical side of Hakluyt, for he urged every argument for planting colonies overseas, to break the Spanish monopoly, to reinforce the naval power of England and to spread the Gospel, and he maintained that effective occupation conferred on the Queen a right to own such territories.

The defeat of the Spanish Armada roused the spirit of the English and not least the patriotism of Hakluyt. He made up

his mind to produce a volume of documents devoted entirely
to the exploits of the English seamen. The first edition of *The
Principal Navigations* appeared in one folio volume in 1589. It
was dedicated to Sir Francis Walsingham and it confined itself
to voyages planned for discovery, colonization and the opening
up of new trade routes. The second edition was published ten
years later in three volumes, dedicated to the Lord High
Admiral, Howard of Effingham. In this edition Hakluyt
greatly extended the field of his researches. He set out to
illustrate the whole history of English navigation, which he
called 'the very walls of this our islands'. He went back to 'the
learned, witty, and profound Geoffrey Chaucer', he drew upon
the antiquarians of his own day, on Camden, he included
stories of warlike raids, sea fights, and especially the defeat of
the Armada. Nor did he neglect foreign sources, Spain,
Portugal and the Netherlands.

Professor Walter Raleigh has called Hakluyt 'the silent man,
seated in the dark corner, who is content to listen and
remember . . . ' But Hakluyt was not content with sitting in
a corner. He was up and about travelling hundreds of miles
to interview some sea captain of whom by chance he had heard.
He examined the records in the Tower; he talked with Don
Antonio, the Portuguese Pretender; he met 'five or six of his
best captains and pilots, one of whom had been born in East
India'; he was in Bristol interviewing the master and master's
mate of the ship *Toby*, who could give him information about
Florida; he talked with Captain Muffett, an English gentleman
who had been a prisoner in Spain. Friends from overseas gave
him gifts of silver ore and stuffed animals. Mr. Pryhouse of
Guernsey explained to him the French plans in Canada.
Hakluyt was one of the greatest ransackers and pillagers of
other men's memories that ever lived and we are his fortunate
heirs. For down it all goes into his book, the factual information
which may help later sailors, deep-sea soundings and sailing
orders: the strange sights of birds and beasts, the crocodiles and
the origin of crocodile tears, the wonderful anatomy of the
camel, exactly suited to its work and its surroundings: the
fearful noise of whales which terrified Anthony Jenkinson:

even the smells do not escape him—the soap from Benin which smelt like 'beaten violets'. Then back to the practical side of things—what are the best exports to take to Russia, a full description of the currency in use there. And how proud he is of the Elizabethan English people: 'What English ships did heretofore ever anchor in the mighty river of the Plate, pass and repass the impassable (in former opinion) Strait of Magellan, range along the coast of Chile, Peru, and all the backside of Nova Hispania, further than any Christian ever passed, traverse the mighty breadth of the South Seas, land upon the Luzones in despite of the enemy, enter into alliance, amity, and traffic with the princes of the Moluccas and the Isle of Java, double the famous Cape of Bona Speranza, arrive at the Isle of Santa Helena, and last of all return home most richly laden with the commodities of China, as the subjects of this now flourishing monarchy have done?' It is said that when Hakluyt died, he left enough material for a fourth volume, some of which Purchas used later in his *Pilgrimes* with less skill as an editor. What Hooker's *Ecclesiastical Polity* was to the beginnings of the Anglican Church: what Foxe's *Book of Martyrs* was to the foundations of the Protestant tradition, that Hakluyt's *Principal Navigations* was and still is to those men who were laying the foundations of English sea power and of England's new Empire overseas.

Richard Hakluyt, *The Principal Navigations, Voyages, Traffiques and Discoveries of the English Nation*, Hakluyt Society, 1903–5.

E. G. R. Taylor, *Late Tudor and Early Stuart Geography, 1583–1650*, 1934.

Professor Walter Raleigh, *The English Voyages of the Sixteenth Century*, section II, being the introduction to the Hakluyt Society's edition of *The Principal Navigations*, 1926.

Sir Keith Feiling, *In Christ Church Hall*, 1960—a vivid portrait to which this biography owes much.

SHAKESPEARE, WILLIAM, poet and dramatist: modern research has greatly increased the evidence for the life of Shakespeare and reasonable deductions from that evidence have further enlarged our knowledge. The following account assumes the truth of both evidence and deductions, but references are given to books which discuss fully the problems involved.

William Shakespeare was baptized in Holy Trinity church at Stratford-upon-Avon on April 26th, 1564. It was usual to hurry children to baptism, because the rate of mortality among babies was so high in the sixteenth century: by convention Shakespeare's birthday is now celebrated on April 23rd, but there is no evidence to justify the choice of that date nor of the room now shewn to the public as the birthplace. (M. M. Reese, *Shakespeare, his world and his work*, p. 9, n. 1. cf. Chambers and Williams, *A Short Life of Shakespeare*, pp. 11 and 133.) He was the third child in the family of eight and the eldest of four sons born to John Shakespeare and Mary Arden. John was a well-to-do yeoman, a glover and curer of soft skins for gloves, at Stratford-upon-Avon, himself a native of Snitterfield who came to, Stratford halfway through the sixteenth century. He became a man of much importance: he bought two houses in 1556, two more in 1575 and by 1590 he owned two contiguous houses in Henley Street. Between 1557 and 1568 he held all the chief municipal offices and reached that of Bailiff. Later he fell on evil days and declined in importance, but all the same in 1596 he was granted a coat of arms. He died in September 1601. There is no evidence to prove that the Shakespeares were either Protestant or Catholic 'recusants', but we know that William became godfather to William Walker in 1608 (and godfathers had to be sound Anglicans) and remembered him in his will ('to my godson William Walker xx^s in gold'). The significance of this is discussed in a chapter entitled 'William Shakespeare, Anglican' in T. W. Baldwin's *William Shakespeare's Petty School* (University of Illinois, 1943). (M. M. Reese, *ib.* pp. 16 *sqq.*)

William's mother was Mary Arden, the youngest of eight daughters of Robert Arden of Wilmcote. She was connected with the Ardens of Park Hall, she married John in 1557 or 1558 and outlived him by seven years.

Of William's education we know nothing for certain, but the probability is that he went to the King's New School in Stratford, but there are no lists existing of these early years.

Certainly at some time or other he acquired a knowledge of the usual subjects taught in the grammar schools of his day. Ben Jonson's famous tag, 'Little Latin and less Greek' means no more than that. Judged by Jonson's own high standard of scholarship, Shakespeare was no scholar, but he was as well educated as any other boy of his standing: he learned and loved Ovid, but he does seem to have disliked the formal education of his time and it is noteworthy that the only people for whom he shews in his writings no sympathy are the schoolmasters. (M. M. Reese, *ib.* pp. 10, 389, *sqq.*)

In 1582 Shakespeare was granted a licence by the Bishop of Worcester to marry Anne Whateley of Temple Grafton. Here lies a problem which has never been solved. Certain it is that William Shakespeare married 'Anne Hathwey of Stratford', though nobody knows when or where. Who then was Anne Whateley? Was she merely a clerical error in the licence? Yet, if it is easy to write Whateley for Hathwey, it is more than difficult to write Temple Grafton for Stratford. (Chambers and Williams, *Short Life of Shakespeare*, pp. 16–17, 140–2.)

Anne Hathaway of Shottery was 26 when she married Shakespeare, eight years older than her husband, and she was already pregnant. A daughter Susanna was baptized on May 26th, 1583, and on February 2nd, 1585, were baptized the twins, Hamnet and Judith. There is no convincing evidence that the marriage was an unhappy one, but if we may judge from the frequent allusions throughout his plays, Shakespeare seems to have held strongly that wedlock must be sanctioned by the Church. (M. M. Reese, *ib.*, pp. 28–31.)

By 1592 Shakespeare was in London. We do not know why he left Stratford. The legend, as now presented, that he made Stratford too hot to hold him by poaching Sir Thomas Lucy's deer in Charlecote Park will not stand up to detailed examination, even if there may be a grain of truth in the episode (M. M. Reese, *ib.* 31–4.) The fact remains that Shakespeare was in London by 1592, he was a professional actor with one, but we know not of which, of the 'Companies' of actors, but it is possible that he may have begun his theatrical life with Alleyn's Company, if the story is true that he started his career by holding gentlemen's horses at the playhouse door, for the only theatres to be reached by horseback were The Theatre and The Curtain, both of which were in the hands of Alleyn in 1590–1. (C. and W. *ib.* p. 40.) By 1592 Shakespeare was successful enough to arouse the jealousy and anger of Greene, who attacked him as 'an upstart Crow, beautified with our feathers'. (C. & W. *ib.* 187.) It is possible that Shakespeare was writing plays for more than one Company between 1592 and 1594, but by 1594 he was a full member of the Chamberlain's Men, with whom he was to spend the rest of his professional life.

Shakespeare was living in London in St. Helen's, Bishopsgate, and the probability is that he had his wife and family with him. In 1596 one of the twins, Hamnet, died and Shakespeare may well have thought that he would move his family to Stratford to avoid the dangers to health in London. Certainly in that year he bought New Place to provide a home for his wife and daughters. He himself moved from Bishopsgate to Bankside. At this time he was closely associated with Francis Langley, owner of the new Swan theatre in Paris Garden in Southwark, and it is possible that his Company was then playing at the Swan. Shakespeare and Langley became involved in a violent quarrel with the notorious Justice of the Peace, William Gardiner, a Puritan who was opposed to play-acting, and Shakespeare was bound over to keep the peace. (Hotson, *Shakespeare versus Shallow.*) From 1596 onwards Shakespeare visited Stratford more frequently and for longer periods, nor was New Place the only property he bought. It is clear that Shakespeare was making a good deal of money and he gradually became the largest property holder in Stratford.

In 1601 his father died and left Shakespeare the houses in Henley Street, which he let. He bought 107 acres of land and a cottage and garden in Chapel Lane. In 1605 he bought for £440 a thirty-two year lease of tithes in Stratford and nearby villages, and for the last ten years of his life Shakespeare was the outstanding citizen in Stratford.

He was in London in 1612, 1613 and 1614, and at some point he moved his London Lodgings to Silver Street in Cripplegate. In 1613 he bought the gatehouse of the Blackfriars Priory for

£140 as an investment. In that year his last play, *Henry VIII*, was produced at the Globe Theatre in June. Tradition has it that he himself spoke the Prologue, so that he would have been present at the fire which destroyed the Globe during that first performance. There is no one moment when Shakespeare retired from the theatre: rather he spent more and more time at Stratford and gradually gave up his theatrical work in London.

In 1608 Shakespeare's mother died. The year before his daughter, Susanna, had married Dr. John Hall, but unhappily there was only one child, a daughter. He made his will either in 1615 or 1616, and that will has become famous for the clause in it by which he left to his wife Anne 'my second-best bed with furniture'—the only mention of his wife in his will. This is no proof of a lack of affection on Shakespeare's part: rather it suggests that he knew that in his happy and united family he could take it for granted that Anne would be properly looked after at New Place to the end of her life. The greater part of his estate went to Susanna, for it is clear that Shakespeare wanted most of his property to pass undivided and to remain within the family. Wealthy widows did not long remain widows in the sixteenth century. Their new husbands saw that they took their wealth with them.

Shakespeare died (tradition has it) on his birthday, April 23rd, 1616. He lies buried in the chancel in front of the altar in Holy Trinity Church, Stratford-upon-Avon.

Lack of space forbids any discussion here of the many problems which surround the dates of composition of the plays.

The generally accepted chronology of his plays is as follows: 1590–1, *2 Henry VI* and *3 Henry VI;* 1591–2, *1 Henry VI*; 1592–3, *Richard III* and *The Comedy of Errors*; 1593–4, *Titus Andronicus* and *The Taming of the Shrew*; 1594–5, *Two Gentlemen of Verona, Love's Labour's Lost* and *Romeo and Juliet*; 1595–6, *Richard II* and *A Midsummer Night's Dream*; 1596–7, *King John* and *The Merchant of Venice*; 1597–8, *1 Henry IV* and *2 Henry IV*; 1598–9, *Much ado about Nothing* and *Henry V*; 1599–1600, *Julius Caesar, As You Like It* and *Twelfth Night*; 1600–1, *Hamlet* and *The Merry Wives of*

Plate 31

'Dr' John Dee

Sir Walter Ralegh

Plate 32

Bess of Hardwick

Sir John Harington of Kelston

Windsor; 1601–2, *Troilus and Cressida*; 1602–3, *All's Well That Ends Well*; 1604–5, *Measure for Measure* and *Othello*; 1605–6, *King Lear* and *Macbeth*; 1606–7, *Antony and Cleopatra*; 1607–8, *Coriolanus* and *Timon of Athens*; 1608–9, *Pericles*; 1609–10, *Cymbeline*; 1610–11, *The Winter's Tale*; 1611–12, *The Tempest*; 1612–13, *Henry VIII*, perhaps part of *The Two Noble Kinsmen.*

Shakespeare also wrote the poems *Venus and Adonis* (1592–3); *The Rape of Lucrece* (1593–4); *The Sonnets* (1595–9); *The Phoenix and The Turtle* (1600).

Equally, it is not possible here to discuss the problem of the *Sonnets*, which were published by a piratical printer in 1609. Who was the 'Mr. W. H.' to whom the sonnets were dedicated? Was it Shakespeare's patron, the Earl of Southampton? Was it William Herbert, son and heir of the Earl of Pembroke? Was it the printer, William Hall? Who was the Dark Lady? (All these problems are discussed in M. M. R. *ib.* pp. 408 *sqq.*)

Many thorny problems surround the dates when the plays were published. By the end of Elizabeth's reign fifteen Shakespearean texts had appeared, of which six, (perhaps seven) were 'bad' quartos: of eight the original texts were 'good' quartos. Not much more printing was done before the issue of the First Folio in 1623 by Heminges and Condell, which covered eighteen of the nineteen plays already issued in quarto. *Pericles* was omitted. The Second Folio was printed in 1632, the Third Folio in 1663 (a second issue of 1664 included *Pericles* and one or two plays not by Shakespeare). The Fourth Folio was printed in 1685. (C. & W. *ib.* pp. 67 *sqq.*) It is one of the tragedies of English literature that not a single MS of Shakespeare's work remains to us. The only handwriting of his which we possess is to be found in six signatures (to one are appended the words 'by me'), three of which are on his will. It is possible that in the MS play, *Sir Thomas More*, one page is in the handwriting of Shakespeare. The difficulties in accepting this view are set out in M. M. R. pp. 280–3: on the other hand a very convincing argument along purely literary lines is to be found in R. W. Chambers, *Man's Unconquerable Mind*, ch VII.

(A. W. Pollard and others: *Shakespeare's Hand in a Play of Sir Thomas More*, 1923.)

Shakespeare's tremendous success arose from the fact that he combined in himself three roles—he was a poet, a playwright and an actor: up to his time the theatre had never known such a trinity in unity. Shakespeare created the theatre as we understand that word. But Shakespeare was first and foremost a poet, before he was a playwright or an actor. We know nothing about his ability as an actor (but cf. M. M. R. pp. 242-6), but he understood the professional needs of the theatre, because he lived with, acted with and wrote for actors—not actresses, because feminine parts were then played by boys. His dramatic work was at first conditioned by the literary conventions of his times—the classical imagery, the use of the soliloquy, the affectations of speech which appear, notably, in the verbal agility in punning. He was also governed by the general views of his time on the nature and purpose of Man, the supernatural, etc. What raises Shakespeare far above all his contemporaries is his ability to emancipate himself from these conventions and yet to transmute them by his own genius to his own use. Shakespeare was a poet who for his living had to write plays. Because he was a poet, and one of the greatest, he could not but produce dramatic poetry: his triumph was that he gave to the theatre poetic drama—every dramatic thought, every dramatic situation was to be presented in the imagery of poetry. (Spurgeon, *Shakespeare's Imagery*: H. Morris, *Elizabethan Literature*, pp. 205 *sqq.*)

Two other points have to be remembered: Shakespeare was never an entirely free agent, for he had to provide suitable parts for the actors in the Company, and also he had to provide the right sort of play for the audience which was going to hear it. A play which would score a success at The Theatre in Finsbury Fields might offend the public at the Globe on the South Bank: a royal command to perform in front of the Queen or a private performance at a nobleman's house would demand a totally different sort of play. (Milton Holmes, *Shakespeare's Public*.)

What sort of a man was this William Shakespeare? 'Without a single dissentient voice his contemporaries testify to his sweetness, gentleness, honesty and "civil demeanour": no famous man has had so little evil spoken of him'. (M. M. R. *ib.* 381, *sqq.*) And, indeed, the width of his sympathy with every sort of human being (except schoolmasters) stands out in all his writings. To him evil is detestable, but the evil doer is an object of compassion, except where the criminal has given himself over to evil, as in Iago. Nothing is more moving in Shakespeare's plays than the defence by Costard of Sir Nathaniel in *Love's Labour's Lost* (Act. V, sc. ii, 569)—and Sir Nathaniel was a schoolmaster. Shakespeare is the most merciful of all the great men. Ben Jonson called him 'my gentle Shakespeare' and 'my beloved author'; 'I lov'd the man, and do honour his memory (on this side Idolatry) as much as any. He was indeed honest and of an open and free nature: had an excellent Phantasy: brave notions and gentle expressions.' In his last years Shakespeare became the best known figure and the most popular in Stratford, so that he was welcome in many homes and welcomed many to his own New Place. Down the centuries and across the continents his name glows ever brighter, so that perhaps Carlyle's claim is no empty boast, 'he is the grandest thing we have yet done'.

There is no authentic portrait of Shakespeare. On the chancel wall in the Stratford church stands a bust, the work of Gheerart Janssen, commissioned and completed a few years after Shakespeare's death, but it is to be hoped that this dull and heavy work reinforces Shakespeare's own verdict, 'there's no art To find the mind's construction in the face'. In the First Folio there was printed a drawing by Martin Droeshout, a Dutch engraver, but as he was only fifteen years old when Shakespeare died he must have copied another picture. The painting now at Stratford was copied from the engraving.

(Plate 30)

E. K. Chambers & C. Williams, *A Short Life of Shakespeare*, 1933.
M. M. Reese, *Shakespeare, His world and his work.* 1953.
Lamborn & Harrison, *Shakespeare, The Man & His Stage.* 1924.
Milton Holmes, *Shakespeare's Public.* 1960.
Granville-Barker & G. B. Harrison, *A Companion to Shakespeare Studies.* 1934.

Ivor Brown, *Shakespeare*. 1949.

H. Morris, *Elizabethan Literature*, contains also a most valuable bibliography.

HOLBEIN, HANS, the younger, was born at Augsburg in 1497, the son of Hans Holbein the elder, a painter. He died in London in 1543, aged 46. We are only concerned here with his life and work in England. He came to England on a first visit from Basle in 1526, driven out by the effects of the Reformation which were making painting there less and less profitable. His friend Erasmus gave him a letter of introduction to Sir Thomas More. During the eighteen months he spent in England he devoted himself wholly to portraiture. There survive of his paintings at this time his 'Archbishop Warham' 1527 (Louvre); 'Sir Thomas More' 1527 (Frick Gallery, New York); 'John and Thomas Godsalve' 1528 (Dresden); 'Niklaus Kratzer' 1528 (Louvre). His greatest work was a group of Sir Thomas More and his family. The original has not survived, but there is at Basle a drawing for the picture and at Windsor drawings for seven of the heads.

In 1528 he went back to Basle, but he returned to England in 1532 and spent the rest of his life here. The first circle from whom he found patrons was that of the merchants of the Hansa steelyard in London, and in 1532 and 1533 he painted many of these prosperous gentlemen in their flat velvet hats. Of these portraits the most famous is 'The Ambassadors', now in the National Gallery. By the end of 1533 he was working for Henry VIII and his courtiers. The portrait of Thomas Cromwell, 1533 (Frick Gallery) was the first in this series; in 1536 he painted Jane Seymour (Vienna), after which he was officially employed by the King. In 1537 he was commissioned to paint a fresco on the wall of the Privy Chamber in the palace of Whitehall of Henry VIII and Jane Seymour with Henry VII and his wife, Elizabeth of York. The original was destroyed in the fire of 1698, but part of the cartoon for the painting survived and is now in the N.P.G. London. Only one other portrait of Henry VIII is accepted as indubitably by

Holbein, in the Thyssen collection at Lugano. The well-known portraits of Henry VIII at Rome, Belvoir, Liverpool, Warwick and Castle Howard are not now generally accepted as being by Holbein. There is at Windsor a grisaille miniature on vellum, 'Solomon and the Queen of Sheba', in which Solomon is personified by Henry VIII. During these years Holbein was also used by the King to travel abroad and paint portraits of possible wives for Henry. Examples of these are the 'Anne, Duchess of Milan' 1538 (National Gallery) and the 'Anne of Cleves' 1539 (Louvre).

Much of his time was occupied in painting the courtiers. Of this work Windsor Castle possesses the splendid collection of drawings which, in spite of damage and attempts at restorations by later and lesser artists, still reveal to us the men and women of the sixteenth century.

Holbein was perhaps the greatest of all portrait painters, certainly he was the greatest of all painters in miniature. He also illustrated books and painted religious subjects, made designs for buildings and for glass, and drew also settings for jewels which appear in many of his portraits.   (*Plate 20*)

Hans Reinhardt, *Holbein*, English translation, Heinemann.
K. T. Parker, *The Drawings of Holbein at Windsor Castle*, Phaidon.

HILLIARD, NICHOLAS, miniaturist, was born about 1547 and died in 1619 at the age of 72. He 'is the central artistic figure of the Elizabethan age, the only English painter whose work reflects . . . the world of Shakespeare's earlier plays' (Waterhouse). The art of painting in miniature was known in the sixteenth century as 'limning': Hilliard at some unknown date was appointed limner and goldsmith—for he was also a worker in gold and in jewels—to Queen Elizabeth I. Hilliard's right to make small portraits of the Queen in limning only probably dates from before 1572. It is possible that he made a miniature of Lady Arabella Stuart for the Duke of Parma at the time when the Catholics were proposing that these two should marry, but the miniature does not now exist. It was Hilliard who designed and executed Queen Elizabeth's second Great

Seal, in 1584. He was friends with Sir Philip Sidney and Sir Christopher Hatton, and from time to time he received large grants of money. All the same, he was frequently in financial difficulties. James I carried on Elizabeth's patronage, but in 1617 Hilliard was imprisoned in Ludgate for debt, and he died two years later. His character is best revealed in his *Treatise concerning the Arte of Limning*, which he published in 1600 where he appears as a gentle, kindly, artistic gentlemen, devoted to his art and a great admirer of the English race: 'Rare beauties are . . . more commonly found in this isle of England than elsewhere.' Hilliard interprets the English of the sixteenth century with complete understanding and sympathy. He must be looked on as one of the leaders of the English Renaissance.

(Plate 20)

E. Waterhouse, *Painting in Britain, 1530-1790*, Pelican History of Art.

C. Winter, *Elizabethan Miniatures*, King Penguin.

DAVIS (or **DAVYS**), **CAPTAIN JOHN,** navigator and explorer, was born about 1550 at Sandridge, near Dartmouth, in Devon, and he died at sea in 1605. Nothing is known of his parentage, but he spent his youth with the Gilbert family, Humphrey, Adrian and Walter Ralegh, and he must have gone to sea early in life. The first mention of him occurs in the diary of 'Dr.' John Dee, the astrologer, in 1579 and again in 1583. In 1584 Adrian Gilbert organized an expedition to find the N.W. Passage to China, which sailed in 1585 under the command of John Davis. The voyage was financed mainly by London merchants and those in the west country, especially by William Sanderson, who became a close friend and unfailing supporter of Davis in all his northern voyages. Davis must by this time have been an experienced seaman and a competent surveyor, for on this voyage he 'platted' the exact position of islands, rocks and harbours 'with lines and scales thereunto convenient'.

This first voyage lasted from July 1585 to the end of September. Davis reached the east coast of Greenland and went up Cumberland Gulf, naming the prominent places after

his friends and places at home—Mount Ralegh, Cape Walsingham, Gilbert Sound, Totnes Road, Exeter Sound.

His second expedition was subscribed chiefly by west
countrymen. It sailed from Dartmouth on May 7th, 1586,
Davis taking with him the *Mermaid* and the *Moonshine*. He
sailed in the same direction as on the previous voyage, up
Davis Strait to Gilbert Sound, but curiously he failed to
recognize some of the places he had visited the year before.
He met many Eskimos who were very friendly, but who
proved great thieves and skilful wrestlers. Davis soon sent the
Mermaid home and went on himself in *Moonshine* westwards to
Labrador, where he caught an immense amount of cod, which
he salted and took home. In October he joined up with
Sunshine, which he had previously sent to explore the east
coast of Greenland. Both ships were back in the Thames in
October. The profits from this voyage were small, and a bale
of cloth was lost, which so seriously disturbed the west country
merchants that they declined to take shares in the next
expedition.

The third voyage (May to September 1587) consisted of
three ships, the *Elizabeth* from Dartmouth, the *Sunshine* and
a small pinnace of about 20 tons. Davis elected to sail in the
pinnace, the *Ellen*, as it was handier for dealing with ice. He
intended to explore in this small vessel, while the other two
ships were to go to the cod fishing grounds. The fleet arrived
in Gilbert Sound in June 1587. The two fishing ships separated
from the *Ellen* in September and Davis sailed north along the
Greenland coast as far as latitude 72 degrees 12 minutes. He
named the most northerly point in Greenland that he reached
Sanderson's Hope, then he turned west and then south to
rejoin the fishing ships, but they had broken their promise
and had gone back to England sixteen days after leaving Davis.

Davis had failed to find the N.W. Passage, but that was not
his fault, as years later in 1616 William Baffin explained. The
voyage had been a very daring one, demanding extreme skill
and high seamanship. David had to meet a good deal of
criticism, to answer which he produced in 1595 his *World's
Hydrographical Description*. His own account of this voyage

became a guide to later navigators, and there is no doubt that it was thanks to what Davis had accomplished that Hudson was able to reach Hudson Strait. Davis also produced his *Traverse Book* (1587), which became the model for all future log books. Davis had also now to reconcile his discoveries with the previous work of Frobisher and with the old Zeno map of the Arctic regions published in 1558. He made a large scale map to show his voyages, but this has been lost. He also delineated his results on the Molyneux globe which is now in the Middle Temple Library (for full description, see A. H. Markham, *The Voyages and Works of John Davis*, pp. xxxiii, *sq.*). His voyages are also recorded on what Shakespeare called 'the new map' of the world prepared by Edward Wright, the first map to be drawn on the projection discovered by him but erroneously attributed to Mercator.

Davis's next employment was with Cumberland's squadron off the Azores in 1589. He was captain of the *Desire* in Cavendish's expedition to the South Sea in 1591, a voyage he undertook because he was eager to sail round America and because Cavendish promised him a bark to explore for the N.W. Passage on the Pacific side of America. The voyage was a disaster, Davis and Cavendish lost touch with each other in bad weather and Cavendish, who died on the way home, accused Davis of deliberately deserting him—a false accusation, for Davis three times tried to break into the Pacific through the Straits of Magellan and three times was driven back by storms. He then went to the rendezvous at Port Desire on the east coast of Patagonia, but Cavendish was not there and Davis was compelled to sail home (June 1593). Out of the 76 men who started out with him only 15 got home. On this voyage Davis discovered the Falkland Islands. The claim to have done this was made by Sir Richard Hawkins, but he arrived there only in 1594.

In 1594 Davis produced his *Seaman's Secrets*, a practical guide for sailors, providing from his own experience all the scientific knowledge necessary for successful navigation. He had also invented the backstaff, an improvement on the old cross-staff, an instrument for calculating the altitude of the heavenly bodies.

In 1596 and 1597 Davis was probably with Essex at Cadiz and the Azores. 1598 saw him in service with the Dutch on a voyage to the East Indies—a disastrous voyage, the only account of which was written by Davis and published later by Purchas in his *Pilgrimes*. The Dutch historian, de Jonge, falsely accused Davis of being an English spy and ruining the voyage, whereas in fact Davis did yeoman service as chief pilot.

In 1600 Davis again joined a Dutch expedition, and then in 1601 he was Pilot Major on the *Red Dragon*, Lancaster's ship in the first expedition sent out by the East India Company. He was home in 1603 and the next year he sailed with Sir Edward Michelbourne in the second venture of the East India Company. He went in the *Tiger* from Cowes in December 1604. The fleet fell in with some Japanese pirates near Bantam who accepted English hospitality and then treacherously attacked the crews. Davis was murdered and died on the 29th or 30th of December, 1605.

John Davis was one of the greatest of English seamen. Not such a notable fighting sailor, strategist and tactician as Drake, not such an able administrator as Hawkins, not such a glamorous figure as Grenville, he was yet as tough and enduring an explorer as Frobisher, as great a seaman and as beloved by his men as were Drake and Hawkins, and he possessed an inventive genius and a scientific knowledge which none of his predecessors could claim. And he, a Puritan, had something else, too—a mystic and fanatical faith in the destiny of the English people: 'There is no doubt but that we of England are this saved people, by the eternal and infallible presence of the Lord predestinated to be sent unto these Gentiles in the sea, to those Isles and famous Kingdoms, there to preach the peace of the Lord: for are not we only set upon Mount Zion to give light to the rest of the world? Have not we the true handmaid of the Lord to rule us, unto whom the eternal majesty of God hath revealed his truth and supreme power of Excellency? . . . It is only we, therefore, that must be these shining messengers of the Lord, and none but we.' (Hakluyt, *Principal Navigations*, Hakluyt Society, 1905, xii, 32, n. 1.)

Capt. A. H. Markham, R.N., *The Voyages and Works of John Davis*, Hakluyt Society, 1880. A work of great learning and interest. Contains a useful criticism of other biographies and shows how totally unreliable is Froude in his *Short Studies on Great Subjects*.

Walter Raleigh, *The English Voyages of the Sixteenth Century*, 1926, pp. 44–7.

GLOSSARY

ANABAPTIST. A comprehensive word to cover various sects on the continent which denied the validity of infant baptism. They were hated and persecuted by both Catholics and Protestants in the sixteenth century, because they took literally the New Testament on communism, pacifism, etc.

ANTI-CLERICALISM. Bitter hostility felt by the laity for the clergy, which in England broke out in the Parliament of 1529.

ATTAINDER. The usual method adopted by the Tudors for getting rid of inconvenient or unwanted persons: an act of Parliament which authorized execution without any trial. The heirs of an attainted noble lost the title and possessions.

AUSTIN FRIARS. An older English form of the word Augustinian.

AUTO-DA-FE (act of faith). The ceremony under the Spanish Inquisition at which heretics underwent the sentences passed on them: used specially to mean the burning of convicted heretics.

BENEVOLENCE. The free or so-called free gifts made by the wealthier people to the Crown: made illegal by Richard III, reappeared under Henry VII and Henry VIII, not used by Elizabeth, unless perhaps in 1568 at the expense of the clergy.

CALVINISM. That form of Protestantism set up by Calvin at Geneva, denying Free Will, asserting Predestination, rejecting Bishops and Transubstantiation: the sort of Church which Presbyterians wanted in England, because (they claimed) it alone had scriptural warrant. Presbyter = Lay Elder.

CONVOCATION. The general assembly of the clergy of England.

COUNCIL, GENERAL. Assemblies of the clergy of the Catholic Church throughout the world, whose decisions were regarded as binding on all Christians.

COUNCIL OF TRENT. A meeting of the General Council at Trent in 1545 to 1563 to counter the growth of Protestantism and to make reforms in the Catholic Church. It launched the Counter-Reformation against Protestantism.

COURT OF ARCHES. The Archbishop's court held at the church of St. Mary-le-Bow (*i.e.*, St. Mary of the Arches, *de arcubus*), so called because the church was built on arches or 'bows' above the marshy ground: heard appeals from diocesan courts and grew into a court of first instance.

COURTS OF AUDIENCE. Archiepiscopal courts of appeal.

COURT OF AUGMENTATIONS. Established by Act of Parliament in 1536 to administer the transfer of ecclesiastical lands to the Crown at the dissolution of the monasteries.

COURT OF CHANCERY. When a decision by Common Law was legal but appeared not to be just, appeal was made to the Court of Chancery, where the Chancellor dispensed a form of law which came to be known as Equity, to rectify the unfairness. In course of time this Court developed so much red tape that it lost its original popularity (see *Bleak House*).

COURT OF STAR CHAMBER. The King's Council sitting as a court in the old starred chamber and exercising the old judicial authority of the Council. It did not arise out of any Act of Parliament. It greatly increased in activity and importance under Wolsey. Most of the cases dealt with were between private individuals, only occasionally on Crown matters. (Elton, *Tudor Constitution*, pp. 158 *sqq.*)

COURT OF WARDS. Established by statute by Henry VIII in 1540 to safeguard the Crown's financial interests in the royal wards and the administration of their lands, their marriages, etc. (Hurstfield, *The Queen's Wards*.)

CROWN MATRIMONIAL. The reversion of the Crown in Scotland on the death of the Queen to her consort and not to her heir.

ERASTIAN. The subordination of the Church to the State: derived from Thomas Erastus (1524–1583), who was not himself an Erastian. (Figgis, *The Divine Right of Kings*.)

GOLDEN ROSE. An ornament in the shape of a rose of gold and jewels, blessed by the Pope on the 4th Sunday in Lent and then presented by him as a mark of special favour to an individual or a community.

HANAPER. The financial department of Chancery responsible for collecting the fees due to the Crown upon the issue of any writs or letters patent.

HUMANIST. In the sixteenth century anyone who studied Greek and Latin and who approached questions of religious reform from a literary or cultural point of view rather than from a religious and ideological point of view.

THE INDEX (*index librorum prohibitorum*). The list of prohibited books by the Papacy which members of the Catholic Church were and are forbidden to read or to possess. Started by Paul IV in 1557.

KING DE FACTO. The actually ruling king, though not the legal king: a usurper.

KING DE JURE. The legal king by lineal descent, though not necessarily the ruling king.

KNIGHT BANNERET. Degree of knighthood superior to that of knight-bachelor, distinguishable by the square banner he carried in place of the pointed pennon. Awarded for bravery in the field. Ranked before all other knights except those of the Garter. Now extinct.

LEGATUS A LATERE. A papal plenipotentiary whose commands could only be resisted by appeal to the Pope: usually appointed for a particular and temporary purpose. Wolsey was appointed with Campeggio in 1518 to preach a crusade and was continued in office with wide powers.

LETTERS OF MARQUE. Authority issued by a ruler or a claimant to a throne (*e.g.*, Don Antonio of Portugal) to a shipmaster to prey upon the merchant shipping of the king's enemies. Often issued in times of peace to enable the holder to recover what he had lost in some previous attack, either from the same attacker or from any of his countrymen.

LORD HIGH STEWARD. In the sixteenth century purely a ceremonial office. Originally a household official who ordered the King's meals.

LUTHERANISM. That form of Protestantism evolved by Martin Luther of which the chief characteristic was that a man is justified by faith alone and not by good works. Luther did not deny transubstantiation.

MASTER OF THE ROLLS. Originally the keeper of the rolls of Chancery, the administrative records of that office. By Tudor times the work was more legal than administrative. The first lay keeper was Thomas Cromwell.

MISPRISION OF TREASON. Knowing that treason is being plotted and not revealing it: having some hand, but only an indirect one, in treason.

PENTATEUCH. The five books of Moses—Genesis, Exodus, Leviticus, Numbers, Deuteronomy.

PETER'S PENCE. A very ancient tax which by the sixteenth century had amounted to £200 paid annually by English bishops to the Pope. The tax was profitable to the bishops, because they collected the sum from their dioceses, but more than was needed and kept the surplus. Payment to Rome was abolished by Act of Parliament in 1534, when Henry VIII broke with Rome, but Henry took the tax.

PIRACY. Unlicensed robbery at sea by men without letters of marque.

PLURALIST. An ecclesiastic who held more than one church office or living and thereby increased his income.

PRAEMUNIRE. A series of acts passed between 1352 and 1359 to protect the king's rights against foreign, especially papal, interference in ecclesiastical property or jurisdiction. Extended later to protect the lay courts against the ecclesiastical courts.

PREBEND (*praebere*, to provide). One who draws an income from a cathedral in return for a limited amount of service (adj. prebendary).

PRIVATEERING. Licensed robbery at sea by men carrying letters of marque.

PURITANISM. A word which covers three groups of people who wanted the Church to be 'purified': (1) the presbyterians (except the Tudor puritans, who did not want to do away with the royal supremacy), who wanted to reconstruct the Church on the lines of the Geneval model of Calvin and to do away with bishops and the royal supremacy; (2) the separatists or sectarians, who would abolish any form of national church and allow freedom of worship and organization to individual congregations, electing their own ministers; (3) the moderates, who wanted changes in ritual and worship, but did not worry much about the government of the Church. (Elton, *Tudor Constitution*, pp. 432, *sqq.*)

SACRAMENTARIES. The name given by Luther to those who held that the bread and wine in the Communion service are only the Body and Blood of Christ in a purely symbolical sense; then used of all who denied the Real Presence.

SEMINARY. Used especially of the English theological colleges established on the continent (Douai, Rome) to plant the seed (*semen*) of Roman Catholicism in Englishmen with a view to their returning to England to save and spread Catholicism there.

ST. PAUL'S CROSS. A pulpit in the N.E. corner of the Close of St. Paul's cathedral, which formed a national centre for sermons and disputations usually arranged by the government for purposes of propaganda (see J. O. W. Haweis, *Sketches of the Reformation and Elizabethan Age*, 1844).

SUBSIDY. A tax made by Parliament to increase the sum produced by the Tenth and the Fifteenth: became fixed at 4s. in the £ on the annual value of land, and 2s. 8d. in the £ on the annual value of goods. No one paid on both. Usually under-assessed by J.P.s who would not return the true value of their own and their friends' wealth.

TENTH AND FIFTEENTH. The normal Parliamentary taxation on landed property. Towns represented in Parliament paid a tenth, others a fifteenth. Never brought in enough, therefore a 'subsidy' (*subsidium*, a help) was granted.

TRANSUBSTANTIATION. The belief that after the prayer of consecration in the Communion service the bread and the wine cease to be bread and wine except in appearance and become the real body and blood of Christ.

VISITATIONS. Periodical inspections of his diocese by the bishop: metropolitical visitation, inspection of every diocese by the Archbishop of the Province—Canterbury or York.

WARDEN OF THE CINQUE PORTS. The governor of the five ports of Hastings, Romney, Hythe, Dover and Sandwich, to which were added Winchelsea and Rye. Allowed to deduct £500 from their share of any Tenth or Fifteenth levied on Sussex or Kent, a privilege confirmed to them by Elizabeth as a reward for their services against the Armada.

ZWINGLIANISM. That form of Protestantism evolved in Zurich by Zwingli of which the chief characteristic was that he denied any form of corporeal presence in the Eucharist. He regarded the Eucharist as purely symbolic.

INDEX

Allen, William, Cardinal (1532–94) **318–23**: and Sir Christopher Hatton, 225; and Robert Parsons, 325–7

Anne Boleyn (1507–36) **35–6**: Henry VIII's love letters to, 20; rumoured poisoning of Henry Fitzroy, 46; Elizabeth Barton's prophecy, 99; patroness of William Barlow, 110; suspected plan to poison Princes Mary, 143; and Cranmer, 155; Udall's celebration of her coronation, 181–2; and Matthew Parker, 268–9, 270

Anne of Cleves (1515–57) **38**; and Cranmer, 155

Arthur, Prince of Wales (1486–1502) **6–7**: Treaty of Medina del Campo, 4; Linacre tutor to, 75

Ascham, Roger (1515–68) **180–1**; tutors Edward VI, 123; on Lady Jane Grey, 133; friend of Ponet, 178; teaches Robert Dudley, 209

Aske, Robert (*ob.* 1537) **95–6**

Askew, Anne (1521–46) **121–2**: friend of Joan Bocher, 122

Babington, Sir Anthony (1561–86) **308–12**

Barlow, William, Bishop (*ob.* 1569) **110–12**: and Robert Fenner, 173

Barnes, Robert (1495–1540) **107–10**: helped by Coverdale, 118

Barrow (Barrowe), Henry (c. 1550–93) **341–2**

Barton, Elizabeth (1506–34) **98–9**

Beaufort, Margaret, Countess of Richmond (1433–1509) **1–2**: and marriage of Henry to Elizabeth of York, 6, 10; friendship with Bishop John Fisher, 79–80

Bess of Hardwick *see* Hardwick, Elizabeth

Bilney, Thomas (*ob.* 1531) **99–101**: converts Latimer, 165

Bocher, Joan (*ob.* 1550) **122–3**: John Foxe pleads for, 300

Boleyn, Anne *see* Anne Boleyn

Bonner, Edmund, Bishop of London (1500?–69) **146–50**: tries to save Anne Askew, 121; his family befriended by Ridley, 162; examines John Dee, 442–3

Bothwell, James Hepburn, 4th Earl of (1535?–78) **247–62**

Browne, Robert (*c.* 1550–1633) **342–4**: and Henry Barrow, 341

Burghley, William Cecil, Lord (1520–98) **198–204**: employs Sir Robert Sadler, 59–60; rescues John Hales, 139; friend of Ponet, 178; and plan to marry Mary Stuart to Norfolk, 190; and Walsingham, 206–7; helped by Thomas Gresham, 234–5; and Matthew Parker, 268, 270; and Whitgift, 278; and Ridolfi, 301–2; 369; and William Parry, 306; and Topcliffe, 327–8; and Barrow, 342 and Browne, 342, 343; and Sir John Hawkins, 389, 391–2; and Sir Richard Hawkins, 398; and Drake, 400–1; and the aristocrats, 417; and John Dee, 442

Cabot, John **344–8**

Cabot, Sebastian (*ob?* 1557) **348–51**

Campion, Edmund (1540–81) **334–6**: his *History of Ireland*, 212; Hatton's help in publishing his *Challenge*, 227; and Parsons, 323–4; and Pound, 324; and Cuthbert Mayne, 329

Cartwright, Thomas (1535–1603) **339–41:** welomed by Whitgift to Warwick, 278; influences Robert Browne, 342–3

Cary, Robert, 1st Earl of Monmouth (?1560–1639) **267–8**

Catherine of Aragon (1485–1536) **33–5:** and Margaret Beaufort, 2; dowry, 4; marriage to Arthur, 7; her children, 20; validity of her marriage to Henry VIII, 21; Mary Tudor's support of, 43; and Henry Standish, 63; championed by Fisher, 82; and Cranmer, 155

Catherine Howard (*ob.* 1542) **39–40:** and Lord Howard of Effingham, 421

Catherine Parr (1512–48) **40–2:** Coverdale's funeral sermon, 120; offended by Seymour's behaviour to Elizabeth, 185

Cavendish, George (?1499–?1562) **56–8**

Cavendish (Candish), Thomas (1560–92) **362–8:** and Captain John Davis, 460

Cecil, William, Lord Burghley *see* Burghley

Chancellor, Richard (*ob.* 1556) **353–5:** and Anthony Jenkinson, 369, 370

Cheke, Sir John (1514—57) **183–4:** friend of Ponet, 178; introduces John Dee to Edward VI, 442

Clifford, George, 3rd Earl of Cumberland *see* Cumberland

Colet, John, Dean of St. Paul's (*c.* 1466–1519) **67–71:** and Linacre, 75; influence on Erasmus, 77; and Sir Thomas More, 85

Coverdale, Miles (?1488–1568) **117–21:** John Rogers' use of his translation, 153; and the Geneva Bible, 283

Cranmer, Thomas, Archbishop of Canterbury (1489–1556) **154–8:** Henry VIII's support of, 27; issues dispensation for marriage to Jane Seymour, 37; reveals Catherine Howard's indiscretions, 40; examines John Frith, 103; and

John Lambert, 106; verdict on William Barlow, 111–12; and Coverdale, 120; and Joan Bocher, 122–3; critic of Bonner, 148–9; and Gardiner, 151–3; and Ridley, 159–61; influence of Ponet on, 178

Cromwell, Thomas (?1485–1540) **63–7:** issues the *Injunctions*, 26; and marriage alliance with Cleves 38; and Bishop Fisher, 83; employs Rowland Lee, 89–90; opposed by Thomas, Lord Darcy, 97–8; and burning of John Forest, 104–5; employs Thomas Barnes, 109; and William Barlow, 110–11; and Tyndale, 116; and Coverdale, 118–20; Cranmer pleads for his life, 156; portrait by Holbein, 456

Cumberland, Geroge Clifford, 3rd Earl of (1558–1605 **426–7:** and Sir James Lancaster, 432; employs Captain John Davis, 460

Darcy, Thomas, Lord (1467–1537) **96–8**

Darnley, Henry Stuart, Lord (1545–67) **251–4:** and Riccio, 255–6; and Bothwell, 258–60

Davies, Richard, Bishop of St. David's (1501–81) **287**

Davis (Davys), Captain John (c. 1550–1605) **458–62:** and Thomas Cavendish, 366–7, 368

Dee, 'Dr.' John (1527–1608) **441–4:** collaborates with Chancellor, 354; and Humphrey Gilbert

Devereux, Robert, 2nd Earl of Essex *see* Essex

Drake, Sir Francis (?1543–96) **398–411:** Essex joins Lisbon expedition, 218; compared with Cavendish, 366; and Sir John Hawkins, 394–5, 407, 408; and Sir Richard Hawkins, 396; and Howard of Effingham, 405–8, 422–3; and Sir Richard Grenville, 418, 419; and Thomas Fenner, 427–8

Dudley Edmund (?1462–1510) **17–18**

Dudley, Jane *see* Grey, Lady Jane
Dudley, John, Earl of Warwick, Duke of Northumberland *see* Northumberland
Dudley, Robert, Earl of Leicester *see* Leicester

Edward VI **123–6:** plans for his marriage, 133; his sister Mary's affection, 144; re-opens St. Thomas' hospital, 163; rewards Cheke, 183–4; and Thomas Gresham, 233; and John Dee, 442; his diary, 444
Elizabeth I **184–198:** treatment of Bonner, 148; and William Cecil, 199–204; and Walsingham, 206–9; and Leicester, 206–17; and Campion, 212, 335–6; and Essex 217–21; and Hatton, 225–8; and Sir Philip Sidney, 229; and Sir Thomas Gresham, 234–6; employs Palavicino, 238; and Peter Wentworth, 240–3; and Mary, Queen of Scots, 245–7, 249–50; offer of marriage to James, Earl of Arran, 246; and Darnley, 252; and Bothwell, 258; and Sir John Harrington, 262–6; and Robert Cary, 267; and Matthew Parker, 269, 270–4; and Grindal, 275–6; and Whitgift, 278–80; and Dean Alexander Nowell's sermons, 289–90; and John Foxe, 299, 300; and William Parry, 306–8; and Babington, 310–11; and Lopez, 312–13; and Thomas Stuckley, 316; and Southwell, 333; and Sir Humphrey Gilbert, 355–60; and Anthony Jenkinson, 370, 372, 374–7; and Sir John Hawkins, 383–6, 391–2, 394–5; and Sir Richard Hawkins, 397; and Drake, 400, 402–4, 406, 408, 409–10; and Frobisher, 412, 414, 415; and Howard of Effingham, 422–4; and Cumberland, 427; and East India Company, 433; and Cathay expedition, 435; letter to Akbar, 437; and John Dee, 442; and Richard Hakluyt,

446; employs Nicholas Hilliard, 457–8
Elizabeth of York (1465–1503) **5–6:** Morton suggests her marriage to Henry Richmond, 10; fresco by Holbein of, 456
Empson, Sir Richard (*ob.* 1510) **17**
Erasmus, Desiderius (1466–1536) **76–9:** and Archbishop Warham, 48; quarrel with Polydore Vergil, 55; and Henry Standish, 63; visits Canterbury with Colet, 70–1; friendship with Grocyn, 72–3; and Linacre, 75; verdict on Fisher, 83; Bilney reads his New Testament, 99–100; introduces Holbein to More, 456
Essex, Robert Devereux, 2nd Earl of (1567–1601) **217–22:** and Ralegh, 223; Sidney's sonnets to his daughter, 230; and Harrington, 264; and Lopez, 313; legend of the flung hat, 420; quarrel with Howard of Effingham, 424; and George Fenner, 429; and Captain John Davis, 461

Feckenham, John de, Abbot of Westminster (?1518–85) **285–7**
Fenner, George (*ob.* 1618) **427–9**
Fenton, Edward (*ob.* 1603) **424–6:** and Walsingham, 209; and Hatton, 228
Ferrar, Robert, Bishop of St. David's (*ob.* 1555) **173–4**
Fisher, John, Bishop of Rochester (1469–1535) **79–84:** and Elizabeth Barton, 99; and Cranmer, 155
Fitch, Ralph (?1550–1611) **438–40:** and Newbery's third expedition, 436–7
Fitzroy, Henry, Duke of Richmond *see* Richmond
Forest, John (*ob.* 1538) **103–5**
Fox, Richard, Bishop of Winchester (*ob.* 1528) **13–14:** won over to Henry Richmond by Morton, 10; quarrel with Warham, 47; and Polydore Vergil's *Anglica Historia*, 55

Foxe (Fox), John (c.1516–87) **297–300**: unfair to Bonner, 147–8

Frith, John (1505–33) **102–3**

Frobisher, Sir Martin (1539–94) **411–16**: and Hatton, 228; and Jenkinson, 377; and Sir John Hawkins, 394; and the Armada, 407; and Fenton, 425

Gardiner, Stephen, Bishop of Winchester (?1482–1555) **150–3**: supports Catherine Howard, 39; and Thomas Cromwell, 66; Fisher in custody of 82; and John Frith, 102–3; and Thomas Barnes 109; and Bonner, 147; examines Rogers, 154; examined by Ridley, 163; and Robert Ferrar, 173; and pronunciation of Greek, 183; quarrel with Parker, 269

Gerard, Father John (1564–1637) **337–9**

Gilbert, Sir Humphrey (?1539–1538) **355–62**: and Walsingham, 209; and Captain John Davis, 458–9

Grenville, Sir Richard (1542–1591) **416–20**: and Walsingham, 209; arrests Mayne, 329; and Thomas Cavendish, 362

Gresham, Sir Thomas (?1518–1579) **230–7**

Grey, Lady Jane (1537–54) **132–6**: and Sir John Cheke, 184; and Feckenham, 286

Grindal, Edmund, Archbishop of Canterbury (1519–83) **274–6**: ordains John Foxe, 299; and Gregorian calendar, 443

Grocyn, William (1446–1519) **71–3**: friendship with Linacre, 74

Hakluyt, Richard (the Younger) (c.1552–1616) **444–8**: dedication to Walsingham, 209; advises Gilbert, 357; and Frobisher, 413; and John Newbery, 434, 436; and Ralph Fitch, 440

Hales (Hayles), John (ob. 1571) **138–40**: and Latimer, 168

Hardwick, Elizabeth (1520–1608) **266–7**

Harrington, Sir John (1561–1612) **262–6**

Hatton, Sir Christopher (1540–91) **224–8**: *The Golden Hind* renamed in his honour, 401–2; and Nicholas Hilliard, 458

Hawkins (Hawkyns) family, **378–98**

Hawkins, Sir John (1532–95) **380–95**: and his brother, William, 380; and his son, Richard, 396; and Drake, 399, 407–8, 410; criticised by Frobisher, 396; and George Fenner, 428

Hawkins, Sir Richard (1560–1622) **395–8**

Hawkins, William (the first) (ob. c. 1553) **378–9**

Hawkins, William (the second) (?1519–89) **379–80**

Henry VII **2–5**: and his mother, 1–2, 6, declines to marry Elizabeth of York, 5; oath to marry her, 6; and death of Prince Arthur, 6; conscious of being Welsh, 6; education of his sons, 7, 19; and Morton, 10–12; treatment of Simnel 15; of Perkin Warbeck, 16–17; and Empson and Dudley, 17–18; and Catherine of Aragon, 33; marriage of Margaret to James IV, 44; and Erasmus, 77; employs Thomas Howard, 92–3; and Sebastian Cabot, 344–7; and John Cabot, 348–9; fresco by Holbein, 456

Henry VIII **18–33**: executes Empson and Dudley, 18; and Catherine of Aragon, 33–5; and Anne Boleyn, 35–6; and Jane Seymour, 36–7; and Anne of Cleves, 38; and Catherine Howard, 39–40; and Catherine Parr, 40–1; and his sister, Mary, 42–3; and his natural son, Fitzroy, 45; relations with Warham, 47–8; and Wolsey, 49–54; employs Sadler, 58–9; and Henry Standish, 62–3; and Thomas Cromwell, 64–7; and Calot, 70; and Linacre, 75; and Bishop John Fisher, 81–4; and Sir Thomas More, 85–8; employs

Thomas Howard, 93–5; and Robert Aske, 95–6; and Lord Darcy, 97–8; and John Frith, 102–3; and John Forest, 104; and Thomas Barnes, 109; and Tyndale, 116–17; his will, 124; treatment of his daughter, Mary, 142–3; employs Bonner, 147; and Stephen Gardiner, 150–1; and Cranmer, 151, 154–6, 158; and Latimer, 166; and Reginald Pole, 174–5; his letter to Tunstal, 292; and Sebastian Cabot, 349–50; and William Hawkins the first, 379; and John Dee, 441; employs Holbein, 456–7; portraits of, 456–7

Hepburn, James, 4th Earl of Bothwell see Bothwell

Hilliard, Nicholas (c. 1547–1619) **457–8**

Holbein, Hans, the younger (1497–1543) **456–7**: illustrates Polydore Vergil, 55: drawing of Colet, 71; illustrates *The Praise of Folly*, 78; portrait of Fisher, 84; drawing of Robert Southwell's grandfather, 331

Hooker, Richard (1553–1600) **293–7**: supported by Whitgift, 279; answers Cartwright, 340

Hooper, John, Bishop of Gloucester and Worcester (*ob.* 1555) **170–3**: and Protector Somerset, 131; and Gardiner 152; and John Rogers, 154; opposed by Cranmer, 156

Howard, Catherine see Catherine Howard

Howard, Charles, Baron Howard of Effingham, 1st Earl of Nottingham 1536–1624) **420–4**: disagrees with Essex, 219; tutored by Foxe, 298; and Sir John Hawkins, 393; and Drake and the Armada, 406–8; and Frobisher, 415; and George Fenner, 429; Hakluyt's dedication to, 447

Howard, Thomas, Earl of Surrey and second Duke of Norfolk see Norfolk

Hunne, Richard (*ob.* 1514) **60–2**

Jane Seymour (?1509–37 **36–7**: depicted by Holbein, 456

Jenkinson, Anthony (*ob.* 1611) **368–78**

Jewel, John, Bishop of Salisbury (1522–71) **280–2**

Joan of Kent see Bocher, Joan

Ket, Robert (*ob.* 1549) **136–8**: and Matthew Parker, 269–70

Knox, John (*ob.* 1572) **140–1** opposes Mary of Guise, 187; and Mary Queen of Scots, 246–7; at Frankfort and Geneva, 283

Lambert, John (*ob.* 1538) **105–7**

Lancaster, Sir James (c. 1554–1618) **429–33**: and Captain John Davies, 461

Latimer, Hugh, Bishop of Worcester (?1485–1555) **164–70**: verdict on John Frost, 104; argues with Lambert, 106; teaches Pole, 174; and Matthew Parker, 268

Lee (Legh), Rowland, Bishop of Coventry and Lichfield (*ob.*? 1543) **87–90**: fines William Barlow, 111

Leicester, Robert Dudley, Earl of (1533–88) **209–17**: opposed to Parker, 272; and Robert Parsons, 325; and Cartwright, 340, 340; and Edward Fenton, 425

Linacre, Thomas (?1460–1524) **73–6**: and Grocyn, 72–3; and Erasmus, 78; and Princess Mary, 142; teaches Pole, 174

Lopez, Rodrigo (*ob.* 1594) **312–14**

Margaret Tudor, Queen of Scotland (1489–1541) **44**: Sadler's mission to, 58

Mary I, Queen of England **141–6**: and Catherine Parr, 41; and Sir Ralph Sadler, 60; Thomas Cromwell's letters to, 67; Linacre tutor to, 75; wishes to save Lady Jane Grey, 135; and Stephen Gardiner 151–2; and Cranmer, 156; and Ridley, 163; and Pole, 176; employs Ascham, 180; and Udall, 182; and her sister Elizabeth, 185; employs William Cecil, 199; and Thomas Gresham, 233–4; Jewel's oration at Oxford, 281; and Muscovy Company, 354; and the Hawkins family, 380, 382–3; and John Dee, 442

Mary Stuart, Queen of Scots (1542–87) **244–51**: attitude of Elizabeth to, 191, 193; and Leicester, 212, 214, 216; Hatton, 226; and Darnley, 252–4; and Riccio, 255–6; and Bothwell, 257–61; and Elizabeth Hardwick, 266–7; and Ridolfi Plot, 302–3; and Throckmorton Plot, 304–5; and William Parry, 306; and Anthony Babington, 308–11; and William Allen, 321; and Lord Howard of Effingham, 421

Mary Tudor, Queen of France (1496–1533) **42–4**: and Thomas Howard, Duke of Norfolk, 93

Mayne, Cuthbert (1544–77) **328–30**

More, Sir Thomas, Lord Chancellor (1478–1535) **84–9**: and *The History of Richard III*, 12; verdict on Wolsey, 54; marriage of George Cavendish to More's neice, 57; letter to Colet, 72; learns Greek from Linacre, 75; and Erasmus' *Praise of Folly*, 78; with Fisher opposes the Divorce and Royal Supremacy, 81–3; canonised, 84; and Elizabeth Barton, 99; and John Lambert, 105; and Thomas Barnes, 109; controversy with Tyndale, 115; on the Bible in English, 149; and Cranmer, 155; dedication of Tunstal's arithmetic, 291; and Holbein, 456

Morgan, William, Bishop of St. Asaph (c. 1541–1604) **288**

Morton, John, Archbishop of Canterbury and Cardinal (?1420–1500) **8–12**

Newbery, John (fl. 1579–84) **434–8**: and Ralph Fitch, 438–9

Norfolk, Thomas Howard, Earl of Surrey and 2nd Duke of Norfolk (1444–1524) **90–5**

Northumberland, John Dudley, Earl of Warwick and Duke of (?1502–53) **129–32**: treatment of Lady Jane Grey, 134; campaign against Ket, 137; and John Knox, 141; outwitted by Princess Mary, 144; and Cranmer, 156; and William Cecil, 199; his son Robert's support, 210; and Stuckley, 315

Nottingham, Earl of *see* Howard, Charles, Baron Howard of Effingham

Nowell (Noel), Alexander, Dean of St. Paul's (*ob.* 1602) **288–90**

Palavicino, Sir Horatio (c. 1540–1600) **237–9**

Parker, Matthew, Archbishop of Canterbury (1504–75) **268–74**: and William Barlow, 111; and Coverdale, 120; and Peter Wentworth, 240; and Grindal, 275 and Whitgift, 277; and Tunstal, 292

Parr, Catherine *see* Catherine Parr

Parry, William (*ob.* 1585) **305–8**

Parsons (Persons), Robert (1546–1610) **323–7**: opposed by Peter Wentworth, 243; and Father Gerard, 337

Penry, John (1563–93) **330–1**

Pole, Reginald, Cardinal and Archbishop of Canterbury (1500–58) **174–7**: and the *Ten Articles*, 26; and Stephen Gardiner, 152

Ponet, John, Bishop of Winchester, (1516–56) **177–80**: his opinion of Bonner, 148

Ralegh, Sir Walter (?1552–1618) **222–4**: and Essex, 218; and Humphrey Gilbert, 357–9; and Thomas Cavendish, 362; off Ireland with Grenville, 419; builds the *Ark*, 422; verdict on Lord Howard of Effingham, 423; and Captain John Davies, 458–9

Riccio (Rizzio), David (?1533–66) **254–7**

Richmond, Henry Fitzroy, Duke of (1519–36) **45–6:** suggested marriage to his half-sister, Mary, 20

Ridley, Nicholas, Bishop of London (?1503–55) **158–64:** examines Joan Bocher, 123; influences Edward VI, 125; and John Rogers, 154; Latimer's words to him at the stake, 169; and Margaret Parker, 269; and Edmund Grindal, 274; and Whitgift, 276–7; ordains Foxe, 298

Ridolfi, Roberto di (1531–1612) **300–3:** and Sir John Hawkins, 389

Rogers, John (c. 1500–55) **153–4**

Sadler (Sadleir), Sir Ralph (1507–87) **58–60**

Salesbury, William (c. 1517–c. 1600) **287–8**

Seymour, Edward see Somerset

Seymour, Jane see Jane Seymour

Shakespeare, William (1564–1616) **448–56:** supposed presence at Kenilworth, 213; and Essex, 221–2; original of Shylock, 313

Sidney, Sir Philip (1554–86) **228–30:** marries Walsingham's daughter, 206; defends Leicester, 214; friend of Hilliard

Simnel, Lambert (?1475–1525) **14–15**

Smith, Sir Thomas, 139, *n*.1

Somerset, Edward Seymour, Earl of Hertford and Duke of (?1506–52) **126–9:** employs Sadler, 59; promotes Barlow, 111; and Joan Bocher, 123; treatment of Edward VI, 124–5; plans marriages for his son and for Edward VI, 133; and Ket's rebellion, 133; and John Hales, 138; treatment of Bonner, 147; employs William Cecil, 199; and Stuckley, 314; supports Sebastian Cabot and Willoughby, 350–1

Southwell, Robert (1561–95) **331–4:** refusal to answer questions, 329

Standish, Henry, Bishop of St. Asaph (*ob.* 1535) **62–3**

Stuart, Henry, Lord Darnley see Darnley

Stuckley, Sir Thomas (*ob.* 1578) **314–18:** and Frobisher, 413

Surrey, Thomas Howard, Earl of see Norfolk

Throckmorton, Francis (1554–84) **303–5**

Topcliffe, Richard (1532–1604) **327–8:** treatment of Southwell, 332; examines Anne Bellamy, 332; on Father Gerard, 338

Tudor, Margaret see Margaret Tudor

Tudor, Mary see Mary Tudor

Tunstal, Cuthbert, Bishop of Durham (1474–1559) **290–3:** examines Bilney, 100–1; deprived of his see, 132; examines Knox, 141; Cranmer's intercession for, 158

Tyndale, William (*ob.* 1536) **112–17:** and John Frith, 102–3; his *New Testament* distributed by Barnes, 108; and Joan Bocher, 122; and John Rogers, 153–4; compared with Coverdale, 119, 121; and Tunstal, 291

Udall, Nicholas (1505–56) **181–3**

Vergil, Polydore (c. 1470–1555) **54–6**

Walsingham, Sir Francis (1532–90) **204–9:** his daughter marries Essex 218; and Throckmorton plot, 304; and Richard Hakluyt, 446

Warbeck, Perkin (?1474–99) **15–17**

Warham, William, Archbishop of Canterbury (?1450–1532) **46–9:** and charges against Colet, 70; and Grocyn, 73; and Erasmus, 77; and Elizabeth Barton, 98; protects Lambert, 105; and Tunstal, 291

Warwick, John Dudley, Earl of see Northumberland

Wentworth, Peter (c. 1524–96) **239–44:** on Sir Humphery Gilbert, 356

Whitgift, John, Archbishop of Canterbury (1530–1604) **276–80:** Hatton co-operates with, 227; supports William Morgan, 288; controversy with Cartwright, 339–40; tutors George Clifford, 426

Whittingham, William, Dean of Durham (?1524–79) **282–5**

Willoughby, Sir Hugh (*ob.* 1554) **351–3:** and Sebastian Cabot, 350

Wolsey, Thomas, Cardinal, Archbishop and Chancellor (?1473–1530) **49–54:** and the divorce from Catherine of Aragon, 21–2; indicated for *praemunire*, 24; devalues the coinage, 30; forbids Anne Boleyn's marriage to Percy, 36; quarrel with Warham, 47; and Polydore Vergil, 55; and George Cavendish, 56–8; employs Thomas Cromwell, 63–4; opposed by Fisher, 81; and Rowland Lee, 89; rivalry with Thomas Howard, 93–4; and Elizabeth Burton, 99; and Robert Bilney, 100–1; and John Firth, 102; and Robert Barnes, 107

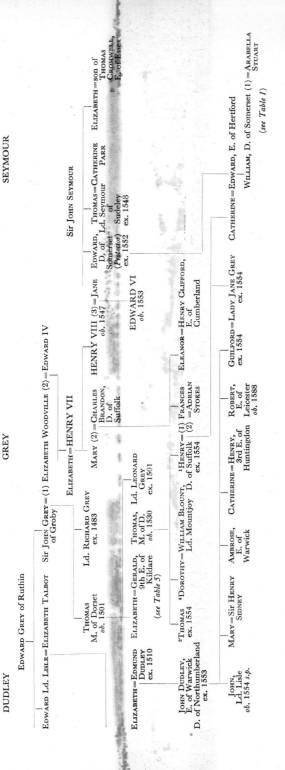

TABLE III.—THE DUDLEY, GREY AND SEYMOUR FAMILIES